HEGEL'S IDEA
OF A
Phenomenology
of Spirit

HEGEL'S IDEA OF A *Phenomenology of Spirit*

MICHAEL N. FORSTER

The University of Chicago Press / Chicago and London

Michael N. Forster is professor and chairman of the Department of Philosophy, University of Chicago. He is the author of *Hegel and Skepticism* (1989).

The University of Chicago Press, Chicago 60637
The University of Chicago Press, Ltd., London
© 1998 by The University of Chicago
All rights reserved. Published 1998
Printed in the United States of America
07 06 05 04 03 02 01 00 99 98   1 2 3 4 5
ISBN: 0-226-25740-1 (cloth)
ISBN: 0-226-25742-8 (paper)

Library of Congress Cataloging-in-Publication Data

Forster, Michael N.
   Hegel's idea of a Phenomenology of spirit / Michael N. Forster.
   p. cm.
   Includes bibliographical references and index.
   ISBN 0-226-25740-1 (hardcover : alk. paper). — ISBN 0-226-25742-8 (pbk. : alk. paper)
   1. Hegel, Georg Wilhelm Friedrich, 1770–1831. Phänomenologie des Geistes. I. Title.
B2929.F67   1998
193—dc21   97-41474
                                                                                 CIP

♾ The paper used in this publication meets the minimum requirements of the American National Standard for Information Sciences—Permanence of Paper for Printed Library Materials, ANSI Z39.48-1992.

For Raymond Geuss

Contents

	Acknowledgments	ix
	Introduction	1
PART ONE	The Official Project of the *Phenomenology*	
Chapter One	The *Phenomenology* as "Introduction" to Hegelian Science	11
Chapter Two	Curing Modern Culture: The Pedagogical Tasks	17
Chapter Three	Justifying Hegelian Science: The Epistemological Tasks	126
Chapter Four	Creating God, Meaning, and Truth: The Metaphysical Tasks	193
PART TWO	The Official Project Continued: The Relation of the *Phenomenology* to Hegelian Science	
Chapter Five	The *Phenomenology* as "Appearance" of Hegelian Science	259
Chapter Six	The *Phenomenology*'s Independence from Hegelian Science	270
Chapter Seven	The *Aufhebung* of the *Phenomenology* to Hegelian Science	282

PART THREE	History and Historicism in the *Phenomenology*	
Chapter Eight	Two Varieties of Historicism	291
Chapter Nine	History in the Chapters *Consciousness* through *Reason*	296
Chapter Ten	Intellectual Historicism in the Chapters *Consciousness* through *Reason*	360
Chapter Eleven	History in the Chapters *Spirit* through *Absolute Knowing*	447
Chapter Twelve	Further Intellectual Historicism in the *Phenomenology*	464
PART FOUR	*Phenomenology* and Ur-*Phenomenology*; *Phenomenology* and Logic	
Chapter Thirteen	The Issues	501
Chapter Fourteen	The Basic Case for a Shift in Plan	505
Chapter Fifteen	The Underlying Logic of the *Phenomenology*	511
Chapter Sixteen	The Effects of the Shift in Plan on the Design of the *Phenomenology*	536
Chapter Seventeen	Hegel's Reasons for the Shift in Plan	540
PART FIVE	Hegel's Later Attitude toward the *Phenomenology*	
Chapter Eighteen	A Fundamental Reinterpretation or Devaluation?	547
Chapter Nineteen	The Historical Relativity of the *Phenomenology*	556
	Appendices	571
	Index	647

Acknowledgements

This book took many years to conceive and write, and I have incurred many large debts of gratitude in the process, which I would like to record here.

Michael Frede (Oxford University) has been a constant source of both intellectual inspiration and support in connection with this project. Hans Friedrich Fulda (Heidelberg University) stimulated my thoughts about Hegel during many hours of conversation, gave me the idea of writing this book through his generous encouragement of an early version of part 1, and provided helpful written comments on an early draft of the whole book. Raymond Geuss (Cambridge University) has been a constant source of intellectual inspiration and support, and provided helpful written comments on a draft of this book—it is dedicated to him with deepest thanks. Susan Hahn (Johns Hopkins University) provided intellectual stimulation, encouragement, and practical help. H. S. Harris (York University) provided helpful written comments on an early draft of the book which were especially important for the development of parts 3 and 4. Michael Inwood (Oxford University), though not directly involved in this project, provided intellectual stimulation through his own work on Hegel, and valued encouragement of related work of mine. Mark Johnston (Princeton University) has been a much appreciated source of stimulation in connection with some of the more strictly philosophical aspects of this project. Saul Kripke (Princeton University), though not directly involved with this project, provided important intellectual stimulation through both his teaching at Princeton and his writings. Richard Rorty (University of Virginia), though not directly involved in this project, provided important intellectual stimulation through his teaching at Princeton and his writings, as well as valued encouragement when I was beginning my work on continental philosophy at Princeton. Alan Ryan (Oxford University) first developed my sense of Hegel as a philosopher deserving of serious attention through lectures and tutorials that he gave at Oxford. Charles Taylor (McGill University), though not directly involved in this project, has been a constant source of enlightenment and stimulation through his writings on Hegel and related subjects (and my several disagreements with him on specific points should be seen against this background). Ralph Walker (Oxford University) played a vital role in developing my interest in philosophy generally and German idealism particularly when I was an undergraduate at Oxford, and also provided helpful written comments on a draft of this book. Allen Wood (Yale University) provided helpful written comments on a draft of this book which were especially valuable for encouraging fuller development of the subject of Hegel's debts to Herder.

Besides the above, I would also like to thank for myriad intellectual stimulations and encouragements the students in seminars I have taught on the *Phenomenology of Spirit* over the past decade or so at the University of Chicago, the University of Michigan at Ann Arbor, and Princeton University; and the audiences of talks I have given on the subjects of this book during the same period at the University of Chicago, Harvard University, Northwestern University, Oxford University, and Princeton University.

I would also like to thank the three fine academic institutions by which this project was mainly nurtured: Oxford University, Princeton University, and the University of Chicago. Special thanks are due to my colleagues at the University of Chicago for providing, to an extraordinary degree, the sort of intellectual stimulation and moral support without which such a project as this would be unthinkable.

Further sincere thanks go to David Brent and his colleagues at the University of Chicago Press for exemplary work in bringing this project to publication; Joanne Grencius of the Philosophy Department at the University of Chicago for very generously and accurately typing the manuscript at one point (and for much else that makes my work possible from day to day); and Megan Moshayedi and Dedi Felman of the University of Chicago for scrupulous work in proofreading the book and preparing the index.

Needless to say, none of the above should be held responsible for the views developed in this book, still less for any mistakes it may contain.

Last, but certainly not least, warmest thanks go to my parents, Michael and Kathleen Forster; my wife, Noha; and my daughter, Alya, for their support and patience during the work on this project, and for making it and everything else worthwhile.

Introduction

Hegel's *Phenomenology of Spirit* has the ambivalent reputation of being simultaneously one of the most obscure and one of the most important works of philosophy—a reputation richly deserved on both counts.[1] In the present book I aim to penetrate some of the *Phenomenology*'s obscurity and to reveal some of its importance. My goal is not to provide a detailed section-by-section commentary on the *Phenomenology*.[2] Rather, it is to explain the *idea* of the *Phenomenology*, by which I mean the more general philosophical and architectonic principles of the work. The aim is to provide an x-ray picture revealing the vital organs and skeleton of the work, so to speak.

---

1. G.W.F. Hegel, *Phenomenology of Spirit*, trans. A.V. Miller (Oxford: Oxford University Press, 1977). References to parts of the *Phenomenology* are henceforth by means of Miller's paragraph numbers. Miller's translation is usually reliable. However, in quoting from the *Phenomenology* I frequently modify it or substitute a translation of my own without specific notice—occasionally in order to correct an outright mistake, more often in order to bring out a relevant nuance of Hegel's much-nuanced German which Miller's translation loses or obscures. A similar policy is followed in relation to all other translations referred to in this book.

2. Readers in search of something more along the lines of such a commentary might consult one or more of the following, all of which are very helpful in their different ways: J. Hyppolite, *Genesis and Structure of Hegel's Phenomenology of Spirit* (Evanston, Ill.: Northwestern University Press, 1974); R. C. Solomon, *In the Spirit of Hegel* (Oxford: Oxford University Press, 1983); C. Taylor, *Hegel* (Cambridge: Cambridge University Press, 1975), parts 1 and 2. Also very useful for particular sections of the work are: R. Norman, *Hegel's Phenomenology: A Philosophical Introduction* (Atlantic Highlands, N.J.: Humanities Press, 1981); M. Westphal, *History and Truth in Hegel's Phenomenology* (Atlantic Highlands, N.J.: Humanities Press, 1982).

To describe the contents of this book in succinct and dry terms: Part 1 addresses the question of what philosophical tasks the *Phenomenology* was originally written to perform and how it was supposed to perform them. Part 2 deals with the question of the originally intended relationship between the *Phenomenology* and Hegel's "Science" proper (i.e., the system comprising Logic, Philosophy of Nature, and Philosophy of Spirit, a version of which he eventually went on to publish in the *Encyclopaedia*). Part 3 addresses the questions of the role of history in the design of the *Phenomenology* and the nature of the work's "historicism." Part 4 deals with two connected questions: first, the question of whether there lies behind or within the published *Phenomenology* an Ur-*Phenomenology,* an originally planned version of more modest scope, and if so what effect Hegel's change of plan had on the coherence of the work's design; second, the question of the *logical* design of the *Phenomenology,* or the way in which Hegel's Logic underlies it as a sort of scaffolding. Finally, part 5 addresses the question of Hegel's attitude toward the *Phenomenology* in his later years.

Four general ambitions have guided this project. A first is to offer an interpretation of the *Phenomenology* which treats it *as a whole* ("top-down" rather than "bottom-up," as it were). There are several good books on the *Phenomenology* already available, but their emphasis and strength lie mainly in their treatments of particular sections of the work. By contrast, the character of the *Phenomenology* as a whole tends to be passed over rather quickly, and where dealt with not dealt with particularly well. This is very unfortunate because many of the most philosophically interesting ideas of the work are to be found at the level of the work as a whole and are not at all clearly visible from the standpoint of particular sections. It is unfortunate also because a lack of clarity about the nature of the work's project as a whole inevitably casts its shadows on the interpretation of particular sections as well. So this is a serious deficit in the existing literature which the present book seeks to remedy.

A second guiding ambition is to demonstrate the fundamental coherence of the *Phenomenology*'s overall conception. Most of the more serious secondary literature on the *Phenomenology* leaves the strong impression of a work whose general conception, if indeed it can be said to have one at all, is marred by deep incoherencies of various kinds—the work is, in Solomon's words, "a slapdash manuscript, . . . bordering on incoherence."³ Thus, it has been argued—by Solomon himself for example—that Hegel never even had a clear idea of what he was trying to accomplish in the *Phenomenology* as a whole: "Hegel did not know what he was trying to do . . . Hegel did not have the opportunity to quietly meditate . . . about the exact aims or intentions of his book. (Thus the belligerent opening of the Preface, in which he tells us that it would be 'inappropriate' to tell us what these are: he didn't know.)"⁴ It has been argued—by Haering and Fulda for example—that Hegel's conception of the relation between the *Phenomenology* and the system of the *Encyclopaedia* was originally inconsistent. It has been argued—by Haym and Pöggeler for example—that history plays only a sporadic and inconsistent role within the work. It has been argued—by Haym, Haering, and Pöggeler for example—that Hegel changed his mind about the scope and character of the *Phenomenology* during its composition, leaving the work without a coherent design. It has been argued—by Lukács for example—that the *Phenomenology*'s views concerning the direction of contemporary historical events and its own relation to modern history are inconsistent with Hegel's later conceptions. It has been argued—by Haering and Fulda for example—that after publishing the *Phenomenology* Hegel drastically reinterpreted the work, and—by Haering and Pöggeler for example—that he eventually, and for good reasons, lost faith in it altogether and abandoned it. And so forth.

In contrast to such interpretations as these, the present book will argue for the fundamental coherence of the *Phenomenology*'s overall conception. Concerning the issues just mentioned, specifically, for instance, I shall argue for the following claims: First, Hegel had a long-developed, clear, elaborate, and very sophisticated conception of the aims and methods of the *Phenomenology* (part 1). Second, Hegel had from the start a well-thought-out and quite coherent conception of the work's relation to the system of the *Encyclopaedia* (part 2). Third, history plays a role in the design of the *Phenomenology* which is both fundamental and fundamentally consistent (part 3). Fourth, although Hegel did indeed change his mind about the scope and character of the *Phenomenology* during its composition, this change, far from leaving it without a coherent design, merely took it from one fundamentally coherent design to another (part

---

3. Solomon, *In the Spirit of Hegel,* p. 156.
4. Ibid.

4). Fifth, the *Phenomenology*'s views concerning the direction of contemporary historical events and its own relation to modern history are perfectly consistent with Hegel's later conceptions (part 3). Sixth, Hegel's interpretation of the *Phenomenology* remained fundamentally unchanged after its publication, and he never lost faith in or abandoned the work (at least not in any sense unforeseen or unintended at the time when he wrote it) (part 5). In short, far from being a work marred by deep incoherence, the *Phenomenology* exhibits rather extraordinary coherence, both at the time of its composition and in relation to Hegel's position in later years.

A third guiding ambition behind this book is to show that, beyond meeting the (perhaps fairly basic) requirement of coherence, the general conception of the *Phenomenology* has quite extraordinary sophistication and depth. This is true both of the more straightforwardly philosophical and of the more architectonic aspects of the work's general conception. Given the thoroughly systematic nature of the *Phenomenology,* and of Hegel's philosophy generally, I shall inevitably be concerned with architectonics throughout much of this book. It is my hope to convey at least the impressiveness, and perhaps even the attractiveness, of the *Phenomenology*'s architectonic conception. The investigation of the work's more straightforwardly philosophical side, by contrast, falls mainly in parts 1 and 3.[5] Among the ideas discussed there which in my view deserve particular emphasis for philosophical interest are the following: Hegel's historically informed diagnosis of the ills of modern culture in terms of the pervasiveness of dualisms within it, and his project for curing them by means of a more monistic standpoint (chapter 2); his commitments and arguments against transcendence of the natural sphere and for naturalism, in theology (where he rejects ideas of a transcendent God in favor of identifying God with man and nature), the philosophy of mind (where he rejects dualism in favor of physicalism and behaviorism), the philosophy of language (where he rejects such items as Platonic forms, instead equating meanings with the linguistic behavior of a community), and the philosophy of causal explanation (where he rejects realism about causal connections and forces in favor of a certain sort of antirealism) (chapters

---

5. These parts are written in such a way that the reader with an interest in philosophical ideas but little tolerance for architectonic matters can, if he or she wishes, read them by themselves.

2 and 4);[6] his conception that the real challenge in epistemology comes from the radical skepticism of the ancients, critique of more contemporary epistemologies in the light of this, and attempt to establish his own philosophical system as by contrast epistemologically secure in the face of it (chapter 3); his theories and supporting arguments concerning the nature, and in particular the *social* nature, of meaning and truth, together with projects arising therefrom of meeting the conditions, and in particular the *social* conditions, of meaningfulness and truth on behalf of his own philosophy (chapter 4); and last, but not least, his development of a broad family of what might be called intellectual historicist ideas, or ideas based on the root insight that human thought changes in fundamental ways over the course of history (chapters 8 to 12).

A fourth and final ambition guiding this book is to provide an instrument to help unlock the mysteries of particular sections of the *Phenomenology*. Much of what has made the *Phenomenology* such an influential work in the history of modern philosophy, and indeed much of its intrinsic value, lies in themes which are more or less confined to particular sections.—Concerning the work's influence on subsequent nineteenth-century German philosophy, for example, Marx found in the *Lordship and Bondage* section and in the section on *Culture* the idea, seminal for his own thought, of man's self-creation through labor, that is, the idea that there is no such thing as a given and unchanging human nature, but human nature undergoes deep changes over the course of history, and these changes are primarily determined by changes in the character of man's economic activity.[7] And Feuerbach drew from the *Unhappy Consciousness* section of the *Phenomenology* the fundamental principles of his own critique of Christianity (thereby laying the foundations for much subsequent nineteenth-century German criticism of religion, for example in Marx and Nietzsche, as well).[8]—If, however, one turns to particular

---

6. This characterization of Hegel's position as naturalistic and opposed to transcendence of nature will in the end require some qualification, but not much. For a discussion of this matter in connection with the crucial theological case, see chapter 4.

7. In the *Economic and Philosophic Manuscripts* Marx writes: "The great thing in Hegel's *Phenomenology* and its final result . . . is simply that Hegel grasps the self-development of man as a process . . . ; that he thus grasps the nature of *work* and comprehends objective man . . . as the result of his *own work*"; "he grasps labor . . . as man's act of self-creation" (*Marx: Selections*, ed. A. W. Wood [New York: Macmillan, 1988], pp. 67, 75).

8. To illustrate Feuerbach's debt briefly: In the *Unhappy Consciousness* section Hegel writes that the Christian consciousness (i) "is the gazing of one self-consciousness into an-

sections of the *Phenomenology,* whether in order to understand their influence on later thinkers or to draw insights from them oneself, without some prior grasp of the work's general philosophic and architectonic principles, one confronts virtually insurmountable difficulties. This is to some extent for the general reason that it is *always* important to have an overview of an original work of philosophy or literature if one is to understand its particular parts properly (a point rightly emphasized in Schleiermacher's theory of interpretation). But in the case of the *Phenomenology* this general need for an overview is amplified far beyond normal bounds by such features of the work as its deliberately *systematic* character, its failure, though, to state its systematic principles explicitly and clearly, and, certainly not least, its general opacity of expression. Thus the reader who approaches a particular section of the *Phenomenology* without an overview of the work at hand will find, or certainly *should* find, his access to it blocked by a host of unanswered general questions: What is the purpose of the account given in this section of the work? Is it given for its own sake merely, or does it serve ulterior philosophical ends, and if so, what are these? In what relation does this section in particular, or the *Phenomenology*'s account generally, stand to the system of the *Encyclopaedia*? Is it, for instance, Hegel's position that we have to know the system, or some part of it, before we can understand the *Phenomenology,* that the latter in this sense presupposes the former? More specifically, does Hegel's Logic underlie the argument of the *Phenomenology,* and if so how exactly? Is the account in this section, or in the *Phenomenology* generally, supposed to be a history, or is it rather a psychology, or something else? If a history, then what sort of history is it, and with which periods, individuals, and episodes is it concerned? If a psychology, then what sort of psychology, and to whom does it apply? Are we to infer from such circumstances as Hegel's later failure to endorse the *Phenomenology* in the *Encyclopaedia* that we are dealing here with

---

other, and itself *is* both . . . But it is not as yet aware . . . that it is the unity of both," and (ii) takes God "to be the *essential* being" and itself "to be the unessential" and "is conscious only of its own nothingness" (pars. 207–9). These Hegelian claims reappear as the fundamental principles of Feuerbach's *The Essence of Christianity,* trans. G. Eliot (Buffalo, N.Y.: Prometheus Books, 1989): (i′) "The divine being is nothing else than the human being, or . . . the human nature purified . . . made objective—i.e., contemplated and revered as another, a distinct being"; (ii′) "As what is positive in the conception of the divine being can only be human, the conception of man . . . can only be negative. To enrich God, man must become poor, that God may be all, man must be nothing" (pp. 14, 26).

mere juvenilia without authority for the mature Hegel? And so forth. I attempt in this book to provide an explanation of the general principles of the *Phenomenology* which answers such questions as these, and thereby to remove this welter of obstacles to a proper understanding of particular sections of the work. I thus aim to establish a framework within which their interpretation can proceed more fruitfully in the future.

One comment, in conclusion, concerning the interpretative approach adopted in this book: The task of determining the general philosophic and architectonic principles of the *Phenomenology* is a difficult one largely because Hegel tends to leave these unexplained, or only obscurely explained, within the *Phenomenology* itself. Fortunately, however, there is much in Hegel's other writings—especially from before, but also from during and after, the *Phenomenology*'s composition—which throws light on the general principles of the *Phenomenology*. To mention one important example: Hegel's prephenomenological writings concerning the discipline of Logic prove to be of great help, because that discipline, as Hegel then conceived it, had functions very similar to those which he would later assign to the *Phenomenology* (more similar to these, indeed, than to the functions of the later Logic, the Logic of the *Science of Logic* and the *Encyclopaedia*). It is above all by drawing on these other writings of Hegel's that we may hope to arrive at an adequate understanding of the overall project of the *Phenomenology*.

In accordance with this methodological principle, I have translated in appendices at the end of the book a number of the most important such writings. Some of these have hitherto been unavailable in translation, and the wide dispersion of the rest has made it difficult for most readers of the *Phenomenology* to consult them.[9]

---

9. In these translations, and throughout the book, I take two modest liberties with Hegel's texts: (i) I sometimes capitalize nouns where this seems desirable in order to signal to the reader that one is dealing with a Hegelian term of art—*Science*, the *Concept*, the *Idea*, etc. This is entirely the translator's device, for, of course, *all* nouns receive an initial capital in German, and, as the saying goes, she who gives herself to all gives herself to none. (ii) I freely omit Hegel's emphases where these distract from rather than clarify his meaning. Emphases in Hegel often have about as much semantic significance as nervous tics, and indeed something of the same character. (On the other hand, *added* emphases are always specified as such.)

PART ONE

The Official Project
of the *Phenomenology*

CHAPTER ONE

The *Phenomenology* as "Introduction" to Hegelian Science

This first part of the book will give an account of what we may call the *official project* of the *Phenomenology*. By this I mean the philosophical purposes which originally motivated the work, and Hegel's conception of the means by which the work would accomplish these purposes. As one might expect, this official project finds prominent expression in the *Phenomenology*'s Introduction and Preface. Its execution occurs almost entirely in the chapters *Consciousness* through *Reason* (the explanation of this being that, as we shall see later, these chapters exhaust the scope of the *Phenomenology* that Hegel originally intended to write).

Most philosophical and other academic works are written with the aim of expounding the truth, or at least a part of the truth, about some subject matter. The *Phenomenology* is different: one must make an "advance from this system [i.e., the *Phenomenology*] to the Science of the *true* in its *true shape*" (par. 38). "The Science of the *true* in its *true shape*" referred to here is the philosophical system, comprising Logic, Philosophy of Nature, and Philosophy of Spirit, which Hegel went on to expound in the *Science of Logic* and the *Encyclopaedia*. This philosophical system, to describe it very briefly, posits Absolute Spirit, Hegel's version of God, as a single principle encompassing everything. Each of the three parts of the system is intended to capture an essential aspect of Absolute Spirit's constitution or self-realization. The Logic expounds Absolute Spirit as a self-developing conceptual hierarchy which pervades and explains all natural and human spiritual phenomena. But it expounds this self-developing conceptual hierarchy in abstraction from natural and human spiritual phenomena, or in Hegel's words as "God as he is in his eternal essence before the creation of nature and a finite spirit."[1] The Philosophy of Nature expounds the realization of this self-developing conceptual hierarchy in nature. Accordingly, nature is here interpreted as a self-developing hierarchy mirroring the self-developing conceptual hierarchy of the Logic. This natural hierarchy includes merely mechanical phenomena at its lower end, and organic ones at its higher end. The Philosophy of Spirit also expounds the realization of the Logic's self-developing conceptual hierarchy, but this time at the higher level of human spiritual or mental phenomena. Accordingly, these are here likewise interpreted as a self-developing hierarchy corresponding to the self-developing conceptual hierarchy of the Logic. The Philosophy of Spirit ascends from the general mental characteristics of individual human beings, to the social and political institutions of the state and their historical development, and finally to art, religion, and philosophy, interpreted as expressions of the truth about Absolute Spirit and hence as its return to itself and achievement of an essential knowledge of its own nature. This whole system is conceived, on one level at least, as a defense or rational reworking of the Christian conception of God. In particular, its three parts are an attempt to make sense of the Christian idea of a God who is three in one—the Logic depicting God as he is in himself, the Philosophy of Nature God the Son, and the Philosophy of Spirit God the Holy Spirit.[2]

Now the official project of the *Phenomenology* is to serve as a sort of *introduction* to this philosophical system wherein the truth is expounded. By the time of the *Phenomenology*'s composition it was already a long-standing belief of Hegel's that his system required an introduction of some sort. During the Jena years immediately preceding the *Phenomenology*'s composition his earlier system—comprising Metaphysics, Philosophy of Nature, and Philosophy of Spirit—had the early Logic as its intro-

---

1. Hegel, *Science of Logic,* trans. A.V. Miller (New York: Humanities Press, 1976), p. 50.
2. Hence Hegel writes: "Christianity contains . . . a revelation of God's spiritual nature. In the first place, he is the Father, a power which is universal but as yet enclosed within itself. Secondly, he is his own object, another version of himself, dividing himself into two so as to produce the Son. But this other version is just as immediate an expression of him as he is himself; he knows himself and contemplates himself in it—and it is this self-knowledge and self-contemplation which constitutes the third element, the Spirit as such . . . It is this doctrine of the Trinity which raises Christianity above the other religions" (*Lectures on the Philosophy of World History: Introduction,* trans. H.B. Nisbet [Cambridge: Cambridge University Press, 1980], p. 51).

duction.³ When he transformed this earlier system into the mature system of Logic, Philosophy of Nature, and Philosophy of Spirit sketched above, at around the time of the *Phenomenology*'s composition, the *Phenomenology* took over the early Logic's introductory role. Hence in a letter to Schelling from 1807 Hegel writes that the *Phenomenology* "is actually the introduction," and he describes it as "the introduction" to his philosophical system in the *Encyclopaedia* as well.⁴

However, if the *Phenomenology* serves as an introduction to Hegel's system and its exposition of the truth, that does not yet tell us what *sort* of introduction the work is supposed to be. Hegel warns us in the Preface that it "will not be what one immediately thinks of when one thinks of an introduction of the unscientific consciousness to Science" (par. 27). And we would do well to take this warning seriously.

The *Phenomenology* in fact serves a multiplicity of distinct introductory tasks.⁵ These introductory tasks prove, on inspection, to be very di-

---

3. On the introductory character of the early Logic, see K. Düsing, "Spekulation und Reflexion. Zur Zusammenarbeit Schellings und Hegels in Jena," *Hegel Studien* 5 (1969).

4. *Briefe von und an Hegel,* ed. J. Hoffmeister (Hamburg: Felix Meiner Verlag, 1969), 1:161, also in appendix XII; Hegel, *Enzyklopädie der philosophischen Wissenschaften* (Frankfurt am Main: Suhrkamp Verlag, 1970), par. 25, also in appendix XVII. Cf. Hegel's remark in a letter to Sinclair from 1810: "The Science itself is to come only after [the *Phenomenology*]" (*Briefe von und an Hegel* 1:332). (Hegel did in places refer to the *Phenomenology* as the first part of his system. However, he explicitly withdrew this designation in a footnote added to the first-edition preface of the *Science of Logic* in 1831, and it was, I think, from the start misleading. We shall consider this matter more closely in part 5.)

5. Westphal, in an otherwise very helpful book on the *Phenomenology,* therefore seems to me to start out, along with several other commentators, on a wrong foot when he opens with the assertion that "we can meaningfully speak of *the* task of the *Phenomenology*; . . . there is a single coherent argument running through its entirety" (*History and Truth,* p. 1).

In loose connection with this point, it is worth noting that *whatever* linguistic unit one chooses in Hegel—whether text (as here), chapter, paragraph, sentence, or word—it is absolutely typical of Hegel's philosophical writing to mean several distinct (though hopefully consistent) things at once. This reflects deliberate policy on Hegel's part, not merely confusion. It is especially important for analytic philosophers to keep this in mind when interpreting Hegel, because analytic philosophy tends to espouse an equally deliberate opposite policy of avoiding such ambiguities at all costs (especially at the level of sentence and word). One can debate the merits of these alternative policies. My own view is that either is compatible with fruitful philosophical work if practised well, but that whatever advantages Hegel's policy may enjoy over analytical philosophy's (e.g., economy of expression) are in the end outweighed by its disadvantages (e.g., loss of clarity and precision). Accordingly, in this book I will be concerned to separate out as far as possible issues which in Hegel's texts are much run together. This situation carries some further consequences for my interpretation as well. For example, when I say that Hegel means such and such by a given

verse, surprising, ambitious, and philosophically interesting (arguably, indeed, more philosophically interesting than the contents of the system itself).[6] They constitute just by themselves a project quite unparalleled in the history of philosophy. The *Phenomenology* is indeed a very unusual kind of "introduction."

In order to give a provisional idea of the nature of these tasks, and an aid to orientation during the detailed explanation of them which is to follow, it may be useful to present them here in the form of a (for the moment, inevitably dogmatic and somewhat cryptic) list. We can think of them as falling into three groups: tasks of a *pedagogical* nature, tasks of an *epistemological* nature, and tasks of what I shall call, for want of a better term, a *metaphysical* nature. The pedagogical tasks of the work are the tasks of teaching modern individuals to understand and accept Hegel's system, in order to bestow on them its theoretical and practical benefits, by (1) discrediting alternative viewpoints, including those initially occupied by these individuals themselves, (2) providing these individuals with a compelling path toward Hegel's system, and (3) along the course of this path giving them a provisional presentation of the contents of the system. The epistemological tasks of the work are the tasks of justifying Hegel's system by (4) defending it against the skeptical problem of "equipollence," (5) defending it against the skeptical problem of "concept-instantiation," and (6) providing a proof of it for all non-Hegelian viewpoints which is compelling to each of them in the light of its own initial views and criteria. Finally, the metaphysical tasks of the work are the tasks of (7) accomplishing Absolute Spirit's essential self-knowledge and thereby its full realization, (8) demonstrating the essentially communal nature of meanings or concepts, (9) establishing the communal conditions of meaningfulness or concepthood on behalf of the concepts of Hegel's own system in order to make possible and actual this system's conceptual articulation, (10) demonstrating that truth is consti-

---

passage, I should never be taken to be implying that he does not mean various other things by it as well; he typically does. Also, I shall sometimes have to return to a single passage of Hegel's more than once in order to draw out distinct strands of thought which co-reside there, in a way that would be unnecessary and tiresome when dealing with most other authors.

6. Like many other commentators (e.g., Dilthey, Royce, and H.S. Harris), I am strongly inclined to think the *Phenomenology*, in Dilthey's words, "Hegel's mightiest work" (*Die Jugendgeschichte Hegels*, in *Wilhelm Dilthey's Gesammelte Schriften* [Leipzig/Berlin: Teubner, 1921], 4:157).

tuted by enduring communal consensus, and (11) establishing an enduring communal consensus in support of Hegel's own system in order to make possible and actual this system's truth. In what follows I shall devote a chapter to each of these groups of tasks—the pedagogical, the epistemological, and the metaphysical—in turn.[7]

---

7. These official tasks of the *Phenomenology* have nowhere in the secondary literature received the sort of complete and detailed treatment for which I aim in this part of the book. However, they have not, of course, gone entirely unnoticed. It may therefore be worth indicating briefly, for bibliographical purposes, some points at which the better secondary literature has touched on them.

One of the best Anglo-American books on the *Phenomenology*, Solomon's *In the Spirit of Hegel*, argues, as we saw in the introduction, that Hegel had no clear idea of the aims of the *Phenomenology* at all. According to Solomon, the most that one can say is that "he knew that he wanted to produce his own system. He knew that its introduction would have to establish 'the absolute' unity of experience, at which point he could begin the study of logic and metaphysics . . . But he had no definite plan how to get there" (p. 156). This account is so vague that it could equally well be said to include all of the tasks distinguished above or none of them. Turning to Taylor's *Hegel*, probably the best general book on Hegel in English, or indeed any language, Taylor mentions three tasks which the *Phenomenology* aims to perform: It aims to provide an introduction to the system for the ordinary consciousness, comprising both a demonstration of contradictions in forms of the ordinary consciousness and a demonstration of the necessity of the development of these forms to the standpoint of the system (pp. 127–28, 134, 136). This corresponds to pedagogical tasks (1) and (2) in my list. In addition, according to Taylor, the *Phenomenology* is supposed to demonstrate the necessity of the principle of Hegel's philosophy, Absolute Spirit, through showing that lesser viewpoints necessarily develop into it by means of an immanent (i.e., not externally imposed) dialectic—thereby avoiding the need to rest that principle on mere faith or overall plausibility (pp. 130, 139–40). This corresponds approximately to epistemological task (6) in my list.

Turning to the best French commentary on the *Phenomenology*, Hyppolite's *Genesis and Structure*, this work too takes note of the tasks mentioned by Taylor (see pp. 7, 41 for the two pedagogical tasks, and pp. 4, 11, 44 for epistemological task [6]). But it also mentions one further important task as well: the *Phenomenology* actually constitutes (does not merely describe) an essential moment in the life of Absolute Spirit, namely, Absolute Spirit's coming to self-knowledge through the individual subject's being led to Hegelian Science or the knowledge of Absolute Spirit (pp. 7–8, 41–43). This is metaphysical task (7) in my classification.

Turning to the German secondary literature, K. Fischer in his *Hegels Leben, Werke, und Lehre* (Heidelberg: Carl Winter, 1911) makes the important point that the *Phenomenology* aims to refute skepticism by showing that the dualism of knowledge and object, or concept and object, which skepticism presupposes as its basis is false (p. 297). This corresponds to epistemological task (5) in my list. R. Haym in his 1857 work *Hegel und seine Zeit* (Hildesheim: Georg Olms, 1962) gives one of the best (but also most critical) short treatments of the *Phenomenology*'s tasks. In addition to recognizing most of the tasks already mentioned, Haym notes that the *Phenomenology* is supposed to provide a justification or proof of Hegelian Science by (i) systematically doubting, testing, and criticizing nonscientific cognition (pp. 232–33), and (ii) showing Hegelian Science to be the highest standpoint in the development of consciousness and the goal of history (p. 240). This identifies central aspects of the three epistemological tasks in my list: (4), (5), and (6). In addition, Haym notes that the *Phenomenology* is supposed to contain a presentation, in some fashion, of all of Hegelian Science's content (pp. 253–55). This is roughly pedagogical task (3) in my classification. Finally, H.F. Fulda in his valuable book *Das Problem einer Einleitung in Hegels Wissenschaft der Logik* (Frankfurt am Main: Vittorio Klostermann, 1975) goes more deeply into the *Phenomenology*'s project, already indicated by Haym, of justifying Hegelian Science by means of, on the one hand, a skeptical destruction of the ordinary consciousness and its presuppositions and, on the other hand, a positive deduction of Hegelian Science (pp. 4–5, 46). In particular, Fulda is more clearly aware than Haym that it is largely in response to *skeptical* difficulties that Hegel undertakes to justify his Science (pp. 4–5). And Fulda also adds the refinement that what is in question here is both a justification of Hegelian Science to itself and a justification of it to the ordinary consciousness (p. 31)—the former part of which is a goal common to epistemological tasks (4), (5), and (6) in my list, while the latter is a goal distinctive of epistemological task (6). In addition, Fulda points to some further aspects of the *metaphysical* tasks of the *Phenomenology* (though without, I think, getting to the bottom of their import): in particular the facts that Hegel considers the *Phenomenology* to be necessary for the genesis of the medium in which his Science completes itself (pp. 114–15), and that he considers the achievement of full self-knowledge by consciousness to be necessary to his Science (pp. 94–101).

CHAPTER TWO

Curing Modern Culture: The Pedagogical Tasks

Prominent among the ambitions of the *Phenomenology* is the pedagogical ambition of teaching the broad generality of modern individuals to understand and accept Hegel's philosophical system. As Hegel puts it in the Preface, his philosophical system is to be made "exoteric, comprehensible, and capable of being learned and appropriated by all," and it is the *Phenomenology* which is to perform this "task of leading the individual from his uneducated standpoint to knowledge [i.e., to the standpoint of the Hegelian system]" (pars. 13, 28).

Certain questions arise immediately concerning this pedagogical project. A first is why Hegel thinks it as important as he obviously does that his system be made accessible and compelling to the general run of his contemporaries.[1] A modern physicist, for example, might have quite as high an opinion of the theory of relativity as Hegel has of his philosophical system, and yet consider it a matter of no great consequence that only a few of his contemporaries will ever really come to understand or believe the principles of the theory. What accounts for Hegel's very different attitude?

In order to answer this question, it is necessary to understand something of the fundamental motivation behind Hegel's philosophy. For Hegel, the purpose of doing philosophy is not only the *theoretical* pur-

---

1. Compare the Jena Hegel's remark, at K. Rosenkranz, *Georg Wilhelm Friedrich Hegels Leben* (Darmstadt: Wissenschaftliche Buchgesellschaft, 1977), p. 186: "Philosophy . . . is according to its very nature *for everybody.*" Also, and especially, Hegel's 1805 letter to Voss (*Briefe von und an Hegel* 1:100–101).

pose of determining the truth. It is also, and perhaps even more fundamentally, the *practical* purpose of enabling modern men to achieve genuine happiness. (In this respect, Hegel's position is reminiscent of the Hellenistic schools of philosophy, which also aimed at the attainment of happiness as their primary objective.) Thus, as Harris shows in his excellent study of Hegel's early theological writings, practical motives, and in particular a concern for human happiness, dominated Hegel's thought in the earliest stages of his career.[2] Likewise, happiness continued to be philosophy's central concern for Hegel in the early Jena period. In the essay *Faith and Knowledge* from 1802, for example, we read that "every [genuine] philosophy sets forth nothing else but the construction of highest bliss [Seligkeit] as idea," or "happiness [Glückseligkeit] conceived as idea."[3] And there is a similar preoccupation with human happiness in the *Phenomenology* as well.[4] Perhaps the clearest expression of this occurs in the middle of the *Reason* chapter, where Hegel characterizes the course of history from the culture of ancient Greece to the culture which he envisages for the modern world as a movement from one "state of happiness [Glücke]" to another (par. 353), indicating that in the interim an inevitable "withdrawal from this state of happiness" into individualism and resulting unhappiness has taken place (pars. 354–55), but that thence the "individual is sent out into the world by his own spirit to seek his own happiness" and will find it in the modern world's "happy state of being the ethical substance" (par. 356).[5]

---

2. H.S. Harris, *Hegel's Development: Toward the Sunlight 1770–1801* (Oxford: Oxford University Press, 1972), esp. pp. 75, 104 n.1, 106 n.2 (on the dominance during this period of Hegel's thought of practical motives generally), 22–25 (on his concern with happiness specifically).

3. Hegel, *Faith and Knowedge*, trans. W. Cerf and H.S. Harris (Albany: State University of New York Press, 1977), p. 59.

4. Solomon rightly remarks: "The *Phenomenology* is not only a book about truth; it is also a treatise on the good life and human happiness" (*In the Spirit of Hegel*, p. 173).

5. For Hegel (as for Hellenistic philosophy) the philosopher's pursuit of happiness must remain within the bounds of the truth, it may not *violate* the truth. However, one should beware of inferring from this that truth constrains the pursuit of happiness in the manner of something quite independent of that pursuit and possessed of a value quite independent of the value of happiness. For, as we shall see in due course, (i) truth is not for Hegel something independent of our volitions, but rather something which we collectively create. And (ii) according to Hegel's conception of happiness, the attainment of truth is an essential component of happiness, so that his respect for truth stems at least in part from his commitment to happiness as a value rather than from a commitment to truth as a value independent of happiness.

It is important, though, to distinguish what "happiness" as a goal of philosophy means for Hegel from various things which it does not. "Happiness" in this context does not mean what many philosophers (and others) have meant by it. In particular, it should not be equated—in the manner of two conceptions of "happiness" which have enjoyed great popularity, especially since the seventeenth century—with either (i) mere feelings, such as presence of pleasure and absence of pain, or (ii) the satisfaction of those obvious, and often individually varying, desires in terms of which we usually explain people and what they do. Thus, in *Faith and Knowledge* Hegel, while indeed saying that every genuine philosophy aims at "the construction of highest bliss as idea," also insists just as emphatically, in rejection of such conceptions as (i) and (ii), that "when happiness is conceived as idea, it ceases to be something empirical and contingent, and it ceases to be something sensuous [in the manner of Enlightenment eudaemonism]."[6] Likewise, the *Phenomenology* repudiates "happiness" in sense (i) in its criticism in the *Pleasure and Necessity* section of the conception of "happiness [Glück]," espoused by Goethe's Faust, as "the enjoyment of pleasure," "just pleasure . . . , or the simple single feeling" (pars. 361–64). And it repudiates "happiness" in sense (ii) in the *Self-consciousness* chapter's argument that the realization of our mundane desires can never provide us with genuine satisfaction (pars. 174–75), and in the *Reason* chapter's observation that the idea that "an immediate will or natural impulse which obtains its satisfaction," or the "goal [of natural impulses,] is the true character and essential nature of self-consciousness" belongs to a consciousness which has "*lost* the happiness of being in the substance" (par. 357; emphasis added).[7]

What then *does* Hegel have in mind when he makes "happiness" the central goal of philosophy? As far as I can see, he nowhere explicitly defines the term in the relevant sense. However, it can be inferred from the way in which he uses the term that what he mainly has in mind is a quite attractively revised form of (ii) which we might succinctly express in the formula: (iii) the satisfaction of our desires, especially *our deepest*

---

6. *Faith and Knowledge*, p. 59; cf. 58–61.

7. Cf. the *Phenomenology*'s critique of the Enlightenment ideal of utility in the *Spirit* chapter. Similarly, the *Philosophy of Right*, trans. T.M. Knox (Oxford: Oxford University Press, 1967), rejects as the true end of man or philosophy "happiness" in the sense of feelings of pleasure and/or satisfaction of the obvious, and frequently varying, desires in terms of which we usually explain people and their behavior (see esp. pars. 20–21, 123, including Hegel's additions).

ones.⁸ In this formula the italicized expression is meant to convey several distinct ideas: that the desires in question are in some sense *strongest;* that they may be *unobvious* enough not to figure in our usual explanations of people and their behavior (even when these are *self*-explanations); and that they are *invariant,* or common to all of us.

The *Phenomenology* identifies three such deep desires as crucial for happiness. First, we have a fundamental and common desire for *agreement,* or (to borrow a term from Rorty) *solidarity, with our community.* Thus Hegel argues in the *Reason* chapter that identifying with one's community in the sense of actively and self-consciously "living in accordance with the customs of one's nation" realizes an individual's "essential character" and that this realization is a "state of happiness" (pars. 351–53). Second, we have a profound and common desire for *knowledge of truth.* This is already implicitly identified as a strong and shared desire by the Introduction, where Hegel argues that each type of consciousness which arises has a conception of truth and aspires to knowledge of truth (pars. 77, 82, 84), and that the result of the frustration of this impulse by skepticism is "despair" (par. 78).⁹ Third, we have a fundamental and common desire for *radical freedom,* that is, for the power to determine, and the actual determination of, what is the case quite generally. The *Self-consciousness* chapter undertakes to unmask this as the deeper impulse underlying our more mundane desires to effect particular changes in reality. It does so by pointing to the peculiar phenomenon that the realization of such desires never leads to lasting satisfaction but only to the emergence of new ones. If one supposed that such desires were *really* what motivated us, Hegel implies, then this phenomenon would be inexplicable, since in that case one would expect their realization to produce lasting satisfaction. If, on the other hand, such desires are merely appearances and surrogates of a deeper impulse to attain the power to determine, and actually to determine, the nature of reality generally, then the phenomenon becomes readily explicable: Realizing our mundane desires by effecting particular changes in mind-independent reality does not realize this impulse to overcome the mind-independence of reality itself, but rather, in requiring the establishment of a new mind-independent state of affairs, depends on its *non*realization. That is why it always leaves us

---

8. *Satisfaction* here, as in the most attractive form of (ii), essentially includes a cognitive component: not only is the goal of one's desire achieved, but also one *recognizes* this.
9. Cf. pars. 347, 349.

dissatisfied.[10] In accordance with this unmasking of our deep desire for radical freedom, Hegel writes in the *Reason* chapter that the satisfaction of this aspiration to radical freedom "means happiness" and that "the individual . . . , knowing that in his actual world he can find nothing else but its unity with himself, or only the certainty of himself in the truth of that world, *can experience only joy in himself*" (pars. 356, 404).

According to Hegel, it in fact turns out, for reasons which we shall consider later, that these three deepest—i.e., strongest, largely unobvious, and invariant—human aspirations, on whose satisfaction our genuine happiness mainly depends, while intensionally distinguishable, really all aim at one and the same condition.[11]

* * *

10. Desire implicitly aims at the unity of the object with itself, at "the unity of self-consciousness with itself," or "the unity of [consciousness] with [the] difference" of "otherness . . . in the form of a being" (par. 167), it implicitly aims at the negation of the object qua independent (par. 168). Desire "destroys the independent object and thereby gives itself the certainty of itself as . . . a certainty which has become explicit for self-consciousness *in an objective manner*. In this satisfaction, however, experience makes it aware that the object has its own independence. Desire and the self-certainty obtained in its gratification are conditioned by the object, for self-certainty comes from superseding this other: in order that this supersession can take place, there must be this other. Thus self-consciousness, by its negative relation to the object, is unable to supersede it; it is really because of that relation that it produces the object again, and the desire as well. It is in fact something other than self-consciousness that is the essence of desire . . . But at the same time [self-consciousness] is . . . *for itself*, and it is so only by superseding the object; and it must experience its satisfaction" (pars. 174–75).

11. The position just ascribed to the *Phenomenology* above might appear to be in sharp disagreement with Hegel's later position in the *Philosophy of Right*, where he explicitly argues that *not happiness* but rather *freedom* is the will's ultimate end (pars. 20–21), though happiness is a *part* of this ultimate end (pars. 123–24). (For a very helpful account of the *Philosophy of Right*'s position on happiness and freedom, see A.W. Wood's excellent book *Hegel's Ethical Thought* [Cambridge: Cambridge University Press, 1990], esp. pp. 53–74.) Two points about this: First, the disagreement is in reality not nearly as sharp as it may seem at first sight. For one thing, the "happiness" which the *Philosophy of Right* subordinates to our ultimate end in this way is "happiness" in senses (i) and/or (ii), *not* in sense (iii) (see pars. 20, 123)—so that this is a subordination with which the *Phenomenology* does not disagree but rather *agrees*. For another thing, the freedom which is the *Philosophy of Right*'s ultimate end is in a sense the *Phenomenology*'s too. For, it is the same sort of radical freedom, or possession of the power to determine, and actual determination of, reality generally, in which the *Phenomenology* is interested (*Philosophy of Right*, pars. 22–23, 27). And moreover, for the *Philosophy of Right*, as for the *Phenomenology*, achieving it turns out to be in some sense *the same thing* as realizing our other deep desires, for communal solidarity and knowledge of truth. Thus for the *Philosophy of Right*, too, the genuinely free will essentially achieves communal identification (pars. 24, 29) and "is . . . truth itself" (par. 23). Second, there do indeed, though, remain some genuine differences between the two works' positions–especially, that the *Phenomenology* conceives the ultimate end as "happi-

It was Hegel's firm conviction from very early in his career that the culture of modern Europe was, in contrast especially to that of ancient Greece, deeply ailing, that it doomed its participants to unhappiness. Thus already in a Tübingen essay of 1793 Hegel, after giving a glowing description of ancient Greek culture (representative terms are *enjoyment, beauty, freedom, joy, gaiety, grace, friendship, love,* and *harmony*), then proceeds to say the following of the Europe of his own day: "A different genius of the nations has the West hatched—his form is aged—beautiful he never was . . . his father is bowed—he dares not stand up straight either to look round gaily at the world nor from a sense of his own dignity—he is short-sighted and can see only little things one at a time—without courage, without confidence in his own strength, he hazards no bold throw, iron fetters raw and" (the text breaks off).[12]

Marx is in a sense right when he claims in the *Economic and Philosophic Manuscripts* that Hegel believes the sources of, and also the cure for, modern Europeans' unhappiness to lie in their *consciousness,* their *mental outlook.*[13] Already long before writing the *Phenomenology* Hegel had come to the view that one of the most distinctive and pervasive characteristics of modern Europeans' outlooks was their conception of reality in terms of sharp and fundamental *dualisms.*[14] In an essay from 1802,

---

ness" in sense (iii), whereas the *Philosophy of Right* refrains from doing so, adopting instead freedom *per se;* that the *Phenomenology* sets our deep aspiration for freedom on an equal footing with our other two deep aspirations, for communal solidarity and knowledge of truth, whereas the *Philosophy of Right* in a way elevates it above them; and that the *Phenomenology* has relatively simple and intuitive grounds for its conception of our ultimate end whereas the *Philosophy of Right* bases its conception of this on a rather elaborate and unintuitive philosophical argument (presented mainly in the work's introduction). However, it seems at least arguable that the *Phenomenology*'s position is in these respects actually more philosophically attractive than the *Philosophy of Right*'s.

12. Harris, *Hegel's Development,* pp. 506–7. This outlook of Hegel's owes something to Rousseau, still more to Herder and Schiller.

13. *Marx: Selections,* pp. 66–69, 74–76 (Marx is of course highly critical of this feature of Hegel's position). Marx is only "in a sense" right because, although Hegel's diagnosis and cure indeed look to consciousness in the first instance, Hegel is also deeply aware that the psychological ills in question have socio-economico-political causes, and that accordingly the necessary psychological cures also require appropriate socio-economico-political changes to underpin them. On this see chapter 12.

14. For helpful general discussions of this theme in Hegel, see esp. Taylor, *Hegel,* parts 1 and 2; also S.B. Smith, *Hegel's Critique of Liberalism* (Chicago: The University of Chicago Press, 1989), chap. 2. Further helpful discussions can be found in M.J. Inwood, *Hegel* (London: Routledge and Kegan Paul, 1983); R. Plant, *Hegel: An Introduction* (London: George Allen and Unwin, 1973); and M. Westphal, *History and Truth.*

for example, he refers to "the universally raging dualism in the culture of the more recent history of our Northwestern world."[15]

In the early theological writings Hegel had particularly identified eight dualisms as distinctive of and pervasive within modern European culture. Four of these had the character of dividing man from other aspects of reality, while the other four had the character, at least in part, of dividing man within himself. Among the former, the first was a sharp division between God, on the one hand, and man and nature, on the other. Hegel was inspired in his treatment of this division largely by Schiller, and in particular Schiller's poem "The Gods of Greece."[16] Hegel describes this division in detail in such early texts as *The Positivity of the Christian Religion* and *The Spirit of Christianity* (1795–1800). The ancient Greeks had conceived their gods as present and perceptible within the human and natural sphere. Thus, they had understood them to appear frequently among and to men in human shape.[17] And they had understood them to

---

15. Hegel, *Jenaer Schriften* (Frankfurt am Main: Suhrkamp, 1970), p. 184.

16. As we shall see in some detail, it was largely through Schiller's influence that the young Hegel developed his conception of modern European culture as distinctively and pathologically dualistic. Schiller's influence on the young Hegel was in general extremely strong. Thus, Hegel praised Schiller's *On the Aesthetic Education of Man* in 1795, the year of its first publication, as "a masterpiece" (*Briefe von und an Hegel* 1:25). And another symptom of Schiller's strong influence on the young Hegel is the fact that much of the latter's philosophical terminology and usage visibly comes from Schiller (in some cases, certainly, among others). Schiller's two essays *On the Aesthetic Education of Man* and *On Naive and Sentimental Poetry* were particularly rich sources in this respect. A few examples of Hegelian terminology already found in these essays in strikingly Hegelian usages: *aufheben* (in the paradoxical double sense of both abolishing and preserving), *Bildung/Kultur* (in the sense of a cultural development accentuating dualisms, and so having ambivalent value), *positiv* (of morality based on divine commands), also *das Absolute, räsonieren/Räsonement, reflektieren/Reflexion, das Unendliche, die Vernunft, der Verstand*.

17. As Hegel puts it in one early fragment, "In ancient times the gods moved among men" (*Hegels theologische Jugendschriften,* ed. H. Nohl [Tübingen: J.C.B. Mohr, 1907], p. 376). This is, of course, an accurate report of Greek conceptions—as can be illustrated both from literary examples, such as Athena's appearance to Achilles during his quarrel with Agamemnon at the beginning of the *Iliad,* or to Odysseus among the Phaeacians in the *Odyssey,* and from historical times, as in Herodotus's story of her appearance to the Greeks at Salamis. Besides certainly thinking of such uncontroversial examples, Hegel also tends to give more controversial ones. For instance, he suggests that in "the pictures, feelings, inspiration, and devotion of Eleusis" the Greeks saw "revelations of god" (Hegel, *Early Theological Writings*, trans. T.M. Knox [Philadelphia: University of Pennsylvania Press, 1981], p. 193; cf. Hegel's 1796 poem "Eleusis," in *Dokumente zu Hegels Entwicklung,* ed. J. Hoffmeister [Stuttgart: Frommanns Verlag, 1936], esp. p. 382). And he implies that the Greeks regarded their statues of the gods as somehow identical with the

be in other cases more or less strictly identical with perceptible natural objects (*Gē* was the earth, *Hēlios* the sun, *Ēōs* the dawn, *Skamandros* a river, and so forth).[18] Moreover, the ancient Greeks had conceived their gods as relatively similar in nature to men—in particular, as susceptible to similar shortcomings, such as moral failings, factual errors and ignorance, and insufficient power to attain their ends.[19] Connectedly, for the ancient Greeks understanding and knowing about the gods had not been especially problematic; the gods were epistemically accessible.[20] By contrast, the Judeo-Christian tradition had established a great rift dividing its single God from man and nature: This tradition had reconceived God as quite removed from the human and natural sphere, and as imperceptible (at least to sight and touch).[21] Moreover, it had reconceived him as

---

gods themselves: "In an Apollo or Venus we must forget the marble, the breakable stone, and see in its shape the immortal only" (*Early Theological Writings*, p. 252; I shall return to this claim later). For the general point, cf. Schiller, "Die Götter Griechenlands," in J.C.F. Schiller, *Sämtliche Werke* (Leipzig: Tempel Verlag, 1911–12), 1:168–69, where the theme of the gods appearing among and to human beings for the Greeks, and having intercourse with them—social and especially sexual—is prominent.

18. Schiller had expressed this point forcefully in "Die Götter Griechenlands": "Everything revealed to initiated eyes, / everything, the trace of a god. / Where now, as our wisemen tell us, only / a ball of fire turns soullessly, / Helios then steered his golden car in silent majesty. / Oreads filled these peaks, / a Dryad died with that tree, / from the vessels of lovely Naiads / sprang forth streams' silvery foam" (*Sämtliche Werke* 1:167).

19. For the ancient Greek or Roman, his gods "too were individual, incomplete beings ... Greeks and Romans were satisfied with gods ... poorly equipped, with gods possessing the weaknesses of human beings" (*The Positivity of the Christian Religion*, in appendix 1; cf. Hegel's *Lectures on the Philosophy of Religion*, trans. E.B. Speirs and J.B. Sanderson [London: Routledge and Kegan Paul, 1974], 2:257). Cf. Schiller, "Die Götter Griechenlands," *Sämtliche Werke* 1:172: "The citizens of Olympus I could reach, / the god whom his sculpture praises / the lofty sculptor could formerly resemble," "the gods were still more human."

20. As Hegel would put this point later at *Lectures on the Philosophy of Religion* 2:257–58: "In this religion there is nothing incomprehensible, nothing which cannot be understood; there is no kind of content in the god which is not known to man."

21. "In ancient times the gods moved among men; the more separation grew, removal, the more the gods too took their leave of men" (*Hegels theologische Jugendschriften*, pp. 376–77); "Your halls have fallen silent, O Goddess! / The circle of the gods has fled from the consecrated altars back to Olympus" ("Eleusis," in *Dokumente zu Hegels Entwicklung*, p. 381). For the Jews, from the time of Abraham on, "God ... was alien to [the whole world]. Nothing in nature was supposed to have any part in God," and "the infinite subject [God] had to be invisible ... An image of God was just stone or wood to them ... [T]here was no concrete shape to be an object of religious feeling ... The holy was always outside [their objects and actions], unseen and unfelt" (*Early Theological Writings*, pp. 187, 191–93). Similarly, in early Christianity God "was put into another world in whose confines we had no part," leaving "the modifications of nature, the relationships of life," as "mundane

quite unlike, and as infinitely superior to, human beings—particularly in virtue of such qualities as moral perfection, omniscience, and omnipotence.[22] And connectedly, it had reconceived him as beyond the power of human comprehension and knowledge; he was now epistemically inaccessible.[23] In these several ways, then, the Judeo-Christian tradition had produced a great division between God, on the one hand, and man and nature, on the other.[24] (One of Hegel's central preoccupations in the early theological writings was the search for an explanation of *why* Greek and

---

realities" for the early Christians as they had already been for the Jews (ibid., pp. 163, 288); and although early Christianity attempted to make the divine appear and become visible through the image of the risen Jesus, this attempt ultimately failed, because it left a mere juxtaposition of the divine and its putative appearance in the natural realm rather than their genuine union (ibid., pp. 291–92, 300). (Hegel is aware of exceptions to the general rule, such as the story of God's appearance to Moses on Mount Sinai [ibid., p. 150 n.].) Cf. Schiller, "Die Götter Griechenlands": the Christian God holds back from intercourse with men, one searches for him "fruitlessly in the world of the senses," now "no deity reveals himself to my view," and nature is a "nature robbed of gods [entgötterte Natur]" (*Sämtliche Werke* 1:169, 171–72).

22. For the Jews, there are "two natures of different kinds, a human nature and a divine one, a human essence and a divine one . . . both remaining two because they are posited as absolutely different" (*Early Theological Writings*, p. 264), "the infinite object [God] is everything, . . . man is nothing" (unpublished note on Judaism, in Harris, *Hegel's Development*, p. 300). Cf. Schiller, "Die Götter Griechenlands": "The citizens of Olympus I could reach, / the god whom his sculpture praises / the lofty sculptor could formerly resemble. / What beside you [God] is the highest spirit / of those who were born to mortals? / Only the first and noblest among worms. / When the gods were still more human / men were more godlike" (*Sämtliche Werke* 1:172).

23. Schiller had already stressed this in "Die Götter Griechenlands": "Does my [creator] reveal his name to the understanding? / . . . With difficulty do I spy [him] out in the ideal world, / fruitlessly in the world of the senses" (ibid., p. 169).

24. There is, of course, a temptation when confronted with claims like the above about "the ancient Greeks" or "the Judeo-Christian tradition" to object indignantly along such lines as, "Which Greeks? Did Anaxagoras, for example, conceive of the sun as a god? Was Greek religion really so monolithic? What about Orphism, for example? etc." For an objection of this sort, see for instance Plant, *Hegel: An Introduction*, p. 37 n.8. As often, Hegel is already a couple of steps ahead of such objections, however. His conscious purpose is to capture the *dominant* position in a culture or period, not the chimera of a position held in it *exceptionlessly*. Hence, for example, in the Berne fragments he notes the possibility of an objection of just this sort against his characterization of Christianity, and responds that it is not his aim to give an account which applies to every single strand and instance of the religion, but rather one which applies to its culturally dominant form, "the line generally taken on the pulpit and in the schools" (Hegel, *Three Essays 1793–95*, trans. P. Fuss and J. Dobbins [Notre Dame: University of Notre Dame Press, 1984], pp. 92–93). In adopting this historical methodology, Hegel is in agreement with, and in all probability following, Herder; see, for example, the latter's *Auch eine Philosophie der Geschichte zur Bildung der Menschheit*, in *Herders Ausgewählte Werke* (Leipzig: Reclam, 1881), 2:640–42.

Roman polytheism had been supplanted by Judeo-Christian religion in the West. The explanation at which he arrived by the time of *The Positivity of the Christian Religion* was strikingly proto-Nietzschean.²⁵ Its essence was that later periods of Greek and Roman history had seen the development of widespread economic, social, and political oppression within Greek and Roman society, and that Judeo-Christian religion corresponded to the wants and habits of oppressed people in ways that polytheism did not. It did so, in particular, by [i] answering with its thesis of a perfect divine realm sharply separate from the secular realm oppressed people's yearnings for a sphere of freedom from the oppression and misery of the latter; [ii] offering promises of rich rewards for the virtuous in an otherworldly afterlife, which corresponded to oppressed people's yearnings for consolation for their earthly miseries; [iii] offering promises of punishment for the wicked in an otherworldly afterlife, which corresponded to oppressed people's yearnings that their oppressors be punished; [iv] introducing a divine-command—or in Hegel's terminology, a *positive*—conception of the nature of morality, which corresponded to oppressed people's habits of slavish obedience; [v] introducing a battery of desire-opposing moral prescriptions, which again corresponded to oppressed people's habits of slavish obedience; and [vi] introducing other moral prescriptions which sanctified and rationalized the fearful impotence of oppressed people, for example, "Blessed are the peacemakers."²⁶ Thus in addition to the above critical characterization of the intellectual consequences of Judeo-Christian religion's ascent over polytheism in the West, the early Hegel also offered this critical explanation of its ascent.²⁷)

---

25. J.G. Gray rightly notes the proto-Nietzscheanism of this text in his *Hegel's Hellenic Ideal*, in *The Philosophy of Hegel*, ed. H.S. Harris (New York: Garland, 1984), pp. 31–33.

26. For (i), (ii), (iv), (v), and (vi), see the extract from *The Positivity of the Christian Religion* in appendix I; also *Three Essays 1793–95*, pp. 101–2. For (iii), see *Hegels theologische Jugendschriften*, pp. 364–65. The *Self-consciousness* chapter of the *Phenomenology* retains a faded version of the same explanation, in the form of its (indirect) transition from slavery and oppression in the *Lordship and Bondage* section to Christianity in the *Unhappy Consciousness* section.

27. Note that the early Hegel's critical characterization and explanation of Christianity concerns orthodox Christianity as *contrasted*, not *identified*, with the viewpoint of Jesus himself. Throughout the sometimes dramatic changes in Hegel's position which occur during the course of the early writings—for example, the shift from the Kantianism of *The Life of Jesus* and *The Positivity of the Christian Religion* to the anti-Kantianism of *The Spirit of Christianity*—one thing remains constant: his insistence on a sharp distinction between the views of the Christian tradition and those of Jesus himself, and estimation of

A second dualism, intimately connected with the first, was a sharp distinction between man and nature. In ancient polytheism virtually all of nature was conceived as permeated by personality and purpose, namely, the personalities and purposes of polytheism's gods. Consequently, nature was conceived as fundamentally like man. For us moderns, by contrast, nature is, to use a vivid term of Weber's, "disenchanted [entzaubert]"—it is no longer generally personal or purposive. Schiller had made this point forcefully in "The Gods of Greece":

> No deity reveals himself to my view,
> ah! of that image warm with life
> was left me only the skeleton . . .
> Unconscious of the joys which she grants,
> never delighted at her splendour,
> never sensible to the arm that steers her,
> never richer by my gratitude . . . ,
> like the dead stroke of the pendulum clock,
> she slavishly obeys the law of gravity,
> this nature robbed of gods [entgötterte Natur].[28]

Hegel makes the same point, more prosaically, in *The Spirit of Christianity:* our "European intellectualism . . . extracts all spirit from the contents of consciousness and crystallizes the latter into absolute objectivities, into realities downright opposed to spirit"; whereas the Greeks conceived "the modifications of nature" as "relationships of life," our tradition has "objectified" this life, turning it into an "object, . . . a cut-and-dried fact," it has "crystallized the modifications of nature, the relationships of life, into mundane realities."[29] (Schiller and Hegel both offer the same explanation of how this development came about. In their view, the *crucial* step was not, as one might suppose, the discrediting of Aristotelian science and its displacement by mechanistic science at the beginning of the seven-

---

the former as misguided and pathological, but the latter as essentially correct and salutary. Herder, whose attitude toward the Christian tradition and Jesus was sharply bifurcated in a similar way, may have been an important influence here (see esp. *Ideen zur Philosophie der Geschichte der Menschheit,* in *Herders Werke* [Leipzig and Vienna: Bibliographisches Institut, 187–], vol. 3, bks. 17, 19).

28. *Sämtliche Werke* 1:171–72.
29. *Early Theological Writings,* pp. 300, 288.

teenth century—Bacon, Galileo, Descartes, et al.³⁰ Rather, it was the displacement of nature-immanent polytheism by the nature-transcendent monotheism of the Judeo-Christian tradition which occurred much earlier in the ancient world. Thus, in "The Gods of Greece" Schiller offers the following explanation of why polytheism's god-infused nature has become disenchanted for us in the manner described above: "To enrich *one* among all [i.e., the single God of Judeo-Christian religion], / this world of gods had to disappear."³¹ Similarly, Hegel argues in *The Spirit of Christianity* that "the Jewish spirit had crystallized the modifications of nature, the relationships of life, into mundane realities . . . The spirit of the Christian communion likewise saw mundane realities in every relationship of self-developing and self-revealing life."³²)

A third dualism dividing man from other aspects of reality which Hegel emphasized in the early theological writings concerned the relation between the individual and his community. In *The Positivity of the Christian Religion* Hegel argues that the early Greek (and Roman) intimately identified himself with his community in two important ways: First, he regarded the community as his highest end: "The idea of his fatherland, of his state, was the invisible thing, the higher thing, for which he worked, which motivated him, this was the final purpose of the world for him, or the final purpose of his world . . . Before this idea his individuality

---

30. Pace Plant, *Hegel: An Introduction,* pp. 37–38, 106.
31. *Sämtliche Werke* 1:171.
32. *Early Theological Writings,* p. 288. Taylor, in his excellent book *Hegel*, recognizes that Hegel attributes disenchantment in the first instance to Judaism, but argues that this is historically wrong (p. 58). For Taylor, the process has much more recent roots in Calvinism (pp. 9, 58) and especially the scientific revolution of the early seventeenth century (pp. 4 ff.). It seems to me that Hegel and Schiller are right here and Taylor mistaken, that the roots of disenchantment *do* lie in Judeo-Christian nature-transcendent monotheism's displacement of nature-immanent polytheism and the immediately consequent leaching out from nature of the personality with which the latter had infused it. It is true that this did not lead immediately to the wholly mechanistic conception of inanimate (and even animate) nature which has emerged since the seventeenth century. The main reason for this was that a resilient compromise position was found, which, while dispensing with nature's full personality, and thereby satisfying the theological demands of Judeo-Christian nature-transcendent monotheism, nevertheless retained the ascription of certain paradigmatically personal traits to nature, in particular purposes. This compromise position was, of course, Aristotelianism. It was indeed the scientific revolution of the early seventeenth century which discredited this compromise position, and thereby ushered in modernity's wholly mechanistic conception of nature. However, in doing so it rather completed a process of disenchantment begun long ago by Judeo-Christian religion than began that process.

vanished, he demanded preservation, life, and endurance only for it."³³ (One thinks here, for example, of the conception of the citizen as an *erastēs* of his *polis* in Pericles' Funeral Speech as reported by Thucydides, or of Herodotus's story that Solon characterized Tellus as the happiest of men because his city was prosperous and he died successfully defending it.) Second, he automatically accepted the community's shared judgments, especially on moral matters: "As free men the Greeks . . . obeyed laws laid down by themselves," and even in the case of those few moral injunctions which they ascribed to the gods rather than directly to the community, "if it had been possible for the question to occur to one of them by what means he proposed to prove the divinity of a command or prohibition, he could have cited no historical fact, but only the feeling of his heart and the agreement of all good men."³⁴ (One thinks here, for example, of Sophocles' *Antigone* and Oedipus cycle more generally, where the theme of the authority of the community's judgments, especially on moral matters, is pervasive, communal opinion being appealed to as an authority not only by Creon in support of explicitly secular laws but also by Antigone and Haemon in support of divine laws.) These two

---

33. *The Positivity of the Christian Religion,* in appendix I.

34. Ibid. Hegel maintains, with historical plausibility, that traditional Greek morality usually did *not* conceive its injunctions as divinely commanded, but rather as directly communal: "The Greeks had their religious sagas almost exclusively for the purpose of having gods to whom they could devote their gratitude, build altars, and offer sacrifices. Our sacred history, on the other hand, is supposed to have many uses; we are supposed to learn and derive from it all sorts of moral truths . . . As free men the Greeks and Romans obeyed laws laid down by themselves . . . In public as in private and domestic life, every individual was a free man, one who lived by his own laws . . . His will was free and obeyed its own laws; he knew no divine commands . . . [Unlike Christians] they were quite unfamiliar with finding in the god what man's duty was" (*Early Theological Writings,* pp. 151–57).

As can be seen from this quotation, however, Hegel also implies at points in this early work, inconsistently with the second of the two passages quoted above, and without historical plausibility, that the Greeks ascribed *no* moral injunctions to the gods at all, that moreover they ascribed them all to themselves *explicitly*, and also that they did so in an *individualistic* spirit. The *Phenomenology* will unequivocally retract these problematic further implications. (For its retraction of the former two, see esp. its treatment of Antigone's "divine law" in the *Spirit* chapter; for its retraction of the third, see esp. par. 355.) This revision in fact has several advantages: besides making the *Phenomenology*'s position internally consistent and more plausible as history, it also gains Hegel the important systematic benefit of leaving the *modern* ethical community with something unequivocally *new* to accomplish, namely, a morality which really *is* wholly free of divine commands, quite explicitly human in origin, and inclusive of a measure of individualism. (For these traits of the *Phenomenology*'s modern ethical community, see esp. pars. 351–52, 436.)

forms of close identification with the community both soon disappeared, however, leaving instead a rift in the individual's mind between himself and his community. Thus, contrary to the first, in the later Greek and Roman world, "all activity, all purposes related now to what was individual, there was no longer any activity for a whole—each person either worked for himself or, through compulsion, for another individual."[35] And, contrary to the second, with the advent of Christianity in the later Greek and Roman world, "the right of legislation [was] conceded to God exclusively," and so taken away from the community.[36] (In *The Positivity of the Christian Religion* Hegel explains both of these developments in terms of the widespread loss of socio-economico-political freedom which, he claims, occurred in later periods of Greek and Roman history. By depriving the individual of the role of free participant in his political community, this undercut his commitment to the community as his end, leading him to reinvest his concern in private ends instead. Moreover, it diminished his respect for the community as an authority in [moral] judgment, and led, in a way described earlier, to the ascent of Christianity, and thereby to the displacement of authority in [moral] judgment away from the community to God.[37])

A fourth dualism touched on in the early theological writings concerned the relation between the self and its thought, on the one hand, and reality (or the rest of reality), on the other. In *The Spirit of Christianity* Hegel implies that the ancient Greeks and the first Christians did not draw a sharp distinction between these spheres, as we moderns do. He writes, for example, that "the apostles lack the European intellectualism which extracts all spirit from the contents of consciousness and crystallizes the latter into absolute objectivities, into realities downright opposed to spirit. Their cognition is more like a vague hovering between reality and spirit."[38] By contrast, modern man—for the early Hegel a para-

---

35. *The Positivity of the Christian Religion*, in appendix I. On the subsequent continuation of this attitude in the modern world, see *Three Essays 1793–95*, p. 101.

36. *The Positivity of the Christian Religion*, in appendix I. There thus arose our sharp modern distinction between socially based custom or law, on the one hand, and a private morality which we deem higher, on the other—a distinction which preoccupies the young Hegel especially in the 1802–3 essay *Natural Law*, trans. T.M. Knox (Philadelphia: University of Pennsylvania Press, 1975).

37. Both parts of this explanation can be found in appendix I.

38. *Early Theological Writings*, p. 300. Hegel sees this attitude of the apostles as manifested above all in their belief in miracles (ibid., pp. 296–300). But he implies the qualification that in the case of the apostles the "hovering" between the self and its thought, on

digmatic example is Fichte—conceives himself and his thought, on the one hand, and reality, on the other, as sharply distinct from one another, "setting [himself] as pure I over the ruins of this body and the shining suns, over the million heavenly bodies and the new solar systems," "as an independent unity for whom everything else is a world external to him."[39]

Besides these four dualisms dividing man from other aspects of reality, the early Hegel also identified as distinctive of modern culture four dualisms which, at least in part, divide man *within himself*.[40] Thus, he argued that, in contrast to early man, modern man is beset by this fifth dualism, or pair of dualisms: modern man distinguishes sharply between facts and human volitions (another dualism dividing the self from reality), and in consequence also conceives himself as sharply divided between a theoretical or fact-discerning side and a practical or volitional side (a first self-internal dualism).[41] Hegel is not entirely clear at this stage of his career

---

the one hand, and reality, on the other, takes the form less of a genuine fusion of the two than of a contradictory vacillation between their fusion and their sharp distinction (ibid., p. 300). In the case of the early Greeks, by contrast, "the two sides coalesce into a pure nature" (ibid., p. 300, read in light of p. 298).

39. From the *Fragment of a System*, in appendix II; and the essay *Love*, in *Early Theological Writings*, p. 303. Cf. Hegel's characterization of the modern viewpoint in the early fragment *Faith and Being* as one for which "what is thought about is something separated, opposed to the thinker" (*Hegels theologische Jugendschriften*, p. 383).

40. The theme of a contrast between early man's (salutary) psychic unity and modern man's (harmful) psychic dividedness was prominent before Hegel in both Herder and Schiller (see esp. Herder, *Vom Erkennen und Empfinden der menschlichen Seele*, in *Herders Ausgewählte Werke*, vol. 3; Schiller, *On the Aesthetic Education of Man*, trans. E.M. Wilkinson and L.A. Willoughby [Oxford: Oxford University Press, 1982]). For all three authors the early condition of (salutary) psychic unity is paradigmatically exemplified by the Greeks (see Herder, ibid., p. 734; Schiller, ibid., pp. 31-33).

Herder and Schiller—but not, as far as I can see, Hegel—offer the same general explanation of why this development has occurred: unlike our ancient counterparts, we moderns experience psychic division, and consequently also reflect this in our psychological theories about ourselves, because, whereas our ancient counterparts were required by their societies to be well-rounded in activities and abilities, and so each developed their mental faculties in harmonious proportion, our society on the contrary requires of us an extreme *division of labor*, so that each of us develops within himself in an exaggerated fashion only some one aspect (or few aspects) of the mind, leaving the rest undeveloped (or underdeveloped) (Herder, ibid., pp. 734-35; Schiller, ibid., pp. 31-39).

41. Hegel's major forerunner in this thought was Herder. Herder argues that in the experience and theory of earlier peoples such as the ancient Greeks the cognitive and the volitional or affective sides of man were not sharply distinguished (*Herders Ausgewählte Werke*, 3:734; cf. 640-42, 670), and that this is the wholesome and correct condition and view to have (pp. 709-10, 724-25), but that modern man on the contrary experiences and

about how exactly early man lacked these dualisms. However, he apparently means to suggest that the ancient Greeks' ways of thinking about their religious art-objects and myths, and the Jews' and early Christians' ways of thinking about their myths and miracles, reveal that for these peoples the distinction between facts and their own volitions, and consequently between their own theoretical and practical sides, was less sharp than it is for us moderns. Thus, in one passage he implies that the Greeks somehow conceived the sculptures of the gods formed by the creative volitions of their sculptors as identical with the gods themselves: "In an Apollo or Venus we must forget the marble, the breakable stone, and see in its shape the immortal only . . . But grind the Apollo or Venus to dust and say '*This* is Apollo, *this* Venus,' and then the dust confronts you and the images of the immortals are in you, but the dust and the divine never coalesce into one."[42] Again, in the following passage, which we have already encountered, Hegel seems to imply that for the Greeks religious facts such as the divine origin of a moral injunction were not sharply distinct from their own feelings: "If it had been possible for the question to occur to one of them by what means he proposed to prove the divinity of a command or prohibition, he could have cited no historical fact, but only the feeling of his heart and the agreement of all good men." Similarly, Hegel says that for the Jews history and God's commands "had truth and spirit, but only *their* truth and *their* spirit; they did not let it

---

conceives them as sharply distinct (pp. 734–35). Schiller too implies at points that cognition and volition or affects were not sharply distinct for the ancient Greeks (*On the Aesthetic Education of Man*, pp. 31–33), that this is the correct and wholesome condition and view to have (pp. 187–89), and that modern man by contrast experiences and conceives them as sharply distinct (pp. 31–33). However, Schiller is less explicit and emphatic about this than Herder, and much more wedded to ideas which cut against it in various ways (such as a typical Enlightenment insistence on sharply distinguishing true cognition from wishful thinking and fiction [pp. 51, 193–99]).

42. *Early Theological Writings*, p. 252. Hegel's suggestion, though controversial, may well be defensible. Consider, for example, Orestes' remark in Aeschylus's *Libation Bearers*, made with a gesture at a statue of the god Hermes, "I call on this fellow [*toutōi*] to watch over things here, directing aright for me my sword-bearing combats" (ll. 583–84, interpreted in agreement with A.F. Garvie); and also a very similar passage in Aristophanes' *Clouds* (ll. 1478–85). One *might*, of course, construe such passages as these, implying a god's identity with his statue, as meant in some nonliteral way (e.g., as analogous to someone today pointing to a picture of Stalin and saying, "This fellow caused the Russians many woes"). However, there is no evidence in the texts supporting such an interpretation. Nor does the obvious fact that there were multiple statues of each god in different locations refute a literalist interpretation—for the Greeks, notoriously, found multiple localizations of a single god unproblematic.

become objective . . . There is a . . . formless hovering between reality and spirit."[43] And in explanation of the early Christians' susceptibility to belief in miracles, he notes that, in contrast with us moderns, "they regarded fewer things as objects and so handed fewer things over to intellectual treatment . . . While we set to work solely with the intellect and see in another person just a factual entity, the early Christians mingled their spirit with his . . . The apostles lack the European intellectualism which extracts all spirit from the contents of consciousness and crystallizes the latter into absolute objectivities, into realities downright opposed to spirit. Their cognition is more like a vague hovering between reality and spirit."[44] (As *we moderns* might put it, for these peoples wishful thinking was the norm rather than the exception.) By contrast, as one can see from the passage just quoted, Hegel thinks that we moderns distinguish sharply between facts and human volitions, and hence also between our theoretical or fact-discerning and our practical or volitional sides. For the early Hegel, a paradigmatic example of the resulting dualistic self-conception is Kant's philosophy, with its sharp distinction between theoretical and practical reason, reflected in its division of philosophical disciplines. The early Hegel, in the essay *Natural Law* from 1802–3 for example, also interprets Fichte as a modern philosopher who is entangled in, and striving unsuccessfully to overcome, this pair of dualisms. Fichte's attempt to overcome them lies in the circumstance that his system makes the *self's act* of self-positing the basis of all fact, and thence of all theoretical representation of fact as well, and moreover explains factuality in terms of its being required in order to give the *self* a sphere for *practical* or moral *activity*. His failure lies in the circumstance that in his system factuality, or the object, is posited by the self in *opposition* to itself and *stays* in opposition to itself, and, worse still, *has* to do so in order to provide the self with a sphere for practical activity.[45]

A sixth distinctive modern dualism to which the early Hegel devoted much attention had again preoccupied Schiller before him: the constant, sharp opposition encountered by modern men—both at the affective level of their practical experience and in their more theoretical understanding

---

43. *Early Theological Writings*, p. 298.
44. Ibid., pp. 297–300.
45. This is the force of Hegel's comment that for Fichte, "although the ideal and the real are identical . . . , the real remains flatly opposed [to the ideal]. This real is essentially posited outside reason, and practical reason resides only in its difference from it" (*Natural Law*, p. 72).

of that experience—between *duty,* on the one hand, and *desire* or inclination, on the other.[46] Morally conscientious ancient Greeks and Romans had, the early Hegel believed, *not* felt a constant, sharp opposition between duty and desire at the affective level of their practical experience.[47] And they had standardly conceived duty and desire as quite of a piece in theory as well—dutiful behavior just *was,* for them, behavior motivated by desires of certain specific sorts.[48] By contrast, modern men both af-

---

46. For this theme in Schiller, see esp. *On the Aesthetic Education of Man,* letters 4 and 6.

47. The theme of the harmony experienced by the Greeks between their morality, on the one hand, and their desires, on the other—in contrast to the disharmony and opposition between these experienced by modern men—is already found in the Tübingen essay of 1793 (Harris, *Hegel's Development,* pp. 505–7). In *The Positivity of the Christian Religion* Hegel remarks, similarly: "As free people [the Greeks and Romans] obeyed laws which they had given themselves, . . . they . . . practised in actions maxims of virtue which they could call completely their own, in public as in private and domestic life each was a free man, each lived in accordance with his own laws" (in appendix I).

Hegel's idea here might seem historically fanciful, but I do not believe that it is. Two points are worth noting in its support, the first defensive, the second more positive. First, this idea is likely to appear dubious particularly because of the prevalence of inner conflict as a theme in ancient tragedy and comedy. Are not Aeschylus's Agamemnon and Orestes inwardly torn when they kill Iphigenia and Clytaemestra? Is not comedy full of characters like Aristophanes' Strepsiades, torn away from duty by their baser desires? Such evidence does not really speak against Hegel's claim, however. The tragic examples do not for two reasons: first, they do not represent normal situations but highly abnormal ones, and second, they concern in the first instance not conflicts between duty and desire (which would be inconsistent with the tragic hero's virtue, and hence with his tragic status) but between duty *and duty* (Agamemnon's duty as father versus his duty as head of state, Orestes' filial duty to his slain father versus his filial duty to his mother). The comic examples likewise fail to tell against Hegel's idea for two reasons: first, they do not concern morally conscientious or virtuous individuals (it being comedy's primary function to lampoon vice), and second, the disposition to vice represented is indeed usually so extreme that there is little or no inner conflict with duty involved, base desires rather holding a virtual monopoly over the individual.

Second, more positively, and more importantly, note that a broad range of very strong human desires common to ancient and modern men alike are sharply opposed by the moral values of the Judeo-Christian tradition which dominates modernity but were in contrast *approved* (or at the very least accepted) by the Homeric value system which dominated ancient Greece and Rome. Examples are: desire for revenge when injured, desire for power, desire to exercise physical aggression, desire for wealth, desire for glorious public reputation, desire to attain one's ends by dishonesty (recall Odysseus the *polytropos*), desire for promiscuous sex.

48. For the ancient Greeks and Romans, "people's will was free, obeyed its own laws, they knew no divine commandments," and the few which they did know derived their authority for an individual not from the historical fact of their having been commanded but from "the feeling of his heart and the agreement of all good men" (*The Positivity of the Christian Religion,* in appendix I). Again, Hegel's idea here might appear historically

fectively experience and theoretically conceive duty as sharply opposed to desires. At the affective level, the feeling of a sharp opposition between duty and desire is a constant feature of modern life. From the time of the Tübingen essay of 1793 at latest, Hegel saw this as true of moral experience within modern Christianity.[49] And by the time he wrote *The Spirit of Christianity*, he saw it as equally characteristic of moral experience within his age's great alternative to orthodox Christianity, Kantianism, as well. Thus he notes in this work, with good textual grounds, that Kant is unable even to *conceive* of a duty not in opposition to desires: for Kant "an 'ideal' in which duties are represented as willingly done is self-contradictory, since duties require an opposition."[50] At a more theoretical level, modern men conceive action from duty and action from desire as quite different in *kind*. Thus, as the young Hegel early and often emphasized, modern Christianity interprets dutifulness not as motivation by desires of certain sorts but as *obedience to divine commands*. This "positive" conception of morality is the central topic of such early works as *The Positivity of the Christian Religion* and *The Spirit of Christianity*.[51] And by the time Hegel wrote the latter work, he was concerned to emphasize that a sharp theoretical distinction between action from duty and action from desire was equally typical of Kantianism as well. For Kantianism of course distinguishes sharply between acting out of respect for the moral law and acting from desire or inclination, assigning moral worth to the former only, to the complete exclusion of the latter. (The early theological writings offer, in addition, an interesting *explanation*

---

implausible at first sight. It will do so especially if one's first thought is of Plato, for whom moral motivation was rational in nature and as such sharply distinct from and opposed to motivation by desires. However, Platonism was very much a minority position even within Greek philosophy, let alone Greek culture generally. And according to a more standard Greek view, represented for example by Protagoras and Aristotle, being moral was indeed essentially a matter of being disposed to act from certain sorts of desires or inclinations (as the result of an appropriate upbringing).

49. See the Tübingen essay, in Harris, *Hegel's Development*, pp. 505–7; cf. *Early Theological Writings*, pp. 139–42.

50. *Early Theological Writings*, p. 213. For the sound textual basis of Hegel's point, see, for example, Kant, *Groundwork of the Metaphysics of Morals*, in *The Moral Law*, trans. H.J. Paton (London: Hutchinson, 1956), p. 62: "The concept of duty . . . includes that of a good will, exposed, however, to certain subjective limitations and obstacles." In Kant the constant modern experience of duty-desire opposition has, so to speak, set into conceptual concrete.

51. Schiller had characterized the Christian conception of morality similarly, likewise employing the term "positive" (*On the Aesthetic Education of Man*, p. 179).

of this whole shift in moral outlook. The explanation lies primarily, according to the early Hegel, in the origins of the Judeo-Christian tradition. For it was ancient Judaism, and following it early Christianity, that introduced the experience at an affective level of duty as sharply opposed to desires.[52] And it was also they that, at the more theoretical level, introduced the interpretation of dutifulness as, not motivation by certain sorts of desires, but obedience to divine commands.[53] According to Hegel, the ancient Jews' and early Christians' affective and theoretical experience of a sharp opposition between duty and desire was explicable as the result of the slavery and other forms of social oppression to which their secular lives had subjected them, and their consequent mental habits of servitude, in particular suppression of their own desires and submission to others' commands. Thus, concerning the ancient Jews, he writes that Moses as the "liberator of his nation [i.e., from slavery in Egypt] was also its lawgiver; this could mean only that the man who had freed it from one yoke had laid on it another. A passive people giving laws to itself would be a self-contradiction."[54] And similarly, he explains the early Christians' receptivity to Judaism's way of feeling and conceiving morality in terms of the socio-economico-political oppression of large segments of the population in the later Greek and especially Roman worlds.[55] It was, ac-

---

52. The ancient Jews experienced moral obligation as a "yoke," "a direct slavery, an obedience without joy, without pleasure or love" (*Early Theological Writings*, pp. 191, 206). Christianity then inherited this experience (pp. 139–42).

53. This is a dominant and pervasive theme in *The Positivity of the Christian Religion* and *The Spirit of Christianity*.

54. *The Spirit of Christianity*, in *Early Theological Writings*, p. 191; cf. 190–99.

55. This explanation is a central theme in the extract from *The Positivity of the Christian Religion* in appendix I.

In thus undertaking to explain the distinctive character of Judeo-Christian morality in terms of slavery and other forms of social oppression in the ancient world, Hegel's account is strikingly Nietzschean in spirit.

It is also worth noting some differences, however: First, Hegel focuses far more than Nietzsche does on explaining the divine-command *form* of Judeo-Christian morality, its "positivity," in such terms. Nietzsche, on the other hand, focuses far more than Hegel does on explaining the prescriptive *content* of Judeo-Christian morality in such terms. The two accounts thus complement each other in a very striking and interesting way.

Second, and connectedly, Nietzsche includes in his explanation of the prescriptive content of Judeo-Christian morality a brilliant (but still not well appreciated) historical thesis which is quite absent from Hegel's account, namely, the thesis that this content can largely be understood as a systematic inversion of standing Greek and Roman valuations, originally motivated by the resentment [*ressentiment*] of people oppressed by the Greeks and Romans, in particular the Jews of Palestine. To give a very brief idea of the deep evidential basis of this thesis: (i) Whereas Homer and the dominant Greek and Roman ethical tradition contin-

cording to Hegel, ultimately this historical development that had led to the modern world's affective and theoretical experience of duty as sharply opposed to desire. This was true not only of the form of this opposition found in modern Christianity [where the causal continuity is obvious], but also of the form of it found in Kantianism [where it is somewhat less so]. Thus in answer to Kant, who had argued that there was no great difference between the man who obeyed secular authorities and the man who obeyed divine commands, but a tremendous difference between either of these and the man who acted out of respect for the moral law

---

uous with him praised the man who was physically assertive and courageous, and despised the man who lacked these traits, for the New Testament, "Blessed are the peacemakers," "Blessed are the poor in spirit . . . Blessed are the meek" (Matt. 5:9, 3–5). Whereas Homer and the dominant Greek and Roman ethical tradition praised the man who had political power and success, and despised the man who lacked them, for the New Testament, "Whosoever exalteth himself shall be abased; and he that humbleth himself shall be exalted," "The kings of the gentiles exercise lordship over them; and they that exercise authority over them are called doers of good [*euergetai*]. But ye shall not be so; but he that is greatest among you, let him be as the younger; and he that is chief, as he that does serve" (Luke 14:11, 22:25–26). Whereas Homer and the dominant Greek and Roman ethical tradition praised wealth and freedom from want, and despised the opposite qualities, for the New Testament, "Blessed be ye poor . . . Blessed are ye that hunger . . . Woe unto you that are rich! . . . Woe unto you that are full!" (Luke 6:20–25). Whereas Homer and the dominant Greek and Roman ethical tradition praised the man who took revenge when injured, as for example when Odysseus took revenge on the suitors, and despised the man who failed to do so, the New Testament enjoins, "Love your enemies, do good to them which hate you. Bless them that curse you, and pray for them that despitefully use you. And unto him that smiteth thee on the one cheek offer also the other" (Luke 6:27–29). Whereas Homer and the dominant Greek and Roman ethical tradition praised good reputation [*timē*] and fame [*kleos*] above virtually all else, and dreaded their absence or loss, for the New Testament, "Blessed are ye when men shall hate you, and when they shall separate you from their company, and shall reproach you, and cast out your name as evil . . . Woe unto you, when men shall speak well of you" (Luke 6:22–26). Whereas Homer and the dominant Greek and Roman ethical tradition praised the man adept in cunning lying, as in the case of Odysseus the *polytropos*, and despised the man unpracticed in it, for the New Testament, "[We] have renounced the hidden things of dishonesty, not walking in craftiness, nor handling the word of God deceitfully; but by manifestation of the truth, commending ourselves to every man's conscience in the sight of God" (2 Cor. 4:2). Whereas Homer and the dominant Greek and Roman ethical tradition praised bodily pleasures, such as sexual pleasure, and dreaded their absence or loss, for the New Testament, "To be carnally minded is death; . . . the carnal mind is enmity against God . . . ; they that are in the flesh cannot please God" (Rom. 8:6–8). Etc. And (ii) this inversion of values was introduced by a people who had for centuries suffered heavy oppression at the immediate hands of the imperial Greeks and Romans, namely, the Jews of Palestine. (Nietzsche's thesis certainly requires qualification—especially in order to take into account anticipations of the evaluative inversions in question by important strands of Greek and Roman moral thought. But Nietzsche is himself well aware of this. And qualification is not abandonment.)

given by his own reason, Hegel replies pointedly that between the latter and both of the former "the difference is not that the former make themselves slaves, while the latter is free, but that the former have their lord outside themselves, while the latter carries his lord in himself, yet at the same time is his own slave."[56] In short, the Judeo-Christian tradition sublimated real slavery into an imaginary moral enslavement to God, and Kant further sublimated it into an imaginary moral enslavement to one's own reason.)

The early Hegel also came to see modern man as subject to a seventh, again self-internal, dualism closely connected to the previous one: a sharp division between virtue and happiness. In *The Positivity of the Christian Religion* Hegel implies that for the Greeks there was an intimate bond between realized virtue and happiness.[57] Since virtue was experienced by them as a species of desire (not as indifferent or opposed to desire), and moreover as their deepest desire, deeper than their more selfish desires, its realization, even when requiring the sacrifice of their more selfish desires, was for them sufficient and necessary for their happiness; this and only this realized their deepest desire. Hegel implies this point in connection with patriotic virtue specifically:

> As free people they obeyed laws which they had given themselves, . . . they . . . practised in actions maxims of virtue which they could call completely their own . . . , in public as in private and domestic life each was a free man, each lived in accordance with his own laws. The idea of his fatherland, of his state, was the invisible thing, the higher thing, for which he worked, which motivated him, this was the final purpose of the world for him, or the final purpose of his world . . . Before this idea his individuality vanished, he demanded preservation, life, and endurance only for it . . . To demand,

---

56. *The Spirit of Christianity*, in *Early Theological Writings*, p. 211; cf. 244, where Hegel speaks of "the self-coercion of Kantian virtue." Hegel's idea here that, continuously with Christianity's experience and conception of morality as slavish obedience to the will of another, Kantianism experiences and conceives it as a sort of *self-enslavement* comes from Schiller, who points both to Kant's rigorism and to the categorical imperatival form of his moral law as evidence of this (see esp. *On the Aesthetic Education of Man*, p. 179 and *Über Anmut und Würde*, in *Sämtliche Werke* 4:118–19).

57. Hegel would therefore regard the Greek philosophers—Socrates, Aristotle, Epicurus, the Stoics—who maintained that virtue (or in Aristotle's case, in closest proximity to Hegel at this time: *realized* virtue) was sufficient and necessary for happiness as in a sense showing deeper cultural self-understanding than Homer, and much of the literary tradition, for whom the relation between the two was quite arbitrary. For example, we read in Homer that "it is Zeus himself, the Olympian, that gives happy fortune to men, both to the good and the evil, to each man as he will" (*Odyssey*, bk. 6, ll. 188–89; cf. bk. 18, ll. 272–76).

or beg for, endurance or eternal life for himself as an individual could not occur to him . . . , he could feel a little more strongly a wish that concerned merely himself only in moments of inactivity, of indolence.[58]

With the intrusion of the Judeo-Christian tradition, however, this intimate bond between realized virtue and happiness was broken. For, as we have noted, this tradition ceased to experience dutifulness as a species of desire, let alone as deepest desire, instead experiencing duty's objectives as contrary or at best indifferent to desire, as objectives to be realized only out of obedience to divine commands: in this tradition, dutiful behavior is "the performance of a mass of *senseless and meaningless* actions, . . . compulsions dictated by dead formulas . . . slavish obedience to laws not made by [people] themselves."[59] This destroyed the Greeks' intimate bond between realized duty and happiness, because now the realization of duty's objectives was a realization of objectives hostile or indifferent to one's desires, not the fulfillment of one's deepest desires—not happiness. Christianity did desperately attempt to heal the breach between realized virtue and happiness which it had thus itself created, namely, by means of the mechanism of a God who judges us, and rewards or punishes us according to our deserts, in an afterlife. However, the early Hegel considers this deus ex machina a feebly inadequate cure for the established breach. First and foremost, it is transparently illusory—merely a comforting self-delusion caused by, and readily explicable in terms of, the human

---

58. In appendix I. This passage should be read in the light of Herodotus's famous account of Solon's insistence that Tellus was the happiest of men because his city was prosperous and he died successfully defending it.

Note that Hegel had earlier taken the opposite view that for the Greeks realized virtue did *not* ensure happiness: "The free republican . . . devoted his energies—indeed his very life to his fatherland; and he did so out of duty, without placing such value on his own efforts that he could presume to expect compensation or reimbursement. He toiled on behalf of his idea, his duty: what could he ever claim in return? . . . So, too, when someone has taken it upon himself, as a maxim of reason, to obey nature and necessity, honoring this law as sacred . . . what claims to compensation are left to him? What indemnification can an Oedipus claim for his undeserved sufferings . . . ?" (*Three Essays 1793–95*, p. 101).

This shift in historical interpretation is connected with a subtle shift in *The Positivity of the Christian Religion* (later made more emphatic and explicit in *The Spirit of Christianity*) away from certain Kantian assumptions still at work in the earlier passage just quoted, in particular the connected assumptions that virtuous motivation is distinct from rather than a species of action from desire (so that realized virtue would not entail realized desire, happiness), and that all desire is selfish (so that realized desire, happiness, would have to take the form of satisfying selfish desires).

59. *Early Theological Writings*, p. 178; emphasis added.

misery and weakness of those who originally invented and those who perpetuate it. Thus, in *The Positivity of the Christian Religion* Hegel explains its origins in terms of the human misery caused by oppression in the Roman Empire: "The despotism of the Roman emperors had chased the human spirit from the face of the earth . . . , the misery which it spread abroad had forced the human spirit to seek and expect happiness in heaven."[60] And elsewhere in the early writings he describes it as a "timorous contrivance," an "artificial system of drives and means of consolation in which so many thousands of weak souls have found comfort."[61] Second, Hegel also sees a number of problems of a more internal nature in Christianity's attempt to achieve by means of this doctrine the summum bonum of pairing virtue with happiness and vice with misery. For example, he argues that Christianity's doctrine of original sin implies that those whom the Christian imagines finding happiness in heaven will in fact violate rather than exemplifying the summum bonum ideal; that the strong strand in Christianity which makes not our virtue but Jesus's death for us and our faith in him the key to our happiness violates this ideal as well; and that in making doctrinal belief the sine qua non of happiness Christianity denies happiness to the many obviously virtuous heathen, such as Socrates, once again in violation of the summum bonum ideal.[62] Implied in this critical account of orthodox Christianity's creation of, and subsequent vain attempt to heal, the virtue-happiness breach is a similar critical account of Kant's position that practical reason requires the postulation of the soul's survival after death and of a judging, justly apportioning God in order to guarantee its presupposition of the summum bonum.[63]

Finally, the early Hegel also identified an eighth, and again self-internal, dualism as distinctive of modern man: a sharp dualism between the mind (and therefore the self), on the one hand, and the body, on the other. The early Hegel's most extensive reflections on this theme occur in the last few pages of *The Spirit of Christianity*. There he argues that the ancient Greeks did not sharply distinguish mind from body: for them, "body and soul persist together in one living shape."[64] This claim would appear

60. In appendix I.
61. *Three Essays 1793–95*, pp. 102–3.
62. Ibid., pp. 94–95.
63. Hence, after having earlier accepted a version of Kant's theory of the postulates, Hegel in the mid-1790s lost faith in it.
64. *Early Theological Writings*, p. 298.

seriously misguided if one took as representative of the ancient Greek position on the relation between mind or self and body the Orphic-Pythagorean-Socratic-Platonic tradition, which conceived the soul [*psychē*] as the locus of mental activity and identical with the self, but as distinct and separable from the body.[65] However, Hegel's view is defensible, for that tradition was very much at odds with an older and more typical tradition of Greek thought about the relation between mind or self and body which did indeed bind these together very intimately. Thus, in Homer, although the *psychē* is likewise conceived as separable from the body, it is not conceived as a mind, a locus of mental activity—"there are no wits [*phrenes*] in it at all" (*Iliad*, bk. 23, l. 104)—but only as a sort of perceptible image [*eidōlon*] of the dead man. And on the other hand, those faculties which *do* perform mental functions, such as the *thumos*, the *kardia*, and the *phrēn*, are virtually all identified with parts of the body—in these cases, the chest, the heart, and the diaphragm, respectively. In consequence, the self too tends to be identified with the body rather than with the separable *psychē*—a point nicely illustrated through a revealing ambiguity of sorts in the opening lines of the *Iliad*, where Homer says that Achilles' wrath "sent forth many mighty souls of warriors to Hades, and made *autous* [their bodies / themselves] a spoil for all the dogs and birds" (bk. 1, ll. 3–4). In Greek philosophy, similarly, there was a strong tradition which conceived the *psychē*, understood now as the locus of mental activity and hence as the self, as indivisibly bound up with the body. For example, we see from the *Phaedo* that *one* strand of Pythagoreanism conceived the *psychē*, so understood, as a harmonious adjustment between the elements of the body, on analogy with the attunement of the parts of a musical instrument.[66] Again, Aristotle—of whom Hegel is perhaps mainly thinking in the passage quoted above from *The Spirit of Christianity*—defined the *psychē* as "the form of a natural body having life potentially within it," and its "actuality," that is, what makes it actually alive.[67] And just as he held generally that the form of a physical thing could not exist separately from matter, but could only be distinguished from it by thought, so he maintained that the soul could not exist separately from the body, but could only be distinguished from it by thought.[68]

65. The locus classicus for this tradition is, of course, Plato's *Phaedo*.
66. Ibid., 85e–86d.
67. *De Anima*, 412a20–23; cf. 413a20–22.
68. Ibid., 413a3–6, 413b24–29, 414a19–22. Oddly, Aristotle recognized one exception: the soul's faculty of reason.

Again, orthodox Stoicism conceived the *psychē* as corporeal, and more specifically as the life-giving breath in a living body.[69] Hegel notes in *The Spirit of Christianity* that the apostles too conceived the mind or self as essentially embodied, indicating as evidence of this the fact that they always conceived of survival after death as *bodily resurrection*: "They look on spirit as embodied. An instance of [this] type of outlook is their way of taking what we call immortality, and in particular the immortality of the soul. To them it appears as a resurrection of the body."[70] Hegel again seems quite correct in this observation.[71] By contrast, Hegel points out, modern Europeans characteristically think of the mind or self as sharply distinct from the body: unlike the apostles, we modern Europeans assume "the separation of spirit and body"; where "they look on spirit as embodied," "we place only spirit unalloyed"; our outlook "sets a soul ... over against the intellect's object, the dead body."[72] For the early Hegel, Fichte is a paradigmatic example of this modern outlook. Thus in some remarks which we have already encountered he describes Fichte, using the latter's own words, as "setting [himself] as pure I over the ruins of this body and the shining suns, over the million heavenly bodies and the new solar systems," "as an independent unity for whom everything else is a world external to him."[73]

* * *

69. See *The Hellenistic Philosophers*, A.A. Long and D.N. Sedley (Cambridge: Cambridge University Press, 1987), 1:272, 315.

70. *Early Theological Writings*, p. 297. Hegel argues, however, that the apostles' position differs from and is inferior to its Greek counterpart in that it involves simultaneously and contradictorily thinking of the body as both dead and living (pp. 298, 300).

71. Note that this interpretation of the apostles simply brings them into line with the dominant strand of pre-Christian *Jewish* thought about the relation between mind or self and body, and about survival after death. Thus compare with the apostles' conception of personal survival as bodily resurrection in passages such as Luke 24:12–43 the Jewish prototype of that conception in such places as Ezekiel 37 and Daniel 12. (There were, certainly, alternative strands of Jewish thought on these matters by the Christian era as well, in particular: (i) an even older view, similar to Homer's, according to which bodily death meant the extinction of the mind and self, leaving only a shadowy existence in a Hades-like Sheol [see, for example, Ps. 6:5]; and (ii) a later view, deriving from the Greek Orphic-Pythagorean-Socratic-Platonic tradition, according to which the soul, understood as a locus of mental activity and hence as the self, was separable from the body and survived the latter's destruction [see esp. the apocryphal text *The Wisdom of Solomon*, and Josephus's report on the Essenes].)

72. *Early Theological Writings*, pp. 297–98; cf. 300. The *Difference* essay of 1801 accordingly includes among the modern dualisms which it is philosophy's purpose to overcome the opposition of "spirit and matter, soul and body" (in appendix IV).

73. Clearly, there is a long story to be told about how the modern world succumbed

Now when one reads the *Phenomenology* in light of these early texts, one can see immediately that it too contains a historical account according to which men have fallen from an earlier condition of relative unity in their conception of the world and themselves into a condition of conceiving the world and themselves in terms of sharp, fundamental dualisms. This is the force, for example, of the picture of history, implied at several points in the Preface, as a process which begins from simplicity or unity but then falls into division: Absolute Spirit is "the bifurcation of the simple," or of "an original or immediate unity," "it is the doubling which sets up opposition" (par. 18; cf. 21). Within the main body of the work this process of division is depicted above all in the *Self-consciousness* chapter, where we see the unified outlook of Life (the unified outlook of the ideal period of Greek culture) give way to the dualistic perspectives of Stoicism (ancient Stoicism) and the Unhappy Consciousness (Christianity).[74]

Moreover, the *Phenomenology*'s historical account is largely the same as that in the earlier writings—with some modest omissions, additions, and revisions. Thus, in the *Unhappy Consciousness* section we encounter once again the Judeo-Christian division of God from man and nature: The section points out that Christianity reconceives God as quite removed from the perceptible sphere of man and nature—"the simple unchangeable" (God) and "the protean changeable" with which it "identifies itself" "are, for the Unhappy Consciousness, alien to one another"; God or the "essence is the unattainable *beyond* which ... flees, or rather has already flown" (pars. 208, 217). The section points out that with the advent of Christianity God becomes reconceived as in character quite different from, and utterly superior to, man—the Christian consciousness "is conscious that its essence [i.e., God] is only its opposite, is conscious of its own nothingness" (par. 209). And the section points out that in reconceiving God in these ways Christianity also renders him fundamentally incomprehensible and unknowable to man—the deity "does not

---

to a dualism of mind or self and body. This story would have to include prominent reference to the Orphic-Pythagorean-Socratic-Platonic tradition's espousal of such a dualism, its perpetuation and dissemination by a dominant strand of Christianity (the Augustinian, as opposed to the Thomistic, strand), and its further entrenchment through the philosophy of Descartes and those influenced by him. Hegel will tell parts of this long story in the *Phenomenology*.

74. Here, and in what follows, I draw freely on a conception of the historical significance of the various sections of the *Phenomenology* which will be demonstrated in part 3.

make its appearance in conceptual form, not as something comprehended . . . Where that 'other' [i.e., God] is sought, it cannot be found, for it is supposed to be just a *beyond*, something that can *not* be found" (par. 217).[75]

We also reencounter in the *Phenomenology* the emergence of the modern world's sharp distinction between man and nature. In its historical dimension, the *Self-consciousness* chapter concerns developments in the ancient Greek and Roman worlds, culminating in the appearance of the Unhappy Consciousness of Christianity. The chapter's historical account begins with a conception of objects as "Life": "What self-consciousness distinguishes from itself as having *being* also has in it . . . not merely the [inanimate] character of Sense-certainty and Perception, but it is being that is reflected into itself, and the object . . . is a *living thing*" (par. 168). By this Hegel means, as when he used the term *life* in a similar way in passages from *The Spirit of Christianity* quoted earlier, the sort of interpretation of nature as wholly permeated by personality and purpose which is found in ancient polytheism. In contrast with this early conception, when we reach Christianity in the *Unhappy Consciousness* section nature has become disenchanted: the realm of natural objects is now a realm of "existence alien to [consciousness], . . . existence in the form of independent things" (par. 218). As in *The Spirit of Christianity*, what has made it so is the extraction of the personality and purpose of polytheism's gods from nature by the advent of nature-transcendent (Judeo-)Christian monotheism: due to "the Unchangeable's [i.e., the deity's] . . . having *surrendered* its embodied form, and having *relinquished* it," human consciousness likewise suffers division, including that of coming to stand in "a *relation* to the world of *actuality*" (par. 220; cf. 486). In the

---

75. Note, though, how much of Hegel's rich account in the early theological writings has been omitted or obscured here in the *Phenomenology*. In particular: (i) The *Unhappy Consciousness* section focuses exclusively on Christianity, without indicating Christianity's debts to Judaism as the early theological writings had done. (ii) The contrast so emphasized in the early theological writings between Christianity and Greek and Roman *polytheism*, though present in the *Self-consciousness* chapter as the contrast between the Unhappy Consciousness and the preceding outlook of Life, is nonetheless much obscured. And (iii), although when read in light of the early theological writings the *Self-consciousness* chapter can be seen to retain a version of the former's explanation of Christianity's triumph over polytheism in the West in terms of the rise of socio-economico-political oppression in the later ancient world, namely, in the form of the (indirect) transition from slavery and oppression in the *Lordship and Bondage* section to Christianity in the *Unhappy Consciousness* section, the explanation is now faded and obscured to the point of near-indiscernibility.

Observing Reason section of the *Reason* chapter Hegel describes how this trend toward the extraction of personality and purpose from nature is carried to completion by the rejection of Aristotelian teleology and its replacement with mechanistic explanations of nature begun in the scientific revolution of the early seventeenth century (Bacon and Galileo are prominent in Hegel's mind).[76]

The *Phenomenology* is much concerned with the emergence of the modern division between individual and community as well. The text contains two distinct (though not necessarily incompatible) accounts of the early development of this division. First, the *Self-consciousness* chapter offers an account similar to that in *The Positivity of the Christian Religion*. According to this account, social oppression in the later ancient world, Lordship and Bondage, led to the outlooks of Stoicism and the Christian Unhappy Consciousness. Within Stoicism the individual then no longer regarded his community as his highest end, but instead sought his happiness in inner ends removed from, and invulnerable to the fate of, the community: "As lord, it [the Stoic consciousness] does not have its truth in the bondsman, nor as bondsman is its truth in the lord's will and in his service; on the contrary, whether on the throne [like Marcus Aurelius] or in chains [like Epictetus], its aim is to be free, and to maintain that lifeless indifference which steadfastly withdraws from the bustle of existence . . . into the simple essentiality of thought" (par. 199). And within Stoicism the individual no longer automatically accepted his community's shared judgments, but instead considered himself capable of thinking and of discovering within his thought a criterion of truth *independently* of other people: "In thinking, I *am free*, because I am not in an *other*, but remain simply and solely in communion with myself, . . . my activity in conceptual thinking is a movement within myself"; "To the question, what is good and true, [Stoicism] . . . gave for answer the contentless thought" (pars. 197, 200). The Christian Unhappy Consciousness then similarly opted for individualism, pursuing as its highest

---

76. See esp. pars. 249–50. This development reaches its climax for Hegel when the scientific revolution, having reduced physical nature to a sphere of impersonal, purposeless things and processes, undertakes to reduce the human mind or self to such a thing or process as well. Hegel sees this as occurring in eighteenth-century physiognomy and especially phrenology (which identifies the mind with the brain and its activity; par. 327): "The unhappy self-consciousness . . . reverted . . . to the consciousness for which the object is something which merely *is*, a thing; but here [in phrenology], what is a thing is self-consciousness" (par. 344).

end not the good of its community but its own salvation, and regarding as the ultimate epistemic authority not the community's shared judgment but its own judgment insofar as inspired by God (pars. 207 ff., esp. 216-25).

Second, the *Spirit* chapter offers an alternative or additional account. In the section *The Ethical World* Hegel describes, as in earlier writings, an ideal stage of Greek culture in which, he supposes, the individual (i) regarded the community as his highest end—"qua ethical consciousness, it is the simple, pure direction of activity toward the essentiality of ethical life" (par. 465)—and also (ii) automatically accepted the community's shared judgment, especially on ethical matters—virtue here consists in a citizen's "knowing that the law of his own heart is the law of all hearts" (par. 461; cf. 352-53), "there is no caprice and . . . no struggle, no indecision, [no] making and testing of law . . . ; on the contrary, the essence of ethical life is for this consciousness immediate, unwavering, without contradiction" (par. 465).[77] The following section, *Ethical Action*, inter-

---

77. Characteristic (ii) might seem inconsistent with Hegel's distinction in this section between the Ethical World's "human law" (championed by Creon) and "divine law" (championed by Antigone), since Hegel suggests that, while the former is communal, the latter is *individual* (pars. 447-49). On reflection, however, the inconsistency proves only apparent. For, as J.N. Shklar has argued in her stimulating book *Freedom and Independence* (Cambridge: Cambridge University Press, 1976), it is Hegel's view that at bottom even the "divine law" is communal (unlike the divine law of the Judeo-Christian tradition) (pp. 82-83). Thus, as we noted earlier, in *The Positivity of the Christian Religion* Hegel had said that even in the case of the few laws which the Greeks ascribed as commandments to their gods, rather than directly to the community, their ultimate authority lay not in their having been commanded but in "the feelings of [the Greek's] heart and the agreement of all good men." Similarly, in the *Phenomenology* he argues that "*each* of the opposite [laws] in which the ethical substance exists contains the entire substance," and that "the two determinations of individuality and universality [i.e., communality] . . . express only the *superficial* antithesis of the two sides" (pars. 450, 446; emphasis added). His position is hence that, although the communal character of the "human law" is more explicit, the "divine law" is implicitly communal as well.

It is interesting to note that this position wins significant support from the Greek texts which were Hegel's main guide in thinking about these matters, namely, Sophocles' *Antigone* and Oedipus cycle generally. Thus, (a) it is not only Creon who appeals to the authority of communal opinion in order to establish the morality of his position in the play (e.g., at ll. 508-10), but Antigone does so as well:

Ant. All these men would say that [my deed] pleased them, did not fear shut up their tongues . . .
Cr. You alone of the Thebans see things thus.
Ant. These men see things so also, but they suppress their speech before you. (ll. 504-11)

(Antigone does, though, go on to imply at l. 511 that even if the Thebans did *not* agree with her she would still think her deed appropriate.) And Haemon similarly appeals to the

prets the Greek tragedy of the fifth century B.C. as reflecting the disintegration of these attitudes in its own time (or shortly before).[78] Tragedy reflects the emergence of a prioritizing of individual over communal ends and the emergence of the individual's reliance upon his own judgment in independence from the judgments of his fellows in society—or in Hegel's words, it reflects the emergence of "the absolute being-for-self of the

---

community's supportive opinion in order to justify Antigone's deed (ll. 683–711, 728–39). Moreover, (b) there is a general stress on the misguidedness of diverging from the community's moral opinion throughout this play and the Oedipus cycle as a whole. See, for instance, in addition to the examples just given, the chorus's reproach that Antigone's temper is *autognōtos*, "disposed to decide/cognize alone" (l. 875); and Creon's plea to Oedipus in *Oedipus The King*, "Do not condemn me apart [*chōris*]," meaning *apart from the opinions of others* (for which sense of *chōris*, cf. *Antigone*, l. 510).

78. I stress "in its own time (or shortly before)." Solomon claims that Hegel understands the tragedies of the fifth century B.C., and in particular Sophocles' *Antigone*, to be concerned not with the *polis* of the fifth century but with what Solomon describes as earlier "tribal society" (*In the Spirit of Hegel*, p. 546). Solomon is consequently puzzled that the *polis* of the fifth century is omitted from the *Phenomenology*'s account in the *Spirit* chapter (p. 546). These are mistakes. Concerning the *historical facts* about the tragedies, to begin with: There is, no doubt, an obvious sense in which the tragedies are—typically, though with exceptions, such as Aeschylus's *Persians*—concerned with what might loosely be described as earlier "tribal society." They are so, namely, in the sense that they take as their raw subject matter ancient myths which originated in and reflect conditions from such a society. However, in a less obvious but no less important sense, they are also very much about their *own age*, for they are concerned with the political and ethical issues of their own time and place. For example, Aeschylus's *Oresteia* is very much concerned with the virtues of *contemporary democracy*, and even of contemporary political alliances (Athens and Argos). Likewise, the *Antigone* is very much concerned with ethical dilemmas which may *now* confront citizens of a state. Much of the best recent work on tragedy stresses this important contemporary reference (see, for example, work by J.P. Vernant, P. Vidal-Naquet, N. Loraux, C. Segal, J.P. Euben, and S. Goldhill). Concerning, next, *Hegel's understanding* of the tragedies: It seems to me that Hegel well recognizes this situation, that while he is of course aware of the obvious way in which the tragedies are typically concerned with earlier "tribal society," he also recognizes that they are simultaneously very much about the politics and ethics of their own times. Hence, for example, at *Phenomenology*, pars. 734–35 he notes that the chorus in tragedy represents the political situation and views of the common people who are spectators at its performance. And in the *Aesthetics* he says that (Greek) drama "posits as the ground and cause of everything the self-conscious and active individual," and that for (Greek) drama "the free self-consciousness of human aims, complications, and fates must have already been completely aroused and developed *in a way possible only in epochs of the half-way or later development of a national life*" (*Aesthetics: Lectures on Fine Art*, trans. T.M. Knox [Oxford: Oxford University Press, 1975], pp. 1159–60; emphasis added). Also, note that it is Hegel's *general* view of art, as of philosophy, that it reflects the *current* life of a nation (see, for example, *Lectures on the Philosophy of World History: Introduction*, p. 146, and *Philosophy of Right*, p. 11). There is, therefore, pace Solomon, no puzzle as to why Hegel's account in the *Spirit* chapter of the *Phenomenology* does not deal with the *polis* of the fifth century; it *does*.

purely individual self-consciousness," of a period in which "the individual has . . . placed himself in opposition to the laws and customs" which "are regarded as mere ideas having no absolute essentiality . . . , while he as this particular 'I' is his own living truth" (pars. 464, 355). In both those respects, therefore, the individual now comes to view himself as radically detached from his fellows in society: "The life of Spirit and this substance which is self-conscious in everyone is lost . . . The simple compactness of their individuality has been shattered into a multitude of separate atoms" (par. 476). This condition is then bequeathed to, and becomes even more extreme within, the Roman Empire, the subject of the next section of the *Spirit* chapter, *Legal Status*.[79] (Instrumental in bringing about this whole change, according to this second account, was the fact that Greek individuals became aware, through their actions, that there were fundamentally conflicting ethical values within their communities—a process paradigmatically represented, in Hegel's view, by Sophocles' play *Antigone*, in which Creon and Antigone become aware through their actions of the stark conflict between the "human law," which Creon represents, and the "divine law," which Antigone represents.[80] Thus the socio-economico-political explanation of the development of individual-

---

79. In Legal Status the "living immediate unity of individuality and substance withdraws" into "the soulless community which has ceased to be the substance . . . of individuals, and in which they now have the value of selves . . . , possessing a separate being-for-self. The universal being thus splits up into a mere multiplicity of individuals"; "They exist, as persons, on their own account, and exclude any continuity with others from the rigid unyieldingness of their atomicity" (pars. 477, 482).

80. See pars. 466 ff., esp. par. 468: "The ethical essence has split itself into two laws, and consciousness . . . is assigned only to one . . . [Self-consciousness], just because it . . . advances to action, raises itself out of simple immediacy, and spontaneously splits itself into two. By this act it gives up the specific quality of the ethical life."

Commentators have sometimes implied that this characterization of ancient tragedy *only* works plausibly for Sophocles' Oedipus cycle (e.g., Solomon, *In the Spirit of Hegel*, p. 610). This seems to me untrue, and indeed arguably the reverse of the truth. Aeschylus's *Oresteia*, for instance, is a very clear example of a representation of the revelation through action of fundamental ethical conflicts within a community. See especially the opening play of the trilogy, the *Agamemnon*, in which each of the main conflicting parties claims, with strong support both in received values and from the gods, to have right on his or her side—a situation encapsulated by the chorus in the comment, "Blame here meets blame; it is hard to decide between them" (ll. 1560–61). On the other hand, it actually seems more doubtful that Sophocles wrote the *Antigone* in this spirit, as Hegel implies he did. The most cogent case known to me for saying that he did *not*, that the play's ethical intuitions are not divided between Antigone with her divine law and Creon with his human law, but rather entirely in sympathy with the former, is R. Jebb, *Sophocles: The Plays and Fragments* (Amsterdam: Hakkert, 1971), pt. 3, pp. xxi–xxvii.

community division which Hegel gave in *The Positivity of the Christian Religion* and again in the *Self-consciousness* chapter of the *Phenomenology*, namely, in terms of a loss of socio-economico-political freedom in later periods of Greek and Roman history, here gets replaced or supplemented by a much more intellectualistic explanation, namely, in terms of the emergence of a consciousness of conflicts between ethical values in fifth-century Greece.[81])

The *Phenomenology* is also concerned with the development of the sharp modern dualism of self or thought, on the one hand, and reality, on the other. However, it provides a much more interesting account of this than was yet to be found in the early theological writings. In the Preface, at paragraph 33, Hegel gives a condensed historical account of how this development occurred from "ancient times" to "modern times" comprising the following stages: (i) Initially, Hegel implies, ancient man was not yet conscious of his own representations or general concepts ("universals") as such, or as distinct from the reality which they represented.[82] (ii) Ancient Greek philosophy then raised the mind to such a self-consciousness—the ancient mind, "philosophizing about everything it encountered, developed itself into a thoroughly active universality." (iii) Finally, in modern times, consciousness of the mind's own general concepts as such, and as sharply distinct from the reality which they represent, has become a given—"in modern times . . . the individual finds the abstract form ready prepared; the effort of grasping it and making it one's own is more the immediate development of what is inner and the detached production of the universal than the emergence of it from the concrete and the manifoldness of the existent." Hegel fleshes out this skeletal historical account in the main course of the *Phenomenology*. The outlooks which he calls Sense-certainty and Perception exemplify stage (i): Sense-certainty, in its fixation on the reality represented, fails to recog-

---

81. The later *Lectures on the Philosophy of World History* continues but also revises this shift in the nature of the explanation offered—like the *Spirit* chapter explaining the emergence of individual-community division in the ancient world in intellectualistic terms, and more specifically in terms of the emergence of fundamental ethical conflicts in fifth-century Greece, but unlike the *Spirit* chapter identifying *the Sophists and Socrates* as the main culprits. See *The Philosophy of History*, trans. J. Sibree (New York: Dover Publications, 1956), pp. 227–71.

82. This is implied especially in the opening lines of par. 33. Cf. Hegel's later observation in the *Lectures on the History of Philosophy*, trans. E.S. Haldane and F.H. Simson (New York: The Humanities Press, 1974), 2:366: the "undeveloped consciousness" "usually knows nothing of what is present in addition to the content."

nize the role of general concepts, "universals," as such altogether; Perception does so, but still conceives them as *in* rather than as distinct from sensible particulars.[83] One can perhaps illustrate Hegel's conception that people saw things this way before the development of Greek philosophy by reference to the earlier Platonic dialogues. When in the dialogues Socrates asks his characteristic "What is X?" questions, seeking definitions of general concepts ("piety," "courage," "virtue," etc.), his interlocutors typically at the outset construe the questions, not as questions about the definitions of general concepts, but as questions about the examples or species of X actually found in reality; they have to be *educated* by Socrates to conceive the questions in the former way.[84] And even Socrates himself in early dialogues like the *Euthyphro* still assumes that the general concepts or forms are *in* their particular instances.[85] Step (ii) is partly spelled out in the *Force and the Understanding* section, where Hegel alludes to Plato's theory of forms from the middle period—when he conceived them as sharply separated from sensible particulars—as a development of a clear recognition of general concepts or "universals" as such and as distinct from the sensible particulars which instantiate them.[86] Partly it is spelled out in the *Stoicism* section, for ancient Stoicism too, as Hegel interprets it, developed an explicit recognition of general concepts as such, and as sharply distinct from reality: for Stoicism, the object presents itself "in *concepts,* i.e., in a distinct being-in-itself or intrinsic being, consciousness being immediately aware that this is not anything distinct from itself" (par. 197). Hegel has in mind here the Stoics' theory that incorporeal "sayables [*lekta*]" (i.e., roughly what we would call predicates and propositions), together with "impressions [*phantasiai*]" in the corporeal soul, constitute a medium distinct from the existent (or strictly, in the case of impressions, the *rest* of the existent) through which cognition of the existent takes place. (Hegel also offers, in the *Self-consciousness* chapter and in the *Legal Status* section of the *Spirit* chapter, an interesting causal explanation of the emergence and enduring appeal of this Stoic outlook in the later ancient world, namely, in terms of the socio-econom-

---

83. "I . . . perceive in [the object which I apprehend] a property which is a *universal*" (par. 117).
84. See for example *Euthyphro,* 6d; *Laches,* 191c–192b; *Meno,* 72a–c; *Hippias Major,* 287d–e; *Theaetetus,* 146e.
85. *Euthyphro,* 5d: holiness is self-identical "*en pasēi praxei.*"
86. See esp. pars. 132, 143–44, 146.

ico-political oppression which he sees as dominating Greece and Rome in that period—an explanation which will be considered in chapter 12.)[87]

The *Phenomenology* is also concerned with the development of our sharp modern distinction between fact and volition, and consequently between the theoretical or fact-discerning and the practical or volitional sides of the self: It is a prominent theme in the *Religion* chapter's treatment of Greek religion, as it had been in the early theological writings, that for the Greeks their volitions were *not* sharply distinct from (religious) fact. Hegel now sees this attitude as revealed above all in the *linguistic* aspects of Greek religion: "The god who has language for the element of his shape is the work of art . . . that possesses immediately in its outer existence pure activity . . . In other words, self-consciousness, in the objectification of its essence, abides immediately with itself" (par. 710).[88] Thus, he discerns this attitude in the Greeks' conceptions of their unwritten laws and of their sacred songs (pars. 712, 715). And above all he discerns it in their conceptions of their poetry, seeing epic, tragic, and comic poetry as steps of increasing explicitness in this attitude.[89] In partic-

---

87. In later years Hegel would revise the *Phenomenology*'s implication that Plato and the Stoics were the *first* to draw a sharp distinction between the subject's conceptual thought, on the one hand, and reality, on the other. He came to believe—rightly, I think—that this step had already been taken earlier by the Sophists of the fifth century. Thus, in the *Lectures on the Philosophy of World History* he writes that in Sophism "through the ascendant inner world of subjectivity the breach with reality occurred" (*The Philosophy of History*, pp. 378–79). And in the *Lectures on the History of Philosophy* he points in particular, and plausibly, to the second and third parts of Gorgias's treatise *Concerning Nature or Concerning the Non-existent* as a place where Sophism drew such a sharp distinction (*Lectures on the History of Philosophy* 1:383–84). In that treatise Gorgias argues for a sharp distinction between thought and language, on the one hand, and the realm of existence (if there were one), on the other, in the course of supporting the last two of three alarmingly skeptical theses which he advances: (i) "nothing exists," (ii) "even if anything exists it is inapprehensible to man," and (iii) "even if anything is apprehensible, yet of a surety it is inexpressible and incommunicable to one's neighbor" (Sextus Empiricus, *Against the Logicians*, trans. R.G. Bury [Cambridge, Mass.: Harvard University Press, 1983], bk. 1, secs. 65–87).

88. By contrast, Greek *sculpture*, which, as we saw, Hegel earlier presented as an example of this Greek attitude as well, is now rather *excluded* (pars. 708–9, 713). On the other hand, Hegel does still recognize certain *other* nonlinguistic manifestations of this attitude in Greek religion—for example, the manner of the Greeks' sacrifice, and dedication of temples and treasures, to their gods (pars. 718–19).

89. See esp. pars. 729, 732–33, 742, 747. In the following I shall pass over what for Hegel is the star example—comedy—because, although comedy undoubtedly involves an explicit awareness of the role of the poet's creative volitions, it seems implausible to suggest that it involves a conception of the products of those creative volitions as *factual*. The cases of epic and tragic poetry are more interesting.

ular, he implies that, at some level of awareness at least, the epic minstrel recognizes himself and is recognized by his community to be the *creator* of the world of religious facts which he describes: "The minstrel is the individual and actual Spirit from whom, as a subject of this world, it [the world] is produced and by whom it is borne" (par. 729).[90] And he argues that in tragedy the explicit involvement of creative actors and the close identification of the spectators with the chorus bespeak a similar awareness of the fusion of human volitions with the facts represented (pars. 733, 742).[91] Hegel implies in the *Stoicism* section that ancient Stoicism,

90. Hegel accordingly sees deep significance in a famous passage of Herodotus's ascribing the discovery of Greek religion to Homer and Hesiod which he interprets as meaning that "the Greek poets *made* the Greeks their gods" (Hegel, *Sämtliche Werke* [Stuttgart: Frommanns Verlag, 1958], 20:106; emphasis added).

It seems to me, however, that the epic poets' explicit attributions of their poetry and its factual insights to the inspiration of the gods (in particular, the Muses) cut significantly against Hegel's whole idea here, or at least show that the level of awareness at which it held true of the epic poets and their community would have to have been a very deeply submerged one.

91. The example of tragedy seems to me the most favorable for Hegel's idea (more so than either comedy or epic poetry), and may therefore be worth expanding on. That the tragedians must have been aware that the situations and events which they depicted had a basis in their own creative volitions seems fairly clear. For they involved substantial modifications and (especially) elaborations of traditional myths undertaken in a highly deliberate way in order to illustrate general ideas—especially of an ethical, political, or psychological sort—and meet complex aesthetic requirements. And (as far as one can tell from the evidence) there was not in the case of tragedy the sort of habitual and literal displacement of responsibility for the artistic process away from the poet to a Muse that is found in epic poetry. How, though, did the tragic poet conceive the resulting situations and events depicted? One popular answer, with a long and imposing history, is that he conceived these as in one degree or another historical *fiction*, written in order to illustrate his general ideas and produce his aesthetic effects. This answer goes back to Aristotle, who argues in the *Poetics* that this is what distinguishes (tragic) poetry from historical writing: "The poet's job is to describe, not what has happened, but what might happen and what is possible in accordance with probability or necessity. The historian and the poet are distinguished . . . by the fact that the one says what has happened, but the other what might happen" (1451a36–b5). And this answer has been swallowed more or less whole by most writers ever since—recently, for example, by J. Annas, who automatically describes Greek (tragic) poetry as "fiction" and its characters as "fictional characters" (*An Introduction to Plato's Republic* [Oxford: Oxford University Press, 1981], p. 96). However, Aristotle is highly unreliable as a historian of ideas in other areas, systematically assimilating past thinkers' positions to his own—as has been shown in connection with his treatment of traditional Greek religion by Jaeger, and in connection with his treatment of the presocratic philosophers by Cherniss, for example. (As we shall see in chapter 10, there are deep and interesting *philosophical reasons* for these interpretative shortcomings lying in his philosophical theories of meaning, understanding, and interpretation—they are not simply the result of carelessness or ignorance.) And one should therefore approach his testimony concerning tragic

in developing the sort of sharp distinction between the subject's thought and reality which was described in the previous paragraph, equally establishes a sharp distinction between the subject's volitions and reality: for the bondsman who develops into the Stoic consciousness "these two moments—itself as an independent object, and this object as a mode of consciousness . . .—fall apart," and for Stoicism "the freedom of self-consciousness is indifferent to natural existence and has . . . *let this equally go free*" (pars. 197, 200). This dualism is then perpetuated in the modern world. Thus the *Morality* section of the *Spirit* chapter finds it epitomized in the outlook of Kant's moral philosophy, for which "the object has . . . become . . . a nature whose laws like its actions belong to itself as a being which is indifferent to moral self-consciousness, just

---

poetry with the greatest of caution. In fact there is very strong evidence that the great tragedians of the fifth century conceived the contents of their tragedies *not* as fiction but as *historically factual:* First, serious poetry *traditionally* conceived itself as conveying not only general ethical, political, and psychological truths but also, and perhaps above all, historical truths about gods and men. Hence, for example, the relentlessly historical spirit of the Catalogue of Ships at *Iliad,* book 2, and the pervasive appeals in epic poetry for the divine inspiration of the Muses to enable the poet to make his account historically accurate (e.g., at the start of the Catalogue of Ships, or at *Theogony,* ll. 1–32). Second, two very insightful authors standing a good deal closer in time, milieu, and intellectual disposition to the tragedians of the fifth century than Aristotle does give evidence of tragedy's intention of stating historical fact. One is Aristophanes, who reveals the tragic poets' common assumption that it is tragedy's function to state historical truths in a brief but telling passage of the *Frogs:*

Euripides Is then this account about Phaedra which I composed untrue?
Aeschylus No, by Zeus, it is true; but the poet must hide from view what is base. (ll. 1052–53)

The other, and still more compelling, witness is Plato. For Plato's extended attack on epic and tragic poetry in *Republic,* books 2 and 3 consists in large part of the charge that they give factually false accounts of the gods and heroes and their activities—a charge which only makes sense on the assumption that epic and tragic poetry *purport* to give factually true accounts of these matters. And Plato's account of epic and tragic poetry in *Republic,* book 10 as aimed at an exact copying or mirroring of reality implies the same assumption (which is why Annas, who approaches Plato's views on this poetry with anachronistic ideas of "fiction" in mind, is baffled by this account—*An Introduction,* pp. 336–38). (Nor does the circumstance that a tragedian will occasionally give inconsistent historical accounts in different places, as Sophocles does in different parts of the Oedipus cycle for example, tell against the factual intentions of tragedy. Change of mind is at least as characteristic of factual as of fictional writing.) It seems, therefore, that we must indeed conclude that the tragedians *both* recognized the fundamental role of their own creative volitions in molding the situations and events which they depicted *and* nevertheless understood these to be historically factual. One can perhaps catch an echo of this—to us very alien—outlook from a passing remark of Plato's in the *Phaedrus:* the inspired madness of the poets, "ordering/adorning [*kosmousa*] countless deeds of the ancients, educates later generations" (245a).

as the latter is indifferent to it," and which experiences "the complete indifference and independence of nature toward moral purposes and activity" (pars. 599–600).[92]

The *Phenomenology* also contains an account of the development of our sharp modern opposition between duty and desire (though its account is less rich than that in the early theological writings). Thus, like the early theological writings, the *Unhappy Consciousness* section emphasizes that the Christian consciousness feels moral duty to be not one with but indifferent or hostile to its desires: "*For itself*, action and its own actual doing remain pitiable, its enjoyment remains pain" (par. 230). And, like the early theological writings, this section emphasizes that, at a more theoretical level, the Christian conceives dutifulness not as a species of action from desire but as obedience to divine commands (communicated through a mediating priest): "This mediator [the priest], having a direct relationship with the unchangeable being [God], ministers by giving advice on what is right. The action, since it follows upon the decision of someone else, ceases, as regards the *willing* of it, to be [consciousness's] own"; consciousness "renounces its *will*" (par. 228). Similarly, the *Morality* section of the *Spirit* chapter, like the later of the early theological writings, ascribes a sharp affective and theoretical opposition between duty and desire to the standpoint of Kant's moral philosophy as well. For this standpoint, "sensuousness, . . . in the shape of volition, as instincts and inclinations . . . is opposed to the pure will and its pure purpose . . . What is explicit for it is the antithesis of itself and impulses and instincts" (par. 603).[93] (The *Phenomenology* also retains a version, albeit a faded one, of the early theological writings' explanation of the development of this moral outlook in terms of slavery and oppression in the

---

92. Hegel goes on to interpret Kant's postulation of the summum bonum as an unsuccessful attempt to overcome this dualism (par. 602), and Fichte's philosophy likewise (esp. pars. 616–17), his diagnosis of Fichte's failure being similar to that which he had given earlier in the *Natural Law* essay.

93. As in *The Spirit of Christianity*, Hegel notes that indeed for the Kantian a felt opposition between duty and desire is a *necessary* feature of moral experience, the idea of a duty which did *not* stand in opposition to desire containing a self-contradiction, because it is part of the very *concept* of a duty that it involve such an opposition: For the Kantian, however much we may and must strive to harmonize duty and desire, "the consummation of this progress has to be projected into a future infinitely remote; for if it actually came about, this would do away with the moral consciousness. For morality is only moral consciousness as negative essence, for whose pure duty sensuousness has only a *negative* significance, is only *not* in conformity with duty" (par. 603; cf. 622).

ancient world. This is implied by the *Self-consciousness* chapter's interpretation of the Christian's conception of God and of his relation to God as derived from the bondsman's experience of the lord and of his relation to the lord [par. 206], and by its characterization of the Christian's way of affectively experiencing and theoretically conceiving duty as a slavish surrender to God analogous to the bondsman's slavish surrender to his lord: "Through these moments of surrender, first of its right to decide for itself, then of its . . . enjoyment, . . . [the Unhappy Consciousness] truly and completely deprives itself of the consciousness of inner and outer freedom, of the actuality in which consciousness exists *for itself*" [par. 229].)

Concerning the development of our sharp modern distinction between virtue and happiness: The *Phenomenology*, like *The Positivity of the Christian Religion* before it, implies that for the ancient Greeks these were closely connected. However, the *Phenomenology* understands this bond in a subtly different way, and as still more intimate. In *The Positivity of the Christian Religion*, it will be recalled, Hegel's thought was that since in the Greeks virtuous impulses were experienced as desires, and indeed as their deepest desires, realizing virtuous impulses was for them sufficient and necessary for the realization of their deepest desires, and so for happiness. The *Phenomenology*, by contrast, argues not that *realized* virtue but that virtue *per se* was sufficient and necessary for their happiness. The reasoning is as follows. For the Greeks, virtue simply consisted in willing in conformity with one's community: for them "virtue" consisted in the citizen's "knowing that the law of his own heart is the law of all hearts" (par. 461).[94] But also, the deepest desire of a Greek—as of men generally—was a desire for agreement between his volitions and those of his community, so that fulfillment of this desire was his true happiness. Thus Hegel argues, generally but with special reference to the Greeks, that in a community where the individual knows the laws "as particularized in his own individuality, and in each of his fellow citizens," "the individual . . . finds his essential character, i.e., his universal and particular nature, expressed . . . and . . . has realized that essential character," so that this is the "state of happiness" of having "realized his essential character" (pars. 351–53). Consequently, for the Greeks virtue and happiness were at bottom *one and the same thing*: volition in agreement with one's com-

---

94. Cf. par. 352: "The wisest men of antiquity have . . . declared that wisdom and virtue consist in living in accordance with the customs of one's nation."

munity. For a Greek, therefore, virtue—and any sacrifice of more selfish desires required to attain it—was necessary and sufficient for happiness: "The necessity in which [the desire/pleasure of the enjoyment of his individuality] passes away is his own self-consciousness as a citizen of his nation. Or, again, it is knowing that the law of his own heart is the law of all hearts, knowing the consciousness of the self as the acknowledged universal order. It is virtue, which *enjoys* the fruits of its sacrifice, which brings about what it sets out to accomplish, viz. to bring forth the essence to actual presence, and its *enjoyment* is this universal life" (par. 461; emphasis added).[95] Now in the *Unhappy Consciousness* section, as in the early theological writings, Hegel argues that Christianity, by introducing its experience of duty as not one with but sharply opposed to desires, destroyed this immediate connection between virtue and happiness enjoyed by the Greeks, creating instead a sharp breach between them—a breach which it then desperately and vainly tried to heal by invoking the deus ex machina of a god passing judgment and apportioning rewards and punishments according to deserts in the afterlife. Thus, toward the end of the *Unhappy Consciousness* section Hegel indicates that once Christianity introduces its experience of a breach between duty and desire (as discussed in the previous paragraph) the Christian consciousness finds itself acting dutifully without thereby satisfying or expecting to satisfy its desires, its "being-for-self," and hence without attaining or expecting to attain happiness (at least in the here-and-now): the "unity of objectivity and being-for-self . . . is not the principle of its action," "for itself, action and its own actual doing remain pitiable, its enjoyment remains pain" (par. 230). And he points out that the Christian consciousness instead, in consolation, "lets the mediating minister express . . . that its misery is . . . in principle the reverse, i.e., that its action brings it . . . in principle self-satisfaction or blessed enjoyment," which however "remains a *beyond*" (par. 230). As in the early theological writings, Hegel in the *Unhappy Consciousness* section indicates several fatal weaknesses in this desperate attempt by Christianity to heal the breach between virtue and

---

95. One could put the shift in interpretation between *The Positivity of the Christian Religion* and the *Phenomenology* in the following way. In the earlier work Hegel thought that a version of Aristotle's theory of the relation between virtue and happiness held true for the Greeks: *realized* virtue was identical with—and so, sufficient and necessary for—their happiness. In the *Phenomenology* he thinks, rather, that a version of the Stoics' theory of the relation between virtue and happiness held true for them: virtue *per se* was identical with—and so, sufficient and necessary for—their happiness.

happiness which it has itself created. First and foremost, as in the earlier writings, he implies that it is illusory.[96] Hence it is *objectively* unsatisfactory. Second, he adds the point that the Christian thesis of God's settling of accounts in a "beyond" has uncertainty even in the eyes of the Christian himself, which makes it an unsatisfactory healing of the breach *subjectively* as well: the Christian consciousness has "a certainty which is . . . incomplete, that its misery is only *in principle* the reverse, i.e., that its action brings it only *in principle* self-satisfaction or blessed enjoyment" (par. 230). The *Phenomenology*'s most extended discussion of the modern world's breach between virtue and happiness concerns its Kantian form, however. This discussion is found in the *Morality* section of the *Spirit* chapter (esp. pars. 601–25). Like orthodox Christianity, Kantianism, because it experiences duty as indifferent or opposed to desire, finds in the here-and-now no necessary connection between virtue and happiness (pars. 601, 618). Having thus, in continuity with orthodox Christianity, itself produced a breach between virtue and happiness, Kantianism, again in continuity with orthodox Christianity, attempts to restore the summum bonum of their connection by means of the postulates of the soul's survival and of a judging, justly apportioning God in a realm beyond (pars. 606, 609, 612). However, this attempted restoration of the broken connection, like its orthodox Christian counterpart, fails. It does so because, like the orthodox Christian version, it is illusory, and moreover succumbs to the problem of its subjective uncertainty as well—only here in a more specific and even more acute form, since Kant's own doctrine of the unknowability of things in themselves entails that knowledge of this solution's truth is in principle impossible.[97] (Hegel sees the Kantian solution as subject to further internal problems as well.)

Finally, the *Phenomenology*, like the early theological writings, is concerned with the development of the sharp modern dualism between mind or self and body. The *Self-consciousness* chapter opens with a perspective which conceives not only objective nature but also the *mind* or *self* as "Life": "The object is a living thing" (par. 168), but also consciousness is an "other life," "a living self-consciousness" (pars. 173, 176; cf. 186).

---

96. Thus, as we just saw, the divine manipulation which Christianity invokes to heal the breach is supposed to occur in "a beyond." But it is one of the central theses of the *Unhappy Consciousness* section that the Christian conception of a God located in a realm beyond is an illusion (see esp. pars. 207, 216).

97. Hegel runs these two points together in his observation that the God of this Kantian solution is "a being existing only in thought" (par. 612).

The former part of this refers, as we have noted, to Greek polytheism's conception of nature as personal and purposive. The latter part, on the other hand, refers to the Greeks' conception of the mind or self and the body as indivisible, as forming a unity. Thus recall *The Spirit of Christianity*'s reference to "the Greek view that body and soul persist together in one *living* shape" (emphasis added). Now the remainder of the *Self-consciousness* chapter, and later parts of the book as well, describe the fragmentation of this unified conception of mind or self and body that has occurred in the subsequent history of Western thought. The first form of a sharp division of the mind or self from the body which Hegel identifies is ancient Stoicism, for which "these two moments—itself as an independent object, and this object as a mode of consciousness, and hence its own essential nature—fall apart" (par. 197; cf. 199–201). This characterization of Stoicism's position would not apply well to early Stoicism, for which, as we noted earlier, the soul was corporeal, the body's life-breath. However, Hegel is thinking here rather of later Stoics, such as Seneca, who did indeed tend to conceive the relation of the mind or self to the body more in conformity with the dualism of the Orphic-Pythagorean-Socratic-Platonic tradition.[98] The next major example of a sharply dualistic conception of the relation of the mind or self to the body is the Unhappy Consciousness of Christianity, which is "divided within itself," appearing as broken up "into a relation to the world of actuality . . . and into a being that is in itself," or in other words into a physical side occupied with "the changing of [actuality] or working on it" and a mental side consisting "of faculties and powers" that "belongs to the Unchangeable beyond" (par. 220). This description might at first seem inconsistent with Hegel's characterization of the apostles' outlook in *The Spirit of Christianity*. However, Hegel is thinking here of a different strand of thought about the relation between the mind or self and the body within the Christian tradition: not the apostolic conception of the former as essentially bound up with the latter (nor Thomism's somewhat similar, neo-Aristotelian, conception of their relation) but the dominant Orphic-Pythagorean-Socratic-Platonic conception of their relation preserved in the Augustinian tradition. The section of the *Reason* chapter *Logical and Psychological Laws*, which is largely concerned with the outlooks of Locke and Hume, attributes to these philosophers a still later

---

98. See, e.g., Seneca, *Letters from a Stoic*, trans. R. Campbell (Harmondsworth: Penguin Books, 1975), pp. 87–88.

version of dualism concerning the mind or self and the body: a conception of the world as falling apart "into a world that in itself is . . . given, and an individuality existing *on its own account*," or of "the mutual indifference" of "actuality" and "self-consciousness" (pars. 308–9). In addition, the *Reason* chapter represents this dualistic conception as subsequently accepted by other modern movements, for example modern physiognomy, which, according to the next section, *Physiognomy and Phrenology*, conceives the relation of the mind or self to the body in such a way that "the externality which the inner obtains through [bodily organs such as mouth and hand] is the action as a reality separated from the individual. Speech and work are outer expressions in which the individual no longer keeps and possesses himself within himself" (par. 312). Finally, Hegel implies that Kant and Fichte too ascribe to mental activity an independence from bodily expression, and to the mind or self an independence from the body, which place them within this dualistic tradition (par. 509).[99] (Hegel also develops in the *Phenomenology* an explanation of *why* the tradition of dualistic thought about the relation between the mind or self and the body superseded the Greek tradition which conceived the former as inseparably bound up with the latter. As already noted, the *Lordship and Bondage* section implicitly reaffirms Hegel's view, stated more explicitly in *The Positivity of the Christian Religion*, that later periods of Greek and Roman antiquity were dominated by slavery and other forms of social oppression. Hegel sees *this* fact as the key to explaining the appeal of the dualism concerning mind or self and body that was propounded by later Stoicism and Augustinian Christianity. In his view, the autonomy of the mind or self from corporeal reality asserted by this dualistic tradition was a metaphysical expression of an oppressed people's yearnings to retreat from a corporeal reality which had become a site of misery and degradation for them. Thus, he already strongly hints at such an explanation in *The Positivity of the Christian Religion*: "The despotism of the Roman emperors had chased the human spirit from the

---

99. A fuller account of the historical development of this dualism than the *Phenomenology* gives would still need to take into account the ancient Orphic-Pythagorean-Socratic-Platonic tradition (which lies behind the later Stoic and Augustinian Christian forms of this dualism dealt with in the *Self-consciousness* chapter), and Descartes (who lies behind the more recent forms of it dealt with in the *Reason* chapter). It is noteworthy that Hegel tends to downplay the mind-body dualism of Plato and Descartes pretty systematically, in large part because he wishes to interpret both thinkers as forerunners of his own antidualistic, monistic philosophy.

face of the earth."[100] And in the *Phenomenology* he explains the Stoic's conception of the independence of the mind or self from the body as a direct outcome of the experience of the bondsman who, "as a consciousness forced back into itself, . . . will withdraw into itself and be transformed into a truly independent consciousness" [par. 193].[101] In *The Positivity of the Christian Religion* he also implies a further part of the explanation, a further, more ambitious step of imaginary retreat from the corporeal realm motivated by oppression in the later ancient world which dualism of mind or self and body had made possible, or at least greatly facilitated: Christianity's salvation of the mind or self from the corporeal realm to bliss in heaven after death.[102] This further part of the explanation is implicit in the *Self-consciousness* chapter of the *Phenomenology* as well.[103] In short, dualism concerning the mind or self and the body won the dominant appeal which it has had for the modern world due to the trauma of slavery and other forms of social oppression in the later ancient world, which generated an incentive to escape from a now miserable and degrading corporeal sphere—an escape which this dualism in part itself effected, and whose more ambitious religious forms it made possible, or at least greatly facilitated.[104])

* * *

100. In appendix I.

101. Cf. par. 197: "For the subservient consciousness [which develops into Stoicism] . . . these two moments—itself as an independent object, and this object as a mode of consciousness, and hence its own essential nature—fall apart."

102. "The despotism of the Roman emperors had chased the human spirit from the face of the earth, its robbery of freedom had forced the human spirit to carry off its eternal aspect, its absolute aspect, to safety in the deity, the misery which it spread abroad had forced the human spirit to seek and expect happiness in heaven" (in appendix I).

103. Strictly speaking, Hegel in the *Phenomenology* believes that the experience of slavery and oppression promotes a dualism of mind or self and body by causing a *double* process of divorce. It not only provides a motive for conceiving the mind or self as liberated from corporeal reality, in the ways just described, but also promotes a more objective, less mind-infused conception of corporeal reality, namely, through the greater appreciation of corporeal objects' autonomy from the mind which comes from laboring on them as the slave must (see esp. par. 190).

104. Note that such an account is more plausible as an explanation of the *perpetuation and spread* of dualism concerning the mind or self and the body in later antiquity than as an explanation of its *origination*. For this dualism had its origins not in later Stoicism and Christianity but earlier in the Orphic-Pythagorean-Socratic-Platonic tradition, and the latter tradition, far from being associated mainly with slaves and the socially oppressed, seems to have been largely *aristocratic*. (In the case of Orphism this is disputed, but for a balanced discussion of the evidence consistent with the view just stated, see W.K.C. Guthrie, *The Greeks and Their Gods* [Boston: Beacon Press, 1955], pp. 326–32.)

These, then, are the eight modern dualisms with which Hegel is centrally concerned in the *Phenomenology*.[105] Now it had already been Hegel's position in the early theological writings that modern men's replacement of the more unified outlook of earlier history with these sharp dualisms was the main source of their endemic unhappiness. Thus in the *Fragment of a System* from 1800 he refers to "peoples whose life is torn and separated apart as little as possible" as "happy peoples," but to those who by contrast live "in . . . separation" as "unhappier peoples," and in another, roughly contemporary, fragment he writes that "in unhappiness separation is present . . . in happiness this separation is gone—what rules is . . . unity."[106] The same position is implicit in the *Phenomenology* as well. Hence, for example, the work's name for the paradigmatically dualistic perspective of Christianity: the "*Unhappy* Consciousness."

Why does Hegel regard a sharply dualistic perspective as a source of unhappiness in this way? He appears to have two distinguishable sorts of reasons. First, he seems to believe that regarding the world and oneself in terms of fundamental dualisms is somehow just *intrinsically* productive of unhappiness.[107] But second, and more interestingly, he also has a variety of reasons specific to each of the dualisms with which he is most concerned.[108]

Thus, to begin with the Judeo-Christian tradition's sharp division between God, on the one hand, and man and nature, on the other, Hegel envisages several ways in which this is productive of unhappiness, among which the following are particularly important. First, like Schiller and Hölderlin before him, Hegel believes that the Greek gods' presence among and intimate involvement with mankind and nature had infused mankind and nature with an extraordinary dignity and beauty for the

---

105. These eight dualisms could reasonably be described as the *Phenomenology*'s theme of *alienation* [Entfremdung], in a broad sense of the term. R. Schacht, in his *Alienation* (Garden City, N.J.: Doubleday, 1970), is quite helpful in connection with certain of these aspects of the *Phenomenology*. Unfortunately, however, he confines himself to the range of the *word* in the text, and consequently considers only the division of individual from society with which the word is mainly associated there (see esp. pp. 40, 43), instead of exploring this far broader *phenomenon* with which the text is concerned. Especially unfortunate are Schacht's actual *denials* that Hegel is concerned with alienation between man and God or between the self and objectivity (pp. 15–16, 64). These denials are, if not merely verbal points, serious mistakes.
106. Appendix II; *Hegels theologische Jugendschriften*, p. 373.
107. This is the sense that one gets from reading his discussion of dualisms in the section of the *Difference* essay "The Need for Philosophy," for example (in appendix IV).
108. The reasons which follow are intended to be illustrative rather than exhaustive.

Greeks, thereby enhancing the Greeks' daily joy.[109] The Judeo-Christian religion, in expelling polytheism's gods from the human and natural sphere, and exalting its own god far above it, eliminated this dignity and beauty, thereby diminishing men's daily joy.[110] The *Unhappy Consciousness* section of the *Phenomenology* expresses this already quite familiar thought allusively in such remarks as that for the Christian the "essence [God] is the unattainable *beyond* which, in being laid hold of flees, or rather has already flown . . . Consciousness, therefore, can only find as a present reality the *grave* of its life" (par. 217). Second, Hegel also believes that Christianity's qualitative exaltation of God above man involves an illusory displacement of virtues and potentials which in fact belong to man himself away from man and onto this imaginary independent being, thus leaving man with undeserved self-contempt and inhibiting him from realizing his potentials.[111] This is a central point in the *Unhappy Consciousness* section: the Christian falsely imagines that there is a deity distinct from himself, and takes it "to be the *essential* being, . . . and . . . itself to be the unessential being" (pars. 207–8), and consequently, "consciousness of life, of its existence and activity, is only an agonizing over this existence and activity, for therein it is conscious that its essence is only its opposite, is conscious only of its own nothingness"

---

109. Schiller, "Die Götter Griechenlands," *Sämtliche Werke* 1:168–69: "Beneath Iris's beautiful bow bloomed / more charmingly the pearled meadow. / More splendid appeared the dawn / in Himeros's rosy folds, / more mellifluous sounded the flute / in the hand of the shepherd-god . . . Higher was valued the gift / which the giver enjoyed together [with man] in friendship." Similarly, the young Hegel: "The brazen bond of his needs fetters [the Greek genius] too to Mother Earth, but he worked over it, refined it, beautified it with feeling and fancy, so that he could delight in these fetters" (1793 Tübingen essay, in Harris, *Hegel's Development*, p. 506; cf. *The Positivity of the Christian Religion*, in appendix I). Nietzsche would later advance a similar view of the effects of traditional Greek religion, most explicitly in *The Birth of Tragedy*, sec. 3.

110. Schiller, "Die Götter Griechenlands," *Sämtliche Werke* 1:167, 192: the Greek gods "guided happier ages of mankind / by joy's light leading-string"; "Yes, [the gods] went home, and everything beautiful, / everything lofty they took with them, / all colors, all life's tones, / and we were left only with the soulless word." See, similarly, the young Hegel's comments on the joylessness of Christianity in the 1793 Tübingen essay (Harris, *Hegel's Development*, pp. 505–7).

111. *Three Essays 1793–95*, p. 102: Christianity "transfer[s] [all that is fine in human nature] onto an alien individual, retaining for ourselves nothing but the loathsomeness of which our nature is capable." In a 1795 letter Hegel writes that Christian "religion . . . has taught . . . contempt for the human race, its incapacity for any good, its incapacity to be something independently" (*Briefe von und an Hegel* 1:24).

(par. 209; cf. 225–30).[112] Third, Hegel also implies that—besides the two processes just mentioned—the distancing and qualitative exaltation of God above man and nature which occur in the Judeo-Christian tradition inevitably entail a corresponding *devaluation* of man and nature, which come to seem "unessential" or "nothing" *in comparison,* thereby again undermining human happiness (pars. 208–9; cf. 225–30).[113] Fourth, Hegel implies that the severe limitations imposed by Judeo-Christian religion on man's capacity to comprehend and know God entail further self-contempt, and also doubt, and hence further unhappiness. Hegel points, as specific examples of this, to the Catholic laity's reception of its religion in Latin, a language which it does not understand, and the self-contempt which inevitably results therefrom (pars. 228–29), and to the Christian's lack of certainty about the afterlife, and the miserable doubt in which this leaves him (par. 230). In these several ways, then, the Judeo-Christian tradition's sharp division of God from man and nature causes human unhappiness.

Consider next modernity's sharp distinction between man and nature, its denial of personality and purpose to the latter. Hegel often uses the word *fremd* [foreign, alien] and cognates to describe a nature so conceived (e.g., pars. 218, 486). This word is meant to suggest several distinguishable features of such a conception of nature, each of them productive of unhappiness. First, and perhaps most obviously, it suggests that in leaving behind a conception of the natural environment as personal and purposive like ourselves we have suffered an experience analogous to that of exile from one's own culture (only in a way more extreme, since in relation to nature we have left behind familiar people and purposes, not, as typically in exile from a culture, for unfamiliar people and purposes, but rather for no people or purposes at all). It is plausible to think that exile from one's own to an alien culture must exact a price of

---

112. It was above all this thought that Feuerbach would later take over and develop in *The Essence of Christianity.*
113. Before the *Phenomenology,* this idea is already present in Schiller's "Die Götter Griechenlands": "What beside You [God] is the highest spirit / of those who were born by mortals? / Only the first and noblest among worms" (*Sämtliche Werke* 1:172). It is also implied in a remark of Hegel's concerning Judaism, from 1798: "If the infinite object is everything, then man is nothing" (in Harris, *Hegel's Development,* p. 300 n.2). After the *Phenomenology,* this idea reappears in Feuerbach's *The Essence of Christianity* (e.g., p. 161). And it takes center stage in Nietzsche, for whom the "slander" on man and nature involved is not only an *effect* of Judeo-Christian theology but also its implicit *purpose.*

unease and unfulfillment.[114] Analogously, Hegel implies, our exile from a natural environment formerly like ourselves to one now quite unlike ourselves has exacted such a price.[115] Second, more specifically, the personality and purposiveness of nature had held open a comforting possibility which closes once nature becomes disenchanted, namely, the possibility that nature in one degree or another shares *our* purposes. A qualified version of this idea was implicit in traditional Greek polytheism all along—for example, Demeter's aim that her corn should grow coincided with the Greeks'. And it was the prospect of a much more ambitious version of it which attracted Socrates in his youth to Anaxagoras's doctrine that mind was the constitutive principle of all nature—for this doctrine raised for Socrates the prospect that, like men (as Socrates conceived them), nature too was purposively directed at the attainment of the highest good.[116] Such an idea, by representing nature as, in one measure or another, man's ally and a guarantor of the fulfillment of his purposes, encouraged in man a sense of being at home in nature and a sense of optimism, thus contributing to his happiness. The disenchantment of nature, by contrast, deprives man of any such comfort: since nature is neither personal nor purposive, a fortiori it does not share *his* purposes.[117] Third, Hegel implies that a disenchanted nature also becomes *fremd* in the sense that we can no longer satisfactorily *understand* it—and this not only in the obvious sense that we can no longer attribute *meanings* to what we now conceive as impersonal and purposeless, but also in the sense that we can no longer satisfactorily *explain* an impersonal, purposeless nature *at all*. In forgoing explanations of nature in terms of personality and final causes, the modern disenchanted worldview has resorted instead to explaining it in terms of efficient causes, and in particular efficiently causing forces. However, according to Hegel, a genuine explanation of nature *cannot* thus stop at the identification of efficient causes, it

---

114. Hegel would certainly say so (see for example pars. 351–53).
115. Note that this problem could be solved in two different ways: either by making physical nature more like us again, or by making us more like physical nature. As we shall see, Hegel addresses it in *both* ways: he undertakes both to repersonalize physical nature and to physically naturalize persons.
116. *Phaedo*, 97c–d.
117. A designing deity *external* to nature might offer a measure of similar comfort—but only a measure, and only, as we have seen, at the cost of *other* negative consequences for happiness.

must include explanation in terms of final causes. The Socrates of the *Phaedo* had held a similar view, but had done little more than simply *assume* it.[118] Hegel, by contrast, offers a substantial *argument* for it. This argument appears in the *Force and the Understanding* and *Observing Reason* sections of the *Phenomenology*.[119] Its central points are as follows. Hegel recognizes that there are, broadly speaking, two alternative ways of construing explanations in terms of efficient causes and efficiently causing forces: either one can be a *realist* about the causal connections and forces, conceiving them as items over and above the sensible occurrences which they are called upon to explain (this was Newton's standard position), or one can be an *antirealist* about them, construing them as, in effect, identical with regularities in those sensible occurrences (this was in essence the position adopted by Hume). Now Hegel's basic strategy of argument is to impale disenchanted explanations on the horns of a dilemma: in *whichever* of these two ways one attempts to make sense of them, insurmountable problems arise. If we construe them in the manner of the *realist,* then we are left without any adequate answer to the question *why* the presence of a particular causal connection or force produces sensible occurrences of the kind which it is adduced to explain. To be sure, in *describing* it as a causal connection or force we *imply* its production of sensible occurrences, and in *describing* it more specifically as a causal connection or force of a certain kind, for example as gravity, we *imply* its production of sensible occurrences of a corresponding kind. So if the question were why *qua falling under such a description* a particular causal connection or force produced sensible occurrences of the kind which it is called upon to explain, then the answer would be the trivial one that its description *implies* this. But since, on the realist model, a causal connection or force is supposed to be something *independent* of the sensible occurrences which it explains, the further question can always be asked why it, not qua falling under such a description, but *simpliciter* produces sensible occurrences of the relevant kind, and *this* question remains unanswered. Hence explanation fails at this point, or, as

---

118. In the *Phaedo* Socrates effectively assumes that it is absurd to try to explain human beings in terms of efficient causes alone, without appeal to final causes, and infers that it is likewise absurd to try to explain nature in such terms (97c–99c). That is barely an argument.

119. For a similar line of argument, but drawn from other texts of Hegel's, see Inwood's extremely insightful book *Hegel*, pp. 60–64.

Hegel puts it, no "necessity" is shown.[120] Besides this problem concerning the *explanatoriness* of the realist's appeal to causal connections and forces, the realist account also, according to Hegel, in conceiving causal connections or forces as *supersensible,* confronts severe problems concerning how we could ever *know* about them.[121] The alternative, antirealist, account faces severe problems as well, according to Hegel. First and foremost, like the realist account, it faces a problem with respect to explanatoriness. Hegel's basic objection here is that if causal connections and forces are just abbreviations for regularities in sensible occurrences, then any appeal to them to explain these regularities will be merely tautologous, so that we will be left without any real explanation of the latter. Moreover, he believes that this vitiates any appeal to them to explain particular sensible occurrences as well. Here his thought seems to be roughly as follows. On the antirealist view, to explain a particular B-event in terms of causation by a preceding A-event is implicitly just to say that it was preceded by an A-event and that A-events are *always* followed by B-events. But then, in the absence of an explanation of *why* A-events are always followed by B-events, how does *that* constitute an *explanation* of the particular B-event (rather than just adding to what requires explanation)?[122] Hegel also notes that, like the realist account, the antirealist account faces an additional problem concerning the possibility of attaining *knowledge* about causes and forces: in this case, the

---

120. The above argument appears at par. 152: "It is usually said . . . that [the force of electricity] *has the property* of expressing itself in this way. It is true that this property is the essential and sole property of this force, or that it belongs to it *necessarily*. But necessity here is an empty word: force *must,* just *because it must,* duplicate itself in this way . . . Electricity, as *simple force,* is indifferent to its law—*to be* positive and negative; and if we call the former its concept but the latter its being, then its concept is indifferent to its being. It merely *has* this property, which just means that this property is not *in itself* necessary to it."

121. See esp. par. 146.

122. The above argument appears at pars. 154–55: "A law is enunciated; from this its implicitly universal element or ground is distinguished as *force;* but it is said that this difference is no difference, rather that the ground is constituted exactly the same as the law. The single occurrence of lightning, e.g., is apprehended as a universal, and this universal is enunciated as the *law* of electricity; the 'explanation' then condenses the *law* into *force* as the essence of the law . . . *Force is constituted exactly the same as law;* there is said to be no difference whatever between them . . . In this tautological movement, . . . the movement falls only within the understanding itself, not within the object. It is an explanation that not only explains nothing, but is so plain that while it pretends to say something different from what has already been said, it really says nothing at all but only repeats the same thing" (cf. pars. 152, 250; also *Science of Logic,* pp. 458–59).

need to rely on induction to general laws from finite evidence, and the notorious fallibility of this procedure.[123] The upshot of this whole dilemma is that any attempt to explain nature in the manner of our modern disenchanted worldview by appeal to efficient causation, and in particular efficiently causing forces, fails both qua *explanation* and qua *knowledge*.[124] In leaving our aspiration to understand nature unsatisfied in this way, the disenchanted worldview makes yet a further contribution to our unhappiness.[125]

Concerning the sharp modern division between the individual and his community, consider first the part of this which consists in the modern individual no longer regarding the community as his highest end. Hegel

---

123. Par. 250: "The assertion that stones fall when raised above the ground and dropped certainly does not require us to make this experiment with every stone; it does perhaps mean that the experiment must have been made with a very great number, and from this we can then *by analogy* draw an inference about the rest . . . But analogy not only does not give a perfect right, but on account of its nature contradicts itself so often that the inference to be drawn from analogy is rather that analogy does not permit an inference to be made."

124. It is worth noting that Hegel's charge, if cogent at all, will not be escaped by someone who, like Newton in nonstandard moods or, less equivocally, Russell in "On the Notion of Cause," maintains that modern science can and should *dispense* with such notions as causation and invoke general laws alone. If Hegel's two arguments against the antirealist position work at all, then they will also work against *this* position.

125. Hegel's own solution to this problem, his recipe for achieving explanations of nature which are both genuinely explanatory and known, will reject the realist's approach altogether, but build upon the antirealist's.—His strong preference for the latter over the former is already well developed before the *Phenomenology* in the 1804–5 *Logik, Metaphysik, und Naturphilosophie* (Hamburg: Felix Meiner, 1982), pp. 46–63; and it persists later, for example at *Encyclopaedia*, par. 136.—He envisages, in effect, complementing the antirealist's efficient causal explanations by adding a teleological component to them. This teleological component will solve the antirealist's *explanatoriness*-problem by furnishing a final cause to serve as the genuine basis of explanation which his explanations lack, and it will solve his *knowledge*-problem by furnishing a criterion for identifying, and a ground for confidence in, reliable inductive generalizations, namely, their teleological intelligibility. Hegel sketches this solution at paragraph 250, immediately after explaining the antirealist's knowledge-problem and alluding to his explanatoriness-problem (reason "does not discern necessity" in his laws): "That a stone falls is true for consciousness because in its heaviness the stone has in and for itself that essential relation to the earth which is expressed in falling. Consciousness thus has in experience the *being* of the law, but it has, too, the law in the form of a *concept* [i.e., a final cause]; and it is only because of the two aspects together that the law is true for consciousness. The law is valid as a law because it is manifested in the world of appearance, and it is also in its own self a concept." As Hegel envisages this solution, it ultimately involves the attribution to nature not only of purposes but also of a personality for these purposes to belong to, namely, the personality of Absolute Spirit (see esp. pars. 161–64).

points out in *The Positivity of the Christian Religion* that as long as the individual did so regard it, this prevented or at least greatly diminished his experience of fear at the prospect of his own death, because his deepest concern was invested not in something contingent on his remaining alive but instead in something which would surely survive his death.[126] When, however, the individual ceased to regard the community as his highest end, he generally reinvested his greatest concern in ends which were self-regarding, in the sense of being realizable only as long as he remained in existence. And in this situation the prospect of death inevitably did become a terrifying one, since it promised to extinguish everything that he most cared about. Thus Hegel remarks that in that period of ancient history in which the individual ceased to regard the community as his highest end, "the phenomenon which tore down for him the whole fabric of his purposes, the activity of his whole life, namely, death, was inevitably something terrible for him, for nothing survived him."[127] Hegel points to the high incidence of avoidance of military service through desertion, bribery, and self-mutilation among the Romans of the Roman Empire as evidence that such a development really did occur in later periods of ancient history.[128] In the *Phenomenology* Hegel

---

126. *The Positivity of the Christian Religion,* in appendix I: "The idea of his fatherland, of his state, was the invisible thing, the higher thing, for which he worked, which motivated him, this was the final purpose of the world for him, or the final purpose of his world . . . Before this idea his individuality vanished, he demanded preservation, life, and endurance only for it . . . To demand, or beg for, endurance or eternal life for himself as an individual could not occur to him . . . The republican was survived by the republic, and the thought hovered before his mind that the republic, his very soul, was something eternal."
127. In appendix I.
128. Ibid. The case of Christianity might seem to be at odds with Hegel's account here in two respects: (i) Is not Christianity typically self-denying, like ancient patriotism, rather than self-regarding? And (ii) does it not, like ancient patriotism, extinguish fear of death, especially through its promise of a happy afterlife? Hegel would contradict both of these suggestions. Contrary to (i), he would say that Christianity's orientation toward personal salvation reveals it to be in fact *deeply* self-regarding, that the Christian's seeming self-denial in this world really represents a profoundly self-regarding concern for his own well-being in the next. Contrary to (ii), as we saw earlier, he regards whatever consolation might be drawn from Christianity's promises concerning an afterlife as severely undercut by the inherent uncertainty of those promises (*Phenomenology,* par. 230). Moreover, he argues in an early fragment that the net effect of Christianity's orientation toward the afterlife, so far from being to *diminish* people's fear of death, has rather been to *exacerbate* it, in particular by increasing their preoccupation with death and with living in preparation for it (*Three Essays 1793-95,* pp. 76-78). There is, of course, some prima facie evidence pointing the other way here—for example, the fearlessness, and even enthusiasm, with which Christian martyrs, such as Polycarp, met their deaths. However, Hegel is well aware of this phenome-

makes the same point about the severe cost of an orientation toward self-regarding desires in a more modern connection. Thus in the *Pleasure and Necessity* section he considers the case of a modern consciousness motivated, like Goethe's Faust, by that paradigmatically self-regarding desire, desire for one's own pleasure, and argues that such a consciousness "experiences the double meaning implicit in what it did, namely, having *taken* its *life*; it took hold of life, but instead it thereby took hold of death" (par. 364).[129] Consider next the other part of the modern division between individual and community: the individual's refusal to accept automatically the community's shared judgments. Hegel believes this to be destructive of happiness mainly because he believes that it necessarily thwarts the three deepest human desires which were mentioned earlier: those for solidarity with one's community, knowledge of truth, and radical freedom. It is perhaps evident enough that it must thwart the deep desire for solidarity with one's community. Why, though, must it thwart the other two deep desires, those for knowledge of truth and radical freedom? The reason lies in a distinctive theory of truth which Hegel holds, and for which the *Phenomenology* furnishes an extended argument. According to this theory, it is a necessary and sufficient condition of a claim's truth that it be agreed upon by an enduring communal consensus: "The absolute pure will of all . . . has the form of immediate being. It is not a commandment which only *ought* to be; it *is* . . . ; it is the universal 'I' . . . which is immediately a reality, and the world *is* only this reality" (par. 436).[130] Because of this theory of truth, the individual's solidarity with his community is, in Hegel's eyes, necessary and sufficient for his attainment of knowledge of truth.[131] Moreover, because of this theory of

---

non (see for example *Early Theological Writings*, p. 162). And it remains arguable, I think, that the net effect of Christianity has been just as he says.

129. Hegel is exploiting a morbid pun in order to make his point here: the phrase translated "having *taken* its *life* [sein *Leben* sich *genommen* zu haben]" could mean either "having taken its [share in] life for itself" (i.e., having acted hedonistically), or "having taken its own life" (i.e., having committed suicide).

130. This theory of truth and Hegel's argument for it will be considered in detail in chapter 4.

131. Pars. 347–49: The individualistic consciousness's "certainty has . . . to be raised to the level of truth . . . To begin with this active Reason is aware of itself merely as an individual . . . Then, however, its consciousness having raised itself into universality, it becomes *universal* Reason, and is conscious of itself as Reason, as a consciousness that is . . . recognized in and for itself, which in its pure consciousness unites all self-consciousness," this "goal" being "the self-consciousness . . . which has its own self-certainty in the other free self-consciousness, and possesses its truth precisely in that 'other.' "

truth, the individual's solidarity with his community is also necessary and sufficient for his attainment of radical freedom, or the power to determine, and the actual determination of, what is the case quite generally. This is why the *Self-consciousness* chapter, immediately after unmasking human beings' deep aspiration to achieve such a freedom, goes on to indicate that it will be, and will only be, through participation in a communal consensus, " 'I' that is 'We' and 'We' that is 'I,' " that individuals will "enjoy perfect freedom and independence" (par. 177; cf. 356, 436).[132] Consequently, when individuals become divided from their community in the sense of ceasing to defer to their community's shared judgments, they doom themselves to unhappiness in each of these fundamental respects: they thwart their deep desire for solidarity with their community, their deep desire for knowledge of truth, and their deep desire for radical freedom. The *Phenomenology* is in large part devoted to recounting how, between the undivided community of ancient Greece and a dawning modern counterpart to it, man has run through a series of forms of such individualism, each incurring these costs.[133]

Concerning the sharp modern division of the subject and his conceptual thought from reality, which was first developed, according to the *Phenomenology*, by Platonism and Stoicism, Hegel sees this as leading inevitably to the epistemological anguish of *skepticism*. Thus in the *Self-consciousness* chapter of the *Phenomenology*, and again later in the *Lectures on the History of Philosophy*, he interprets this aspect of Stoicism as the immediate cause of ancient skepticism (with some historical plausibility).[134] And one can see from the 1802 essay *The Relation of Skepticism to Philosophy* that he would ultimately trace modern skepticism back to the same source as well.[135] Skepticism causes anguish because it frustrates

---

132. This equation of communal solidarity with both knowledge of truth and attainment of radical freedom helps to explain why Hegel describes communal solidarity as the individual's "essential character," and its realization as the "state of happiness," *simpliciter* (pars. 352–53). It was this equation that I had in mind when I said earlier that for Hegel, although our three deep human desires are intensionally distinguishable, they turn out to aim at one and the same condition.

133. For a general statement of this conception of history's course, see esp. pars. 352–56.

134. In particular, it is plausible to see ancient skepticism as indebted to this aspect of Stoicism in connection with what I shall be calling its "concept-instantiation" problems (rather than its "equipollence" problems in general). See chapter 3 for this distinction.

135. "According to this newest skepticism the human cognitive faculty is a thing which has concepts, and because it has only concepts, it cannot get to the things which are outside; it cannot *investigate* or *discover* them—for the two are *specifically* different"; but "the

human beings' deep desire to know the truth. Thus the Introduction says that "the natural consciousness . . . presses forward to true knowledge," and that the frustration of this aspiration through "skepticism" produces "despair" (pars. 77–78).[136]

Consider next our sharp modern distinction between fact and volition, and hence also between the theoretical and the practical sides of the mind. It is perhaps evident enough, to begin with, that the experience, and indeed even the mere prospect, of finding that the facts can balk however we may will them to be are productive of unhappiness. Hence, in one early fragment, for example, Hegel writes that "where the separation between the impulse and actuality is . . . great, . . . actual pain arises."[137] In addition, though, as we have seen, the *Self-consciousness* chapter of the *Phenomenology* unveils it as one of our deepest human aspirations to overcome the volition-independence of facts altogether.[138] And Hegel accordingly characterizes the satisfaction of this deep aspiration as fundamental to human happiness.[139] For both of these reasons, then, a sharp fact-volition distinction such as modernity assumes inevitably generates unhappiness. Furthermore, Hegel certainly agrees with Herder, who had argued that the second, self-internal, aspect of this dualism is also a potent cause of unhappiness.[140]

Concerning modern man's constant sharp opposition, both at an affective and at a more theoretical level, between his duty and his desires: First, it is perhaps obvious enough that the inner strife, and perpetual choice between moral guilt and unsatisfied desire, which this inflicts upon him must produce unhappiness.[141] Additionally, though, Hegel in the early theological writings indicates certain less obvious, more subtle ways in which this opposition is productive of unhappiness. Thus, second, con-

---

invention of this opposition [of concept and object] is . . . in itself older than the newest skepticism" (*Jenaer Schriften*, pp. 253, 251; also in appendix VI).

136. Hegel has in mind in this passage a specific sort of "skepticism," namely, the *Phenomenology*'s own. But his remark also has broader significance.

137. *Hegels theologische Jugendschriften*, p. 377.

138. Pars. 167–68, 174–75.

139. Par. 356.

140. See esp. *Vom Erkennen und Empfinden der menschlichen Seele*, in *Herders Ausgewählte Werke* 3:724–25, 734–35.

141. Schiller had put this unsavoury choice as follows: "Since the sense-drive exerts a physical, the form-drive a moral constraint, the first will leave our formal, the second our material disposition at the mercy of the contingent" (*On the Aesthetic Education of Man*, pp. 97–99).

trary to a long tradition—of which the earliest representative is perhaps Plato's *Phaedo* and the most recent (for Hegel) the Kantian conception of the *heter*onomy of all desires—according to which all desires are *extraneous* or *accidental* to the real self, Hegel believes that a person's identity and sense of his own identity essentially include desires. Thus in one passage he notes that, although "it is so often ignored," "a human being is a being composed of sensuousness and reason"; in another he refers to the desiring, as opposed to the moral, side of the individual as "the ordinary self"; and in a third he ventures the equation "your sensuous side or your individuality."[142] Consequently, if one feels and conceives duty as standing above and in sharp opposition to desires, in the manner of the Christian or the Kantian, then it will inevitably appear to one to be in some measure both alien to and coercive of oneself. Hegel characterizes the experience of alienness here as a form of what we would today call multiple personality disorder: in the Christian "the ordinary self goes on acting as before alongside the spiritual [i.e., the morally dutiful] self . . . the man is not a unity at all"; the Kantian "carries" a "lord in himself."[143] And concerning the experience of coerciveness, Hegel writes that Christianity represents, like Judaism before it, "bondage to law," and he speaks of "the self-coercion of Kantian virtue," stating that the Kantian "carries his lord in himself, yet at the same time is his own slave."[144] In this way too, then, unhappiness is generated. Third, Hegel implies, moreover, that one's sense of a *meaningful life* is essentially dependent on one's having *unconditional desires* or commitments of certain specific sorts. In *The Positivity of the Christian Religion* he emphasizes an unconditional desire for the welfare of one's community (patriotism), in *The Spirit of Christianity* an unconditional desire for the welfare of one's family members

---

142. *Hegels theologische Jugendschriften*, p. 357; *Early Theological Writings*, pp. 141, 238.

143. *Early Theological Writings*, pp. 141, 211. Schiller had already taken a view very similar to Hegel's here (*On the Aesthetic Education of Man*, p. 179; *Über Anmut und Würde*, in *Sämtliche Werke* 4:119). Note that Kant explicitly gives a "personify[ing]" description of our moral experience as "the fight of the good mind with a bad mind" (*Preisschrift über die Fortschritte der Metaphysik*, in *Kants gesammelte Schriften* [Berlin: de Gruyter, 1942], 20:346). Similarly, in a note from the critical period he writes: "Twofold self, to the extent that I am passive or active, animal or human. That is why I govern myself, reprimand and quarrel with myself" (*Reflexionen Kants zur Kritik der reinen Vernunft*, ed. B. Erdmann [Leipzig: Fues's Verlag, 1884], p. 379, no. 1321).

144. *Early Theological Writings*, pp. 139, 244, 211. Again, Schiller had already held a view very similar to Hegel's here (*On the Aesthetic Education of Man*, p. 179; *Über Anmut und Würde*, in *Sämtliche Werke* 4:118–19).

(love).¹⁴⁵ The *Spirit* chapter of the *Phenomenology* in its description of the ideal community of ancient Greece, and the *Philosophy of Right* in its description of the ideal modern community, incorporate both of these unconditional desires, distributing them along gender lines: unconditional commitment to the community is characteristic of the ideal male citizen, unconditional commitment to the family of the ideal female citizen.¹⁴⁶ Consequently, if one feels and conceives duty as standing above

---

145. Hegel considers both narrower and broader candidates but finds them all wanting. The narrower candidate of *oneself* leads to the problem of terror at the prospect of one's death (as we saw earlier). The broader candidate of *humanity as a whole* is incapable of sustaining deep commitment, and is only embraced as a reaction against narrower candidates: "The shapelessness of cosmopolitanism, . . . the void of the Rights of Man, or the like void of a league of nations or a world republic . . . are abstractions and formalisms filled with exactly the opposite of ethical vitality and which in their essence are protestants against individuality" (*Natural Law*, pp. 132–33). Also, as one can see from this passage, *general principles* are incapable of playing the meaning-giving role in question according to Hegel, for similar reasons. (This component of Hegel's intuition would later be repeated by Windelband as the provocative thesis that we can only truly value the "particular," not the "universal.")

146. *Phenomenology*, pars. 446 ff.; *Philosophy of Right*, par. 166. These ideals are quite likely to seem unattractive, or even pernicious, at first hearing, and it may therefore be worth saying a few words in Hegel's defense: (i) His insistence on these unconditional commitments and on their distribution between the sexes is generally explained by commentators mainly in terms of social-functional and logico-metaphysical motives (for a general example of these types of explanation, see Taylor, *Hegel*, pp. 434–35; for an example of their application to this case specifically, see Wood, *Hegel's Ethical Thought*, pp. 243–44). These are certainly important parts of Hegel's motivation. But they are unlikely by themselves to make his position seem appealing to many of us. However, once one understands his position in the way suggested above one can see that there is also a much more direct concern with the meaningfulness of individual lives at work behind it: in order to have a meaningful life, an individual must have one or the other of these unconditional commitments; and if the commitment is to be truly *unconditional* in the way required in order for it to provide meaning, rather than vitiated by divided loyalties, then he or she can only have *one* of them. Of course, that still leaves the question of why these commitments should be divided along gender lines and why men should get the politics while women get the family. But once Hegel's vital concern for meaningfulness in the lives of all parties is recognized, such a view at least loses its appearance of offensiveness, and perhaps even begins to look plausibly defensible.

(ii) One can, of course, all too easily imagine such unconditional commitments taking extreme and barbaric forms. It is important, however, to note that they *need not* do so and furthermore *do not* on Hegel's conception of them. Unconditional commitments to the welfare of one's own community or family need not entail the exclusion of commitments to the welfare of *other* communities or families, nor even a preference for the interests of one's own community or family on every occasion when these conflict with those of another (though, to be meaningful, they presumably *must* entail such a preference when the interests of one's own community or family at stake are sufficiently *fundamental* ones). In this humane spirit, Hegel endorses, for instance, a commitment to mankind at large, only insisting

and in opposition to one's desires, in the manner of the modern Christian or Kantian, then this will inevitably undermine the meaningfulness of one's life. Accordingly, Hegel criticizes Judaism and Christianity on the ground that their experience and conception of duty as divine commands entails a sort of conditionality for all other commitments (at best) which is incompatible with such an essentially unconditional commitment as genuine love. An early fragment on Judaism expresses this thought in the remark that "nothing is more opposed to the beautiful relations which are naturally grounded in love than lordship and bondage."[147] Hegel sees this flaw in Judaism as epitomized by the biblical story of Abraham's readiness to sacrifice his own son Isaac for God.[148] Similarly, Hegel notes

---

that this must not be allowed to undermine the unconditionality of the citizen's commitment to his state: "A man counts as a man in virtue of his manhood alone, not because he is a Jew, Catholic, Protestant, German, Italian, etc. This is an assertion which thinking ratifies and to be conscious of it is of infinite importance. It is defective only when it is crystallized, e.g., as a cosmopolitanism in opposition to the concrete life of the state" (*Philosophy of Right*, par. 209). Nor need unconditional commitments to the welfare of one's community or family entail support for one's own community or family *whatever it may do*, "My country right or wrong" (at least, not in any sense at odds with usual moral intuitions). This implication would be avoided if one included in one's conception of its *welfare* conformity to certain norms of ethical behavior, for example. Hegel's position avoids it mainly in a subtly different way: by including conformity to certain ethical norms in the ideal individual's conception of the very *identity* of the community or family to which he is unconditionally committed. Such an inclusion is part of the force, for instance, of Hegel's general preference for describing the ideal citizen's unconditional commitment as one to "ethical life" or "ethical substance," rather than, say, to "Athens" (e.g., *Phenomenology*, pars. 349–57). Hence in the *Philosophy of Right* Hegel accords the state a "supreme right" (pars. 258, 261) but insists that "an oriental despotism is not a state, or at any rate not the self-conscious form of state which is alone worthy of mind, the form which is organically developed and where there are rights and a free ethical life" (par. 270, addition). That Hegel adopts a similar position vis-à-vis the family is evident, for example, from the *Phenomenology*'s thesis—based partly on a notorious, and perhaps spurious, passage in the *Antigone* (ll. 909–15)—that the Greek woman's commitment to her family was a commitment to it, not simply qua a certain group of human beings, but *qua realizing a certain ethical function*: "The family is . . . within itself an *ethical* entity only so far as it is not the *natural* relationship of its members"; "In the ethical household, it is not a question of *this* particular husband, *this* particular child, but simply of husband and children generally; the relationships of the woman are based, not on feeling, but on the universal" (par. 457). If the community or family to which the ideal Hegelian individual is unconditionally committed were to behave in sufficiently despicable ways, therefore, his or her unconditional commitment would not require continued support for it; rather *it* (in the sense of its identity relevant to his or her commitment) would thereby cease to exist.

147. Unpublished fragment, quoted in Harris, *Hegel's Development,* p. 290 n.2.

148. "Love alone was beyond [Abraham's] power; even the one love he had, his love for his son . . . could depress him, trouble his all-exclusive heart and disquiet it to such an extent that even this love he once wished to destroy; and his heart was quieted only through

the many disparaging pronouncements about family ties in favor of religious ones in the New Testament.[149] And he comments on them: "A terrible tearing-apart of all natural bonds, the destruction of all nature."[150] The Jews, and by implication the Christians too, are left with "the performance of a countless mass of *senseless and meaningless* actions, . . . compulsions dictated by dead formulas . . . slavish obedience to laws not made by themselves."[151] In a similar vein, Hegel writes in criticism of Kantianism: "For the particular—impulses, inclinations, pathological love . . .—the universal is necessarily and always something alien and objective . . . Woe to the human relations which are not unquestionably found in the concept of duty; for this concept . . . excludes or dominates all other relations."[152] In this third way too, then, modernity's sharp opposition between duty and desire generates unhappiness.[153]

---

the certainty of the feeling that this love was not so strong as to render him unable to slay his beloved son with his own hand" (*Early Theological Writings*, p. 187).

149. These pronouncements (curiously underemphasized in Sunday schools) are very frequent and emphatic in the New Testament. See for example Luke 14:26: "If any man come to me, and hate not his father and mother, and wife, and children, and brethren, and sisters . . . he cannot be my disciple" (cf. Luke 18:29–30, 20:34–35; Matt. 19:29; Mark 10:29–30). Hegel first draws attention to this aspect of the biblical Jesus's position (uncritically) in *The Life of Jesus*, in *Three Essays 1793–95*, p. 138, and then later (and much more critically) in a fragment at *Hegels theologische Jugendschriften*, p. 396.

150. *Hegels theologische Jugendschriften*, p. 396.

151. *Early Theological Writings*, p. 178; emphasis added. Cf. *Phenomenology*, par. 228: for the Christian consciousness, "what it does is foreign to it, a thinking and speaking of what is meaningless to it."

152. *Early Theological Writings*, pp. 211–12. Note Hegel's significant elaboration here "excludes *or dominates*." The problem with which he is concerned is, of course, clearest in cases where duty is understood actually to proscribe solicitude for one's community or family. However, it remains in cases where duty is understood to permit or even to prescribe such solicitude. For in such cases commitment to one's community or family still loses its *unconditionality*, becoming instead conditional upon duty's permission or endorsement— and that is enough to preclude the sort of genuine patriotism or love which can alone, in Hegel's view, give life real meaning. To adapt an example from Williams in illustration of the point, there is a major difference between the man who, faced with the choice between saving his wife from a burning building and saving a stranger, chooses to save his wife *just because she is his wife*, and the man who chooses to do so partly or wholly *on the basis of having determined that moral duty permits or requires him to*. As Williams puts it, the latter scenario "provides the agent with one thought too many: it might have been hoped by some (for instance, by his wife) that his motivating thought, fully spelled out, would be the thought that it was his wife, not that it was his wife and that in situations of this kind it is permissible [or morally required] to save one's wife" (B.A.O. Williams, *Moral Luck* [Cambridge: Cambridge University Press, 1981], p. 18).

153. The Hegelian argument just presented bears a striking resemblance to what I take to be Williams's best case against Kantian impartial morality in *Moral Luck*, chap. 1,

Concerning the sharp modern division between virtue and happiness, which the Judeo-Christian-Kantian tradition first created and then unsuccessfully attempted to heal, Hegel implies that this inevitably produces unhappiness because it leaves the agent on the horns of the following dilemma: *either* he can pursue virtue, but in that case, given the desire-opposing character of virtue in this tradition, unhappiness will inevitably follow,[154] *or* he can pursue happiness by seeking satisfaction of his desires, but in that case, given the desire-opposing character of virtue in this tradition, he will have to sacrifice virtue, and consequently suffer the pains of bad conscience, thus rendering the pursuit futile—once again he incurs unhappiness.[155] In addition, Hegel points out, to the extent that a person confronts the breach between virtue and happiness within the theological framework of the Judeo-Christian-Kantian tradition, he will inevitably experience a sense of divine injustice, and thence feelings of bitterness and guilt—thereby reaping a still further harvest of unhappiness.[156]

Consider, finally, the dualism of mind or self and body. As we noted earlier, the *Phenomenology* explains modern adherence to this dualism as largely the *effect* of unhappiness (namely, the unhappiness of slaves and the socially oppressed in later antiquity). But the work also sees this dualism as the *cause* of—or at least a significant contributing cause of—further unhappiness. The work develops this theme most fully in its discussion of the Christian version of this dualism in the *Unhappy Consciousness* section (though the points made there would apply to

---

namely, his argument from the necessity to a meaningful life of such specific sorts of "ground projects" as love, and the incompatibility of these with Kantian impartial morality, to Kantian impartial morality's incompatibility with a meaningful life (see esp. pp. 17–18).

I call this Williams's "best case" because his chapter also contains a significantly different argument which he himself rather tends to emphasize, namely, from the *general* necessity of a ground project for a meaningful life, and the possibility that it will conflict with Kantian impartial morality, to the irrationality in such cases of sacrificing one's ground project to Kantian impartial morality, contrary to the latter's essential claim to win any possible conflict (pp. 11–14); but as it stands this argument is vulnerable to an obvious and inevitable Kantian rejoinder that Kantian impartial morality can, and as a condition of rationality must, *be* the ground project which gives one's life meaning.

154. *Phenomenology*, pars. 228–30: for the consciousness which does "what is right," "action and its own actual doing remain pitiable, its enjoyment remains pain."

155. Thus Hegel comments on the position of Goethe's Faust which aims at "just pleasure itself, or the simple single feeling," that "the transition from the moment of this its purpose into the moment of its true essence is for it a sheer leap into its antithesis. For these moments are not contained and linked together in feeling" (*Phenomenology*, par. 365).

156. Ibid., par. 601.

some other versions of the dualism as well, such as those in the Orphic-Pythagorean-Socratic-Platonic tradition, and if suitably modified might perhaps be extended to cover all versions of it). As we saw earlier, the *Unhappy Consciousness* section represents Christianity as distinguishing sharply between the body and its activities, on the one hand, and the mind or self, on the other, and additionally as associating the former with a corporeal nature divorced from God and the latter with God (pars. 220, 226). Hegel argues that such a conception inevitably leads to contempt for, or even a bedeviling of, the body and its activities: one's "actual doing . . . becomes a doing of nothing. Work and enjoyment . . . lose all universal content and significance"; the animal functions "are no longer performed naturally and without embarrassment . . . ; instead, . . . it is in them that the enemy reveals himself in his characteristic shape" (par. 225). In Hegel's view, this contempt for or bedeviling of the body and its activities is a potent destroyer of happiness, and this in several ways. First, according to Hegel, the mind or self is *not* in fact distinct from the body and its activities, but rather identical with them (I shall discuss Hegel's reasons for this view shortly). Consequently, this contempt for or bedeviling of the body and its activities is really a form of *self*-contempt or *self*-bedeviling: "Consciousness, in fixing its attention on [the devil which it sees in the body's animal functions], far from freeing itself from him, really remains forever in contact with him, and forever sees itself as defiled" (par. 225). This is one way in which unhappiness is generated. Second, this contempt for or bedeviling of the body and its activities inevitably leads to an attempt to *free* the mind or self from them. The Christian consciousness aims at "freeing itself from" the devil of the body's animal functions (par. 225), and engages in a systematic effort to renounce its bodily actions by, for example, handing over the decisions and volitions behind them to someone else (the priest, as God's representative), forgoing even an understanding of these decisions and volitions (by accepting them in Latin, a language which it does not comprehend), giving up the goods produced by its actions (as in tithing and charity), and rejecting all pleasure in the results of its actions (as in fasting and mortification) (par. 228).[157] These renunciations of the body and its activities generate

---

157. Par. 228: "In the mediator [i.e., the priest] . . . this consciousness frees itself from action and enjoyment so far as they are regarded as its own . . . It rejects the essence of its will, and casts upon the mediator or minister its own freedom of decision, and herewith the responsibility for its own action. This mediator, having a direct relationship with the unchangeable being [God], ministers by giving advice on what is right. The action, since

unhappiness in two further ways. On the one hand, most obviously, they deny the individual his former this-worldly forms of self-realization and satisfaction. On the other hand, less obviously, since the body and bodily activity are in fact identical with the mind or self according to Hegel, the Christian consciousness's attempt to free itself of its body and its bodily activities in fact amounts to a project of destroying itself, and therewith any possible form of self-realization: its attempt to free itself from its body is in fact "the attempted destruction of what [consciousness] actually is"; in its renunciation of its own bodily actions it in fact "truly and completely deprives itself of the consciousness of inner and outer freedom, of the actuality in which consciousness exists *for itself*. It has the certainty of having truly divested itself of its 'I' " (pars. 226, 229). In these several ways, the Christian's version of a dualism of mind or self and body contributes to the destruction of his happiness, to his "misery" (par. 230).

These, in short, are some of Hegel's major reasons for thinking modernity's distinctive dualisms productive of unhappiness. Before proceeding further, let me say explicitly that Hegel's historical diagnosis of modern man's distinctive unhappiness seems to me deep and in large measure defensible, both in its claims about man's development over the course of history from a more unified perspective to one rent by dualisms, and in its claims about the contribution which this development has made to modern man's unhappiness.[158]

* * *

In accordance with this diagnosis of the sources of modern man's unhappiness, Hegel, beginning in the early theological writings, developed

---

it follows upon the decision of someone else, ceases, as regards the doing or the *willing* of it, to be its own . . . [The fruit of its labor, and its enjoyment] it rejects as well. It renounces them, partly . . . in as much as what it does is foreign to it, a thinking and speaking of what is meaningless to it; partly as identified with *external possessions*—when it gives away part of what it has acquired through work; and partly, also, as identified with the enjoyment it has had—when, in its fasting and mortifications, it once more completely denies itself that enjoyment."

158. Of course, much more could be said about these issues. I do hope, though, that the above explanation of Hegel's position may at least have lent it enough plausibility to call into doubt Williams's initially tempting judgment in connection with Hegel that "one of the most persistent fantasies, at least of the Western world, is that there was a time when things were both more beautiful and less fragmented . . . But it is always a fantasy, and no serious study of the ancient world should encourage us to go back to that world to search for a lost unity" (*Shame and Necessity* [Berkeley: University of California Press, 1993], pp. 166–67).

the position that the required cure for this unhappiness was to overcome the offending dualisms. His primary means for accomplishing this was to be the establishment in modern culture of a fundamentally monistic conception of reality. As he already put this goal in the early fragment *Love*, from 1797–98, in connection with an early version of his unifying principle, "love": "In love the separate does still remain, but as something united and no longer as something separate."[159] As can perhaps already be seen from this remark, the aim was not so much to eliminate the dualisms altogether, but rather to mitigate them by conceiving them against the background of a deeper unity.[160] The fundamentally monistic conception of reality which Hegel went on to develop in his first philosophical system in the Jena years preceding the publication of the *Phenomenology* had the same purpose. Thus in the section of the *Difference* essay of 1801 entitled "The Need for Philosophy"—in many ways the locus classicus for the issues with which we are concerned here—he refers to the dualisms or divisions which I have been discussing and argues that "division is the source of *the need for philosophy*," and that "the task of philosophy consists in unifying [the Absolute and division], in setting . . . division in

---

159. *Early Theological Writings*, p. 305. In the early theological writings Hegel variously calls his unifying principle "love" (as in this fragment and, with more qualification, *The Spirit of Christianity*), "life" (in *The Spirit of Christianity* and the *Fragment of a System*), and "One Being" (in the strongly Hölderlin-influenced fragment *Faith and Being*).

160. Indeed, by 1800 or thereabouts Hegel had become quite emphatic about the need not only to overcome dualisms but also to *preserve* them in some fashion, and he remained so ever henceforth. This is the force, for example, of his rejection in the *Fragment of a System* of an *unqualified* monism in favor of "the union of union and non-union" (*Early Theological Writings*, p. 312), and of his rejection in the *Difference* essay of an *unqualified* principle of identity in favor of the principle of "the identity of identity and non-identity" (*Jenaer Schriften*, pp. 35–41, 96). Schiller was an important source of this insistence on the need to preserve dualisms within a restored unity in some fashion (see for example *On the Aesthetic Education of Man*, pp. 33, 39–41; and esp. *Über naive und sentimentalische Dichtung*, in *Sämtliche Werke* 4:425–27). For discussion of Hegel's motives in seeking to preserve dualisms in some fashion, see Taylor, *Hegel*, and Plant, *Hegel: An Introduction*; in chapter 4 I shall discuss a central motive which arises in connection with his theology specifically. On the other hand, it is very important to realize that the idea of unity or identity remains the *dominant* or overarching one for Hegel here—as can be seen, for example, from the very expressions "the *union* of union and non-union," "the *identity* of identity and non-identity" (as also from the *Difference* essay's equivalent expression, "absolute *identity*"). Consequently, however exactly one must in the end construe this paradoxical-sounding position (a question which I shall discuss in connection with the crucial theological case in chapter 4), it is at least clear that it is meant to remain in some pretty strong sense monistic.

the Absolute . . . as its appearance" (i.e., in revealing division to be merely the appearance of a deeper unity, that of the Absolute).[161] The same motivation would remain active behind the mature Hegel's philosophy as well. In an 1818 speech, for example, he again explains "the need for philosophy" as arising from the dualisms which I have discussed.[162]

Not surprisingly, therefore, the *Phenomenology* likewise has the ambition of overcoming these dualisms so that human happiness may become possible. Hence, for example, the work's historical schema, mentioned earlier, of a fall from simplicity or unity into division has a crucial last step: "The bifurcation of the simple," or of "an original or immediate unity," "is the doubling which sets up opposition, *and then again the negation of this indifferent diversity*" (par. 18; emphasis added; cf. 21).[163] (This is a central schema for the interpretation of history in the *Phenomenology*, though only one of several which we shall encounter.)[164]

As for the writings of the early Jena period such as the *Difference* essay, and for mature works such as the speech from 1818, it is, of course, for the *Phenomenology* Hegel's own philosophical system which is to

---

161. In appendix IV. This section of the *Difference* essay refers explicitly to almost all of the eight dualisms which I have distinguished as central to Hegel's concerns: that between God, on the one hand, and man and nature, on the other (here "Absolute" and "appearance"), that between man and nature (here "spirit and matter," "intelligence and nature"), that between the self and its thought, on the one hand, and reality, on the other (here "absolute subjectivity and absolute objectivity," "intelligence and nature"), that between volition and fact (here "freedom and necessity"), that between duty and desire (here "reason and sensuousness"), and that between mind or self and body (here "soul and body," "spirit and matter").

162. *Enzyklopädie der philosophischen Wissenschaften* 3:406–8. This speech refers in particular to the dualisms between God, on the one hand, and man and nature, on the other (here the "infinite" and the "finite"), fact and volition (here "objectivity and freedom"), and duty and desire (here "reason" and "impulses").

163. Like Hegel's previous writings, the *Phenomenology* envisages this overcoming of dualisms, not as eliminating them altogether, but rather as overcoming them while also in some fashion preserving them. Hence, the sentence just quoted continues: "and then again the negation of this indifferent diversity *and of its antithesis*" (emphasis added)—meaning that *undifferentiated* unity is to be superseded as well. Similarly, in the same paragraph Hegel writes that "only . . . reflection of otherness within itself—not an *original* or *immediate* unity as such—is the true." Note in this vein also the work's emphasis on the essential role in Absolute Spirit of the separating activity of the Understanding (par. 32), and the work's criticism of Schelling for failing to preserve division in his monistic principle, his rendering the "Absolute as the night in which, as the saying goes, all cows are black" (par. 16).

164. Schiller was the main source of this schema. See, for example, *Über naive und sentimentalische Dichtung*, in *Sämtliche Werke* 4:386: "Nature makes [man] one with her-

achieve this overcoming of dualisms (i.e., the system which he eventually went on to publish in its mature form in the *Encyclopaedia*). One way in which the *Phenomenology* expects the system to accomplish this lies in the latter's monism, its interpretation of all features of reality as merely aspects of a single principle, Absolute Spirit (in the manner sketched briefly in chapter 1). For, as the *Difference* essay had already indicated, this automatically sets any dualisms against the background of a deeper unity—or "set[s] . . . division in the Absolute . . . as appearance"—thereby diminishing their sharpness.[165] However, there are also numerous more specific features of the philosophical position toward which the *Phenomenology* is arguing which are aimed in more specific ways at overcoming each of the dualisms that most concern Hegel, and these are especially interesting and worthy of attention.

Thus, in answer to the division of God from man and nature, to begin with this, the philosophy envisaged by the *Phenomenology* includes a rather elegant account according to which God is actually in some sense *identical* with man and nature. This identity is the point behind the work's criticism of the Unhappy Consciousness of Christianity: "What it does *not* know is that . . . its object, the unchangeable [God], which it knows . . . in the form of individuality, is *its own self*, is itself the individuality of consciousness" (par. 216).[166] Furthermore, according to Hegel's philosophical position, God, far from being epistemically inaccessible to man, is fully intelligible and knowable by him, and is indeed fully understood and known by him in Hegelian philosophy itself.[167] With these two doctrines—which are among the most novel and distinctive features of Hegel's theology, and his most dramatic departures from orthodox Christian beliefs—the traditional dualistic conception of God's

---

self, art separates and divides him, through the ideal he returns to unity." Also, and especially, *On the Aesthetic Education of Man*, letter 6.

165. The *Phenomenology* expresses this conception in, for example, its descriptions of Absolute Spirit as "this reflection in otherness within itself," and as that which "in its self-externality abides within itself" (pars. 18, 25).

166. A version of this position can already be found in the early theological writings. Thus already in *The Spirit of Christianity* Hegel interprets and endorses Jesus as rejecting the Jews' assumption "of their opposition to the divine, of an impassable gulf between the being of God and the being of men," commenting that "the hill and the eye which sees it are object and subject, but between man and God, between spirit and spirit, there is no such cleft . . . ; both are one" (*Early Theological Writings*, p. 265).

167. For an especially forceful statement of this position, see Hegel's *Vorrede zu Hinrichs Religionsphilosophie*, in Hegel, *Sämtliche Werke* 20:25–27.

relation to man and nature is overcome.[168] And the several forms of unhappiness which were generated by that conception are thereby overcome as well. (I shall consider this Hegelian theology in some more detail in chapter 4.)

Concerning modernity's sharp distinction between man and nature, its denial of personality and purpose to the latter, the philosophical position toward which the *Phenomenology* is arguing restores both purpose and personality to nature, namely, the purpose and personality of Absolute Spirit, with whom it identifies (man and) nature.[169] This interpretation of nature is worked out in detail in the *Encyclopaedia*'s Philosophy of Nature. Within the *Phenomenology* itself it emerges as a sort of subtext of the development of modern natural science as this is described by the *Observing Reason* section—ironically, since the *text* of that development is rather the unfolding of the disenchanted worldview to its most extreme form. Thus, on the one hand, according to the *Observing Reason* section, at the textual or explicit level that development begins with the emergence of disenchanted scientific explanations of inanimate nature in the early seventeenth century (Bacon and Galileo), then extends such explanations to organic nature (the Accademia dei Lincei), and then finally extends them even to the human mind itself (most radically in the eighteenth century pseudoscience of phrenology, which identifies the mind with the brain and its activity). But on the other hand, the *Observing Reason* section implies, at a more subtextual or implicit level the same development simultaneously represents a sort of *reversal* of the whole process of disenchantment: beginning from disenchanted scientific explanations of inanimate nature in the early seventeenth century, the focus then shifts to organic nature, and the implicit moral of this shift is the superiority of *teleological* explanations of nature (pars. 249–50, 253–54), and then finally the focus shifts to the human mind, and the implicit moral of *this* shift is the superiority of explanations of nature which are not only teleological but also *personal*, and indeed

---

168. Note that—in marked tension with, though not necessarily contradicting, his ambition to preserve dualisms in some fashion—Hegel indeed with these two doctrines in a way bridges the gulf between God and man/nature even more completely than it was bridged by the Greeks. We shall see that this feature recurs in his responses to other dualisms as well.

169. Note again here that Hegel's philosophy indeed in a way bridges the gap between man and nature even more completely than it was bridged in Greek polytheism: Greek polytheism bridged it only in the sense of making nature *like* mankind; Hegel's philosophy, on the other hand, since it identifies Absolute Spirit not only with nature but also with mankind, in a sense makes nature not just like but also *identical with* mankind.

humanly personal (pars. 258–59, 347).[170] This subtext in the development of modern natural science has prepared the ground for Hegel's own explicit execution of such teleological and personal explanations of nature within his Philosophy of Nature.[171] By reversing the process of disenchantment in this way, Hegel's philosophy will eliminate the three sorts of "alienness" in nature which were described earlier, and with them the unhappiness which they have generated.[172]

Consider next the modern division between individual and community. Hegel believes that the modern individualist's division between himself and his community rests on an implicit assumption of his ontological and practical autonomy from his community: an assumption that he is not dependent on his community or on conformity with it either for his own existence and identity or for the realization of his deepest aspirations (at least, not essentially). The *Phenomenology* addresses the individual-community division largely by arguing that, on the contrary, the very existence and identity of the individual and the realization of all his deepest aspirations do depend essentially on his community and on his conformity with it. Thus, concerning first the individual's *very existence and identity*, the *Phenomenology* argues forcefully that (i) conceptual thought of any kind essentially requires possession of a corresponding language, and (ii) possession of a language essentially requires participation in a corresponding linguistic community.[173] Consequently, (iii) a human indi-

---

170. As illustrative of the final steps of these two contrary readings, and of Hegel's idea of the different levels of opposed significance in modern science's development generally, note the double significance which he ascribes to the phrenologist's identification of the human mind with a natural object (the brain and its activity) in the following passage: "Self-consciousness found the thing to be like itself, and itself to be like a thing; i.e., it is aware that it is in itself the objectively real world. It is . . . a certainty for which the immediate in general has the form of something superseded, so that the objectivity of the immediate still has only the value of something superficial, its inner being and essence being self-consciousness itself" (par. 347).

171. Connectedly, the development of modern natural science, as Hegel interprets it, has also prepared the ground for his own Philosophy of Nature by taking up subject matters in the same order as the latter: beginning with inanimate nature, then turning to organic nature, then finally to the human mind (as in the Philosophy of Nature's climactic transition to the Philosophy of Spirit).

172. The most difficult aspect of this, namely, how it will eliminate the third sort of "alienness," our inability to *understand* a disenchanted nature, was explained in footnote 125 above.

173. These views play major roles in the *Sense-certainty* section. (i) is Hegel's reason for assuming there, as he does, that it is damning of Sense-certainty's claim to know (and so to think) in the way that it purports to that such putative knowledge (and so thought)

vidual, as the sort of being who could not exist at all without conceptual thought, nor be the particular person he is without (much of) the specific conceptual thought which he has,[174] depends essentially for his existence and identity on participation in his linguistic community. Thus in a paragraph of the *Spirit* chapter devoted to the question of the "characteristic significance" of language Hegel writes:

> [The power of speech] is the *real existence* of the pure self as self; in speech, self-consciousness's autonomous individuality comes into existence as such, so that it exists *for others*. Otherwise, the "I" . . . is non-existent, is not *there* . . . Language . . . contains [the "I"] in its purity, it alone expresses the "I," the "I" itself. This *real* existence of the "I" is, qua real existence, an objectivity which has in it the true nature of the "I." The "I" is this particular "I"—but equally the *universal* "I" . . . The "I" that expresses itself . . . is an infectious bondedness [eine Ansteckung] in which it has immediately passed into unity with those for whom it is a real existence, and is a universal self-consciousness. (par. 508)[175]

Concerning second *the realization of all his deepest aspirations*, as has already been mentioned, the *Phenomenology* contains an extended argument for the theory that truth consists in a judgment's endorsement by an enduring communal consensus, so that the individual's realization of his deep aspirations not only to communal solidarity itself but also to

---

would be in principle inexpressible. (ii) is part of the force of the *Sense-certainty* section's conclusion that one cannot say what one merely *meint*, i.e., means *by oneself*, because language is inherently *allgemein*, i.e., involves general concepts *common to all selves*. I shall return to these views and consider Hegel's arguments for them later in this chapter and in chapter 4.

174. This idea that the human individual essentially depends for his existence on conceptual thought and for his particular identity on (much of) the specific conceptual thought which he has is intuitively plausible and reasonably uncontroversial. It is worth noting, however, that Hegel also holds some less common views which lend his version of the idea a distinctive character. In particular, (a) his model of what it is to be a self or a consciousness essentially includes possession of a set of rather specific conceptual thoughts, including for example thinking of oneself as a self. (On this, see for instance *Encyclopaedia*, par. 24, addition 1. I shall consider this model in some detail later in the present chapter.) And (b) he believes that not only conceptual and propositional attitudes, such as thinking of and thinking that, but *all* human mental contents are in essential part constituted by conceptual thought. (On this, see for example ibid., pars. 2 and 24, addition 1.)

175. Language plays a central role in Hegel's philosophy generally and in the *Phenomenology* in particular. Some helpful general treatments of the subject are: T. Bodammer, *Hegels Deutung der Sprache* (Hamburg: Felix Meiner, 1969); D.J. Cook, *Language in the Philosophy of Hegel* (The Hague: Mouton and Co., 1973); and M.J. Inwood, *A Hegel Dictionary* (Oxford: Blackwell, 1992).

knowledge of truth and to radical freedom essentially depends on, and is ensured by, his community and his conformity with it. Hegelian man, through coming to recognize in these ways that his very existence and identity, and also the realization of all his deepest aspirations, depend essentially on his community and his conformity with it, loses all sense of himself as a being ontologically or practically autonomous of his community. His conception of his relation to his community instead becomes more like one of identity: "I regard them as myself and myself as them," " 'I' that is 'We' and 'We' that is 'I' " (pars. 352, 177).[176] Hegel envisages it as a consequence of the modern Hegelian individual's attainment of these insights that he will be restored to the two attitudes of close identification with his community which were characteristic of the Greeks, and whose rupture constituted the individual-community division: First, he will be restored to a commitment to his community as his highest end. Thus Hegel writes at the beginning of the *Spirit* chapter concerning the standpoint of modern Hegelian individuals: "Spirit, being the substance and the universal, self-identical, and abiding essence, is the unmoved solid ground and starting-point for the action of all, and it is their purpose and goal" (par. 439).[177] In this way, the obstacles to happiness caused by the individualist's rejection of the community as his highest end, such as terror at the prospect of his own death, will be overcome. Second, the modern Hegelian individual will be restored to that automatic identification with his community's judgments, especially on ethical matters, which was the other aspect of the Greek's sense of closeness to his community (in contrast to the later accordance of ultimate authority to the individu-

---

176. As in the case of the previous dualisms, note that this Hegelian bridging of the division between the individual and his community in a way brings them even closer together than they were for the Greeks, whose awareness of such a thoroughgoing ontological and practical dependence of the individual on his community could presumably only have been implicit at best.

177. The Hegelian individual's attainment of insight into his essential ontological and practical dependence on his community and his conformity with it should perhaps, strictly speaking, be interpreted as advancing him *toward* this valuation of his community as his highest end, rather than as taking him all the way there. An individualist who discovered that his very existence and identity, and the realization of all his deepest aspirations, depended essentially on his community and his conformity with it would certainly thereby be moved *closer* to regarding his community as his highest end. In particular, it would now be irrational of him to value anything *more highly* than his community. However, one can still imagine him without breach of rationality valuing it only *instrumentally* rather than as an *end* (albeit now as an *essentially* required instrument, not a merely causally required or dispensable one).

al's judgment in autonomy of the judgments of his fellows in society, whether as interpreting God's, in the manner of Judeo-Christian religion, or as self-standing, in the manner of Stoicism for example). Thus, sketching the attitude of his own philosophy at the climax of the *Reason* chapter, Hegel writes:

> The law . . . is not grounded in the will of a particular individual . . . ; it is the absolute *pure will of all* which has the form of immediate being . . . The obedience of self-consciousness is not the serving of a master whose commands were arbitrary and in which it would not recognize itself [i.e., as in the Judeo-Christian conception] . . . If [the laws] are supposed to be validated by *my* insight, then I have already denied their unshakeable, intrinsic being . . . Ethical disposition consists just in sticking steadfastly to what is right, and abstaining from all attempts to move or shake it, or derive it. (pars. 436–37)[178]

The *Phenomenology* contains an interesting causal account of how such a conformism in judgment has become possible for the modern world. It has become so as the result of a long historical process that has disciplined individuals to judge conformably with their fellows, a process in which the experience of slavery and other forms of social oppression in the later ancient world—the experience of the bondsman in the *Lordship and Bondage* section—played a key role.[179] However, the modern Hegelian individual's conformism in judgment is not therefore merely slavish or irrational. For, he *wants* to conform in this way, and indeed wholeheartedly so, without contrary individualistic wants.[180] And he does so for

---

178. Hence the modern distinction between social law or custom, on the one hand, and private morality, on the other, disappears—morality becomes once again, as it was for the Greeks (as Hegel interprets them), entirely social. (For this theme, cf. *Natural Law*, esp. pp. 112–15.) Note, indeed, that, as in other cases, the distinction is now in a sense healed even more completely than it was for the Greeks: As we saw earlier, according to the *Phenomenology*, although the Greeks' laws were all *at bottom* social—the Greeks had no genuinely private morality as we moderns have—there were nevertheless marked differences in the degrees of explicitness with which their laws were recognized to be socially based; while the "human law" was explicitly recognized to be so, the "divine law" was only implicitly recognized to be so. The modern Hegelian standpoint removes even this modicum of asociality in the Greeks' conception of some of their laws; all laws are now recognized to be socially based with full and equal explicitness, none are in any way attributed to a deity distinct from us.

179. I shall consider the details of this causal account in chapters 4 and 9.

180. Par. 436: "The obedience of self-consciousness is not the serving of a master . . . in which it would not recognize itself. On the contrary, laws are . . . thoughts which are immediately its *own*," it "has put its merely individual aspect behind it."

compelling *reasons*—in particular, his recognition now, in light of the enduring communal consensus theory of truth which the *Phenomenology* has established, that this, done in concert with the other members of his community, is necessary and sufficient for the realization of all his deepest aspirations, those for solidarity with the community per se, for knowledge of truth, and for radical freedom. (In addition, as we shall see later in this and the next chapter, he has reasons of certain sorts furnished by the *Phenomenology* for converging with his fellows in society on the standpoint of Hegelian philosophy *specifically*.)[181] Through achieving such conformism in judgment, modern Hegelian individuals eliminate the obstacle posed by individualism in judgment to the realization of their three deepest aspirations, and thereby to their happiness. And more positively, they ensure the realization of those aspirations, and thereby of the very core of their happiness. As Hegel puts this thought in his discussion of the standpoint of his own philosophy at the end of the *Reason* chapter: "The law . . . is the absolute pure will of all . . . It is not a commandment, which only ought to be: it *is* and is *valid;* it is the universal 'I' . . . which is immediately a reality, and the world *is* only this reality. But since this existent law is valid unconditionally, the obedience of self-consciousness is not the serving of a master whose commands were arbitrary, and in which it would not recognize itself. On the contrary, laws are the thoughts of its own absolute consciousness, thoughts which are immediately its own" (par. 436).

Concerning the modern dualism of the self and its conceptual thought, on the one hand, and reality, on the other, the renunciation of any sharp distinction between these is a fundamental tenet of the philosophy toward which the *Phenomenology* is arguing. As Hegel puts it in the *Phenomenology,* "Whereas in the Phenomenology of Spirit each moment is the

---

181. It is noteworthy, though, that these reasons are not particularly oriented to the detailed *ethical* content of Hegelian philosophy, and that indeed Hegel's presentation of his own ethical outlook at paragraphs 436–37, as just quoted above, seems to speak against rather than for its inclusion of reasons grounding its specific ethical laws (cf. the immediately preceding dismissal of both law-giving and law-testing reason). By contrast, later works such as the *Philosophy of Right* will accord a clear role to law-specific reasons in ethics. On the other hand, as Wood points out, this change will not involve any abandonment of the *Phenomenology*'s ideal of an individual's automatic identification with his community's judgments, because this remains for the later Hegel a sine qua non of ethical disposition, and is merely *reinforced* by the law-specific reasons in question, not *supplanted* by them as the basis of ethical decision (*Hegel's Ethical Thought*, pp. 217–18). This is also the way to think of the role of the reasons mentioned above which the *Phenomenology* does already have in view.

difference of knowledge and truth, . . . Science on the other hand does not contain this difference . . . On the contrary, . . . the moment . . . unites the objective form of truth and the form of the knowing self in an immediate unity" (par. 805). Or as he puts it in the *Science of Logic*, "Pure Science presupposes the liberation from the opposition of consciousness. It contains *thought insofar as it is equally the matter in itself, or the matter in itself insofar as it is equally pure thought.*"[182] Indeed, as we shall see in chapter 3, it is one of the central purposes of the *Phenomenology* to discredit the distinction between concepts and their real instances and to prove the identity of the two sides through showing that all possible ways of articulating such a distinction are implicitly self-contradictory. And, as we shall see in chapter 4, it is another central purpose of the work to discredit the distinction between propositional representations and independent facts and the conception resting upon this distinction that truth consists in a relation of correspondence between the two, and to show that truth instead consists just in enduring communal agreement, again by showing that all possible ways of articulating such a distinction are implicitly self-contradictory. In these (and other) ways Hegel's philosophy aims to undercut the epistemological doubts of the skeptic and to restore *certainty*, thereby eliminating the skeptic's epistemological anguish: "In absolute knowing . . . the separation of the object from self-certainty has dissolved itself completely and the truth has become equal to this certainty and this certainty to the truth."[183] (These and other epistemological matters will be considered in some more detail in chapter 3.)

182. In appendix XV. H.P. Kainz is therefore mistaken when he writes: "As far as Hegel was concerned . . . [subject and object] are irreducible to each other . . . He maintains the distinction in its rigor . . . He recognizes that there is something really objective outside of and other than the ego" (*Hegel's Phenomenology, Part One: Analysis and Commentary* [Tuscaloosa: University of Alabama Press, 1976], p. 21; cf. 22, 163).
183. From the *Science of Logic*, in appendix XV. The general idea of dispelling skepticism by discrediting as self-contradictory the assumption of a sharp opposition between thought and reality on which it rests, and so establishing their unity, was first developed by Hegel as early as the 1798 fragment *Faith and Being*. Thus, in this fragment Hegel implies that skepticism arises on the basis of a sharp distinction between thought and reality, or between two sorts of being (that of the former and that of the latter): "What is thought about is something separated, opposed to the thinker . . . From this source alone can there arise a misunderstanding, that there are different types of unification, of being, and that one can therefore to this extent say: there is something, but it is not necessary for that reason that I believe it—with one sort of being it does not necessarily follow that another sort of being belongs to it; moreover, belief is not being, but a reflected being; to this extent one can also say that what is need not for that reason 'be' reflected, come to consciousness" (*Hegels theologische Jugendschriften*, p. 383). But Hegel then indicates that this basis of

Concerning the sharp modern distinction between fact and volition, and consequently also between the theoretical and the practical sides of the self: In the *Phenomenology*'s *Reason* chapter, as we approach the standpoint of Hegel's own philosophy presented in paragraphs 435–37 at the very end of the chapter, and specifically from the section *Pleasure and Necessity* (the perspective of Goethe's Faust) onwards, we encounter viewpoints for which facts are not independent of but dependent upon the self and its practical activity, and the latter consequently enjoy priority. By the section *The Spiritual Animalkingdom* (Herder's perspective), the sharp distinction between fact and volition is explicitly erased: for this perspective, there is a "unity of *doing* and *being,* of willing and achieving" (par. 409).[184] More specifically, for the outlook of this section, and thereafter for the Hegelian standpoint at paragraphs 435–37 itself as well, there is simply no distinction between the self's willing X together with a community of other selves and X's being a fact: "The nature of the matter itself [die Sache selbst]" "is such that its *being* is the *action* of the *single* individual and of all individuals" (par. 418); "The absolute pure will of all . . . has the form of immediate being. It is not a commandment, which only *ought* to be: it *is* . . . ; it is the universal 'I' . . . which is immediately a reality, and the world *is* only this reality" (par. 436). The reason for this lies in these viewpoints' acceptance, in one form or another, of the Hegelian theory of truth, according to which enduring communal consensus is necessary and sufficient for truth, so that all and only what we collectively and enduringly decide to be the case really is the case. Nor is the direct translatability of volitions into facts thus envisaged by these viewpoints understood to be a bare possibility. For, as Hegel describes these viewpoints, coming after the long historical process of disciplining individuals toward conformism which began with slavery and other forms of social oppression in the later ancient world (Lordship and Bondage), and in particular immediately after the disciplining of un-

---

skepticism is implicitly self-contradictory, and that the two sides must therefore be unified in "One Being": "What is separated finds its unification only in One Being; for a different being of one sort would presuppose a nature which was also not nature, or in other words a contradiction" (ibid., p. 383). This early version of Hegel's argument against skepticism is heavily indebted to Hölderlin and von Sinclair—concerning which, see my *Hegel and Skepticism* (Cambridge, Mass.: Harvard University Press, 1989), pp. 118 ff.

184. Cf. the prominence in this section of the phrase *die Sache selbst* in the intentionally double sense of "the *thing* itself " and "the *cause* itself " (in the volitional sense of "cause," as when we speak of a political cause).

bridled modern individualism effected by Frederick the Great (Virtue), and moreover possessing insight, thanks to their enduring communal consensus theory of truth, into the necessity and sufficiency of conformism for the realization of their deepest desires, they constitute a historical context in which the sort of convergence in volitions that is required for direct truth-constitution is a reality. Hence Hegel writes of the Herderian standpoint of the Spiritual Animalkingdom that here "being is the action of the single individual and of all individuals, and [its] action is immediately . . . a thing as the action of each and everyone" (par. 418), and of his own standpoint at paragraphs 435–37, similarly, that here "the law . . . is grounded not in the will of a particular individual . . . ; it is the absolute pure will of all . . . It is not a commandment, which only ought to be: it *is* and is *valid*; it is the universal 'I' . . . which is immediately a reality, and the world *is* only this reality" (par. 436). For these viewpoints, therefore, the sharp distinction between fact and volition is overcome in a quite thorough way. And accordingly, the unhappiness caused by such a sharp distinction is eliminated. In addition, the Hegelian individual who attains such a standpoint ceases either to have, or to conceive himself as having, beliefs, a theoretical perspective. For belief essentially includes a conception of objectivity, or of its object's independence from the self and the self's mental representations.[185] But any such conception has been eliminated by the Hegelian individual's distinctive theory of truth. Hence Hegel writes that this individual "does not *believe* . . . for . . . [belief] perceives [essential being] as something alien to itself" (par. 436).[186] The Hegelian individual's attempts at the truth rather have, and are conceived by him to have, the character of creative volitions. This is one reason why his perspective is consistently characterized in the para-

---

185. Par. 85: "The distinction between the in-itself and cognition is already present in the very fact that consciousness has cognition of an object at all. Something is *for it* the *in-itself*; and cognition, or the being of the object for consciousness, is, *for it*, another moment." (Note that by "cognition" in this context Hegel means what we would usually call *belief*, rather than knowledge; "false cognition" is no oxymoron for the Introduction.)

186. Similarly, and consistently, Hegel implies that the early Greeks, who had not yet *developed* a sharp fact-volition distinction, did not yet *believe* in our sense of the word either (*Early Theological Writings*, pp. 196–97). And he implies the same of the ancient Jews—though in their case not because they inserted their *own* wills into their factual views like the Greeks, but because they subjected their factual views wholly to the will of *another*, namely, God (ibid.). Hegel's ideas that belief itself in our sense of the word is a much more historically localized phenomenon than we generally suppose, and an activity which we should ourselves dispense with, strike me as philosophically pregnant.

graphs at the end of the *Reason* chapter presently under discussion as a form of *willing*. And it also helps to explain why Hegel elsewhere characterizes the acceptance of his own philosophy's standpoint by such expressions as "the decision to will pure thought."[187] Or alternatively, since there does remain for this Hegelian perspective a sort of weakened analogue of the constraint of the individual's judgments by objective facts, in the form of their constraint by the judgments of the rest of the community, one could say that the Hegelian individual's attempts at the truth now have, and are conceived by him to have, the character of neither beliefs nor volitions, but a sort of synthesis of the two. In this alternative vein, Hegel writes in the 1805–6 Philosophy of Spirit: "Spirit is actual neither as intelligence nor as will but as *will which is intelligence.*"[188] Either way, modernity's sharp distinction between the theoretical and the practical sides of the self is overcome. And the forms of unhappiness caused by this self-internal aspect of the dualism, such as Herder had emphasized, are thereby eliminated as well. In sum, for the Hegelian standpoint sketched at the end of the *Reason* chapter both the sharp opposition between fact and volition and the sharp opposition between the theoretical and the practical sides of the self disappear, and with them the various forms of unhappiness which they produce.[189]

Consider next the modern opposition, both at an affective and at a more theoretical level, between duty and desire. For the perspective of Hegel's philosophy sketched at the end of the *Reason* chapter, there is no general distinction between duty and desire in theory, because duty is conceived just as a special sort of desire, namely, desire in which all members of society are in agreement: "The law . . . is the absolute *pure will of all*" (par. 436).[190] Nor is there any opposition between duty and desire at the affective level of practical experience; the Hegelian individual does not find himself struggling against contrary inclinations when he follows duty. Instead, he immediately and wholeheartedly wills in agree-

---

187. *Encyclopaedia*, par. 78.
188. Hegel, *Jenaer Realphilosophie* (Hamburg: Felix Meiner, 1969), p. 213.
189. For the above reasons, J.G. Gray seems to me mistaken when he writes that Hegel "opposed the whole modern emphasis on the creativity of will . . . Will in his philosophy is subsumed under intellect, and the intellect is governed largely by the capacity to know and understand rather than to create" (*Hegel's Hellenic Ideal*, in *The Philosophy of Hegel*, p. 67).
190. This represents for Hegel a return to the conception of duty held by the Greeks, for whom "virtue" consisted in the citizen's "knowing that the law of his own heart is the law of all hearts" (par. 461).

ment with his fellows: "Laws are . . . thoughts which are immediately [self-consciousness's] own . . . Ethical self-consciousness is immediately one with essential being through the universality of its self . . . [It] has put its merely individual aspect behind it" (par. 436). As we have noted, the *Phenomenology* explains this condition of the modern Hegelian individual as both *causally* supported, namely, through history having disciplined modern individuals to will conformably with their fellows by a long process which began with slavery and other forms of social oppression in the later ancient world, and *rationally* supported, namely, through the modern Hegelian individual's recognition, in light of his enduring communal consensus theory of truth, that all of his deepest desires, not only that for solidarity with his community per se, but also those for knowledge of truth and radical freedom, can be realized by and only by thus willing in conformity with his fellows in society. Through overcoming modernity's sharp duty-desire opposition in this way, the modern Hegelian individual is freed of the several forms of unhappiness which it generated.[191]

Concerning our sharp modern division between virtue and happiness, the Hegelian position toward which the *Phenomenology* argues restores a very intimate connection between these, and one similar to that which the work ascribes to the Greeks. As we have noted, for this Hegelian position virtue consists in solidarity with the community: "The law . . . is the absolute pure will of all." At the same time, this position also recognizes that our deepest human desires are for solidarity with the community, knowledge of truth, and radical freedom, and that, because of the identity of truth with enduring communal consensus, the realization of the first of these, solidarity with the community, is sufficient and necessary for the realization of the other two as well. Consequently, for this Hegelian position virtue is sufficient and necessary for the realization of

---

191. The project of overcoming the duty-desire opposition already had a fairly long history behind it by the time Hegel developed this solution in the *Phenomenology*. The goal of overcoming this opposition was already central to Schiller's philosophy, the solution in his case taking the form of the development of an *aesthetic* standpoint (see esp. *On the Aesthetic Education of Man*, pp. 17–19, 97–99, 119–21; *Über Anmut und Würde*, in *Sämtliche Werke* 4:112–17, 120–21). Also, Hegel's own project of overcoming it was already strongly developed in *The Spirit of Christianity*, though in a way notably different from either Schiller's or the *Phenomenology*'s: in *The Spirit of Christianity* he interpreted and endorsed Jesus's ethical principle of *love* as an attempt to overcome the Jewish opposition between divine law and desire, and as a way of overcoming the Kantian opposition between self-given moral law and desire as well (see esp. *Early Theological Writings*, pp. 214 ff., 225, 247).

all three of our deepest desires, and hence for the very core of our happiness. This is why the *Reason* chapter equates virtue, solidarity with one's community, and happiness, not only for the Greek standpoint, the standpoint from which "self-consciousness . . . has withdrawn," but also for the emerging Hegelian standpoint, the standpoint which "self-consciousness . . . has not yet realized": "The wisest men of antiquity have . . . declared that wisdom and virtue consist in living in accordance with the customs of one's nation. But from this state of happiness of having realized its essential character . . . self-consciousness . . . has withdrawn, or else has not yet realized it; for both may equally well be said" (pars. 352–53). Modernity's sharp virtue-happiness division therefore disappears for the modern Hegelian individual, and with it the unhappiness which it has generated as well.[192]

Concerning finally the modern dualism of mind or self and body, as we noted earlier, the *Logical and Psychological Laws* section and the first part of the *Physiognomy and Phrenology* section, dealing with physiognomy, depict modern secular forms of this dualism (respectively, those

---

192. Hegel's ways of resolving the last five dualisms just considered—individual-community, thought-reality, fact-volition and cognition-practice, duty-desire, and virtue-happiness—owe much of their inspiration, I believe, to a passage from Herder's *Vom Erkennen und Empfinden der menschlichen Seele* in which Herder implies the equations true cognition = moral volition = moral feeling = cognizing/willing/feeling in agreement with other people = freedom: "Just as our cognition is only *human* and must be so if it is to be *right*, our volition too can only be *human*, and so from and full of *human* feeling. Humanity is the noble measure in accordance with which we cognize and act: *feeling for self and for others* are the two expressions of our will's elasticity. *Love* is thus the noblest cognition, as it is the noblest feeling. The great impetus in one to enter into loving empathy with others and then to follow this sure pull—this is moral feeling, this is conscience. It stands in opposition only to empty speculation, but not to cognition, for true cognition is *love*, is *feeling* in a human way. Look at the whole of nature, observe the great analogy of creation. Everything feels itself and its own kind, life flows with life. Each string quivers to its note, each fibre binds itself with its mate, animal feels with animal. Why should not human being feel with human being? . . . True cognition and good volition are but one in kind, *one force* and *effectiveness* of the soul . . . Where spirit is master, there is freedom. The deeper, purer, and diviner our cognition is, the purer, diviner, and more universal our action is too, and so the freer our freedom" (*Herders Ausgewählte Schriften* 3:724–26). As will become clear in due course, Hegel's debts to Herder in his solutions to dualisms also go well beyond those visible from this passage. For example, his solution to the individual-community dualism is deeply indebted to Herder, not only in its reflections on the realization of our deepest desires, but also in its reflections on the individual's very existence and identity, its position that conceptualization essentially depends on language, and language on linguistic community, so that the individual, as essentially concept-using, depends essentially on his linguistic community. Again, Hegel's way of overcoming the mind/self-body dualism, to which we are about to turn, is also deeply indebted to Herder.

found in Locke and Hume, and in the physiognomy of Lavater). The *Physiognomy and Phrenology* section also begins, however, and the section *The Spiritual Animalkingdom* continues, Hegel's *critique* of any such dualism, and his argument, instead, for a conception of the mind or self and its psychological conditions which can quite properly be described as physicalist and behaviorist.[193] Hegel's case may conveniently be divided into six parts: (i) Hegel offers a critique of the idea that such *affective* aspects of the mind or self as its purposes or character traits can be identified, in the manner envisaged by the dualist, with states or processes only contingently related to the body and its activities, and known through introspection. Hegel argues, in effect, that whatever states or processes of such a sort might occur in us, they are neither sufficient nor necessary for the presence of our purposes or character traits, and so cannot be identified with the latter. They are not *sufficient*, because, whatever such states or processes an individual might undergo, and however sincerely and forcefully he might affirm on this basis that he had such and such a purpose or character trait, his *behavior* can decisively refute any such attribution: "When his performance and his inner possibility, capacity, or intention are contrasted, it is the former alone which is to be regarded as [the individual's] true actuality, even if he deceives himself on the point, and turning away from his action into himself, fancies that in this inner self he is something else than what he is in the deed"; "The deed . . . does away with . . . what is meant privately [das Gemeinte]" (par. 322). Nor are such states or processes *necessary* either. For, even in the absence of any such state or process, just so long as *behavior* of a certain sort occurs, that is sufficient to warrant ascribing to the individual a corresponding

---

193. Hegel's physicalist and behaviorist conception of the mind or self and its psychological conditions has frequently been completely overlooked by commentators, who have tended to assume, quite falsely, that his conception of their relation to the body is Cartesian or Fichtean in spirit. A good example of this mistake is Marx, *Economic and Philosophic Manuscripts*, in *Marx: Selections*, pp. 69–71. Hegel's *real* debt in his conception of their relation to the body is instead to Aristotle and above all Herder—though Hegel's physicalism and behaviorism are even more radical than Herder's (concerning which see chapter 9). The most suggestive literature on this whole topic is: Taylor, *Hegel*; "Hegel and the Philosophy of Action," in *Hegel's Philosophy of Action*, ed. L.S. Stepelevich and D. Lamb (Atlantic Highlands, N.J.: Humanities Press, 1983); "Hegel's Philosophy of Mind," in Taylor, *Human Agency and Language: Philosophical Papers I* (Cambridge: Cambridge University Press, 1996); A. MacIntyre, "Hegel on Faces and Skulls," in *Hegel: A Collection of Critical Essays*, ed. MacIntyre (Notre Dame, Ind.: University of Notre Dame Press, 1976). The promising-sounding recent book by W.A. deVries, *Hegel's Theory of Mental Activity* (Ithaca, N.Y.: Cornell University Press, 1988), by contrast, is disappointing; through brack-

purpose or character trait: "The deed . . . is murder, theft, a good action, a brave deed, and so on . . . It *is* this, and its being is not merely a sign, but the fact itself" (par. 322; cf. 401).[194] (ii) Hegel implies that a precisely analogous argument holds good concerning more *cognitive* aspects of the mind or self as well, such as understanding concepts and holding beliefs. Thus paragraph 322, though focused in the first instance on affective conditions, also presents itself as a refutation of the dualist's conception of *meinen*, a term which usually connotes for Hegel private meaning or belief.[195] Concerning meaning, or understanding concepts, specifically, Hegel goes on to indicate explicitly how the first half of the argument would go for this case: the sort of state or process only contingently related to behavior, and known through introspection, with which the dual-

eting the *Phenomenology* out of consideration in favor of later works, and imputing to the current notion of the "supervenience" of the mental on the physical a power as a philosophical explanation which it in fact lacks, it fails to penetrate to what is most original and interesting in Hegel's position on this issue (and other issues in the philosophy of mind).

194. Cf. *Encyclopaedia*, par. 140: "As a man is outwardly, i.e., in his action (not of course in his merely bodily outwardness [i.e., nonbehavioral bodily conditions, such as facial characteristics or the shape of the skull]), so is he inwardly . . . One can . . . infer what to think when someone, faced with his miserable achievements or even despicable acts, appeals to the inwardness of his allegedly splendid intentions and dispositions which should be distinguished from them. It may indeed happen in individual cases that well-meant intentions are brought to nothing by unfavorable outward circumstances, or well-purposed plans frustrated in their execution. In general, though, the essential unity of the inner and the outer holds good here too, so that one must say: what a man *does*, that he *is*, and one must answer the deceptive vanity which warms itself by the consciousness of inner excellence with the saying of the Gospels: 'By their fruits ye shall know them.' This great saying applies, as initially in relation to morals and religion, so also in relation to scientific and artistic achievements. Hence, concerning the latter, a sharp-eyed teacher may, from perceiving in a boy marked talents, express the opinion that there is a Raphael or Mozart in him, and the outcome will then teach to what extent such an opinion was grounded. But if an inept painter and a bad poet consoled themselves with the claim that they were inwardly full of high ideals, that would be a bad consolation, and if they demand that one not judge them by their achievements but by their intentions, it is right to dismiss this pretension as empty and groundless. Conversely, it also often happens that people employ the untrue distinction between inner and outer in judging other people who have achieved something right and good, in order to allege that this is only their outer side, but that inwardly they were concerned with something quite different, with the satisfaction of their vanity or other contemptible passions. This is the attitude of envy . . . And if in cases of other people's praiseworthy achievements someone speaks of hypocrisy in order to spoil them, one must counter that a man can to be sure conceal himself and hide things in individual cases, but not his inner side in general, which inevitably reveals itself in the decursus vitae, so that also in this connection it must be said that a man is nothing but the series of his deeds."

195. Note also in this connection that Hegel explicitly includes in the passage from the *Encyclopaedia* quoted in the preceding note "*scientific* . . . achievements."

ist would have us identify conceptual understanding is not *sufficient* for it, because whatever such state or process an individual might be in, and however sincerely and forcefully he might affirm on the basis of it that he understood such and such a concept, his *behavior* can decisively refute any such attribution, and in particular a failure to achieve appropriate *linguistic* behavior will do so. Thus Hegel writes that "although it is commonly said that reasonable men pay attention not to the word but to the thing itself, . . . this is at once incompetence and deceit, to fancy and to pretend that one merely has not the right *word,* and to hide from oneself that really one has failed to get hold of the thing itself, i.e., the concept. *If one had the concept, then one would also have the right word*" (par. 328; emphasis added).[196] Similarly, Hegel assumes in the *Sense-certainty* section that in order genuinely to mean or believe anything an individual must be able to *express* what he means or believes *behaviorally* in *language* (or at least in some analogous mode of behavioral expression such as pointing).[197] The other half of the argument in this case would, of course, be that the sort of state or process only contingently related to behavior, and known through introspection, with which the dualist proposes to identify conceptual understanding is not *necessary* for the latter either, since even in the absence of any such state or process, just so long as *behavior* of certain kinds occurs, and in particular appropriate *linguistic* behavior, that is sufficient to warrant ascribing to the individual a corresponding conceptual understanding.[198] (iii) Hegel implies that the above arguments against identifying such affective conditions as purposes

---

196. Cf. *Encyclopaedia,* par. 462: "It is in names that we *think* . . . We . . . only have determinate, genuine thoughts when we give them the form of objectivity, of being distinguished from our inwardness, i.e., the form of externality, and indeed of such an externality as at the same time bears the imprint of the greatest inwardness. Only the *articulated sound,* the *word,* is such an inward external thing. To want to think without words, as Mesmer once tried to, is therefore clearly an absurdity . . . The inexpressible is in truth only something dark, fermenting, which only achieves clarity when it is able to attain verbal expression [zu Worte zu kommen vermag]."

197. That Hegel makes this assumption in the *Sense-certainty* section is clear from the fact that his critique there of Sense-certainty's standpoint consists in showing that the sort of cognition which it supposes itself to have would be *in principle inexpressible in language* (or by pointing). For *that* is only a telling criticism of Sense-certainty if such expressibility is in some way *essential* to cognition—which of course it is on the assumption that meaning and belief are necessarily behaviorally expressible in language (or by pointing).

198. The above arguments are very similar in spirit to, though less richly developed in detail than, the later Wittgenstein's arguments in the *Philosophical Investigations,* trans. G.E.M. Anscombe (Oxford: Blackwell, 1976), pt. 1 against identifying such conditions as intending and understanding with inner mental states or processes.

and character traits or such cognitive conditions as conceptual understanding and belief with states or processes of the sort envisaged by the dualist work equally well, mutatis mutandis, against attempts to identify them with *any other* nonbehavioral states or processes as well. Hence, for example, paragraph 322 deploys the same arguments against identifying such conditions with the facial characteristics in which the physiognomist is interested. And when, more interestingly, Hegel takes up the phrenologist's identification of the mind with the brain and spinal cord and their activity (pars. 327, 331), he implies that this identification too is unacceptable because of the decisiveness of behavioral criteria (pars. 337, 339).[199] (iv) Hegel infers from the availability of these arguments that *behavior itself constitutes such psychological conditions*. This is the force of his remark that "the deed ... is murder, theft, or a good action, a brave deed, and so on ... It *is* this, and its being is not merely a sign, but the fact itself" (par. 322; cf. 401).[200] Consequently, the existence and character of such conditions in an individual can only be known from his behavior, and this is as true of *his* knowledge of them as of other people's: "Consciousness must act in order that what it is *in itself* [i.e., potentially and unconsciously] may become *for it* [i.e., actual and consciously known by it] ... What it is *in itself*, it knows therefore from what it *actually* is [aus seiner Wirklichkeit]. Accordingly, an individual

---

199. Cf. the later Wittgenstein's argument at *Philosophical Investigations,* par. 149 against identifying such psychological conditions as understanding with states of the brain.
200. Cf. *Encyclopaedia,* pars. 140, 383: "As a man is outwardly, i.e., in his actions (not of course in his merely bodily outwardness [i.e., nonbehavioral bodily conditions such as facial characteristics or the shape of the skull]), so is he inwardly"; "The determinacy of the mind is ... *manifestation*. The mind is not some determinacy or content whose expression or outwardness was only a form distinct from it. So it does not reveal *something,* but its determinacy and content is this revelation itself ... The self-revelation is ... itself the content of the mind and not merely some form added externally to mind's content. Consequently, the mind reveals in its revelation, not a content different from its form, but its form expressing the mind's whole content, its self-revelation. Form and content are therefore identical with one another in the mind. Certainly, one usually imagines revelation to be an empty form, which requires a content to be added from outside in addition, and one here understands by 'content' something which exists in itself, something which keeps itself within itself, and by 'form' on the other hand the external manner of the content's relation to something else. But ... in truth the content is not merely something which exists in itself, but something which through itself steps into relation with something else, just as conversely form must be understood, not merely as something lacking independence and external to the content, but rather as that which makes the content into a content, into something existing in itself, into something distinct from something else. Hence the true content contains the form in itself, and the true form is its own content."

cannot know what he is until he has made himself an actuality through action" (par. 401). (v) Hegel conceives this whole position in the following more specific ways, I believe. Concerning, first, the *ontology* of psychological conditions: While there is indeed nothing more to these than bodily behavior, so that in this sense bodily behavior constitutes them, on the other hand, so long as an individual is in a position to produce new bodily behavior, no amount or quality of his accomplished bodily behavior is ever sufficient for their existence. It is only, at best, sufficient for a justified ascription of them to him, but one which remains in principle revisable in the light of further behavior by him.[201] For, however copious and compelling the behavioral grounds available at a given time for saying that an individual has or had in the past such and such a purpose, character trait, conceptual understanding, belief, etc. may be, so long as he can produce new behavior it always remains possible that he will go on to do so in ways which compel revision of that judgment (for instance, that his linguistic behavior will take an unexpected turn, as in Kripke's *quus* case or Goodman's *grue* case, forcing us to revise our earlier assessments of his conceptual understanding, and consequently also of the purposes, character traits, and beliefs which rest upon it). This revisability-in-principle-in-the-light-of-further-behavior of psychological judgments is not merely epistemic (as though there were, after all, something over and above bodily behavior which *really* constituted the presence of the conditions in question, and of which bodily behavior was merely fallible evidence). It is rather—to use the tempting, though dangerously paradoxical, terms which Hegel himself tends to favor—*ontological*, a revisability-in-principle in the *facts*. (Or to put the point in safer terms: it is simply the nature of these psychological concepts that their application is entirely conceptually tied to bodily behavior, but in such a way that, whatever bodily behavior has occurred, their application in principle always remains revisable in the light of further bodily behavior.) I take this position to be an important part of what Hegel means to convey by such statements as the following in the *Phenomenology* concerning the mind and its conditions: they cannot be described as having being, as real, as things, as fixed or immovable (pars. 337, 339, 343); their nature is instead becoming, movement, unrest (pars. 21–22); it is the mind's nature to negate

---

201. This is why in explaining Hegel's anti-dualist arguments above I used the circumspect formulation that certain sorts of behavior are "sufficient to warrant ascribing" corresponding psychological conditions.

and abolish being in its deeds, "the individuality, in the deed, exhibits itself . . . as the negative essence, which abolishes being" (pars. 322, 339); "The being of spirit cannot . . . be taken as something fixed and immovable. Man is free . . . The freedom of the individual . . . [is] indifferent to being as such . . . The individual can be something else than he is" (par. 337).[202] It follows from this position that there is only one circumstance in which an individual's psychological conditions could be said to be really definite, namely, when it is no longer possible for him to produce any further behavior, that is, at the end of his life. This explains why Hegel says of the absolute mind—for his theory of mental conditions applies as much to the *absolute* mind and *national* minds as to individual human minds—that "of the Absolute it must be said that it is essentially a *result, that only in the end* is it what it truly is" (par. 20). Concerning next the *epistemology* of psychological conditions: In consequence, it is impossible to arrive at a definitive judgment about an individual's psychological conditions as long as the individual can produce further behavior, that is, as long as he remains alive. It is only possible to do so once the individual cannot produce any further behavior, that is, upon his death. This explains why Hegel in the *Phenomenology* implies approval of "Solon, who thought he could only know [someone's particular individuality] from and after the course of the whole life" (par. 315).[203] It also explains Hegel's famous position in the *Philosophy of Right* that knowledge of a *national* mind can only be achieved at the end of *its* life (namely, by philosophy): philosophy "appears only when actuality is already there cut and dried after its process of formation has been completed . . . When philosophy paints its grey in grey, then has a shape of life grown old . . . The owl of Minerva spreads its wings only with the falling of the dusk."[204] It also explains why Hegel in the *Phenomenology* equates the *absolute* mind's attainment of self-knowledge with the end of *its* temporal existence: "Spirit . . . appears in time just so long as it has not *grasped* its pure Concept . . . , i.e., has not annulled time" (par. 801; cf. 803).[205] This, then, is Hegel's physicalist and behaviorist theory of psychological

---

202. This Hegelian conception of the relation of behavior to psychological conditions strikingly resembles the later Wittgenstein's conception of their relation as *criterial*.
203. Hegel is of course exercising some poetic licence in his interpretation of Solon's point here.
204. *Philosophy of Right*, pp. 12–13.
205. We can see in the ontological and epistemological positions concerning the mind just explained and their application to Absolute Spirit specifically a large part of the motiva-

conditions.²⁰⁶ (vi) Since the mind or self is *constituted* by such psychological conditions as these, it too consists of, and is known from, bodily behavior: "The true being of a man is . . . his deed; in this the individual

---

tion behind the *Phenomenology*'s otherwise quite mysterious doctrine in passages such as this one that time itself comes to an end as the standpoint of Hegelian philosophy is reached in the modern world. For, by those positions, Absolute Spirit, in order to attain definite existence or be known—specifically, by Hegelian philosophy, and therein also by itself—must have come to an end. But the only conceivable way for that to happen is for time itself to come to an end, because an Absolute Spirit which came to an end while time continued on would ipso facto not be an *Absolute* Spirit.

206. This theory about the nature and our knowledge of psychological conditions is sharply at odds with some common intuitions about such matters. (a) As Hegel himself points out, it conflicts with a common intuition that the psychological conditions such as purposes and beliefs in terms of which we explain people's bodily behavior in normal action-explanations must and do *precede* the bodily behavior which they explain: it conflicts with the intuition that an agent "in order to act . . . must have [the] purpose beforehand" (par. 401). (This intuition is of course especially compelling in cases where, as we would usually put it, a good deal of conscious deliberation precedes the behavior.) Hegel responds that the action *constitutes* the purpose, that "the . . . action does not go outside itself . . . as purpose" (par. 401). But this merely identifies the *source* of the theory's conflict with the common intuition; it does nothing to resolve the conflict. Wittgenstein, whose account of psychological conditions faces just the same conflict with the same common intuition, attempts to resolve it by suggesting, in effect, that our common habit of ascribing psychological conditions to times prior to the behavior which on his account too in some sense constitutes them is merely a sort of *façon de parler*, and so only superficially at odds with their constitution by that behavior. This, I take it, is the implication of such remarks as the following: " 'You said, "It'll stop soon."'—Were you thinking of the noise or of your pain?' If he answers 'I was thinking of the piano-tuning'—is he observing that the connexion existed, or is he making it by means of these words?—Can't I say *both*? If what he said was true, didn't the connexion exist—and is he not for all that making one which did not exist?" (*Philosophical Investigations*, par. 682); " 'But I don't mean that what I do now (in grasping a sense) determines the future use *causally* and as a matter of experience, but that in a *queer* way, the use itself is in some sense present.' But of course it is, 'in *some* sense'! (And don't we also say: 'the events of the years that are past are present to me'?) Really the only thing wrong with what you say is the expression 'in a queer way.' The rest is correct" (*Remarks on the Foundations of Mathematics*, trans. G.E.M. Anscombe [Oxford: Blackwell, 1978], pt. 1, par. 126). This suggestion of Wittgenstein's that our common assignments of temporal locations to psychological conditions are meant nonliterally seems quite interpretatively implausible, however. (b) As Taylor notes in his illuminating essay "Hegel and the Philosophy of Action," Hegel's theory involves a rejection of the common intuition that explanations of behavior by reference to purposes and beliefs succeed in virtue of identifying the latter as *efficient causes* of the former. For on Hegel's account purposes and beliefs lack both the temporal priority to and the ontological independence of the behavior explained which would be required in order for them to be its efficient causes. Again, a similar point applies to Wittgenstein's theory, as I understand it. (c) Perhaps the sharpest conflict between such a theory of psychological conditions as Hegel's—or Wittgenstein's, as I read him—and common intuitions lies in its apparent implication that there could not be a psychological condition which entirely lacked behavioral manifestation. For we

is *actual* [wirklich] . . . The individual human being *is* what the *deed is*" (par. 322; cf., concerning knowledge, par. 401, the passage quoted under [iv] above).[207] This, in sum, is Hegel's physicalist and behaviorist theory of the mind or self and its psychological conditions.[208] With this theory

---

commonly think that this not only is quite possible but also happens with some frequency. (d) Hegel's theory—and Wittgenstein's too (though in a different way)—implies a denial of the common intuition that people have incorrigible knowledge of and privileged cognitive access to their own (current) psychological conditions. For on Hegel's theory, one's assessments of one's own current mental conditions are always corrigible in the light of what one goes on to *do*, and the basis of one's cognition of one's own mental conditions is the same as the basis of other people's cognition of them, namely, observation of one's bodily behavior. (On the other hand, it would perhaps be possible, within the general framework of Hegel's theory, to do *more* justice to the ideas of first-person incorrigibility and privileged access than he attempts to; one can imagine ways in which weakened analogues of these might be preserved within such a theory.)

It is not my intention to evaluate these conflicts between Hegel's theory and common intuitions here. However, one general point may be worth making: To the extent that these are genuine conflicts with common sense and common usage/concepts (not merely with philosophers' theories), Hegel is in a much more comfortable position than Wittgenstein. For whereas Wittgenstein has strong commitments to the propriety of common sense and common usage/concepts—"Philosophy may in no way interfere with the actual use of language; it can in the end only describe it . . . It leaves everything as it is" (*Philosophical Investigations,* par. 124)—Hegel does *not*. Hegel does, certainly, in his theory attempt to do justice to central aspects of common sense and common usage/concepts—in particular, for example, to common intuitions concerning the decisiveness of behavioral criteria in the ascription of psychological conditions when such criteria conflict with other evidence. But this is not from any *general* deference toward common sense and common usage/concepts. Should it turn out, therefore, that in order to do them justice in a self-consistent, defensible theory Hegel has to contradict *other* aspects of common sense and common usage/concepts, such as the four listed above, then nothing in his general philosophical position will cause him any compunction about doing so. On the contrary—as we shall see more clearly in a moment—for Hegel this will just be business as usual.

Note, finally, that if this is indeed the sort of position that Hegel is committed to in his philosophy of mind, then, surprising as this may sound, his position might reasonably be described as, not only a form of physicalism and behaviorism, but moreover a form of eliminative materialism, in that it incorporates a denial that our received mentalistic concepts have application to reality (albeit, unlike some more recent and familiar forms of eliminative materialism, with the qualification that quite close analogues of our received mentalistic concepts do have application to reality).

207. Hegel retains this position in later works: "What a man *does*, that he *is* . . . A man is nothing but the series of his deeds" (*Encyclopaedia,* par. 140, addition). "What the subject is, is the series of his actions" (*Philosophy of Right,* par. 124; cf. 343). "Man is realized for himself by practical activity, inasmuch as he has the impulse, in the medium which is directly given to him, to produce himself, and therein at the same time to recognize himself" (Hegel, *On Art, Religion, Philosophy,* trans. J.G. Gray [New York: Harper Torchbooks, 1970], p. 58).

208. Hegel's application of this theory to the *absolute* mind or self, Absolute Spirit, specifically—as much as to individual human minds—helps to explain why for him Abso-

Hegel introduces a conception of the mind or self and its psychological conditions which overcomes the dualistic conception of them as sharply distinct from the body, and restores something more like "the Greek view that body and soul persist together in one living shape" of which he had written approvingly in *The Spirit of Christianity*.[209] The various forms of unhappiness which mind-body dualism produces are consequently eliminated for the modern Hegelian individual.

Both in virtue of its general monism and in these various more specific ways, then, the *Phenomenology* aims to overcome through Hegelian philosophy all eight of the dualisms which beset modern men and cause their unhappiness, and thereby to make possible at last their attainment of genuine happiness.[210]

---

lute Spirit, unlike the God of traditional theism, is in its existence and psychological conditions essentially dependent upon and indeed in some sense identical with *nature and mankind*. For more on this, see chapter 4.

209. As I have tried to show in the preceding with the help of collateral footnotes, this whole theory of the relation of the mind or self and its psychological conditions to the body is not only found in the *Phenomenology* but also represents a prominent strand in Hegel's later thought on the subject. Whether the later Hegel remains *consistently* committed to it is, though, another matter. As cause for some doubt that he does, see for example *Encyclopaedia*, par. 389.

210. The above account has, I hope, made it clear that Shklar and Hyppolite are quite mistaken when they interpret the *Phenomenology* as a work pessimistic or at best agnostic about the possibility of overcoming modernity's divisions (Shklar, *Freedom and Independence*, pp. 41, 45, 48, 96, 140–41, 204–5, and "Hegel's *Phenomenology*: an Elegy for Hellas," in *Hegel's Political Philosophy*, ed. Z.A. Pelczynski [Cambridge: Cambridge University Press, 1976], pp. 81, 89; Hyppolite, "The Significance of the French Revolution in Hegel's *Phenomenology*," in *Studies on Marx and Hegel* [New York: Basic Books, 1969], p. 61; Shklar and Hyppolite are especially concerned with the division between individual and community).

A number of further errors which have contributed to this serious misinterpretation may be worth briefly noting here: (i) In order clearly to perceive that the work depicts history as a process of development from unity through divisions toward the eventual overcoming of divisions in the modern age, and specifically in Hegel's own standpoint, it is crucial to have recognized (a) that the chapters *Consciousness* through to the end of *Reason* contain a chronological treatment of history from ancient times up to Hegel's own age and standpoint, and in particular (b) that paragraphs 435–37 at the very end of the *Reason* chapter represent Hegel's own age and standpoint (these facts will be demonstrated in chapter 9). Shklar and Hyppolite fail to do so. Thus, contrary to (a), both authors deny that the chapters in question are chronologically historical in the way described (Shklar, *Freedom and Independence*, pp. 8–9; Hyppolite, *Genesis and Structure*, pp. 36–37). And contrary to (b), Hyppolite's treatment of paragraphs 435–37 is brief and entirely vague about their significance (ibid., p. 318), while Shklar, misled by Hegel's quotation there from the *Antigone*, misconstrues them as representing, not Hegel's age and standpoint, but the ancient Greeks' (*Freedom and Independence*, pp. 100–102, 140–41). (ii) Shklar and Hyppo-

Now, to return at last to our original question, it is largely this whole *practical* motive behind Hegel's philosophy which explains why he thinks it as vitally important as he does in the *Phenomenology* that his philosophy be made accessible and compelling to the general run of his contemporaries. Because this practical motive of curing modern men of unhappiness is paramount, and because the envisaged cure lies in their adoption

---

lite both lose sight of the important fact that the *Phenomenology* is conceived merely as an "introduction" to Hegel's philosophy, or its "appearance" (pars. 38, 76), not as Hegelian philosophy itself. This introductory character of the work fully explains the relative lack of explicitness in the work's indications of how divisions are to be overcome by Hegelian philosophy. This lack of explicitness ought not, therefore, to be read, as Shklar and Hyppolite read it, as a sign that the work is pessimistic or agnostic about overcoming them. The merely introductory character of the *Phenomenology* also makes it fallacious to infer, as Shklar and Hyppolite do, from the fact that the work already holds the later Hegel's conception of *philosophy* as by nature merely descriptive/explanatory and retrospective rather than activist and forward-looking (as it in fact does), that it therefore conceives its *own* role in such terms (Shklar, *Freedom and Independence*, p. 146; Hyppolite, "The Significance of the French Revolution," pp. 41–42). As we shall see in chapter 12, an activist, forward-looking attitude dominated Hegel's thought in the years preceding the *Phenomenology*'s composition, and in the year after its publication he could still write: "Theoretical work, I become daily more convinced, accomplishes more in the world than practical work; when the realm of representation is once revolutionized, reality cannot hold out" (*Briefe von und an Hegel* 1:253). (iii) Shklar supports her contention that the *Phenomenology* does not envisage a modern overcoming of individual-community division by noting that at the time of the work's composition Hegel had not yet written the *Philosophy of Right,* where a modern reconciliation of individual and community is worked out (*Freedom and Independence*, pp. 204–6). This argument overlooks the fact that Hegel had already written a substantial body of reconciling political writings in the period immediately preceding the *Phenomenology*'s composition—in particular, the prescriptions for a united Germany at the end of *The German Constitution,* and the sketches for a modern reconciled political community in the *System of Ethical Life* and the 1805–6 Philosophy of Spirit. (iv) Shklar interprets the *Phenomenology* as holding that the French Revolution accomplished "absolutely nothing" (*Freedom and Independence*, pp. 177–79). This reading is incorrect. The *Phenomenology*'s position is rather that the French Revolution, with its ideal of the "general will," represented an important groping toward that synthesis of individualism with collectivism which is Hegel's own ideal for modernity (pars. 584, 587), and that, although it failed to achieve this synthesis *immediately* due to its rejection of mediating political structures and social roles/classes (pars. 584–85, 588), it thereby led to the hard lesson of the Terror which disciplined men to accept these (par. 593), and has hence made possible an *eventual* achievement of the synthesis in question (par. 595). (Cf. Taylor, *Hegel,* pp. 418–19 for some further aspects of the French Revolution's positive achievement as Hegel sees it at the time of the *Phenomenology*.)

Note, finally, that the *Phenomenology*'s optimism for the future is in keeping with the cautiously optimistic attitudes of the two thinkers who, as we have seen, were the main inspiration behind its project of cultural reform, namely, Herder and Schiller (see esp. Herder, *Auch eine Philosophie der Geschichte zur Bildung der Menschheit*, in *Herders Ausgewählte Werke* 2:692–93; Schiller, *On the Aesthetic Education of Man*).

of the outlook of Hegelian philosophy, clearly the broad dissemination of this philosophy is of crucial importance.[211]

* * *

A further question which arises immediately concerning the pedagogical project of the *Phenomenology* is this: Why does Hegel believe that in order to make his contemporaries understand and accept his philosophical system it is necessary (or even appropriate) to develop the sort of elaborate pedagogical pathway which we find in the *Phenomenology*? Why does he not simply set forth his philosophical system as accessibly and clearly as possible and leave it at that?

Now Hegel does in fact make efforts to present his philosophical system as accessibly and clearly as he can (however odd this may sound to those of us who have struggled hard to understand it).[212] But doing so

---

211. As we shall see in chapters 3 and 4, there are, in Hegel's view, also further very important reasons why it is crucial that his philosophy be made accessible and compelling to the general run of his contemporaries: this is in a sense required for its justification (chapter 3), and especially it is required for the full realization of its subject matter (Absolute Spirit), its conceptual articulability, and its truth (chapter 4).

212. Two examples of these efforts: (i) Hegel's choice of philosophical language. Already quite early in his career Hegel developed, explicitly in response to the need to make his philosophy broadly accessible, a policy of avoiding as far as possible in its articulation the use of terminology borrowed from foreign languages, such as Greek and Latin, or artificially constructed, in the manner of Kant or Schelling, and instead employing familiar German terms in ways at least rooted in (though not bound to) their familiar usage. Hence, for example, in a letter from 1805 he inveighs against the "current lack of publicity in the sciences," the "schools which shut themselves off and . . . withhold [their essence] from publicity," "these privileged circles of authorities and pretensions . . . [through] which laymen who are concerned to acquire the science and knowledge which belong to general education are subjected to delusive obscurantism," expresses his own contrary "hope of an activation of art and science which is more efficacious, has an impact on general education," and announces that in pursuit of this objective, "I want to try to teach philosophy to speak German" (*Briefe von und an Hegel* 1:100–101; cf. Rosenkranz, *Hegels Leben*, pp. 181–85). Accordingly, Hegel's basic approach in writing philosophy is to begin from familiar German terminology and usage, and then *modify* this usage in the ways that are necessary in order to make possible the expression of the novel concepts required by his philosophy. Hence, for example, in the *Science of Logic* he remarks that "philosophy has the right to select from the language of common life . . . such expressions as seem to approximate to the determinations of the Concept," although "there cannot be any question of demonstrating for a word selected from the language of common life that in common life, too, one associates with it the same concept for which philosophy employs it" (p. 708). Ironically, therefore, what might at first sight seem to be merely the distinctive quality of Hegel's obscurity as a philosophical writer, namely his use of familiar words in largely unfamiliar ways, is in fact deeply motivated by an aspiration to make an inevitably conceptually innovative philosophy as accessible as possible. (ii) In versions of his philosophical system from the 1808 ff. *Encyclopaedia* onwards, including especially the three editions of

cannot, he thinks, suffice to make it generally understood and accepted, because (like his sometime mentor Schelling) he believes that there is a sharp disagreement in both concepts and doctrines between the everyday viewpoints of modern men and the viewpoint of his philosophical system. Hegel is not one of those philosophers who, like Aristotle, Berkeley, Kant, and the later Wittgenstein in their various ways, wish to deny or to minimize their philosophy's disagreement with prevailing common sense.[213] Thus, concerning concepts to begin with, Hegel implies at *Phenomenology,* paragraph 39 the inadequacy to the expression of his own philosophical position of even such fundamental everyday concepts as those of truth and falsehood, subject and object, finite and infinite, and being and thought.[214] And in the *Science of Logic* he writes more generally that "there cannot be any question of demonstrating for a word selected from the language of common life that in common life, too, one associates with it the same concept for which philosophy employs it."[215] Likewise, concerning doctrines, Hegel notes in an essay from 1802 that philosophy is "precisely opposed to the Understanding and still more to the healthy human Understanding . . . ; in relation to this the world of philosophy is fundamentally a perverted world."[216] And in the *Phenomenology* he observes similarly that "the standpoint of consciousness . . . is for Science the antithesis of its own standpoint. The situation in which consciousness

---

the published *Encyclopaedia,* Hegel is at pains to make its presentation as accessible and clear as possible by means of such devices as conciseness, relative simplicity in formulation, careful division of subjects into sections and numbered paragraphs, cross-referencing, and so forth. Indeed the pedagogical orientation of these versions of the system is reflected in their very title: *EncycloPAEDIA.*

213. Some modest qualifications of this point in order to forestall misunderstanding: (i) Hegel does think that everyday viewpoints contain *obscure anticipations* of his philosophical concepts and truths. For example, he remarks that the categories of the Logic are "present in everyday speech," although "mixed and covered in quite concrete materials" (Rosenkranz, *Hegels Leben,* p. 183), the 1801–2 *Logic and Metaphysics* sees "speculative meaning" in our everyday forms of syllogism (appendix V), and the *Phenomenology* argues that the everyday subject-predicate form of judgments can be construed in a "speculative" way (pars. 60 ff.). (ii) As we saw in the preceding note, Hegel, despite envisaging a conceptual discrepancy between everyday viewpoints and his philosophy, does not think that his philosophy needs to, or should, have recourse to *words* different from those employed in everyday German, or even to *usages* of them which are *wholly* divorced from their usages in everyday German.

214. On the inadequacy to philosophy of the everyday concept of truth, and philosophy's need for a different concept of truth, in particular, cf. *Encyclopaedia,* par. 24, addition 2.

215. *Science of Logic,* p. 708.

216. *Jenaer Schriften,* p. 182.

knows itself to be at home is for Science one marked by the absence of Spirit. Conversely, the element of Science is for consciousness a remote beyond in which it no longer possesses itself" (par. 26). Summing up the whole situation, Hegel writes in an 1812 letter that "to the uninitiated, speculative philosophy must . . . present itself as the upside-down world, contradicting all their accustomed concepts and whatever else appeared valid to them according to so-called common sense."[217] There is, in short, a deep conceptual and doctrinal opposition between everyday viewpoints and Hegelian philosophy.[218]

The reason for the *doctrinal* opposition here is perhaps already clear enough: whereas everyday viewpoints conceive everything in terms of sharp dualisms, Hegelian philosophy overcomes those sharply dualistic conceptions in favor of monistic ones. Why, though, should there be a *conceptual* disagreement? In order to see why, it is important, first of all, to note that it is a quite general characteristic of Hegel's position to regard a lot of "theory" as internal to concepts or meanings.[219] Because of this, the sorts of fundamental doctrinal differences just mentioned translate,

---

217. *Hegel: The Letters,* trans. C. Butler and C. Seiler (Bloomington, Ind.: Indiana University Press, 1984), p. 591.

218. This conceptual and doctrinal opposition was not only a matter of philosophical principle for Hegel; it was also something of which he was constantly (and one imagines painfully) reminded by his activities as a teacher in the years preceding the *Phenomenology*'s composition. Thus Rosenkranz reports concerning Hegel's attempts to teach his philosophical system during this period: "Hegel had in Jena at first presented his system in all the roughness of its original conception, but had in several years been able to learn sufficiently that such a form was not suited to academic presentation. He was forced to a lively awareness of the need for a more *popular* presentation. The rift between the deep spirit which unfolded itself in that system with the boldest abstraction and the consciousness which the student brought with him at the start to the lecture was too great" (*Hegels Leben,* p. 178).

219. To give an example of this, in an early argument where he is attempting to show that the concepts of attraction and repulsion are implicitly self-contradictory, Hegel relies in order to do so on an assumption that Newton's third law of motion—the law that to every action there is an equal and opposite reaction—is internal to these concepts, part of the very meanings of these terms: "If the increased density or specific weight of a body is explained as an increase in the force of attraction, the same phenomenon can be explained with equal ease as an increase in the force of repulsion, *for there can only be as much attraction as there is repulsion . . . the one has meaning only with reference to the other. To the extent that one were greater than the other, to that same extent it would not exist at all*" (*Natural Law,* p. 119; emphasis added). For a much later, and different type of, illustration of Hegel's commitment to the position in question, see his reflections on the interpretation of culturally alien concepts in the 1826 work *Rezension der Schrift "Über die unter dem Namen Bhagavad-Gita bekannte Episode des Mahabharata. Von Wilhelm von Humboldt,"* in Hegel, *Sämtliche Werke,* vol. 20, esp. pp. 67–68, 75–78, 115–16.

for Hegel, more or less automatically into thoroughgoing conceptual differences as well. Thus he understands even the most basic concepts which belong to everyday viewpoints to be *of their essence* sharply dualistic in nature, so that abandoning the relevant sharp dualisms in the manner of monistic Hegelian philosophy ipso facto involves abandoning those concepts: "Forms of division [Entzweiung] . . . , the categories of the finite, are in their very nature unusable for grasping and connoting what is in itself unitary, the true."[220] For example, he implies that even such fundamental everyday concepts as those of subject and object, or being and thought, *essentially* involve the sort of sharp distinction between these items which (as we noted earlier) his own philosophy abandons: "To talk of the *unity* of subject and object, . . . of being and thought, etc. is inept, since object and subject, etc. signify what they are *outside* of their unity" (par. 39). And, as we saw previously, he indicates, with special reference to Kant in whom this is explicit, that the conception of a sharp opposition between duty and desire, such as his own philosophy abandons, is part of modernity's very concept of a duty.[221]

Because of this sharp disagreement, in both concepts and doctrines, between the everyday viewpoints of Hegel's contemporaries and his own philosophical system, merely giving an optimally accessible and clear exposition of this system would not by itself be enough to bring his contemporaries to understand and accept it. Something more had to be done to bridge the yawning conceptual and doctrinal opposition. Incipit the *Phenomenology of Spirit!*

* * *

It was, then, largely because of these two features of his position—the practical motive behind his philosophy, and the awareness of a deep conceptual and doctrinal opposition between the everyday viewpoints of his contemporaries and his philosophy—that Hegel was driven to develop the sort of pedagogical project which we find in the *Phenomenology*.

As it happens, we can date the birth of such a project from these two features of his position fairly exactly. In a letter to Schelling from 1800

---

220. *Sämtliche Werke* 20:281.
221. My suggestion in footnote 206 that Hegel conceives his physicalist and behaviorist theory of the mind as doctrinally and conceptually revisionist of common sense, and hence as incorporating an element of eliminative materialism, should be viewed in light of these general considerations.

Hegel writes that his own educational development began from a concern for "men's less exalted needs" but has driven him "inevitably . . . to Science" or "a system" (this alludes to the practical motive behind his philosophy). And with this Science before him, at least in conception, he ponders, "I wonder now, while I am still occupied with it, what return is to be found to an impact on [zum Eingreifen in] the life of men" (this alludes to the conceptual and doctrinal opposition between the everyday viewpoints of his contemporaries and his philosophy's standpoint, and to the challenge of bridging it).[222]

In answer to this challenge, Hegel immediately set about developing a discipline which would bring his contemporaries to understand and accept the standpoint of his philosophical system. Thus in the *Difference* essay of 1801 he announced the ambition that "the Absolute should be constructed for consciousness," and sketched a discipline which he called Logic as the means to accomplish this.[223] He continued developing this discipline over the next several years (as we see from the several sketches and drafts of it which have survived). Eventually he gave up this early introductory Logic and assigned the same function to the *Phenomenology* instead, which, as we have seen, likewise has "the task of leading the individual from his uneducated standpoint to knowledge [i.e., to the standpoint of Hegel's system]."

In order to meet the challenge identified in his letter of 1800 by means of these disciplines, Hegel had to reject a series of assumptions which had been made by Schelling, who, though chronologically younger, was very much the senior partner in their collaborations during the early Jena period. This marks one of Hegel's earliest and most striking displays of independence from Schelling during this period. Schelling had held that the essence of doing genuine philosophy was a synthesizing faculty, or activity, of "intellectual intuition" which *could not be taught or learned*: "It is clear that [intellectual intuition] is nothing teachable; thus all attempts to teach it are quite useless in scientific philosophy"; philosophy "as such cannot be learned . . . Only the knowledge of its particular forms can be attained in this way."[224] For Schelling the ability to philosophize

---

222. Appendix III.
223. *Jenaer Schriften*, pp. 25 ff.
224. F.W.J. Schelling, *Fernere Darstellungen aus dem System der Philosophie*, in *Ausgewählte Schriften* (Frankfurt am Main: Suhrkamp, 1985), vol. 2, par. 11; *Vorlesungen über die Methode des akademischen Studiums* (Hamburg: Felix Meiner, 1974), lecture 6.

was, on the contrary, "an innate capacity, a free gift, and awarded by destiny," and as such *the preserve of a few select individuals*.[225] In particular, therefore, there could be, for Schelling, *no pedagogical bridge between the ordinary consciousness and philosophy*: "It is unintelligible . . . why philosophy should have any obligation to be considerate of incompetence. It is rather appropriate to cut off the approach to philosophy sharply and to isolate it on all sides from common cognition in such a way that no path or pavement can lead from common cognition to philosophy. Here begins philosophy, and whoever is not already there or is afraid to reach this point—let him stay away or flee back."[226]

Hegel's pedagogical project in the early Logic and the *Phenomenology* involves an unequivocal rejection of all three of these Schellingian assumptions. Hegel believes, pace Schelling, that philosophy *can be taught and learned,* and indeed can be taught to and learned by more or less *all individuals,* and that this can be accomplished precisely by constructing a *pedagogical bridge* between their ordinary cognition and philosophy. Evidence of this sort of reversal of positions can already be seen as early as 1801–2, when Hegel writes in a fragment that "if philosophy is complete and round, philosophizing is on the contrary something empirical which [can] proceed from various standpoints and diverse forms of culture and subjectivity, and . . . in connection with the empirical beginnings of philosophizing an introduction to philosophy is possible, which constitutes a sort of bonding and bridge between the subjective forms and the objective, absolute philosophy."[227] Hegel's rejection of Schelling's assumptions is expressed still more comprehensively and forcefully in the *Phenomenology,* where he writes: "Without . . . articulation, Science lacks universal intelligibility, and gives the appearance of being the esoteric possession of a few individuals . . . Only what is completely determined is at once exoteric, comprehensible, and capable of being learned and appropriated by all. The Understanding's [verständige] form of Science is the way [Weg] to Science open and equally accessible to everyone, and consciousness as it approaches Science justly demands that it be able

---

225. Ibid., lecture 6; cf. *Fernere Darstellungen aus dem System der Philosophie,* par. 11.
226. Ibid., par. 11.
227. Hegel, "Introductio in Philosophiam. Diese Vorlesungen . . . ," unpublished ms., forthcoming in *Gesammelte Werke* (Hamburg: Felix Meiner), vol. 5.

to attain rational [vernünftig] knowledge by way of the ordinary Understanding [Verstand]" (par. 13).[228]

We can already see from these passages that Hegel's pedagogical strategy in the early Logic and the *Phenomenology* will involve constructing some sort of pedagogical bridge leading from the everyday viewpoints of his contemporaries to his own philosophical system. What, though, does this mean in less metaphorical terms?

The *Phenomenology*'s pedagogical strategy can best be understood against the background of the early Logic's, so we should begin by considering the latter. The early Logic's strategy is stated most clearly and concisely in a sketch of the discipline from 1801–2. In this sketch Hegel explains that the Logic's approach is to "begin from what is finite . . . in order to proceed from this, namely, insofar as it is first destroyed, to the infinite."[229] Thus the strategy has two sides: First there is a *destructive* side, where "finite" cognition, or the everyday viewpoints of Hegel's contemporaries, gets "destroyed," or discredited. Second, there is a *constructive* side, where the "finite" viewpoint which has just seen all of its cognition discredited gets initiated into "infinite" cognition, or Hegelian philosophy. We shall see that the *Phenomenology* retains this two-sided strategy for teaching Hegel's system.

What is the character of the first side of the Logic's strategy, its "destruction" or discrediting of "finite" cognition, more specifically? Hegel explains the basic approach in illuminating metaphorical terms in the *Natural Law* essay of 1802–3, where he writes, with the Logic in mind, that the proof of the "nullity [Nichtigkeit]" of nonscientific positions "is

---

228. Hegel's position here is strongly influenced by Herder. In the *Fragmente* Herder observes that the usual manner of proceeding in philosophy is to expect pupils to leap directly from their ordinary way of thought and language to another way of thought and language, thereby creating major problems for understanding and justifying the latter (*Johann Gottfried Herder Werke* [Frankfurt am Main: Deutscher Klassiker Verlag, 1985–], 1:641). In contrast to this, he recommends the following manner of proceeding instead: "That presentation is without question best which begins where I wanted to begin: from the ideas which I already have; and from the words in which I preserve them. It proceeds forth on the course of the good healthy Understanding [Vertandes], and so I still find myself on familiar paths [Wegen]: I approach the field of Reason [Vernunft]; but my guide does not let me yet lose the land of my origin from view: I finally step, aware of the path [Weges] behind me, of my own accord higher step by step until I have an overview of everything in a language which I suppose myself to have thought out for myself. That is a textbook of philosophical education" (1:640–41; cf. 398, 425). Note that Hegel echoes not only Herder's thoughts here but also his very words.

229. Appendix V.

presented most convincingly by showing the unreal basis and ground from which they grow, and whose flavor and nature they absorb."[230] The identity of the "basis and ground" in question here is made clear by the sketch of 1801–2, which indicates that the discrediting of finite cognition is to take the form of discrediting finite cognition's "concepts, judgments, and syllogisms," by which Hegel means its most fundamental concepts, forms of judgment, and forms of syllogism.[231] What does this approach amount to in more detail? Hegel wishes to discredit all of the concepts, judgments, and theories which constitute the everyday viewpoints of his contemporaries. Since, however, the stock of everyday concepts, judgments, and theories which have actually been employed is huge and, worse, infinitely expandable, to attempt to do so *directly* would be to take on an impossibly large task—it would not be, as Hegel puts it, "convincing." Hegel therefore proposes to adopt instead an *indirect* approach, to discredit their "basis and ground." For, although the stock of everyday concepts, judgments, and theories is huge and infinitely expandable, there is a finite and manageable stock of fundamental concepts, forms of judgment, and forms of syllogism which must be drawn on for the articulation of any everyday concept, judgment, or theory, which in this sense constitutes the "basis and ground" of our everyday concepts, judgments, and theories. Thus, all of our everyday *concepts* are either themselves fundamental categorial concepts or else implicitly draw on these—as, for example, the concept "blue" implicitly draws on the fundamental categorial concept of "quality," and the concept "table" on the fundamental categorial concept of "substance."[232] All of our everyday *judgments* draw, not only on the same stock of fundamental concepts, via their conceptual content, but additionally on one or another of the fundamental forms of judgment—as, for example, the judgment "If it rains this afternoon, then the grass will be hard to cut" draws on the hypothetical form of judgment "If X then Y." All of our everyday *theories* draw, not only on the same stock of fundamental concepts and forms of judgment, via the judgments which they contain, but additionally on one or more of the fundamental forms of syllogism or inference which establish logical relations between

---

230. *Natural Law*, p. 61.
231. Appendix V.
232. For a statement of the idea that a very specific concept like "blue" implicitly draws on more general concepts, see Hegel, *Jenenser Realphilosophie* (Leipzig: Felix Meiner, 1932), 1:212–15.

those judgments. Moreover, it is Hegel's idea that the fundamental concepts, forms of judgment, and forms of syllogism relied upon by any particular everyday concept, judgment, or theory enter into its very meaning—that it in this sense "absorbs their flavor and nature." Consequently, if the fundamental concepts, forms of judgment, or forms of syllogism relied upon by a particular concept, judgment, or theory prove to be essentially defective in some way, then the latter will be so too.[233] Since it "absorbs their flavor and nature," their "unreality" will prove its "nullity" too. Therefore, if *all* of the finite and manageable stock of fundamental concepts, forms of judgment, and forms of syllogism can be shown to be essentially defective in some way, then it will thereby be shown that *all* everyday concepts, judgments, and theories are likewise defective. Showing the entire "basis and ground" to be "unreal" is a "convincing" way of showing the "nullity" of all everyday positions. The early Logic's means of discrediting as essentially defective all of finite cognition's fundamental concepts, forms of judgment, and forms of syllogism, and thereby the rest of finite cognition as well, was to show them to be implicitly *self-contradictory*—this is the nature of the "unreality" of the "basis and ground," and of the "nullity" of what rests upon it. Copious examples of the early Logic's attempts to demonstrate self-contradictions in fundamental concepts, forms of judgment, and forms of syllogism can be found in texts from the period.[234] As we shall see, the early Logic's indirect

---

233. Strictly, this inference is a little hasty. The essential defect in fundamental concepts, etc. which Hegel has in mind is self-contradictoriness. Now it does not actually follow from the fact that a concept is self-contradictory that *all* judgments made using it will also be self-contradictory and so false. For example, let "squarenot" mean the self-contradictory property of being both square and not square. Many judgments which use this concept will indeed thereby be self-contradictory and so false, e.g., "Some things are squarenot," or "This object is squarenot." Other judgments, however, will not, e.g., "There are no squarenot things," or "This object is not squarenot," both of which judgments are on the contrary self-consistent and true. This qualification is not damaging to Hegel's project, however. For it is Hegel's idea that *all* concepts which enter into judgments are implicitly self-contradictory—including, as we see especially from the beginning of the later Logic, the concept of *not being* (or "nothing"). And if *that* is so, then the self-contradictoriness of concepts really will guarantee the self-contradictoriness and falsehood of the judgments in which they are used.

234. See especially the version of the Logic from 1801–2 in *Schellings und Hegels erste absolute Metaphysik (1801–2)*, ed. K. Düsing (Cologne: Jürgen Dinter, 1988); the several demonstrations in the 1802–3 *Natural Law* essay of self-contradictions in concepts such as attraction and repulsion, which demonstrations are drawn from Hegel's Logic of the period; and the 1804–5 version of the Logic in Hegel's *Logik, Metaphysik, und Naturphilosophie*. It is, of course, much clearer how this approach could be applied to fundamental

approach to discrediting everyday views, and its employment of the discovery of implicit self-contradictions as the means of discrediting them, remain central to the pedagogical strategy of the *Phenomenology*.

Hegel's approach on the *constructive* side of the early Logic rested in large part on an important assumption which he made: among the false, self-contradictory materials of "finite" cognition there exists a *hierarchy* in which some are, despite their falseness and self-contradictoriness, *better* expressions of "infinite" cognition, or philosophical truth, than others.[235] Given this situation, the early Logic, having shown the occupant of the finite viewpoint its self-contradictoriness, could then supply him with a positive bridge from that viewpoint to philosophical truth by having him focus on its *highest* forms of self-contradictory falsehood and thereby providing him with a sort of provisional insight into philosophical truth within the false, self-contradictory medium of his own thought. It is this strategy that Hegel has in mind when he writes in the sketch from 1801–2 that the Logic "hold[s] forth the image of the Absolute in a reflection, so to speak, and make[s] people familiar with it." Hegel gives as a specific example of this approach the Logic's focus on finite cognition's forms of syllogism, which are, he claims, "an imitation of Reason by the Understanding."[236] Once again, as we shall see, this constructive approach survives as part of the pedagogical strategy of the *Phenomenology*.

Finally, we should note another important feature of both the destruc-

---

concepts than to forms of judgment and forms of syllogism. This is no great threat to Hegel's project, however. For, as that project has just been explained, fundamental concepts are a foundation of *all* finite cognition's contents—its concepts, judgments, and theories alike—so that showing fundamental concepts alone to be through and through self-contradictory would be enough by itself to discredit all finite cognition. Accordingly, Hegel does in fact sometimes imply that all of finite cognition can be discredited by discrediting its concepts alone. For example, in the 1802 essay *The Relation of Skepticism to Philosophy* he praises Plato's *Parmenides*, on which he modeled versions of his own early Logic, on the ground that it "encompasses the whole sphere [of finite cognition] through concepts of the Understanding and destroys it" (in appendix VI).

235. This assumption is reflected, for example, in Hegel's remark in the *Difference* essay of 1801 that the "law of [causal] ground," by which he means Spinoza's conception of substance as causa sui, although an "expression of antinomy," or in other words self-contradictory, is nevertheless "the highest possible expression of Reason through the Understanding" (*Jenaer Schriften*, p. 39). The earliest example of this assumption that I have encountered in Hegel occurs in his discussion of John's gospel in *The Spirit of Christianity* (*Early Theological Writings*, pp. 255–58).

236. Appendix V.

114   The Official Project of the *Phenomenology*

tive and the constructive sides of the early Logic (at least in its last version, that in the 1804–5 *Logic, Metaphysics, and Philosophy of Nature*). This is the use of Hegel's famous *dialectical method*. This method consists in alternately demonstrating implicit self-contradictions in earlier concepts and then their necessary resolutions in subsequent ones. By so proceeding the method serves both to discredit fundamental concepts through revealing their implicit self-contradictions (in fulfillment of the destructive side of Hegel's pedagogical project) and to construct a positive bridge toward philosophical truth which is compelling for the "finite" pupil through demonstrating to him the necessity of following its course in search of refuge from the self-contradictions in which it has shown him to be entangled (in advancement of the constructive side of Hegel's pedagogical project).[237] Once again, the *Phenomenology* retains this use of the dialectical method as a means of realizing both the destructive and the constructive sides of its pedagogical project.

Let us now observe how all of these aspects of the pedagogical strategy of the early Logic survive within the *Phenomenology*. It is clear enough, to begin with, that the *Phenomenology* is designed to have a destructive side, to discredit everyday viewpoints. Thus the Introduction tells us that the pathway of the *Phenomenology* has "a negative significance" for the "natural consciousness," that it represents for this consciousness "the loss of its own self; for it does lose its truth on this path," that it is a "way of despair" which shows "the untruth of phenomenal cognition," that it is a "self-completing skepticism" (par. 78).[238]

Moreover, it is clear that this destructive side of the *Phenomenology* pursues the early Logic's strategy of showing the "nullity" of everyday views by "showing the unreal basis and ground from which they grow, and whose flavor and nature they absorb," that is, the strategy of discred-

---

237. Within the early Logic the dialectic only led *toward*, not all the way to, philosophical truth, this being reached at the end of the dialectic through a dialectically unguided step of "postulation" (as Hegel characterizes it in the *Difference* essay).

238. Cf. Heidelberg *Encyclopaedia* (Heidelberg: August Oswalds Universitätsbuchhandlung, 1817), pars. 35–36 (in appendix xvi): the *Phenomenology* effects a giving-up of all his "presuppositions" by the individual who is to reach the standpoint of Hegelian philosophy. Note that the *Phenomenology* indeed aims at nothing less than a discrediting and consequent abandonment of *consciousness itself* (not merely particular types or contents of it): "The standpoint of consciousness which knows objects in their antithesis to itself, and itself in antithesis to them, is for Science the antithesis to its own standpoint" (par. 26); "Pure Science presupposes liberation from the opposition of consciousness," as achieved by the *Phenomenology* (*Science of Logic*, pp. 48–49).

iting them by demonstrating self-contradictions in each member of a finite stock of items which must be drawn on for the articulation of any such view and which enter into the meanings of any view articulated through them. For the Introduction indicates, and the main body of the work confirms, that the *Phenomenology*'s "way of despair," which shows "the untruth of phenomenal cognition" quite generally, will consist in the demonstration of the self-contradictoriness of each member of a finite series of general viewpoints, or "shapes of consciousness," treated in the course of the work. As described in the Introduction, the self-contradictions will have the character of contradictions within each "shape of consciousness" between two of its essential components: its consciousness of an object, and its consciousness of its "cognition," or representation, of an object (pars. 84–85). How, more precisely, the early Logic's strategy is supposed to be replicated in the *Phenomenology* is a difficult question which I shall pursue further shortly.

That the *Phenomenology* has a *constructive* side as well is especially clear from remarks in the Preface. Thus, as we have seen, Hegel there assigns the work "the task of leading the individual from his uneducated standpoint to knowledge." And similarly, he there insists, with the *Phenomenology* in mind as the "ladder," that "the individual has the right to demand that Science should . . . provide him with a ladder to this standpoint [i.e., Science's standpoint]" (par. 26).

Moreover, the constructive side of the *Phenomenology*, like the constructive side of the early Logic, includes building a pedagogical bridge from ordinary cognition to philosophical truth containing a provisional presentation of philosophical truth in the false, self-contradictory medium of ordinary cognition itself, in exploitation of the assumed circumstance that some sorts of self-contradictory falsehood are better approximations to philosophical truth than others. This is part of Hegel's idea when he asserts that the ordinary consciousness should "be able to attain rational knowledge by way of the ordinary Understanding" or via "the Understanding's form of Science" (par. 13), and that Science should "show [the individual] this standpoint [Science's] *within himself*" (par. 26; emphasis added). As we shall see in chapter 5, it is also part of the force of Hegel's characterization of the *Phenomenology* as presenting an *appearance* of Science (pars. 38, 76).

Finally, the destructive and constructive sides of the *Phenomenology*, like those of (at least the last version of) the early Logic, employ the dialectical method as their means of discrediting everyday views and constructing a positive bridge toward philosophical truth which is compelling for the pupil. Hegel describes the dialectical method of the *Phenomenology*, where it is applied to "shapes of consciousness," in paragraphs 85–87 of the Introduction. This method's alternating demonstrations of implicit self-contradictions in earlier "shapes of consciousness" and of their necessary resolutions in subsequent "shapes of consciousness" both display the self-contradictoriness of "shapes of consciousness" (in realization of the destructive project) and compel the pupil undergoing education to proceed along the work's path toward philosophical truth (in realization of the constructive project).

So much for continuities between the pedagogical strategies of the early Logic and the *Phenomenology*. There are, however, also significant *dis*continuities, and in order to arrive at a more precise understanding of the *Phenomenology*'s pedagogical approach we must now consider these. Perhaps the most obvious discontinuity is this: The early Logic sought to undermine finite cognition by showing the self-contradictoriness of finite cognition's *fundamental concepts, forms of judgment, and forms of syllogism,* and used *these* materials to form a positive bridge toward philosophical truth. The *Phenomenology,* on the other hand, seeks to undermine finite cognition by discovering self-contradictions in, and forms a positive bridge toward philosophical truth out of, finite cognition's fundamental *shapes of consciousness.*

Two questions which we must ask, then, are what exactly Hegel means by "shapes of consciousness" and how exactly he envisages these playing the role which had been played in the early Logic by fundamental concepts, forms of judgment, and forms of syllogism (especially in relation to the destructive side of the pedagogical project)?[239]

In order to understand what Hegel means by "shapes of consciousness," it is important, first of all, to realize that he presupposes a certain contemporary theory about the essential structure of all consciousness, a theory originally developed by his predecessors Kant, Reinhold, and Fichte.[240] According to this theory, all consciousness essentially includes three interdependent elements: consciousness of *consciousness* itself, or

---

239. Some central aspects of the *constructive* side of the *Phenomenology*'s pedagogical project will be pursued in subsequent chapters. See especially chapters 3 (for the dialectical method) and 5 (for the idea of different degrees of approximation to philosophical truth within self-contradictory falsehood).

240. Agreement with Kant, Reinhold, and Fichte on the *structure* of consciousness does not of course require agreement with them on its *constitution*. Hegel agrees with them on

of the *self*, as such; consciousness of *something other than oneself*, or of an *object*, as such; and consciousness of one's *representation* of this other something or object as such.[241] Thus, concerning the first two of these three elements, Hegel writes in the Introduction that "consciousness is, on the one hand, consciousness of the object and, on the other, consciousness of itself" (par. 85).[242] And concerning also the third, he writes that "consciousness is . . . consciousness of what for it is the true, *and consciousness of its cognition* [i.e., its representation] *of the truth* . . . The distinction between the in-itself and cognition is already present in the very fact that consciousness has cognition of an object at all. Something is for it the in-itself; and cognition, or the being of the object for consciousness, is, for it, another moment" (par. 85; emphasis added).[243]

Hegel tends to take the correctness of this theory of consciousness somewhat for granted (no doubt partly due to its widespread acceptance by his immediate predecessors). Nevertheless, it does seem possible to

---

the former, but in his physicalism and behaviorism parts company with them sharply on the latter.

241. The beginnings of this theory lay in Kant's transcendental deduction of the categories in the *Critique of Pure Reason*. Reinhold's *Elementarphilosophie*, an attempt to systematize Kant's philosophy, set forth as its fundamental principle a "proposition of consciousness" which clearly implied the essentiality of all three of the elements just mentioned to consciousness: "In consciousness the representation is distinguished by the subject from the subject and the object and is related to both" (K.L. Reinhold, *Neue Darstellung der Elementarphilosophie*, in *Beiträge zur Berichtigung bisheriger Mißverständnisse der Philosophen* [Jena: Widtmann and Mauke, 1790–94], 1:167). Fichte brought this model of consciousness to still greater prominence by accepting Reinhold's fundamental principle in the *Science of Knowledge*—making two of its three elements, the self's self-positing and the self's positing of a not-self, respectively the first and second principles of the *Science of Knowledge*, and the third, consciousness of one's representation, derivative from them. The best account of these matters known to me is to be found in two essays by D. Breazeale, "Fichte's *Aenesidemus* Review and the Transformation of German Idealism," *Review of Metaphysics* 34 (1981), and "Between Kant and Fichte: Karl Leonhard Reinhold's 'Elementary Philosophy,' " *Review of Metaphysics* 35 (1982).

242. Cf. *Science of Logic*, p. 63: "Consciousness embraces within itself the opposition of the ego and its object."

243. The source of this Hegelian model of consciousness in Kant, Reinhold, and Fichte is evident not only from the striking similarity of the ideas involved but also from verbal echoes. For example, Reinhold's "proposition of consciousness" reads: "In consciousness the representation is distinguished [unterschieden] by the subject from the subject and the object and is related [bezogen] to both." Echoing this, Hegel begins his account of the nature of consciousness in the Introduction with the observation that consciousness "distinguishes [unterscheidet] . . . something from itself, to which it at the same time relates [bezieht] itself" (par. 82). One can also trace the model back to Kant, Reinhold, and Fichte through Hegel's correspondence with Hölderlin and Schelling in the 1790s.

generate quite a forceful argument for it in the general spirit of his remarks: All consciousness worthy of the name must involve thinking of something or other as objective (real, being).[244] Now in order to think of something as objective (real, being) one must have the *concept* of objectivity (reality, being). Thus Hegel remarks in the *Lectures on the History of Philosophy* that "each act of consciousness has and requires the whole abstract thought determination of being."[245] But the concept of objectivity (reality, being) is surely in essential part the concept of *not being merely for representations*. Hence Hegel's remark at paragraph 85 that "the distinction between the in-itself and cognition [i.e., representation] is already present in the very fact that consciousness has cognition of an object at all."[246] And the concept of a representation is surely in essential part the concept of a representation *by a consciousness* or *self*. And so it turns out that all consciousness worthy of the name must include possession of the three concepts of objectivity, representation, and self. Moreover, each of these concepts seems to require the other two, since not only are the concepts of representation and selfhood essentially involved in the concept of objectivity in the ways just indicated, but equally: the concept of a representation is in essential part the concept of a representation *by a self* (as was just mentioned), and also in essential part the concept of a representation of something *as objective;* and the concept of the self is in essential part the concept of a viewpoint or a *locus of representations*, and the concept of a representation is in turn (as was just mentioned) in essential part the concept of a representation of something *as objective*. If, in response to this line of argument supporting Hegel's model of consciousness, it be asked whether one could not have consciousness of something as objective, and therefore as not being the way that it is merely for the representations of selves, without having consciousness of one's *own* representations or of one's *own* self as such,

---

244. Even if one is conscious only of one's own mental states, still one must think of them as objectively or really mental states, as mental states which are; even if one is conscious only of fictional objects or events, for example while watching a cartoon film, although one need not *believe* them to be objective, real, or existent, still one must *think of* them as such.

245. Hegel, *On Art, Religion, Philosophy*, p. 262.

246. Cf. *Faith and Being*: Being "is certainly taken to be, but the mere fact of its being does not, it is held, make it for us; the independence of being is held to consist in the fact that it is, whether for us or not for us. Being is taken to be capable of being something quite separate from us, in which there lies no necessity that we should come into relation with it" (*Hegels theologische Jugendschriften*, p. 383).

then it seems plausible to give a negative answer to this question. For, surely, possession of the concept of a representation requires that one know *from one's own case* what it is to represent things as being a certain way, and possession of the concept of a self requires that one know *from one's own case* what it is to be a self.[247]

Unlike his predecessors, however, Hegel believes that this theory of consciousness only captures consciousness as a *genus*. There exist also different *species* of consciousness, and in order to instantiate the generic model an individual must belong to one or another of these species. Each of these species of consciousness is defined by a more specific model as essentially comprising a *particular type* of each of the three elements in the generic model, in interdependence with one another: a *particular type* of consciousness of self, distinguished by a particular conception and concept of the self; a *particular type* of consciousness of object, distinguished by a particular conception and concept of objectivity; and a *particular type* of consciousness of representation of object, distinguished by a particular conception and concept of representation. These different species of consciousness are what Hegel in the *Phenomenology* calls "shapes of consciousness" (pars. 84–89).[248]

Two aspects of these specific models require further explanation. First,

---

247. Note that it would be consistent with this claim to say that one must also know from *others'* cases, that one must also identify *others* as selves. Fichte had already argued for such a position—for a helpful account of which, see Wood, *Hegel's Ethical Thought*, pp. 78–80. Hegel at first sight appears to argue for a similar view in the Lordship and Bondage section of the *Phenomenology*—and has been interpreted along these lines by for example J. Royce in his *Lectures on Modern Idealism* (New Haven, Conn.: Yale University Press, 1964), pp. 158, 177. However, on closer inspection the intentions of the section in this regard are quite equivocal (see for example par. 186, which could be read as speaking either for or against the view in question). For a more contemporary version of such a view, see P.F. Strawson, *Individuals* (London: Methuen, 1977), chap. 3.

248. For specific examples of the *Phenomenology*'s shapes of consciousness, see chapter 9, where I have in particular explained the three shapes from the *Consciousness* chapter—Sense-certainty, Perception, and Force and the Understanding—in such a way as to exhibit their instantiation of Hegel's model. As we shall see in chapter 9, Hegel believes that (i) each shape of consciousness arises within and is distinctive of a particular culture and historical period (e.g., Stoicism arises within and is distinctive of Greek and Roman culture in a period of later antiquity, Physiognomy within and of German culture in a period in the late eighteenth century), and (ii) shapes of consciousness may arise from or be paradigmatically represented by a number of different areas of culture (e.g., Perception arises from or is paradigmatically represented by theoretical common sense, Stoicism from or by philosophy, Unhappy Consciousness from or by religion, Pleasure and Necessity from or by literature).

one might be puzzled by the suggestion that what distinguishes a shape of consciousness's particular types of consciousness of self, object, and representation are particular *conceptions and concepts* of self, object, and representation. The immediate textual evidence for this reading is the fact that the Introduction moves back and forth between locutions which suggest that what define a shape of consciousness are *conceptions,* that is, beliefs, about these items and locutions which suggest that what do so are *concepts* of these items. For example, the following expression at paragraph 84 seems to imply that *beliefs* about them are in question: "what consciousness *affirms from within itself* as being-in-itself or the true" (emphasis added). But this expression at paragraph 85 seems to imply rather that *concepts* of them are in question: "the abstract *determinations* [Bestimmungen] of cognition and truth as they occur in consciousness" (emphasis added). This apparent equivocation is not, I think, careless or accidental. Rather, it is Hegel's idea that what defines a shape of consciousness and sets it apart from other shapes is always a set of *distinctive conceptions of self, objectivity, and representation which at the same time amount to distinctive concepts of them.* Thus, if we consider Hegel's actual examples of shapes of consciousness in the main body of the *Phenomenology* (as we shall in chapter 9), we find that the differences in conceptions of self, objectivity, and representation which he picks out as distinguishing one shape of consciousness from another are in general sufficiently *fundamental* in character to be seen with plausibility as constituting differences also in the very *concepts* of self, objectivity, and representation. For instance, what distinguishes Perception's conception of objectivity from the conception of objectivity belonging to Force and the Understanding is not merely some more or less minor disagreement—a disagreement about which of two types of particle or force is objectively real, for instance. Rather, it is the very fundamental disagreement that, roughly, Perception believes objective reality to be identical with the sensibly perceptible, whereas Force and the Understanding believes it to be identical with supersensible forces or constitutions of which the sensibly perceptible is only a superficial appearance. (It is also significant in this connection to recall the fact noted earlier that Hegel quite generally regards a lot of "theory" as internal to concepts or meanings.)

The second feature of these specific models which requires further explanation is Hegel's idea that the distinctive conceptions of self, object, and representation which define a shape of consciousness are *interdepen-*

dent. The immediate textual evidence for this reading lies in such remarks as that a shape of consciousness's conception of its object "essentially belong[s]" to its conception of its "cognition," or representation, so that when consciousness alters its conception of its "cognition" automatically "the object itself alters for it too," and any testing of its conception of its "cognition" is "also a testing of the criterion," that is, of its conception of the object (par. 85). Now if a shape of consciousness's distinctive conceptions of self, object, and representation were just any old distinctive conceptions, then this idea of their interdependence would be quite mysterious. But when we realize that the conceptions of self, object, and representation which distinguish a shape of consciousness are understood by Hegel to be not only distinctive conceptions but also distinctive *concepts* of these items, then it becomes readily intelligible. For in that case their interdependence derives from their being implicitly interdefined, in accordance with the arguments which I gave recently to account for the interdependence of the concepts of self, objectivity, and representation in the generic model.

This theory of consciousness is of considerable intrinsic interest (especially when developed in historical detail as it is by the *Phenomenology*). Moreover, and of more immediate relevance here, it enables us to make good exegetical and philosophical sense of Hegel's transference to the *Phenomenology* of his earlier destructive strategy—his strategy of proving the "nullity" of everyday views by "showing the unreal basis and ground from which they grow, and whose flavor and nature they absorb," or in other words discrediting them by demonstrating self-contradictions in each member of a finite stock of items which must be drawn on for the articulation of any such view, and which enter into the meanings of the views articulated through them, thereby infecting these with self-contradictions also.

We need to answer three main questions here: (i) Why do all everyday views have to draw on shapes of consciousness for their articulation? (ii) How does a shape of consciousness enter into the meaning of any view articulated through it? (iii) How does a self-contradiction in a shape of consciousness infect any view articulated through that shape, so that the view too becomes self-contradictory?

An exegetically and philosophically plausible answer to question (i) is this: Everyday views are essentially composed of concepts and judgments. But a concept of an X is always implicitly a concept of a *real* X, and a judgment that Y is always implicitly a judgment that Y is *really* the case.[249] Hence any everyday view must include a concept of *reality*. But now, by an argument given earlier, the concept of reality is implicitly interdefined with the concepts of *representation* and *self*. And, again by an argument given earlier, possession of these latter two concepts requires knowing that they apply in one's own case. And so it turns out that the entertainment of any everyday view requires, not only a consciousness of something as real, but also a consciousness of one's own representations as such and of oneself as such. In other words, it requires possession of some shape of consciousness or other.

An exegetically and philosophically plausible answer to question (ii) is this: Any everyday concept or judgment is (as was just suggested) implicitly a concept of something as, or a judgment that something is, *really* a certain way. Now we have seen that a shape of consciousness is always, for Hegel, constituted in essential part by a *distinctive concept of reality*, together with the distinctive concepts of representation and self with which it is implicitly interdefined. Hence, a concept or judgment which is articulated through a particular shape of consciousness will always implicitly be a concept of something as, or a judgment that something is, *really* a certain way *in the distinctive sense of "real" belonging to that shape*. Moreover, since that sense of "real" is implicitly interdefined with the other concepts which together with it constitute the shape, the whole shape thereby implicitly enters into the meaning of the concept or judgment in question.

An exegetically and philosophically plausible answer to question (iii) is this: Hegel claims that there will always turn out to be an implicit contradiction between a shape of consciousness's conception/concept of objectivity and its conception/concept of representation (pars. 84–85). Now since (as we have seen) each of these elements of a shape of consciousness is implicitly defined in terms of the other, this means that each will, implicitly, be *individually self-contradictory* as well. Hence, in particular, the shape's concept of objectivity or reality will be implicitly self-contradictory.[250] And so all concepts articulated through the shape, be-

---

249. Aristotle sometimes seems to imply a view of the former kind (e.g., *Metaphysics*, 1003b27–30). And concerning the latter, note Hegel's comment in *Faith and Being*: "In every proposition the connecting word 'is' expresses . . . a being . . . Belief presupposes a being" (*Hegels theologische Jugendschriften*, p. 383).

250. For some specific examples of how Hegel envisages this situation, see the discussions of Perception in chapter 4 below and of the Spiritual Animalkingdom in chapter 9.

cause they are always implicitly concepts of things as *really* a certain way *in the same sense of "real,"* and all judgments articulated through the shape, because they are always implicitly judgments that such and such is *really* the case again *in the same sense of "real,"* will also be implicitly self-contradictory.

A further difference between the execution of the pedagogical project in the early Logic and its execution in the *Phenomenology* is the following. Although the constructive side of the early Logic used a dialectical exposition which led *toward* philosophical truth, this dialectical exposition stopped short of philosophical truth itself, which was instead reached by an act of dialectically unguided "postulation" at the end of the Logic.[251] In the *Phenomenology*, by contrast, the dialectical exposition eventually leads the ordinary consciousness undergoing education all the way to philosophical truth itself. Thus note the wording in the Preface: "Science should at least provide [the individual] with the ladder *to this standpoint*" (par. 26; emphasis added). And note also Hegel's remark in the *Encyclopaedia* that the *Phenomenology* develops its dialectic "*up to* the standpoint of philosophical Science."[252]

A final difference between the executions of the pedagogical project in the early Logic and in the *Phenomenology* is that on its constructive side the latter attempts, unlike the former, to give not only a provisional presentation of philosophical truth, but moreover a provisional presentation of the *whole* of philosophical truth, a provisional presentation of the *entire content* of the Hegelian system.[253] In the *Encyclopaedia* Hegel explains the presence of the later parts of the *Phenomenology* within the text in terms of the need to do justice to precisely this aspiration: "It was not possible [in the *Phenomenology*] to remain at the formal aspect of mere consciousness [i.e., the contents of the chapters *Consciousness* through *Reason*]; for the standpoint of philosophical knowing is at the same time within itself the most contentful and concrete standpoint, so that in being produced as a result it presupposed also the concrete shapes

---

251. This is most explicit in the first version of the early Logic, sketched in the *Difference* essay of 1801 (*Jenaer Schriften*, pp. 43–44). It also applies, though, to the final version in the 1804–5 *Logic, Metaphysics, and Philosophy of Nature* (on which see my *Hegel and Skepticism*, pp. 162–64).

252. In appendix XVII; emphasis added.

253. This is well noted by Haym, *Hegel und seine Zeit*, pp. 253–55. We shall see later that, while it is indeed true of the published version of the *Phenomenology*, it was not true of the version of the work which Hegel originally planned to write.

of consciousness, for example those of morality, ethical life, art, and religion [i.e., the contents of the *Spirit* and *Religion* chapters]."[254] Accordingly, within the *Phenomenology* we find a provisional presentation of virtually all parts of the Hegelian system of the *Encyclopaedia:* As Hegel implies in remarks at paragraphs 89 and 805 (and as we shall see in detail in chapter 15), the whole of the later Logic is given a sort of provisional presentation in the form of shapes of consciousness in the chapters *Consciousness* through *Reason*. The Philosophy of Nature receives a sort of provisional presentation in the *Observing Reason* section of the *Reason* chapter—where the development proceeds, as in the Philosophy of Nature and its culminating transition to the Philosophy of Spirit, from inanimate nature, to organic nature, and eventually to the human mind (in the subsections *Logical and Psychological Laws* and *Physiognomy and Phrenology*). The section of the Philosophy of Spirit which in the *Encyclopaedia* bears the same title as the *Phenomenology,* "Phenomenology of Spirit," receives a sort of provisional presentation in the chapters *Consciousness* through *Reason.*[255] The section of the Philosophy of Spirit entitled "Objective Spirit" in the *Encyclopaedia* finds a sort of provisional presentation in the *Phenomenology* as well: its parts on Morality and Ethical Life or The State are anticipated in the *Spirit* chapter of the *Phenomenology,* and its part on World History is anticipated in the *Phenomenology* as a whole, since in its entirety the *Phenomenology* constitutes a sort of provisional philosophy of world history (see esp. par. 808).[256] Finally, the Philosophy of Spirit's concluding section, entitled "Absolute Spirit" in the *Encyclopaedia,* and dealing with art, religion, and philosophy, finds a provisional presentation in the *Phenomenology*'s *Religion* chapter (art and religion) and *Absolute Knowing* chapter (philosophy).[257]

---

254. In appendix XVII.
255. Note that the Philosophy of Spirit already contained a "Phenomenology of Spirit" section in the *Encyclopaedia* of 1808 ff. (Hegel, *Nürnberger und Heidelberger Schriften* [Frankfurt am Main: Suhrkamp, 1979], p. 42, pars. 128–29). There is therefore no anachronism in interpreting the *Phenomenology* of 1807 as deliberately giving a provisional presentation of such a section.
256. All these parts of the mature Philosophy of Spirit—Morality, The State, and World History or "Philosophical History"—are already present in the Philosophy of Spirit of the 1808 ff. *Encyclopaedia* (though not yet under the title "Objective Spirit"). So, once again, there is no anachronism in interpreting the *Phenomenology* of 1807 as deliberately giving a provisional presentation of this material.
257. The title "Absolute Spirit" comes from the published *Encyclopaedia,* but the contents in question were already part of the Philosophy of Spirit in the 1808 ff. *Encyclopaedia* (and indeed earlier, in Hegel's Jena system). So, once again, there is no anachronism in

Taking all of these continuities and discontinuities between the early Logic and the *Phenomenology* into account, we may now summarize the basic pedagogical strategy of the *Phenomenology* as follows. The work seeks to make Hegel's contemporaries understand and accept his philosophical system, thereby bestowing on them not only the theoretical benefit of knowing the truth but also, and perhaps especially, the practical benefit of happiness, through these means: (1) It discredits alternative viewpoints, including the viewpoints which these contemporaries themselves currently occupy, by demonstrating the self-contradictoriness of their "shapes of consciousness" with the help of the dialectical method. (2) It provides these contemporaries with a compelling pathway from their own viewpoints toward, and indeed right up to, Hegel's system, namely, the *Phenomenology*'s dialectical pathway, which compels them to follow it in their efforts to escape the self-contradictions in their current viewpoints which it reveals to them, and which eventually culminates in Hegel's system. (3) It affords these contemporaries along the course of the pathway a provisional presentation of Hegel's system, and indeed of the *whole* of Hegel's system, by exploiting the assumed circumstance that even false, self-contradictory views may contain *relatively* good approximations to philosophical truth, and building such relatively good approximations to the truth of Hegel's system into the pathway of the work.[258]

---

interpreting the *Phenomenology* of 1807 as deliberately giving a provisional presentation of this material.

258. This is the *basic* pedagogical strategy of the work. Many of the features of the work to be explained in the next two chapters can be seen as elaborating this basic pedagogical strategy in various ways.

CHAPTER THREE

Justifying Hegelian Science: The Epistemological Tasks

So much for the pedagogical tasks of the *Phenomenology*. We may now turn to the epistemological tasks, the tasks of justifying Hegelian Science's claim to truth by (4) defending Hegelian Science against the skeptical problem of "equipollence," (5) defending it against the skeptical problem of "concept-instantiation," and (6) giving a proof of it for all non-Hegelian viewpoints which is compelling to each of them in the light of its own initial views and criteria.[1]

That the *Phenomenology* was from the start conceived in large measure as a work of epistemology can be seen from its preoccupation with epistemological themes especially in the Introduction, and also to some extent in the Preface.[2] The Introduction opens with a critique of an epistemological conception due to Lambert, Kant, and others influenced by them according to which knowledge constitutes a sort of instrument [Werkzeug] or medium [Mittel/Medium] by means of or through which we ascertain truth and which requires an investigation prior to our use of it to do so (pars. 73–76).[3] The Introduction goes on to criticize the

---

1. Some of the epistemological themes of this chapter are discussed more fully in my *Hegel and Skepticism*.
2. For a very helpful commentary on the Introduction specifically which emphasizes epistemological themes there, see Hegel, *Einleitung zur Phänomenologie des Geistes*, ed. A. Graeser (Stuttgart: Reclam, 1988).
3. J.H. Lambert, in his 1764 work *Neues Organon* (Hildesheim: Georg Olms Verlagsbuchhandlung, 1965), characterizes sciences as "Mittel und Werkzeuge" (cf. the title *Organon*) and develops a systematic project of investigating human cognition (see esp. vol. 1, the *Vorrede*). Hegel explicitly associates the conception of knowledge as an instrument which must be investigated prior to use with Kant at *Lectures on the History of Philosophy*

epistemological dogmatism of Schelling, whose response, when confronted with viewpoints which disagree with that of his own "Science," is simply to "reject [them] as an ordinary way of looking at things, while assuring us that . . . Science is a quite different sort of knowledge for which that ordinary cognition is of no account whatever" (par. 76; cf. 27). The Introduction next proceeds to reject as inadequate the epistemological technique of "critique" which Hegel had himself developed in cooperation with Schelling in their *Critical Journal of Philosophy* during the earlier Jena period—the technique of, in effect, assuming the truth of their own philosophy and then looking for anticipations of it in other philosophers' theories as a means to the latter's critical evaluation and its own validation.[4] This is the point of the Introduction's comment: "Still less can Science appeal to whatever intimations of something better it may detect in the cognition that is without truth, to the signs which point in the direction of Science" (par. 76). The Introduction then proceeds to reject Descartes's epistemological strategy of preemptive skepticism, "the skepticism with which an earnest zeal for truth and science fancies it has prepared and equipped itself in their service: the resolve, in science, not to give oneself over to the thoughts of others, upon mere authority, but to examine everything for oneself and follow only one's own conviction, or better still, to produce everything oneself and accept only one's own

---

3:428, and *Encyclopaedia,* par. 10. The conception of knowledge as an *instrument* to be investigated prior to use is not exactly obvious in Kant. However, he does speak of the need to "prepare the ground [for metaphysics] beforehand by a critique of the organ, that is, of pure reason itself" (*Critique of Pure Reason,* trans. N. Kemp Smith [London: Macmillan, 1978], Bxxxvi–xxxvii), of an "organon of pure reason" (A11/B25), and frequently also of "employing" our cognition (e.g., Bxxiii–xxv), "applying" it to objects (e.g., Bxxx), and using it as a "means" (e.g., A22–23). Another person whom Hegel may well have in mind here is K.L. Reinhold, for whose expression of relevant ideas, and in particular the conception of cognition as a medium, see Reinhold, *Versuch einer neuen Theorie des menschlichen Vorstellungsvermögens* (Prague: Widtmann and Mauke, 1789), pp. 366 ff., 374 ff.

4. Hegel explains the *theory* of this technique of "critique" in the 1802 essay *On the Nature of Philosophical Critique,* in *Jenaer Schriften;* the essential passages are excerpted in appendix VII. The technique's *practice* is paradigmatically exemplified by Hegel's treatment of the philosophies of Kant, Fichte, and Jacobi in the contemporary essay *Faith and Knowledge,* in *Jenaer Schriften.*

Incidentally, failure to understand the character of this technique properly has contributed to some quite serious misinterpretations of Hegel. For example, interpreters who have seen in early Jena essays such as *Faith and Knowledge* evidence of the birth of Hegel's mature philosophy out of a sort of immanent critique of Kant's conception of transcendental apperception need to reflect harder on the distinctive character of this technique (as well as on the fact that the main lines of Hegel's mature philosophy antedate these essays).

deed as what is true [i.e., one's own mental "deed," one's *cogitatio* in Descartes's idiom]" (par. 78). In the Preface, written later, Hegel adds a repudiation of the epistemology of the Romantics, who advocate intuition, immediate knowledge, or feeling as the criterion of truth, holding that "the true exists only in or rather as what is called now intuition, now immediate knowledge . . . The Absolute is not to be understood, but felt and intuited, not its concept, but the feeling and intuition of it should have authority and be expressed" (par. 6).

Why does Hegel reject these earlier epistemological approaches, and with what epistemological concerns and strategies does he intend to replace them? In order to answer these questions it is vital, above all, to have understood Hegel's stance toward *skepticism*. Especially illuminating in this connection are his 1802 essay *The Relation of Skepticism to Philosophy* and his discussions of ancient Academic and Pyrrhonian skepticism in the *Lectures on the History of Philosophy*. Consideration of these texts reveals that Hegel takes the challenge of skepticism very seriously indeed, but also that he understands this challenge to lie in the difficulties raised by the *ancient* skeptics rather than in those raised by their modern counterparts. The tendency of much discussion of skepticism in the modern period has been to regard the relatively restrained modern varieties of skepticism, such as Hume's, as philosophically superior to the more radical skepticism of the ancient skeptics, and in particular the Pyrrhonists. Among Hegel's predecessors, Hume himself famously held this view.[5] So too did people who were for Hegel closer to home in time and place, such as the neo-Humean "Aenesidemus" Schulze, and Fichte.[6] Against this orthodoxy, Hegel argues that radical ancient skepticism, and in particular Pyrrhonism, is philosophically far superior to the

---

5. See esp. Hume, *An Enquiry Concerning Human Understanding* (1748) (Oxford: Oxford University Press, 1975), sec. 12, pt. 2, where Hume contrasts ancient Pyrrhonism unfavorably as a "popular" form of skepticism with a skepticism which raises "philosophical objections" in his own manner.

6. Schulze is Hegel's own prime example of this view—see *The Relation of Skepticism to Philosophy*, in *Jenaer Schriften*, pp. 222–23, 225–26, 231; also in appendix VI. In the *Science of Knowledge*, trans. P. Heath and J. Lachs (Cambridge: Cambridge University Press, 1982), Fichte had similarly written of an extreme skepticism "which doubts whether it doubts," in the manner of the ancient Pyrrhonists: "Never yet, in good earnest, has there been a skeptic of this kind. A critical skepticism, such as that of Hume, Maimon, or Aenesidemus [i.e., Schulze, not the ancient Pyrrhonist], is another matter; for it points out the inadequacy of the grounds so far accepted, and shows in doing so, where better are to be found. And if knowledge gains nothing as to content from this, it certainly does as to form" (p. 118).

more restrained modern forms of skepticism. Thus in *The Relation of Skepticism to Philosophy* he gives a highly respectful exposition of ancient Pyrrhonism, but remarks that by contrast "the ideas about skepticism in common circulation are extremely formal and the noble nature which skepticism possesses when in its true form is habitually perverted into a general hidingplace and excuse for unphilosophy [Unphilosophie] in the most recent times."[7]

What, for Hegel, is the great difference between ancient and modern skepticism which renders the former philosophically compelling but the latter philosophically worthless? In Hegel's view—and I think also in fact—the great strength of ancient skepticism lies in its possession of the method of equipollence [*isostheneia*—literally, "equal force on both sides"], that is, the method of setting into opposition equally strong propositions or arguments on both sides of any issue that arises, and thereby producing an equal balance of justification on both sides of the issue.[8] The ancient skeptics used this method as their means of inducing suspension of belief [*epochē*] about any issue that arose. The centrality of this method to ancient Pyrrhonism can be seen both from Sextus Empiricus's skeptical practice, and from his programmatic statement: "The main basic principle of the skeptic system is that of opposing to every proposition/argument [*logos*] an equal proposition/argument; for we believe that as a consequence of this we end by ceasing to dogmatize."[9]

In Hegel's view, this method has two closely connected distinguishing virtues. (i) It avoids any essential reliance on beliefs; the use of the method to attack particular beliefs does not require a retention or holding firm of *other* beliefs as a basis for the attack. (ii) Consequently, it enjoys general applicability; it is a method which can be used to attack any and all beliefs

---

7. *Jenaer Schriften*, p. 214; also in appendix VI.

8. Ibid., pp. 240, 246; also in appendix VI.

9. Sextus Empiricus, *Outlines of Pyrrhonism*, trans. R.G. Bury (London: Loeb Classical Library, 1976), bk. 1, chap. 6. Bury translates *logos* here simply as "proposition," but it is important to preserve the ambiguity in the Greek between "proposition" and "argument." For, on the one hand, Sextus Empiricus's practice is usually one of balancing opposed *arguments*, not merely propositions, so that he must surely have this sense of *logos* in mind in this definition of Pyrrhonian procedure. But, on the other hand, one cannot therefore simply substitute "argument" for Bury's "proposition," for Sextus Empiricus does not *always* insist on balancing opposed arguments, but does envisage in certain cases merely balancing opposed propositions, namely, cases where dogmatists have themselves advanced propositions without supporting arguments (this is the skeptical method of the fourth trope of Agrippa; see *Outlines of Pyrrhonism*, bk. 1, chap. 15).

regardless of content, rather than being restricted in applicability to some subset of beliefs having a specific kind of content. Hegel describes the equipollence method, emphasizing these two distinctive virtues, in the *Lectures on the History of Philosophy:* "We must now consider . . . the method in which the skeptics proceed, and it consists in this, that they have brought the universal principle that each definite assertion has to be set over against its 'other' into certain forms, not propositions . . . In view of the nature of skepticism, we cannot ask for any system of propositions . . . Sextus hence says that skepticism is no selection . . . of dogmas, it is not a preference for certain propositions, . . . it is . . . rather a method or manner by which only universal modes of that opposition are shown."[10]

The general thrust of Hegel's interpretation of ancient skepticism in *The Relation of Skepticism to Philosophy* is to see it as, and commend it for, attacking *all* beliefs by means of the equipollence method.[11] In particular, contrary to other interpreters, such as Schulze (or Kant in his Logic lectures), who had interpreted ancient skepticism as wisely attacking only scientific or philosophical beliefs, but not commonsense beliefs, Hegel interprets it as and approves it for attacking *both*.[12] Moreover, as we shall see below, Hegel goes so far as to interpret ancient skepticism as, and approve it for, attacking a subject's beliefs about his own current mental states. And elsewhere he interprets it as, and approves it for, attacking beliefs in the principles of formal logic.[13]

The ancient skeptics could use the equipollence method to motivate a quite general suspension of belief because the method's strategy of setting

---

10. *Lectures on the History of Philosophy* 2:345.
11. This claim requires certain qualifications: (i) Hegel draws distinctions between different phases of ancient Pyrrhonism—seeing the early ten tropes of Aenesidemus as directed solely against common sense, rather than against the sciences or philosophy, and only the later five tropes of Agrippa as directed against *all* beliefs. (ii) Hegel's approval of the radicalism of the five tropes of Agrippa has one very firm exception: their direction against genuine philosophy is, he thinks, misconceived and futile.
12. This is a dominant theme in *The Relation of Skepticism to Philosophy*. Note that the interpretative dispute still rages unabated today, with some authorities, for example M. Frede, defending an interpretation roughly along the lines of Schulze and Kant, while others, for example M.F. Burnyeat, defend one roughly along Hegel's lines. The textual issues here are very complex (as the longevity of the debate testifies). However, my own view is that the Hegel-Burnyeat reading is ultimately the more defensible. For further discussion see my *Hegel and Skepticism*, chap. 1, n.58.
13. For a sympathetic account of this aspect of Hegel's interpretation, see my *Hegel and Skepticism*, chap. 1, n.49.

up opposing propositions or arguments of equal weight on each issue in order to induce suspension of belief did not require belief in any of the propositions or arguments thus deployed. When the ancient skeptic set up an argument hostile to some piece of dogmatic theory (such as the Stoics' theory that "cataleptic impressions" provided a criterion of truth or the theory that there were gods having such and such a nature) this was never because he believed or sought to induce belief in the destructive argument, regarding or hoping to make others regard it as decisive against the dogmatic theory in question, or as more convincing than the dogmatists' arguments in favor of the theory. On the contrary, he no more identified or sought to induce identification with the destructive argument than with the constructive arguments which the dogmatists had provided in support of the theory. For the whole point of the ancient skeptic's procedure of adducing propositions or arguments on both sides of an issue was that he and his audience should find those on neither side more convincing than those on the other. If the ancient skeptic's practice laid greater emphasis on the development of destructive than of constructive arguments, this was merely because the constructive cases had already been sufficiently well argued by the dogmatists themselves, so that the skeptic could concentrate on developing the destructive cases required for establishing an equal balance of plausibility on each issue. Thus Sextus Empiricus, as too often goes unnoticed, will conclude a thoroughly destructive argument against the existence of a criterion of truth which has extended over many pages of his text with the following brief but vital reminder: "But one should notice that we do not propose to assert that the criterion of truth is unreal (for that would be dogmatism); but since the dogmatists appear to have established plausibly that there really is a criterion of truth, we have set up counterarguments which appear to be plausible; and although we do not positively affirm either that they are true or that they are more plausible than their opposites, yet because of the apparently equal plausibility of these arguments and of those propounded by the dogmatists we deduce suspension of judgment."[14]

Hegel argues, plausibly, that modern skepticism, by contrast, has

---

14. *Outlines of Pyrrhonism*, bk. 2, chap. 7. One might wonder whether this procedure does not at least require the skeptic and his audience to believe in the equal plausibility of the arguments set into opposition, thus forcing the exemption of at least these beliefs from attack by means of the equipollence method. But, as Hegel notes in *The Relation of Skepticism to Philosophy* (*Jenaer Schriften,* pp. 231, 249; also in appendix VI), Sextus Empiricus argues not: such "formulas" of the skeptic if positively affirmed as truths are subject to

abandoned ancient skepticism's equipollence method, and has in consequence lost ancient skepticism's distinguishing virtues: modern skepticism essentially relies, in attacking those beliefs which it does attack, on a presupposition of other beliefs, and as a result it lacks general applicability, instead attacking only some beliefs without being in a position to attack others. For, in place of equipollence problems, modern skepticism typically raises problems concerning the legitimacy of proceeding from propositions about one subject matter *knowledge of which it assumes to be absolutely or relatively unproblematic* to propositions about a second subject matter knowledge of which it does not find thus unproblematic. In some cases the supposedly unproblematic subject matter is the sphere of one's own (current) mental states, and the problematic subject matter the mind-external world.[15] In other cases the supposedly unproblematic subject matter is the realm of the human mind and physical nature, and the problematic subject matter the objects of religious belief.[16] (In yet

---

equipollence attack as much as any other positive affirmations, and are accepted by the skeptic only as *appearances* (*Outlines of Pyrrhonism*, bk. 1, chap. 7).

15. In *The Relation of Skepticism to Philosophy* "Aenesidemus" Schulze is Hegel's paradigmatic example of this sort of modern skepticism. For the sound basis of this reading of Schulze, see for instance Schulze's work *Aenesidemus*, in *Between Kant and Hegel*, trans. G. di Giovanni and H.S. Harris (Albany: State University of New York Press, 1985), esp. pp. 105, 116, 133. Schulze's avowed model here is, though, Hume, who raises the same sort of skeptical problem in *An Enquiry Concerning Human Understanding*: "By what argument can it be proved that the perceptions of the mind must be caused by external objects, entirely different from them though resembling them . . . ? Here experience is and must be entirely silent. The mind has never anything present to it but the perceptions, and cannot possibly reach any experience of their connexion with objects" (pp. 152–53). And accordingly, Hegel indicates in the *Encyclopaedia* that he considers Hume an example of this sort of modern skepticism as well (par. 39; cf. 81, addition).

16. In the seventh of the theses for his *Habilitationsdisputation* of 1801 Hegel identified Kant's critical philosophy as an "imperfect skepticism" of this sort ("imperfect" because, as the eighth thesis implies, although it attacks claims to *know* the objects of religion, it defends claims to *justified belief* in them, namely, through its doctrine of the postulates) (Rosenkranz, *Hegels Leben*, p. 159). In *The Relation of Skepticism to Philosophy* Hegel associates this sort of skepticism above all with "Aenesidemus" Schulze (*Jenaer Schriften*, pp. 222–23, 225–26, 250 ff.; also in appendix VI). Hume too provides an example of this sort of skeptical problem, in the *Dialogues Concerning Natural Religion* (written in the 1750s) (New York: Hafner, 1966), in the person of Philo, the work's most radical skeptic: "So long as we confine our speculations to trade, or morals, or politics, or criticism, we make appeals every moment to common sense and experience, which strengthen our philosophical conclusions . . . But in theological reasonings, we have not this advantage, while at the same time we are employed upon objects which, we must be sensible, are too large for our grasp" (pp. 9–10). And accordingly, Hegel in the *Encyclopaedia* associates Hume with this sort of modern skepticism as well (par. 50; also in appendix XVII).

other cases, modern skepticism substitutes for equipollence problems a sort of negative theorizing again essentially shot through with beliefs.[17])

The problem which Hegel sees in modern skepticism's essential reliance on certain beliefs for its attack on other beliefs, and sparing of the former from skeptical attack, is that this makes modern skepticism fundamentally *dogmatic*—in the sense of being essentially founded on the acceptance of beliefs which are in fact vulnerable to skeptical attack. Hence the sorry tale which Hegel tells in *The Relation of Skepticism to Philosophy* of a gradual degeneration of the skeptical tradition over the course of history into dogmatism. The tradition began with "the old and genuine skepticism" of early Pyrrhonism but later declined into dogmatism "until [skepticism] finally in the most recent times sinks so far with dogmatism that now for both the facts of consciousness possess undeniable certainty and for both truth lies in the temporal sphere, so that because the extremes touch each other in these happy times the great goal is . . . attained by them that dogmatism and skepticism fall together in their decline and each reaches out to the other most warmly the hand of friendship."[18]

In order to illustrate this charge in more detail, let us focus on the more radical of the two modern skeptical problems mentioned above, the problem of knowledge of the mind-external world, or what Berkeley called the problem of a "veil of perception."[19] This problem can be for-

---

17. Hume's skepticism, for example, often takes the form of generating arguments against commonly believed propositions in such a way that he believes and intends his readers to believe the premises, the validity of the inferences, and the negative conclusions of the arguments. For instance, in *An Enquiry Concerning Human Understanding*, sec. 7 Hume believes and intends his readers to believe such premises as that every idea requires an antecedent impression, the validity of various inferences from these premises, and the negative conclusion drawn that the common belief that a causal relation between two events A and B consists in a connection between events A and B themselves is false (and indeed also the more positive conclusion drawn that it instead essentially includes such facts as the regular conjunction of A-like and B-like events in the past, and the mind's consequent propensity to anticipate that A-like and B-like events will continue to be conjoined in cases as yet unobserved). This is entirely different from the ancient skeptic's equipollence method, in which the ancient skeptic who generates negative arguments does not believe or intend his audience to believe their premises or the validity of the inferences therefrom, but rather finds and intends his audience to find these just equally plausible with contrary propositions and inferences, and does not believe or intend his audience to believe the negative conclusions drawn, but instead embraces and aims to induce in his audience suspension of judgment concerning them.
18. *Jenaer Schriften*, pp. 237–38; also in appendix VI.
19. As the more radical of the two modern skeptical problems mentioned, this is of course the one more *favorable* for the modern skeptic as he faces Hegel's charge. Hegel is still more scathing in his criticisms on the score of dogmatism of the other modern skeptical

mulated roughly as follows: How, given the fact that I have immediate knowledge of, but only of, the contents of my own mind, am I ever to know that these contents represent matters outside my mind as they really are, or indeed even that there is anything outside my own mind at all—since everything of which I have immediate knowledge, and which I might therefore use in order to decide this question, could be just as it is regardless of how, or even whether, matters are outside my mind?[20] This problem looms so large in modern formulations of skepticism—both by skeptics, such as Hume and Schulze, and by antiskeptics, such as Descartes, Berkeley, and Moore—that skepticism at times comes close to being simply equated with it. However, in Hegel's view, to the extent that one's skepticism includes or is exhausted by this problem, it is based on dogmatic assumptions—assumptions which an ancient skeptic, so far from sharing, would subject to compelling skeptical attack by means of the equipollence method.

Hegel identifies three such dogmatic assumptions underpinning "veil of perception" skepticism. Let us consider these in turn, determining in each case how he envisages the ancient skeptic's stance to be different. The first dogmatic assumption made by "veil of perception" skepticism is that we have certain knowledge of at least one kind of fact, namely, facts concerning our own (current) mental contents. Modern "veil of perception" skeptics assume that no skeptical difficulty can arise concerning their beliefs about their own (current) mental contents, and so feel themselves justified in retaining these beliefs as part of the basis for their skeptical attack on beliefs about the mind-external world. That this assumption is quite dogmatic was the point of Hegel's recently quoted remark, in charging modern skepticism with dogmatism, that modern skepticism has sunk so far together with dogmatism that for both "the facts of consciousness possess undeniable certainty."[21] This assumption is dogmatic, in

---

problem (see for example *Jenaer Schriften*, pp. 225–26, 249–50; also in appendix VI).

20. In *The Relation of Skepticism to Philosophy* Hegel states this problem, which, as we noted, he associates with Schulze and Hume, as follows: "According to this newest skepticism the human faculty of knowledge is a thing which has concepts, and because it has nothing more than concepts it cannot go out to the things which are outside it. It cannot find out about them or explore them—for the two things are . . . different in kind. No rational person in possession of the representation of something will imagine himself at the same time to possess this something itself" (*Jenaer Schriften*, pp. 253–54; also in appendix VI).

21. In *The Relation of Skepticism to Philosophy* Schulze is the skeptic with whom Hegel mainly associates this assumption. Accordingly, in his *Aenesidemus* Schulze had written:

Hegel's view, because it is not shared, but instead effectively controverted, by ancient skepticism.[22]

This complaint against "veil of perception" skepticism is, I believe, ultimately justified, but it is not by any means *obviously* so. Two objections which might naturally be raised against it are these: First, someone might object that the ancient skeptic is in fact in exactly the same position as the modern "veil of perception" skeptic with regard to his own current mental states. For does not Sextus Empiricus, in a chapter specially devoted to the question of whether or not the skeptics abolish appearances, write that "when we question whether the underlying object is such as it appears, we grant . . . that it appears, and our doubt does not concern the appearance itself"?[23] Second, someone might object that there really

---

"No skeptic denies that there are in man intuitions, concepts, or ideas . . . This is a matter of fact" (*Between Kant and Hegel*, p. 108). In the *Encyclopaedia* Hegel explicitly includes Schulze's model, Hume, as well: "Hume assumes the truth of the empirical element, feeling and sensation" (par. 39). Accordingly, Hume never, even in his most skeptical moods, questions his own currently experienced impressions. For example, even in one of the most skeptical parts of *A Treatise of Human Nature* (1739) (Harmondsworth: Pelican Books, 1969), he still writes of "those perceptions which are immediately present to our consciousness" as a point beyond which skeptical doubts can be pushed no further (bk. 1, pt. 4, sec. 7).

22. As we shall see, this is a central theme in *The Relation of Skepticism to Philosophy*. Cf. *Encyclopaedia*, par. 39: "The skepticism of Hume . . . should be clearly marked off from Greek skepticism. Hume assumes the truth of the empirical element, feeling and sensation . . . So far was ancient skepticism from making feeling and sensation the canon of truth, that it turned against the deliverances of sense first of all."

23. *Outlines of Pyrrhonism*, bk. 1, chap. 10. Note, moreover, that this exemption of appearances is fundamental to the Pyrrhonist's whole position. This is so in at least two ways: First, acceptance of his own appearances is essential for the Pyrrhonist's retention of a philosophical position at all. For it is only by identifying with the propositions which constitute his philosophical position—for example, that such and such arguments are counterbalanced by such and such others, or that suspension of belief is the way to achieve mental quietude and so happiness—as propositions expressing how matters *appear* to him that he can hope, consistently with his official renunciation of all claims that matters really are a certain way, to retain a philosophical position at all. (Sextus Empiricus attributes this appearance-expressing status to all of his claims, and in particular to his distinctive skeptical formulas, including those which express the counterbalancing of arguments, and to his doctrines concerning the relation between suspension of judgment, mental quietude, and happiness [bk. 1, chaps. 1, 7, 33].) Second, acceptance of his own appearances is essential to the Pyrrhonist's solution to the problem of how, having given up all beliefs about the way matters really are, he is going to sustain action and life. For his solution to this problem is to allow himself to be guided in his daily life by appearances of certain specific sorts: "Adhering, then, to appearances, we live in accordance with the normal rules of life, undogmatically, seeing that we cannot remain wholly inactive. And it would seem that this regulation of life is fourfold . . ." (bk. 1, chap. 11).

is no way of generating a skeptical doubt about one's own current mental states, so that to condemn beliefs in these as dogmatic is unjustified.

Hegel's response to the first of these objections is to *deny* that the ancient and the modern skeptic really take the same position on their own current mental states. Hegel seems, at first sight, to vacillate between two incompatible ways of arguing this case. According to one argument, presented in the *Lectures on the History of Philosophy,* what distinguishes the ancient skeptic's position from the modern skeptic's, and allows him room to object to the latter, is that whereas the modern skeptic envisages his own current mental states as a sort of certain reality, the ancient skeptic does not envisage them as a sort of certain *reality*. According to Hegel's other argument, presented earlier in *The Relation of Skepticism to Philosophy,* it is rather that whereas the modern skeptic envisages his own current mental states as a sort of certain reality, the ancient skeptic does not envisage them as a sort of *certain* reality. Both of these arguments are very interesting and insightful, and they can, with only a modicum of interpretative charity, be reconciled into a single consistent and powerful case for denying that the ancient and modern skeptics' positions regarding their own current mental states are the same. Let us, therefore, consider each argument in turn.

Hegel's first argument is that, although the ancient skeptics did indeed, like their modern counterparts, accord their avowals of their own current mental states a sort of certainty, unlike their modern counterparts they never conceived these avowals to be expressions of *reality* or *truth*. Thus in the *Lectures on the History of Philosophy* Hegel states that "to assert [what is in our immediate consciousness] to be the truth did not occur to [the older skeptics]," for whom "certainty alone is in question, and not truth"; their appearances "did not have the significance of a truth for them, but only of a certainty."[24] In *The Relation of Skepticism to Philosophy* Hegel characterizes this outlook as one of "mere subjectivity," and notes that it entails that the skeptics' avowals of their own mental states were neither genuine assertions nor expressive of beliefs: "They are merely a formal illusion of an assertion"; the ancient skeptic "means his expressions to be understood as absolutely no objective thought or judgment."[25] For, of course, to assert or believe that p is necessarily to assert or believe p to be *reality, truth*. This interpretation of ancient skep-

---

24. *Lectures on the History of Philosophy* 2:331, 332, 343.
25. *Jenaer Schriften,* pp. 248–49; also in appendix VI.

ticism has great merit. Besides generally conforming well with Sextus Empiricus's texts, it in particular explains how he can, without falling into crass inconsistency, both liberally avow his own appearances and completely renounce assertions of reality or truth, and beliefs. And it also explains how he can consistently condemn as dogmatic and open to skeptical attack the Cyrenaic position that our mental affections and nothing beyond these furnish us with a criterion of truth, despite the superficial similarity of this position to his own privileging of his own appearances.[26] This Hegelian interpretation of ancient skepticism has recently been endorsed, through repetition, by a leading authority on ancient skepticism, Burnyeat.[27] On this first argument, then, the similarity between the modern skeptic's and the ancient skeptic's stances toward their own current mental states is only superficial, leaving room for the ancient skeptic to attack the modern skeptic's stance, because, whereas the modern skeptic conceives these states as real, so that his avowals of them have the status of assertions and expressions of beliefs, this is not true of the ancient skeptic.[28]

26. Sextus Empiricus, *Against the Logicians*, bk. 1, secs. 190–200.
27. M.F. Burnyeat, "Can the Skeptic Live his Skepticism?" in *The Skeptical Tradition*, ed. Burnyeat (Berkeley: University of California Press, 1983), pp. 121, 142–43: "When the skeptic doubts that anything is true . . . he has exclusively in view claims as to real existence. Statements which merely record how things appear are not in question—they are not called true or false—only statements which say that things are thus and so in reality . . . If the modern reader finds this an arbitrary terminological narrowing, on the grounds that if I say how things appear to me my statement ought to count as true if, and only if, things really do appear as I say they do . . . the answer is that this objection, though natural, is anachronistic. The idea that truth can be attained without going outside subjective experience was not always the philosophical commonplace it has come to be. It was Descartes who made it so, who (in the Second Meditation) laid the basis for our broader use of the predicates 'true' and 'false' whereby they can apply to statements of appearance without reference to real existence . . . If *epochē* is suspending belief about real existence as contrasted with appearance, that will amount to suspending all belief, since belief is the acceptance of something as true. There can be no question of belief about appearance, as opposed to real existence, if statements recording how things appear cannot be described as true or false, only statements making claims as to how they really are." Cf. Burnyeat, "Idealism and Greek Philosophy: What Descartes Saw and Berkeley Missed," in *Idealism Past and Present*, Royal Institute of Philosophy Lectures 13 (1982), pp. 26–27. As far as I know, Burnyeat is not aware that he is repeating Hegel's interpretation.
28. Hegel's insight that the ancient skeptics did not conceive their own mental contents as parts of reality was, I suspect, facilitated by his sympathetic acquaintance with the relevantly similar Fichtean idea that a self's mental act of self-positing is metaphysically prior to reality or existence: "When all existence of or for the subject is taken away, it has nothing left but an act" (*Science of Knowledge*, p. 33). (Hegel defends this Fichtean conception of the mental, against its denial by Krug, in the 1802 essay *How the Common Human*

According to Hegel's second, and seemingly incompatible, argument, formulated in *The Relation of Skepticism to Philosophy,* what distinguishes the ancient skeptic's attitude toward his own current mental states from the modern skeptic's, and gives him reason to object to the latter, is that, whereas the modern skeptic assumes his own current mental states to be a sphere of certain reality, the ancient skeptic, while likewise conceiving his own current mental states to be real in nature, does not regard them as *certain,* but rather as vulnerable to skeptical attack by means of the equipollence method. Thus in *The Relation of Skepticism to Philosophy* Hegel says of ancient skepticism that "through its turning against knowledge in general it finds itself, because it here opposes one thinking to another and combats the 'is' of philosophical thinking, driven likewise to overcome the 'is' of its own thinking."[29]

There appear at first sight to be two problems with this second argument. First, it seems to conflict with the former argument, in that it implies that the ancient skeptics initially conceived of their mental states as real in nature but regarded their avowals of them as uncertain, whereas the former argument implied that they did *not* initially conceive of their mental states as real in nature and regarded their avowals of them as *certain* (this is the seeming incompatibility mentioned earlier). Second, as I have noted, there is good textual evidence that Sextus Empiricus did not consider his appearances to be parts of reality, and moreover quite explicit evidence that he exempted them from skeptical attack, so that this second argument also seems to involve a brute misinterpretation of Sextus Empiricus's texts.

Despite these prima facie problems for Hegel's second argument, it seems to me that, far from being just an embarrassing slip, it represents one of his philosophically and exegetically deepest insights into skepticism. The prima facie conflicts with his other interpretative argument and with Sextus Empiricus's texts disappear when we realize two things:

Understanding Takes Philosophy, in *Jenaer Schriften,* pp. 197, 200.) Thus it is striking that in his discussions of skepticism and cognition of one's own mental states Hegel often describes these states in terms reminiscent of Fichte, for example as "the activity of thought [Denktätigkeit]," "expressed activity [ausgesprochene Tätigkeit]" (*The Relation of Skepticism to Philosophy,* in *Jenaer Schriften,* p. 248; also in appendix VI), or the subject's "deed [Tat]" (*Phenomenology,* par. 78). Fichte's view will have predisposed Hegel to realize that the ancient skeptics could have coherently conceived their own mental contents as mental acts prior to reality rather than as parts of reality.

29. *Jenaer Schriften,* p. 248; also in appendix VI.

(i) This second argument is primarily about what the logic of the Pyrrhonist's position *would* require him to say concerning his own appearances *if* he conceived them as real in nature, rather than about what he *in fact* says concerning his own appearances. And (ii) insofar as it *is* about what the Pyrrhonist *in fact* says concerning his own appearances, it is compatible with Hegel's first argument and with the seemingly contrary evidence in the Pyrrhonian texts *if these texts themselves contain inconsistent strands*. Let us pursue each of these points in turn.

That Hegel's primary concern is to make a normative point about what a consistent ancient skeptic *would* say concerning his own mental states *if* he conceived them as real in nature, rather than a more narrowly interpretative point about what the ancient skeptic did in fact say, can be seen from some remarks in *The Relation of Skepticism to Philosophy* where he criticizes modern skepticism for assuming that we have certain knowledge of our own mental contents conceived as real in nature:

> We nowhere see this skepticism being consistent enough to show that no reasonable man would imagine himself to be in *possession of a representation* of something either. Since of course the representation is a something as well, a reasonable man can imagine himself to possess only the representation of the representation, not the representation itself, and again not the representation of the representation either, since this representation to the second power is a something too, but only the representation of the representation of the representation, and so on ad infinitum. Or since the situation is here so represented that there are two different pockets, of which one is the something which contains representations, and the other the something which contains things, one cannot see why the former should remain the full one and the latter the eternally empty one. The reason why the former *is* full, and why we only imagine the latter to be full, could only be that the former is the shirt of the subject, the latter his jacket, that the representation-pocket lies closer to him, but the thing-pocket further away from him. But in this way the proof would be conducted by means of a presupposition of what should be proved. For the question precisely concerns the advantage in reality between the subjective and the objective.[30]

So construed, the main burden of Hegel's second argument is that if the ancient skeptic were to conceive his own appearances as real in nature, then his use of the equipollence method in combating claims about reality generally would "drive," or require, him to apply it against his

---

30. Ibid., p. 254; also in appendix VI.

claims about his own appearances specifically. This point seems very plausible. The equipollence method in a very real sense defines the character of ancient skepticism—in Sextus Empiricus's own words, it is "the main basic principle of the skeptic system." There is hence a clear sense in which, if the ancient skeptic could effectively use the equipollence method to attack a claim, then the logic of his position would require him to do so. The fact, therefore, if it is a fact, that the method lends itself no less to attacks on claims about one's own appearances (conceived as real in nature) than to claims about any other subject matter affords a clear sense in which the logic of his position would require an ancient skeptic to combat claims about his own appearances (so conceived) by means of the method. Hegel mentions an illuminating analogy in this connection: it is because the equipollence method proves applicable to the skeptic's own formulas ("No more one thing than another," "I determine nothing," etc.) when these are advanced as claims about how matters really are, that the skeptic finds himself compelled to attack them by means of the method, and to accept them only as expressions of how matters appear to him.[31] The rhetorical question implied by Hegel's second argument is why, given that the equipollence method would be equally applicable against a skeptic's avowals of his own appearances (conceived as real in nature), the skeptic would not be equally compelled to attack these too?

The crucial question, then, is whether the equipollence method *is* applicable against a person's avowals of his own current mental states (conceived as real in nature). We might usefully subdivide this into two further questions: (i) Are there any effective *obstacles* preventing its application in this case? (ii) If not, then how might it actually be applied?

Hegel does not explicitly address the first of these questions, but his position of course implies a negative answer to it. Is this implication justified? Sextus Empiricus himself suggests two reasons for thinking that no skeptical attack can be mounted against a person's avowals of his own appearances. However, these reasons do not seem at all compelling upon examination. And so, to this extent at least, Hegel's implication seems correct. Sextus Empiricus's first point is that conscientious statements about one's own appearances are agreed to by everybody and are for this

---

31. Ibid., p. 249, cf. 231; also in appendix VI. The most relevant passage in Sextus Empiricus is *Outlines of Pyrrhonism*, bk. 1, chap. 7.

reason invulnerable to skeptical attack.[32] There are two problems with this argument. First, its presupposition of the skeptic's deference to views generally shared is problematic. To the extent that such deference is just a brute commitment here, it seems to be little more than a random and tenuous accretion to Sextus Empiricus's position from external sources, not part of the essence of his position like the equipollence method. Thus, its occurrence here, and in a few other places in his texts, appears to be merely an uncritical inheritance from Aenesidemus, who had espoused a principle of the truth of views held in common by all men as a Heraclitean component of his skepticism.[33] And Sextus Empiricus in fact argues in other contexts *against* deferring to views generally shared.[34] Nor does general agreement on an issue prevent application of the equipollence method to it by depriving the skeptic of the counterarguments which he requires in order to achieve equipollence. For, as Sextus Empiricus's own practice richly shows, the skeptic can always himself construct *new* arguments against propositions never in fact argued against before.[35] Second, at least if appearances are being considered qua real in nature, it is by no means clear that everybody known to Sextus Empiricus *had* agreed that people had the appearances they claimed to have. For example, Gorgias had argued that *nothing* existed—an argument which Sextus Empiricus does not scruple to call upon in counterargument elsewhere.[36] And, more interestingly, Sextus Empiricus notes in *Against the Logicians* that "some of the physicists, like Democritus, have abolished all appearances."[37]

---

32. *Outlines of Pyrrhonism*, bk. 1, chap. 29: "We declare that the view about the same thing having opposite appearances is not a dogma of the skeptics but a fact which is experienced not by the skeptics alone but by the rest of philosophers and by all mankind; for certainly no one would venture to say that honey does not taste sweet to people in sound health or that it does not taste bitter to those suffering from jaundice."
33. See J.M. Rist, "The Heracliteanism of Aenesidemus," *Phoenix* 24 (1970).
34. *Outlines of Pyrrhonism*, bk. 2, chap. 5, secs. 43–45.
35. Cf. ibid., bk. 1, chap. 13, where Sextus Empiricus warns against the acceptance of an argument which presently appears sound, on the ground that someone might later furnish an equally plausible counterargument.
36. Ibid., bk. 2, chap. 6, sec. 57.
37. *Against the Logicians*, bk. 1, sec. 369. Democritus had famously argued that all that existed were atoms and the void. (I am here construing Sextus Empiricus's remark about Democritus in the light of the attack on the existence of sense-impressions which follows immediately afterwards in the text. Absent this, one might argue that he was attributing to Democritus a less radical position than I imply.)

A second reason suggested by Sextus Empiricus for thinking that a skeptic's claims about his own current appearances are invulnerable to skeptical attack by him is that a person's current possession of appearances *necessitates* his acknowledgement of them, so that he *cannot* question them: the skeptic does not refrain from all avowal, "for the skeptic assents to the feelings necessitated in sense-impression, and he would not, for example, say when feeling hot or cold, 'I think that I do not feel hot or cold' "; the appearance or sense-impression, "since [it] lies in feeling and involuntary affection . . . is not open to question."[38] This reason for thinking the skeptic incapable of raising a skeptical doubt about his own current appearances does not seem compelling either. First, the principle that one's current possession of appearances necessitates one's acknowledgement of them looks like just the sort of dogmatic principle that the skeptic is most adept at calling into question through counterargument. Second, the inference from this principle as a premise to the intermediate conclusion that the skeptic must acknowledge that he currently possesses appearances would require the further premise that *he currently possesses appearances*. But, of course, in relation to a skeptic who proposes to call into question his own current appearances such a premise is flagrantly question-begging.[39] Third, the inference from the intermediate conclusion that the skeptic must acknowledge possession of his own current appearances to the further conclusion that he cannot skeptically question them is dubious. People quite often find themselves in a condition which would

---

38. *Outlines of Pyrrhonism*, bk. 1, chaps. 7, 11 (Bury's translation slightly amended). The key doctrine here that current possession of appearances necessitates acknowledgement of them is more familiar as a part of the Cartesian conception of the mind's self-transparency: the principle that if one is in some mental state S having character C then one necessarily believes and knows this. (This may conveniently be called, following B.A.O. Williams, the principle of *evidence*.) The other part of the Cartesian conception of the mind's self-transparency is the principle that if one believes oneself to be in a mental state S having character C then necessarily one is in such a state and one's belief constitutes knowledge. (This may conveniently be called, again following Williams, the principle of *incorrigibility*.)

39. Problems similar to the above would face any attempt to counter a skeptic inclined to skepticism about his own current mental states by means of the Cartesian principle of *incorrigibility*—along the lines of inviting him to infer, "Since I at least *believe* that I am currently in mental states X, Y, and Z, and since the principle of incorrigibility is true, I must really currently *be* in mental states X, Y, and Z." First, the principle of incorrigibility assumed here is again just the sort of dogmatic principle that the skeptic is most adept at undermining through counterargument. Second, the other essential premise, "I believe that I am currently in mental states X, Y, and Z," is again flagrantly question-begging in relation to such a skeptic. For *belief* is itself a mental state, and so precisely the sort of thing whose current existence in himself he is proposing to call into question.

naturally be described as one of both believing that p and suspending belief on the question whether or not p. Consider, for example, the scientist or philosopher who simultaneously believes in an unreflective way that the car parked outside his office is really yellow (that it does not merely seem so because of today's unusually bright sunlight, for example) and in a more reflective way, due to scientific or philosophical considerations about secondary qualities, suspends belief on the question whether objects such as cars really possess secondary qualities such as yellowness. It is not at all clear that either the attribution or the occupation of such a psychological condition must involve absurdity; for example, it may be that there are two slightly different senses of "believe" or of "really" involved on the two apparently conflicting sides. Now could not a skeptic, similarly, and likewise without absurdity, both believe in an unreflective way that he possessed such and such current appearances and, in his role as skeptic, in a more reflective way suspend belief on that question? Fourth, and more generally, it is indicative of the implausibility of the argument which we are considering for thinking a skeptical questioning of one's own current appearances impossible that figures such as Democritus, and our own modern eliminative materialists, have seriously *denied* that there are appearances in reality—generally, and therefore in their own current cases in particular. For if such serious *denials* are possible, it is surely hard to believe that serious doubt is not.

If there are indeed no effective obstacles preventing an extension of the equipollence method to attack claims about one's own current mental contents (conceived as real in nature), how could the method actually be applied in this case? Hegel unfortunately says little about this in *The Relation of Skepticism to Philosophy*, beyond implying that it can. However, the grounds for his optimism are not too difficult to see. Hegel argues in the essay that Plato's *Parmenides* does away with all "facts of consciousness."[40] This reveals that Hegel is thinking of his *own philosophy's* inclusion of a discrediting as false of all our claims about our own mental contents on its way to the establishment of its own true standpoint. For at this date he conceives Plato's *Parmenides* as virtually indistinguishable from the discrediting enterprise of his own early Logic, and the monistic Platonic standpoint to which the *Parmenides* seems to lead as virtually indistinguishable from the true Hegelian standpoint to which the Logic leads. This inclusion of a discrediting as false of all our individual self-

---

40. *Jenaer Schriften*, pp. 227–28; also in appendix VI.

attributions of mental contents is especially clear in the early Logic's successor discipline, the *Phenomenology*. For, as we can see from its Preface and Introduction, the *Phenomenology* undertakes to discredit the very perspective of the individual consciousness as thoroughly false, to establish that "the standpoint of consciousness . . . is for Science the antithesis to its own standpoint" (par. 26), by demonstrating that the cognitive structure essential to any individual consciousness—a consciousness of self, object, and representation as such—turns out to be in all its possible forms implicitly self-contradictory (pars. 82–89). Such a result implies that all claims which essentially express the perspective of the individual consciousness will be implicitly false and self-contradictory as well, including in particular all individual self-attributions of mental contents (of "cognition," as the Introduction has it).[41] The problem here will lie most obviously in their attribution to *myself*. However, if the reconstruction of Hegel's ideas about the self-contradictions involved which was offered in chapter 2 was correct, then it will extend deeper as well. In particular, the very concept of a *mental content* ("cognition") invoked in individual self-attributions of mental contents will also turn out to be implicitly self-contradictory, and so too will the very concept of *reality* in terms of which the mental contents in question are therein conceived (along with other items).[42] With the attainment of the true standpoint of Hegelian philosophy, the perspective of the individual consciousness is abandoned—"the standpoint of consciousness . . . is for Science the antithesis to its own standpoint"—and therewith all of our individual self-attributions of mental contents as well.[43]

41. Note that—as Graeser points out in *Einleitung zur Phänomenologie des Geistes*, pp. 104–5—cognitive words like "cognition" are sometimes used by the Hegel of the *Phenomenology* to cover mental contents more *generally* (cf. *Encyclopaedia*, par. 3). (Descartes had earlier effected a similar broadening of reference for the word *cogitatio*.)

42. These points are quite important because they rule out the possibility of salvaging "no-ownership" or "alternative-ownership" substitutes for our individual self-ascriptions of mental contents.

43. Note that it would be consistent with this position that *close analogues* of individual consciousness and individual self-attributions of mental contents should reappear within Hegel's philosophical standpoint. Such is indeed the sort of thing that *typically* occurs when non-Hegelian claims are discredited on the way to Hegel's philosophical standpoint—in which connection recall his ubiquitous concept of *Aufhebung*, in the sense of elimination, but also preservation, namely, with a modified meaning. A close analogue of consciousness certainly survives at the *supra*-individual level of the all-embracing Absolute Spirit (as we shall see in chapter 4). Hegel may well already have both of these thoughts in mind when he writes in an 1802 essay that philosophy performs "the sublation [Aufhebung] of con-

The potential for some such argument seems to be Hegel's primary source of optimism about skepticism's prospects in this area. However, he probably has a second source of such optimism as well. For on the account of his views concerning the relation between mind and body which I sketched in the text and notes of chapter 2, he argues for a behaviorist form of physicalism which, rather than analyzing and vindicating our preexisting mentalistic concepts, implies their inadequacy to reality and revises them, and hence for what could reasonably be described as a form of *eliminative materialism*. In this way too, then, he is committed to discrediting all of our individual self-attributions of mental contents as false.[44]

An ancient Pyrrhonist or his twentieth century follower would be likely to find some form of eliminative materialism especially attractive for the task of counterbalancing convictions in one's own current mental contents (conceived as real in nature). For, as was mentioned earlier, Sextus Empiricus at one point in *Against the Logicians* adduces the counterargument that through their materialism "the physicists, like Democritus, have abolished all appearances." And there are nowadays several quite plausibly argued cases for one or another version of eliminative materialism on the philosophical market (by authors such as Feyerabend and the Churchlands).

Through arguing in one of Hegel's two general ways, and perhaps especially in his second (eliminative materialist) way, against the truth of individual self-attributions of mental states altogether, and a fortiori against the truth of any self-attributions of current mental states by himself, the equipollence skeptic might very well hope to counterbalance whatever reasons he has for thinking that he is currently in certain mental states, and thereby to arrive at his habitual suspension of judgment on this issue.[45]

So much for Hegel's primary claim, the normative claim that *if* the

---

sciousness and its preservation in one and the very same act" (*Jenaer Schriften*, p. 202).

44. As in the case of the former line of argument, it would be consistent with this line of argument that *close analogues* of individual self-attributions of mental contents should be recognized as valid by Hegel's philosophical standpoint. It is indeed pretty evident that this is part of his intention from our discussion of his philosophy of mind in chapter 2.

45. Note that both of the strategies of counterargument against one's self-attributions of current mental states in question here would work by arguing against the truth of individual self-attributions of mental states *altogether*. This seems the most plausible approach, and perhaps the only really plausible approach, for a skeptic to adopt in this case.

ancient skeptic conceived his appearances as real in nature then the logic of his position *would* require him to extend the equipollence method to attack his claims about his own appearances as much as any other claims. As we saw, though, Hegel also implies something further as well—namely, that the ancient skeptics actually *did* conceive their appearances as real in nature and actually *did* discredit their claims about them (so conceived) by means of the equipollence method. Even this further claim can be squared with Hegel's seemingly incompatible first argument and with the seemingly contrary evidence in the ancient texts when we recognize that the ancient texts may themselves contain inconsistent strands.[46] Thus, (i) although, as has been indicated, Sextus Empiricus *standardly* does not conceive his appearances as real in nature, there are nevertheless points at which he seems to do so. In this connection, note, to begin with, that it would be incorrect to suggest, as Burnyeat does, that *no one* at this period (or even until the time of Descartes) thought of a subject's appearances as real in nature or of accurate reports of them as true.[47] For the Stoics considered sense-impressions to be physical and so real, and the Cyrenaics considered accurate reports of their own affections to be true. And both of these positions were, moreover, very well known to Sextus Empiricus. In addition, Sextus Empiricus says at one point that the name "appearance" is given by the skeptics "to what is virtually the sense-impression [*tēn phantasian*]," borrowing this term from the Stoic tradition which—as was just mentioned—considered the items in question to be real in nature and indeed physical.[48] Also, the very fact that Sextus Empiricus even raises the question of whether or not the skeptics abolish appearances, and offers the two reasons discussed earlier for not doing so, seems to suggest that he in some measure conceives them as real in nature. Furthermore, (ii) although (as we have noted) Sextus Empiricus standardly declines to attack appearances, in *Against the Logicians* he does generate several counterarguments with a view to equipollence against the positions of such philosophers as the Stoics and the Cyrenaics who conceived their own sense-impressions or affections as real in nature

---

46. Note that the inconsistency in question here need not be, and in fact is not, of a *deep* sort that would seriously undermine the ancient skeptic's philosophical position.
47. For Burnyeat's suggestion to this effect see the passage from "Can the Skeptic Live his Skepticism?" quoted in footnote 27 above.
48. *Outlines of Pyrrhonism*, bk. 1, chap. 11.

and a source of truth.⁴⁹ Thus, reminiscently of Hegel's first line of counterargument, he generates a counterargument that we have no genuine concept of man (or the self), implying that all of our self-attributions of such mental conditions are without genuine meaning.⁵⁰ And he implies that the problem here lies not only in the concept of man (or the self) appealed to in any such self-attribution, but also in the concept of the mental conditions themselves, since these are *essentially* conceptualized as properties of man (or the self).⁵¹ Again, as has been mentioned, reminiscently of Hegel's second line of counterargument, he adduces the counterargument that through their materialism "the physicists, like Democritus, have abolished all appearances."⁵² And finally, he generates further counterarguments aimed at the conclusion that there are, in particular, no sense-impressions.⁵³ Now is it not plausible to see this whole equipollence attack as equally undermining his own occasional, nonstandard conceptions of his own appearances as real in nature (albeit unintentionally)?⁵⁴ Moreover, if we look beyond the texts of Sextus Empiricus himself, we find that Galen reports on the existence of a group of radical Pyrrhonists who, unlike Sextus Empiricus himself, quite explicitly sought to generate suspension of judgment on the subject of their own appearances.⁵⁵ And in another place Galen implies, in a similar vein, that the Pyrrhonists went as far as to call into question whether we think.⁵⁶

---

49. These positions are set up as targets at *Against the Logicians,* bk. 1, secs. 190–260.
50. Ibid., bk. 1, secs. 263–83.
51. Ibid., bk. 1, sec. 263: "I suppose that when we have cast doubt on [man] . . . there will no longer be any need to proceed to further discussion of the other criteria [i.e., reason, the senses, and sense-impressions]; for these are either parts or actions or affections of man." So, as in Hegel's similar first counterargument, there will be no room for a retreat to a "no-ownership" or "alternative-ownership" substitute for self-ascriptions of mental conditions if this counterargument is persuasive.
52. Ibid., bk. 1, sec. 369.
53. Ibid., bk. 1, secs. 370–82.
54. These materials in *Against the Logicians* have, it seems to me, a far better claim to being an equipollence attack on "facts of consciousness" than the material from Sextus Empiricus which Hegel himself cites as such, namely, the ten tropes of Aenesidemus (*Jenaer Schriften,* p. 240).
55. C.G. Kühn, *Galeni Opera Omnia* (Leipzig: Knobloch, 1821–33), 8:711: "Of these people, then, some say that they do not even know their own affections [*pathē*] surely, whom they reasonably call rustic Pyrrhonists." Cf. 14:628.
56. K. Deichgräber, *Die Griechische Empirikerschule* (Berlin: Weidmannsche Buchhandlung, 1930), p. 133: "Let them then accept this as agreed upon by us as well—for I wish

This, then, is a defense of Hegel's charge that modern "veil of perception" skepticism, unlike ancient skepticism, is dogmatic on the subject of one's own current mental states against the counterobjection that the modern and the ancient skeptic take the same view of this subject. In the course of developing this defense we have also generated at least the beginnings of a defense of Hegel's charge against the second counterobjection which was mentioned earlier, namely, that there really is no way of raising a skeptical doubt about one's own current mental states. For, as we have seen, the obstacles which at first sight seem to stand in the way of doing so prove on closer inspection to be ineffective, and the skeptic might very well produce a skeptical doubt here by, for example, drawing on arguments for a form of eliminative materialism in order to establish equal weight on both sides of the question of whether or not our mentalistic self-descriptions have any application to reality at all.

A second dogmatic assumption which Hegel detects in modern "veil of perception" skepticism is the assumption that the mental states which it holds us to have immediate knowledge of are a sort of mental *thing* existing in a sort of inner *space* and known to us through a sort of inner *perception*. It is, I think, true that modern ways of formulating skepticism have been strongly influenced by a (more or less literal) understanding of mental states and our acquaintance with them in these terms (rather than, say, more vaguely but quite naturally, as states of persons who are their conscious bearers). In thus conceiving mental states and our acquaintance with them in terms of this set of concepts originally drawn from discourse about physical things and our sensory perception of them, modern skeptics (and antiskeptics) have been guided above all by Descartes. Thus in Descartes we encounter statements like the following from the *Meditations:* "But what did I perceive clearly concerning [the earth, sky, stars, and everything else that I apprehended by means of the senses]? Certainly that the ideas of such things themselves, or the thoughts, were observed by my mind. But not even now do I deny that these ideas are in me . . . It is clear to me by the light of nature that the ideas in me are like pictures."[57] The same sort of language used to describe the mental

---

to grant them every favor—even that we know neither whether there really is a sun or moon or earth, nor a sea, nor whether we are awake, nor even whether we think [*phronoumen*] or are alive, nor really concerning anything how it is by nature."

57. *Ouevres de Descartes*, ed. C. Adam and P. Tannery (Paris: J. Vrin, 1973), 7:35–42.

and our acquaintance with it was subsequently absorbed by a whole tradition of modern skeptics and antiskeptics, such as Hume and Berkeley. However literally or metaphorically such language has been understood by this tradition, it has exercised a powerful influence on the modern conception of skeptical problems. In relation to the "veil of perception" problem specifically, the conception of mental states as things has firmly secured the modern skeptic's conception of them as parts of reality. Also, the conception of them as things immediately confronting an individual's faculty of perception has entered into the modern skeptic's conception of the crux of the problem, adding seductive force to it by infusing it with the disturbing picture of mental states as mental objects obstructing our line of (visual) perception to other objects which lie beyond them (Berkeley's metaphor of a "veil of perception" is less metaphorical than it might at first sight appear).[58] Hegel argues that, in contrast with this thoroughly dogmatic modern skeptical conception of the mental and our acquaintance with it, ancient skepticism, since it did not conceive mental states as parts of reality, *a fortiori* did not conceive them as things, existing in an inner space, or apprehended by an immediate perception: "What the newest skepticism always brings with it is . . . the concept of a thing, which lies behind and underneath the appearance-things . . . [Ancient skepticism] for its part stops short at the subjectivity of appearance. But this appearance is not a sensuous *thing* for it, behind which dogmatism and philosophy would claim there to be yet other things, namely, the supersensuous ones. Since it refrains altogether from expressing a certainty and reality, it certainly has for itself no thing . . . about which it could have knowledge."[59]

A third and final dogmatic assumption which Hegel detects in modern "veil of perception" skepticism is the assumption that there is a general

---

58. This way of conceiving mental states and our acquaintance with them has decisively contributed to other modern skeptical problems as well, for example Hume's skepticism about the self in the *Treatise*. This skepticism rests on the assumed coherence of the suggestion that the self is nothing more than "a heap or collection of different perceptions" (*A Treatise of Human Nature*, bk. 1, pt. 4, sec. 2), or even that the collection of perceptions is *all* that there is (bk. 3, appendix). The idea here that mental states might exist without there being a self over and above them which had them as its properties, or even without there being a self at all, seems coherent enough so long as one thinks of mental states as *things* or *objects*. But how coherent does it seem if, instead, one reverts to the vague but natural conception of them as states of persons?
59. *The Relation of Skepticism to Philosophy*, in *Jenaer Schriften*, p. 248; also in appendix VI.

and sharp distinction between concepts, on the one hand, and their instances in reality, on the other, of a sort making it conceivable that any concept might exist without having or ever having had instances in reality. For it is assumed by the "veil of perception" skeptic that those many of our mental items which are clearly *essentially* articulated through concepts—such as our thoughts, beliefs, and intentions—could be just as they are without there being or ever having been anything in reality instantiating the concepts which articulate them, or even without there being or ever having been anything in reality at all (beyond the mental items themselves). In *The Relation of Skepticism to Philosophy* Hegel identifies this dogmatic assumption of modern "veil of perception" skepticism in terms such as the following: "According to this newest skepticism the human faculty of cognition is a thing which has concepts, and because it has nothing more than concepts it cannot go out to the things which are outside it. It cannot find out about them or explore them—for the two things are . . . 'different in kind.' "[60]

Now Hegel holds—rightly, I think—that this third assumption is one which the modern skeptic in a way *shares* with the ancient skeptic; the ancient skeptic, too, in a way assumes a general and sharp distinction between concepts and their real instances of a sort making it conceivable that any concept might exist without having or ever having had real instances. This is hinted at in *The Relation of Skepticism to Philosophy*.[61] It is more explicit in the *Phenomenology,* where the shape of consciousness Skepticism (i.e., ancient skepticism) is made to arise out of a shape which is distinguished above all by its establishment of such a sharp distinction between concepts and reality, namely, Stoicism (i.e., ancient Stoicism). In the *Lectures on the History of Philosophy* Hegel particularly associates this assumption with the ancient Academic skeptic Arcesilaus (ancient Academic and Pyrrhonian skepticism being virtually indistinguishable as Hegel interprets them).[62] That Hegel is in general correct to associate this assumption with ancient skepticism can be seen from the key case of Sex-

---

60. Ibid., pp. 253–54; also in appendix VI.
61. The hint lies in Hegel's remark that the assumption of a sharp concept-object distinction is older than its deployment by Schulzean skepticism or Kantianism (*Jenaer Schriften*, p. 251; also in appendix VI).
62. *Lectures on the History of Philosophy* 2:311–28; the most important passages are excerpted in appendix VI. (Concerning Hegel's general assimilation to one another of the Academic and Pyrrhonian positions, and the sound textual basis for this, see my *Hegel and Skepticism*, chap. 1, n.57.)

tus Empiricus, who quite frequently deploys it as a background assumption on the basis of which to advance equipollence arguments. For instance, in *Against the Physicists* he prefaces an inquiry into the question of whether or not gods exist—an inquiry in the course of which in wonted equipollence fashion he sets arguments for and against their existence into balanced opposition to one another—with this comment: "Since not everything which is conceived partakes also in existence, but it is possible for a thing to be conceived and not exist—like a Hyppocentaur and Scylla—after our inquiry about the conception of the gods we shall have to examine also the question of their existence."[63]

But if modern "veil of perception" skepticism and ancient skepticism *share* this assumption, then how can it be pointed to as another example of modern "veil of perception" skepticism being dogmatic in comparison with ancient skepticism? Hegel does not explicitly address this question. However, his likely answer to it can easily be inferred from *The Relation of Skepticism to Philosophy:* There is bound to be a major difference between the ways in which the modern and the ancient skeptic make this assumption. The modern "veil of perception" skeptic simply assumes it to be true, and is thereby guilty of dogmatism. The ancient skeptic, by contrast, is bound to "assume" it only in the very qualified sense in which, as *The Relation of Skepticism to Philosophy* argues, he "assumes" anything else, for example his own formulas and his own appearances: he

---

63. Sextus Empiricus, *Against the Physicists,* trans. R.G. Bury (London: Loeb Classical Library, 1968), bk. 1, sec. 49; cf. *Outlines of Pyrrhonism,* bk. 1, chap. 2, sec. 10. Note that the assumption in this passage that we might always be in possession of a concept which corresponded to nothing in reality is not advanced merely as part of one side of an equipollence argument, without any identification on the part of the skeptic. For it is stated by Sextus Empiricus in propria persona *before* he proceeds to set forth equally balanced arguments on both sides of the issue. It is instead an assumption with which the skeptic himself identifies (presumably in the same manner in which he identifies with his own formulas, "No more one thing than another," "I determine nothing," and so forth). Skeptical arguments which follow the same pattern as this one about the existence of the gods include those in the *Outlines of Pyrrhonism* about the existence of the intellect (bk. 2, chap. 6, sec. 57) and the existence of the Stoic *lekton* (bk. 2, chap. 11, sec. 107). I shall henceforth distinguish skeptical difficulties which follow this pattern from equipollence difficulties more generally as "concept-instantiation" difficulties. As we shall see shortly, together with equipollence difficulties generally, they constitute the aspect of skepticism which has the deepest impact on Hegel's own epistemology. (Closely related to, but distinguishable from, this pattern of ancient skeptical argument is a further pattern in which the existence of a kind of thing is called into question by making a case for the *incoherence* of its concept or definition as one side of the equipollence procedure. See for example the arguments concerning cause, motion, space, and time at *Outlines of Pyrrhonism,* bk. 3.)

152   The Official Project of the *Phenomenology*

will recognize that if positively asserted as truth this assumption would be as susceptible to skeptical attack by means of the equipollence method as any other assertion of truth, will in consequence suspend judgment on the question of its truth, and will identify with it only qua subjective appearance.

This, then, is Hegel's case for saying that modern "veil of perception" skepticism is essentially dogmatic in a way that ancient skepticism was not. To summarize his specific charges: Modern "veil of perception" skepticism dogmatically assumes that we have certain knowledge of at least one kind of fact, namely, facts concerning our own current mental states. Moreover, it dogmatically conceives these mental states as a sort of thing, existing in a sort of inner space, and grasped by a sort of inner perception. Finally, in implying that we might have our present mental states, and hence also the concepts essential for their articulation, without there existing anything in reality corresponding to those concepts, or indeed any mind-external reality at all, it dogmatically assumes a general and sharp distinction between concepts and their real instances.

* * *

It is, therefore, ancient skepticism with its equipollence problems, rather than modern skepticism with *its* characteristic problems, such as the "veil of perception" problem, which in Hegel's view deserves to be taken seriously.

Hegel tends to concentrate on a particular form of the equipollence method, namely, the form in which it is applied to a claim advanced by a dogmatist without supporting argument. In such a case the skeptic finds a contradictory or contrary claim which he likewise advances without supporting argument, and, just for this reason, with equal right. This form of the method appears in the ancient texts as the fourth of the Pyrrhonian tropes of Agrippa.[64] Hegel correctly characterizes this trope in *The Relation of Skepticism to Philosophy*, as follows: it "concerns presuppositions [Voraussetzungen]—[and is] against the dogmatists who in order to avoid being driven into an infinite regress posit something as simply first and unproven, and whom the skeptics immediately imitate by positing the opposite of that presupposition without proof with just the same right."[65]

---

64. See *Outlines of Pyrrhonism*, bk. 1, chap. 15.

65. *Jenaer Schriften*, p. 244; also in appendix VI. It is crucial for a proper understanding of Hegel's epistemology to realize that when he speaks in other contexts of "presuppositions [Voraussetzungen]" or "presupposing [voraussetzen]," as he frequently does, he almost

The main reason for Hegel's concentration on the fourth trope of Agrippa's form of the equipollence problem is that he follows the tropes of Agrippa in thinking that any theory is bound at *some* point to advance a claim without supporting argument, on pain of otherwise falling into the equally bad or worse problems of either infinite regress (the second trope of Agrippa) or vicious circularity (the fifth trope of Agrippa).[66] Hence, in the *Lectures on the History of Philosophy* he praises the tropes of Agrippa for their exhaustion of the possibilities.[67] And in the *Phenomenology,* where, as we shall see, he focuses heavily on the phenomenon of unproven presuppositions, he also notes the second trope's threat of infinite regress confronting the attempt to avoid them by giving proofs: "In ordinary proof . . . the reasons given are themselves in need of further reasons, and so on ad infinitum" (par. 66).

If the dogmatist should make the somewhat natural reply to the fourth trope of Agrippa that some claims, though advanced without supporting arguments, nevertheless have a quality of immediate self-evidence or intuitive compellingness lacking in other, and in particular opposite, claims,

---

always has in mind, not just the everyday sense of *advancing claims without supporting proofs,* but the more specific sense deriving from this fourth trope of Agrippa of doing so *and then being confronted by a contradictory or contrary claim advanced in the same way.* To give an example of the vital importance of realizing this: Hegel often inveighs against the acceptance of "presuppositions" in philosophy (e.g., *Encyclopaedia,* par. 1). Now if, with most of the secondary literature, one understands him to mean in such contexts by "presuppositions" the everyday sense of claims advanced without supporting proofs *simpliciter,* then one will of course immediately infer that the only alternative is for his philosophy to be furnished with a supporting proof of some sort (e.g., a transcendental argument). In this spirit, Taylor, for instance, remarks at one point: "Perhaps out of deference to Hegel's shade I should not use the word 'assumption' [i.e., presupposition, *Voraussetzung*], since for Hegel everything is ultimately demonstrated" ("Hegel's Philosophy of Mind," in *Human Agency and Language,* p. 95). However, when one realizes that Hegel instead means in such contexts by "presuppositions" the more specific phenomenon envisaged in the fourth trope of Agrippa, one can see that there is *another* way in which his philosophy might avoid presuppositions, namely, not by being furnished with a supporting proof, but by being somehow shown *not to face the competition of any contradictory or contrary claim.* As we shall see in detail shortly, this is in fact Hegel's preferred solution to the challenge of avoiding presuppositions in philosophy. It so happens that he also makes this point pretty explicitly in the course of discussing the fourth trope of Agrippa in *The Relation of Skepticism to Philosophy:* the claim made by his own philosophy, "the Rational," is immune to the fourth trope of Agrippa because "the Rational has no opposite"; but the "demand for a ground" is not "of any concern to Reason" (*Jenaer Schriften,* p. 247; also in appendix VI).

66. Hegel correctly records these two further tropes of Agrippa in *The Relation of Skepticism to Philosophy* (*Jenaer Schriften,* p. 244; also in appendix VI).

67. *Lectures on the History of Philosophy* 2:357–65.

which shows them to be true, Hegel will not be impressed by this response. This is already clear from his sharp rejection in the Preface of the *Phenomenology* of the Romantics' appeal to immediate knowledge, intuition, or feeling as a criterion of truth. His most forceful *arguments* against such a response to the fourth trope of Agrippa appear, though, in the *Encyclopaedia*, where he makes two particularly significant points. First, he observes, in effect, that the mere discovery that some of our convictions had a certain introspectible quality which we chose to call "immediate self-evidence," "intuitive compellingness," or whatnot would do nothing to prove that these convictions were actually true of the world: "Since [in such theories] the criterion of truth is found, not in the nature of the content, but in the mere fact of consciousness, every alleged truth has no other basis than subjective certitude and the assertion that we discover a certain fact in our consciousness."[68] Second, he points out that, since these same introspectible qualities are evidently associated in the minds of different people with quite different and indeed inconsistent propositions, if we were to take them to be the criterion of truth, then we would thereby be forced to admit the truth of all sorts of claims made by other people which we find quite unacceptable, and, worse still, we would be forced to admit the truth of contradictions: "A . . . corollary which results from holding immediacy of consciousness to be the criterion of truth is that all superstition or idolatry is allowed to be truth . . . It is because he believes in them . . . that the Hindu finds God in the cow, the monkey, the Brahmin, or the Lama"; "The form of immediacy is altogether abstract. It has no preference for one set of contents more than another, but is equally susceptible to all. It may as well sanction what is idolatrous and immoral as the reverse."[69]

We are now in a better position to understand why in the Introduction and Preface of the *Phenomenology* Hegel dismisses the various epistemological approaches of previous philosophy which he considers there. His reasons for dismissing the Romantics' appeals to immediate knowledge, intuition, or feeling as a criterion of truth have just been explained. We can now also see why he dismisses Descartes's preemptive "skepticism

---

68. *Encyclopaedia*, par. 71.
69. Ibid., pars. 72, 74; cf. Hegel's *Vorrede zu Hinrichs Religionsphilosophie*, in *Sämtliche Werke* 20:20–21. Or is the criterion of truth to be immediate self-evidence or intuitive compellingness for *us* or for *me* only?!

with which an earnest zeal for truth and science fancies it has prepared and equipped itself in their service," and its resolve to "accept only one's own deed [i.e., one's own mental "deed," one's *cogitatio*] as what is true"—that is, Descartes's project of forestalling real skepticism by a method of doubt which arrives at the indubitability of truths concerning one's own current mental states, in preparation for establishing on this supposedly secure foundation the existence of the self, and of God, and thence still other matters questioned by real skeptics. Hegel's fundamental objection to this project is that if one's mental states are conceived as real in nature, and their expressions as truths, and hence as possible bases for proofs of other truths, in the manner of Descartes, then they are quite as vulnerable to skeptical attack as anything else, and that a genuine skepticism like that of the ancient skeptics spares the subject's expressions of his own mental states only insofar as it does *not* conceive these mental states as real in nature or their expressions as truths, and so not as possible bases for proofs of further truths either. Thus, in *The Relation of Skepticism to Philosophy* Hegel had indicated with approval that the ancient skeptics skeptically attacked claims about their own mental states insofar as they conceived these as real in nature and instead accepted such claims only in a purely "subjective" way (as we have noted).[70] And he had then immediately gone on to imply that the Cartesian was therefore guilty of misunderstanding the position and underestimating the skeptical resources of the ancient skeptics when he responded to the ancient skeptics "that if they doubt everything yet this 'I doubt,' 'It seems to me,' and so forth is certain—or in other words, in that the reality and objectivity of the activity of thought is pointed out to them in reply."[71] Similarly, it is mainly because—like the supposed Cartesian bulwark against skepticism—they fall victim to the powerful equipollence method of the ancient skeptics that Hegel rejects the other epistemological approaches which he considers in the Introduction and Preface of the *Phenomenology*. Thus, against the Lambert-Kant epistemological project he develops two lines of criticism: First, he tries to show, in the manner of an internal critique, that their conception of knowledge as an instrument or medium implies that knowledge of truth is in fact impossible—first arguing, against Lambert but in sympathy with Kant, that if knowledge had this character

---

70. *Jenaer Schriften*, p. 248; also in appendix VI.
71. Ibid., p. 248; also in appendix VI.

then it would be unable to know things as they are in themselves (par. 73),[72] and then, against Kant as well, that if it were unable to know things as they are in themselves then it could not be true (pars. 74–75).[73] But

72. Lambert in fact himself suggests such a skepticism at one point (*Neues Organon* 2:233). But his project of "Phenomenology" is conceived as a means of enabling us to abstract from the appearances which arise in us the contribution due to the operation of our cognitive faculties and their relation to objects so as to yield knowledge of the objects as they are in themselves (vol. 1, *Vorrede;* 2:270–72). In paragraph 73 of the Introduction Hegel argues, to the contrary, that the model of knowledge as an instrument or medium, if meant seriously at all, implies that our cognition always presents objects *as they are affected/conveyed by our cognition,* not as they are in themselves (i.e., independently of our cognition). And he criticizes Lambert's attempt to resist this conclusion through the project of "Phenomenology" on the ground that, accordingly, on this model of knowledge the attempt to subtract from our cognition any contribution made by our cognition—as contrasted with some *specific* contribution made by it, "not the refraction of the ray, but the ray itself"—would simply leave us without any cognition at all: "The thing... becomes for us exactly what it was before this, consequently superfluous, effort"; "All that would be indicated would be a pure direction or a blank space." This leaves us with Kant's conclusion that things as they are in themselves are unknowable by us. (Of course, this is not the reasoning by which Kant himself explicitly arrived at that conclusion; his explicit arguments were quite different. However, it is not clear that this harms Hegel's case at all. For one thing, Hegel is at this point concerned mainly with Lambert. For another, Kant's conclusion may be overdetermined.)

73. Kant maintains that *things as they are in themselves* are unknowable but that we can nevertheless quite well know *truths,* namely, truths concerning things as they appear to us. At paragraphs 74–75 in the Introduction Hegel characterizes this position as the view "that cognition which... is excluded from the Absolute [i.e., from things as they are in themselves]... is nevertheless true," "that there is a type of cognition which, though it does not cognize the Absolute, is still capable of grasping other kinds of truth." Hegel's central objection to this position is that cognition, "since it is excluded from the Absolute [i.e., from things as they are in themselves], is surely outside of the truth as well" (par. 74), or in other words, that truth is *necessarily* of things as they are in themselves, not of things qua mind-dependent, so that if we cannot know things as they are in themselves, then we cannot know truth either. The basis of this objection is the following quite plausible line of thought. It is part of the everyday concept of truth that truth consists in a correspondence between representations and mind-independent facts: "Whatever is related to knowledge is also distinguished from it, and posited as existing outside this relationship as well," "in what consciousness affirms from within itself as being-in-itself... we have the standard which consciousness itself sets up by which to measure what it knows" (pars. 82, 84); "We usually give the name of truth to the agreement of a self-standing object [eines Gegenstandes] with our representation," this is the ordinary "meaning of truth" (*Encyclopaedia,* par. 24, addition 2). Kant, furthermore, evidently means to adhere to this everyday concept of truth; for he advertises no departure from it, and in the *Critique of Pure Reason* he quite similarly defines truth as "the agreement of knowledge with its object" (A58/B82). Consequently, Kant must concede, not only that we are unable to know things as they are in themselves, but also, ipso facto, that we are unable to know truth. Interestingly enough, there are a few nonstandard passages in Kant which seem to concede as much. For example, in one note he writes that "there are [in the sequence of the sensible] not true things and true

second, and more fundamentally, Hegel objects that the Lambert-Kant epistemology is unacceptable because it rests on "presuppositions," by which he means unproven assumptions vulnerable to the equipollence method in the form of the fourth trope of Agrippa. In particular, Hegel identifies as such presuppositions the very conception of knowledge as an instrument or medium, and in addition two further conceptions which he takes to be implicit in this model of knowledge, namely, that the knowing self and its knowledge are distinct, and especially that knowledge and the object to which it is applied or which it mediates are distinct. Thus he complains that the Kant-Lambert position "presupposes [*voraussetzen* is the verb] something, and indeed many things, as truth and rests its scruples and inferences thereon . . . It presupposes, namely, ideas about cognition as an instrument and medium; also a distinction between ourselves and this cognition; but above all that the Absolute stands on the one side and that cognition, on the other side, independent and separated from the Absolute, is nevertheless something real" (par. 74).[74] The same problem dooms Schelling's dogmatic assurance that his "Science is a quite different sort of knowledge for which . . . ordinary cognition is of no account whatever." Hegel points out that such an unproven assurance can quite well be mimicked in contradiction by ordinary cognition—"the untrue cognition likewise appeals to the fact that *it is,* and *assures* us that for it Science is of no account"—and that this leaves us with precisely the situation envisaged in the fourth trope of Agrippa: "*One* bare assurance is worth just as much as another" (par. 76). The same problem is also the core of Hegel's reason for rejecting his own and Schelling's earlier technique of "critique" as an adequate epistemology. In such a technique Science would again be left assuming its own truth without proof—or as Hegel puts it, "It would only be appealing again to what merely is" (par. 76). And Hegel implies that this would once again expose it to being

---

causes but only appearances" (*Reflexionen Kants zur Kritik der reinen Vernunft*, p. 415, no. 1436).

74. For this sort of point against Kant, cf. the Heidelberg *Encyclopaedia*, par. 36; in appendix XVI. The charge that Kant's epistemology rested on "presuppositions" had already been raised to prominence before Hegel by Reinhold, whose attempt in his *Elementarphilosophie* to derive Kant's position from a single self-evident "proposition of consciousness" was largely motivated by a desire to rectify this perceived weakness (on which see for example Reinhold's remarks at *Between Kant and Hegel*, pp. 92–93). One may, I think, reasonably have some misgivings about Hegel's attempts to *identify* the fundamental presuppositions of Kant's epistemology; but the crucial point for Hegel is *that* there are such, rather than *what* they are, and on this crucial point he is surely correct.

contradicted in a similar manner,[75] thereby once again leaving it in the untenable position of "*one* bare assurance . . . worth just as much as another."

* * *

Now, as it happens, Hegel believes that *his own Science cannot be proved by deducing it as a conclusion from true premises.* This is a constant feature of his position throughout his career. For example, before the *Phenomenology*, in the *Difference* essay he sharply criticizes the "tendency to give grounds and to establish by grounds [Begründungs- und Ergründungstendenz]" in philosophy,[76] and in *The Relation of Skepticism to Philosophy* he accordingly denies that his own and Schelling's philosophy attempts to ground its principle of identity: "There is . . . no truth in the claim that the new philosophy attempts to ground [ergründen] the possibility of the identity . . . , for it does nothing but express and recognize that presupposed identity."[77] Similarly, after the *Phenomenology*, the *Encyclopaedia* sharply criticizes the traditional manner of undertaking to prove a viewpoint true, wherein "the relation of the starting-point to the end-point to which the advance is made is represented as only affirmative, as an inference from one thing that exists and remains to an other that likewise exists as well,"[78] and the *Encyclopaedia* insists, accordingly, that in Hegel's own Science "the first beginning cannot be mediated by anything."[79] Precisely the same position is implied by the *Phenomenology*'s insistence that it "will . . . be quite different from the 'grounding' [Begründung] of Science" (par. 27).

Why does Hegel hold this position? One reason is that, as was recently mentioned, he believes that the attempt to avoid unproven assumptions is futile, because it can only lead to the equal or greater evils of infinite regress or vicious circularity. Another reason is rooted in more distinctive features of his philosophical standpoint: Hegel believes that truth is only expressible *as a whole*—"the true is the whole" (par. 20), "the true . . .

---

75. The full thought, I take it, is that just as in "critique" Science's truth is assumed and then anticipations of it are identified in other viewpoints as a means to validating Science and measuring the degree of the other viewpoints' inadequacy, so the other viewpoints could assume their truth and then identify anticipations of themselves in Science as a means to validating themselves and measuring the degree of Science's inadequacy.
76. *Jenaer Schriften*, p. 122.
77. Ibid, p. 255; also in appendix VI.
78. *Encyclopaedia*, par. 50; in appendix XVII.
79. Ibid., par. 86.

exists only ... as totality" (*Encyclopaedia,* par. 14).⁸⁰ And accordingly he believes that his own philosophy must and does express, not only *nothing but* truth, but also *all* truth. It follows from this position that any attempt to prove his philosophy by deducing it from true premises must fail, since in order even to hope to qualify as a *proof* of his philosophy such an attempt would obviously have to proceed from premises which were either independent of his philosophy or expressive only of some part of it ("p, therefore p" is not a proof), but, given the position just described, that would inevitably mean proceeding from *untrue* premises.

Now, of course, this appears to leave Hegel's own philosophical Science *itself exposed to the fourth trope of Agrippa's version of the equipollence problem*. Accordingly, one of the main epistemological challenges which Hegel sees himself as facing in the *Phenomenology* is that of defending his own philosophical Science against this form of the equipollence problem. Thus, in the Preface he points out that his Science seems to find itself in just the sort of predicament envisaged by the fourth trope of Agrippa: "The standpoint of consciousness ... is for Science the antithesis of its standpoint ... Conversely, the element of Science is for consciousness a remote beyond in which it no longer possesses itself. Each of these two aspects appears to the other as the inversion of the truth" (par. 26; cf. the criticism of Schelling's position at par. 76). And he goes on to indicate that it is one of the main tasks of the *Phenomenology* to solve this problem (pars. 26–27). Again, he raises the same apparent problem for his Science, though in a slightly different form, at paragraphs 81–84 in the Introduction. He indicates there that it seems as though his Science, if it attempts to evaluate ordinary cognition, must do so by applying a criterion to it, but that ordinary cognition may well reject this criterion (pars. 81–83), and that this leaves his Science with an appearance of "presupposition [Voraussetzung]" (par. 84), or in other words lands his Science back in the unacceptable situation already described at paragraph 76 of giving one bare assurance and finding this confronted by another opposing one. The thought, to unpack it a little, is this: One very natural way for Science to attempt to deal with the equipollence

---

80. This doctrine about truth is not just a dogmatic assertion or an arbitrary redefinition of the concept of truth. Rather, it is something which Hegel considers demonstrated by the fact that all attempts to express something *less* than the whole truth prove to be self-contradictory, as for example each of the partial expressions of the Absolute Idea considered in turn in the Logic proves to be self-contradictory.

problem in the basic form stated in paragraphs 26 and 76, the form of finding its own flatly affirmed view flatly contradicted by ordinary cognition, would be for it to undertake a critical evaluation of ordinary cognition. However, such a response threatens to land Science right back in the same problem again, namely, with respect to whatever criterion or standard it proposes to use in the evaluation. Hegel goes on to sketch his solution to this apparent impasse at paragraphs 84–85.

Equipollence difficulties, then, constitute one part of the challenge from skepticism which Hegel takes seriously, and against which he consequently sees himself as bound to defend his own philosophical system in the *Phenomenology*. There is, though, also a second sort of difficulty associated with ancient skepticism—and in more dogmatic forms with later skepticism as well—which he takes seriously as a threat to his own system. This is the problem of how one can be sure that the descriptive meanings or concepts which one uses have any instances in reality at all. How can one be sure that they are not empty—like the concept of phlogiston, for example? I shall refer to this as the "concept-instantiation" problem. As noted earlier, Hegel has ancient skepticism's version of this problem in mind in the *Stoicism* and *Skepticism* sections of the *Phenomenology*, where he interprets Stoicism's generation of a sharp concept-reality distinction as leading to this problem in ancient skepticism (pars. 197, 202–4), and in the *Lectures on the History of Philosophy* he associates this problem with the Academic skeptic Arcesilaus in particular, although it is also very typical of the ancient skepticism of Sextus Empiricus.[81] Hegel in addition sees this sort of skeptical problem as, in more dogmatic forms, typical of modern skepticism. Thus, as noted earlier, in *The Relation of Skepticism to Philosophy* he identifies a form of this problem as implicit in modern "veil of perception" skepticism. And in the same essay he also interprets Kant's objections against the Ontological Argument for God's existence as a version of this problem (concerning the instantiation of the concept of God), and several of Schulze's arguments as variations on the same theme.[82] Hegel's intention to address this second sort of skeptical problem on behalf of his own philosophical sys-

---

81. The mature Hegel came to see anticipations of this sort of skeptical problem in the Sophists as well. Thus in the *Lectures on the History of Philosophy* he interprets the later parts of Gorgias's treatise *Concerning Nature or Concerning the Non-Existent* as an example, and in the *Lectures on the Philosophy of World History* he alludes to Protagoras's agnosticism about the existence of the gods as an example.

82. *Jenaer Schriften*, esp. pp. 250–52; also in appendix VI.

tem in the *Phenomenology* is not quite as evident as his intention to address equipollence difficulties in general there. However, it is reflected, for example, in such remarks as that the *Phenomenology* is concerned with an examination of whether "the concept corresponds to the object" (par. 84).

Now in *The Relation of Skepticism to Philosophy* and the *Lectures on the History of Philosophy* Hegel argues firmly that the philosophically significant challenge posed by ancient skepticism, and embodied in these problems of equipollence and concept-instantiation, is effective against the "dogmatic cognition of the Understanding," but that "its attacks against the true infinite of the speculative Idea are most feeble and unsatisfactory."[83] In other words, while non-Hegelian viewpoints *are* vulnerable to ancient skepticism's equipollence and concept-instantiation problems, the standpoint of Hegelian Science itself is *not*. We should therefore now turn to consider the question of *how* Hegelian Science is supposed to be invulnerable to these problems, and in particular the *Phenomenology*'s contributions toward showing that it is—or in other words the *Phenomenology*'s ways of performing epistemological tasks (4) and (5).

* * *

Before doing so positively, however, it is worth pausing to indicate a form which the *Phenomenology*'s answer to skepticism will *not* take. Certain authors—especially Taylor in his influential essay "The Opening Arguments of the *Phenomenology*"—have claimed that the epistemological strategy of the *Phenomenology* is one of *transcendental argumentation* in the manner of Kant.[84]

Kantian transcendental arguments, such as those in the *Critique of Pure Reason*'s Transcendental Deduction of the Categories and Analogies of Experience, have the following distinctive character: They aim to establish claims which a skeptic—in particular a Humean skeptic—has called into question, such as that we have a priori concepts enjoying application to objects, or know synthetic a priori principles to be true,[85] and

---

83. *Lectures on the History of Philosophy* 2:367. Cf. *Jenaer Schriften*, pp. 240, 245–46; also in appendix VI.

84. Taylor's essay is in *Hegel: A Collection of Critical Essays*. Taylor's reading has since been followed by others, for example, with qualifications, R.B. Pippin, *Hegel's Idealism* (Cambridge: Cambridge University Press, 1989), and J.C. Flay, *Hegel's Quest for Certainty* (Albany, N.Y.: SUNY Press, 1984).

85. Hume's "no impression, no idea" principle implies that there cannot even *be* concepts which are a priori, still less ones enjoying application to objects; Hume's "fork" implies that we cannot know any synthetic a priori propositions to be true.

to do so in a manner which is compelling not only for the Kantian himself but also for the skeptic. In order to accomplish this they undertake to demonstrate indubitably that such claims being true, of the sphere of experience, is a *condition of the possibility of experience* (this is the force of the epithet *transcendental*). In other words they attempt to demonstrate indubitably the truth of principles of the form "Necessarily if there is experience then C (the contended claim) is true of the sphere of experience." In Kant's arguments, the experience in question here is sometimes objective experience, sometimes subjective experience (arguments of the latter sort having the attraction of being potentially capable of persuading a more radical skeptic). The major work in a transcendental argument always goes into demonstrating a principle of this form. Note, however, that this helps because, and only because, if such a principle is established as indubitably true, then it can be added to another premise which both the Kantian and the (Humean) skeptic find indubitably true, namely, "There is experience," or "I have experience," in order to yield by modus ponendo ponens—a principle of logical inference which both the Kantian and the (Humean) skeptic are again assumed to find indubitably valid—the truth of the contended claim C of the sphere of experience as a conclusion. Hence all transcendental arguments, whether or not they bother to make this explicit (in Kant they rarely do), share the general form: "Necessarily if there is experience then C is true of the sphere of experience. There is experience. Therefore, C is true of the sphere of experience."[86]

Now, given that this is the character of transcendental arguments, we can see immediately from what has already been established in this chapter concerning Hegel's epistemological position two compelling reasons why it must be a mistake to assimilate the *Phenomenology*'s epistemological strategy to one of transcendental argumentation. First, as we have noted, neither Hegel himself nor any skeptic who in his view deserves to be answered by philosophy assumes that the proposition "There is experience," or "I have experience," is true, still less indubitably true—not even if the experience in question is merely subjective experience, that is, concerns only a subject's own mental states, let alone if it is objective experience. On the contrary, for the skepticism which Hegel thinks deserving of a response such supposed "facts of consciousness" fall squarely

---

86. The above explanation of the nature of transcendental arguments is mine rather than Taylor's. However, it does not disagree with the little that Taylor says on the subject in "The Opening Arguments of the *Phenomenology*" (pp. 151–55).

within the domain of the skeptically dubitable, and so they do for Hegel himself too, who indeed, as we saw, thinks them not only dubitable but in fact false. Second, as we just saw, it is essential to the character of a transcendental argument that it prove its conclusion by deducing it from true premises. Yet, as we have noted, Hegel categorically rejects the idea of proving his philosophical standpoint true by deducing it from true premises (especially because if the premises were independent of or less than his philosophical standpoint itself, as they would have to be in order to prove it, then they would inevitably be untrue). (Also significant here is Hegel's general sympathy with skepticism about logic.)[87]

87. It may be worth adding to the above general explanation of why any interpretation like Taylor's of the epistemological approach of the *Phenomenology* as one of transcendental argumentation must be mistaken some critical observations concerning the more detailed readings of the text on which Taylor has based this interpretation.

(i) Taylor implies that the fact that the *Phenomenology* begins with Sense-*certainty* is indicative of a transcendental argument's strategy of proceeding from the *indubitability* of (aspects of) experience: Kantian transcendental arguments rest on the idea that "we can delineate facets of experience that are basic and pervasive enough to be undeniable, and these can be the starting points for our arguments. Kant's first *Critique* thus opened a two-century-long hunting season on empiricism, in the course of which a great many philosophers have joined in. In terms of bent, Hegel is undoubtedly of that company . . . for Hegel starts off in the first chapter of the *Phenomenology* examining 'sensible certainty'" ("The Opening Arguments of the *Phenomenology*," pp. 156–57). This is a mistake, because it implies that in calling the work's first shape of consciousness "Sense-certainty" or "sensible certainty" Hegel means to say that this outlook really *has* certain knowledge of (aspects of) its experience. On the contrary, the "certain knowledge" of Sense-certainty is merely something that it *ascribes* to itself, in Hegel's view, not something that it actually possesses. Thus in the Introduction Hegel tells us that the *Phenomenology* is quite generally a "way of despair" for the ordinary consciousness along which it "loses its truth," that the work shows "the untruth of phenomenal knowledge," that in its course each shape of consciousness "finds that its knowledge does not correspond to its object" (pars. 78, 85). And accordingly, with respect to Sense-certainty in particular, he states as the moral of the *Sense-certainty* section that "immediate certainty does not achieve for itself the true" (par. 111, cf. 91: "Sense-certainty appears to be the *truest* knowledge . . . But, in the event, this very *certainty* turns out to be the most abstract and poorest *truth*"—where, note, the word *truth* is being used in a merely inverted-commas sense, as can be seen from the gloss of it which follows at par. 92 as "[that] which this certainty pronounces to be its truth").

(ii) Taylor implies that according to Hegel Sense-certainty enjoys a true knowledge of sensible particulars ("The Opening Arguments of the *Phenomenology*," pp. 163–68), and quite generally the shapes of consciousness in the *Consciousness* chapter possess some such true knowledge: "The dialectic of Consciousness in the *Phenomenology* will take us through a critique of inadequate conceptions of knowledge *considered as a realized standard*"; "Essential to the dialectical argument is the notion that *the standard . . . is already met*. It is because we know this that we know that any conception of the . . . standard which shows it as unrealizable must be a faulty conception" (*Hegel*, pp. 131–32; emphasis added). This interpretation is once again inconsistent with such passages as those from the Introduction

* * *

What, then, *is* the *Phenomenology*'s antiskeptical strategy? To begin with, note that Hegel had already affirmed in works prior to the *Phenomenology* in explicit response to the skeptical problems of equipollence

and the *Sense-certainty* section just quoted in (i), in which Hegel on the contrary *denies* that shapes of consciousness have true knowledge. The aim of the *Phenomenology* is to show that people do *not* yet have any true knowledge, and that is quite incompatible with the strategy imputed to the work by Taylor of acknowledging that they do have some with a view to showing that conceptions which they have of the nature of knowledge which would make this impossible must therefore be mistaken.

(iii) Taylor's error here stems largely from a failure to realize that when Hegel in the Introduction and in particular sections of the *Phenomenology* speaks of "knowledge [Wissen, Erkenntnis]" in connection with shapes of consciousness, he is not using this word as a success-word, implying truth (as it is often, and indeed typically, used in both English and German). Rather he means by it "belief" or "belief which the believing consciousness *takes to be* true knowledge." Thus he can without the least sense of oxymoron speak of "knowing which is not true" and of "untrue knowing" (par. 76), and say that in the course of the *Phenomenology* consciousness "finds that its knowledge does not correspond to its object" (par. 85), that the work shows "the untruth . . . of phenomenal knowledge" (par. 78), and that "one can of course know something falsely" (par. 39).

(iv) Taylor's reading has obviously been strongly encouraged by Hegel's description of the *Phenomenology*'s contents as "the experience of consciousness" (see esp. "The Opening Arguments of the *Phenomenology*," pp. 156–60). Is this description not indeed indicative of Hegel's concession of and interest in a sphere of indubitably known experience suitable to serve as a basis for transcendental argumentation? The answer is quite emphatically no. For, as we have observed, Hegel had already in *The Relation of Skepticism to Philosophy* dismissed any idea that there was a sphere of indubitably knowable "facts of consciousness," and when we look closely at the *Phenomenology* we see that the work indeed understands each shape of consciousness to be *false* in all of its conceptions, including its conceptions not only of objects but also of itself and of its own mental contents. In addition, Hegel notes at paragraph 87 that his conception of "experience" includes within a shape of consciousness's "experience" components of which it is not itself in any manner aware. "The experience of consciousness," as Hegel conceives it, would thus afford barren soil indeed for transcendental arguments.

(v) Taylor interprets Hegel's methodological remarks toward the end of the *Phenomenology*'s Introduction as saying (a) that a contradiction occurs between a form of "effective experience," its "reality," on the one hand, and the " 'yardstick,' " "idea of what it is to know an object," or "model of itself" which it intrinsically contains, on the other, so that this " 'yardstick,' " "idea of what it is to know an object," or "model of itself," and it alone, is thereby discredited; and (b) that in order to ensure that this contradiction shows that the "model" *cannot* be realized, Hegel proposes to identify the latter's contradiction of "effective experience" as a contradiction of "basic and pervasive facets of experience," "undeniable characteristics of experience." And Taylor infers from this alleged evidence that (c) Hegel's argument "to the extent that it follows the plan of the Introduction, has many affinities to transcendental arguments." ("The Opening Arguments of the *Phenomenology*," pp. 158–60). This is all highly misleading. Concerning step (a) to begin with, the "yardstick [Maßstab]" of which Hegel speaks in the Introduction is not, as Taylor interprets it, a form of experience's "idea of what it is to know an object" or "model of itself," but

and concept-instantiation two doctrines concerning the Absolute and its expression in his Science whose truth he understood to render his Science invulnerable to these skeptical problems, and that the *Phenomenology* refers to these doctrines as well, though without explicitly mentioning their antiskeptical function, so that in this somewhat qualified sense they may be considered part of the work's response to skepticism.

The first of these doctrines was intended to thwart any use of the equipollence problem to attack Hegelian Science. The thought was as follows. In order for an equipollence problem genuinely to arise for a claim, there must be a *contradictory* claim which has equal plausibility with it, either outright or as the conclusion of an argument having equal plausibility with an argument in favor of it (this simply follows from the definition of *equipollence*). But in *The Relation of Skepticism to Philosophy* Hegel had argued that where his own Science's claim, "the Rational," was concerned this necessary condition for the occurrence of an equipollence problem was not met, for "the Rational has no opposite [hat kein Gegenteil]."[88] This doctrine reappears in the *Phenomenology*, though without

---

rather its *conception of an object or truth* (pars. 81–85). Moreover, what it contradicts is not, as Taylor has it, a form of experience's "effective experience" or "reality," but rather its *conception of its own cognition* (i.e., something like the "idea of what it is to know an object" or "model of itself" with which Taylor mistakenly identifies the yardstick itself). Taylor's mistake here is in part just about Hegel's terminology, but it also has a substantive side: whereas Hegel is envisaging a contradiction between a form of experience's *conception of an object or truth* and its conception of its cognition, Taylor has substituted for the former its "effective experience" or its "reality" (in the sense not of its *conception* of reality, but of the reality which it *is*). Moreover, contrary to Taylor's implication that what is discredited by this contradiction is just the "model," since what it contradicts is the "reality" of experience—"The contradiction between model and reality is a determinate one; as such, it calls for a particular transformation to overcome it; and of course, the transformation must be in the model" ("The Opening Arguments of the *Phenomenology*," p. 159)—Hegel argues at paragraph 85 that ultimately the discrediting extends to *both* sides of the contradiction, that is, not only to a form of experience's conception of its own cognition but also to its conception of an object or truth. In sum, pace Taylor, there is for Hegel no question of a contradiction between a form of experience's *"effective experience"* or the *"reality"* of its experience and its conception of its knowledge, and no question of its conception of its knowledge being discredited by contradicting something which itself remains *undiscredited*. Instead, the contradiction is one between a form of experience's *conception of an object or truth* and its conception of its knowledge, and in this contradiction *both* sides get discredited (in a way which I have tried to make philosophical sense of in chapter 2). Step (b) develops this misreading of what Hegel says in the Introduction in a way which, as far as I can see, simply has no textual basis there *at all*. Consequently, step (c), Taylor's inference from (a) and (b) to the *Phenomenology*'s pursuit of a strategy of transcendental argumentation, is quite groundless.

88. *Jenaer Schriften*, p. 247; also in appendix VI. Hegel here explicitly offers this as his answer on behalf of his Science to the equipollence problem in the form of the

explicit mention of its bearing on skepticism. For the *Phenomenology* similarly denies that there "*is* such a thing as the false" in the sense that "the false . . . would be the other, the negative of the substance, which as the content of knowledge is the true" (par. 39).[89]

Hegel's second antiskeptical doctrine was directed against the concept-instantiation problem. The thought was as follows. The concept-instantiation problem rests on an implicit assumption that the concepts in connection with which it arises are distinct from their instances in the real world in such a way that they could exist without in fact having or ever having had any such instances. In *The Relation of Skepticism to Philosophy*, however, Hegel had argued that this assumption was false for the single concept which articulated his own Science's claim, "the Rational," since that concept was absolutely identical with its instantiation in reality. Thus he had written in that essay that it was a mere dogma, untrue of "the Rational," that "concept and being are not one."[90] This doctrine might seem, at first sight, a rather weak answer to a skeptic threatening to raise a concept-instantiation problem against Hegelian Science's concept, because the skeptic could raise a skeptical doubt about the truth of this doctrine itself, and moreover need only be able to *conceive* of Hegelian Science's concept as distinct from its instantiation in reality in order to generate a concept-instantiation problem concerning it, without their actually *being* distinct. However, Hegel means this doctrine in a sense which includes an implication that in order even to understand Hegelian Science's concept a person must affirm its oneness with its instantiation in reality.[91] Therefore a skeptic who skeptically attacked this doctrine or

---

fourth trope of Agrippa, and as an explanation of how his Science can avoid falling victim to that trope without needing to be established by grounds or arguments in order to do so.

89. This doctrine is a Hegelian version of Spinoza's view that, though determinate realities are defined by negation, namely, negation of the rest of reality, the all-encompassing substance is entirely free of negation. Hegel discusses this view of Spinoza's at *Lectures on the History of Philosophy* 3:261–62, 285–86. If Hegel has an *argument* for the doctrine, as I think he does, it is his Parmenides-inspired argument for the ultimate incoherence of the concept of "nothing" or "not-being" at the beginning of the mature Logic.

90. *Jenaer Schriften*, p. 257. This doctrine is a prominent and repeated theme in the essay. Hegel originally received the doctrine from Schelling's Spinozistic Philosophy of Identity, in which it is salient, and of which he was at this time a partisan.

91. Thus, in *The Relation of Skepticism to Philosophy* Hegel approvingly quotes Spinoza, who thought that one could not even understand the concept of God without affirming God's existence: "Spinoza begins his *Ethics* with the declaration: 'By a cause of itself I mean that whose essence includes existence within it, or that whose nature can only

who otherwise failed to affirm it would simply, in Hegel's view, be evincing a failure to comprehend what Hegel was talking about.[92] Once again, this doctrine is subsequently alluded to in the *Phenomenology* as well, though without explicit mention of its bearing on skepticism (it also remains prominent in Hegel's later works). Consider, for example, Hegel's observations in the *Phenomenology* that "the standpoint of consciousness which knows objects in their antithesis to itself, and itself in antithesis to them, is for Science the antithesis of its standpoint," and that in Science "the moment . . . unites the objective form of truth and the form of the knowing self in an immediate unity" (pars. 26, 805). As we shall see shortly, the *Phenomenology* also aims to *prove* this second antiskeptical doctrine.

* * *

So much for these relatively allusive aspects of the *Phenomenology*'s answer to epistemological tasks (4) and (5). But the *Phenomenology* also plays a much more substantial role in Hegel's efforts to accomplish these tasks, a role which it inherited from its predecessor discipline the early Logic.

Let us begin with the *Phenomenology*'s more substantial strategy against the equipollence problem. Since this strategy was first developed in connection with the early Logic, we might usefully start by considering its appearance in this earlier context. Hegel's earliest sketch of the strategy occurs in the 1802 essay *On the Nature of Philosophical Critique*. In this essay he raises the problem that his philosophy is opposed by viewpoints sharing nothing in common with it, so that "because reciprocal recognition is hereby eliminated there appear just two subjectivities opposed to one another. Positions which have nothing in common come forth for just that reason with equal right."[93] Clearly, this is an application of the equipollence problem in the manner of the fourth trope of

---

be conceived [begriffen] as existing'" (*Jenaer Schriften*, p. 229; cf. 251). Similarly, later in life Hegel comments approvingly on Spinoza's characterization of God as "that . . . which cannot be conceived without being" (*Vorlesungen über die Beweise vom Dasein Gottes* [Hamburg: Felix Meiner, 1973], pp. 174–75).

92. In one form or another the general idea that conceptual understanding requires belief, so that a skeptic must choose between, on the one hand, believing, and so forgoing skepticism in *this* way, or, on the other hand, lapsing into meaninglessness, and so forgoing skepticism in *this* way, has had a long tradition among antiskeptics. Besides Hegel, versions of this idea can be found in such diverse antiskeptics as Aristotle (e.g., in *Metaphysics*, bk. Gamma), Spinoza, and the Wittgenstein of *On Certainty*.

93. In appendix VII.

Agrippa.[94] How does the early Hegel propose to deal with this equipollence problem apparently facing his philosophy? His solution in the essay mentioned is to show that the viewpoints which seem to stand in opposition to his philosophy in fact prove to be "nothing," or in other words self-contradictory: "The only thing that can be done is to recount how this negative side [i.e., the opposing viewpoints] expresses itself and confesses its nothingness [Nichtssein] . . . It cannot fail to happen that what is nothing in the beginning appears in its development ever more and more as nothing, so that it can be pretty universally recognized as such."[95] The discipline in which Hegel at this date envisaged demonstrating the "nothingness," or self-contradictoriness, of all viewpoints that seemed to stand in opposition to his own philosophy was his early Logic.

Now, as we have seen, the *Phenomenology* is much concerned with essentially the same problem—a threat to Hegelian Science from the equipollence method in the manner of the fourth trope of Agrippa. Moreover, it proposes a remarkably similar strategy for solving the problem: Hegel indicates in the Introduction that it would be futile for his Science to respond by criticizing the opposing viewpoints on the basis of some criterion of its own, since this would just leave it vulnerable to the same problem with respect to this criterion (pars. 81–83). Fortunately, however, there is an alternative to this, for "consciousness"—that is, the opposing viewpoints—"provides its own criterion from within itself, so that the investigation becomes a comparison of consciousness with itself" (par. 84), namely, one in which it always proves to come into conflict with its own criterion or with itself (par. 85). In other words, each viewpoint standing opposed to Hegelian Science contains as an essential part of its own constitution a criterion of adequacy with which it is itself in contra-

---

94. Strictly speaking, one should probably rather say that it is an application of a very close variant of the fourth trope of Agrippa's problem. Since, as we have seen, Hegel maintains that his own philosophy's claim has no contradictory, so that it can have no contraries either, it cannot strictly be his position that the viewpoints which compete with it are logically inconsistent with it in the way envisaged in the fourth trope of Agrippa. Recall in this connection also his view, mentioned in the previous chapter, that there is a complete conceptual gulf between his own philosophy and other viewpoints, which similarly implies that there cannot strictly be logical inconsistency between its position and theirs. The problem is therefore, strictly speaking, one of finding that his philosophy's claim, advanced without supporting argument, is faced with *claims which though not logically inconsistent with it are otherwise incompatible with it* advanced in the same way, and hence with equal right.

95. Appendix VII.

diction. Or, as the *Science of Logic* puts it, each "has for its result its own negation."[96] So the strategy in the *Phenomenology* is essentially the same as that in *On the Nature of Philosophical Critique:* the alternative viewpoints which seem to create equipollence difficulties for Hegelian Science will turn out not in fact to do so because they will all prove to be implicitly self-contradictory. The *Phenomenology*, like the early Logic before it, has the job of demonstrating these self-contradictions within each non-Hegelian viewpoint. Hence it is a "way of despair" for the ordinary consciousness and "the conscious insight into the untruth of phenomenal knowledge" (par. 78).

As one might expect, both in the early Logic and in the *Phenomenology* this general strategy becomes a good deal more complicated in its details. Some of the most important complications have already been explained in the previous chapter in connection with the two disciplines' pedagogical projects. In particular, we saw there that both in the early Logic and in the *Phenomenology* Hegel avoids the need to take on the impossibly large task of demonstrating the self-contradictoriness of each non-Hegelian claim *directly,* by instead undertaking to show directly the self-contradictoriness of each member of a finite and manageable stock of fundamental items—in the Logic, fundamental concepts, forms of judgment, and forms of syllogism; in the *Phenomenology*, "shapes of consciousness"—through which any non-Hegelian claim must be articulated, and which enter into the meaning of any non-Hegelian claim articulated through them, thereby *indirectly* showing the self-contradictoriness of all non-Hegelian claims. And we also noted there that the direct demonstration of the self-contradictoriness of the fundamental items in question is effected both in the early Logic and in the *Phenomenology* by means of the dialectical method.

A further refinement on the general strategy responds to the fact that both in the early Logic and in the *Phenomenology* Hegel intends his answer to the skeptic's equipollence problem to meet a certain very ambitious standard. It is not sufficient, in Hegel's view, that it be shown that all non-Hegelian claims which have actually been advanced or which we happen to be able to think of are self-contradictory, so that no equipollence problem can arise for Hegelian Science from these sources. We must in addition show that there *cannot* be a self-consistent non-Hegelian claim, so that it is *impossible* for an equipollence problem to arise for

96. *Science of Logic*, p. 54.

Hegelian Science.[97] The *Phenomenology* employs two complementary techniques in the service of this ambitious goal, one inherited from the early Logic, the other peculiar to itself.

Given that any non-Hegelian claim must be articulated through some shape of consciousness or other, and that the self-contradictoriness of a shape of consciousness infects any claim articulated through it, the problem of showing that all possible non-Hegelian claims are self-contradictory becomes the problem of demonstrating that all (possible) shapes of consciousness are self-contradictory. How does Hegel propose to demonstrate this?

Let us consider first the technique which the *Phenomenology* inherited from the early Logic.[98] To begin with, the *Phenomenology* strives to achieve an exhaustive collection of, and demonstration of self-contradictions in, all *known* shapes of consciousness. The early Logic had sought to accomplish something similar with respect to fundamental concepts, forms of judgment, and forms of syllogism. However, in its methodical scouring of the whole known history of thought the *Phenomenology* approaches the task with a new order of seriousness.[99]

Still, this is not by itself enough. Hegel must in addition show that these shapes of consciousness constitute all the shapes there are (or could be). How can he hope to accomplish this? His strategy for doing so exploits a suggestion due ultimately to Kant: the way to show that the collected aggregate of all known items of a certain kind—in Kant's case, pure categories of the understanding; in Hegel's, shapes of conscious-

---

97. One might interpret this as Hegel's response to Sextus Empiricus's warning at *Outlines of Pyrrhonism*, bk. 1, chap. 13 that one should not accept an argument which presently appears sound because someone might later find an equally plausible counterargument.

98. I shall discuss only the *Phenomenology*'s version of this technique here. For a discussion of the early Logic's version, see my *Hegel and Skepticism*, chap. 8.

99. The deeply *historical* character of the *Phenomenology*'s investigation of shapes of consciousness stands in contrast to the basically ahistorical character of the early Logic's investigation of fundamental concepts, forms of judgment, and forms of syllogism. In recognizing that fundamental differences in human thought have occurred over history, perceiving in them a particularly potent source of skeptical problems, and attempting nevertheless to thwart skepticism in the face of them, the *Phenomenology*'s project is strikingly continuous with Herder's *Auch eine Philosophie der Geschichte zur Bildung der Menschheit* (see esp. *Herders Ausgewählte Werke* 2:646–47)—though Hegel's strategy for combatting the skepticism in question is much more sophisticated than Herder's. Herder and Hegel had thus not only already perceived the threat of skepticism posed by intellectual historicism which Troeltsch would make much of early in the twentieth century, but also developed strategies for dealing with it.

ness—constitutes a *complete* collection of items of that kind is to demonstrate that they constitute together an *entire system*.[100] This is a large part of the reason why Hegel is so concerned to claim that the series of shapes of consciousness exhibited in the *Phenomenology* comprehends "nothing less than the *entire system* of consciousness" (par. 89; emphasis added).[101]

But if their constitution of an entire system is to be used as a means of showing that the shapes of consciousness covered in the *Phenomenology* include all the shapes there are (or could be), Hegel needs a way of demonstrating that the shapes covered in the work really *do* constitute an entire system. How does he propose to accomplish this? His technique for doing so is to use the *dialectical method* to show that each shape of consciousness not only is self-contradictory but also necessarily develops through its self-contradiction into the next shape, thus displaying them as an entire connected series or system: "The *completeness* of the forms of the unreal consciousness will result from the necessity of the progression and interconnection itself" (par. 79).[102]

There seems to be a difficulty here, though. Someone might concede that demonstrating that each known shape of consciousness necessarily developed into the next to form a single series would prove that they all belonged to a single system, but yet deny that it would prove that they constituted that system *in its entirety*. "Perhaps," he might object, "they constitute only a segment of some larger series or system, whose remaining shapes remain unknown to us." Hegel has a solution to this difficulty: the entireness of the series or system of shapes revealed by the dialectic of the *Phenomenology* will be shown by the fact that this dialectic *takes a circular course, eventually returning to the shape from which it started*, having taken in all the other shapes known. Thus, if we follow the dialectic of the *Phenomenology* we find that, having begun from Sense-certainty, it extends all the way to Hegel's system, which then, as Hegel explains near the end of the *Phenomenology*, "contains within itself [the] necessity of externalizing itself from the form of the pure Con-

---

100. Kant explains this strategy most clearly at *Prolegomena to Any Future Metaphysics*, par. 39. Note that the inference from "entire system" to "complete collection" is not a trivial one.
101. It is therefore quite false to Hegel's intentions to say, as Kainz does, that "Hegel does not choose just any forms of consciousness [i.e., shapes of consciousness]" but selects only certain ones (*Hegel's Phenomenology, Part One*, p. 17).
102. On the necessity of the development from one shape of consciousness to the next, see esp. pars. 86–88.

cept, and contains the passage of the Concept into consciousness. For the self-knowing Spirit, just because it grasps its Concept, is the immediate identity with itself which, in its difference, is the certainty of immediacy, or sense-consciousness [i.e., Sense-certainty]—the beginning from which we started" (par. 806). In other words, the *Phenomenology*'s dialectic, which began from Sense-certainty, and then took in all other known shapes of consciousness, eventually, when it reaches Hegel's system, returns to Sense-certainty again.[103]

---

103. At the time of writing the *Phenomenology* Hegel seems to have thought of this return as occurring from *two* points within the system, but later only from *one*.

First, both the wording of the passage just quoted from *Phenomenology*, paragraph 806 and the following passage in the 1812 edition of the *Science of Logic* seem to imply a return to Sense-certainty from the end of the system's Logic: "Spirit will also at the *end* of the development of pure knowing freely externalize itself and release itself into the shape of an *immediate* consciousness as consciousness of a being which stands over against it as an other" (in appendix XV). However, Hegel appears later to have withdrawn the idea of *this* return. Thus, as Fulda points out (*Das Problem einer Einleitung*, p. 100), this idea does not get implemented at the end of the 1812 *Science of Logic*. And moreover, in the 1831 edition Hegel deliberately alters the passage just quoted from the 1812 edition beyond all recognition to the following: "It is still more so that Absolute Spirit, which emerges as the concrete truth and the last and highest truth of all being, gets recognized as externalizing itself with freedom at the *end* of the development and releasing itself to the shape of an *immediate being*—resolving on the creation of a world which contains everything which fell within the development which preceded that result and which together with its beginning gets changed due to this reversed position into something dependent on the result qua the principle" (in appendix XVIII).

Second, Hegel implies at *Phenomenology*, paragraph 807 that there will be a return to Sense-certainty from the system through Spirit's "sacrifice of itself" into nature (i.e., through the transition from the end of the Logic to the Philosophy of Nature) and thence through the "reinstatement of the subject" (i.e., through the transition from the Philosophy of Nature to the Philosophy of Spirit). We can see immediately what this means when we turn to the *Encyclopaedia*'s exposition of Logic, Philosophy of Nature, and Philosophy of Spirit. For there within the Philosophy of Spirit we find a section which bears the very same title as the *Phenomenology* and which re-treats the *Phenomenology*'s shapes of consciousness, beginning with Sense-certainty. Moreover, we can be fairly confident that the system was already conceived in this way at the time of the *Phenomenology*'s composition, because the 1808 ff. *Encyclopaedia* already includes such a section (*Nürnberger und Heidelberger Schriften*, p. 42, pars 128–29). In keeping with this reading of paragraph 807, note that the altered passage from the 1831 edition of the *Science of Logic* quoted above refers, pace Fulda (*Das Problem einer Einleitung*, p. 100), not to the end of the whole system and its return to the Logic's beginning with Being, but rather to the end of the Logic and its transition to the Philosophy of Nature and thence to the Philosophy of Spirit, where the contents of the *Phenomenology* are reencountered. Thus note: (i) The phrases "externalizing itself with freedom" and "resolving on the creation of a world" make it clear that Hegel is thinking of the transition from the end of the Logic to the Philosophy of Nature, of which such phrases are characteristic, not the transition from the end of the whole system to the begin-

This, then, is one technique by means of which the *Phenomenology* strives to prove that it has found self-contradictions in *all* shapes of consciousness. There is, though, a readily apparent weakness in this technique as it stands. The weakness concerns its Kantian step. For demonstrating that an aggregate of all known items of a particular kind constitutes an entire system does not by any means *guarantee*, even if it may strongly suggest, that the aggregate constitutes a complete collection of items of that kind. There could, after all, be some as yet unknown second system of such items or some as yet unknown "loners" without systematic connections.

The *Phenomenology* has a second technique, without precedent in the early Logic, which promises to overcome this weakness in the first technique. The *Phenomenology* undertakes to reinforce its proof of the completeness of its collection of shapes of consciousness by adding to the demonstration that they constitute not only all known shapes but also

---

ning of the Logic, of which they are not. (ii) The immediate context of the passage shows that it is supposed to be explaining a way in which we return from the system to the "immediacy with which [consciousness] begins" in the *Phenomenology*: "Consciousness, on its path from the immediacy with which it begins, gets led back to absolute knowing as its innermost *truth*. This last thing, the ground, is, then, also that from which the first thing comes forth, though the latter initially made its appearance as something immediate" (in appendix XVIII). (iii) The term "Absolute Spirit" in the passage in question, while it *could* signify the end of the Philosophy of Spirit, as Fulda understands it to, can equally well refer to the Absolute Idea of the Logic (compare, for example, Hegel's use of the term "self-knowing Spirit" at *Phenomenology*, par. 806). (iv) The term "immediate being" in this passage, while it *could* signify the Logic's beginning with Being, as Fulda understands it to, can equally well signify the beginning of the Philosophy of Nature, which corresponds to Being in the Logic. Now Hegel never withdraws the idea of *this* return from the system to Sense-certainty. Indeed, if the reading just given of the altered passage in the 1831 edition of the *Science of Logic* is correct, he *reaffirms the idea of this return in 1831.*

The question naturally arises *why* Hegel changed his mind about having a twofold return from the system to Sense-certainty, opting instead for just a single return. I would suggest that this was probably a delayed result of a shift in the intended scope of the *Phenomenology* which, as I shall argue in part 4, took place during the process of composition, a shift from an originally planned Ur-*Phenomenology* comprising just the chapters *Consciousness* through *Reason* to the much larger published *Phenomenology*. Within the Ur-*Phenomenology* there was no *general* anticipation of the contents of the system of the kind found in the published work—it only really strove to anticipate the Logic and the Philosophy of Spirit's "Phenomenology of Spirit" section. Consequently, within this conception it was natural to have both of these parts of the system make a return to the Ur-*Phenomenology*. In the published version of the *Phenomenology*, by contrast, there are, as we saw in the previous chapter, deliberate anticipations of virtually *all* parts of the system. Consequently, in the context of the published version of the work the original twofold return ceased to seem natural.

an entire system a demonstration that, moreover, the necessary unfolding of this particular entire system over time, and its culmination in self-consistent Hegelian Science, has been the whole purpose of history, which becomes fully intelligible as just such a teleological process (see esp. par. 808). If Hegel can accomplish this further demonstration, then considerable force is lent to the claim that the entire system of shapes of consciousness exhibited in the *Phenomenology* is *the* system of such items—that there is no second system, nor any "loners."[104]

* * *

We now turn to the *Phenomenology*'s substantial strategy for dispelling the second skeptical problem which seems to threaten Hegelian Science, the concept-instantiation problem. The form of this problem which both the early Logic and the *Phenomenology* seem designed to address could be stated as follows: How can one know that the concept of Hegelian Science corresponds to anything in reality, given that (i) it is distinct from any instances it might have in reality and could therefore exist without having any, and (ii) there are incompatible, competing concepts which appear to have no less plausible a claim than this concept has to depict reality as it is?

The early Logic's strategy for dispelling this problem was to refute both of the assumptions on which it rests. The refutation of (i) took the form of an attempt to *prove* the doctrine mentioned earlier that the concept of Hegelian Science is identical with its instantiation in reality. In the early Logic of the *Logic, Metaphysics, and Philosophy of Nature* the method for accomplishing this was to begin by positing Hegelian Science's concept in *separation* from its instantiation in reality—or as this text, modeled on Plato's *Parmenides,* has it: unity in separation from the real many—and then show by means of a dialectical deduction from this assumption that it led to a series of unresolvable contradictions. The intention was, in effect, to provide a reductio ad absurdum of the original assumption that Hegelian Science's concept was separate from its instantiation in reality, and thereby an indirect proof of their identity.[105]

---

104. Hegel nowhere explains this second technique explicitly, so one cannot be *sure* that he consciously intended it. However, the circumstantial evidence suggests to me that he did.

105. To illustrate this strategy briefly from the text of the *Logik, Metaphysik, und Naturphilosophie*: The Logic begins with the concept of unity. Thus, although the relevant pages at the beginning of the text are lost, Hegel remarks later that "the Logic began with unity itself" (p. 136). But this concept of unity is posited in opposition to the real many: "Multiplicity remains opposed to it"; "Unity and multiplicity [are] . . . still independent

The early Logic's refutation of (ii) took the form of an attempt to show by means of successive steps of dialectic performed on fundamental concepts that all concepts other than the concept of Hegelian Science were self-contradictory and therefore only illusory competition for the concept of Hegelian Science.

Viewed against this background, the *Phenomenology* can be seen to pursue a rather similar strategy. Like the early Logic, it aims to defend Hegelian Science against the concept-instantiation problem by refuting both of the assumptions on which the problem rests. It seeks to refute assumption (i) by showing through a series of steps of dialectic that *all ways* of positing a concept in distinction from its real instance or object—that is, all shapes of consciousness—involve implicit self-contradic-

---

existents [noch für sich Bestehende]"; this unity is posited within an assumed opposition between the ideal and the real and on the ideal side of this opposition, so that "the ideal activity . . . means the same as unity" (p. 3). The fact that the concept of unity at the start of the Logic is a concept of unity in opposition to the real many distinguishes it from *absolute* unity, a unity in which they are identical: "One of the things in opposition is necessarily unity itself; but this unity is because of this very fact not absolute unity" (p. 3). The opposition between the concept of unity and the real many is the principle underlying the whole of the Logic, "the general principle of the Logic of the Understanding" (p. 3). The Logic is, as a consequence, unlike the Metaphysics which follows it, through and through dialectical—thus the transition from the former to the latter is described as "the sublation of the Logic itself, as of dialectic" (p. 134). For the opposition between the concept of unity and the real many is a source of dialectic or self-contradictions in all of the concepts posited in the Logic, including the abstract concept of unity itself. Thus, in the nearly contemporary *Natural Law* essay, where Hegel draws essentially the same distinction between a concept of unity in opposition to the real many and absolute unity, he says that the former unity has as "its essence . . . nothing but to be the unmediated opposite of itself" and "shows itself in its essence to be its own opposite" (pp. 71, 82). And in the *Logik, Metaphysik, und Naturphilosophie* he says similarly that this "negative unity . . . abolishes its own determinacy" and implies that it infects the concepts based on it with self-contradictions also so that in the Logic "in the realization of a concept always something other than itself arose" (p. 125). By being shown to lead unavoidably to the self-contradictions of the Logic, the principle of a concept of unity in opposition to the real many "is recognized as not ultimately valid [nicht für sich seiend], and by this means is sublated" (p. 3). The positive moral drawn from this is the need to posit an absolute unity, a concept of unity not abstracted from but rather in identity with the real many, in order to restore self-consistency. Thus Hegel contrasts with the abstract concept of unity which is self-contradictory and a source of self-contradiction in the concepts based upon it absolute unity or "pure unity" which is self-consistent, which "remains the same as itself in its totality" (p. 125). And accordingly, with the conclusion of the Logic the nondialectical or self-consistent Metaphysics establishes absolute unity, unity not posited in opposition to the real many and so not self-contradictory, as its principle: unity or "the in-itself posits itself here as a self-sameness," as something which "has destroyed the possibility of the many, of being different" (p. 136).

tions.[106] This reduces to absurdity the assumption that concepts are distinct from their real instantiation. And Hegel takes this to show, more positively, that we must identify a concept with its real instantiation in order to restore self-consistency, which is precisely what he therefore proceeds to do in connection with the concept of his own Science. One can think of the strategy of proof here as following the "skeptical paradox, skeptical solution" model familiar from Hume and from Kripke's exposition of the Wittgensteinian rule-following argument: Hegel begins from a commonsense conception of concepts, in this case the conception that they are distinct from their real instances. He then shows that all ways of articulating such a conception prove to be implicitly incoherent. This seems to lead to a skeptical paradox: there are no concepts. In order to avoid this paradoxical conclusion, however, Hegel offers as an alternative a skeptical solution: renounce the commonsense conception which leads to the skeptical paradox in order to avoid the paradox, that is, in this case, give up the conception of concepts as distinct from their real instances, instead identifying a concept with its real instantiation. In the text of the *Phenomenology* the "skeptical paradox" part of this proof is the work's critique of the series of shapes of consciousness in the sections *Sense-certainty* to *The Spiritual Animalkingdom*. Upon reaching the latter section Hegel infers the "skeptical solution" of a concept's identity with its real instantiation: "Self-consciousness has now grasped its concept, . . . namely, of being in its own self-certainty all reality, and its . . . essence is now the . . . interfusion of the universal . . . and individuality . . . [Self-consciousness] has for its object the pure category . . . In all [moments] it holds fast to the simple unity of being and self"; "The pure matter itself is . . . 'the category,' being that is 'I' or 'I' that is being" (pars. 394–95, 418).[107]

---

106. That Hegel conceives shapes of consciousness as ways of positing a concept in distinction from its real instance or object can be seen from paragraphs 82 and 84. Thus paragraph 84 notes that "these two moments, concept and object . . . both fall *within* that knowledge [i.e., the shapes of consciousness] which we are investigating," and paragraph 82 makes it clear that this means *as distinguished from one another*. That, and how, the *Phenomenology* aims to show that it has covered *all* shapes of consciousness we saw earlier in this chapter.

107. In close connection with this argument realized over the course of the sections *Sense-certainty* to *The Spiritual Animalkingdom*, we shall in chapter 4 find the same stretch of text arguing in a similar way for the incoherence of the commonsense conception that our propositional representations stand over against independent facts and that their truth consists in a relation of correspondence to the latter, and for their truth consisting instead

The *Phenomenology*, like the early Logic, seeks to refute assumption (ii) by showing that all concepts which appear to compete with the concept of Hegelian Science are implicitly self-contradictory and therefore only illusory as competitors. In contrast to the early Logic, however, the *Phenomenology* attempts to accomplish this by focusing directly, not on apparently competing concepts themselves, but instead on the shapes of consciousness presupposed by such concepts. The aim is to show that all of the shapes of consciousness which such concepts presuppose are self-contradictory, so that such concepts are themselves all infected with self-contradictions as well.[108]

This concludes my explanation of how the *Phenomenology* is supposed to accomplish the epistemological tasks of (4) defending Hegelian Science against the skeptical problem of equipollence and (5) defending it against the skeptical problem of concept-instantiation.[109]

* * *

Finally, we should consider the *Phenomenology*'s commitment to, and efforts to accomplish, epistemological task (6): the task of providing a proof of Hegelian Science for all non-Hegelian viewpoints which is compelling for each of them in the light of its own initial views and criteria (or what one might alternatively describe as a universally successful ad hominem argument for Hegelian Science's truth).

One can perhaps already discern at least the beginnings of a commitment to this task in a statement of Hegel's from 1801–2 regarding the early Logic: "If philosophy is complete and round, philosophizing is on

---

in an enduring communal consensus. This argument and its conclusion will carry certain additional antiskeptical implications. For example, they would rule out a skeptical worry that even if all human beings agreed in some belief, still that belief might fail to be true through failing to correspond to independent facts.

108. The key assumptions behind this strategy, that such concepts presuppose shapes of consciousness and that a self-contradiction in a shape of consciousness must infect all concepts articulated through it, were explained in chapter 2.

109. Note that, ironically, but with only a superficial appearance of paradox, the *Phenomenology* not only aims in the ways just explained to *defeat* skepticism, but also conceives itself and its manner of doing so *as* a form of skepticism: the *Phenomenology* is a "self-completing skepticism" (par. 78), which, moreover, like Pyrrhonism, includes a systematic critique of "criteria" of truth (pars. 84–85), and, again like Pyrrhonian arguments, constitutes a "ladder" which will be cast away upon the attainment of the satisfactory standpoint (par. 26; compare Sextus Empiricus's famous characterization of the Pyrrhonist's argument as a ladder which once climbed gets kicked away, at *Against the Logicians*, bk. 2, sec. 481). This second side of the work's relation to skepticism is indeed a good deal more textually obvious than the first side emphasized above.

the contrary something empirical which [can] proceed from various stand-points and diverse forms of culture and subjectivity, and . . . in connection with the empirical beginnings of philosophizing an introduction to philosophy is possible, which constitutes a sort of bonding and bridge between the subjective forms and the objective, absolute philosophy."[110]

The *Phenomenology* is emphatically committed to the task in question.[111] Thus, the work's ambition of providing a proof which is compelling for *all* non-Hegelian viewpoints is reflected in such features as its attempt to include on its "ladder" toward Hegelian Science a rung corresponding to every viewpoint or "shape of consciousness" that has arisen during the whole course of human history, and its explicit stipulation that these must include every shape of consciousness or "the entire system of consciousness" (par. 89). And it can also be seen from the *Science of Logic*'s statement that the *Phenomenology* shows that consciousness's "shapes *all* dissolve into the Concept [i.e., the content of Hegelian Science] as the truth."[112] That this proof is moreover intended to be compelling for the non-Hegelian viewpoints *on the basis of their own initial views and criteria* can be seen from such statements in the work as that "consciousness as it approaches Science justly demands that it be able to attain to rational knowledge *by way of the ordinary Understanding,*" and that "the individual has the right to demand that Science should . . . provide him with the ladder to this standpoint [i.e., to Science's standpoint], *should show him this standpoint within himself*" (pars. 13, 26; emphasis added).

It might be asked how this task differs from the pedagogical project of the *Phenomenology* discussed in the previous chapter. The answer is that—although the work realizes both by means of a single procedure, and does not distinguish between them very clearly even in theory—they differ in that task (6) is both more ambitious and otherwise motivated than the pedagogical project. Task (6) is more ambitious in that it (i) demands a way of persuading *all* non-Hegelian viewpoints of the truth of Hegelian Science, not merely all *contemporary* non-Hegelian view-

---

110. "Introductio in Philosophiam. Diese Vorlesungen . . . "
111. Pace Baillie, who writes that although Hegel gives a justification of his philosophy, "it is a justification in terms of and satisfactory to philosophy itself, *not one that any other form of knowledge would accept*" (Hegel, *The Phenomenology of Mind*, trans. J.B. Baillie [London: Allen and Unwin, 1931], p. 33; emphasis added).
112. Appendix XV; emphasis added.

points, and (ii) demands that this persuasion take the form of providing an argument to Hegelian Science which is not only compelling for these viewpoints but compelling for each of them *in the light of its own initial views and criteria*. Task (6) has different motives, as well. One might, and indeed in part should, attribute the *Phenomenology*'s aspiration to meet demand (ii) to pedagogical motives.[113] But the work's aspiration to meet demand (i) cannot plausibly be explained in terms of such motives. Why insist on giving, and go to the enormous trouble of giving, a proof compelling for *all* non-Hegelian viewpoints in the light of their own initial views and criteria if one's only motive were the pedagogical motive of convincing one's contemporaries?[114] That the *Phenomenology*'s attempt to accomplish task (6) thus cannot be fully explained by pedagogical motives alone is indicative of the fact that there is an important further motive behind it: an epistemological or *justificatory* motive. And that Hegel does indeed understand the accomplishment of task (6) to be part of the justification or proof of his Science is confirmed by remarks in the *Science of Logic*. For he writes there that the path of the *Phenomenology* takes in every form of consciousness and culminates in the content of Science, the Concept, and that this "therefore needs . . . no justification here, because it has received it in [the *Phenomenology*]. And it admits of no

---

113. As we shall see shortly, when the early Logic was Hegel's pedagogical discipline, at least at the time of the sketch from 1801-2 (appendix V), it made no serious effort to meet demand (ii). Instead, it required a pupil to accept much information from the scientific standpoint on authority before raising him to this standpoint. The result was not a pedagogical success—as one can infer from Hegel's lament in a Jena aphorism that "the dividing wall between the terminology of philosophy and the ordinary consciousness still has to be broken through" (Rosenkranz, *Hegels Leben*, p. 552), and from Rosenkranz's report that "Hegel had in Jena at first presented his system in all the roughness of its original conception, but had in several years been able to learn sufficiently that such a form was not suited to academic presentation. He was forced to a lively awareness of the need for a more *popular* presentation. The rift between the deep spirit, which unfolded itself in that system with the boldest abstraction, and the consciousness which the student brought with him at the start to the lecture, was too great" (p. 178). The natural step for Hegel to take in order to remedy this pedagogical failure was to narrow the gap between the presuppositions which the pupil was required to accept as a precondition of education by the pedagogical discipline of Logic and the pupil's own initial views and criteria, that is, to move in the direction of meeting demand (ii). Thus the *Phenomenology*'s attempt to meet demand (ii) can, and in part should, be explained in terms of pedagogical motives.

114. It is true that *some* of the older shapes of consciousness covered by the work remain live options for Hegel's contemporaries—e.g., the Christian outlook of the Unhappy Consciousness and the natural scientific outlook of Observing Reason—so that they might properly be covered for pedagogical reasons. But surely not *all* of them.

other justification than just this bringing forth of it through consciousness, whose own shapes all dissolve into the Concept as the truth"; Hegelian Science "has its proof solely in [this] necessity of its coming forth."[115]

It is important not to confuse Hegel's idea here of contributing to the justification or proof of Hegelian Science by accomplishing task (6) with the much more familiar idea of providing a justification or proof of a position by deducing it from true premises. Hegel does not think that the "premises" of the *Phenomenology*—its shapes of consciousness—*are* true, or even self-consistent. And, as we saw earlier, he always rejects the idea of justifying or proving his Science in this familiar way. Rather, it is Hegel's thought that the ideal embodied in task (6) of being able to provide a universally successful ad hominem argument for Hegelian Science in itself has justificatory force, that this would not only be pedagogically fortunate but also *indicative of truth*. This is quite an original thought.[116] It also seems quite plausible; if, in addition to answering the equipollence and concept-instantiation threats, Hegel really could show that his Science was provable to all non-Hegelian viewpoints on the basis of their own initial views and criteria, then this surely *would* lend it an additional measure of certainty.

How, then, does the *Phenomenology* attempt to accomplish task (6)? In order to throw its attempts to do so into starker relief we should begin by observing how very far short of accomplishing this task Hegel still was in 1801–2 when he first began to hint at an interest in it. The early Logic of that period fell short of accomplishing task (6) in two ways. First, it did not make a really strenuous effort to be effective for *all* non-Hegelian viewpoints—in particular, because it failed to make any concessions to intellectually remote viewpoints from historically distant periods. Second, and more strikingly, it made no attempt to be compelling for the viewpoints which it addressed *purely on the basis of their own initial views and criteria*—instead requiring their acceptance of much extraneous information on authority as a precondition of the success of its instruction. To make this second point in a little more textual detail: The

---

115. Appendix XV. Cf. *Encyclopaedia*, par. 25, where Hegel says that the method of the *Phenomenology* is one of "beginning from the first, simplest appearance of Spirit, the immediate consciousness, and developing its dialectic up to the standpoint of philosophical Science, the necessity of which is demonstrated through this progression" (appendix XVII).

116. It is at least not easy to think of precedents in the history of philosophy. Perhaps the most plausible candidate would be the Platonic Socrates—especially in the dialogues *Gorgias*, *Protagoras*, and *Euthydemus*.

sketch of the Logic from 1801–2 implies that the Logic's insight into the self-contradictions in "finite" concepts essentially relied on a presupposed knowledge of the categories expounded in the Metaphysics, on the basis of which knowledge the Logic recognized that "finite" concepts were merely one-sided abstractions from those categories and that in those categories they were identical with their opposites: "Finite cognition or Reflection only abstracts from the absolute identity of what in rational cognition [i.e., the content of Metaphysics] is related to one another or equated with one another, and only through this abstraction does it become a finite cognition. In rational cognition or philosophy . . . [the] finitude [of the finite forms] is destroyed due to the fact that in Speculation [i.e., Metaphysics] they are related to one another."[117] Likewise, the Logic's insight into the *systematic* nature of its collection of "finite" concepts relied essentially on a presupposed knowledge of the system of categories expounded in the Metaphysics, on the basis of which knowledge the "finite" concepts were seen to be a system of one-sided abstractions from that system of categories. This is the implication of Hegel's observation that the "finite" concepts are set up in the Logic "as they proceed forth from Reason."[118] Again, in order for the "finite" pupil to take this Logic's path toward Hegelian philosophy—a path which, as we noted previously, consisted in a pointing-out of anticipations or imitations of Hegelian philosophy's standpoint within the pupil's "finite" cognition—he had to accept on authority the claim that the aspects of his "finite" cognition in question *were* imitations of philosophical truth, for "in order to recognize the Understanding as imitative [of Reason] we must at the same time hold constantly before us the original model which the Understanding copies, the expression of Reason itself."[119] Summing up the pervasive requirement in this Logic that the pupil accept information from the standpoint of Hegelian philosophy on authority before he can enjoy the benefit of the Logic's introduction to this standpoint, Hegel writes that "Logic can serve as an introduction to philosophy . . . only from this speculative side."[120]

In contrast to this earlier work, the *Phenomenology* makes a determined effort to accomplish task (6). How, in general terms? First, it at-

---

117. Appendix V.
118. Ibid.
119. Ibid.
120. Ibid.

tempts to articulate its demonstrations of the invulnerability of Hegelian Science to skeptical equipollence and concept-instantiation problems in such a way that these demonstrations are compelling for every non-Hegelian viewpoint in the light of its own initial views and criteria. Second, it attempts to demonstrate to every non-Hegelian viewpoint in the light of its own initial views and criteria both that that viewpoint itself necessarily develops into Hegelian Science and that every other non-Hegelian viewpoint necessarily does so too. The work seeks to accomplish this whole ambitious project by articulating the several demonstrations in question in the form of a dialectical "ladder" (to use Hegel's own metaphor) on which every non-Hegelian viewpoint, including even those from remote historical periods, finds a rung representing its own views and criteria, starting from which it is gradually compelled, by having the consequences of those views and criteria unfolded, to develop the demonstrations in question in their entirety.[121]

In order to see more clearly how this is supposed to work, let us consider how the *Phenomenology* will attempt to prove Hegelian Science for an individual occupying some randomly chosen non-Hegelian viewpoint—say, one represented half way up the "ladder." The *Phenomenology* implies that its proof of Hegelian Science for such an individual, even if it begins by acquainting him with the rung half way up the ladder which represents his own viewpoint, will not immediately lead him thence to the contemplation of higher rungs lying in the direction of Hegelian Science, but will first lead him back to contemplate all of the more primitive viewpoints represented on lower rungs of the ladder, which are, as the *Phenomenology* conceives things, in a way contained within his own viewpoint: "The individual whose substance is the more advanced Spirit runs through [the] past just as one who takes up a higher science goes through the preparatory studies he has long since absorbed, in order to bring their content to mind: he recalls them to the inward eye but has no lasting interest in them" (par. 28). Arriving at the most primitive rung of the ladder, Sense-certainty, he will be shown the self-contradiction implicit in this primitive viewpoint and the necessity of development to the

---

121. The universal ad hominem proof therefore does not, in case the question has crossed the reader's mind, take the simple—but, from the point of view of contributing something *new* to the justification of Hegelian Science, probably vacuous—form of deducing Hegelian Science from the self-contradiction in each shape of consciousness by exploiting the circumstance familiar to formal logicians that a contradiction implies anything whatever.

next viewpoint, Perception, and so on until he arrives at his own viewpoint half way up the ladder.

So far the individual's course of education will have been relatively easy, since the viewpoints considered were more primitive than his own and in some sense already contained within his own, and it will have been relatively painless, since they were ones which he had already superseded. From now on, though, his education will be more difficult, since it will involve him learning viewpoints not already contained within his own but more sophisticated than it, and it will be more painful—a genuine "way of despair," as the Introduction calls it—since the self-contradictions discovered will now be ones afflicting either his own viewpoint or more sophisticated viewpoints for which he has exchanged his own having found his own discredited. But in principle the process of education will proceed much as hitherto: having arrived at the depiction of his own viewpoint, he will be shown the self-contradiction within it and the necessity of development beyond it to a new, more sophisticated viewpoint, and this process will then repeat itself at successive further levels. In this way he will eventually find himself driven to reach the self-consistent (though dialectically articulated) standpoint of Hegelian Science, comprising Logic, Philosophy of Nature, and Philosophy of Spirit.

So far so good. But the individual will only grasp the proof of Hegelian Science which has been constructed for him in its entirety when, progressing beyond the dialectic of the *Phenomenology* itself into Hegelian Science, he follows the connecting dialectical exposition of Hegelian Science. Doing so will eventually return him through an unbroken course of dialectic begun in the *Phenomenology* with the viewpoint of Sense-certainty, continued through the remaining viewpoints in the *Phenomenology,* and subsequently through the connecting disciplines of Hegelian Science, to the viewpoint of Sense-certainty from which the dialectic of the *Phenomenology* started (namely, in the section of the Philosophy of Spirit bearing the same title as the *Phenomenology*). This return to Sense-certainty is the keystone in the *Phenomenology*'s proof of Hegelian Science for the non-Hegelian individual. For it is by thus being shown the circularity in the *Phenomenology*'s dialectical exposition of all known shapes of consciousness that he is enabled to recognize that this exposition represents an entire system of shapes of consciousness ("the entire system of consciousness"). And his recognition of this, together with his recognition now that the genesis of this particular system of shapes of consciousness and its culmination in self-consistent Hegelian Science has constituted the very purpose of history, proves to him beyond reasonable doubt that the shapes of consciousness collected in the *Phenomenology* are all the shapes of consciousness that there are.

With this information secured, the non-Hegelian individual now has at hand the several demonstrations referred to earlier: He now recognizes that Hegelian Science faces no equipollence problem. For he sees that all shapes of consciousness, on which any non-Hegelian claim must draw in order to be articulated, are self-contradictory, thereby infecting all non-Hegelian claims with self-contradictions. And this shows him that all claims which might be set up in opposition to Hegelian Science are self-contradictory, and consequently no genuine competition for Hegelian Science. Moreover, he now recognizes that Hegelian Science faces no concept-instantiation problem. For, on the one hand, he sees that all viewpoints which posit a distinction between concept and instance or object of the kind required for such a problem to arise—all shapes of consciousness—are self-contradictory, and that there therefore cannot be such a distinction between Hegelian Science's concept and its object in particular, but these must be identical. And, on the other hand, he sees that all non-Hegelian concepts are implicitly self-contradictory and so represent no competition for Hegelian Science's concept. For he sees that all shapes of consciousness, which must be drawn on for the articulation of any non-Hegelian concept, are self-contradictory, thereby infecting all non-Hegelian concepts with self-contradiction. Finally, he now recognizes both that his own non-Hegelian viewpoint necessarily develops into Hegelian Science, and also that all other non-Hegelian viewpoints necessarily do so too. He recognizes this because he now sees that all of the non-Hegelian viewpoints presented in the *Phenomenology*, including his own, dialectically develop into Hegelian Science, and also that these constitute all the non-Hegelian viewpoints that there are.

Such, then, is the grand design of the *Phenomenology* as a work of epistemology. In sum, the *Phenomenology* aspires to justify Hegelian Science's claim to truth by achieving epistemological tasks (4), (5), and (6) through the elaborate strategies explained above.

* * *

We might now usefully conclude this chapter with a few appended observations concerning the viability of this ambitious epistemological project, and also its broader significance.

The viability of this project—as well as of the *Phenomenology*'s pedagogical and metaphysical projects—depends essentially and above all on the cogency of the work's *dialectic*. I have argued elsewhere with special reference to the dialectic of the Logic that the dialectical method is perfectly intelligible and unobjectionable *in principle*, that there are no good reasons for dismissing it *a priori*, and that if problems do arise for it then they stem rather from the brute nature of the categories to which we attempt to apply it, their being as a brute matter of fact so constituted as to resist the method's application. More specifically, I have argued that one can make good sense of the method's fundamental ideas that there are implicit self-contradictions in categories and that there is a necessity of transition from one self-contradictory category to the next (in a sense of "necessity" suitable to Hegel's philosophical purposes), but that it may yet turn out that as a brute matter of fact the dialectical pattern of self-contradictions and necessary transitions is not to be found among the categories which we actually possess.[122] I suggest that the same holds true, mutatis mutandis, of the dialectic of the *Phenomenology*.

Thus, I suggest that we can make perfectly good sense *in principle* of the idea that shapes of consciousness might be dialectical in nature. In particular, (i) there seems to be no difficulty in making sense of the idea that there might prove to be an implicit contradiction within a shape of consciousness between two of its essential elements, its conceptions of cognition and of objectivity, as Hegel implies there to be (pars. 84–85). Moreover, (ii) we can also, I think, make good sense of the idea that there might be necessary transitions between shapes of consciousness, as Hegel implies there to be (pars. 86–87).

The latter is an especially controversial assertion, and therefore calls for some explanation. In order to approach the question of the nature and defensibility of Hegel's idea of such a dialectical necessity fruitfully, it is important, I suggest, not to assume that Hegel must have in mind one or another of the sorts of necessity with which we are already familiar—for example, causal necessity, teleological necessity (necessity for a purpose), or the necessity of formal logical or analytical implication.[123] Rather, we should ask whether it is possible to find a conception of "necessity" which (a) fits with what Hegel says concerning dialectical "neces-

---

122. For this case, see my "Hegel's Dialectical Method," in *The Cambridge Companion to Hegel*, ed. F.C. Beiser (Cambridge: Cambridge University Press, 1993).
123. By formal logical implication I mean the sort of implication that leads from "Socrates is a man" and "All men are mortal" to "Socrates is mortal," by analytical implication the sort of implication that leads from "Smith is a bachelor" to "Smith is unmarried."

sity" in the text, (b) in particular would be adequate to the philosophical purposes for which the text requires dialectical "necessity," and (c) makes reasonable philosophical sense.

I suggest that we can indeed find a conception of "necessity" which satisfies those three criteria: the "necessity" of a transition from a shape of consciousness A to a shape of consciousness B just consists in the complex fact that while shape A proves to be implicitly self-contradictory, shape B preserves shape A's constitutive conceptions/concepts but in a way which modifies them so as to eliminate the self-contradiction, and moreover does so while departing less from the meanings of A's constitutive conceptions/concepts than any other known shape which performs that function.[124] This interpretation of dialectical "necessity" in the *Phenomenology* satisfies the three criteria just mentioned: (a) it fits well what the text says concerning dialectical "necessity";[125] (b) in particular it

---

124. This interpretation is modeled on a similar interpretation of dialectical "necessity" in the Logic for which I have argued in "Hegel's Dialectical Method."

125. For the idea that in dialectical transitions from one shape of consciousness to the next the latter *preserves the former while modifying it to eliminate its self-contradiction*, see esp. paragraphs 28, 84–87, and also the particular transitions in the *Phenomenology*. This is also a perfectly *general* characteristic of dialectical transitions in Hegel, epitomized for example in his application to them of the term *aufheben* in the triple sense: to preserve, abolish, and elevate. The further criterion of *minimal departure in meaning* is required because Hegel believes that there will typically be *multiple* new shapes which preserve a self-contradictory shape while modifying it in such a way as to eliminate its self-contradiction, and indeed that any later shape in a dialectical sequence will do this for any earlier one. Hegel does not make this further criterion explicit in the *Phenomenology*, but the work's actual transitions conform to it well (see for example the transitions from Sense-certainty to Perception to Force and the Understanding).

Someone might perhaps wonder whether the suggested interpretation of dialectical "necessity" does not violate Hegel's text in implying that, when a shape A dialectically necessitates a shape B, A does not contain B in the sense that excogitation from A alone could furnish acquaintance with B and insight into the necessity of transition to B (as in analytical implication, for example), but rather an individual occupying shape A must become acquainted with shape B in some other way in order for either acquaintance with B or recognition of the necessity of transition to B to take place. For does not paragraph 26 imply that in showing the occupant of a nonscientific viewpoint the dialectical ladder leading from his viewpoint to Science the *Phenomenology* will "show him this standpoint [i.e., Science's] *within* himself" (emphasis added)? However, "within" is here only an as yet uninterpreted metaphor. And the interpretation of dialectical "necessity" which I have suggested fits perfectly in the relevant respects with what the *Phenomenology* says about dialectical transitions in its more detailed remarks in the Introduction: the individual who occupies a given shape experiences the transition to a higher shape and its new conception of the object as a transition to "a second object which we come upon by chance and externally"; the "necessity . . . proceeds . . . , as it were, behind the back of consciousness"; it is only "for us" who have already made acquaintance with the higher shape that the emergence of this shape yields a type of "necessity" which seems capable of performing the philosophical functions for which the *Phenomenology* requires dialectical "necessity"—namely, compelling non-Hegelian individuals to move from their current non-Hegelian viewpoints to other viewpoints lying in the direction of Hegelian Science, and revealing the systematicity (and thence completeness) of the shapes of consciousness covered in the work; and (c) it seems to make perfectly reasonable philosophical sense.

Still, the intelligibility and unobjectionableness of the *Phenomenology*'s dialectical method *in principle* by no means ensure that its *applications* in the work are successful, that the work really does (or could) succeed in identifying in the history of thought a series of shapes of consciousness which display self-contradictions and necessary transitions of the sort envisaged by the method. If the work does not (and could not), then the epistemological project sketched in this chapter—and likewise the pedagogical project sketched in the last and the metaphysical project sketched in the next—are in deep trouble, and we may in the end have to agree with Kierkegaard, who wrote in connection with the dialectical method that we should "hold [Hegel] in honor, as one who has willed something great, though without having achieved it."[126] However, this is a large question which could only be satisfactorily decided by a detailed commentary (ideally, one written with an eye, not only to the text as it stands, but also to ways in which it might be reconstructed).

* * *

Finally, a few observations are in order concerning the broader significance of the epistemological project which we have explored in this chapter. The importance of this project for a proper understanding of the *Phenomenology* should require no further comment. But the project is also important for several further reasons.

First, this aspect of the *Phenomenology* shows how deeply mistaken is the very damaging reputation which Hegel suffered until recently as a thinker careless about matters of epistemology in general and skepticism

---

and its new conception of the object "appears at the same time as movement and a process of becoming," that is, as necessary (par. 87). We should therefore, I suggest, use our interpretation of dialectical "necessity" to cash out the literal value of the metaphor at par. 26 of a dialectically necessitated standpoint being "within" the viewpoint which dialectically necessitates it, rather than seeing that mere metaphor as grounds for a contrary interpretation.

126. S.A. Kierkegaard, *Concluding Unscientific Postscript*, trans. D.F. Swenson and W. Lowrie (Princeton, N.J.: Princeton University Press, 1974), p. 100.

in particular. Such an interpretation has been common among Hegel specialists. For example, according to Baillie, "Whether thought is able to know, or how far it can know being at all, is a problem which from the start [Hegel] never seems to have considered"; Hegel "at once assumes that the knowledge which philosophy professes to furnish is possible, is not to be sought or justified by a preliminary inquiry, but has simply to be expounded and exhibited."[127] Similarly, Solomon states that Hegel's position is characterized by a "refusal to take skepticism seriously," a "commonsensical insistence that skepticism is an absurdity, not a position worth refuting."[128] And this reading of Hegel has been quite as deeply entrenched, and probably more so, among non-specialists. For example, Scruton has recently written: "Much of Hegel's metaphysics develops independently of any epistemological basis . . . This makes Hegel's metaphysics so vulnerable to skeptical attack that it has now little to bequeath us but its poetry."[129] Contrary to such interpretations, we have seen that Hegel has very clearly and cogently thought-out views about which skeptical and other epistemological challenges have philosophical merit and which do not, and that he goes to great and ingenious lengths to address those which, in his view, do on behalf of his own philosophical system.

Second, whether or not one ultimately finds his *responses* to them on behalf of his philosophical system convincing, Hegel's views concerning which skeptical and other epistemological challenges are philosophically important and which not are cogent and important in their own right. This is especially true of the sharp distinction which he draws between ancient and modern forms of skepticism, and his positive assessment of the former and negative assessment of the latter—as argued for in *The*

---

127. Baillie, *The Origin and Significance of Hegel's Logic* (London: Macmillan, 1901), p. 42.

128. Solomon, *In the Spirit of Hegel*, pp. 184–85. In fairness, Solomon does go on to qualify this, noting—correctly—that it is truer of Hegel's attitude to modern than of his attitude to ancient skepticism. However, it turns out that Solomon only sees Hegel as taking ancient skepticism more seriously in the minimal sense that he offers the criticisms of it found in the *Skepticism* section of the *Phenomenology* (pp. 461–65). This falls far short of the sort of deep preoccupation with and elaborate defense against ancient skepticism which has been delineated in this chapter.

129. R. Scruton, *From Descartes to Wittgenstein* (New York: Harper and Row, 1982), p. 178. Scruton sees evidence of this in the fact that Hegel "avoids the first-person standpoint of Descartes" (ibid., p. 178). But, as we have noted, that avoidance, far from bespeaking a carelessness about epistemology and skepticism, is largely the product of an unusually deep understanding of and concern to do justice to the same.

Relation of Skepticism to Philosophy and reflected in the *Phenomenology*.

Third, this issue goes to the very heart of the difference between the continental and the Anglo-Saxon traditions in philosophy. If one had to name a single feature which has distinguished the approaches to philosophy in these two traditions, a prime candidate, it seems to me, would be the fact that continental philosophers have, by and large, retained a sensitivity to the ancient conception of the skeptical challenge to belief, in particular the ancient skeptical equipollence problem, while Anglo-Saxon philosophers have generally lost touch with this skeptical tradition and substituted for it alternative skeptical problems such as the "veil of perception" problem instead.

This characterization of the continental tradition holds true *before* Hegel not only of such obvious cases as Montaigne and Bayle, in whom the dominating influence of ancient skepticism and in particular the equipollence problem is impossible to miss, but also of such philosophers as Descartes, Kant, and Fichte, whose debt to the ancients in their conception of the skeptical challenge which philosophy must address is less obvious and has generally been overlooked, especially by Anglo-Saxon interpreters.

Thus, to run through these figures briefly, Descartes's fundamental conception of the skeptical challenge to belief was, I would argue, equipollence skepticism.[130] This is easily overlooked because the "skeptical" method of doubt which he deploys in the First Meditation is *not* equipol-

---

130. Some prima facie evidence for this claim: (i) This is what one would expect given the dominance of ancient equipollence skepticism in the conceptions of skepticism belonging to Descartes's immediate predecessors—above all Montaigne, especially in his *Apology for Raymond Sebond*. (ii) We can see Descartes's early interest in and facility with equipollence arguments from a public display which he gave in this manner at the home of Cardinal Bagni around 1628 (on which see R.H. Popkin, *The History of Skepticism from Erasmus to Spinoza* [Berkeley: University of California Press, 1979], pp. 174–75). (iii) That Descartes's fundamental conception of skepticism was equipollence skepticism is confirmed by his allusions to equipollence skepticism in his texts. For example, in the *Rules* he writes that "since scarce anything has been asserted by one man the contrary of which has not been alleged by another, we should be eternally uncertain which of the two to believe" (*The Philosophical Works of Descartes,* trans. E.S. Haldane and G.R.T. Ross [Cambridge: Cambridge University Press, 1911], 1:6). And in the *Discourse* he writes similarly that "[philosophy] has been cultivated by the most outstanding minds of several centuries, and . . . nevertheless up to now there is no point but is disputed and consequently doubtful" (*Descartes: Philosophical Writings,* trans. G.E.M. Anscombe and P.T. Geach [London: Nelson University Paperbacks, 1971], p. 12).

lence skepticism, not the procedure of generating *equally strong* arguments for and against propositions in order to motivate suspension of judgment about them, but instead a procedure of suspending judgment on any proposition for which one can find "*some* reason for doubt" rendering it "not entirely certain and indubitable," such as the dream-hypothesis or the evil-genius-hypothesis, even if this leaves the proposition, as Descartes concedes, only "doubtful in a way . . . but . . . yet highly probable, and far more reasonably believed than denied."[131] However, this method of doubt is not Descartes's conception of skepticism itself, and hence does not show that he has a conception of skepticism different from equipollence skepticism. Rather, it is a procedure which he has devised as part of a strategy for defeating, precisely, equipollence skepticism. This procedure is motivated by the ambition of setting aside in as efficient a way as possible *at least* all those beliefs which an equipollence skeptic could call into question (for if one can generate an argument against a proposition as strong as any argument for it, *a fortiori* one can generate "*some* reason for doubt" about it rendering it "not entirely certain and indubitable"), in the hope and expectation that when this is done there will prove to be a residue of beliefs which are left over (in particular, beliefs about one's own *cogitatio*), and which the equipollence skeptic therefore could not possibly call into question.[132]

Kant too was deeply influenced by equipollence skepticism.[133] Thus, long before the development of the critical philosophy was influenced by concerns about "veil of perception" skepticism (which played hardly any role in its original motivation, and emerged with real force only in the second edition of the *Critique of Pure Reason*), and even before it was influenced by the Humean skeptical thoughts concerning the concept of causal necessitation and the principle of sufficient reason to which the *Prolegomena to Any Future Metaphysics* famously pays tribute as a "reminder" which woke Kant from "dogmatic slumber" in metaphysics and set him on the path toward the critical philosophy (some time in the early

---

131. *Descartes: Philosophical Writings*, pp. 61, 65; emphasis added.

132. Note that it is a virtue of this interpretation of Descartes's intentions that it fundamentally absolves him of the commonly leveled charge that he has just arbitrarily and illegitimately raised our usual standards for appropriate belief and/or claims to knowledge.

133. On the complicated question of the role played by various sorts of skepticism, including equipollence skepticism, in motivating and shaping the critical philosophy, see my "Kant and Skepticism concerning Metaphysics" (unpub.).

1770s), it was Pyrrhonian equipollence skepticism which in the mid-1760s first really shook Kant's faith in the precritical discipline of metaphysics, leading him to the despair of the discipline which we find in the 1766 work *Dreams of a Spirit Seer,* and thence eventually to the radical reconception of it which produced the critical philosophy.[134] Moreover, the ambition of overcoming equipollence skepticism in connection with metaphysics remains prominent within the texts of the critical philosophy themselves.[135]

Fichte too is deeply concerned with and motivated by equipollence skepticism at points in his work. Thus in *The Science of Knowledge* he argues that (i) there are two and only two alternative philosophical principles available for explaining experience, "idealism" and "dogmatism" (i.e., realism),[136] but (ii) since this is a disagreement between first principles it cannot be decided theoretically (this is clearly an application of

---

134. Thus, in a letter from the year of the *Critique of Pure Reason*'s first publication, 1781, Kant writes of the year 1765: "I saw at that time that this putative science [of metaphysics] lacked a touchstone with which to distinguish truth from deception, since different but equally persuasive metaphysical propositions lead inescapably to contradictory conclusions, with the result that one proposition inevitably casts doubt on the other" (*Emmanuel Kant: Philosophical Correspondence 1759–99,* trans. A. Zweig [Chicago: University of Chicago Press, 1967], p. 97). And we read in Kant's *Information Concerning the Structure of Lectures in the Winter Semester 1765–66* from the very period in question that existing metaphysics constitutes just "an illusion of science" and that "the special method of instruction in [metaphysical] philosophy is zetetic, as some ancients called it (from *zētein*), that is to say investigative" (*Kants Werke* [Berlin: de Gruyter, 1968], 2:307), where by a "zetetic" method Kant can only mean the equipollence method of the Pyrrhonists (cf. his observation in the *Blomberg Logic* of 1771 that the Pyrrhonists described themselves as "zetetici").

135. Thus the *Critique of Pure Reason* opens with reflections on the "darkness and contradictions," the "battlefield of endless controversies," in which metaphysics embroils itself in transcending the limits of experience, noting that reason's "dogmatic employment . . . lands us in dogmatic assertions to which other assertions, equally specious, can always be opposed—that is, in skepticism," and promises that by contrast the critical philosophy will lead to "scientific knowledge" in the discipline (Aviii, B22–23; cf. similar remarks in the preface and preamble of the *Prolegomena to Any Future Metaphysics;* Kant is of course thinking here largely of the Antinomies, but there is also rather more to his thought than that). (Note also in this connection that Kant's usual conception of skepticism *simpliciter* in the texts of the critical philosophy is equipollence skepticism: "A skeptical objection sets assertion and counter-assertion in mutual opposition to each other as having equal weight, treating each in turn as dogma and the other as the objection thereto. And the conflict, as the being thus seemingly dogmatic on both the opposing sides, is taken as showing that all judgment in regard to the object is completely null and void" [*Critique of Pure Reason,* A388–89].)

136. *The Science of Knowledge,* pp. 8–9.

the equipollence problem in the version of the fourth trope of Agrippa),[137] so that (iii) inclination and interest must decide between them instead.[138]

Again, *after* Hegel one can point to such diverse figures as Kierkegaard and the later Wittgenstein as examples of continental thinkers who retain a strong sensitivity to the equipollence difficulties raised by the ancient skeptics.[139]

Hegel can therefore be seen as in a sense representing the continental tradition as a whole in his conception of skepticism. Moreover, as I have attempted to show in this chapter, he is an unusually self-aware and cogent representative of it against such alternative conceptions of skepticism as have predominated in the Anglo-Saxon world.[140]

---

137. Ibid., p. 12: "Neither of these two systems can directly refute its opposite, for their quarrel is about the first principle, which admits of no derivation from anything beyond it; each of the two, if only its first principle is granted, refutes that of the other; each denies everything in its opposite, and they have no point at all in common from which they could arrive at mutual understanding and unity."

138. Ibid., pp. 14–15: "Reason provides no principle of choice . . . Hence the choice is governed by caprice, and since even a capricious decision must have some source, it is governed by *inclination* and *interest*. The ultimate basis of the difference between idealists and dogmatists is thus the difference of their interests."

139. See for example Kierkegaard's conception in *Either/Or* of a fundamental conflict between an "aesthetic" and an "ethical" view of life which is not resolvable by rational means, but only by a non-rational choice; and Wittgenstein's position in *On Certainty* that such fundamental disagreements as those between people who support and people who oppose the biblical story of the creation, or between physicists and oracle-users, are not derived from or resolvable by reasons, but rather rooted in and decided by action and forms of life. In both of these positions one can see the strong influence of the equipollence problem in the form of the fourth trope of Agrippa. In this, and in their ultimate resort to non-rational choice or to the affective side of man, both positions stand in a direct line of descent from Fichte.

140. To end this chapter on and in a suitably equipollent note, Hegel's closest counterpart in the opposing Anglo-Saxon tradition would perhaps be Hume, who not only paradigmatically exemplifies the alternative conception of skepticism, but also in a self-conscious and plausible way contrasts it favorably with the Pyrrhonian skeptical tradition (see esp. *An Enquiry concerning Human Understanding*, bk. 12).

CHAPTER FOUR

Creating God, Meaning, and
Truth: The Metaphysical
Tasks

We have now considered the pedagogical and the epistemological tasks of the *Phenomenology*. In this chapter we shall turn to what, for want of a better term, I am calling the *metaphysical* tasks of the work.[1] These are the tasks of (7) accomplishing Absolute Spirit's essential self-knowledge and thereby its full realization, (8) demonstrating the essentially communal nature of meanings or concepts, (9) establishing the communal conditions of concepthood for Hegelian Science in order to make possible and actual Hegelian Science's conceptual articulation, (10) demonstrating that truth is constituted by enduring communal consensus, and (11) establishing an enduring communal consensus in favor of Hegelian Science in order to make possible and actual Hegelian Science's truth.

Hegel indicates task (7) in the Preface of the *Phenomenology* when he explains that Absolute Spirit is essentially both *what* it is and *aware* of what it is, or in Hegel's terms both "in and for itself," and that while at first it is only *what* it is and so is this only *potentially*, or in Hegel's terms is only "in itself," it must also be what it is *actually* and so must be *aware* of or *know* what it is, or in Hegel's terms "it must also be this for itself,

---

1. I am using the term *metaphysical* here mainly just as a convenient label. It will be quite misleading, however, if the reader thinks of traditional *metaphysica specialis*, which was defined by a concern with supersensuous objects. He or she should rather think of traditional *metaphysica generalis*, which was defined by a concern with the most general and fundamental concepts and principles of things, or of the connected use of the term *metaphysics* common in current British and American philosophy.

193

it must be the knowledge of the spiritual, and the knowledge of itself as Spirit" (par. 25).[2]

This task may best be understood via an explanation of the *Phenomenology*'s central doctrine that "everything turns on grasping and expressing the true [i.e., the Absolute], not only as *substance*, but equally as *subject*" (par. 17)—a doctrine which, Hegel tells us, is the force of his "representation of the Absolute as *Spirit*" (par. 25). This doctrine has two different senses, both of which are crucial for understanding task (7).

In its first sense this doctrine means that the Absolute is itself essentially a self or person. Hegel emphatically rejects conceptions of the Absolute which deny this, such as Spinoza's identification of God with the one substance. Thus he goes on to say at paragraph 17 in allusion to Spinoza: "If the conception of God as the one substance shocked the age in which it was proclaimed, the reason for this was . . . an instinctive awareness that, in this definition, self-consciousness was only submerged and not preserved."[3] Now, for Hegel, the claim that the Absolute is essentially a self automatically carries with it several implications deriving from the model of the essential structure of all selfhood or consciousness which he takes over from his predecessors Kant, Reinhold, and Fichte. According to that model, it will be recalled, selfhood or consciousness essentially comprises three interdependent conditions: consciousness of oneself as such, consciousness of a not-self or object as such, and consciousness of one's representation of a not-self or object as such. Given that he accepts this general model of selfhood, Hegel's claim that the Absolute is essentially a self implies that the Absolute essentially meets each of these

---

2. The contrasting pair of terms "in itself" and "for itself" is used to mark two different distinctions in Hegel: (i) the distinction between merely being ("in itself"$_1$) and being aware that one is ("for itself"$_1$), and (ii) the Aristotelian distinction between being potentially ("in itself"$_2$) and being actually ("for itself"$_2$). In passages such as the one quoted here, Hegel runs these distinctions together. The justification for doing so is that in the case of *consciousness* (whether divine, as here, or human) self-awareness is an essential trait, a necessary condition of existence. Consequently, in the case of consciousness the two distinctions coincide to the extent that a consciousness which *only is* (is only "in itself"$_1$) ipso facto *is only potentially* (is only "in itself"$_2$); and a consciousness which *is actually* (is "for itself"$_2$) ipso facto *is aware* or *knows that it is* (is "for itself"$_1$). (Hegel also uses the terms "in itself" and "for itself" in certain further senses.)

3. Cf. par. 23; also *Encyclopaedia*, par. 573, where Hegel says of the Spinozist and Eleatic apprehension of the Absolute "only as substance," and of similar views in the oriental religions, that "the fault of all these modes of thought and systems is that they stop short of defining substance as subject and as Spirit."

three conditions.⁴ This explains, in particular, his insistence that Absolute Spirit necessarily has consciousness of itself as such, that it must be what it is "for itself, it must be the knowledge of the spiritual, and the knowledge of itself as Spirit," "the Spirit that . . . knows itself as Spirit" (par. 25; cf. Hegel's insistence on God's self-consciousness in criticizing Spinoza at par. 17).⁵ Thus if we want to know why self-consciousness or self-knowledge is for Hegel an essential characteristic of the Absolute, the answer is that this follows from Hegel's conception of the Absolute as essentially a self together with his general model of selfhood. (To digress from our main theme for a moment: Hegel's conception of the Absolute as essentially a self together with his general model of selfhood also explains his insistence that Absolute Spirit must have consciousness of a not-self or object as such: "Spirit . . . is . . . [the] movement of becoming an other to itself, i.e., becoming an object to itself" [par. 36].)⁶

4. For this reason, Solomon is incorrect in thinking it enough to refute Hegel's criticism of Spinoza in such passages as *Phenomenology*, paragraph 17 simply to point out that Spinoza considers thought to be an attribute of substance (*In the Spirit of Hegel*, pp. 256, 633).

5. Note that in the case of Absolute Spirit, or God, Hegel considers an inference from the essentiality of self-*consciousness* to the essentiality of *true* self-*knowledge* admissible, because *God*'s self-consciousness could not but be *true knowledge*. In the case of *human* consciousness, by contrast, Hegel would not consider such an inference admissible (as we have seen).

6. The paradoxical further idea implied in this sentence that Absolute Spirit must *itself* become its own not-self or object is required because of Hegel's fundamental principle that an *Absolute* Spirit must encompass *everything* ("become," not merely "appear to itself as," because, once again, *God*'s conceptions cannot but be *true*). We have here one of the original and fundamental motives behind Hegel's paradoxical doctrine, to be considered further shortly, that God's relation to the sphere of natural objects is one of "the identity of identity and non-identity" (a doctrine reflected at *Phenomenology*, par. 780, for example). Schelling and Hölderlin had presented the general model of selfhood in question here and its inclusion of the positing of a not-self, together with the requirement that the Absolute be exhaustive of everything, as a decisive objection against conceiving the Absolute as a self or consciousness in letters which they wrote to Hegel in 1795 (*Hegel: The Letters*, p. 33), thereby stimulating Hegel to develop this paradoxical doctrine as a way of preserving the Absolute's selfhood or consciousness. Note that this novel and paradoxical aspect of the selfhood or consciousness that Hegel attributes to Absolute Spirit makes it better, strictly, to speak of a *close analogue* of selfhood or consciousness here rather than of selfhood or consciousness *simpliciter*. (The same could be said of the element of conceptual reform implied by Hegel's physicalist and behaviorist theory of the mind.) Such a qualification may indeed already be part of what Hegel means when he writes in 1802 of his philosophy performing "the sublation [Aufhebung] of consciousness and its preservation in one and the very same act" (*Jenaer Schriften*, p. 202). In this connection note also the ambiguity in the *Phenomenol-*

This still leaves it unclear how the *Phenomenology* can have the task of accomplishing Absolute Spirit's essential self-knowledge. How are we to understand this extraordinary suggestion that the *Phenomenology*, this work of Hegel's, contributes something essential to God, something without which God would not be fully real? Here the *second* sense of Hegel's doctrine that the true or Absolute must be grasped not only as substance but also as subject is crucial. In its second sense this doctrine means that the Absolute is identical with, or has as an essential aspect, the *human* subject. One major reason for this is that, in Hegel's view, *the Absolute's essential accomplishment of self-knowledge is identical with the historical process of human subjects progressing toward that knowledge of the nature of the Absolute expressed in Hegelian Science.*[7] Thus the Preface of the *Phenomenology* states that the education of human individuals toward the standpoint of Hegelian Science, "regarded from the side of universal Spirit as substance, ... is nothing but its acquisition of self-consciousness" (par. 28).[8] Because of this identity between the Absolute's essential accomplishment of self-knowledge and the progress of human individuals through history to a grasp of Hegelian Science, the *Phenomenology*'s activity in the modern world of "leading the individual from his uneducated standpoint to knowledge [i.e., to Hegelian Science]" is in Hegel's eyes *identical with the culmination of the Absolute's essential accomplishment of self-knowledge.* Hence the momentous significance ascribed to the *Phenomenology* by task (7)—the significance of achieving Absolute Spirit's essential self-knowledge, of bringing Absolute Spirit or

---

ogy's remark that "the standpoint of consciousness . . . is for Science the antithesis of its own standpoint." *Individual* consciousness or consciousness *tout court*? Mainly the former, certainly, but probably in some degree also the latter.

7. Note that for Hegel, as for Fichte before him, the self-consciousness required for selfhood is essentially an *activity* or *process*. Hence he talks in Fichtean terms of Spirit being "the movement of positing itself" (par. 18), criticizes Schelling's conception of the Absolute's self-consciousness as consisting in "intellectual intuition" on the ground that this "fall[s] back into inert simplicity and . . . depict[s] actuality itself in a non-actual manner" (par. 17), and complains of theories in which "God is only posited *immediately* as subject, but is not represented as the movement of reflecting itself into itself," that "it is only through . . . movement that the content could be represented as subject" (par. 23). (As we saw in chapter 2, for Hegel, *unlike* for Fichte, this position ultimately rests on a theory that mental conditions, such as self-consciousness, are constituted by *physical* activity.)

8. Cf. *Lectures on the Philosophy of World History: Introduction*, p. 95: "The universal Spirit is essentially present as human consciousness. Knowledge attains existence and being for itself in man."

God to full reality for the first time. (To digress briefly from our main theme again: A second reason why the human subject is identical with, or an essential aspect of, the Absolute, for Hegel, is that the Absolute's essential positing of a *not-self* or *object* is identical with the positing of a not-self or object by human consciousness [on which see esp. *Phenomenology*, par. 36].)

Two questions naturally arise at this point. A first is how exactly we are supposed to construe the (rather elegant) theory of the nature of God and his relation to man encapsulated in the two senses of the doctrine that the Absolute is not only substance but also subject. Up to a point the import of this theory is clear; it is clear, in particular, that it involves a rejection of the traditional Judeo-Christian conception of God as *wholly transcendent* of, that is, wholly distinct and independent from, the human and natural sphere (in such a way that he could, for example, fully preexist it before the creation).[9] However, prima facie, this still leaves us with a decision to make between two very different ways of construing the theory: what one might call the *partially transcendent* and the *naturalistic* readings. On the partially transcendent reading, Hegel's idea would be that there is a personal God of whom the human and natural sphere is an essential constituent or aspect, but who in other constituents or aspects transcends this sphere.[10] On the naturalistic reading, by contrast, Hegel would be identifying God with man and nature outright, saying in effect, "Traditional religion has spoken of a supreme person, God; well, if you reflect on what constitutes personhood, namely, the structure articulated in the Kant-Reinhold-Fichte model of consciousness, then you will see that without going beyond the sphere of man and nature you can find a quite sufficient basis for such a conception, since taken as a whole this sphere instantiates that structure in the way explained by my theory."

If we were forced to choose between these two options, we would have to say, it seems to me, that the *Phenomenology* shows a clear preference

---

9. In this respect, Hegel's theory is very much continuous with Spinoza and the Spinoza-revival which swept Germany in the later eighteenth and earlier nineteenth centuries. To take a proximate example, Schelling had already written in 1800 that God "does not exist independently of us, but reveals and discloses himself successively only through the very play of our own freedom, so that without that freedom even he himself *would not be* . . . The absolute acts through each single intelligence whose action is thus *itself* absolute" (*System of Transcendental Idealism* [1800], trans. P. Heath and M. Vater [Charlottesville, Va.: University Press of Virginia, 1981], p. 210).

10. This is Taylor's reading of Hegel's position in the *Phenomenology* and in later works (*Hegel*, esp. pp. 44–45, 100–102, 207).

for the naturalistic over the partially transcendent option (which is certainly a preference for the more original and interesting of the two alternatives).[11] This is just what one would expect given the *Phenomenology*'s general philosophy of mind, which, as we saw in chapter 2, identifies the mind or self and its psychological conditions with physical behavior. For, applied to the divine mind or self, that conception implies an identity of the divine mind or self and its psychological conditions with its physical expression in the human and natural sphere.[12] In accordance with this expectation, the *Phenomenology* is largely conceived as an attempt to dispel as an *illusion* the idea of a (partially) transcendent God and to show that, insofar as there is a God, he is to be found entirely at the level of man and his world.[13] This ambition is epitomized in the *Unhappy Consciousness* section's critique of the transcendent conception of God belonging to the orthodox Christian consciousness: "What it does *not* know is that . . . its object, the unchangeable [i.e., God], which it knows . . . in the form of individuality, is *its own self,* is itself the individuality of consciousness" (par. 216; cf. 207). The same ambition is evident in Hegel's otherwise strikingly different (and much more sympathetic) assessment of Christianity in the *Revealed Religion* section, where he praises it on the ground that its doctrine of God's incarnation as Christ brings it about that "God is sensuously and directly beheld as a self, as an actual individual man . . . There is something hidden from consciousness in its object if the object is for consciousness an '*other*' or something

---

11. I am therefore much in sympathy with Solomon's rejection of Taylor's partially transcendent reading of the *Phenomenology* (*In the Spirit of Hegel,* pp. 5–6). However, Solomon goes too far when he argues further that "Hegel was essentially an atheist . . . There is no God, only man," and that Hegel's "Absolute is in no interesting sense God" (pp. 582, 630). It is so at least in the interesting sense of being a subject who is over and above any particular human subject and who encompasses everything—and indeed also in certain further interesting senses, for example it is in a way both omniscient and omnipotent. (Whether Hegel is really a *Christian* is another matter.) For a more exegetically sensitive corrective to Taylor's reading than Solomon's, see Westphal, *History and Truth,* chap. 7.

12. It will be recalled that Hegel's conception of the identity of the mind or self and its psychological conditions with physical behavior was qualified in certain ways. However, this qualification was not in the direction of conceding there to be something *more* to the mind or self and its psychological conditions than physical behavior—that is, not in the direction of conceiving them as partially transcending physical behavior.

13. In this respect the *Phenomenology* is very much continuous in spirit with Hegel's earlier writings, which, as Taylor himself notes, from the mid-1790s on strove to develop a man-centered theology (*Hegel,* pp. 71–72). In particular, it is continuous with the emphatically antitranscendent Philosophy of Spirit of 1805-6 (*Jenaer Realphilosophie,* pp. 267–72).

alien, and if it does not know it as *its own self* . . . [Consciousness's] object now is the self, but the self is nothing alien; on the contrary, it is the indissoluble unity with itself" (pars. 758–59). Hegel goes on to add that the Christian conception of Christ's death, and the attendant shift in focus from Christ to the Holy Spirit and the Holy Spirit's immanence in the Christian community, refine this message of God's oneness with man into the still more accurate message of God's oneness with human *community* (pars. 779, 781, 787; some of Hegel's reasons for insisting in this way on the vital role of *community* will become clear as the present chapter proceeds).[14]

That is not quite the end of the matter, however. For if we were actually to offer Hegel the choice between the partially transcendent and the

---

14. Hegel's treatment of religion in the intervening *Spirit* chapter seems to me to reflect just the same antitranscendent position. Taylor therefore seems to me mistaken when he offers the following as a summary of the *Spirit* chapter's diagnosis of "the basic error" of the Enlightenment generally and the French Revolution in particular: "It is right to perceive that ultimately rational subjectivity is dominant. But it is wrong in thinking that this subjectivity is simply human, in leaving no place for a cosmic *Geist*" (*Hegel,* p. 182; cf. 185, 373, 402–18, 505, 507, 528). It is not, I think, any part of the *Spirit* chapter's *criticism* of the Enlightenment and the French Revolution that they eliminate (or attenuate) the conception of a God who transcends human subjectivity. On the contrary, that they do so is on Hegel's account one of the greatest marks of their *progress*. Hence, for example, he writes of the Enlightenment: "In *insight* as such, consciousness apprehends an object in such a way that it . . . becomes an object which consciousness permeates, in which consciousness preserves itself, abides with itself, and remains present to itself, and since it is thus the movement of the object, brings it into existence. It is just this that Enlightenment rightly declares faith to be, when it says that what is for faith the absolute being is a being of its own consciousness, is its own thought, something that is a creation of consciousness itself" (par. 549). And he concludes the section on the Enlightenment with the approving observation that "the two worlds are reconciled and heaven is transplanted to earth below" (par. 581). Again, in a similar vein he writes of the French Revolution's principle of absolute freedom that "it is self-consciousness which grasps the fact that its certainty of itself is the essence . . . of the real world as well as of the supersensible world, or conversely that essence and actuality are consciousness's knowledge of *itself* . . . The world is for it simply its own will, and this is a general will" (par. 584). Where the Enlightenment and the French Revolution *do* fall short, in Hegel's eyes, is rather in certain defects at the level of the human community which obstruct the full realization there of a demystified analogue of the debunked transcendent deity—in particular the failure to establish there a satisfactory synthesis of individualism with collectivism. The French Revolution indeed aimed to achieve such a synthesis (pars. 584, 587), but it failed to do so due to its Rousseauian rejection of mediating political structures (pars. 584, 588), and of the restriction of individuals to particular social roles and classes (pars. 585, 588), both of which Hegel regards as necessary conditions for achieving such a synthesis. Only the hard lesson of the Terror has restored men to the acceptance of political mediation and social limitation (par. 593), thereby making possible an eventual attainment of a satisfactory synthesis of individualism and collectivism (par. 595).

naturalistic options, he would, I am confident, decline both, accusing us of remaining wedded here to intrinsically inadequate notions of identity and non-identity, and insisting instead on the need, in thinking of God's relation to man and nature, to raise ourselves to the higher standpoint of "the identity of identity and non-identity," or "*absolute* identity."[15]

However, this doctrine represents a qualification rather than an outright rejection of the naturalistic option, and the degree of qualification involved is, moreover, modest. In this connection three points deserve notice: First, there might be a temptation to understand the doctrine that God's relation to man and nature is one of "the identity of identity and non-identity" as an expression of the partially transcendent option—as though it meant that God was in certain aspects identical with and in others non-identical with man and nature. This temptation should be firmly resisted. For Hegel does not understand the doctrine in this way, and indeed in the course of expounding it explicitly rejects this idea that, as he disparagingly puts it, "God is *composed* [zusammengesetzt] of God and the world."[16]

Second, the doctrine in question not only expresses Hegel's conception of the relation of God to man and nature specifically, but is also a corollary of a novel analysis which Hegel gives of the notion of identity *generally*. It consequently, so to speak, leaves God and man/nature as identical as things could *ever* be for Hegel. In this connection the following details are of central importance: (i) Hegel believes that it is *informative* identity statements, such as that which identifies God with man and nature, that are the fundamental and proper ones; *uninformative* identity statements, such as "God is God," are by contrast merely abuses of language parasitic

---

15. *Difference* essay, *Jenaer Schriften*, pp. 96, 35–41; emphasis added. For this conception in the *Phenomenology*, see esp. pars. 39, 54, 61, 780. In later writings, see for example *Encyclopaedia*, par. 115, addition: "It is very important to arrive at a proper understanding of the true meaning of identity, to which belongs above all else that it not be grasped merely as abstract identity, i.e., not as identity to the exclusion of difference . . . One can say that the true knowledge of God begins with knowing him as identity—as absolute identity." Hegel's most explicit employment of this notion to chart a sort of via media between the idea that God (partially) transcends the sphere of man and nature and the idea that God is simply identical with that sphere is at *Encyclopaedia*, par. 573.

16. *Encyclopaedia*, par. 573. Cf. Hegel's *rejection* in his review of Göschel's *Aphorismen* of an interpretation of his own position as one which implies "not only . . . that God is in man, but also . . . that man is in God, but *only* that man is *in* God, not that man is God," and his *contrasting* there of such a conception with his own doctrine of the identity and difference of God and man (*Sämtliche Werke* 20:293–95).

upon the former.[17] Accordingly, Hegel's analysis of the notion of identity is concerned exclusively with informative identity statements. (ii) Hegel insists on "the identity of identity and non-identity" as the proper analysis of the notion of identity *generally*. This is mainly because he believes all informative identity statements to have the following two characteristics (characteristics which, in each case, he is encouraged to perceive by his inclusion of much "theory" in meaning). (a) He believes that because they involve such a fundamental change in the *conceptions* of the two items involved as that from thinking of them as distinct to thinking of them as the same, they must change the *concepts* of the two items involved as well. In the case of the identification of God with man and nature specifically, therefore, neither the concept of God nor the concepts of man and nature remain the same once the two sides are identified. Hegel makes both the general and the specific points as follows in the *Phenomenology*: "To talk of the *unity* of subject and object, of finite [i.e., man and nature] and infinite [i.e., God], of being and thought, etc. is inept, since object and subject, etc. signify what they are *outside* of their unity, and since in their unity they are not meant to be what their expression says they are" (par. 39).[18] (b) Hegel notes that when we formulate or entertain an informative identity statement we inevitably undergo a psychological transition from thinking of the two items in question as different to thinking of them as identical, and he infers from this that informative identity statements inevitably *express* not only identity but also difference and a transition from difference to identity.[19] His idea that

17. *Science of Logic*, p. 415; *Encyclopaedia*, par. 115.
18. This position is the basis of Hegel's distinction in the *Encyclopaedia* between his own conception of the identity of God with man and nature and the conception of their identity usually attributed to pantheism: his own conception of their identity does not simply identify God with man and nature *as preconceived*, that is, as an "aggregate of finitude" or mere "everything [Alles]," but is rather an "acosmism," a surrender of the idea that man and nature as so preconceived have reality (pars. 50, 573), a "transfiguration [Verklärung] of the natural and spiritual," in which they are "sublated [aufgehoben]" (pars. 573, 115), their reconception "only as the appearance of [God's] power and [God's] splendour," as the appearance of this "pure unity" or "Absolute" (pars. 115, 573).
19. *Science of Logic*, pp. 413–16: "Identity is the reflection-into-self that is identity only as internal repulsion, and is this repulsion as reflection-into-self, repulsion which immediately takes itself back into itself. Thus it is identity as difference that is identical with itself . . . The concrete and application are, in fact, precisely the connection of the simple identical with a manifold that is different from it. Expressed as a proposition, the concrete would at first be a synthetic proposition . . . The fact is that experience contains identity in unity with difference and is the immediate refutation of the assertion that abstract identity as such is something true, for the exact opposite, namely, identity only in union with differ-

the psychological transition is reflected at the semantic level in the very meaning of identity statements derives (once again) from his assumption that much "theory" enters into meaning. For, given this assumption, the fact that a person at first thinks of the two items in question as different from one another is just the sort of fundamental theoretical conception about them that could not but enter into their very concepts, so that at that point their difference is implied in their very concepts; while the subsequent thought of their identity occurs at the semantic level explicitly. (iii) The second part of Hegel's analysis of informative identity statements just mentioned, (b), might seem to render them all implicitly *self-contradictory*, because affirming both non-identity and identity of the same items. However, Hegel argues that this is not the case but only an illusion which arises for the standpoint of common sense.[20] The way to make sense of his claim here to preserve the logical consistency of informative identity statements is to note that part (a) of his analysis implies that to the extent that an informative identity statement involves a transition from the thought of the non-identity of X and Y to the thought of their identity *the meanings of these terms also change,* so that, strictly speaking, no logical contradiction arises.[21] (iv) In Hegel's view, the *commonsense* conception/concept of identity is merely the result of a failure to comprehend this full meaning which informative identity statements implicitly have, their transition from affirming difference to affirming identity, merely the result of abstracting the terminus ad quem from the terminus a quo and the transition—for which reason he often refers to the commonsense conception/concept of identity as "*abstract* identity."[22]

---

ence, occurs in every experience . . . The law of identity itself contains the movement of reflection, identity as a vanishing of otherness."

20. "Reflection [i.e., the standpoint of common sense] is not able to express the absolute synthesis in one proposition . . . To the extent that Speculation [i.e., Hegel's standpoint] is considered from the standpoint of mere Reflection, absolute identity appears in syntheses of opposites, i.e., in antinomies" (*Difference* essay, in *Jenaer Schriften,* pp. 37, 41).

21. The above general analysis of informative identity statements has, in addition to the general motivation just explained, also major theological attractions for Hegel when applied to the identification of God with man and nature specifically. In particular, it promises a way of self-consistently satisfying with this identification both of the two seemingly contradictory requirements that the Absolute or God (α) in order to be a self must posit a *not-self,* and since this is *God* the positing must be *true,* there must really *be* something which is other than the Absolute, yet (β) in order to be *Absolute* must encompass *everything.*

22. The above helps to show one way in which, as I suggested in chapter 2, Hegel's bridging of the dualism between God and man/nature can be even more complete than that envisaged by the Greeks consistently with at the same time nonetheless preserving dualism

Third, Hegel understands his concept of "absolute identity" as, in a way, a synthesis of common sense's abstract concept of identity and contrarily defined concept of non-identity into a new unified but self-consistent concept.[23] Now within such syntheses Hegel generally allows a certain priority to one of the two commonsense concepts synthesized over the other in the outcome.[24] So he does too in this synthesis of common sense's abstract concepts of identity and non-identity into the concept of absolute identity. And the point to be stressed here is that he clearly understands it to be the commonsense concept of *identity* rather than that of non-identity which predominates in the outcome of their synthesis. This can be seen from the fact that it is the idea of identity, rather than that of non-identity, which he conceives as the terminus ad quem in an absolute identity statement, and also from his very choice of such expressions as the "*identity* of identity and non-identity" and "absolute *identity*."

For these three reasons, then, Hegel's insistence that the identity of

---

in some fashion. Roughly, the dualism is bridged more completely than by the Greeks in the sense that an outright identity between God and man/nature is now asserted, but dualism is preserved in the sense that the notion of identity now itself explicitly contains an element of distinguishing.

23. *Difference* essay, in *Jenaer Schriften*, pp. 37–41: "Reflection [i.e., the standpoint of common sense] is not able to express the absolute synthesis in one proposition . . . Reflection must separate what is one in the absolute identity, and express synthesis and antithesis separately in two propositions—in one the identity, in the other the division . . . The first proposition, that of identity, states that contradiction [i.e., non-identity] is =0. The second . . . says that contradiction [i.e., non-identity] is just as necessary as non-contradiction [i.e., identity] . . . To the extent that Speculation [i.e., Hegel's standpoint] is considered from the standpoint of mere Reflection, absolute identity appears in syntheses of opposites, i.e., in antinomies."

To put the point in other terms, Hegel aims to effect an *Aufhebung* of common sense's contrary abstract concepts of identity and non-identity to the concept of "absolute identity," in his usual technical sense of an *elevation* of them to a single more adequate concept, in the course of which they are in a way *preserved*, but a way which also *abolishes* them or in other words modifies their meanings, thereby rendering them no longer contraries and their combination therefore not self-contradictory (an *Aufhebung* analogous to such *Aufhebungen* in the Logic as that from "being" and "nothing" to "becoming").

24. To illustrate this point from a different example, Hegel considers the concept of the Absolute Idea or Absolute Spirit to be a synthesis of the two commonsense concepts of thought or subjectivity and being or objectivity, but he clearly conceives it to accord a certain priority to the former of the two concepts over the latter. One can see this from his very choice of expressions for it: "Absolute *Idea*," "Absolute *Spirit*," "the *Concept*," "*Reason*," etc. And he also makes the point explicitly, arguing, for example, in the *Encyclopaedia* that it would be wrong to call the Absolute Idea the "unity of thought and being" because in the Absolute Idea "thought [encompasses] being, subjectivity [encompasses] ob-

God with man and nature is an "identity of identity and non-identity" or an "absolute identity" represents a qualification rather than a rejection of the naturalistic option, and a relatively modest qualification at that.

A second question which naturally arises is this: Why, if the Absolute's essential accomplishment of self-knowledge is identical with man's attainment of the knowledge of the Absolute contained in Hegelian Science, could it not be achieved by Hegel *alone* coming to understand and know his Science—thus rendering the communication of such understanding and knowledge to other individuals by the *Phenomenology* superfluous? The short answer to this question is that Hegel believes his own, and indeed any other individual's, understanding and knowledge of Hegelian Science to be impossible without a more *general* acquisition of such understanding and knowledge. An investigation of the remaining metaphysical tasks of the *Phenomenology* will now show why he believes this.

* * *

Hegel makes some very puzzling statements about the role of the *Phenomenology* in the Preface of the work. He indicates that the *Phenomenology* prepares the "element" of Science: "What [Spirit] prepares for itself in [the *Phenomenology*] is the element of knowing" (par. 37; cf. 25–27). And he implies that the *Phenomenology* is "the coming-to-be of Science" (par. 27).[25] What are we to make of these puzzling statements? A clue to their meaning is found in an excerpt from a late Jena lecture which Rosenkranz quotes in connection with the *Phenomenology*. In this excerpt Hegel describes "knowing" or Science as the "unity of the universal and the individual self-consciousness," and this unity as the "element" of the Absolute in which Science, beginning with the Logic, develops itself.[26] So we may infer that the *Phenomenology*'s role of preparing Science's "element" and serving as the "coming-to-be of Science" involves the establishment of a "unity of the universal and the individual self-

---

jectivity," though this "encompassing subjectivity, thought . . . is to be distinguished from onesided subjectivity, onesided thought" (par. 215).

25. Cf. the similar statement in Hegel's published Announcement, in appendix XIII. In both contexts Hegel uses the verb *darstellen* which, like its English counterpart "to represent," is ambiguous: it can mean either "depicts" or simply "is." The former is clearly *part* of what Hegel has in mind: the *Phenomenology* depicts the coming-to-be of Science (through shapes of consciousness). But he also means that the work itself *is* the coming-to-be of Science—as can be seen, for example, from the fact that at paragraph 17 he refers to the work itself as "this coming-to-be."

26. Appendix X. Cf. *Phenomenology*, par. 405, where Hegel writes of "the element of universality," qua "not the particular, but the universal, consciousness"; also, par. 417.

consciousness," by which Hegel evidently means some sort of agreement among all individuals in society. That this inference is correct can be seen from the fact that the *Phenomenology* itself advertises its culmination in "the unity of the different independent self-consciousnesses . . . : 'I' that is 'We' and 'We' that is 'I' " (par. 177).

Hegel in fact has two distinguishable concerns in mind when he thus assigns the *Phenomenology* the role of preparing Science's "element" and serving as a "coming-to-be of Science" by establishing communal agreement—one a concern about the *conceptual articulability* of his Science, the other a concern about its *truth*. I shall pursue each of these concerns in turn.

By the time that Hegel wrote the *Phenomenology* he had already for some time held two views about meanings or concepts which quite strikingly anticipate views held by the later Wittgenstein in our own century: (i) In order to possess concepts or to think at all, an individual must possess meaningful *language,* and the scope of his capacity for conceptualization or thought coincides with the scope of his capacity for linguistic articulation. (ii) Meaningful language essentially requires a linguistic *community,* and could not be possessed by an individual in isolation. These two doctrines find early expression in Hegel's Philosophy of Spirit from 1803–4: "Language [Sprache] only exists as the language of a people, and Understanding and Reason likewise . . . Language is something universal [ein Allgemeines] . . . something resounding in the same way in the consciousness of all; every speaking consciousness [jedes sprechende Bewußtsein] immediately comes to be another consciousness in it. In respect of its content too, language for the first time comes to be true language, to express what each person means [meint], in a people."[27] The same doctrines are implied in the *Sense-certainty* section and elsewhere in the *Phenomenology.* Thus, concerning (i), as was noted earlier, the argument of the *Sense-certainty* section assumes that meaning and thought require linguistic expressibility (including pointing as a form of language), and later in the *Phenomenology* Hegel argues explicitly that "if one had the concept, then one would also have the right word" (par. 328).[28] And concerning (ii), Hegel implies in the *Sense-certainty* sec-

---

27. Appendix VIII.
28. Cf. *Encyclopaedia,* par. 462: "It is in names that we *think* . . . We only have determinate, genuine thoughts when we give them the form of objectivity, . . . i.e., the form of externality, and indeed of such an externality as at the same time bears the imprint of the greatest inwardness. Only the *articulated sound,* the *word,* is such an inward external thing.

tion, in a complex piece of wordplay, that any attempt to *meinen* something, that is, to *mean* it *by myself*, must fail because of the fact that "language ... is inherently *allgemein*," that is, employs *general concepts* which are *common to a whole community* (par. 110; cf. 508).[29]

Hegel's commitment to doctrine (i) places him among an important group of thinkers from late eighteenth- and early nineteenth-century Germany who adopted this doctrine, thereby breaking with the dominant Enlightenment position shared by such thinkers as Locke, Hume, and Kant that linguistic ability was inessential to, and no constraint on the scope of, conceptualization and thought, but merely an in-principle-dispensable means for the communication of their autonomous inner realm, and in the process establishing the foundations of modern philosophy of language. Besides Hegel himself, this group prominently included Hamann, Herder, von Humboldt, and Schleiermacher.

Hegel's immediate debt here was almost certainly to Herder, who had written in *On the Cognition and Sensation of the Human Soul*, for instance, that the "medium of our self-feeling and our mental consciousness is—*language* ... Word, language had to come to our aid in order to awaken and guide our innermost vision and hearing ... Thus, as we see, does the child attain its mental constitution [sammelt sich], it learns to speak ... and precisely as a result and in the same way [genau dem zu Folge] to think ... In the deepest languages, also, *reason* and *word* are one single *concept*, one single thing: logos."[30] As in other cases, however, Hegel was no *mere* follower of Herder here, but developed his own arguments for this Herderian position. In the essay just mentioned, Herder's main arguments for it were *empirical* in nature: he argued that deaf and dumb people, that is, people who do *not* have language, lack reason

---

To want to think without words ... is therefore clearly an absurdity ... The inexpressible is in truth only something dark, fermenting, which only achieves clarity when it is able to attain verbal expression."

29. To explain the relevant wordplay: The word *meinen* is used here both in the idiomatic sense "to mean" and in the artificial sense "to appropriate to myself"—an artificial sense based on the first person singular possessive pronoun *mein*, as in *mein Buch*, "my book"; thus Hegel writes at *Encyclopaedia*, par. 20, "What I only *meine* is *mein*, belongs to me as this particular individual" (cf. *Phenomenology*, par. 558). The word *allgemein* is used here in two senses both deriving from its basic etymological meaning of *allen gemein(sam)*, or "common to all," namely, first, in the sense "universal concept" or "general concept" and, second, in the sense "common to all people," in which second sense it also echoes such words as *Gemeinschaft, Gemeinde*, and *Gemeine*, meaning "society" or "community."

30. *Herders Ausgewählte Werke* 3:722–23.

and self-consciousness; and that children develop thought in step with, and in a way which mirrors, their acquisition of language.[31] Hegel's argument, by contrast, is *conceptual* in character, namely, the argument of the *Physiognomy and Phrenology* section considered in chapter 2 for a form of behaviorism concerning mental conditions generally, and in particular for the view that *linguistic* behavioral criteria are central behavioral criteria of conceptual understanding (and hence of any other mental conditions and activities which are *essentially* conceptual as well, such as thought).[32]

Doctrine (ii), the doctrine of the essential *communality* of meaningful language, is only implied, not proved, in the *Sense-certainty* section of the *Phenomenology*. However, it is no mere unproven assumption within the *Phenomenology* as a whole. On the contrary, the work develops an extremely elaborate and interesting argument in support of it. The demonstration of this doctrine is task (8) in our list of the work's tasks, and we should now consider how the work goes about accomplishing it.

Like doctrine (ii) itself, Hegel's argument for it bears a striking resemblance to a line of thought found in the later Wittgenstein, namely, the notorious "rule-following" cum "private language" argument which Wittgenstein gives in support of the same conclusion in the *Philosophical Investigations*. Indeed, this proves to be so to a degree quite undreamed-of even by those commentators who have noted resemblances between Hegel's and Wittgenstein's views in this area.[33]

As Kripke has lucidly explained, the general strategy of Wittgenstein's argument is essentially as follows.[34] Wittgenstein starts out from what is (or at least appears to be) the commonsense conception of the nature of

---

31. Ibid.: "Those born deaf and dumb demonstrate in special tests how deeply reason, self-consciousness, slumbers, when they cannot imitate"; "Thus, as we see, does the child attain its mental constitution, it learns to speak . . . and precisely as a result and in the same way to think. Whoever has observed children, how they learn to speak and think, the peculiar anomalies and analogies which are expressed in the process, will hardly have any further doubts."

32. In his earlier work *Über den Ursprung der Sprache* Herder too had argued for an intimate connection between thought and language on conceptual grounds. But this was merely through the philosophically much less interesting, and later abandoned, maneuver of in effect just deciding to *call* certain fundamental mental operations "language" (specifically, the recognition of distinguishing characteristics, or *Merkmale*). See ibid., esp. pp. 629–30.

33. For example, Taylor, "The Opening Arguments of the *Phenomenology*."

34. S.A. Kripke, *Wittgenstein on Rules and Private Language* (Cambridge, Mass.: Harvard University Press, 1982).

concept-possession, which includes in particular a conception that it is the sort of thing that an individual could in principle accomplish alone. He then undertakes to show that none of the various ways in which one might try to make good sense of this commonsense conception is tenable. This generates a "skeptical paradox": concept-possession cannot occur, at least not as conceived by common sense. To this skeptical paradox he then offers a "skeptical solution," a way of saving the claim that concept-possession occurs, but at the cost of contradicting certain central features of the commonsense conception of the nature of concept-possession, *and in particular the notion that concept-possession is the sort of thing that an individual could in principle accomplish alone*. This, in broad outline, is the strategy of the "rule-following" argument. The "private language" argument then addresses an especially imposing apparent counterexample to the skeptical solution's claim that concept-possession is essentially communal, namely, the apparent possibility of using language meaningfully in ways intelligible only to oneself in the case of one's own sensations. The "private language" argument attempts to show that this is *not* in fact possible, and that the idea that it is so rests upon various misconceptions about the nature of language generally and sensation-language in particular.[35]

Now Hegel, it seems to me, offers in the *Phenomenology*, over the course of the sections from *Sense-certainty* to *The Spiritual Animalkingdom*, an argument for the doctrine that concept-possession essentially requires participation in a linguistic community which is *virtually indistinguishable* from Wittgenstein's in general strategy (and indeed in many details as well). The only significant differences from Wittgenstein's argument in respect of general strategy are the following, which enhance rather than detract from the interest of Hegel's argument: (a) Insofar as Hegel's argument addresses the errors in the conception of a "private language," it does so *at the start* and as an integral *part* of its version of the "rule-following" argument—namely, in the opening *Sense-certainty* section—rather than, as in Wittgenstein, at the end of that argument and as an addendum to it. This is a difference of presentation rather than of substance. (b) As Kripke points out, Wittgenstein, due to a deep convic-

---

35. Among the former, misconceptions about the nature and role of ostensive definition in language are especially salient for Wittgenstein; among the latter, the misconception that first-person avowals of sensations are descriptive in nature, and the failure to recognize that sensation-language depends essentially on behavioral criteria.

tion that common sense and common language are all right as they are, is loath to present his conclusion as one which *really* contradicts common sense or common language, and this basic inconsistency leads him into various contortions and interpretative implausibilities in his statement of the argument.[36] By contrast, Hegel, as we have noted, has no scruples about departing from common sense or common language, and is therefore quite happy to see his conclusion diverge from them in propositional and even conceptual content. He consequently avoids the basic inconsistency and the ensuing contortions and interpretative implausibilities found in Wittgenstein's version of the argument.[37] (c) Hegel in his version of the "rule-following" argument makes a much more serious attempt than Wittgenstein does to demonstrate that he has considered, and shown untenable, *all* ways in which one might try to make good sense of the commonsense conception of concept-possession as something that an individual could in principle accomplish alone. (d) Wittgenstein's serial critique of various attempts to make good sense of this commonsense conception, and his eventual inference to the conclusion that concept-possession is essentially communal, proceed without any particular regard to *history*. Hegel, by contrast, conceives his version of the argument very much in historical terms. Indeed, he believes that in a way the whole argument has already been developed in its proper order by history before him, so that his task in the *Phenomenology* is simply to recapitulate and comprehend what history has already unfolded. Thus, he understands the serial critique of various attempts to make good sense of common sense's individualistic conception of concept-possession which is undertaken in the sections *Sense-certainty* to *The Spiritual Animalkingdom* to run through those attempts in the order of their actual historical emergence. And he understands the conclusion of the argument, the doctrine of the essential communality of concept-possession presented in the section *The Spiritual Animalkingdom*, as a culminating step in that chronological sequence—specifically, as a standpoint developed in modern times by Herder (and then, in continuity with Herder, by Hegel himself).

The central interpretative claim here that Hegel constructs over the

---

36. Kripke, *Wittgenstein on Rules*, esp. pp. 63–66, 69–71.
37. Readers of Wittgenstein who do not believe that he is torn between seeing his conclusion as contradicting common sense or language and denying this, but interpret him as holding the latter position consistently and therefore as consistently directing his argument exclusively against philosophers, are welcome to substitute for "basic inconsistency" in the above sentences "basic implausibility."

course of the sections *Sense-certainty* to *The Spiritual Animalkingdom* an argument for the doctrine that meaning is essentially communal which follows the "skeptical paradox, skeptical solution" pattern should not be altogether surprising. For, as we saw in the last chapter, the very same stretch of text contains *another* argument following this pattern, namely, the argument for concept-object identity. Let us, though, turn to the text in order to illustrate this interpretative claim in some detail.

Consider, to begin with, the "skeptical paradox" part of the argument. A first point to note in this connection is that Hegel understands each of the various "shapes of consciousness" treated in the chapters *Consciousness* through *Reason* to include as one of its essential components a particular conception of its own representations (as we have seen), and in consequence, more specifically, a particular conception of its own *concepts*. Hence the Introduction states in explication of the idea of a "shape of consciousness" that "these two moments, *concept* and object . . . both fall within that knowledge [i.e., the shapes of consciousness] which we are investigating" (par. 84; emphasis added). Moreover, Hegel implies that the shapes of consciousness treated in these chapters are *individualistic,* in the sense that they do not recognize the individual consciousness to be essentially dependent on a community with respect to any of its fundamental components. As Hegel puts the point at the conclusion of these chapters, "All previous shapes of consciousness are abstract forms of [Spirit] . . . In this isolation they have the appearance of existing as such" (par. 440). This implies, in particular, that they conceive their *concepts* in individualistic terms, as the sort of thing that an individual consciousness could at least in principle possess without participating in a community. Accordingly, in his treatment of the specific shapes of consciousness in the chapters *Consciousness* through *Reason* Hegel repeatedly stresses this feature. Thus, as already noted, Sense-certainty is said to conceive of its acts of meaning as a *meinen,* a *meaning by oneself.* Similarly, for Stoicism "the concept is for me straightway *my* concept . . . In thinking I am not in an *other,* but remain simply and solely in communion with myself" (par. 197). Again, the conception of consciousness and meaning belonging to Logical and Psychological Laws (the perspective of Locke and Hume) is depicted as starkly individualistic (pars. 301 ff.). And likewise, Physiognomy is once again said to conceive its own acts of meaning as a *meinen,* a *meaning by oneself* (pars. 319–22). Furthermore, the Introduction promises (pars. 78, 84–85), and we actually find in the specific sections, that the work methodically undertakes to show the essential components of each shape of consciousness, including in particular its conception of its own representations or concepts, to be untenable. In sum, the chapters *Consciousness* through *Reason* are in important part designed to be a survey of a series of different ways of conceiving concept-possession in individualistic terms, as the sort of thing that an individual could in principle accomplish without belonging to a community, in the course of which each of these individualistic conceptions of concept-possession undergoes refutation. This, in general terms, is the "skeptical paradox" part of Hegel's argument.[38] Let us now consider its contents in more detail.

In the *Philosophical Investigations* Wittgenstein implies that a particularly strong temptation to the idea that meaning is something which one could achieve alone, or which could even be unshareable *in principle*, emanates from the conception that meaning is based on, or at least capable of being based on, *the pure ostension of particulars*—whether through acts of pointing (as in the Augustinian model of the nature of language), or through entirely internal analogues of these, acts of concentrating on particulars (as in the conception of a private language).[39] Hegel has a very similar idea in mind when in the *Sense-certainty* section of the *Phenomenology* he depicts a viewpoint which thinks it possible to *meinen*, to mean *by oneself*—and even to do so in ways unshareable *in principle* (par. 105)—by confining oneself to pure acts of pointing to particulars (pars. 105 ff.), or to linguistic analogues of these, pure acts of picking out particulars by means of demonstratives such as "This," "Now," and "Here" (pars. 91 ff.). Wittgenstein's objection to yielding to this temptation to an individualistic conception of meaning is that in fact meaning *is not and could not be* based on a pure ostension of particulars, because in order for acts of ostension to have any definite reference the person who performs them must make their reference definite by construing them in accordance with general concepts—so that *pure* ostension

---

38. Concerning in addition two of Hegel's above-mentioned interest-enhancing elaborations upon the basic strategy which he shares with Wittgenstein in this "skeptical paradox" part of the argument: (α) The *Phenomenology* aims to demonstrate that it has covered *all* individualistic conceptions of concepts, that is, *all* shapes of consciousness—"the entire system of consciousness" (par. 89). (We saw in the last chapter how it aims to demonstrate such complete coverage.) (β) The *Phenomenology*'s treatment of these individualistic conceptions of concepts, or these shapes of consciousness, takes them up in the order of their historical emergence—"the series of configurations which consciousness goes through along this road is, in reality, the detailed history of the education of consciousness" (par. 78).

39. *Philosophical Investigations*, pars. 1, 32, 257 ff.

of particulars is an impossibility, and ostension of particulars is not and could not be the *basis* of other forms of meaning such as possession of general concepts, since it in fact *presupposes* these.[40] Hegel makes fundamentally the same objection in the *Sense-certainty* section. He argues that any attempt to *meinen*, to mean by oneself, through signifying particulars by pure acts of ostension—acts of ostension free of mediation by "universals," or general concepts—is bound to fail because such acts would inevitably lack definite reference, they would inevitably remain indefinite as to reference between any number of particulars. Thus, for example, he argues that any attempt to perform a pure pointing-out of a spatial location must fail because "the here pointed out . . . is . . . a this here which, in fact, is not this here, but a before and behind, an above and below, a right and left. The above is itself similarly this manifold otherness of above, below, etc. The here which was supposed to have been pointed out vanishes in other heres" (par. 108; cf. 107 on times; 110 on contents of space and time).[41] And many of his remarks earlier in the section concerning the verbal analogues of pure acts of pointing, namely, pure uses of demonstratives, can be understood along similar lines (see esp. pars. 96–99).[42]

Sense-certainty is, however, only the first of the series of individualistic

---

40. Ibid., pars. 28–32, 257. This is an orthodox interpretation of Wittgenstein's point. Kripke happens to reject it, appealing to paragraphs 28–29 for textual support (*Wittgenstein on Rules*, p. 84). But paragraphs 30–32 show pretty clearly that Kripke's heterodox reading is untenable.

41. Hegel also makes this point about the inevitable indefiniteness of reference afflicting attempts at a pure pointing-out of particulars by saying that such attempts signify the "universal": "The pointing-out shows itself to be not an immediate knowing, but a movement from the here that is meant through many heres into the universal here which is a simple plurality of heres"; "The pointing-out is the experience of learning that now is a universal" (pars. 108, 107). For Hegel's mention here of the "universal" is largely a way of expressing the idea of indefiniteness of reference among a multiplicity of particulars, as can be seen from some of his other remarks about the "universal" in the *Sense-certainty* section, for example: "A simple thing . . . which is neither this nor that, a not-this, and is with equal indifference this as well as that—such a thing we call a universal"; " 'Here' . . . is indifferently house or tree. Again, therefore, the 'this' shows itself to be . . . a universality" (pars. 96, 98).

42. Note that in accordance with this diagnosis of Sense-certainty's error, the *next* conception of meaning presented in the *Phenomenology*, that belonging to Perception, *recognizes* that "universals," or general concepts, are fundamental to meaning: "Perception . . . takes what is present to it as a universal . . . Universality is its principle in general" (par. 111). And in particular it recognizes that they are required in order for acts of ostension such as uses of demonstratives to pick out particulars: "The sense-element is . . . present . . . as a universal, or as that which will be defined as a property . . . This salt is a simple

conceptions of meaning which the *Phenomenology* sets out to refute in order to generate its "skeptical paradox." Since the idea that meaning could occur without "universals" or general concepts has now been discredited, henceforth the individualistic conceptions of meaning dealt with will be ones which acknowledge, or at least do not deny, the fundamental role of "universals" or general concepts in meaning, though while still attempting to explain these and their possession in individualistic terms. The first is Perception. Perception conceives "universals" or general concepts as *in and constitutive of* sensible particulars: "The object which I apprehend presents itself as a one; but I also perceive in it a property which is a universal"; "This salt is a simple 'here,' and at the same time manifold; it is white and also tart, also cubical in shape, of a specific gravity, etc. All these properties are in a single simple 'here' " (pars. 117, 113). Aristotle is a good example of such a conception of "universals" or general concepts, and Hegel no doubt has him partly in mind here.[43] However, Aristotle was not the first to adopt this conception; as noted in chapter 2, it can already be found in the early Platonic dialogue the *Euthyphro,* for example.[44] And Hegel apparently regards it as in some fashion common sense's preferred conception of "universals."[45] This conception remains individualistic in that its account of "universals" and their comprehension does not preclude, but rather suggests, that they could exist for and be understood by a solitary individual. Hegel could have raised a number of familiar objections against this conception of "universals" or general concepts (e.g., its difficulties in accounting for the existence of general concepts which altogether lack instances in sensible particulars, or for the continued existence at later times of general concepts which have at earlier times ceased to have them). Instead, however, he attempts to demonstrate that this conception of "universals" entails a self-contradictory conception of sensible particulars, so that it is itself implicitly self-contradictory also. The general thrust of his argument for the claim that a conception of "universals" as in and constitutive of sensible particulars entails a self-contradictory conception of sensible particu-

---

here, and at the same time manifold; it is white and also tart, also cubical in shape . . . etc." (par. 113).

43. This is further suggested by Hegel's invocation of the Aristotelian distinction between a thing's essential and accidental properties at paragraphs 124 ff.

44. *Euthyphro,* 5d.

45. Perception's standpoint is one of what is "often called 'sound common sense' " (par. 131).

lars is that (a) it entails the essential dependence of each sensible particular, via its constitutive "universals," on the existence of other sensible particulars, its "being-for-another," because the "universals" in question would by their nature have to be in more than one particular, and in addition require in order to be determinate the existence of contrary "universals" which would in turn have to be in a further multiplicity of particulars, but (b) this contradicts a fundamental conception of the sensible particular as something that is essentially independent, or "for itself" (pars. 114, 117, 123–28). Due to this implicit self-contradiction in Perception's conception of sensible particulars, its conception of "universals" as in and constitutive of sensible particulars is implicitly self-contradictory as well (pars. 129–30).[46]

The next individualistic conception of meaning occurs in the section *Force and the Understanding*. This is Platonism, the theory that "universals" or general concepts are a kind of object existing in a supersensible realm separate from the realm of sensible appearances where we find ourselves and the general run of *instances* of general concepts (a supersensible realm which on Plato's conception is alone genuinely real, in contrast to the realm of sensible appearances, which is self-contradictory), and that conceptual understanding consists in some sort of mental link between us and these supersensible objects. Hegel describes this conception as follows in the section *Force and the Understanding:* "There now opens up above the sensuous world, which is the world of appearance, a supersensible world which henceforth is the true world"; "[The] true essence of things has now the character of not being immediately for consciousness; on the contrary, consciousness has a mediated relation to the inner being ... The middle term which unites the two extremes, the Understanding and the inner world ... is ... called appearance, for we call being that is directly and in its own self a non-being a surface show ... [The] truth is the positive, viz. the universal, the object that, in itself, possesses being. The being of this object for consciousness is mediated by the movement of appearance ... This inner is ... for consciousness an extreme over against it ... The inner is for it certainly concept" (pars. 143–44; cf. 132,

---

46. This criticism of Perception's individualistic conception of meaning is especially noteworthy for its clear exhibition of a feature which, strictly speaking, Hegel intends each of his criticisms of individualistic conceptions of meaning in the *Phenomenology* to have: it convicts the conception in question not just of being untenable but of being untenable *because implicitly self-contradictory*.

and also the allusions to the *Republic*'s Cave and Sun metaphors at par. 146). This theory of concepts and conceptual understanding is once again individualistic in the sense that it does not preclude, but rather suggests, that concepts could exist for and be comprehended by a solitary individual. In the section *Force and the Understanding* Hegel combines his presentation and critique of this Platonist conception of meaning with the presentation and critique of the realist conception of force which I discussed in chapter 2—for he (plausibly) sees a strong resemblance between these two conceptions, and believes them guilty of similar shortcomings. One part of his critique of the Platonist conception of meaning (developed with primary reference to this conception, and only secondary reference to the realist conception of force) is that if "universals" or general concepts were supposed to exist in a supersensible realm separate from and differently constituted than the realm of sensible appearances, as Platonism maintains, then it would be very unclear how we could ever achieve the knowledge of them which, according to Platonism, constitutes conceptual understanding (par. 146). Hegel's other, and most interesting, objection (developed with primary reference to the realist conception of force, and only secondary reference to Platonism) is that the Platonist conception of meaning leaves the connection between conceptual understanding, on the one hand, and its characteristic manifestations in behavior, on the other, *too contingent*.[47] To spell out this objection a little more fully: Platonism, in conceiving a person's understanding of a general concept as consisting in some sort of mental link between him and a supersensible form, implies that the connection between a person's understanding of a general concept and his correct employment of the word(s) for it in linguistic behavior (e.g., in application to particulars) is entirely contingent. However, as Hegel argues explicitly in the *Physiognomy and Phrenology* section, this connection, like the connections between other mental conditions and their characteristic behavioral manifestations, is *not* in fact contingent but rather *necessary*: "If one had the concept, then one would also have the right word" (par. 328). The Platonist conception of meaning must therefore be false.

---

47. At paragraph 152 Hegel makes this point, with primary reference to the realist conception of force, as follows: "Necessity here is an empty word . . . Electricity, as simple force, is indifferent to its law . . . ; and if we call the former its concept but the latter its being, then its concept is indifferent to its being. It merely *has* this property [of expressing itself in this way], which just means that this property is not in itself necessary to it." Note

The next noteworthy individualistic conception of meaning occurs in the *Stoicism* section, and is the conception belonging to ancient Stoicism. Unlike Perception, but like the Platonism of Force and the Understanding, Stoicism, according to Hegel, conceives concepts as sharply distinct from their instances in the sphere of sensible particulars: "Here the concept as an abstraction cuts itself off from the multiplicity of things" (par. 200). Hegel has in mind here the Stoic conception of the meanings expressed by meaningful speech as *lekta*—roughly what we would call predicates and propositions—of an incorporeal nature sharply distinct from the corporeal nature of sensible particulars.[48] As we noted earlier, the *Stoicism* section stresses the *individualistic* character of this Stoic conception of meaning. For this is once again a conception which envisages conceptual understanding as the sort of thing that an individual could in principle accomplish alone. Hegel does not, it seems, offer any special critique of this conception of meaning in the *Stoicism* section. However, the reason for that is pretty clear, and it represents no real omission. For, obviously, this conception of meaning is vulnerable to exactly the same objections as were raised against the Platonist conception of meaning in the section *Force and the Understanding*.[49]

---

the allusions here to the "concept," indicative of the secondary reference to the Platonist theory of meaning.

48. The main *difference* which Hegel sees between Platonism's and Stoicism's conceptions of meaning is that Stoicism thinks of concepts in less metaphysically and theologically extravagant terms than Platonism, and therefore as more intimately present to human minds: in Stoicism "the concept is for me straightway *my* concept," "my activity in conceptual thinking is a movement within myself" (par. 197). On the other hand, this intimacy does not yet go as far as it will later for the empiricist theory of meaning which Hegel proceeds to consider in the *Logical and Psychological Laws* and *Physiognomy and Phrenology* sections, for which concepts have no autonomy from individual minds at all, but are merely "ideas" within them. In Stoicism, "consciousness does indeed destroy the content as an alien being when it thinks it; but the concept is a determinate concept, and this determinateness of the concept is the alien element which it has within it" (par. 200).

49. Having considered the development in conceptions of meaning depicted in the sections *Sense-certainty, Perception, Force and the Understanding,* and *Stoicism,* we can now see more clearly what Hegel meant when he wrote in paragraph 33 of the Preface that "in ancient times" the "proper and complete formation of the natural conciousness" consisted in "purging the individual of an immediate, sensuous mode of apprehension," in "the fact that the object represented becomes the property of pure self-consciousness, its elevation to universality in general," "philosophizing about everything it came across, [consciousness] made itself into a universality," so that in more "modern times . . . the individual finds the abstract form ready-made."

Conversely, these remarks in the Preface provide some confirmation of several points which have been made or implied above concerning the *historical* character of the sequence

The next noteworthy individualistic conception of meaning occurs in the section *Logical and Psychological Laws,* which is mainly concerned with the empiricists Locke and Hume, and in the first part of the section *Physiognomy and Phrenology,* which is concerned with Lavater's physiognomy. According to Hegel's interpretation, Locke and Hume develop, and Lavater's physiognomy then takes over, a model of mental conditions in general, and of meaning or conceptual understanding in particular, which is individualistic, dualistic, and introspectivist. For these thinkers, meaning or conceptual understanding, like other mental conditions, occurs entirely within the mind of the individual, has a merely contingent relation to any physical expressions of it which may occur, and is authoritatively known through and only through the individual's introspection: this perspective "regards as the unessential outer the deed itself and the performance, whether it be that of speech or a more durable reality; but it is the being-within-self of the individual which is for it the essential inner . . . Among the two sides which the practical consciousness has . . . —what it *means alone* [Meinen] by its deed and the *deed* itself— [this perspective] selects the former as the true inner; this is supposed to have its more or less *unessential* expression in the deed" (par. 319). This characterization well captures the position of Locke and Hume and their eighteenth-century followers, for whom meanings were "ideas" located entirely within individual minds, only contingently related to their expressions in linguistic or other forms of physical behavior, and authoritatively knowable through and only through the individual's introspection. In the section *Physiognomy and Phrenology* Hegel recurs to his term of art *meinen,* "to mean by oneself," in order to describe this model of the mind—thereby emphasizing both that acts of meaning are included among the mental items to which the model is applied, and that they are conceived by this model in purely *individualistic* terms, as the sort of thing that could in principle quite well occur within a solitary individual. Hegel's criticisms of this empiricist conception of meaning are essentially

---

of conceptions of meaning in the sections *Sense-certainty* to *Stoicism:* (a) They confirm that Hegel understands these as a historical development, a chronological sequence. (b) They confirm that he understands them to fall within ancient history specifically, and the later ones to belong to ancient philosophical movements such as Platonism and Stoicism ("ancient times," "philosophizing about everything it came across"). (c) They thereby confirm that Perception, falling as it does *before* the treatment of Platonism in the section *Force and the Understanding,* must be conceived by Hegel as an outlook which at least in part antedates Aristotelianism.

(a) that it is mistaken in conceiving the relation between acts of meaning and their expressions in physical behavior (and especially *linguistic* physical behavior) as merely contingent, since the latter are on the contrary necessary and sufficient for justified ascription of the former, and (b) that consequently it is also mistaken in conceiving an individual's introspection as authoritative in assessing his meaning, rather than the observation of his physical behavior (especially his *linguistic* physical behavior). Thus, concerning (a), Hegel argues that appropriate physical behavior (especially linguistic physical behavior) is *necessary* for justified ascription of meaning: "The deed does away with what is meant privately [das Gemeinte]"; "If one had the concept, then one would also have the right word" (pars. 322, 328). And he argues that it is *sufficient* as well: "[The deed's] being is not merely a sign, but the fact itself" (par. 322). And concerning (b), he argues, accordingly, that it is not an individual's introspection but the observation of his physical behavior (especially his linguistic physical behavior) which is authoritative in assessing his meaning: "When his performance and his inner possibility, capacity, or intention are contrasted, it is the former alone which is to be regarded as [the individual's] true actuality, even if he deceives himself on the point, and turning away from his action into himself, fancies that in this inner self he is something other than what he is in deed"; "This is at once incompetence and deceit, to fancy and to pretend that one merely has not the right word, and to hide from oneself that really one has failed to get hold of the thing itself, i.e., the concept. If one had the concept, then one would also have the right word" (pars. 322, 328). The empiricist's individualistic conception of meaning is for these reasons untenable.

Finally, Hegel considers the conception that the mind and its mental conditions, including by implication conceptual understanding, are identical with the brain and spinal cord and their activity, a conception which he ascribes to the phrenologist in the second part of the *Physiognomy and Phrenology* section (pars. 327, 331). This conception of mental conditions such as conceptual understanding is once again individualistic in the sense that it does not preclude, but rather suggests, that they could in principle occur in a solitary individual. Hegel devotes little space to refuting this physicalist conception.[50] However, that is because his critique of the dualist conception in the course of dealing with physiognomy

---

50. He instead concentrates his critical attack mainly on the phrenologist's additional views concerning the relation between the mind = brain and the skull.

has already made clear enough the nature of his objection to it: in this physicalist conception mental conditions such as conceptual understanding are once again identified with something which has only a *contingent* relation to physical *behavior,* but that cannot be squared with the fact that the satisfaction of appropriate behavioral criteria (including in particular linguistic behavioral criteria) is in reality necessary and sufficient for justified ascription of mental conditions such as conceptual understanding.[51] Indeed, it is by this point clear enough that Hegel would deploy this argument from the decisiveness of behavioral criteria (including in particular linguistic behavioral criteria) against *any* account which identified such mental conditions as conceptual understanding with conditions or activities of an individual other than his physical behavior.[52]

The above steps constitute the "skeptical paradox" part of Hegel's argument: none of the various ways in which one might attempt to make good sense of the phenomenon of meaning within the *individualistic* framework of common sense proves tenable, not Sense-certainty's pure-ostension model of the basis of meaning, nor Perception's proto-Aristotelian model, nor Force and the Understanding's Platonist model, nor Stoicism's *lekta*-model, nor the empiricist model of Logical and Psychological Laws and Physiognomy, nor Phrenology's physicalist model, nor for that matter any other model which identified conceptual understanding with a nonbehavioral condition of the individual. As far as the

---

51. One can see that Hegel conceives this argument from the decisiveness of behavioral criteria as disposing, not only of the dualist conception of mental conditions such as conceptual understanding advanced by Locke, Hume, and Lavater, but also of physicalist conceptions of them which identify them with physical items or processes other than physical behavior, like the phrenologist's conception, from the fact that he deploys the argument at paragraph 322, not only against the physiognomist's official dualist identification of such mental conditions with inner mental processes, but also against any tendency in the physiognomist to identify them with the facial characteristics which according to the physiognomist's *official* position are merely their signs. For further hints that Hegel would extend the argument against the physicalism of the phrenologist, see pars. 337, 339.

52. In relying so heavily on this argument from the decisiveness of physical behavioral criteria (including especially linguistic ones), Hegel's version of the "rule-following" argument once again—as in its criticism of the individualistic theory of meaning advanced by Sense-certainty—strikingly resembles Wittgenstein's not only in general strategy but also in *detail*. For Wittgenstein too standardly deploys an argument from the decisiveness of behavioral criteria (including especially linguistic ones) in order to discredit the various individualistic accounts of conceptual understanding which he considers in the course of the "rule-following" argument. (It is, incidentally, a shortcoming of Kripke's treatment of the "rule-following" argument, considered as *exegesis* of Wittgenstein, that it obscures this fact.)

individual goes, all that we have that is of relevance to his meaning is his physical behavior (including his linguistic behavior). But that does away with individualistic meaning altogether: "The true being of a man is . . . his deed; in this the individual is actual, and it is the deed which does away with what is meant privately [das Gemeinte]" (par. 322).[53]

> 53. We should pause at this point to ask *why*, after the failure of all other individualistic conceptions of meaning, restriction to the individual's physical behavior (including his linguistic behavior) alone does away with individualistic meaning. For someone might suggest that, on the contrary, precisely herein lies the *salvation* of individualistic meaning, that an individual's conceptual understanding just *consists in* regularities in his own physical behavior (especially his own linguistic behavior).
>
> Hegel does not explicitly address this question. However, one can perhaps infer his answer to it from things that he says in the *Force and the Understanding* section and elsewhere. As noted above, in that section he sees a strong analogy between the Platonist conception of meaning and the realist conception of force: just as the Platonist conception of meaning construes meanings as items over and above the observable regularities in a person's (linguistic) physical behavior which they are adduced to explain, so the realist conception of force construes forces as items over and above the observable regularites in physical nature which *they* are adduced to explain. This analogy would obviously extend to include all of the other individualistic accounts of meaning considered in the *Phenomenology* which conceive meanings as items over and above the observable regularities in a person's (linguistic) physical behavior as well, such as the Stoic and the empiricist accounts. Now this analogy suggests that Hegel would, correspondingly, see an analogy between a conception of meaning as identical with regularities in an individual's (linguistic) physical behavior and the antirealist conception of force: just as the former identifies meanings with the observable regularities in an individual's (linguistic) physical behavior which they are adduced to explain, so the latter identifies forces with the observable regularities in physical nature which *they* are adduced to explain. We might therefore reasonably hope to infer from Hegel's stated objections to the antirealist conception of force his unstated objections to such a conception of meaning.
>
> Hegel's primary objection to the antirealist conception of force, it will be recalled, was that it renders putative explanations of observable regularities in nature in terms of necessitation by forces implicitly "tautological" so that the "necessity . . . is merely verbal" and the "explanation . . . explains nothing" (pars. 154–55). This immediately suggests a first problem with the conception that an individual's meanings are identical with the regularities in his (linguistic) physical behavior which we adduce them to explain: such a conception would, similarly, render all such explanations implicitly tautological and so explanatorily vacuous.
>
> In addition, it suggests a second problem for such a conception of meaning, a problem concerning not *necessitation* and *explanation* but their close normative relatives *requirement* and *justification*. It is fundamental to our ideas about meaning that the meanings of an individual's words *require* certain linguistic behaviors of him (and proscribe others), that they *justify* certain linguistic behaviors by him (and render others illegitimate). Now, in order for such normative notions to be applicable, it must not only be possible for an individual to *conform* to what is required and would be justified, but also to *fail* to conform. And indeed, it is *independently* a fundamental part of our thinking about meaning that people can and often do fail to conform in their linguistic behavior to what meaning requires

Having thus concluded the development of the "skeptical paradox" at paragraph 322 of the section *Physiognomy and Phrenology,* Hegel immediately goes on to indicate his "skeptical solution" to it: an individual's conceptual understanding is constituted by his (linguistic) physical behavior *together with that of a like-behaving community*. Thus paragraph 322 argues that while *meinen,* or meaning *by oneself,* is indeed done away with, this does not do away with meaning per se because the individual's deed "is not merely a sign, but the fact itself," namely, insofar as "the deed . . . is something *universal,*" or "the individual is *for others a universal being* who really is, and who ceases to be something only privately meant [nur ein Gemeintes]" (emphasis added). This "skeptical solution" becomes still more explicit a little further on in the text in the section *The Spiritual Animalkingdom,* which represents Herder's outlook.[54] For this outlook, "the moments of the individuality which . . . unthinking consciousness regarded as subject . . . coalesce into simple individuality which as this particular individuality is no less immediately universal [i.e., communal] . . . The individual is a self in the form of a

---

and would justify. A problem seems to arise here for the conception that an individual's meaning is identical with regularities in his (linguistic) physical behavior, however. For it seems that, just as on the antirealist conception of force *whatever* observable regularities might occur would be "necessitated by forces," thus rendering the notion of "necessitation" vacuous, so on this conception of meaning *whatever* regular linguistic behavior an individual might perform—and *any* linguistic behavior performed by him will be regular under some description—would be "required/justified by meaning," that on this conception of meaning the individual *could not fail* to conform to "what meaning requires/justifies"—which both renders such normative notions as "requirement" and "justification" vacuous in connection with meaning, and also violates our independently fundamental conviction that people can and often do fail so to conform.

Finally, Hegel had, it will be recalled, a further objection to the antirealist conception of force as well as that just mentioned: the epistemological objection that induction is unreliable, and that the antirealist conception leaves us without a criterion for deciding which of the indefinitely many regularities hitherto observed should, and which should not, be inductively generalized (par. 250). This suggests a third problem with a conception of meaning which identifies it with regularities in an individual's (linguistic) physical behavior: considered in itself, such behavior will exhibit indefinitely many regularities, some of which should be generalized to infer rules constitutive of meaning, but many of which should not, and the individual's behavior taken by itself will yield no criterion for deciding which are which. Thus Hegel writes that "self-conscious individuality . . . in meaning by itself . . . is infinitely determined and determinable" and implies that this "bad infinity" needs to be "destroyed" (par. 322).

These, then, are three lines of objection to a proposal to identify meaning with regularities in an individual's (linguistic) physical behavior which Hegel may have had in mind.

54. That this section represents Herder's outlook will be demonstrated in chapter 9 below.

universal self," "the universal [i.e., the general concept] is an existent thing as [the] action of all and each," "the category is in itself as the universal [i.e., the communal]" (pars. 418–19).[55] Thus, as I mentioned earlier, Hegel conceives, not only the "skeptical paradox" part of his argument, but also its "skeptical solution" part to have been in a sense developed by history before him, namely, in Herder's philosophy.[56] This, then, is Hegel's "skeptical solution."[57]

* * *

55. For further expressions in the *Phenomenology* of the idea that meaningful language (and consequently the mind or self, too) is essentially communal, see esp. the *Sense-certainty* section (as discussed earlier) and pars. 349, 508.

56. In his earlier work Herder is in fact somewhat equivocal on the question of whether community is fundamental to meaningful language. In *Über den Ursprung der Sprache* some passages suggest that it *is* (see for example *Herders Ausgewählte Werke* 3:611–13, where Herder emphasizes the other-directed and species character of *animal* languages, and pp. 671–74, where he argues that man is by nature a herd- or social-creature and that no man is an individual unto himself but all are woven into the species, illustrating this claim by reference to our acquisition of language, and with it our way of thinking and feeling, from other people). Other passages, on the other hand, suggest that it is *not* (e.g., ibid., pp. 631, 637, 638, 670–71). In his later work, however, Herder emphasizes the fundamental communality of meaningful language more unequivocally (e.g., *Vom Erkennen und Empfinden der menschlichen Seele*, ibid., pp. 722–23; *Briefe zu Beförderung der Humanität* [Riga: Hartknoch, 1793], 5:59–62).

57. To pursue a little further the analogy suggested in footnote 53 between Hegel's implicit response to a temptation at the end of the "skeptical paradox" part of his argument to reduce meanings to regularities in individual (linguistic) physical behavior and his explicit response to the antirealist conception of force: As we saw in chapter 2, having detected the problems which he finds in the antirealist conception of force, his reaction is not to reject that conception out of hand but rather to supplement it in such a way as to make the problems solvable—specifically, by adding a reference to final causes. Similarly, having detected the problems in the conception that meaning is reducible to regularities in individual (linguistic) physical behavior which my previous note suggested he has in mind, he reacts not by rejecting that conception out of hand but rather by supplementing it in such a way as to make them solvable—namely, by adding to that conception's reference to regularities in *individual* (linguistic) physical behavior a reference to regularities in the (linguistic) physical behavior of the *community*. This makes possible solutions to each of the three problems in question, as follows.

First, explaining an individual's regular (linguistic) physical behavior by reference to his meaning is no longer tautologous or explanatorily vacuous, because his meaning no longer consists simply in *his* regular (linguistic) physical behavior but in *its conformity to that of his community*.

Second, the possibility of failing to conform to meaning in one's regular (linguistic) physical behavior, and the normativity of meaning which presupposes this, are no longer precluded, but can now be accounted for: since the regularity in (linguistic) physical behavior which constitutes meaning and sets the normative standard is no longer regularity in the *individual*'s (linguistic) physical behavior but rather in the *community*'s, the individual's regular (linguistic) physical behavior can now very well violate this standard.

So much for the *Phenomenology*'s demonstration of doctrine (ii). Now, as noted in chapter 2, doctrines (i) and (ii) and their demonstration by the *Phenomenology* serve, in Hegel's eyes, the important *positive* function of helping to overcome the modern individual's conception of himself as sharply distinct from his community. However, they also generate a *problem and challenge* for Hegel. For, alongside these doctrines of the essential dependence of concepts and thought on language and the essential communality of language, Hegel also, as we saw in chapter 2, holds another belief at the time of the *Phenomenology,* namely, a belief that the concepts required in order to express his own Science must be different from any currently expressed by the community's language. Taken together, these positions immediately generate the following problem and challenge for Hegel's would-be Science at the time of the *Phenomenology*: since this Science's concepts are bound to be different from any currently expressed by communal language, and yet in order even to exist as concepts they must be the common property of a linguistic community, *they cannot yet exist, they have yet to be constructed.* The *Phenomenology* is, I suggest, in important part designed to address precisely this problem and challenge, that is, to construct the concepts of Hegelian Science by establishing a community-wide Hegelian usage of the linguistic terms which are to express them of a sort making possible and actual their existence as concepts. This is metaphysical task (9) in our list of the work's tasks.

This helps to explain why Hegel describes the *Phenomenology* at Heidelberg *Encyclopaedia,* paragraph 36—and in virtually the same words at *Phenomenology,* paragraph 27—as "the production [Erzeugung] of [Science's] concept."[58] Actually, in Hegel's German this phrase expresses the project just sketched still more exactly than my somewhat conservative English translation would suggest. For, in addition to bearing its idiomatic meaning "produce," the verb *erzeugen* here in all probability also bears the artificial sense "bring about through witnessing" (an artificial sense made possible by the fact that the basic verb *zeugen* can mean not

---

Third, the epistemological problem of deciding which of the indefinitely many regularities in an individual's (linguistic) physical behavior are, and which are not, indicative of meaning now finds a solution: roughly, those and only those which he shares with the linguistic community as a whole are so. Hence at paragraph 322 Hegel writes that, although "self-conscious individuality in meaning by itself [in der Meinung] is infinitely determined and determinable," "in the accomplished deed this bad infinity is destroyed. The deed is something simply determined, universal [i.e., communal]."

58. Appendix XVI.

only "produce" or "beget" but also "bear witness to" or "testify to"). Hence we could translate this phrase "the production through witnessing of [Science's] concept"—which rather neatly captures the project just sketched of constituting the concepts of Science through establishing their acknowledgement by a linguistic community.

It is, therefore, I think, no accident or flaw that, as some commentators have pointed out in a spirit of complaint,[59] the meanings of certain key terms appear to undergo a transformation over the course of the *Phenomenology*. For it is part of the *purpose* of the work to lead the reader gradually from familiar uses of terms toward less familiar and richer uses of them which will be more adequate to the expression of Hegelian Science. Take the term *allgemein* itself, for example. When first encountered in the *Sense-certainty* section this term seems to mean something like "universal concept" or "general concept" (as opposed to "proper name" or "demonstrative," for instance)—a meaning already familiar from the term's preexisting use. The following passage is typical: "The pointing-out of the now is . . . the movement which expresses what the now is in truth, viz. a plurality of nows all taken together; and the pointing-out is the experience of learning that now is a *universal* [Allgemeines]" (par. 107). As we proceed through the book, however, we are made aware that the term has—and implicitly had all along—additional implications as well, such as that of *community*. Consider, for example, this later passage: "Actualization is . . . a display of what is one's own in the element of universality [in das allgemeine Element] whereby it becomes . . . the affair of everyone" (par. 417).

Now someone might at this point raise the following objection (either against my interpretation or, granting that, against Hegel): "The project of the *Phenomenology* seems, in various ways, to presuppose that Hegel *already understands* his own Science. For example, the *Phenomenology* is written with the purpose of teaching and justifying this Science, and—as we have noted, and shall see in more detail in part 4—in the belief that contents of the *Phenomenology* correspond one-to-one with the categories of this Science's Logic. How can this be consistent with the view just attributed to Hegel that the concepts of Hegelian Science do not even exist at the time when he writes the *Phenomenology*, that the *Phenomenology* has the job of bringing them into existence for the first time?"

---

59. For example, O. Pöggeler, "Zur Deutung der *Phänomenologie des Geistes*," in *Hegel Studien* 1 (1961), p. 289.

The answer to this objection is, I think, that Hegel believes—and not implausibly so—that a term's expression of a certain meaning is a matter which admits of *degrees,* so that even before a term achieves the community-wide usage required for it to express a concept with perfect clarity it can *approximately* express that concept. Thus, it is a familiar part of Hegel's theory of philosophy, religion, and art that these domains employ different representational media expressing the same ideas but with different degrees of clarity (philosophy's purely conceptual medium expresses them more clearly than religion's medium of *Vorstellung,* or metaphorical representation, and this in turn does so more clearly than art's sensuous medium). And, still more significantly, in a passage from the Philosophy of Spirit of 1803–4 Hegel remarks that barbarians who lack a proper linguistic community "do not know how to say what they mean; they only half say it" (but note that they *do* half say it).[60] In consequence, Hegel can consistently—and with some plausibility—believe at the time of writing the *Phenomenology* that his Science's terms, even though they have not yet attained that community-wide scientific usage which is required for the perfect clarity of his Science's concepts, and which it is the *Phenomenology*'s function to effect, can nevertheless already *approximately* express his Science's concepts, so that a sort of provisional understanding of his Science is already possible.

That Hegel does in fact see himself as in this sort of situation at the time of writing the *Phenomenology* is strongly suggested by a number of things which he says in the work. For example, he implies that the existence of his Science's conceptual element is not an all or nothing matter but comes about by degrees: "This element ... achieves its own perfection and transparency only through the movement of its becoming" (par. 26). He implies that the *Phenomenology* is itself a last phase in that process: it is the preparation of Science's conceptual "element," and "the coming-to-be of Science" (pars. 37, 27). And he implies, accordingly, that the *Phenomenology,* although it does not yet quite express Science itself, *is* nevertheless the "appearance" of Science (pars. 38, 76).[61]

---

60. Appendix VIII.
61. It also supports the psychological plausibility of attributing such a self-understanding to Hegel at the time of the *Phenomenology* that at that time he had probably not yet developed his Science in much detail either orally or on paper; it still remained very much "in his head"—a fact especially significant given his views on the indeterminacy of thought prior to explicit behavioral expression stated at *Phenomenology,* par. 322. (Hegel *had* already lectured copiously on and written detailed versions of his *early* system, comprising—

Hegel's presupposition in the *Phenomenology* of a good deal of information about his Science does not, therefore, on closer inspection, conflict with his pursuit of task (9) in the work. He already has a clear enough grasp of his Science's concepts to allow him a good provisional idea of its contents and structure—good enough that he can form the intention to teach and justify it, recognize that its Logic has such and such contents and structure, and so forth. But he has not yet attained that complete conceptual clarity with respect to Science which must await the establishment of the community-wide scientific usage of terms which the *Phenomenology* is intended to effect.

* * *

Hegel's second concern when he assigns the *Phenomenology* the role of serving as a preparation of Science's "element," or of the "unity of the universal and the individual self-consciousness," and as a "coming-to-be of Science," is a concern about Science's *truth*. By the date of writing the *Phenomenology* Hegel had already for some time held what might be called an *enduring communal consensus theory of truth*—a theory according to which the very nature of truth is such that it is necessary and sufficient for a claim's truth that it be agreed upon and continue to be agreed upon by a community or a communal tradition. One can already discern an inclination to equate truth with enduring communal consensus in this way in later parts of *The Positivity of the Christian Religion*. In this essay Hegel argues in favor of the sort of "religious imagination" of peoples, exemplified above all in Greek polytheism, which finds expression in stories of "gods, angels, devils, or saints, which live on in the traditions of the people," and against Christianity which "has depopulated Valhalla, cut down the holy groves, and exterminated the imagination of the people as a shameful superstition, as a devilish poison."[62] What, for our purposes, is striking about this is that Hegel seems to assume that if only one could establish a system of "religious imagination" as a tradition in the life of a modern people, then the question of the *truth* of that system of belief would somehow just look after itself.

---

after an introductory Logic—Metaphysics, Philosophy of Nature, and Philosophy of Spirit. But he abandoned that system at the time of the *Phenomenology* in favor of his very different mature system, comprising—after an introductory Phenomenology of Spirit—Logic, Philosophy of Nature, and Philosophy of Spirit. And *this* system he only began to lecture on in the summer of 1806 after the composition of the *Phenomenology* was already well underway [see Rosenkranz, *Hegels Leben*, p. 162] and to write out in real detail still later.)

62. *Hegels theologische Jugendschriften*, pp. 214–15.

Furthermore, in this essay Hegel comments disparagingly on Christianity's conception of its doctrines as objective and exclusive of other views, and contrasts favorably with this the conception which he supposes the ancient Greeks to have had of the doctrines of their religion and ethics as instead dependent for their authority only on general acceptance by their community. Thus in a passage which we have already encountered he remarks that for the ancient Greeks the ground for believing their religion's principles was not any supposition of objective fact, but rather, "if it had been possible for the question to occur to one of them by what means he proposed to prove the divinity of a command or prohibition, he could have cited no historical fact, but only the feeling of his heart and the agreement of all good men."[63] The same inclination to equate truth with enduring communal consensus persists in texts from the early Jena period, such as the *System of Ethical Life* from 1802–3.[64] One of Hegel's most explicit expressions of the enduring communal consensus theory of truth is found in an aphorism from the later Jena period: "Science. Whether the individual possesses it is something he can make assurances to himself and others about. Whether that is true is something which his immediate context decides, his contemporaries [die Mitwelt] and then posterity [die Nachwelt] after his contemporaries have already indicated their approval."[65] Within the *Phenomenology* itself, Hegel expresses this theory of truth in such remarks as that "it is the nature of truth to prevail when its time has come . . . The individual needs that this should be so in order to verify what is as yet a matter for himself alone, and to experience the conviction, which in the first place belongs only to a particular individual, as something universally held"; and that "the absolute pure will of all . . . has the form of immediate being. It is not a commandment which only *ought* to be; it *is* . . . ; it is the universal 'I' . . . which is immediately a reality, and the world *is* only this reality" (pars. 71, 436).

This theory of truth is no mere dogmatic assumption in Hegel, but instead rests upon *argument*. As we shall see, the *Phenomenology* is par-

---

63. Ibid., p. 229; also in appendix I.
64. For example, Hegel, *System der Sittlichkeit* (Hamburg: Felix Meiner, 1967), pp. 54–55: "The particular, the individual, is as a particular consciousness simply equal to the universal [i.e., there is complete agreement between individual and community]; and this universality, which has simply unified particularity with itself, is the divinity of the people [implying, among other things, its power to determine what is true quite generally]."
65. Appendix IX.

ticularly concerned with its demonstration—this is task (10) in our list of the tasks undertaken by the work. Hegel had already provided an argument for this theory of truth much earlier, however, namely, in the later parts of *The Positivity of the Christian Religion*. And we should begin by considering this earlier argument first.

This earlier argument arrives at such a theory of truth through a well-motivated revision of a position of Kant's. In the *Prolegomena to Any Future Metaphysics* Kant had argued that the concept of truth or objective validity was analyzable as necessary and universal intersubjective agreement, that "true" or "objectively valid" implicitly just meant "necessarily and universally intersubjectively agreed on," and that necessary and universal intersubjective agreement was hence a defining necessary and sufficient condition of truth or objective validity: "The objective validity of the experiential judgment means nothing but its necessary universal validity [notwendige Allgemeingültigkeit] . . . Objective validity and necessary universal validity (for everyone) are equivalent concepts, and . . . when we consider a judgment to be universally valid and so necessary, precisely thereby its objective validity is understood"; "If a judgment agrees with an object, all judgments about the same object must also agree with one another . . . But conversely, too, if we find cause to consider a judgment necessarily universally valid . . . , we must also consider it objective."[66] Now during his early Kantian phase in the early- to mid-1790s Hegel evidently *accepted* this Kantian analysis and criterion of truth. For example, in one especially Kant-inspired fragment from the period he writes: "As rational [a religion] should be universally valid [allgemeingültig], and each finds for himself a confirmation of his own belief in the fact that he can convince others of the truth of his belief as well."[67]

---

66. Kant, *Prolegomena zu einer jeden künftigen Metaphysik* (Hamburg: Felix Meiner, 1976), pars. 18–19. That Kant's remarks here about *objective validity* equally concern *truth* can be seen from his definition of truth in the *Critique of Pure Reason* as "the agreement of knowledge with its object" (A58/B52).

Note that the *Prolegomena* is more radical in this area than the *Critique of Pure Reason* in that, although the latter work agrees with the former in holding necessary and universal intersubjective agreement to be a necessary and sufficient condition, and hence a "touchstone," of truth (A820–21, B848–49), it does not like the former work make it a *defining* necessary and sufficient condition of truth. The *Critique of Judgment* makes the connection between necessary and universal intersubjective agreement and truth or objective validity still more tenuous—implying that the former is not even a sufficient condition of the latter, since judgments of taste have the former characteristic but not the latter.

67. *Hegels theologische Jugendschriften*, p. 364. Note that Hegel's confederate Schelling also embraced a version of the Kantian account of truth at points in his early work.

By the time of writing the later parts of *The Positivity of the Christian Religion*, however, Hegel had discovered a serious problem with Kant's analysis and criterion of truth, as they stood—namely, that they rested on an assumption that human nature, and in particular human *cognitive* nature, was basically the same in everybody. Hegel now realized, in light of a much greater interest in, and knowledge of, the actual history of human thought than Kant ever had, that this assumption was a mistake, that if there was such a thing as a common human cognitive nature at all, then it was so attenuated, consisted of such few and highly general traits, that it left the class of judgments which were necessarily and universally intersubjectively valid virtually empty. The Kantian analysis and criterion of truth were therefore unacceptable as they stood. To illustrate this line of thought from Hegel's text: In his revised version of the beginning of *The Positivity of the Christian Religion* Hegel opens with a rough characterization of the Kantian conception of human nature and the Kantian criterion of truth and error based upon it: in modern times "we find the conviction that the infinite multiplicity of manifestations of human nature had been comprised in the unity of a few universal concepts. Because these concepts are universal, they also become necessary concepts and characteristics of humanity as a whole. Since these characteristics are fixed, the variations in national or individual manners, customs, and opinions become accidents, prejudices, and errors."[68] But Hegel then goes on to criticize this Kantian position on the grounds that human nature is in fact much more diverse, much less shared in common, than it assumes, and that, consequently, if we were to follow the criterion of truth and error which this position offers, then we would have to judge the class of truths virtually empty, so that this position's criterion of truth and error is unacceptable as well:

> The general concept of human nature admits of infinite modifications, and it is no mere expedient to appeal to the experience that modifications are necessary, that human nature was never found in its purity, but this can be strictly proved. All one needs to do is to determine what, then, "pure

---

Thus in the *System of Transcendental Idealism* (1800) he writes: "For the individual, other intelligences are, as it were, the eternal bearers of the universe . . . The world, though it is posited solely through the self, is independent of me, since it resides for me in the intuition of other intelligences; their common world is the archetype, whose agreement with my own presentations is the sole criterion of truth" (p. 174).

68. *Early Theological Writings*, p. 168.

human nature" would be? This expression is supposed to comprise no more than adequacy to the universal concept. But living nature is always something other than its concept, and therefore that which was for the concept mere modification, pure contingency, something superfluous, becomes the necessary, the living, perhaps the only thing natural and beautiful. The criterion . . . originally put forth thereby receives a quite different appearance. The universal concept of human nature will no longer be adequate . . . The universal concepts of human nature are too empty to serve as a criterion.[69]

Hegel therefore rejects the Kantian criterion of truth and error for the purposes of his own inquiry: "In the following essay the doctrines and commands of the Christian religion will not be measured by the criterion of universal concepts."[70] However, and this is crucial, Hegel's rejection

69. *Hegels theologische Jugendschriften*, pp. 140–41. Knox's translation of this passage in *Early Theological Writings* is misleading in that it makes Hegel's *defense* of empirical scrupulousness in considering human nature sound like a *rejection* of empiricism.
Hegel's empirically motivated skepticism here about the idea that much is universally shared by human minds, and even his concession that there is nonetheless *something*, in all probability echo Herder, and indeed a specific passage from Herder's *Vom Erkennen und Empfinden der menschlichen Seele*: "All respect to 'human reason' and 'universal human understanding' and 'human feeling'; but, my dear friend, these things are something different from your sleeping cap. I could tell you many a fairy tale here about the 'universal human understanding,' as for example of that clever man who believed all the ships in the harbor at Athens his, and was very happy about it . . . To be sure there must be a universal human understanding just as there must be a universal lions' and beasts' understanding; but I fear that an individual . . . could with difficulty give any information about it . . . The 'universal human reason,' as people would like to understand the term, is a cover for our favorite fancies, idolatry, blindness, and laziness. And we shut our eyes and ears to what true human reason, human feeling and need is and always will be" (*Herders Ausgewählte Werke* 3:731–32).
70. *Early Theological Writings*, p. 177. The whole change in the early Hegel's position just described, from an initial acceptance to a rejection of Kant's analysis and criterion of truth as necessary and universal intersubjective agreement, and of the assumption of the uniformity of human cognitive nature on which Kant's analysis and criterion rested, is also reflected in Hegel's changing views about moral principles during the same period, as follows.
In *The Life of Jesus* from 1795 Hegel still accepts the Kantian position on truth and human nature, and accordingly (like Kant) conceives the true moral principles as implicitly agreed upon by all men. Hence he makes the Jesus who represents his own position in the text say, "I never wanted to impose anything arbitrary or alien on mankind, but have instead taught only your law which silently dwells, however misunderstood by most men, within each and every heart" (*Three Essays 1793–95*, p. 156).
By the time of writing the main body of *The Positivity of the Christian Religion*, however, Hegel is beginning to be torn between the Kantian position on truth and human nature and its rejection, and accordingly his views on moral principles are now torn between the position taken in *The Life of Jesus* and its rejection. Thus within the space of a single page in the main body of the essay Hegel can, on the one hand, repeat the position on moral

of the Kantian analysis and criterion of truth in terms of necessary and universal intersubjective agreement, motivated by his recognition that, due to the variability of human cognitive nature, truth so defined would be a more or less empty concept, did not take the form of an *unqualified* rejection of them, but instead of a *revision* of them aimed at preserving them to the greatest extent compatible with overcoming this problem. Hegel's solution was, accordingly, to dispense with Kant's offending insistence that the intersubjective validity equated with truth be *necessary* and *universal,* and to reconceive it instead as something more like de facto intersubjective validity *within a communal tradition.* Hence the passages recently cited from later parts of The Positivity of the Christian Religion in which Hegel implies his commitment to a form of the enduring communal consensus theory of truth.[71]

---

principles taken in The Life of Jesus—"Reason sets up moral, necessary, and universally valid laws"—while also, on the other hand, inconsistently, implying that it is a *mistake* to ascribe universal validity to moral principles: "In the Christian church, or in any other whose underlying principle is a pure morality, the moral commands of Reason, which are subjective, are treated exactly as if they were . . . objective rules"; "Kant calls [Reason's moral laws] 'objective' . . . Now the problem is to make these laws subjective" (*Early Theological Writings,* p. 143).

Finally, when Hegel later writes the materials for a continuation and revision of The Positivity of the Christian Religion, he has wholly rejected the Kantian position on truth and human nature, as we have just seen from the revised version of the beginning of the essay, and accordingly he now unequivocally opposes the Kantian ascription of universal validity to moral principles, instead praising the ancient Greeks and Romans for *refusing* to see their moral principles in such terms: "As free people they obeyed laws which they had given themselves . . . In public life as in private and domestic life each was a free man, each lived in accordance with his own laws . . . People's will was free, obeyed its own laws . . . They recognized the right of each person to have his own will, be it good or bad. Good people recognized the duty of being good for themselves, but at the same time they honored the freedom of another person to be able not to be so as well, so that they set up neither a divine morality nor one made by or abstracted from themselves which they expected others to follow" (ibid., pp. 154–55; also in appendix I).

71. This early argument for the enduring communal consensus theory of truth can once again be understood as following the "skeptical paradox, skeptical solution" pattern: Hegel begins from an assumption that Kant's analysis and criterion of truth in terms of necessary and universal intersubjective agreement capture something basic in our intuitions about truth. He finds, however, that the sort of uniformity in human cognitive nature which would be required for this analysis and criterion to be satisfied by any significant number of propositions is lacking, so that this analysis and criterion would force us to the paradoxical conclusion that there is no significant amount of truth. This is the "skeptical paradox." He then devises a "skeptical solution": we can save at least the *core* of the original Kantian analysis and criterion of truth, in particular their assignment of a key role to intersubjective agreement, but without incurring the skeptical paradox, if only we revise that analysis and

Of course, this early argument for the enduring communal consensus theory of truth has an obvious weakness: it is compelling only to the extent that one is initially inclined to accept the rather unintuitive and controversial Kantian analysis of truth as necessary and universal intersubjective validity. The *Phenomenology,* as we shall see, provides an argument for the theory which avoids this weakness, an argument which presupposes instead only an initial inclination to accept a much more intuitive and uncontroversial analysis of truth as *correspondence to independent fact.* In this sense, the earlier argument will be superseded in the *Phenomenology.* On the other hand, it continues to play an important supporting role. For, to begin with, it is not obviously *contradicted* by the *Phenomenology*'s argument.[72] And, more importantly, it is, as we shall see, in a sense presupposed by the *Phenomenology*'s argument, namely, in that it explains why, when the *Phenomenology*'s argument has shown that we must abandon the conception of truth as correspondence to independent fact in favor of a conception of truth as intersubjective agreement, the subjects in question have to be *a communal tradition,* rather than *all human beings.*[73] The earlier argument therefore remains quite important.

The *Phenomenology*'s own central argument for the enduring communal consensus theory of truth once again follows the "skeptical paradox, skeptical solution" pattern: Hegel starts out from what he rather plausi-

---

criterion from *necessary* and *universal* intersubjective agreement to *de facto* intersubjective agreement *within a communal tradition.* And so that is what he does.

72. It might *seem* that it was so because it might seem that the two arguments' initial analyses of the concept of truth as necessary and universal intersubjective validity, on the one hand, and correspondence to independent fact, on the other, were inconsistent with one another. But it is far from clear that they *are* inconsistent. Thus Kant himself analyzes the concept of truth not only in terms of necessary and universal intersubjective validity, but also in terms of correspondence to fact, "the agreement of knowledge with its object" (*Critique of Pure Reason,* A58/B82). And his position in the *Prolegomena* seems to be the quite coherent one that these two analyses are *consistent* with one another and *both correct,* though *at different levels of conceptual analysis:* At the most immediate level of conceptual analysis "truth" means a representation's correspondence to fact or "agreement . . . with its object," as the analysis in the *Critique of Pure Reason* indicates. But this notion of a representation's agreement with an object can *in its turn* be analyzed, thereby yielding the analysis in terms of necessary and universal intersubjective validity given in the *Prolegomena.* Hence when the *Prolegomena* offers this analysis it does so not as an analysis of the concept of truth *directly* but rather as a direct analysis of the notion of "objective validity," that is, the notion of a representation's agreement with an object.

73. Hence, for example, Hegel implies at *Phenomenology,* paragraph 350 that the Hegelian finds truth "in the life of a people or nation."

bly takes to be the commonsense conception/concept of truth as the correspondence of representations to independent facts. He then undertakes to demonstrate through a serial critique that none of the various ways in which one might try to articulate the idea of such a correspondence is tenable, or even coherent. This produces a "skeptical paradox": it seems as though there is and can be no such thing as truth. Finally, he offers a "skeptical solution" to this "skeptical paradox": we can avoid the paradox, while at the same time preserving many central features of the commonsense conception/concept of truth (such as a distinction between true and false representations), if only we partially reconceive/reconceptualize "truth," dropping the offending idea that truth consists in the correspondence of representations to independent facts, and instead substituting for this the idea that it consists in representations being agreed upon by an enduring communal consensus (and falsehood in their failure to be agreed upon by such a consensus).

Like Hegel's "skeptical paradox, skeptical solution" argument for the essential communality of linguistic meaning, this argument has in addition the following two further noteworthy features. First, it makes a serious effort to demonstrate the *completeness* of its collection of ways of articulating a conception/concept of truth as the correspondence of representations to independent facts. Second, it has a *historical* dimension: Hegel understands both its "skeptical paradox" and its "skeptical solution" parts to have been already unfolded in chronological order by history. Thus, he conceives all of the versions of the correspondence theory of truth which he undertakes to refute in the "skeptical paradox" part of the argument to have been already articulated in past ages, and takes them up there in the order of their historical occurrence. And he also conceives the "skeptical solution" of an enduring communal consensus theory of truth to have been developed before him by history, and at the conclusion of that historical sequence of correspondence theories, namely, (once again) in the philosophy of Herder.

Let us now consider how this argument appears in the text, beginning with its "skeptical paradox" part. Note, to begin with, that the Introduction attributes to "the natural consciousness," or the commonsense standpoint, whose various "shapes" the *Phenomenology* considers a conception/concept of truth as the correspondence of representations to independent facts. Thus, the Introduction implies that the natural consciousness conceives the facts which "knowledge" or representations depict as *independent* of "knowledge" or representations: "Whatever is related to knowledge is also distinguished from it, and posited as existing outside of this relationship as well" (par. 82). And the Introduction also implies that the natural consciousness conceives truth as consisting in the *correspondence* of "knowledge" or representations to such facts: "In what consciousness affirms from within itself as being-in-itself [i.e., as independent fact] . . . we have the standard which consciousness itself sets up by which to measure what it knows. If we designate knowledge as the concept . . . then the examination consists in seeing whether the concept corresponds to the object" (par. 84). Accordingly, the natural consciousness's very *concept* of truth is also one of a correspondence of representations to independent facts or objects. Thus in the *Encyclopaedia* Hegel defines the ordinary concept of truth as follows: "We usually give the name truth to the agreement of a self-standing object [eines Gegenstandes] with our representation [Vorstellung]," this is the ordinary "meaning of truth."[74] Consequently, the various "shapes" of the natural consciousness considered in the *Phenomenology* are understood to be (among other things) a sequence of different ways of articulating a conception/concept of truth as correspondence between representations and independent facts—ways distinguished from one another by their different conceptions/concepts of the two terms of the correspondence relation (representations and independent facts). As we have in effect already seen, it is also part of Hegel's idea that the *Phenomenology* demonstrates the *completeness* of this collection of different ways of articulating a conception/concept of truth as correspondence of representations to independent facts, the completeness of this collection of "shapes of consciousness" (their constitution of an "entire system of consciousness," as the Introduction puts it). It is Hegel's claim, however, and a major purpose of his text to demonstrate, that none of these various ways of articulating a conception/concept of truth as correspondence between representations and independent facts is tenable, or even coherent. For, as we have seen, he believes and undertakes to show that in each case the general conceptions/concepts of the two terms of the correspondence relation, "knowledge" or representations and "objects" or independent facts, implicitly contradict one another (and are consequently, for reasons indicated in chapter 2, individually self-contradictory as well). In each

---

74. *Encyclopaedia*, par. 24, addition 2.

case, therefore, the existence of a relation of correspondence between instances of the two terms in question would be an impossibility. The Introduction expresses this two-step strategy for discrediting conceptions/concepts of truth as correspondence between representations and independent facts in a compressed formula which runs the two steps together by means of a deliberately ambiguous use of the term *correspond* to mean both (i) *logical consistency,* namely, between general conceptions/concepts of "knowledge" or representations and "objects" or independent facts, and (ii) *correspondence* of the kind posited by the correspondence theory of truth, namely, of particular pieces of "knowledge" or representations to particular "objects" or independent facts: "Consciousness finds that its knowledge does not correspond to its object" (par. 85).[75] As we have already in effect seen, the Introduction proposes to undertake this serial survey and critique of different ways of articulating a conception/concept of truth as correspondence between representations and independent facts, or different "shapes of consciousness," in the order of their historical occurrence (it will be, in the words of the Introduction, a "detailed history of the education of consciousness").

The sections *Sense-certainty* to *The Spiritual Animalkingdom* in the main body of the *Phenomenology* execute this plan articulated in the Introduction, attempting to present in the order of their historical emergence and demonstrate the completeness of a series of different ways of articulating the conception/concept of truth as the correspondence of representations to independent facts, or different "shapes of consciousness," and to show in each case that the conceptions/concepts of the two terms of the correspondence relation, representations and independent facts,

---

75 Recognizing the ambiguity here and the two-step strategy of critique behind it is the key to making sense of a particularly puzzling passage in paragraph 85. Hegel there raises what at first sight appears to be a telling objection against his idea that consciousness can test its own representations for correspondence with facts or objects, namely, that "it seems that consciousness cannot, as it were, get behind the object as it exists for consciousness so as to examine what the object is in itself." But he dismisses this objection and implies that such a self-testing by consciousness *is* in fact possible after all. Now, if the only sense of "correspondence" in play here were sense (ii), then the objection would be unanswerable, and Hegel's dismissal of it consequently misconceived. However, we *can,* it seems, make sense of the idea that a form of consciousness might convict itself of a failure of "correspondence" between representations and facts or objects in *sense (i)* and *consequently* also in sense (ii). And this is what Hegel has in mind.

implicitly contradict one another, so that no correspondence of the sort envisaged would be possible.[76]

Hegel believes that this serial critique in the sections *Sense-certainty* to *The Spiritual Animalkingdom* shows there to be no coherent way of articulating a conception of representations standing over against independent facts. Consequently, as the section *The Spiritual Animalkingdom* is reached, he concludes that the "self-consciousness [which] came face to face with a reality supposedly the negative of it" "is set aside," that "consciousness has cast away all opposition . . . ; it . . . is not occupied with an *other*" (pars. 394, 396). But he notes that, given the commonsense conception/concept of truth as the correspondence of representations to independent facts, this seems to do away with *truth:* "What was supposed to give experience . . . its supremacy over individuality's own concept of itself is the *objective reality*. Objective reality, however, is a moment which itself no longer possesses any truth on its own account in this consciousness" (par. 409). This is the "skeptical paradox"—it seems as though we have been forced to the paradoxical conclusion that there is no such thing as truth.

Hegel immediately proceeds in the section *The Spiritual Animalkingdom* to offer a "skeptical solution" to this "skeptical paradox," however. His recommendation is that we should reconceive/reconceptualize a representation's truth or "reality" as its enjoyment of enduring intersubjective agreement in a community, a new conception/concept of truth which preserves much in the commonsense conception/concept, such as the idea that truth is autonomous of any *individual*'s judgment, so that it is possible for individuals to make false judgments as well as true, but which by dispensing with the commonsense conception/concept of truth as the correspondence of representations to independent facts escapes the "skeptical paradox" of there being no truth:

> Reality therefore has for consciousness only the value of a being . . . whose universality is one with the action [of consciousness]. This unity is the true product; it is the matter itself, which simply maintains itself in being asserted [welche sich schlechthin behauptet] and is experienced as something which endures, independently of the matter which is the contingency of the individual action as such . . . The matter itself is thus an expression of

---

76. For an idea of the different versions of the conception/concept of truth as the correspondence of representations to independent facts covered in these sections of the *Phenomenology*, see chapter 9.

spiritual essentiality [glossed a little later at par. 418 as "the action of the single individual and of all individuals, . . . the action of each and everyone"], in which all . . . moments are sublated [aufgehoben] as autonomous, and so are only valid qua universal, and in which consciousness's certainty of itself is . . . the object born of self-consciousness as its own, but without ceasing to be a free, real object. (pars. 409–10)[77]

Or as Hegel had anticipated the same "skeptical solution" a little earlier in the text: the *Phenomenology*'s goal is "self-consciousness which has its own self-certainty in the other free self-consciousness, and possesses its truth precisely in that 'other' . . . It is . . . in the life of a people or nation that the concept of . . . beholding in the independence of the 'other' complete unity with it, or having for my object the free thinghood of an 'other' which confronts me and is the negative of myself as my own being-for-myself, has its complete reality" (pars. 349–50).[78] Hegel's earlier argument from *The Positivity of the Christian Religion* shows its continued importance here, in that it explains why the "skeptical solution" has to take the precise form that it does here, namely, an equation of truth with enduring agreement in a community rather than with agreement among all human beings. Given Hegel's general position on the relation between "theory" and meaning, he inevitably understands this profound reconception of truth to involve a reconceptualization of it as well, a change in the very meaning of the word *true*. Accordingly, in the *Encyclopaedia* he notes that the "philosophical meaning" of "truth" yields "a quite different meaning of truth than" common sense's.[79] Like

---

77. Note that the verb *aufheben*, in its standard threefold Hegelian sense of an *elevation* to a more adequate standpoint through an *abolition*, or in other words modification of the propositional/conceptual content, of a preceding standpoint, which however at the same time *preserves* it, namely, as so modified, is ideally suited for encapsulating the idea of a transition from a commonsense conception/concept via a "skeptical paradox" to which it succumbs to a "skeptical solution" which modifies the commonsense conception/concept while still preserving core aspects of it and thereby both retains advantages that it had and avoids the "skeptical paradox." The above passage well exemplifies the verb's use to this effect.

78. Note that Hegel here emphasizes an important virtue which he sees in the envisaged "skeptical solution" and which I touched on in chapter 2: it promises to make possible the realization of our impulse to *radical freedom*.

79. *Encyclopaedia*, par. 24, addition 2. Cf. *Phenomenology*, par. 38, where Hegel argues that, due to his philosophy's novel conceptions about truth and falsehood, "the expressions true and false must . . . no longer be used." (I do not mean to imply here that these passages have prominently in mind the specific aspect of Hegel's multifaceted reconception of truth with which we are presently concerned. They happen not to.)

the conceptions/concepts of truth as the correspondence of representations to independent facts dealt with in generating the "skeptical paradox," this "skeptical solution" of a reconception/reconceptualization of truth as enduring communal consensus is understood by Hegel to have been already developed before him by history, and at the chronological conclusion of the former—namely, in the philosophy of Herder, which the section *The Spiritual Animalkingdom* represents.[80] This, in sum, is the general form of Hegel's central argument in the *Phenomenology* for a conception/concept of truth as enduring communal consensus.[81]

---

80. Hegel's implied ascription to Herder of a conception/concept of truth as enduring communal consensus has a significant basis in Herder's texts. Thus, in *Vom Erkennen und Empfinden der menschlichen Seele* Herder writes: "Our cognition is only human and must be so if it is to be *right* . . . Humanity is the proper measure in accordance with which we cognize . . . The great impetus in one to enter into loving empathy with others and then to follow this sure pull . . . stands in opposition only to empty speculation, but not to cognition, for true cognition is love, is feeling in a human way"; "We live in a world which we ourselves create" (*Herders Ausgewählte Werke* 3:724–25; *Sämtliche Werke* [Berlin: Weidmann, 1877–1913], 8:252 [an earlier version of the same essay]). And in the *Briefe zu Beförderung der Humanität* Herder writes that a "public" in the sense of "a universal judgment, or at least a majority of the voices in the sphere in which one speaks, writes, or acts" is "a reasonable, moral entity, which participates in our thoughts, our speech, our acts, and is able to assess their value or lack of it," and that the "public" of all times and places is a "universal concilium . . . which alone, and indeed only in constantly developing votes, can be a judge of the true and the false" (5:52–53, 113; cf. 1:7).
81. Hegel's conception/concept of truth as enduring communal consensus, and the argument for it which has just been sketched, bear a striking resemblance to a position recently developed by R. Rorty, especially in his *Objectivity, Relativism, and Truth* (Cambridge: Cambridge University Press, 1991). The following similarities are especially noteworthy: (i) Like Hegel, Rorty proposes that "one reinterprets objectivity as intersubjectivity, or as solidarity," that one "think of truth . . . as entirely a matter of solidarity," meaning by this solidarity within a specific community (pp. 13, 32, 22–23, 38). (Note, though, that Rorty equivocates between this proposal of *reinterpreting* objectivity or truth as solidarity and the slightly different proposal of *substituting* the ideal of solidarity for that of objectivity or truth [pp. 24, 27–28, 38–42].) (ii) Rorty's main argument in support of this proposal is very similar in general strategy to the Hegelian argument which we have just considered. Like Hegel, Rorty criticizes as untenable the distinction between representations and representation-independent reality, and consequently the correspondence theory of truth which rests upon this distinction (pp. 8–11). And like Hegel, he therefore proposes that we should reinterpret the notion of truth or objectivity as communal solidarity in order to avoid its present commitment to those untenable ideas, while yet preserving what is valuable in the received notion of truth or objectivity, such as a distinction between true and false judgments and the striving for better judgments which this distinction grounds (pp. 12–13; cf. 41). (On the other hand, Rorty's specific reasons for rejecting the distinction between representations and representation-independent reality, and hence the correspondence theory of truth, are different from Hegel's.) (iii) For Rorty, as for Hegel, moreover, one of the great positive attractions of this reinterpretation of the notions of truth or objectivity as

Finally, it is likely (though less clear from the text) that Hegel in the *Phenomenology* intends a further argument for the enduring communal consensus theory of truth as well: The work's extended argument for the conclusion that meaning is constituted by the shared linguistic behavior of a community can plausibly be understood to imply this further conclusion that a community's shared judgment is necessary and sufficient for truth as well. For, intuitively, the truth of a judgment in a particular context consists in its accordance in that context with the rules for judgment given by its meaning. But then, if the community's shared linguistic behavior constitutes meaning and its rules for judgment, it seems to follow that no judgment could be true which had not in some way been collectively endorsed by the community (that the community's shared judgment is necessary for truth), and moreover that any judgment which was collectively endorsed by the community would ipso facto be true (that the community's shared judgment is sufficient for truth).[82] Besides the naturalness

---

communal solidarity is that it opens up the prospect of a sort of *radical freedom:* "the change from a sense of [human beings'] dependence upon something antecedently present to a sense of the utopian possibility of the future, the growth of their ability to mitigate their finitude by a talent for self-creation," "there would be nothing to be responsible to except ourselves" (pp. 17, 41). Given Rorty's acknowledged early obsession with the *Phenomenology* (see his "Trotsky and the Wild Orchids," in *Wild Orchids and Trotsky: Messages from American Universities* [New York: Viking Press, 1993]), it seems very probable that these striking similarities between his position and the *Phenomenology*'s represent not only common ground with it but also an intellectual debt to it.

82. It is noteworthy in this connection that Wittgenstein in the *Philosophical Investigations* recognizes the naturalness of inferring from the rule-following argument's conclusion that communal practice constitutes meaning the further conclusion that communal agreement decides truth and falsehood. For immediately after the rule-following argument he has his imaginary interlocutor ask, "So you are saying that human agreement decides what is true and what is false?" (par. 241). Wittgenstein in fact wants to *resist* the inference: "It is what human beings *say* that is true and false; and they agree in the *language* they use. That is not agreement in opinions but in form of life" (par. 241). However, it seems doubtful that he can do so consistently. His position, if I understand it correctly, is that the communally shared judgments which constitute all of the meanings of a language concern only a subset of individually specifiable propositions, namely, those which he calls "grammatical" (such as the propositions of logic and mathematics), together with an individually unspecifiable large number of "empirical" propositions, and that in relation to *these* therefore something like the idea that communal endorsement is necessary and sufficient for truth holds good, but that the meaning of any specific "empirical" proposition neither requires nor would be dictated by communal agreement concerning it, so that communal endorsement of it is neither necessary nor sufficient for its truth (ibid., pars. 240–42, pp. 226e–27e; cf. *Remarks on the Foundations of Mathematics*, pt. 3, pars. 67, 69; pt. 6, par. 39). The problem with this position, it seems to me, is that it implicitly rests on an idea that meanings or rules—albeit ones created by actual communal practice—can somehow extend

of developing the argument for the essential communality of meaning into an argument for the enduring communal consensus theory of truth in this way, there are two more specific textual reasons for believing this to be part of Hegel's intention in the *Phenomenology:* (i) At the very beginning of his extended proof of the communal constitution of meaning, in the *Sense-certainty* section, Hegel points forward to that conclusion in formulations which also seem to imply the communal constitution of truth: "I experience what the truth of Sense-certainty is in fact: . . . a universal [ein Allgemeines]"; "Immediate certainty does not obtain for itself the true, for its truth is the universal [das Allgemeine]" (pars. 110–11). (ii) As we have seen, the conclusion that truth is constituted by enduring communal consensus is drawn at precisely the same point in the text as the conclusion that meaning is communally constituted—namely, in the section *The Spiritual Animalkingdom*.[83]

In sum, one can distinguish either behind or within the *Phenomenology* as many as three different arguments all converging on the enduring communal consensus theory of truth as their conclusion.

Before proceeding further, we should pause to consider briefly the question of the *tenability* of this enduring communal consensus theory of truth argued for by the *Phenomenology*. For the theory might seem vulnerable to certain fairly obvious and damning objections. Consider, to begin with, the part of the theory which maintains that enduring communal consensus is a *necessary* condition of truth. Two objections might naturally be raised against such a thesis, neither of which, however, seems in the end telling against Hegel's version of it: (i) Such a thesis contradicts the commonsense conviction that there can be, and are, many true propositions about which an enduring communal consensus never has been and never will be reached—for example, propositions known by only one person and taken to the grave, or propositions concerning events in prehistorical times or unobserved regions which are experienced by no one,

---

their judgment beyond actual communal practice to cases unconsidered in that practice, and indeed in such a way that their judgment has authority over any actual judgments on those cases by the community which might occur. For this idea, while certainly conventional enough, seems quite inconsistent with the thrust of the rule-following argument.

83. It is perhaps also significant in this connection that Herder, whose standpoint the section *The Spiritual Animalkingdom* represents, offers one of his clearest statements of a communal consensus theory of truth immediately after one of his clearest statements of a communal theory of meaning (*Vom Erkennen und Empfinden der menschlichen Seele*, in *Herders Ausgewählte Werke* 3:723–25).

leave no trace, and consequently never were or will be known by anyone. Hegel would be unimpressed by this objection, and reasonably so. For, as can be seen from the destructive or discrediting sides of his pedagogical and epistemological projects in the *Phenomenology*, he would not allow that mundane propositions of this sort *were* true. And the sorts of propositions to which, by contrast, he *would* be prepared to accord a measure of truth, namely, those expressed by great art, religion, and philosophy, are propositions which *could* more plausibly be claimed to enjoy the endorsement of an enduring communal consensus (especially if one reads the histories of great art, religion, and philosophy in the way that Hegel does). (ii) Again, it might seem that the thesis in question runs into the following objection: Where is the enduring communal consensus in favor of the enduring communal consensus theory of truth itself, and if there is none then how can the theory be true by its own lights? Hegel would reasonably be unimpressed by this objection as well. He would argue, I think, that the theory in fact *does* have, or is at least on the verge of achieving, enduring communal recognition among modern individuals. For, as he represents them toward the end of the *Reason* chapter of the *Phenomenology*, specifically from the section *The Spiritual Animalkingdom* (Herder and his age) through to the concluding paragraphs 435–37 (Hegel and his age), recent German perspectives are already implicitly committed to one or another close variant of the theory, in one way or another treating intersubjective agreement as the ultimate criterion of truth.[84] And elsewhere he implies that the theory has even deeper roots in modern Germany than this, in that a close variant of it is implicit in Protestantism.[85] Moreover, whatever finishing touches to an enduring communal consensus in Germany in support of the theory may still be

---

84. We have already seen this in connection with the first and last of these recent German perspectives, *The Spiritual Animalkingdom* (Herder and his age) and paragraphs 435–37 (Hegel and his age). Note, however, that the intervening sections *Reason as Lawgiver* and *Reason as Testing Laws* depict modern German viewpoints committed to one or another close variant of such a theory of truth as well. For, as we shall see in chapter 9, the section *Reason as Lawgiver* is concerned with the German *Popularphilosophie* of the later eighteenth century, which was based on the Scottish philosophy of common sense and so considered *common* sense the ultimate criterion of truth; and the section *Reason as Testing Laws* is concerned with Kant's philosophy, whose equation of truth with intersubjective agreement has already been discussed.

85. Thus in letters from 1816 Hegel writes that Protestantism, unlike Catholicism, "lies solely in general insight and culture" and allows that "*all* members of the community have the same right and role in the determination and preservation of church affairs and doctrine . . . Our safeguard . . . is . . . only the collective culture of the community . . . The sole

needed are in the process of being realized by the *Phenomenology* itself, namely, through its public dissemination of its own arguments in support of the theory.

Consider next the part of the theory which holds that enduring communal consensus is a *sufficient* condition of truth. Once again two objections naturally arise against this thesis, but once again neither of them seems telling against Hegel's version of it: (i) This thesis seems to imply that if only enough people could be brought to believe and to continue to believe that, for example, two plus two was five, or the earth was one foot in diameter, then these things would indeed be so. Is such an implication not patently absurd? In response to this objection two points deserve notice. First, the fact that the thesis conflicts with commonsense intuitions in this way is not in itself a flaw, in Hegel's eyes, for, as we have seen, his standard view is that common sense is deeply misguided and in need of correction by philosophy. Second, such a counterintuitive corollary as that mentioned is moreover not only *acceptable,* in Hegel's eyes, but positively *desirable*—for this is what constitutes the *radical freedom,* or power to determine what is the case quite generally, which he aspires to vindicate in his philosophy. (ii) The thesis that enduring communal consensus is sufficient for truth might seem open to the even more damning objection that it implies the truth of contradictions. For if a community's consensus is held to be sufficient for truth, does this not imply that, for example, the late medieval community's consensus that there are such things as witches and the modern community's consensus that there are no such things as witches are both true? Several features of Hegel's position arguably block such an inference, however. First, the objection, as stated, overlooks the fact that the communal consensus which according to Hegel is sufficient for truth is an *enduring* one. Indeed, it seems likely that Hegel's inclusion of the idea of *endurance* in his reconception/reconceptualization of truth as communal consensus is in part motivated precisely by the aim of avoiding objections of this sort. Second, though, this does not dispose of the objection entirely, because the objector might still point to *enduring* consensuses which take inconsistent positions on the same issues—for example, the Hindu tradition's conception of God versus the Christian tradition's incompatible conception of God. Hegel would probably reply to such a reformulation of the

---

authority is the intellectual and moral culture of all . . . *General* intellectual and moral culture is what is holy to Protestants" (*Hegel: The Letters,* pp. 327–28).

objection that in order to be truth-constituting a consensus must endure among *historically relevant* communities. For the *Phenomenology* implies, and the *Lectures on the Philosophy of World History* reiterates more explicitly, that there is, and in some sense *necessarily* is, only *one* national community which has historical relevance in any given age—namely, the one national community which, as the latter work puts it, "carries the torch of world history" in that age.[86] An insistence on the *historical relevance* of the communities among which a consensus must endure in order to be truth-constituting would therefore decisively extinguish the charge of endorsing contradictions, since it would imply that conflicting enduring consensuses of a kind relevant to Hegel's theory of truth do not, and in some sense cannot, arise.[87]

So much, then, for task (10) of the *Phenomenology*, the task of demonstrating the enduring communal consensus theory of truth.[88]

* * *

86. Concerning the *uniqueness* in question here, see for example *Phenomenology*, par. 808: "History . . . is Spirit emptied out into time . . . This becoming presents a slow-moving succession of Spirits . . . The realm of Spirits which is formed . . . constitutes a succession in time in which one Spirit relieved another of its charge and each took over the empire of the world from its predecessor." Concerning the *necessity* in question here, see for example pars. 5, 29.

87. This solution no doubt sounds contrived, but that is no vice, for to *contrive* a consistent and defensible conception/concept of truth is precisely Hegel's aim (not, for example, simply to offer an analysis of our preexisting conception/concept of truth).

88. Inwood (*Hegel*, pp. 74–75) has rightly pointed out that the mature Hegel tends to conflate truth and intersubjective agreement in certain passages of the *Encyclopaedia*, such as this one from paragraph 22, addition: "The truth is the objective and should be the rule for the conviction of everyone, so that the conviction of the individual is bad insofar as it does not correspond to this rule . . . If we have said . . . that it is the ancient conviction of human beings that it is spirit's destiny to know the truth, then there is also this point implicit therein: that objects, external and internal nature, in general the object as it is in itself is as it is thought, that therefore thought is the truth of the objective. Philosophy's business consists solely in bringing explicitly to consciousness what has had validity for human beings with respect to their thought from time immemorial. Hence philosophy presents nothing new; what we have here brought forth by our reflection is already the immediate preexisting judgment of everyone." We can now see, though, that this conflation is no mere accident or dogma, but instead represents positive doctrine, and moreover positive doctrine with quite substantial arguments behind it.

On the other hand, a qualification is required here concerning the precise *breadth* of the intersubjective agreement that is in question. As we have noted, the main core of the *Phenomenology* seems on the side of seeing this as intersubjective agreement within *a communal tradition* rather than among *all human beings*—as paragraph 350 puts it, the Hegelian finds truth "in the life of a people or nation." However, already in the *Phenomenology* the distinction between these two options appears to be less sharp than it was for Hegel at the time of the revised beginning of *The Positivity of the Christian Religion*. Thus contrast

As we have already seen in chapter 2, the establishment of this theory of truth plays a number of vitally important *positive* roles for the Hegel of the *Phenomenology*. We should now also note, however, that it creates a *problem and challenge* for him as well: since at the time of the *Phenome-*

---

with relatively early passages in the text like paragraph 350 passages written later where it rather sounds as though the subjects in question *are* all human beings—for instance, at paragraphs 70–71: "all self-conscious Reason," "universally held." In later texts, such as the passage from the *Encyclopaedia* quoted above, one detects a still more decided shift in the same direction: "everyone," "human beings . . . from time immemorial."

In the later parts of the *Phenomenology* this shift might just be due to the fact that Hegel, while perhaps still believing in the sorts of radical differences in human cognitive nature posited by *The Positivity of the Christian Religion*, now—as we saw in chapter 3—believes all outlooks except one, his own, to be implicitly self-contradictory and *in a way* implicitly committed to the truth of that one outlook (namely, in a dialectical way). The shift is probably, though, also due to a deeper change of outlook which becomes more emphatic in later works like the *Encyclopaedia*.

In the *Encyclopaedia* the shift in question seems to be closely connected with a shift in Hegel's estimation of how much all human beings share intellectually which occurs between the revised beginning of *The Positivity of the Christian Religion* and the main core of the *Phenomenology*, on the one hand, and later parts of the *Phenomenology* and later texts like the *Encyclopaedia*, on the other, and which we shall explore in chapter 10—a shift, roughly, from the answer *very little* to the answer *quite a lot*. As we have noted, Hegel's primary reason in the main core of the *Phenomenology* for preferring to equate truth with intersubjective agreement within a communal tradition rather than intersubjective agreement among all human beings appears to be his view from the revised beginning of *The Positivity of the Christian Religion* that very little is shared intellectually by all human beings. This view entails that the latter equation would leave the class of the true virtually empty. And it also confines the shared linguistic behavior relevant to the constitution of meaning, and hence the shared judgments determinative of truth because of the constitution of meaning by shared linguistic behavior, to a particular community or communal tradition rather than humanity at large. When in later parts of the *Phenomenology* and in subsequent texts Hegel retracts the view in question, coming instead to see all human beings as sharing quite a lot intellectually, he loses these reasons for preferring the former equation over the latter, so that nothing any longer stands in the way of embracing a version of the latter equation—specifically, as one sees from the passage of the *Encyclopaedia* quoted above, a version which equates truth with not only explicit endorsement by an enduring communal consensus but also the implicit agreement of humanity at large.

It would be hasty, however, to infer that this is all simply a change of mind on Hegel's part. For, on the interpretation which will be suggested in chapter 10, his mentioned shift from the answer *very little* to the answer *quite a lot* is not a straightforward self-contradiction across time, as it might appear to be, but rather a product of his adoption of different criteria and concepts of meaning in different theoretical contexts to suit different theoretical purposes. And if that is correct, then his shift from equating truth with the enduring agreement of a communal tradition to equating it instead with that plus the implicit endorsement of all human beings is probably likewise no simple self-contradiction across time but rather something more complex and systematic. (This suggestion will be pursued further in the notes to chapter 10.)

nology's composition there is certainly not yet an enduring communal consensus in favor of his Science, *his Science cannot yet be true, it can only become so if such a consensus is established.* It is, I suggest, an important part of the intended function of the *Phenomenology* to address this problem and challenge, to establish an enduring communal consensus in support of Hegelian Science in the modern world, and thereby to make possible and actual Hegelian Science's truth. The work has two main means for accomplishing this task. The first is its pedagogical/epistemological procedure, already considered in the last two chapters, for "leading the individual from his uneducated standpoint to knowledge," or Hegelian Science, specifically. The second is its general case for the enduring communal consensus theory of truth, and hence for participation in an enduring communal consensus being necessary and sufficient for realizing all three of one's deepest aspirations—those for communal solidarity per se, knowledge of truth, and radical freedom—and so the very core of one's happiness.[89] This is task (11) in our list of the work's tasks.[90]

This idea that, as a consequence of the enduring communal consensus theory of truth, Hegelian Science must achieve enduring communal acceptance if it is to become true, and that it is the *Phenomenology*'s task to effect this acceptance, is reflected in many remarks in the Preface of the *Phenomenology*. For example, it lies behind the Preface's insistence that Hegelian Science cannot remain "the esoteric possession of a few individuals" but must become, through the *Phenomenology,* "exoteric, comprehensible, and capable of being learned and appropriated by all";

---

89. There is also a second and perhaps more obvious sense in which the *Phenomenology* has the task of making Hegelian Science true by leading people to accept it: As we have seen, task (7) of the work is to lead people to the standpoint of Hegelian Science in order to accomplish Absolute Spirit's essential self-knowledge and thereby its full realization. Since Hegelian Science postulates Absolute Spirit as *real,* it is only thanks to the *Phenomenology*'s performance of that task that Hegelian Science is true.

90. This task may help to explain a further part of the motivation behind the *Phenomenology*'s startling doctrine at paragraphs 801 ff. that with the attainment of Hegelian Science *time ends.* If time did *not* end, then, however successful the *Phenomenology* might be in establishing a communal consensus in Hegelian Science's support in the modern world, Hegelian Science's truth would still, by the lights of the enduring communal consensus theory of truth, remain forever an indeterminate matter and not certainly knowable, because forever vulnerable to a future lapse in communal support for Hegelian Science—neither of which corollaries would be acceptable to Hegel, who aspires to determinate and certainly known truth. If time *does* end, on the other hand, and moreover does so with Hegelian Science communally endorsed (as Hegel envisages), then this can reasonably be understood to render Hegelian Science, by the lights of the enduring communal consensus theory of truth, determinately true and knowable with certainty at that point.

that Hegelian "Science . . . requires that self-consciousness should have raised itself . . . in order to be able to live—and [actually] to live—with Science and in Science"; and that Hegelian Science must be "ripened to its properly matured form so as to be capable of being the property of all self-conscious Reason" (pars. 13, 26, 70). Again, Hegel's concern to establish through the *Phenomenology* an enduring communal consensus in support of his Science in order to make possible and actual his Science's truth explains his pondering at the end of the Preface the question of his work's acceptance by "contemporaries" and "posterity," and his reassurance to himself that the speedy judgment which gets passed on an "author [Schriftsteller]" by the "public [Publikum]," and particularly by its self-appointed representatives, must be distinguished from "the more gradual effect which corrects the attention extorted by imposing assurances and corrects, too, contemptuous censure, and gives some writers contemporaries [eine Mitwelt] only after a time, while others after a time have no posterity [keine Nachwelt] left" (par. 71). These remarks are not merely, as they might seem, expressions of vainglorious yearnings for lasting good repute. Rather, it is Hegel's idea that nothing less than the truth of his Science depends upon its acceptance by a contemporary world and then a posterity. Thus, he prefaces these remarks with the observation that "it is the nature of truth to prevail when its time has come . . . The individual needs that this should be so in order to verify what is as yet a matter for himself alone, and to experience the conviction, which in the first place belongs only to a particular individual, as something universally held" (par. 71). And they should also be read in the light of the late Jena aphorism quoted earlier in which Hegel indicates that the truth of a position is decided by the verdict of *die Mitwelt* and then *die Nachwelt*.[91]

Note finally that, as Hegel conceives matters, the *Phenomenology*'s achievement of metaphysical task (11), its realization in the modern

---

91. It is also illuminating in this connection to compare the above remarks from paragraph 71 with some passages from Herder's *Briefe zu Beförderung der Humanität* which clearly provided their inspiration. Herder writes there that the "public [Publikum]" of all times and places is a "universal concilium . . . which alone, and indeed only in constantly developing votes, can be judge of the true and the false," and that it is hence the "contemporaries and posterity [Welt und Nachwelt]" of an "author [Schriftsteller]" who have ultimate authority, but that it is not immediate popularity with "the numerically strongest . . . public" which matters but rather "the most intelligent public" whose "judgment survives and continues to have influence," and that "an author often finds these readers only after his death" (5:113–19).

world of an enduring communal consensus supporting Hegelian Science, and thereby of Hegelian Science's truth, will simultaneously be an achievement for the first time of genuine communal solidarity, knowledge of truth, and radical freedom—that is, of human beings' three deepest aspirations, and hence the very core of human happiness. Nor are the work's *means* to these two achievements sharply distinct (namely, in both cases mainly the two means mentioned in the paragraph before last).

* * *

The above are the essential points to note concerning the metaphysical tasks of the *Phenomenology*. Before we proceed to a new topic, however, it is worth noting that the *Phenomenology*'s commitment to the enduring communal consensus theory of truth, and consequent demand and expectation—both because of the need to make Hegelian Science true, and because of the need to realize our three deepest human aspirations, to solidarity, knowledge of truth, and radical freedom—that an enduring communal consensus is to be achieved in the modern world, are also reflected in the work's *historical* account. For the main body of the *Phenomenology*—in particular the chapters *Consciousness* through *Reason*, which, as we shall see in parts 3 and 4, contain a treatment of the whole course of human history from ancient times up to Hegel's present, and constitute a sort of Ur-*Phenomenology*, or the entirety of the work which Hegel originally planned to write—is conceived largely as an account of history's gradual genesis of and eventual culmination in an enduring communal consensus in the modern world. (This is another of the several general schemas for the interpretation of history operative in the *Phenomenology*.)

Thus, the Preface tells us that "it is the nature of humanity to press onward to agreement with others; human nature only really exists in an achieved community of minds" (par. 69). And if we follow the course of the chapters *Consciousness* through *Reason* we find just such a development toward enduring communal consensus depicted there. Thus, early in the *Self-consciousness* chapter Hegel looks ahead to the eventual experience of "absolute substance which is the unity of different independent self-consciousnesses . . . : 'I' that is 'We' and 'We' that is 'I' " (par. 177). By early in the *Reason* chapter he indicates that, although this goal has still not been attained at the stage of history now under consideration, it will be attained during the remaining historical course of the chapter: "To begin with . . . active Reason is aware of itself merely as an individual . . . Then, however, consciousness having raised itself into universality, it becomes *universal* Reason . . . which in its pure consciousness unites all self-consciousness" (par. 348). And as we near the end of the *Reason* chapter, this predicted achievement of enduring communal consensus is represented as realized in the modern world. Hence, by the section *The Spiritual Animalkingdom*—on Herder and his age—Hegel writes that now a thing's "being is the action of the single individual and of all individuals, and [its] action is immediately . . . a thing as the action of each and everyone" (par. 418). And when we reach paragraphs 435–37 at the very end of the *Reason* chapter—on Hegel's own standpoint and age—we read similarly that now "the law . . . is grounded not in the will of a particular individual . . . ; it is the absolute *pure will of all*" (par. 436).

This depiction in the main body of the *Phenomenology* of history's gradual genesis of and eventual culmination in an enduring communal consensus in the modern world can be viewed from another angle as well. Kojève, in his well-known *Introduction to the Reading of Hegel*, attributes to the *Phenomenology* a conception of history, centered in the *Lordship and Bondage* [Herrschaft und Knechtschaft] section, as a process of the gradual diminishing and eventual overcoming of the socioeconomic opposition of master and slave depicted in that section, a process mediated by labor, and culminating in the emergence of the harmonious, freedom-providing institutions of the modern state, which both sustain and require the overcoming of the master-slave opposition.[92] This reading of the *Phenomenology* is, I think, broadly justified—in the sense that it does succeed in identifying one important strand in the work's interpretation of history.[93] Hegel was, I believe, inspired to this strand of his interpretation of history by a little known work published in 1789 by the German classical historian J.F. Reitemeier, *The History and Condition of Slavery and Bondage in Greece*.[94] For in this work Reitemeier advances the strik-

---

92. A. Kojève, *Introduction to the Reading of Hegel* (Ithaca, N.Y.: Cornell University Press, 1980), esp. chaps. 1 and 2.

93. Pace G.A. Kelly in his influential essay "Notes on Hegel's *Lordship and Bondage*," in *Hegel: A Collection of Critical Essays*, who objects to Kojève's reading that it (i) anachronistically imputes to Hegel a Marxian belief in the primacy of socioeconomic factors in historical explanation (pp. 191–93) and (ii) wrongly reads the *Phenomenology* as a philosophy of history (pp. 199–200). These objections are both misconceived, for, as we shall see in part 3, the *Phenomenology* in fact *does* espouse a (qualified) belief in the primacy of socioeconomic (and political) factors in historical explanation, and *is* (among other things) a philosophy of history.

94. J.F. Reitemeier, *Geschichte und Zustand der Sklaverei und Leibeigenschaft in Griechenland* (Berlin: August Mylius, 1789).

ingly similar historical thesis that ancient slavery was an early and extreme form of more general socioeconomic relations of "lordship [Herrschaft]" and "subordinate service [Dienstbarkeit]," which have gradually become less extreme over the course of subsequent history, until now "universal freedom" has been achieved among "the present German and other European countries," a situation better both for the "serving class" and for the state as a whole.[95] However, Kojève's interpretation of the *Lordship and Bondage* section and of the conception of history centered in it is seriously incomplete. For one thing, as Kelly rightly points out, it neglects an important *psychological* aspect of Hegel's conception: the idea that the social opposition of master and slave has had over the course of history profound effects on the constitution of the individual mind, awakening within it an opposition between psychological faculties which is required for human development, eventually leading to their higher synthesis and harmony within the modern individual mind.[96] More specifically, this social opposition adds to the attitude of "being-for-self," or self-assertiveness, which initially monopolizes the individual mind a contrary attitude of "being-for-another," or deference, and eventually leads to the synthesis and harmony of these attitudes within the modern mind. This psychological account is a close variant of a theory originally developed by Schiller, for whom the eventual achievement of psychic synthesis and harmony in itself constituted the attainment of a sort of *freedom*, as it does for Hegel too.[97] We might call this aspect of the eventual goal of history

---

95. Ibid., pp. 3–4, 175. Note in addition the following respects in which Hegel's account resembles and was probably influenced by Reitemeier's: (i) As we shall see in chapter 9, Hegel's *Lordship and Bondage* section refers primarily to slavery in classical Greece and under Rome. This is the great age of slavery in Reitemeier's account as well. (ii) The *Lordship and Bondage* section depicts the early origins of slavery as occurring among individuals who have a character of unrestrained wilfullness or "simple being-for-self" and in terms of feuds between pairs of such individuals in the course of which the weaker submits to the stronger as his *Knecht*. Similarly, Reitemeier gives an account of the early origins of slavery according to which it emerges among individuals whose wills are unrestrained by higher authority, each being its own law, and through conflicts between them which typically take the form of feuds, and lead to the weaker succumbing to the stronger, and yielding to him his property and powers, becoming his *Knecht* (pp. 8–9, 12–13).
96. Kelly, "Notes," pp. 194–97, 202–3, 214–16.
97. Thus an important strand of Schiller's *On the Aesthetic Education of Man* argues that the egoistic "sense-drive" is initially present in man by itself, that it is later complemented in him by the other-regarding "form-drive" (p. 139), and that freedom requires the development of both, consisting in the eventual development out of them of a "play-drive" which synthesizes and harmonizes them: Freedom "arises only when man is a *complete* being, when *both* his fundamental drives [i.e., the sense-drive and the form-drive] are fully

envisaged by the interpretation of history centered in the *Lordship and Bondage* section *psychological freedom* in order to distinguish it from the *socioeconomic freedom* emphasized by Kojève's reading. In addition, though, and most importantly for our present purposes, Kojève's reading also omits a crucial *metaphysical* dimension of Hegel's conception of the master-slave opposition and its attenuation and eventual overcoming through history. There is yet a third sort of freedom whose realization through history Hegel is here concerned to describe and explain: *metaphysical freedom* (or what I have previously been calling *radical freedom*).

What I mean by the *metaphysical* dimension of Hegel's conception is the following. In the paragraphs which preface the *Lordship and Bondage* section Hegel tells us that "self-consciousness is *desire*," and as such is "certain of itself only by superseding the other," "certain of the nothingness of this other," and that self-consciousness achieves only an imperfect realization of this desire when it "destroys the independent object" in a merely "objective" or natural manner (pars. 174–75). An important part of Hegel's thought here is that there is an impulse within man to attain the power to determine, and actually to determine, what is the case quite generally—and in this sense "perfect freedom" (par. 177). Hegel goes on to say that self-consciousness, as "desire," "achieves its satisfaction only in another self-consciousness," and that the goal which lies ahead is "the unity of the different independent self-consciousnesses which . . . enjoy perfect freedom and independence: 'I' that is 'We' and 'We' that is 'I' " (pars. 175, 177). An important part of his thought here is that the individual will, and will only, satisfy his "desire" for the power to determine, and the actual determination of, what is the case quite generally, or in other words for "perfect freedom," through becoming a participant in a stable community of individuals judging in agreement with one another. And the implicit reason for this is the enduring communal consensus theory of truth, which entails that an individual can attain the power to

---

developed; it will, therefore, be lacking as long as he is incomplete, as long as one of the two drives is excluded"; "Both drives . . . exert constraint upon the psyche; the [sense-drive] through the laws of nature, the [form-drive] through the laws of reason. The play-drive . . . , as the one in which both the others act in concert, will exert upon the psyche at once a moral and a physical constraint; it will, therefore, since it annuls all contingency, annul all constraint too, and set man free both physically and morally" (pp. 139, 97). Note that Hegel's commitment to a conception of freedom of this sort is already implicit in *The Spirit of Christianity*'s characterization of the still inwardly divided and antagonistic self of Kantian moral theory as "his own *slave*," a victim of "self-*coercion*."

determine, and actually determine, what is true quite generally by, and only by, participating in a stable community with shared judgments.

The *Lordship and Bondage* section and subsequent sections of the *Phenomenology* are in large part conceived as an account of the long and arduous historical route from conditions in ancient society which prevented the establishment of such a stable community with shared judgments to conditions in the modern world which do make this possible, and which hence at last make possible the individual's realization of his "desire" for the power to determine, and the actual determination of, what is the case quite generally, or for "perfect freedom."

Thus, the *Lordship and Bondage* section opens with an account of a period of antiquity in which all individuals exemplified in an extreme form a psychological attitude which Hegel calls "being-for-self," that is, an attitude of pure self-assertiveness, of treating other men and things alike as wholly subject to one's will: "Self-consciousness is, to begin with, simple being-for-self, self-equal through the exclusion from itself of everything else. For it, its essence and absolute object is 'I' . . . What is 'other' for it is an unessential, negatively characterized object. But the 'other' is also a self-consciousness; one individual is confronted by another individual. Appearing thus immediately on the scene, they are for one another like ordinary objects" (par. 186). It is Hegel's idea that such a psychological condition of individuals precludes their formation of a stable community with shared judgments of the sort necessary if they are to attain the power to determine, and actually to determine, truth. Thus he goes on to imply that in a society of such individuals that mutual recognition or deference toward each other which would enable them to constitute a stable community with shared judgments of the sort required for them to determine truth is inevitably absent, so that they fail to determine truth: "They are for one another like ordinary objects" and as a consequence the individual's "own self-certainty has no truth," since "its own being-for-self" can "confront[] it as an independent object" "only when each [individual] is for the other what the other is for it, only when each in its own self through its own action, and again through the action of the other, realizes this pure abstraction of being-for-self" (par. 186).

According to Hegel, a society of such individuals inevitably falls into harsh conflicts (par. 187). These conflicts may result in the death of one of the conflicting parties, an outcome which, for obvious reasons, brings this society no closer to mutual recognition, and so no closer to a stable community with shared judgments, and thence to the determination of truth, than before: "This trial by death ... does away with the truth which was supposed to issue from it ... For death is the *natural* negation of consciousness ... which thus remains without the required significance of recognition" (par. 188). Alternatively, these conflicts may result in one of the conflicting parties submitting to the will of the other in order to save his life, and accepting a position of social subordination or enslavement (par. 189). With this second outcome a new psychological attitude emerges among those who are subordinated or enslaved, an attitude opposite in character to the pure "being-for-self" which initially characterized all individuals and continues to characterize the victorious lord, an attitude of pure "being-for-another," or pure deference: "There is posited a pure self-consciousness, and a consciousness which is not purely for itself but for another ... They exist as two opposed shapes of consciousness; one is the independent consciousness whose essential nature is to be for itself, the other is the dependent consciousness whose essential nature is simply to live or to be for another. The former is lord, the other is bondsman" (par. 189).[98] It might seem as though this second outcome held out more promise of establishing mutual recognition and a stable community with shared judgments—"Here ... is present this moment of recognition, viz. that the other consciousness [i.e., the bondsman] sets aside its own being-for-self ... Similarly ... what the bondsman does is really the action of the lord" (par. 191). However, Hegel argues that that is not really the case, or at least not *directly*. For the sort of recognition established under these conditions is at best one-sided, a recognition of the lord by the bondsman but not vice versa: "For recognition proper the moment is lacking that what the lord does to the other he also does to himself, and what the bondsman does to himself he should also do to the other. The outcome is a recognition that is one-sided and unequal" (par. 191). It therefore turns out that, like the original society made up entirely of purely self-assertive master types, the society which emerges therefrom divided between purely self-assertive master types and purely deferential slave types makes mutual recognition and a stable community with shared judgments impossible.

Nevertheless, it is Hegel's idea that the emergence of the latter society,

---

98. The deference here is in part toward the lord, of course, but also in part toward the brute factuality of the objects on which the subjugated individual labors for the lord. Unlike for the lord, "the thing is independent vis-à-vis the bondsman ... he only works on it" (par. 190).

although it does not make the achievement of mutual recognition and a stable community with shared judgments possible *directly*, does, by its addition to the original purely self-assertive master types of a class of purely deferential slave types, make their achievement possible *indirectly*. As long as there existed only purely self-assertive individuals, their achievement was quite impossible. With the arrival of the subjugated individual, however, there has emerged a psychological attitude of pure "being-for-another" or deference which can be synthesized with the pure "being-for-self" or self-assertiveness of the lord in the course of subsequent history to yield individuals of a psychological type capable of participating in mutual recognition and a stable community with shared judgments, and thence of attaining the power to determine, and actually determining, truth, or in other words achieving "perfect freedom."[99] Thus, the *Lordship and Bondage* section already implicitly looks forward to such a psychological synthesis,[100] and the middle of the *Reason* chapter explicitly ascribes it to the individuals who make up the ideal modern community to which it looks forward: this community is a "unity of being-for-another, or making oneself a thing, and of being-for-self," in it "there is nothing which would not be reciprocal, nothing in relation to which the independence of the individual would not in the dissolution of its being-for-self in the *negation* of itself, give itself its *positive* significance of being *for* itself" (par. 351).[101] And the broader thought is summed up succinctly in the *Encyclopaedia*'s discussion of Lordship and Bondage: "Without having experienced this disciplining which breaks

---

99. Hegel's idea here that the individual's attainment of *psychological* wholeness and harmony is the key to the achievement of a unified and harmonious *society* was already part of Schiller's forerunner of Hegel's account (see *On the Aesthetic Education of Man*, pp. 215–17).

100. At pars. 194–96 Hegel argues that, although the bondsman is dominated by the attitude of being-for-another, his experience of fearing death, with the melting-away of everything objective which this involves, implicitly preserves within him, and his subsequent experience of shaping things by his labor develops within him more explicitly, an element of being-for-self, or of regarding things as quite subject to his will. As Hegel puts this idea at paragraph 196, "In fear, the being-for-self is present in the bondsman himself; in fashioning the thing, he becomes aware that being-for-self belongs to *him*."

101. The need for this modern tempering of individuals' original "being-for-self" through synthesis with "being-for-another" in order for them to become capable of participating in an enduring communal consensus capable of sustaining truth, and in particular the truth of Hegelian Science, lies behind Hegel's remark in the Preface that "the nature of Science implies and requires" that "the individual must ... forget himself, ... [he] may demand less for himself" (par. 72).

willfulness, no one ... becomes reasonable ... For that reason all peoples in order to become free ... have had first to go through the strict discipline of subjection to a lord ... Bondage and tyranny are therefore a necessary step in the history of peoples and therefore something *relatively* justified" (par. 435, addition). In other words, there is a need for a historical process of disciplining individual self-assertiveness in order to render men eventually "reasonable," or capable of mutual recognition and participation in a stable community with shared judgments, so that they may "become free," particularly in the sense of possessing the power to determine, and actually determining, truth.[102]

In accordance with this conception of the function of the historical development described in the *Lordship and Bondage* section, the *Phenomenology* eventually depicts an overcoming and synthesis in the modern world of the opposed psychological attitudes of pure "being-for-self" or self-assertiveness and pure "being-for-another" or deference characteristic of the lord and the bondsman respectively, the emergence in the modern world of a new psychological attitude different from but owing something to each of these earlier extremes, which by contrast with them is capable of sustaining the sort of mutual recognition and stable community with shared judgments required for the determination of truth, or for

---

102. Interestingly, the application of this idea in the *Phenomenology* is not confined to the *Lordship and Bondage* section and its theme of social oppression and slavery in the ancient world. The *Phenomenology* does indeed represent this as the historically earliest and most important example of such a disciplining process. But it also goes on to interpret various later and quite different historical developments as, in effect, repeating or reinforcing the same disciplining function in various ways. Thus, the *Unhappy Consciousness* section interprets the subordination of the laity to God and his intermediating priests within Catholic Christianity as playing a similar role: "The surrender of one's own will is only from one aspect negative; in principle, however, or in itself, it is at the same time positive, viz. the positing of will as the will of an 'other,' and specifically of will, not as particular, but as universal will" (par. 230). Again, according to the section *Virtue and the Way of the World*, which, as we shall see, concerns the theory and practice of Frederick the Great ("Virtue") in its opposition to and disciplining of individualism ("The Way of the World"), it is part of Frederick's achievement that "individuality's *being-for-self*" which "was opposed to essence or the universal" "has ... been conquered and has vanished" (par. 392). Finally, the *Spirit* chapter interprets the Terror which followed the French Revolution as serving a similar function of disciplining the rampant individualism of its time and place: "These individuals who have felt the fear of death, of their absolute master, again submit to negation and distinctions, arrange themselves in various spheres, and return to an apportioned and limited task, but thereby to their substantial reality" (par. 593; note the deliberate echo of the *Lordship and Bondage* section in the first few words here, which should be compared in this regard with par. 194).

"perfect freedom." This occurs in the later parts of the *Reason* chapter, beginning with the section *The Spiritual Animalkingdom,* which is concerned with Herder and his age. Thus in this section Hegel describes a modern psychological attitude which he calls "action" as a synthesis of "being-for-self" and "being-for-another" (par. 418); he describes it as lending itself to mutual recognition and a stable community with shared judgments—it is "the action of each and everyone" (par. 418); and he consequently characterizes it as possessing the power to determine truth—the "limitation of being . . . cannot limit the action of consciousness" (par. 398). With this outcome, individuals finally realize that "desire" for the power to determine, and the actual determination of, what is the case quite generally, or for "perfect freedom," which has implicitly driven them since earlier periods of history, but hitherto been frustrated.[103]

It is, then, not only in a *socioeconomic* sense and a *psychological* sense, but also, and indeed above all, in a *metaphysical* sense—a truth-determining sense based on the enduring communal consensus theory of truth—that the *Phenomenology*'s history of the master-slave opposition and its eventual overcoming is conceived by Hegel as a history of the realization of *freedom*. In interpreting the *Phenomenology*'s account of history centered in the *Lordship and Bondage* section, we must add to the socioeconomic thread which Kojève disentangled, and the psychological thread which Kelly noted, also, and especially, this metaphysical thread. (Doing so yields yet another important schema for the interpretation of history operative in the *Phenomenology*.)

This concludes our investigation of the metaphysical tasks of the *Phenomenology*, and therewith our investigation of the work's official tasks as an "introduction" to Hegelian Science generally.

---

103. Hegel's account of how men were originally motivated by "desire" wholly in a mode of "being-for-self" or wilful self-assertion, and were thereby deprived of true community and true freedom, but by undergoing enslavement or subjugation have become disciplined into a measure of social deference which makes possible true community, " 'I' that is 'We' and 'We' that is 'I,' " and with it "perfect freedom," owes something to Rousseau. Thus in *The Social Contract* Rousseau argues that in the state of nature man was ruled by "instinct" or "physical impulse," and thereby deprived of community and freedom (*Rousseau: Selections,* ed. M. Cranston [New York: Macmillan, 1988], p. 127), that he has since subjugated himself and his property to the community, in forms of enslavement often worse than that of the state of nature (p. 127; cf. 118), but that this process of subjugation was necessary for and served to bring about the formation of a true community or general will (p. 125) and with it the freedom which only this makes possible (p. 127).

PART TWO

The Official Project Continued:
The Relation of the *Phenomenology* to
Hegelian Science

CHAPTER FIVE

The *Phenomenology* as "Appearance" of Hegelian Science

In this and the next two chapters we shall pursue the (largely architectonic) question of the officially intended relation between the *Phenomenology* and Hegelian Science proper (i.e., the system comprising Logic, Philosophy of Nature, and Philosophy of Spirit, of which Hegel went on to publish a version in the *Encyclopaedia*).[1] A large part of the answer to this question has already been given in part 1, where we have seen that the *Phenomenology* is officially intended to serve as an "introduction" to Hegelian Science of a certain highly novel and complex sort. There do, though, remain some further aspects of the officially intended relation between the *Phenomenology* and Hegelian Science still to be specified. In the course of specifying these in this and the next two chapters we will also have an opportunity to determine Hegel's solutions to a series of problems which might still seem to threaten the work's official function as an "introduction" to Hegelian Science in various ways.

The first of the further aspects of the officially intended relation between the *Phenomenology* and Hegelian Science which demand notice is Hegel's conception that the *Phenomenology* gives us, not "the Science of the true in its true shape," but instead only an "appearance [Erscheinung]" of Science (or of Science's principle, Absolute Spirit). This conception is implied by the Introduction's statements that "Science, just because it comes on the scene, is itself an appearance: it is not yet Science

---

1. The secondary literature contains a wide variety of answers to this question. For a helpful survey of some of the most significant, see Fulda, *Das Problem einer Einleitung*, pp. 57–78.

in its developed and unfolded truth," and that "an exposition of how Science makes its appearance will here be undertaken [i.e., in the *Phenomenology*]" (par. 76). The same conception is also implied by the Preface, where Hegel contrasts his own procedure of beginning with the *Phenomenology* in order to prepare the ground for Science with an alternative procedure which someone might advocate of beginning with Science straightaway, and articulates the case that might be made for the latter procedure in the following terms: "Now, because the system of the experience of Spirit [i.e., the *Phenomenology*] embraces only the appearance of Spirit, the advance from this system to the Science of the true in its true shape seems to be merely negative, and one might wish to be spared the negative as something false, and demand to be led to the truth without more ado" (par. 38). For, although Hegel goes on to criticize this case, on the ground that it mistakenly assumes a sharp opposition between truth and falsehood (par. 39), this criticism leaves standing the implication that, in contrast to straightforwardly true Science, the *Phenomenology* presents mere appearance, which is less than straightforwardly true. Finally, the same conception of the *Phenomenology* is also implied by the very title of the work, *Phenomenology of Spirit*—the word *phenomenology* coming from the Greek *phainomai*, meaning to appear.

Hegel really has two ideas here which should be distinguished. First, he is thinking of the viewpoints, the "shapes of consciousness," which constitute the principal *subject matter* of the *Phenomenology* as an "appearance" of Science (or of Science's principle, Absolute Spirit). In this vein, he refers in the *Science of Logic* to consciousness as "the appearing [erscheinende] Spirit."[2] (This is the more textually obvious and philosophically unsurprising of Hegel's two ideas.) But second, and no less importantly, he is also thinking of the standpoint of the *Phenomenology itself*, in which those shapes of consciousness culminate, and which treats them as its principal subject matter, as, likewise, an "appearance" of Science (or of Science's principle, Absolute Spirit).

What then, more precisely, does Hegel mean by characterizing the *Phenomenology* as in these two ways presenting merely the "appearance" of Science? In order to answer this question, we need to consider the sense that he assigns to the category of Appearance in the mature Logic. In the *Science of Logic* this category follows the lower category of Existence [Existenz] and is in turn followed by the higher category of Essential Rela-

2. *Science of Logic*, p. 28; also in appendix XV.

The *Phenomenology* as "Appearance" of Hegelian Science 261

tion. Its character is that of both a *transitional category between* and (to put the thought a little crudely perhaps) a *mixture of* the abstraction, impurity, and instability of mere Existence, on the one hand, and the concretion, purity, and stability of Essence or Law, on the other. Thus the *Science of Logic* tells us that "the world of appearance has in the essential world its negative unity . . . into which it withdraws as into its ground," that "existence withdraws into law as into its ground; appearance contains these two, the simple ground, and the dissolving movement of the appearing universe whose essentiality it is," and that "the realm of laws is the *stable* content of appearance; appearance is the same content but presenting itself in restless flux and as reflection-into-other. It is law as the negative, simply alterable existence."[3] In the Nuremberg *Logic* of 1810–11, which, due to its slightly earlier date, is more likely to reflect accurately the position of the *Phenomenology*, the category of Appearance has basically the same character, except that it is conceived as a transition between and mixture of *Determinate Being* [Dasein] and Essence or Law, rather than *Existence* and Essence or Law. Hence Hegel writes in this version of the Logic that "essence must appear . . . because determinate being [Dasein] dissolves in it and returns to its ground—negative appearance."[4]

When Hegel in the *Phenomenology* characterizes the work as presenting just an "appearance" of Science he has this technical sense of the word *appearance* in mind. One can see in a general way that he does so as he writes the *Phenomenology* from his evident use of it in this sense in such passages as the following: Law "is the stable image of unstable appearance . . . The supersensible world is an inert realm of laws which, though beyond the perceived world—for this exhibits law only through incessant change—is equally present in it" (par. 149).[5] And that he specifically conceives the *Phenomenology* as presenting an "appearance" of Science in the same technical sense can be seen from his statements that "the element of determinate being [Dasein] is . . . what distinguishes this part of Science [i.e., the *Phenomenology*] from the others," and that the *Phenomenology* will culminate "at a point where appearance becomes identical with essence, so that [consciousness's] exposition will coincide with just this point of the authentic Science of Spirit [i.e., with the Logic,

---

3. Ibid., pp. 508, 503–4.
4. *Nürnberger und Heidelberger Schriften*, p. 175.
5. Hegel is here characterizing the shape of consciousness Force and the Understanding.

whose categories Hegel sometimes refers to as "essences," e.g., at par. 34]" (pars. 35, 89).[6]

In characterizing the *Phenomenology* as presenting an "appearance" of Science Hegel therefore means to say that what it presents *effects a transition between, and itself constitutes a mixture of, the abstract, impure, unstable "determinate being" of nonscientific perspectives, on the one hand, and the concrete, pure, stable "essence" of Hegelian Science, and in particular the Hegelian Logic, on the other.*

The first part of this conception, the idea that what the *Phenomenology* presents effects a *transition* from the imperfection of nonscientific perspectives to the perfection of Hegelian Science, requires no further explanation here. For we have just explored the various facets of this idea in some detail in part 1—that is, the various ways in which the shapes of consciousness treated in the work as its subject matter and the standpoint of the work itself serve to effect such a transition.

The second part of the above conception, though, the idea that what the *Phenomenology* presents constitutes a *mixture* of the imperfection of nonscientific perspectives and the perfection of Hegelian Science, still calls for an explanation. To say that the *Phenomenology* presents an "appearance" of Science in this second sense is to say that the shapes of consciousness which it treats as its subject matter and even the standpoint of the work itself express the same content as Science but in a form which includes the imperfection of nonscientific perspectives. Thus Hegel indicates that even the standpoint of the work itself is not "the Science of the true in its true shape" but instead merely "the Understanding's form of Science [die verständige Form der Wissenschaft]" (pars. 38, 13). Since Science alone is true, this implies that the shapes of consciousness treated by the work as its subject matter and even the standpoint of the work itself combine Science's truth with the *falsehood* of nonscientific perspectives. Hence Hegel indicates that even the standpoint of the work itself combines truth with falsehood—rejecting a characterization of the work as simply false, not on the ground that it is simply true, but on the ground that it is a mistake to suppose that " 'True' and 'False' belong to those determinate ideas which qualify as inert and motionless essences of which the one stands isolated and firm there and the other here, without sharing anything with the former. On the contrary, one must hold that truth is

---

6. I follow Pöggeler in retaining the original text of the latter passage rather than amending it.

no fully minted coin which can be given finished and pocketed that way" (pars. 38–39).⁷ Indeed, one may properly infer further that in characterizing what the *Phenomenology* presents as an "appearance" of Science Hegel is implying that the shapes of consciousness treated by the work as its subject matter and even the standpoint of the work itself combine Science's truth with the *self-contradictory* falsehood of nonscientific perspectives. For it will be recalled that part of Hegel's epistemological strategy in the work is to show that *all* perspectives other than that of Science itself are self-contradictory. Accordingly, Hegel characterizes even the standpoint of the *Phenomenology* itself as an example of "the negative" (par. 38), a term which for him invariably implies self-contradictoriness.⁸ This suggestion that Hegel understands the shapes of consciousness treated by the *Phenomenology* as its subject matter and even the standpoint of the work itself to express Science's truth through self-contradiction should come as no great surprise. For, as we saw in part 1, the *Phenomenology*'s predecessor discipline, the early Logic, rested squarely on an assumption that self-contradictory viewpoints form a *hierarchy* whose upper ranks are distinguished by being, despite their self-contradictoriness, nonetheless relatively good expressions of Hegelian Science's truth. Hegel's conception that the *Phenomenology* presents in the shapes of con-

---

7. J.H. Lambert, the first philosopher to have conceived of a philosophical discipline of "Phenomenology," had argued similarly—though with reference only to the subject matter of the discipline, not the standpoint of the discipline itself as well—that there was "no error without truth mixed in with it" (*Neues Organon* 1:553) and that in "appearance [Schein]" truth and falsehood were mixed: "We should . . . not simply oppose the True to the False, but there exists in our cognition between these two a middle-thing which we call *appearance* [Schein]" (2:217). However, Lambert had also, in some inconsistency with both of these points, drawn a distinction between, on the one hand, "*Schein* in general" and, on the other hand, "what we call *mere Schein*" in which "nothing real lies at the basis" (2:236). And we can see in the wish to preserve such a distinction as this but without falling into Lambert's inconsistencies the motivation behind two subtle modifications which Hegel has effected in his version of Lambert's two points: (i) Hegel's idea is not that there is *never* error without truth mixed in with it, but rather that error in *some* cases has truth mixed in with it. And (ii) Hegel draws a terminological distinction between *Erscheinung* and *Schein*—roughly corresponding to Lambert's first sort of *Schein*, "*Schein* in general," and his second sort of *Schein*, "*mere Schein*," respectively—and reconceives Lambert's doctrine about appearance containing truth as well as falsehood as a doctrine strictly about *Erscheinung*, but not *Schein*.

8. Note in this connection that Lambert too had conceived appearance [Schein] and (self-)contradiction as intimately connected: "If one . . . accepts as completely true an appearance which is in fact different from the true, then this is an error from which it is consequently always possible to deduce contradictions" (ibid., 2:247).

sciousness which are its subject matter and even in its own standpoint an "appearance" of Science rests on the same assumption, implying that the work presents therein relatively high forms of self-contradiction, forms of self-contradiction which are relatively good expressions of Hegelian Science's truth—indeed, in the case of its own standpoint, the *highest* form of self-contradiction, that form of self-contradiction which *best* expresses Hegelian Science's truth.[9]

This basic explanation of Hegel's conception of the *Phenomenology* as presenting an "appearance" of Science in the second sense of a *mixture* of Science with nonscientific perspectives requires some further elaboration, however. There are, especially, two ideas here which may still seem in one or another degree obscure and controversial: (i) the idea of viewpoints mixing truth with falsehood, and in particular with self-contradictory falsehood, and (ii) the idea of their doing so in differing proportions, as it were, so that some viewpoints which do so are better and some worse as expressions of truth. How are we to make sense of these ideas?

I suggest that in connection with the *Phenomenology* Hegel conceives idea (i) in the following ways. When in the 1801–2 sketch of the early Logic he had deployed a version of idea (i), arguing that the Understanding's forms of syllogism, though false and self-contradictory, nevertheless had "speculative meaning," or signified true Hegelian Science, his thought had evidently been, not that they strictly meant or implied this—how could they?—but rather that they functioned as effective *metaphors* for it. His application of idea (i) to the *Phenomenology* should in part, I suggest, be understood in a similar way: the *Phenomenology*'s self-contradictory falsehoods express true Hegelian Science by standing as effective *metaphors* for it. However, metaphors can be of different sorts, and in particular a metaphor may be more or less distant in literal sense from the idea for which it stands. In many, and indeed most, cases the semantic distance is great—as, for example, when Shakespeare ponders, "Shall I compare thee to a summer's day?" In other cases, though, the semantic distance may be quite modest. For example, a physicist who believed that such concepts as "mass" and "force" had changed subtly in the transition from Newtonian to Einsteinian physics might choose

---

9. The implied contrasting class of false, self-contradictory views which *fail* to express truth or do so in only a negligible degree (in Hegel's terminology, cases of *Schein* rather than of *Erscheinung*) would include many, and indeed probably most, of the particular claims made *within* shapes of consciousness.

to characterize a certain Einsteinian law for the benefit of a Newtonian audience by saying that it was *like* a corresponding law of Newton's. The 1801–2 sketch's interpretation of the Understanding's forms of syllogism as having "speculative meaning" evidently involves an interpretation of them as metaphors for true Hegelian Science of the first, semantically distant, sort. By contrast, when the *Phenomenology* conceives the viewpoints which it contains as subject matter and its own standpoint as expressing true Hegelian Science, this seems to involve an interpretation of them as (especially in the latter case) metaphors for true Hegelian Science of the second, semantically close, sort.

There is, though, in addition, a further component to idea (i) in the context of the *Phenomenology*. This is the thought that a self-contradictory falsehood can express truth by *dialectically implying* it. The notion of a self-contradictory falsehood X dialectically implying a truth Y as a matter of fact *includes* the notion that X can stand as a metaphor for Y, or at least for some aspect(s) of Y. For dialectical implication of Y by X essentially involves what Hegel calls the *Aufhebung* of X by Y, that is, (paradoxically glossed) the *preservation* and *abolition* of X in Y, or (non-paradoxically cashed out) X's preservation in Y but with a modified meaning—a situation of the same general sort as we envisaged in our Newton/Einstein example. However, the idea of a self-contradictory falsehood's dialectical implication of a truth also includes a good deal more than just the idea of its suitability as a metaphor for the latter: in particular, in order for self-contradictory falsehood X to imply dialectically truth Y, there must also be a *necessary transition* from self-contradictory falsehood X to some new proposition which either is truth Y itself or else eventually leads through a finite sequence of such necessary transitions to truth Y.[10]

In short, in connection with the *Phenomenology* idea (i) should be understood in terms of self-contradictory falsehoods (a) serving as semantically close metaphors for the truth, and (b) dialectically implying the truth.

How, next, are we to explain in connection with the *Phenomenology* idea (ii), the idea that viewpoints may mix falsehood, and indeed self-contradictory falsehood, with truth in differing proportions, so that some which do so are better and some worse as expressions of truth? The two respects just indicated in which the *Phenomenology*'s self-contradictory

---

10. Concerning the nature of this dialectical "necessity" see chapter 3.

falsehoods may express the truth, namely, by serving as semantically close metaphors for the truth and by dialectically implying the truth, suggest an answer to this question. For different self-contradictory falsehoods might satisfy these two conditions in significantly different ways. Thus, concerning, to begin with, their role as semantically close metaphors for the truth, the degree of *precision* with which they play this role might vary, thereby yielding a first criterion for judging some self-contradictory falsehoods' expressions of the truth more successful than others'. This general criterion of precision can be subdivided into three more specific criteria: (a) the number of self-contradictions which have to be resolved in a self-contradictory falsehood in order to bring it to self-consistency—ceteris paribus, the fewer, the more precise the metaphor for the truth, and so the more successful the expression of the truth; (b) the degree of a self-contradictory falsehood's semantic proximity to the truth—ceteris paribus, the closer, the more precise the metaphor for the truth, and so the more successful the expression of the truth; and (c) the amount of the truth, or the number of aspects of the truth, captured by a self-contradictory falsehood's metaphor—ceteris paribus, the more, the more precise the metaphor for the truth, and so the more successful the expression of the truth. Concerning, next, self-contradictory falsehoods' dialectical implication of the truth, the number of dialectical transitions required in order for them to generate the truth dialectically may vary, thereby yielding a further criterion of self-contradictory falsehoods' relative success in expressing the truth: (d) the number of dialectical transitions required in order for a self-contradictory falsehood to generate the truth—ceteris paribus, the fewer, the more successful the expression of the truth.

Hegel in fact believes, at least in the context of the *Phenomenology*, that these four criteria (a)–(d) always coincide with one another, that whenever a self-contradictory falsehood A is more successful at expressing the truth than a self-contradictory falsehood B judged by *one* of these criteria, then it is so judged by *any* of them. Thus, the dialectical development of false and self-contradictory viewpoints toward true Science depicted within the *Phenomenology* begins from Sense-certainty, a viewpoint which (a′) has the most implicit self-contradictions in need of resolution in order to yield self-consistency, (b′) has the least semantic proximity to true Science, (c′) serves as a metaphor for the fewest aspects of true Science (due to its simplicity), and (d′) has the most dialectical steps to go through before it dialectically generates true Science. And as we proceed through the remaining course of the work these weaknesses gradually diminish with the attainment of each new viewpoint in step with one another. The standpoint of the *Phenomenology* itself, coming at the summit of this hierarchy, has each of these weaknesses in the lowest degree possible for any position short of true Science itself.

This, I suggest, is how we should understand ideas (i) and (ii) implied by Hegel's conception of the *Phenomenology* as presenting an "appearance" of Hegelian Science in the second sense of a *mixture* of Hegelian Science with nonscientific perspectives.

The *Phenomenology*'s status as a presentation of Science's "appearance" in the second sense of a *mixture* of Science with nonscientific perspectives of the sort just described has motives deeply rooted in the official project of the work which we investigated in part 1. For it constitutes Hegel's solution to a certain problem, or family of problems, which seems to confront that project: On the one hand, as we saw, the *Phenomenology*'s whole pedagogical project presupposes there to be a propositional and conceptual gulf between Hegelian Science and nonscientific viewpoints. And, as we saw in connection with pedagogical task (1) and epistemological task (4), Hegel believes his Science alone to be true, and all nonscientific viewpoints to be by contrast false and self-contradictory. But on the other hand, it is an essential part of the *Phenomenology*'s project *to convey Science and truth at the level of nonscientific viewpoints*. In particular, pedagogical task (3) requires that the work give a provisional presentation of true Science at the level of nonscientific viewpoints. And epistemological task (6) requires that the work provide a demonstration of Science purely in the light of the initial views and criteria of nonscientific viewpoints—a demonstration which, however, Hegel clearly understands to be more than merely specious, to be in some manner genuinely revealing of facts supportive of Science (such as the self-contradictoriness of all nonscientific viewpoints, and Science's consequent invulnerability to skeptical equipollence problems), and therefore in some manner true. How can these two sides of Hegel's position be reconciled? How can he purport to convey Science and truth at the level of nonscientific viewpoints, while simultaneously believing that there is a propositional and conceptual gulf between Science and nonscientific viewpoints, and that only Science itself is true, and every nonscientific viewpoint by contrast false and self-contradictory? Enter the doctrine that the *Phenomenology* presents an "appearance" of Science in the second sense of a *mixture* of Science with nonscientific viewpoints of the sort that has been described above.[11]

We might usefully conclude with some concrete examples of how Hegel conceives this status of the work in connection with pedagogical task (3) and epistemological task (6). Relevant to both cases is the fact that in the Introduction Hegel implies, more specifically, that the *Phenomenology*'s presentation of its series of shapes of consciousness is an "appearance" of the *Logic*'s presentation of its series of categories (par. 89).[12] Consequently, concerning pedagogical task (3), although the *Phe-*

---

11. Versions of the above problem have been raised at several points in the secondary literature. However, to my knowledge, only one author has recognized this direction in which Hegel's answer to it lies, namely, Fulda. Thus, Haym raises an epistemological form of the problem (with characteristic irony) in *Hegel und seine Zeit:* "There is of course no true cognition except from the standpoint of Absolute Knowing. Thus Hegel stood before a new . . . problem which he had to solve through the composition of the *Phenomenology*. He had the difficult task of *combining the proof of the absolute standpoint with its nonproof.* It was a matter of both for the first time leading up to this standpoint and yet at the same time making this movement proceed in no other element than that of Absolute Knowing" (p. 251). But Haym overlooks the function of Hegel's notion of Science's or Absolute Knowing's "appearance" in reconciling these two seemingly irreconcilable aspirations—instead interpreting Hegel as ultimately choosing in favor of preventing the *Phenomenology* from failing as a proof because untrue by making it work from the standpoint of Absolute Knowing from the start, and thus in effect sacrificing the goal of "for the first time leading up to this standpoint" in the work, a solution which, however, according to Haym, was to no avail because it made the resulting "proof" viciously circular (pp. 252–56). Fulda recognizes an epistemological form of the problem as well. Thus, he notes that the *Phenomenology* aspires to provide the sort of proof of Science for nonscientific viewpoints purely in the light of their own initial views and criteria which I have classified as task (6): "an *introduction* to [Science] which is at the same time a real *access route,* or in other words leads to Science without making the presupposition of Science," an access route which "the nonscientific consciousness must acknowledge; since it does not require [that consciousness] to concern itself with the demands which Science makes of it and satisfies its own claim to independence" (*Das Problem einer Einleitung,* p. 165). But he points out that such an aspiration confronts the problem that it is unclear how Hegel can possibly operate on this basis with "other than merely rhetorical means—persuasion and shock" (p. 167). Unlike Haym, however, Fulda hints in the direction of Hegel's real solution to this problem, noting that in order to decide whether Hegel's aspiration to include in the *Phenomenology* an access route to Hegelian Science of the sort described is capable of realization "it would be necessary to undertake an exact analysis of speculative thought with respect to the side of its *appearance,*" and designating this "one of the most important tasks in the interpretation of Hegel" (p. 165; emphasis added). The present chapter attempts to make some progress in this direction.

12. Cf. Hegel's remark at paragraph 805 that "to know the pure concepts of Science in [the] form of shapes of consciousness constitutes the side of their reality" (that is, mixes with the "Essence" of those concepts the "Determinate Being" of nonscientific perspectives).

nomenology's presentation of its sequence of shapes of consciousness occurs at the level of nonscientific viewpoints, and is therefore strictly speaking false and even self-contradictory, it nevertheless succeeds in giving relatively good provisional expression to at least the logical part of true Science. Similarly, concerning epistemological task (6), specifically in its task (4) component: We have seen that the *Phenomenology* offers a demonstration of Hegelian Science's invulnerability to the skeptical equipollence problem which consists in showing that each member of a series of shapes of consciousness is self-contradictory, and moreover necessarily develops into the next to form a circle which manifests their constitution of an entire system and hence their complete collection. Now, as Hegel conceives matters, this demonstration occurs at the level of nonscientific viewpoints, and is therefore, strictly speaking, false and even self-contradictory, and so in a way no genuine demonstration. However, it is also an "appearance" of certain scientific truths which really do show his Science's invulnerability to the equipollence problem: namely, the true state of affairs exhibited in the Logic that each of the logical categories which underlie the *Phenomenology*'s shapes of consciousness is self-contradictory, and moreover necessarily develops into the next to form a circle which manifests their constitution of an entire system and hence their complete collection.[13] Hence, even though the *Phenomenology*'s demonstration of his Science's invulnerability to the equipollence problem works at the level of nonscientific viewpoints, and is therefore strictly speaking false and even self-contradictory, and so in one way no genuine demonstration, it nevertheless succeeds in being a genuine demonstration in another way, namely, by at the same time giving relatively good expression to a true state of affairs which really does show his Science's invulnerability to the equipollence problem.[14]

---

13. Hegel explicitly indicates this *logical* version of his answer on behalf of Hegelian Science to the skeptical equipollence problem (as the problem of "presupposition") at *Encyclopaedia*, pars. 1, 78, and *Vorlesungen über die Beweise vom Dasein Gottes*, p. 175. For a discussion of this logical version of his answer, see my *Hegel and Skepticism*, chap. 8.

14. A similar situation obtains in connection with the task (5) component of task (6). For Hegel has a logical version of his answer to task (5) as well—concerning which see my *Hegel and Skepticism*, chap. 8.

CHAPTER SIX

The *Phenomenology*'s Independence from Hegelian Science

According to a very popular reading, Hegel conceives the *Phenomenology* to depend in important respects for intelligibility and cogency on information drawn from Hegelian Science proper—the system comprising Logic, Philosophy of Nature, and Philosophy of Spirit—and in particular from the Logic. It is relatively uncontroversial that the *Phenomenology* seeks to demonstrate of a sequence of shapes of consciousness (i) that they are all self-contradictory and (ii) that each necessarily develops into the next in a continuous series. But many commentators have in addition claimed that, although the work may seek to demonstrate (i) without presupposing information from Hegelian Science proper, its demonstration of (ii) does essentially presuppose such information—and in particular, information from the Logic—and is therefore intelligible and compelling only for a viewpoint which is already scientific. For example, making the more general version of this point, Hyppolite writes that "there are two necessities: the necessity of the negation of the object, effected by consciousness itself in its experience, in the testing of its knowledge, and the necessity of the appearance of the new object which takes place through the prior experience. The latter necessity pertains only to the philosopher ... The *Phenomenology* is simultaneously a *theory of knowledge* and a *speculative philosophy*."[1] And similarly, but with more specific reference to the Logic, Pöggeler writes: "In the progressive formation of consciousness in the *Phenomenology* one does not yet perceive the

---

1. Hyppolite, *Genesis and Structure*, p. 25.

necessity of the progressive formation. This necessity is perceived only in the Logic."[2] This, then, is the popular reading.[3]

This reading is very natural because of the following four pieces of evidence which seem at first sight to speak strongly in its favor. Concerning the dependence of the *Phenomenology* on Science proper in general: (a) The Introduction informs us that the "experience" of consciousness exhibited in the *Phenomenology* includes the necessary origination of a new object for consciousness—and hence a new shape of consciousness—at each level, but that this necessity is perceived only "by us," not by the consciousness depicted in the *Phenomenology* itself, for which the necessity is, on the contrary, "as it were, behind [its] back" (par. 87). (b) Moreover, the Introduction goes on to say that because the *Phenomenology* includes the exhibition of this necessity it is "itself already Science" (par. 88). Concerning the dependence of the *Phenomenology* more specifically on the Logic: (c) Both in the Introduction and toward the end of the *Phenomenology* Hegel implies that the shapes of consciousness treated in the work stand in a one-to-one correspondence with the categories of the Logic, and indeed that the latter are somehow the underlying reality of the former: "In [Science] the moments of [Spirit's] movement no longer exhibit themselves as specific shapes of consciousness, but . . . as specific concepts . . . Conversely, to each abstract moment of Science corresponds a shape of manifest Spirit [i.e., a shape of consciousness] as such" (par. 805; cf. 89). Moreover, he implies that the necessity of the development from one shape of consciousness to the next in the *Phenomenology* obtains in virtue of, or is even in some sense identical with, the necessity of the development into one another of the underlying categories of the Logic. Thus, we read in the Preface that the movement of the categories of the Logic constitutes their necessary expansion to an organic

---

2. O. Pöggeler, "Qu'est-ce que la *Phénoménologie de l'Esprit?*" in *Archives de Philosophie*, Apr.–June 1966, p. 222.

3. Some further examples of the popular reading are: Baillie, translator's introduction to Hegel, *Phenomenology of Mind*, pp. 35, 58; W. Purpus, *Die Dialektik der sinnlichen Gewißheit bei Hegel* (Nuremberg: Sebald, 1905), pp. 3–4, and *Zur Dialektik des Bewußtseins nach Hegel* (Berlin: Trowitzsch, 1908), p. 16; R. Kroner, *Von Kant bis Hegel* (Tübingen: J.C.B. Mohr, 1924), 2:369–70; Kojève, *Introduction*, pp. 261–63; Fulda, *Das Problem einer Einleitung*, esp. pp. 110–11, 163–64 (Fulda, however, regards this only as Hegel's *considered* conception of the modus operandi of the *Phenomenology*, the conception at which he arrived after an alleged *Umdeutung* or reinterpretation of the work following its composition); S. Rosen, *Hegel: An Introduction to the Science of Wisdom* (New Haven, Conn.: Yale University Press, 1974), pp. xx, 126, 129.

whole and that "through this movement the path by which the Concept of knowledge is reached [i.e., the path of the shapes of consciousness in the *Phenomenology*] becomes likewise a necessary and complete process of becoming" (par. 34; cf. 5). And we read in the *Science of Logic* concerning the *Phenomenology* that consciousness's "advance rests solely ... on the nature of the *pure essentialities* which constitute the content of Logic."[4] (d) In the course of its detailed execution, the *Phenomenology* evidently quite often appeals to information from a version of the Logic, especially in order to demonstrate the necessity of the transition from one shape of consciousness to the next. At least in these cases Hegel clearly seems to be identifying the "us" said in the Introduction to perceive the necessity "behind the back of consciousness" with a viewpoint in possession of a knowledge of the Logic. For example, the following passage evidently relies on information concerning the Logic's transition from the category Being-for-self to the category Essence in order to justify the transition from Perception to Force and the Understanding, ascribing this information to "us": "*We* must step into [consciousness's] place and be the concept which develops that which is contained in the result ... The result has implicitly the positive significance that in it the unity of being-for-self and being-for-another is posited or that absolute opposition is immediately posited as self-identical essence" (pars. 133–34).[5]

The problem arises, however, that if the *Phenomenology* were indeed supposed to work as the popular reading says, then this would conflict with the official project of the work described in part 1 in certain fundamental ways. First, if the popular reading were correct, then the *Phenomenology* would be in principle incapable of providing the sort of proof of Hegelian Science for all nonscientific viewpoints based purely on their own initial views and criteria which is required by task (6). For that proof essentially includes making the necessary development from each shape of consciousness to the next intelligible and compelling for all nonscientific viewpoints purely on the basis of their own initial views and criteria (specifically, in order to enable them to perceive the completeness of the collection of nonscientific viewpoints discredited in the work in response to

---

4. *Science of Logic*, p. 28; also in appendix XV.
5. Another example of the *Phenomenology* evidently identifying "our" viewpoint with the viewpoint of the Logic: "What is, for the Understanding, an object in a sensuous covering, is for us in its essential form as a pure concept. This apprehension of the difference as it is in truth, or the apprehension of infinity as such, is for us ... The exposition of its concept belongs to Science" (par. 164; "infinity" is a category in Hegel's Logic).

The *Phenomenology*'s Independence from Hegelian Science 273

the skeptical equipollence and concept-instantiation problems, and the necessity of their own and all other nonscientific viewpoints' development into Hegelian Science). But this could not be achieved if the popular reading were correct. Or to restate part of this problem in more directly textual terms: In the Preface Hegel says that "the individual has the right to demand that Science should at least provide him with the ladder to this standpoint [i.e., Science's standpoint], should show him this standpoint within himself" (par. 26). But it seems that on the popular reading the *Phenomenology* would *not* provide the nonscientific individual with a "ladder to this standpoint." It would provide him only with an unconnected heap of rungs (the shapes of consciousness and their self-contradictions), not with the uprights which hold the rungs together in a fixed sequence leading to Science (the necessity of the development from each shape of consciousness to the next). And it seems that on the popular reading the *Phenomenology* would therefore also *not* show the nonscientific individual Science's "standpoint within himself." For it is only by showing him the necessity of the development from one shape of consciousness to the next, and in particular the necessity of the development from his own shape of consciousness through subsequent shapes to the standpoint of Science, that this could be achieved.[6]

---

6. Accordingly, it seems to me that Fulda's interpretation of the *Phenomenology* falls into inconsistency because he simultaneously claims (rightly) that the work aspires to give a proof of Hegelian Science for nonscientific viewpoints of the sort involved in task (6) and claims (mistakenly, as I am arguing) that the text is supposed, on Hegel's considered conception of its modus operandi, to function in the manner of the popular reading. Thus, Fulda notes that the work is supposed to give the nonscientific viewpoint more than a merely "skeptical" introduction to Hegelian Science, that is, an introduction which dialectically discredits nonscientific viewpoints but provides no necessary principle of development from one discredited viewpoint to the next (*Das Problem einer Einleitung*, pp. 36–37). According to Fulda, such an introduction would fail to satisfy "the modern yearning for an unshakeable certainty" (p. 50). And it would do so for at least two reasons: First, a nonscientific viewpoint which merely saw all nonscientific viewpoints known to it dialectically discredited, without seeing the necessity of their development into one another and eventually into Hegelian Science, would still lack a justification for accepting the remaining viewpoint of Hegelian Science, which could still seem arbitrary to it (pp. 46–47). Second, such a nonscientific viewpoint would still lack any insight into the constitution by the viewpoints discredited of a complete whole (pp. 49–50), so that for it " 'all' forms of finite cognition . . . can . . . only mean all known ones" (p. 37). Fulda seems to me quite correct in imputing to the Hegel of the *Phenomenology* an insight into these shortcomings of a merely "skeptical" introduction, and an intention to overcome them by providing an introduction that is more than merely "skeptical." A problem arises for Fulda's interpretation, however, when he goes on to argue that the *Phenomenology*, on Hegel's considered conception of the work, functions as the popular reading says it does (pp. 163–64). For if it did so, then it would

Second, if the *Phenomenology* were supposed to function as the popular reading says, then this would conflict with its role of serving as "the coming-to-be of Science," that is, as a work which accomplishes metaphysical tasks (9) and (11), the tasks of for the first time constructing the concepts of Hegelian Science and making Hegelian Science true. For this role implies that Hegelian Science is not yet articulable or true until the *Phenomenology* has done its work. But if that were so, then how could the *Phenomenology* presuppose information from Hegelian Science as an essential part of its method, as the popular reading maintains?[7]

I want to suggest that these two problems threatening the official project described in part 1 are in fact illusory, because the popular reading which would generate them does *not* represent Hegel's considered conception of the *Phenomenology*'s method. Hegel's considered conception of the work's method is instead that the work *in no respect essentially presupposes Hegelian Science for intelligibility or cogency, but is entirely independent of Hegelian Science.*[8]

The first, and perhaps most important, advantage of this reading over the popular reading is of course precisely that it frees the *Phenomenology* from the two problems for its official project to which the popular reading inevitably leads. This reading is also supported over its rival by evidence of other sorts, however. For example, it is supported by Hegel's implica-

---

after all give the nonscientific viewpoint no more insight into the necessary development from one nonscientific viewpoint to the next than a merely "skeptical" introduction to Hegelian Science does. And it would therefore be just as inadequate an introduction of the nonscientific viewpoint to Hegelian Science as a merely "skeptical" introduction, falling just as short of meeting the two requirements which need to be met in order to satisfy "the modern yearning for an unshakeable certainty": that the final step from the discredited nonscientific viewpoints to Hegelian Science be shown to be nonarbitrary, and that the discredited viewpoints be shown to constitute a complete whole and therefore really all the nonscientific viewpoints there are. As far as I can see, Fulda neither perceives nor offers any solution to this problem facing his interpretation.

7. Fulda makes this point well (with respect to Hegel's conception of the *Phenomenology before* his alleged *Umdeutung* or reinterpretation of the work). According to Fulda, the popular reading could not (at that time) have represented Hegel's official view of the work, because he (then) understood the work to be "the coming-to-be of the medium in which Science completes itself" or the place in which Science establishes "the final, still missing [condition of its existence]," so that the *Phenomenology* was "not only a condition of the communication and recognition of Science, but at the same time the condition of its existence" (*Das Problem einer Einleitung,* p. 161).

8. One commentator who has clearly perceived this is K. Dove, "Hegel's Phenomenological Method," *New Studies in Hegel's Philosophy,* ed. W. Steinkraus (New York: Holt, Rinehart, and Winston, 1971).

tion that the *Phenomenology* is not "the Science of the true in its true shape" but only the "appearance" of Science, and moreover that this is so *without exception:* "The system of the experience of Spirit [i.e., the *Phenomenology*] embraces *only* the appearance of Spirit" (par. 38; emphasis added). Also, it is supported by the trend of development discernible in the *Phenomenology*'s predecessor discipline, the early Logic, which was away from a thoroughgoing dependence on Hegelian Science proper (in the versions of the discipline from the early Jena period) and toward complete independence from Hegelian Science proper (in the last version of the discipline from the period immediately before the *Phenomenology*'s composition).⁹

This still leaves the four pieces of evidence (a)–(d) which seemed to speak strongly in favor of the popular reading, however. I want to argue that on closer inspection these do *not* in fact require that we accept the popular reading as capturing Hegel's considered position, but can plausibly, and therefore for the above reasons should, be read in ways conformable to the alternative reading of his considered position just suggested.

Consider first evidence (a), Hegel's indication in the Introduction that the necessary origination of the new shape of consciousness at each stage along the course of the *Phenomenology* occurs, "as it were, behind the back of consciousness" and is only perceived "by us." If this meant that the necessary origination of the new shape of consciousness at each stage occurred behind the back of *any* consciousness, then it would indeed require the popular reading. For in that case it would imply that the necessary origination of the new shape of consciousness was only perceptible by those of "us" who had overcome consciousness (by overcoming consciousness's essential opposition of subject and object), and this would for Hegel be equivalent to saying those of us who had attained the standpoint of Hegelian Science. But that is *not* what Hegel means. Hegel is not here contrasting "us" with consciousness *in general,* but instead more

---

9. The terminus a quo in this development is the Logic of the sketch from 1801–2, which, as we saw in part 1, essentially depends, through and through, on a presupposition of information from the first part of Hegelian Science proper, the Metaphysics. The terminus ad quem is the Logic of the *Logic, Metaphysics, and Philosophy of Nature* from 1804–5 which, as I read it (in agreement with Baillie, in *The Origin and Significance of Hegel's Logic,* but in disagreement with some more recent commentators, such as Pöggeler and Trede), involves no essential presupposition of information from Hegelian Science proper at all, and particularly not in its demonstrations of the necessity of the transitions from each category to the next. For more details, see my *Hegel and Skepticism,* chap. 9.

specifically with the consciousness which is *merely an object observed* in the *Phenomenology*'s "detailed history of the education of consciousness ... to the standpoint of Science" (par. 85). He therefore leaves quite open the possibility that among "us" who do perceive the necessary origination of a new shape of consciousness there may be nonscientific consciousnesses, namely, ones which are *more* than mere objects of observation, because they are being led by the *Phenomenology* toward Hegelian Science (in the manner described in the Preface at pars. 28–29).[10]

Consider next evidence (b), Hegel's claim in the Introduction that because of its inclusion of the necessity of the origination of each new shape of consciousness, the *Phenomenology* is "itself already Science." At first sight this seems to speak strongly for the popular reading. However, on closer inspection it turns out not to do so, for the following reasons. First, Hegel went on in the several editions of the *Encyclopaedia* to explain what he had meant by referring to the *Phenomenology* in its title as "the first part of the system of Science," and by implication what he had meant by calling the work "itself already Science" in its Introduction as well. And his explanations make it quite clear that the status of the *Phenomenology* as "itself already Science" neither implies nor is even consistent with its presupposition of information from Hegelian Science proper. Thus in the Heidelberg *Encyclopaedia*, for example, he writes: "I earlier treated the *Phenomenology of Spirit,* the scientific history of consciousness, as the first part of philosophy [i.e., of Hegelian Science] *in the sense that it should precede pure Science, since it is the production of pure Science's Concept.*"[11] Second, the Introduction's claim that the *Phenomenology*, due to its inclusion of the necessity of the origination of each new shape of consciousness, is "itself already Science" is, taken alone, ambiguous in an important way. It could be interpreted—and this is how the popular reading interprets it—as an explanation of the nature of the *necessity* involved in the *Phenomenology*. In this case Hegel would be taking for granted what it was for something to be Science, namely, to belong to the system of Logic, Philosophy of Nature, and Philosophy of Spirit, and would be explaining the nature of the necessity in the *Phenom-*

---

10. Heinrichs seems to me right to distinguish between the consciousness observed by the work and the consciousness instructed by the work, and to suggest that the "us" of whom Hegel speaks are the latter rather than individuals at the standpoint of Science proper (*Die Logik der Phänomenologie des Geistes* [Bonn: Bouvier Verlag, 1974], pp. 13–14). Cf. Dove, "Hegel's Phenomenological Method," p. 639.

11. Par. 36, emphasis added; cf. Berlin *Encyclopaedia,* par. 25.

enology as the necessity pertaining to Science in that sense. On the other hand, the Introduction's claim could instead be interpreted—and I suggest really *should* be interpreted—as an explanation of what it means to say that the *Phenomenology* is *scientific,* an explanation of why the *Phenomenology* can reasonably be given the title "Science" in common with Hegelian Science proper. In this case Hegel would be taking for granted the nature of the necessity in the *Phenomenology*—a very natural and reasonable thing for him to do in this context, since he has just before given an extended account of the nature of this necessity (pars. 84–87)—and would be explaining that the scientific status of the *Phenomenology,* the propriety of according the work the title "Science" in common with Hegelian Science proper, derives from its inclusion of just this necessity. This second reading of the Introduction's claim is strongly supported over the first by a reformulation which Hegel gives of the same claim in the 1808–9 *Doctrine of Consciousness,* where, after noting that an introduction to Science must observe the constitutions and activities through which Spirit goes in order to reach Science, he writes: "By virtue of the fact that these spiritual constitutions and activities stand in necessary interconnection, this self-knowledge likewise constitutes a Science."[12] We can see more clearly what Hegel has in mind on this second reading by recalling his doctrine that the *Phenomenology* is an "appearance" of Science proper. For, this status implies, as we have seen, that the work contains the Essence or *Law* of Science proper mixed with the impurity of nonscientific perspectives. And it is above all the work's *necessity* that manifests its share in the Essence or *Law* of Science proper. On this second reading, unlike the first, the Introduction's claim carries no implication that the *Phenomenology*'s presentation of the necessary origination of a new shape of consciousness presupposes information from Hegelian Science proper.

Consider next evidence (c), Hegel's indications that the shapes of consciousness in the *Phenomenology*'s presentation stand in one-to-one correspondence with, and are even in some sense identical with, the categories of the Logic, and that the necessary development into one another of the shapes of consciousness in the *Phenomenology*'s presentation obtains because of, or is even in some sense identical with, the necessary development into one another of the categories of the Logic. Pace the popular reading, this evidence does not show that the *Phenomenology*'s presenta-

---

12. *Nürnberger und Heidelberger Schriften,* p. 73.

tion of the necessary development of shapes of consciousness into one another can only be understood and accepted by someone who presupposes information from the Logic. For, it is sufficiently explained by (i) the sort of ontological fundamentalness of the Logic's categories and their self-development to human spiritual phenomena that is posited by Hegel's system, as this was sketched in chapter 1, together with (ii) the fact noted in the last chapter that Hegel conceives the *Phenomenology*'s presentation of shapes of consciousness and their necessary development to be an "appearance" of the Logic's presentation of categories and their necessary development. But, (i) does not imply that any awareness of the human spiritual phenomena in question must inevitably be mediated by an understanding of the underlying logical categories and their self-development. And, as we saw in the last chapter, (ii) permits, and indeed implies, that there is an *intensional difference* between the two presentations in question, so that it would be quite possible for someone to understand and have conviction in the *Phenomenology*'s presentation of shapes of consciousness and their necessary development without understanding or having conviction in the Logic's presentation of categories and their necessary development.[13]

Finally, we must consider evidence (d), the fact that in the course of its detailed execution the *Phenomenology* sometimes appeals to information from a version of the Logic, especially in order to effect its necessary transitions from one shape of consciousness to the next. It seems to me undeniable that the work does at points rely on a version of the Logic in this way. However, I would suggest that this does not reflect, but rather constitutes a deviation from, a flaw in the execution of, the work's considered method, which is instead to develop the work's contents, including the necessary transitions from one shape of consciousness to the next, in an entirely *immanent* manner, a manner involving no essential presupposition of information from Hegelian Science proper.[14] Several consider-

---

13. J. Habermas therefore seems to me mistaken when he asserts that there is a conflict between, on the one hand, the understanding which the *Phenomenology* has of itself as based on the pure essences of the Logic and, on the other hand, the work's task as a presuppositionless introduction to Hegelian Science, which requires that the phenomenological observer not be assumed to have attained the standpoint of the Logic (*Knowledge and Human Interests* [Boston: Beacon Press, 1971], p. 22).

14. I am here in substantial agreement with Fulda, who argues that before Hegel's alleged *Umdeutung* or reinterpretation of the *Phenomenology*, at a time when its official method allowed no presupposition of information from Hegelian Science proper, its execution did nevertheless illicitly rely at points on "the construction from the already existing

ations support this view. First, although *some* of the necessary transitions in the *Phenomenology* depend on an appeal to the Logic, it is not the case that they all do so. And in particular, the very first transition, that from Sense-certainty to Perception, *where if anywhere one would expect to find the official method of the work practised,* does not. Thus, in effecting this transition, the *Sense-certainty* section reaches without any evident reliance on the Logic the conclusion that "it is in fact the universal that is the true [content] of Sense-certainty," and the *Perception* section then takes this result as a sufficient basis for inferring the nature of the object belonging to the next shape of consciousness, Perception: "For us . . . the universal as principle is the essence of Perception . . . Since the principle [of Perception's object], the universal, is in its simplicity something *mediated,* [Perception's object] must express this as its own nature in itself. In this way it shows itself to be *the thing with many properties*" (pars. 96, 111–12). Second, it would not be surprising if Hegel had sometimes in his execution of the work succumbed to an illicit temptation to evade the required task of working out an immanent demonstration of the necessity of the transition from one shape of consciousness to the next by instead pointing to a corresponding transition in preexisting or emerging versions of his Logic. For this particular step in the dialectical method, the notorious "negation of the negation," is the one which he invariably finds it most difficult to make convincing.[15] Third, much later in life Hegel wrote in a note concerning the revision of the *Phenomenology* for a second edition: "Make the object develop independently, the Logic is *behind* consciousness [Gegenstand für sich fortbestimmen, Logik hinter dem Bewußtsein]."[16] This remark is most plausibly interpreted, I suggest, as a self-critical self-admonition that the necessary transitions from one shape of consciousness to the next in the *Phenomenology* had to be made immanent because the Logic on which the first edition had tended to rely at these points was unavailable to the viewpoint of the ordinary consciousness for which the work was written—that is, as an acknowledgement of the flaw which I have hypothesized and a resolution to correct it. Fourth, the several versions of the Nuremberg *Doctrine of*

Logic and Real Philosophy [i.e., Philosophies of Nature and Spirit]" (*Das Problem einer Einleitung,* p. 161).

15. Inwood aptly comments that "the transitions from one element to the next are often among the most difficult parts of [Hegel's] text, difficult both to understand and accept" (*Hegel,* p. 130).

16. Appendix XIX.

280   The Relation of the *Phenomenology* to Hegelian Science

Consciousness, which Hegel wrote immediately after the *Phenomenology*, and in which he gave a condensed restatement of much of the *Phenomenology*, actually attempt, in accordance with the self-admonition just quoted, to demonstrate the transitions from each shape of consciousness to the next in an immanent fashion even at those points where this had not been seriously attempted by the *Phenomenology* itself. For example, in the *Doctrine of Consciousness* of 1809 the transition from Perception to (Force and the) Understanding, which, as we saw earlier, in the *Phenomenology* itself relies on an appeal to a corresponding transition from the category of Being-for-self to the category of Essence in the Logic, is effected immanently, without any essential appeal to the Logic. Thus, the *Perception* section of the 1809 *Doctrine of Consciousness* argues in an immanent fashion that "in that [Perception's thing's] properties are essentially mediated, their existence lies in an other [in einem Anderen] and they change [verändern sich]. They are only accidents. But the things ... cease to exist when [their properties] change ... In this change not only something is overcome and becomes an other, but the other passes away as well. But the other of the other or the change of the changeable is the *becoming of the unchanging*." And, having in this immanent fashion derived both the accidental character of the properties of Perception's object and the emergence of the unchanging, Hegel then goes on in the section *(Force and the) Understanding* to treat these two traits as sufficient to define the nature of this new shape of consciousness's object: "The object has now the determination of having (α) a simply accidental side, but (β) also an essence and something unchanging. In that consciousness's object has for it this determination, consciousness is the Understanding."[17] Hegel had therefore already begun to undertake in these Nuremberg writings the task to which he later committed a second edition of the *Phenomenology* in the note recently quoted, the task of eliminating all dependence of the *Phenomenology*'s transitions from one shape of consciousness to the next on the Logic, and instead making them entirely immanent.[18] It seems reasonable to infer from these four facts that the *Phenomenology*'s reliance on a version of the Logic at certain points,

    17. *Nürnberger und Heidelberger Schriften*, p. 115. Whether this attempt at an immanent transition is philosophically plausible is of course quite another question.
    18. It therefore seems to me that Fulda and Habermas, who argue in their already cited works that Hegel reconceived the *Phenomenology* after its publication away from having it independent of, and toward having it dependent on, Hegelian Science proper, therein precisely *reverse* the true direction of Hegel's afterthoughts on the work.

although it initially appears to support the popular reading, does not in fact show that reading to reflect Hegel's considered conception of the work's method, but is instead merely a flaw in the work's execution of its considered method, which on the contrary requires the work to operate without any essential appeal to the Logic.

In sum, the four pieces of textual evidence (a)–(d) which at first sight seemed to demand the popular reading prove on closer inspection not in fact to do so. We should therefore, I suggest, for the several positive reasons indicated earlier, reject that reading, and instead understand the considered method of the *Phenomenology* to be that the work makes no essential presupposition of information from Hegelian Science proper, but rather functions quite independently of Hegelian Science proper.

CHAPTER SEVEN

The *Aufhebung* of the *Phenomenology* to Hegelian Science

A final component of Hegel's official conception of the *Phenomenology*'s relation to Hegelian Science proper is that the *Phenomenology* undergoes an *Aufhebung* to the level of Hegelian Science proper, in Hegel's technical sense of (i) an *abolition,* but also (ii) a *preservation* at a *higher level* in a modified meaning (a technical sense derived by running together the three idiomatic senses of the verb *aufheben*: to abolish, to preserve, to elevate).[1]

It had always been Hegel's conception of the *Phenomenology*'s predecessor discipline, the early Logic, that it would undergo an *Aufhebung* to the level of Hegelian Science proper (which began at that time with the Metaphysics). Thus, in the *Difference* essay of 1801 the several elements of the Logic's *Aufhebung* to Hegelian Science proper are described as follows: After deriving its oppositional content, the Logic will abolish itself—the "highest law" of "Reflection" (the faculty whose philosophical variety articulates the Logic) is "its destruction."[2] The abolition of the Logic will then lead to the postulation of the higher viewpoint of "Intuition" which expresses "Reason," that is, the Metaphysics.[3] This higher viewpoint will then preserve the oppositional content of the Logic as the content of "Reason" or Metaphysics, though in a synthesized, nonoppositional form.[4] And in the *Logic, Metaphysics, and Philosophy of*

---

1. One commentator who has clearly perceived this is W. Maker, "Hegel's *Phenomenology* as Introduction to Science," *Clio* 10 (1981), esp. pp. 388–90.
2. *Jenaer Schriften,* pp. 44, 28.
3. Ibid., pp. 43–44.
4. Ibid., p. 44.

The *Aufhebung* of the *Phenomenology* to Hegelian Science 283

Nature of 1804–5 Hegel writes more explicitly and simply that the final category of the Logic which effects the transition from Logic to Metaphysics, namely, Cognition, "is as the transition to the Metaphysics the *Aufheben* of the Logic itself."⁵

Not surprisingly, therefore, Hegel understands the *Phenomenology* too to undergo an *Aufhebung* to the level of Hegelian Science proper. Thus, both editions of the *Science of Logic* indicate that the *Phenomenology*'s transition to a different standpoint "just as much *aufhebt* itself again [so hebt es sich ebensosehr wieder auf]," and the 1831 edition adds in the same vein that the *Phenomenology*, as the mediation through which the beginning of the Logic is reached, is the "*Aufheben* of itself."⁶ Again, the *Encyclopaedia* ascribes the function of elevating the mind to the absolute standpoint to a course of education which, while not explicitly identified with the *Phenomenology*, bears a very striking resemblance to it (pars. 12, 50),⁷ and insists that "in being a *transition* and *mediation*, this elevation is just as much an *Aufheben* of the *transition* and mediation," and that "what exists as the mediator vanishes and hence in this mediation even the mediation gets *aufgehoben*" (par. 50).⁸

Consider more closely, to begin with, the *negative* side of this intended *Aufhebung* of the *Phenomenology*, the discipline's *abolition*. Hegel characterizes the *Phenomenology* in its Introduction as a "self-completing skepticism" (par. 78) which systematically criticizes "criteria" of truth (pars. 84–85). This is clearly a modeling of the discipline on ancient skepticism. And this modeling continues in the Preface when Hegel describes the discipline as the "ladder" to the standpoint of Science (par. 26). For

---

5. *Logik, Metaphysik, und Naturphilosophie*, p. 134.
6. Appendices XV, XVIII.
7. Appendix XVII. Note in particular how much of the terminology used at par. 12 to describe this course of education is borrowed from the technical vocabulary of the *Phenomenology* and deployed in similar ways—especially, the words *Erfahrung, Bewußtsein*, and *Erscheinung*. For example, we read there: "The emergence of philosophy which results from the need [for philosophy] has experience [Erfahrung], the immediate and rationalizing consciousness [Bewußtsein], as its starting point. Aroused by this need as a stimulus, thought's behavior is essentially to elevate itself above the natural, sensuous, and rationalizing consciousness into its own pure element . . . In this way thought initially finds its satisfaction in itself, in the idea of the universal essence of these appearances [Erscheinungen]."
8. Pippin therefore seems to me mistaken when he argues against the view that Hegel conceives the *Phenomenology* as self-sublating that "Hegel had abandoned the idea of a 'negative' or wholly self-destructive introduction after 1804 and never returned to it" (*Hegel's Idealism*, p. 279).

this description recalls Sextus Empiricus's famous characterization of the skeptic's argument in *Against the Logicians:* "Just as it is not impossible for the man who has ascended to a high place by a ladder to overturn the ladder with his foot after his ascent, so also it is not unlikely that the skeptic after he has arrived at the demonstration of his thesis by means of the argument proving the non-existence of proof, as it were by a stepladder, should then abolish this very argument."[9] We may reasonably infer from this that it is part of Hegel's conception of the *Phenomenology* that, just as the ancient skeptic uses an argument to call into question proof which in its culmination calls itself into question as well, so too the *Phenomenology*'s "skeptical" discrediting of nonscientific viewpoints culminates in its own self-discrediting as well.[10] This conception is just what one would expect given the work's self-understanding as not "the Science of the true in its true shape" but only an "appearance" of Science, a version of Science at the level of false and self-contradictory nonscientific viewpoints. And it is encapsulated in the doctrine that the work undergoes an *Aufhebung* in the negative sense of an *abolition*. Hegel thus belongs to a long line of thinkers—beginning, perhaps, with the historical Parmenides, running through Sextus Empiricus, and including in our own century the Wittgenstein of the *Tractatus*—who have thought that the argument which discredits the received views of things and leads to the correct philosophical standpoint ends by discrediting itself as well.

What, next, of the *positive* side of the *Aufhebung* of the *Phenomenology* to Hegelian Science, the *preservation* of the discipline at the *higher level* of Hegelian Science (in a modified meaning)? Such a preservation is implied not only by this doctrine of the work's *Aufhebung* to Hegelian Science, but also by the doctrine that the work is the "appearance" of Hegelian Science. Toward the end of the *Phenomenology* Hegel indicates two places at the higher level of Hegelian Science where the content of the work will be preserved (in a modified meaning). First, he indicates

---

9. *Against the Logicians*, bk. 2, sec. 481.
10. Habermas is one of the few to have understood this aspect of Hegel's conception of the relation between the *Phenomenology* and Hegelian Science. Habermas argues that when the *Phenomenology*, as a radicalized critique of knowledge forgoing all presuppositions, reaches Hegelian Science, it makes itself superfluous, and "indeed it refutes the perspective of inquiry held by the critique of knowledge as such," so that it is to be regarded as "a ladder which we must throw away after climbing it to the standpoint of the Logic" (*Knowledge and Human Interests*, p. 22).

that the work's self-developing shapes of consciousness will be preserved in the Logic in a purified form as the self-developing logical categories which are their underlying reality: "In [Science] the moments of [Spirit's] movement no longer exhibit themselves as specific shapes of consciousness, but . . . as specific concepts and as their organic self-grounded movement" (par. 805). Second, he refers to a part of Hegelian Science where the *Phenomenology*'s shapes of consciousness will be preserved qua shapes of consciousness, namely, after Spirit's "sacrifice of itself" into nature, or in other words the transition from the end of the Logic to the Philosophy of Nature, and thence the "reinstatement of the subject," or in other words the transition from the Philosophy of Nature to the Philosophy of Spirit (pars. 806–7)—meaning, specifically, the section of the Philosophy of Spirit which bears the same title as the *Phenomenology*, and which re-treats the latter's shapes of consciousness from a scientific standpoint.[11] However, since the *Phenomenology* is supposed, at least in its finally published form, to give a provisional treatment of virtually *all* aspects of Hegelian Science, as the *Encyclopaedia* indicates (par. 25), these two parts of Hegelian Science to which the *Phenomenology* itself points forward as places where its content will be preserved at the higher level of Hegelian Science do not exhaust the list. In principle virtually *all* parts of Hegelian Science are to be seen as preserving content from the *Phenomenology* at the higher level of Hegelian Science (in a modified meaning).

Recognizing this conception that the *Phenomenology* undergoes an *Aufhebung* to the level of Hegelian Science proper enables us to solve an exegetical problem, or family of exegetical problems, which arises in connection with the official project of the work described in part 1. On the one hand, the *Science of Logic* and the *Encyclopaedia* characterize the *Phenomenology* as the "justification," "proof," and "deduction" of Hegelian Science.[12] But on the other hand, the *Difference* essay emphatically rejected the "tendency to give grounds and to establish by grounds" in philosophizing; the *Phenomenology* itself indicates that it is not a "grounding" of Science (par. 27); and the *Encyclopaedia* and the *Science*

---

11. This re-treatment has a modified meaning relative to the treatment in the *Phenomenology* because shapes of consciousness are now explicitly understood through their underlying logical basis, rather than implicitly vice versa as in the *Phenomenology*.

12. Appendices XV, XVII.

of Logic insist that Science must be presuppositionless, that its "first beginning [in the Logic] . . . cannot be something mediated," and that its Logic makes an "absolute beginning" which "may presuppose nothing, must be mediated by nothing, and must have no ground."[13] Are these two sets of statements not flatly inconsistent with each other? Haering, for one, was so convinced that they were that he called on these apparent inconsistencies as a major part of his evidence for interpreting the *Phenomenology* as a rushed and makeshift work which Hegel subsequently had to reinterpret and eventually gave up.[14]

A first point to note about these apparent inconsistencies is that they were by no means new with the emergence of the *Phenomenology*. On the contrary, they had already existed for years in connection with the early Logic. For example, in the period 1801–2: On the one hand, as we have noted, the *Difference* essay rejected the "tendency to give grounds and to establish by grounds" in philosophy, and *The Relation of Skepticism to Philosophy* stated that Hegelian Science did not attempt to ground its principle of identity but "only expresses and recognizes that presupposed identity." But on the other hand, at the same time the *Difference* essay also assigned to the early Logic the task of giving a "deduction" of the "Rational," or the content of Hegelian Science.[15] The fact that these apparent inconsistencies already had such a long career in Hegel's thought behind them by the time of the *Phenomenology* makes it, prima facie, rather unlikely that they were merely hasty blunders, as Haering supposes. Is it not much more likely that Hegel was aware of them but believed that he had a way of resolving them, a way of showing them to be *merely* apparent?

Once we recognize that Hegel conceives the *Phenomenology* (and conceived the early Logic before it) to undergo an *Aufhebung* to Hegelian

---

13. *Encyclopaedia*, pars. 1, 10, 78, 86; *Science of Logic*, pp. 43, 70. Cf. *Encyclopaedia*, par. 10, where Hegel notoriously criticizes Kant for seeking to investigate our cognitive capacity for Science prior to expounding Science itself, rather than beginning with Science itself straightaway.

14. Haering argues that Hegel, in embarrassment at such inconsistencies, first changed the work from being an external introduction to his system to being merely a part of his system, and then finally gave up the work altogether and treated its subject matter in the *Encyclopaedia* instead (T. Haering, *Hegel: sein Wollen und sein Werk* [Leipzig and Berlin: Teubner, 1929–38], 2:480–81; "Die Entstehungsgeschichte der *Phänomenologie des Geistes*," in *Verhandlungen des dritten Hegelkongresses in Rom* [Tübingen: J.C.B. Mohr, 1934], pp. 132–35).

15. *Jenaer Schriften*, p. 44.

Science proper, we can see that this is indeed the case. How can Hegel simultaneously present the *Phenomenology* as the "justification," "proof," and "deduction" of Hegelian Science, and also deny the propriety of, or any involvement in, "grounding" Hegelian Science and insist that Hegelian Science makes no "presupposition," is not "mediated," makes an "absolute beginning"? *Part* of the answer to this question lies in the fact that the "justification" of Hegelian Science offered by the *Phenomenology* consists, not in deducing it from true premises, but instead in defending it against skeptical objections, and motivating its positions on meaning and truth, through *negative* procedures (and also providing a universal *ad hominem* argument for it). Hence the *Encyclopaedia* urges that Hegelian Science, in being mediated through an ascent above a sensuous starting-point against which it has a negative relation, is "no less independent, indeed it gives itself its independence essentially through this negation and ascent" (par. 12). However, someone might still object that even such a negative "justification" of Hegelian Science would still in a fairly strong, and for Hegel problematic, sense "ground" Hegelian Science, give it a "presupposition," make it "mediated," deny it an "absolute beginning." After all, he might urge, would it not still work by exhibiting various *truths* in support of Hegelian Science, such as truths about the inadequacies of nonscientific viewpoints? It is here that Hegel's conception of the *Phenomenology* as itself subject to an *Aufhebung,* in the negative sense of an *abolition,* or a discrediting as false and self-contradictory, comes to the rescue. As Hegel puts the thought in the *Encyclopaedia*, "What exists as the mediator vanishes and hence in this mediation even the mediation gets *aufgehoben*" (par. 50). The objector might now, shifting foot, concede that this avoids subjecting Hegelian Science to "grounding," "presupposition," "mediation," and the lack of an "absolute beginning" all right, but complain that it does so only at the cost of preventing the *Phenomenology* from being a genuine "justification," "proof," or "deduction" of Hegelian Science. However, this would be to overlook Hegel's conception of the work as subject to an *Aufhebung* to Hegelian Science also in the *positive* sense of a preservation there (in a modified meaning), or equivalently his conception of the work as an "appearance" of Hegelian Science, an expression of scientific truth though still in a false and self-contradictory nonscientific form. For, as we noted in chapter 5, on such a conception the work can, despite its falseness and self-contradictoriness, nonetheless give relatively good expression to genuine justifications of Hegelian Science.

This concludes my account of the officially intended relation of the *Phenomenology* to Hegelian Science proper. To sum up: besides being understood to serve as an "introduction" to Hegelian Science of the novel and complex sort explained in part 1, the *Phenomenology* is conceived as presenting an "appearance" of Hegelian Science, as independent of Hegelian Science, and as subject to an *Aufhebung* to Hegelian Science.

PART THREE

History and Historicism
in the *Phenomenology*

CHAPTER EIGHT

Two Varieties of Historicism

Much, if not most, of the interest shown in the *Phenomenology* since it was first published in 1807 has focused on the historical and historicist aspects of the work. There is a certain irony in this. For one thing, these aspects of the work play a subordinate role within, and are even in part superfluous to, the work's official project, the project which has been explained in parts 1 and 2.[1] For another thing, the ontological status of time, and a fortiori of history, is ultimately a very equivocal one for Hegel. Time is, to be sure, the form in which Absolute Spirit or the Concept (Hegel's version of God) appears: "Time is the Concept itself that *is there* . . . Spirit necessarily appears in time" (par. 801; cf. 46). But somehow time is *merely* the form in which Absolute Spirit or the Concept *appears,* and the latter is, au fond, atemporal.[2] Consequently, Hegel writes that Spirit "appears in time just so long as it has not *grasped* its

---

1. To be more precise, the historical and historicist aspects of the chapters *Consciousness* through *Reason* are required for, though subordinate within, this official project, while the historical and historicist aspects of the chapters *Spirit* through *Absolute Knowing* are more or less superfluous to it.
2. This is especially explicit in some of Hegel's later remarks. *Encyclopaedia,* par. 258: "Time . . . has no power over the Concept, nor is the Concept in time or temporal . . . Only the natural . . . is subject to time insofar as it is finite; the true, on the other hand, the Idea, Spirit, is *eternal.*" *Lectures on the Philosophy of World History: Introduction,* p. 209: "Temporal duration is something entirely relative and the Spirit belongs to eternity" (cf. p. 150). *Hegel in Berichten seiner Zeitgenossen,* ed. G. Nicolin (Hamburg: Felix Meiner, 1970), p. 153: "There is no time at all—or an eternal time." Remarks such as these show that Findlay is mistaken when he flatly asserts that "Hegel is not teaching any doctrine of the 'unreality' of time" (*Hegel: A Re-examination* [New York: Oxford University Press, 1976], p. 146).

pure Concept [in other words, has not achieved proper self-understanding], i.e., has not annulled time" (par. 801), and that as we leave behind the inadequate perspectives depicted in the *Phenomenology* and approach the true perspective of his own system "unresting and unhalting time collapses . . . within itself" (par. 803).³ These qualifications made, though, it remains the case that history and historicism are among the most prominent and interesting themes in the *Phenomenology*. And it is therefore appropriate that we should now turn to consider them in some detail.

The secondary literature contains an extraordinary diversity of opinions concerning the role of history in the design of the *Phenomenology*. At one extreme, Solomon, for example, claims flatly that "the *Phenomenology* is not a book about history, and its structure is not historical, as even the most superficial scan of its contents will reveal."⁴ At another extreme, Lukács argues that the whole work is designed to give a grand threefold treatment of history and is structured accordingly.⁵ One of our main tasks in this part of the book will therefore be to determine whether, and if so how, history enters into the general design of the *Phenomenology*. It will turn out that on this question Solomon is fundamentally wrong and Lukács fundamentally right.

Our second main task in this part of the book will be to explain the historicism of the *Phenomenology*. The term *historicism* (one not used by Hegel himself) is vague and polysemic. For our purposes it is particularly important to distinguish the following two senses which it commonly bears. On the one hand, it sometimes signifies a position based on the

---

3. If these doctrines of the mere apparentness of time, and of the eventual overcoming of the appearance of time in Hegel's own age and philosophy, be found surprising, one should recall that Hegel is writing shortly after Kant had argued that time was merely a mind-imposed form of appearances, not a property of things as they are in themselves, and Schiller (whose strong influence on Hegel we have noted) had added to that Kantian thesis the claim that man's highest goal was the "annulment [Aufheben]" of time (*On the Aesthetic Education of Man*, pp. 73–77, 81–83, 97). Besides these precedents, and philosophical motives associated with them, Hegel has some interesting philosophical motives of his own for the doctrines in question. For example, as noted in chapters 2 and 4, he has interesting philosophical motives for the doctrine that (the appearance of) time comes to an end with his own age and philosophy arising from his distinctive philosophy of mind and theory of truth.

4. *In the Spirit of Hegel*, p. 211; cf. 228.

5. G. Lukács, *The Young Hegel* (Cambridge, Mass.: MIT Press, 1976), esp. pp. 470–72.

recognition that human thought undergoes fundamental changes during the course of history. This is a large part of what Troeltsch and Mannheim have in mind when they argue for the significance of "historicism," for example.[6] On the other hand, it sometimes signifies the idea that history is subject to a general law of development in light of which at least its major steps can be seen to be necessary and/or that history is a teleological process aimed at the achievement of some final goal or purpose. This is a large part of what Popper has in mind when he criticizes "historicism" in *The Poverty of Historicism*, for example.[7] Let us distinguish these two types of historicism as "intellectual historicism" and "law and purpose historicism," respectively.

Now, clearly, these positions are in principle quite distinct and separable; one could quite consistently be an intellectual historicist without being a law and purpose historicist, and vice versa. Nietzsche provides a good example of intellectual historicism without law and purpose historicism, while Kant provides a fairly good example of the converse.[8] The *Phenomenology* in fact combines both sorts of historicism, however. It is committed to a form of intellectual historicism, for it undertakes to show that history has contained a succession of human perspectives which have differed from one another in fundamental ways. But it marries with this a full-blooded law and purpose historicism. For, in addition, it tries to show that the development of that succession of human perspectives has been dictated by a dialectical law in accordance with which each one, due to a self-contradiction implicit within it, necessarily developed into the next (pars. 5, 29, 84–87). And it tries to show that the development of this sequence of perspectives has aimed at the achievement of a final goal or purpose, namely, the emergence of Hegel's own philosophical standpoint in the modern world—a standpoint which, in contrast to the self-contradictoriness of all preceding perspectives, is at last self-consistent, reveals the true nature of Absolute Spirit or the Concept (God), and, on a still more exalted plane, constitutes Absolute Spirit's

---

6. See E. Troeltsch, *Der Historismus und seine Probleme* (Tübingen: J.C.B. Mohr, 1922), and "Die Krisis des Historismus," *Die Neue Rundschau* 33 (1922); K. Mannheim, "Historismus," *Archiv für Sozialwissenschaft und Sozialpolitik* 52 (1924).

7. K.R. Popper, *The Poverty of Historicism* (London and New York: Ark Paperbacks, 1986).

8. The two aspects of "law and purpose" historicism are in principle distinct and separable from one another as well.

attainment of the self-knowledge which is essential to it: "The realm of Spirits . . . constitutes a succession in time . . . Their goal is the revelation of the depth of Spirit, and this is *the absolute Concept* . . . The goal [is] Absolute Knowing, or Spirit that knows itself as Spirit" (par. 808).[9]

In what follows, though, I shall bracket off the law and purpose historicism of the *Phenomenology* in order to focus on its intellectual historicism. Several reasons have motivated this decision, and may be worth stating briefly. Two are broadly exegetical in character: First, whereas the *Phenomenology*'s law and purpose historicism is relatively easy to recognize and understand, and has accordingly been reasonably well explained in the literature, its intellectual historicism is less easily recognized and understood, and has accordingly been only poorly explained in the literature. Second, whereas the best statement of Hegel's law and purpose historicism occurs not in the *Phenomenology* but rather in later works such as the *Lectures on the Philosophy of World History,* his intellectual historicism nowhere receives such an interesting and radical statement as in the *Phenomenology*. A third reason is more philosophical in character: In the final analysis, it seems to me that one must judge law and purpose historicism—whether in Hegel's version of it or in any of the other versions of it developed by eighteenth- and nineteenth-century German philosophy, such as those of Kant and Marx—philosophically indefensible, merely one of the more seductive and persistent of the many philosophical damp squibs developed during this period, alongside other ideas of real value.[10] Intellectual historicism, by contrast, seems to me to be one of those ideas of real value.[11]

We have, then, two main tasks to perform: first, we must clarify the role of history in the general design of the *Phenomenology*, and second,

---

9. In thus *combining* intellectual historicism with law and purpose historicism the *Phenomenology* owes much to Herder, who, especially in *Auch eine Philosophie der Geschichte zur Bildung der Menschheit,* had developed both the view that thought changes in fundamental ways from epoch to epoch and the view that, as he puts it there, this is not mere "Penelope-work," but the progressive realization of a divine plan.

10. As Nietzsche implies in *The Uses and Disadvantages of History for Life,* the popularity of this sort of historicism during the period in question is all too easily explained in terms of its perpetuation in a modified guise of recently discredited Christian theological dogmas, and gratification thereby of the culturally habitual emotional wants formerly satisfied by them.

11. I am accordingly very much in sympathy with Dilthey's judgment that much of Hegel's greatness lies in his role, played out in the *Phenomenology* above all, as a "founder of the history of the innerness of the human spirit" (*Die Jugendgeschichte Hegels,* in *Gesammelte Schriften* 4:157).

we must explain the work's intellectual historicism. These two tasks are deeply interdependent. However, of the two, the former is the one *more* capable of independent treatment. My general approach in the following chapters will accordingly be to determine aspects of the role of history in the work's design first, and then to discuss the intellectual historicist ideas bound up with them subsequently.

CHAPTER NINE

History in the Chapters
Consciousness through *Reason*

Lukács deserves great credit as the first scholar to have understood clearly, in essentials at least, the role of history in the general design of the *Phenomenology*. As he saw, the *Phenomenology* is designed to treat the whole course of human history in chronological order not just once but three times, each time with a different focus. First, we have in the chapters *Consciousness* through *Reason* a treatment of the whole course of history focusing on the general shapes of consciousness which have arisen in different historical periods. Second, we have in the *Spirit* chapter a treatment of the whole course of history focusing on the sequence of "Spirits" or social contexts within which those shapes of consciousness arose. Third, we have in the chapters *Religion* and *Absolute Knowing* a treatment of the whole course of history focusing on the attempts associated with those shapes of consciousness and social contexts to express the nature of God or the Absolute, through art and religion (the *Religion* chapter) and eventually Hegel's own philosophy (the *Absolute Knowing* chapter).[1]

---

1. Lukács, *The Young Hegel*, pp. 470–72: "The various aspects of history that are treated do not occur arbitrarily, as has often been thought; in fact they occur in their correct historical sequence, which, however, is repeated three times in the course of the work . . . Hegel's point of departure is . . . the ordinary natural consciousness of the individual . . . As the individual works his way individually from the immediate perception of objective reality to the point where its rationality is discerned, he traverses all the phases of man's history up to the present . . . The second phase repeats the entire course of history from its beginnings up to the present—*real* history in its concrete social totality . . . The historical survey in the third stage once again recapitulates the past *in its entirety*. Thus the course of history is repeated for the third time. However, on this occasion we no longer find the

It is crucial to recognize this fundamental principle of the *Phenomenology*'s design if one is to make decent sense of the work. Yet, before Lukács scholars of the text had failed to do so, as he himself points out.[2] And, less forgivably, since Lukács most scholarship on the work has gone out of its way to *deny* that the work operates in accordance with this principle, thereby plunging readers back from Lukács's hard-won light into darkness once again.

In this and the following chapter, I shall investigate in some detail the *Phenomenology*'s first treatment of history, the treatment in the chapters *Consciousness* through *Reason*. In chapters 11 and 12 I shall consider more briefly the *Phenomenology*'s second and third treatments of history, that in the *Spirit* chapter and that in the *Religion* and *Absolute Knowing* chapters. The chapters *Consciousness* through *Reason* deserve the especially close attention to be devoted to them for four main reasons: First, it is only the historical and historicist aspects of *these* chapters, not those of the remaining chapters, which are strictly required by the official project of the work described in parts 1 and 2. Second and connectedly, as we shall see in part 4, the chapters *Consciousness* through *Reason* constitute the whole originally planned scope of the *Phenomenology,* a sort of Ur-*Phenomenology,* to which the remaining chapters were only added as an afterthought—so that in this sense too they constitute the very core of the book. Third, it is in connection with the chapters *Consciousness* through *Reason* that Lukács's case for his interpretation of the work as chronologically structured is least well made and has been most vehemently disputed. Fourth, this is the part of the book which is most rich in, and therefore most important for understanding, the book's intellectual historicism.

The thesis to be developed in this chapter is, then, that the opening three chapters *Consciousness* through *Reason* are designed to give (no doubt among other things) a chronological history of the development

---

actual series of events, but a summary of mankind's efforts to comprehend reality. Art, religion, and philosophy are for Hegel the three great instruments by which man cognizes the world . . . This, in the crudest outline, is the basic structure of the *Phenomenology of Spirit*." Using Hegel's later distinction between "subjective," "objective," and "absolute" Spirit to distinguish the different subject matters of these three treatments of history, this gives us "the following division of the *Phenomenology*: A. *Subjective Spirit:* Chapters I–V: Consciousness, Self-consciousness, Reason; B. *Objective Spirit:* Chapter VI: Spirit; C. *Absolute Spirit:* Chapters VII–VIII: Religion, Absolute Knowing."

2. Ibid., p. 471. An arguable but unclear exception is Purpus, *Zur Dialektik des Bewußtseins nach Hegel,* pp. 72, 124, 174–75.

of consciousness from ancient times up to the modern age. Now Lukács's own case for this interpretation is, it must be said, highly unsatisfactory. To mention its more egregious shortcomings: First, Lukács gives no real explanation of what, for Hegel, a chronological history of consciousness would be.[3] Second, Lukács makes no serious or convincing effort to justify ascribing this project to the chapters *Consciousness* through *Reason*. In particular, he fails to offer any account of how large stretches of these chapters can be read as chronological history—for example, the *Consciousness* chapter and the first half of the *Reason* chapter. And among the historical identifications which he does venture, many prove, on closer inspection, to be merely fanciful.[4] In fact, the only stretch of these chapters for which he does manage to give a plausible reading as chronological history is the *Self-consciousness* chapter.[5] Third, Lukács makes no attempt to answer, and his account affords no resources for answering, several quite plausible objections which can be raised against an attempt to understand the chapters *Consciousness* through *Reason* as a chronological history (objections which we shall consider later). In short, Lukács's version of the interpretation in question remains at the level of little more than a vague and inexact, if inspired, guess.

It is, therefore, perhaps after all not *so* surprising that later commentators have almost universally rejected this interpretation of the chapters *Consciousness* through *Reason*. For example, Hyppolite writes: "In . . . the first part of the *Phenomenology,* including the major sections 'Consciousness,' 'Self-consciousness,' 'Reason' . . . history plays little more than the role of example . . . Hegel clearly insists that the three moments Consciousness, Self-consciousness, and Reason, are not to be considered as a succession. They are not in time."[6] Solomon writes, in a similar vein: "The progression of the first five chapters [i.e., *Consciousness* through *Reason*] is emphatically *not* chronological."[7] Kainz, in his book on the

---

3. This omission is largely a consequence of Lukács's misguided attempt to interpret Hegel as concerned primarily with economic matters.
4. Examples are his identifications of the sections *Virtue and the Way of the World* and *The Spiritual Animalkingdom* with modern capitalism as characterized by Adam Smith, and of the section *Reason as Lawgiver* with the perspectives of Kant and Fichte (*The Young Hegel,* pp. 482–84; cf. 498). We shall see later in this chapter what these sections really do represent historically.
5. Ibid., pp. 477–78, 327–28.
6. Hyppolite, *Genesis and Structure,* pp. 35–36. As we shall see shortly, Hegel "clearly insists" on no such thing.
7. Solomon, *In the Spirit of Hegel,* p. 320; cf. 211, 228.

chapters *Consciousness* through *Reason*, remarks similarly that "Hegel . . . does not proceed in any specifically temporal order in his reminiscences."[8] And Pöggeler too denies that these chapters give a chronological history, arguing in one essay, for example, that the *Self-consciousness* chapter does not continue a history begun in the *Consciousness* chapter but makes a new historical beginning, and that the *Reason* chapter is not chronologically ordered.[9]

It will be my task in this chapter, therefore, to attempt to develop a more cogent case for interpreting the chapters *Consciousness* through *Reason* as a chronological history of consciousness from ancient times up to the modern age—a case plugging each of the gaping holes in Lukács's case which were just listed in turn.

We should ask, then, to begin with, what it would *mean* for Hegel to be giving in these chapters a chronological history of consciousness? The explanation of Hegel's notion of a "shape of consciousness" which I developed in chapter 2 affords the basis for an answer to this question. To recapitulate the main points of that explanation: Hegel accepts the generic model of consciousness developed by his immediate predecessors, according to which all consciousness essentially includes the three interdependent elements: consciousness of *oneself* as such, consciousness of something other than oneself or of an *object* as such, and consciousness of one's *representation* of this other something or object as such. But unlike his predecessors he distinguishes different *species* of consciousness, each defined by a more specific model as essentially comprising a *particular type* of each of the three elements described in the generic model, in interdependence with one another: a particular type of consciousness of self, distinguished by a particular conception and concept of the self; a particular type of consciousness of object, distinguished by a particular conception and concept of objectivity; and a particular type of consciousness of representation, distinguished by a particular conception and concept of representation. These different species of consciousness are what Hegel means by "shapes of consciousness." Now Hegel's idea in the *Phenomenology* is that each of these species or shapes of consciousness, with

---

8. Kainz, *Hegel's Phenomenology, Part One*, p. 8; cf. 10–11, 43.
9. Pöggeler, "Zur Deutung der *Phänomenologie des Geistes*," pp. 268 ff. In a later essay Pöggeler argues that the *Self-consciousness* chapter is not historical at all (*Hegels Idee einer Phänomenologie des Geistes* [Freiburg/Munich: Verlag Karl Alber, 1973], pp. 248, 264).

its distinctive interdependent conceptions and concepts of self, objectivity, and representation, emerges within and is characteristic of a particular period of human history, so that a chronological history of their succession in time can be told. This, in brief, is what, for Hegel, a chronological history of consciousness would be.

Having established this much, we should next develop a case for saying that the chapters *Consciousness* through *Reason* are supposed to give such a history. A first argument for this thesis rests on two sets of evidence: (i) That the *Phenomenology* was, from the very start of its composition, and consistently thereafter, conceived as a chronological history of the development of consciousness up to the achievement of Hegel's philosophy or "Science" in the modern age (no doubt among other things), is indicated by a series of remarks which begin in the Introduction, the part of the work which Hegel wrote first, and continue through the later parts of the work, and beyond the *Phenomenology* into subsequent texts. Thus, the Introduction tells us that the series of shapes of consciousness depicted in the work "is, in reality, the detailed history [Geschichte] of the formative education of consciousness itself to the standpoint of Science" (par. 78). The *Reason* chapter informs us, similarly, that "the system of structured shapes assumed by consciousness . . . that we are considering here . . . has its objective existence as world-history" (par. 295). Again, the *Religion* chapter states that the "totality of Spirit," whose moments included "Consciousness, Self-consciousness, Reason," each of which in turn "assumed different 'shapes': as, e.g., in Consciousness, Sense-certainty and Perception were distinct from each other," "is in time, and the 'shapes,' which are 'shapes' of the totality of Spirit, display themselves in a temporal succession" (par. 679).[10] The

---

10. It is quite ironic, therefore, that Hyppolite appeals to a passage from this very paragraph in order to *refute* the reading of the chapters *Consciousness* through *Reason* as chronological history. Hyppolite asserts: "Hegel clearly insists that the three moments, Consciousness, Self-consciousness, and Reason, are not to be considered as a succession. They are not in time . . . Hegel clearly says that with regard to Religion nothing that precedes it is to be considered as a historical development." And Hyppolite quotes in support of this assertion a passage from paragraph 679 in which Hegel writes that "the course traversed by these moments [i.e., Consciousness, Self-consciousness, Reason] is . . . , in relation to Religion, not to be represented as occurring in time" (*Genesis and Structure,* pp. 36–38). What Hyppolite has failed to realize here is that Hegel's qualification in this passage "in relation to Religion" does real work. Hegel's thought is, roughly, that the moments and their shapes in question, which, as he *explicitly says* in the part of paragraph 679 quoted in my main text above, "display themselves in a temporal succession," *also* have an exis-

same chronologically historical project is implied by the Preface, the part of the work which Hegel wrote last (pars. 28–29).[11] And, beyond the *Phenomenology* itself, in the Heidelberg *Encyclopaedia* Hegel once again characterizes the *Phenomenology* as "the scientific *history* [Geschichte] of consciousness" (par. 36; emphasis added).[12] (ii) The *Phenomenology*'s treatment of shapes of consciousness covers (officially at least) all and

---

tence sub specie aeternitatis as aspects of Absolute Spirit, and that it is *thus*, rather than in their historical existence, that *Religion* relates to them.

11. Thus Hegel writes at paragraphs 28–29 concerning the way in which the work introduces a modern individual to the standpoint of Hegelian philosophy: "The individual whose substance is the more advanced Spirit runs through [the] past just as one who takes up a higher science goes through the preparatory studies he has long since absorbed . . . The single individual must . . . pass through the formative stages of universal Spirit so far as their content is concerned, but as shapes which Spirit has already left behind . . . [We] will recognize in the pedagogical development the history of the formative education of the world as though traced out in silhouette . . . Since the Substance of the individual, the World Spirit itself, has had the patience to pass through these shapes over the long passage of time, and to take upon itself the enormous labor of world-history . . . and since it could not have attained consciousness of itself by any lesser effort, the individual certainly cannot in the nature of the case comprehend his substance in an easier fashion."

12. Two points about the above evidence: (a) Someone might object that in some or all of these passages the word *Geschichte* does not simply mean chronological history, but connotes, in continuity with a use of the word begun by Platner and developed by Fichte and Schelling, an ahistorical psychology. As we shall see later, this claim is correct. However, it constitutes no objection to the interpretation offered here, for the interpretation offered here requires only that the word means *at least* that much, not that it means *only* that much—and that it does so is shown clearly by the passages from pars. 295, 679, and 28–29. (b) Someone might, though, still attempt to drive a wedge between these three passages, written relatively late in the process of the *Phenomenology*'s composition, and the passage from paragraph 78, written early in the process of composition, and to argue that the word *Geschichte* has come to mean something different in the former from what it meant in the latter, so that one cannot, as I have implied, interpret the latter as showing that Hegel had the project of a chronological history of consciousness in mind *from the start* of the work's composition. Pöggeler in effect argues in this way at "Die Komposition der *Phänomenologie des Geistes*," *Hegel Studien* 3 (1966), pp. 64–65. Such an argument seems very implausible to me. For, first, while such a change in meaning is no doubt, here as always, a bare *possibility*, quite general principles of interpretation surely speak against denying a word its normal meaning in a passage, when similar contexts in the same text clearly use it in that meaning, and the denial entails attributing to the author a change of mind from one position to another inconsistent position, in the absence of *very* strong textual grounds for doing so—and, as we shall see shortly, the only textual ground offered by Pöggeler which could conceivably justify doing so in this case, namely, his claim that it is impossible actually to read the chapters *Consciousness* through *Reason* as a chronological history, proves to be quite mistaken. Moreover, second, as we shall see later, Schelling had already some years before the *Phenomenology* in his *System of Transcendental Idealism* of 1800, a work which deeply influenced the *Phenomenology*, conceived the project of a *Geschichte* of consciousness in a sense which *included* the idea of a chronological history of consciousness.

only the chapters *Consciousness* through *Reason*. For immediately after concluding the *Reason* chapter Hegel informs us that the book will henceforth be concerned, not with shapes of consciousness, as hitherto, but with what he distinguishes from these as "real Spirits" or "shapes of a world": "These [coming] shapes . . . are distinguished from the previous ones by the fact that they are real Spirits . . . and, instead of being shapes merely of consciousness, are shapes of a world" (par. 441). Putting these two sets of evidence, (i) and (ii), together gives us strong prima facie grounds for believing that the chapters *Consciousness* through *Reason* constitute a chronological history of the development of consciousness from early times up to the achievement of Hegel's philosophy or "Science" in the modern age.[13]

Still, this is only a strong prima facie case. It might yet be overturned were it to prove impossible actually to read a chronological history of consciousness out of the chapters in question. On the other hand, if that *does* prove possible, then the correctness of the interpretation will be placed beyond much doubt. Most of the secondary literature argues that it is impossible to read the chapters in that way. I believe that, on the contrary, it is quite possible to do so. Let us now turn to see in some detail how.[14]

* * *

We begin with the *Consciousness* chapter. This chapter is by far the most challenging for an interpretation of the chapters *Consciousness* through *Reason* as a chronological history. Accordingly, it has usually been considered altogether recalcitrant to a reading as chronological history. Solomon's view is representative: "The first chapters [i.e., the sections of *Consciousness*] . . . are written more or less without reference to history of any kind."[15] And as we noted earlier, even Lukács, although

---

13. Note that on this interpretation it *cannot* be Hegel's aim to show that the shapes of consciousness treated in the *Phenomenology* are impossible perspectives—as, for example, Solomon implies when he writes that "Sense-certainty is not only an inadequate form of consciousness; it could not possibly be a form of consciousness at all" (*In the Spirit of Hegel*, p. 327). It is important to distinguish between (a) proving perspectives to be incoherent, and (b) proving it incoherent to suppose that perspectives exist. Hegel *is* engaged in (a), but *not* in (b).

14. It will be convenient, for various purposes, to dwell in the course of the following exposition on certain of the contents of these chapters in a little more detail than is strictly required in order to demonstrate their chronological ordering.

15. Solomon, *In the Spirit of Hegel*, p. 216. Cf. Haym's influential reading of this chapter as transcendental psychology, and not history, in *Hegel und seine Zeit*. Even Taylor,

he does regard the chapter as chronological history, is unable to provide any proof that or explanation how it is so.

Nonetheless, the chapter is, I think, intended to be chronologically historical. In addition to the general prima facie case which was stated above, there are two more specific textual reasons for a measure of confidence that this is so. First, when Hegel in the *Religion* chapter remarks on the chronologically historical character of the work's sequence of shapes of consciousness he explicitly includes, and indeed emphasizes, those in the *Consciousness* chapter: the "totality of Spirit," whose moments included "*Consciousness,* Self-consciousness, Reason," each of which in turn "assumed different 'shapes': as, e.g., in *Consciousness, Sense-certainty* and *Perception* were distinct from each other," "is in time, and the 'shapes' . . . display themselves in a temporal succession" (par. 679; emphasis added). Second, as we saw in chapter 4, within the *Consciousness* chapter Sense-certainty is depicted as not yet recognizing "universals" or general concepts as such, but rather conceiving meanings as intimately bound up with sensible particulars, Perception then as recognizing "universals" as such, but still conceiving them as intimately bound up with the sensible particulars which instantiate them, and Force and the Understanding then as not only recognizing "universals" as such but also embracing a Platonism which sharply distinguishes them from the sensible particulars which instantiate them. Now, in the Preface Hegel makes it clear that he conceives this development to be *chronologically historical,* and to fall within *ancient times.* For he says there that, in contrast to "modern times" in which "the individual finds the abstract form ready-made," "in ancient times" the "proper and complete formation of the natural consciousness" consisted in "purging the individual of an immediate, sensuous mode of apprehension," in "the fact that the object represented becomes the property of pure self consciousness, its elevation to universality in general," and that "putting itself to the test at every point of its existence, and philosophizing about everything it came across, [consciousness] made itself into a universality" (par. 33).

The evidence just considered rather vaguely locates the chronological development of the *Consciousness* chapter in "ancient times," and implies its culmination in Greek philosophy (and specifically, the Platonism of the *Force and the Understanding* section). At the time of writing the

---

who is generally quite sensitive to the historical design of the *Phenomenology,* regards this chapter as ahistorical (*Hegel,* p. 131).

chapter Hegel's conception of its historical reference was, I suspect, little more precise than this.[16] As we shall see in chapter 10, his theory in the *Phenomenology* about how one achieves a knowledge of the occurrence and character of past shapes of consciousness would have made it perfectly coherent and natural for him to have believed at the time of writing the chapter that he knew its earlier shapes to have occurred in ancient times but without knowing anything much more specific about when or among whom.

However, evidence in the text from beyond the *Consciousness* chapter itself indicates that Hegel's *eventual and considered* conception in the *Phenomenology* of the chapter's contents is the more precise one that they begin in the *Sense-certainty* and *Perception* sections with shapes of consciousness which originated in the ancient Orient (Persia and India, respectively), and culminate in the section *Force and the Understanding* with a shape which originated in ancient Egypt and then underwent further development among the ancient Greeks (specifically, in Homeric theology and, eventually, Greek rationalist philosophies such as Platonism).[17] Let us consider each of the sections of the *Consciousness* chapter in turn in order to illustrate this conception.

The first section of the chapter, *Sense-certainty*, describes a shape of consciousness distinguished mainly by the following characteristics.[18] From the perspective of this shape of consciousness, its *representation* of reality appears to be sensuous, certain, immediate, and simple—simple specifically in the sense of not yet being articulated in terms of an ontology of things possessing qualities (as later in Perception). Correlatively, the *self* appears to be a locus of just this sort of representation of reality,

---

16. Purpus's attempts to retrieve a detailed history of philosophy from the *Sense-certainty* and *Perception* sections seem to me largely unsuccessful; some of the historical allusions which he claims to identify are plausible, but many are not.

17. Hegel only arrived at this more precise historical conception at the time of writing the *Religion* chapter. Among the facts which show that he did not have it in mind earlier, the following are the most important: (i) The *Consciousness* chapter itself contains clear allusions only to the last part of the historical sequence just outlined, namely, Greek rationalist philosophy. (ii) The *Spirit* chapter, which is designed to retrace the historical steps of the chapters *Consciousness* through *Reason*, contains at its start no treatment of pre-Greek oriental and Egyptian history.

18. The description which follows, and those of the remaining shapes from the *Consciousness* chapter, are designed to serve a secondary purpose of illustrating Hegel's conception of a "shape of consciousness" in some of its concrete applications. These, and subsequent, descriptions simplify considerably in abstracting from the *developments* which Hegel depicts *within* each shape of consciousness.

and in particular is not yet conceived as a locus of representations which are independent of reality. And correlatively again, reality or the *object* appears to be sensuous, certain, immediate, and simple—simple again specifically in the sense that it is not yet articulated in terms of an ontology of things possessing qualities.[19]

I suggest that Hegel from the start conceived this shape of consciousness to have existed at the dawn of human prehistory, at a time when men were still very primitive. This is certainly his *considered* view of it in the *Phenomenology*. For in the *Religion* chapter, which is generally recognized to be chronologically historical in design, he explicitly associates Sense-certainty with the historically first and most primitive form of religion, God as Light (par. 686). He associates this form of religion with the Zoroastrian tradition of ancient Persia.[20] It is therefore reasonable to infer that his considered view of Sense-certainty is that it too has its source in ancient Persia.[21]

---

19. Thus, for example, Hegel describes Sense-certainty's conception of its representations as including, in addition to the sensuousness and certainty implied by its very name, the idea of "immediate knowledge, a knowledge of the immediate or of what simply is" (par. 90). And he says of its conception of the self and its object: "I, this particular I, am certain of this particular thing, not because I, qua consciousness, in knowing it have developed myself or thought about it in various ways; and also not because the thing of which I am certain, in virtue of a host of distinct qualities, would be in its own self a rich complex of connections, or related in various ways to other things . . . Here neither I nor the thing has the significance of a complex process of mediation; the 'I' does not have the significance of a manifold imagining or thinking; nor does the 'thing' signify something that has a host of qualities" (par. 91).

20. In addition to the strong hints of this in the *God as Light* section itself, see *Lectures on the Philosophy of Religion* 2:77 ff.

21. In this connection, the following may be significant: As we saw earlier, one of the major themes of the *Sense-certainty* section is that the "universal," the general concept, is fundamental to language, that the particular can only be referred to by means of the "universal," and that accordingly the primitive perspective of Sense-certainty, even if it believes otherwise, from the start expresses the "universal." Now, Herder, who deeply influenced Hegel's conception of history, had argued similarly that the "universal" was fundamental to language and necessary for reference to the particular: "The goal of our senses, our Reason, our Understanding is *to create for ourselves from an obscure cloud of universals* [Allgemeinem] *the clearer image of a particular* . . . [The Understanding] could only find . . . the particular in the universal" (*Eine Metakritik zur Kritik der reinen Vernunft*, in *Sämtliche Werke* 21:208–9). And Herder had argued in support of this view, and as a phenomenon explained by it, that in the historical development of languages "universals" had preceded terms for particulars—"Thus in human language *the universal* preceded the particular" (ibid., p. 208)—and that this was shown by the fact that the basic roots of the *ancient oriental* languages (Herder locates the origins of mankind in the Orient) are verbs (*Über den Ursprung der Sprache*, in *Herders Ausgewählte Werke* 3:639–40). Here, then,

The *Perception* section of the *Consciousness* chapter goes on to describe a shape of consciousness distinguished mainly by the following characteristics. From the perspective of this shape of consciousness, its *representation* of reality still appears sensuous, but it no longer appears possessed of the degree of certainty and immediacy assumed by Sense-certainty, for it is now recognized to be subject to error in some cases and (a connected fact) is more sharply distinguished from reality.[22] On the other hand, Perception's sensuous representation still seems to it *relatively* certain and immediate—accurate in the normal course of events, a reflection of a reality fundamentally open to view.[23] In addition, for this shape of consciousness its representation of reality no longer seems simple, as it did for Sense-certainty, but instead complex—in the correlative sense of now being articulated in terms of an ontology of things possessing properties. Correspondingly, from the perspective of this shape of consciousness, unlike that of Sense-certainty, the *self* appears to be a locus of representations which can be mistaken and which are distinguished from reality (though still *relatively* certain and in a *relatively* immediate relation to reality), and to be a locus of complex rather than of simple representations. And from the perspective of this shape of consciousness, unlike that of Sense-certainty, reality or the *object,* though it still appears sensuous and *relatively* certain and immediate, no longer appears to have *perfect* certainty and immediacy, but instead to be capable of being misjudged and to be distinct from representations.[24] And in addition the object no longer appears to be simple, but instead complex, articulated in terms of an ontology of things possessing properties.[25]

I suggest again that Hegel from the start considered Perception to be a shape of consciousness which emerged very early in human prehistory,

---

we can see one specific reason why Hegel might have been inclined to identify the perspective of Sense-certainty with the ancient Orient.

22. Thus Hegel writes that for Perception, "since the object is the true and universal, ... while consciousness is alterable and inessential, it can happen that consciousness apprehends the object incorrectly and deceives itself. The percipient is aware of the possibility of deception" (par. 116). Cf. the subtitle of the section, "The Thing *and Deception.*"

23. Hence Hegel writes that in Perception consciousness "only has to *take* [the thing], to confine itself to a pure apprehension of it, and what is thus yielded is the true" (par. 116).

24. Hegel writes, for example, that for Perception "the object ... is the essence regardless of whether it is perceived or not; but the act of perceiving ... is the unessential moment" (par. 111).

25. The object "[shows] itself to be the thing with many properties" (par. 112).

though this time after Sense-certainty. This is clearly his *considered* view of it. For in the uncontroversially historical *Religion* chapter he explicitly associates Perception with the second earliest and most primitive form of religion, Plant and Animal (par. 689). He seems to associate this early form of religion with ancient India.[26] It is therefore reasonable to infer that on his considered view Perception has its source in ancient India as well.

The last section of the *Consciousness* chapter, *Force and the Understanding*, depicts a shape of consciousness distinguished mainly by the following characteristics. It replaces Perception's naive conception of its *representation* of reality as sensuous and relatively certain and immediate with the more sophisticated view that sensuous representation's realm of things and their properties is only a superficial *appearance* of a reality which is au fond quite different in character, namely, a realm of supersensible constitutions and causal principles underlying the sensuous appearances, which is accessible only to a more extraordinary mode of representation than the sensuous possessing the power to penetrate beyond sensuous appearances to it.[27] Correspondingly, from the perspective of this shape of consciousness, the *self* is no longer conceived as the sort of being who stands in a sensuous and relatively certain and immediate cognitive relation to reality, as in Perception, but instead as the sort of being who enjoys such a relation only to superficial appearances, and who must penetrate beyond these appearances by more extraordinary cognitive means in order to discover reality itself. And from the perspective of this shape of consciousness, reality or the *object* is no longer conceived as sensuous, relatively certain, and relatively immediate, as in Perception, but as supersensible, liable to be wholly misjudged, and quite alien.[28]

---

26. For this association, see esp. *The Philosophy of History,* p. 141.
27. Hence the subtitle of the section is "Appearance and the Supersensible World," and Hegel gives the following characterization of this shape of consciousness's conception of its representation: "[The] true essence of things has now the character of not being immediately for consciousness; on the contrary, consciousness has a mediated relation to the inner being and, as the Understanding, looks through [the] mediating play . . . into the true background of things"; "Raised above Perception, consciousness exhibits itself closed in a unity with the supersensible world through the mediating term of appearance, through which it gazes into this background" (pars. 143, 165).
28. Hence Hegel writes, for example, that "there now opens up above the *sensuous* world, which is the world of *appearance,* a *supersensible* world which henceforth is the *true* world, above the vanishing *present* world there opens up a permanent *beyond*" (par. 144).

The *Phenomenology* as a whole identifies three distinct historical phases and forms of Force and the Understanding in the ancient world. The *Force and the Understanding* section itself alludes only to the latest of these, however. So let us begin with this and work backwards historically to the earlier two. The *Force and the Understanding* section implies that this shape of consciousness was instantiated in the ancient world by Greek rationalism—a movement which Hegel in the *Lectures on the History of Philosophy* traces back to Thales in the late seventh to early sixth centuries B.C. as its earliest representative.[29] Several facts show this to be the case. First, it is clear that the distinguishing features of Force and the Understanding, as described above, well capture the distinctive outlook shared by the Greek rationalists (Parmenides, Plato, Democritus, and the rest). Second, near the beginning of the section *Force and the Understanding* there are specific allusions to Parmenides' monism (in its relation to pluralism), as Hegel understood this from his reading of Plato's *Parmenides*. Thus, near the beginning of the section the issue is raised of "on the one side, a universal medium of many subsistent 'matters' and, on the other side, a One reflected into itself, in which their independence is extinguished," and the outcome is stated that "the 'matters' posited as independent directly pass over into their unity, and their unity directly unfolds its diversity, and this once again reduces itself to unity" (pars. 135–36). Compare this with Hegel's summary of the moral of Plato's *Parmenides* in the *Lectures on the History of Philosophy*: "In the proposition 'the One is' it is also implied that 'the One is not One but many'; and conversely, 'the many is' also indicates that 'the many is not many, but One.' They show themselves dialectically and are really the identity with their 'other'; and this is the truth."[30] Third, later in the section there are even clearer allusions to Plato's rationalism, particularly as articulated in the *Republic*. Thus, besides emphasizing the characteristically Platonic distinction between sensible appearances and supersensible reality, Hegel also alludes there specifically to Plato's theory of supersensible forms,[31] to the *Republic*'s view that sensible appearances are

---

29. *Lectures on the History of Philosophy*, esp. 1:177–78.
30. Ibid., 2:59–60. Note that Hegel dates Parmenides somewhat earlier than scholars would today, placing his flourishing at the end of the sixth century B.C. (ibid., 1:249).
31. Par. 143: "The inner is for [consciousness] certainly the concept." Cf. my earlier discussion of this in chapter 4.

contradictory, partaking of both being and not-being,[32] and to the Cave and Sun metaphors of the *Republic*.[33] Fourth, in the *Spirit* chapter Hegel correlates the contents of the *Consciousness* chapter—implying at least this culminating phase Force and the Understanding—with the "Ethical World" of ancient Greece.[34]

The *Force and the Understanding* section therefore implies a rather interesting historical claim: that it was the Greek rationalists who first superseded the sort of naive realist outlook which Hegel calls Perception by developing the view that sensuous appearances concealed supersensible constitutions and causal principles requiring a special mode of representation over and above mere sensuous representation in order to be known. Such a claim would require some significant qualifications if it were to be historically plausible, however. And it is therefore interesting that Hegel goes on in later parts of the *Phenomenology* (and in subsequent works) to enter the requisite qualifications—thereby unfolding an account of the outlook of Force and the Understanding which is both historically richer and more compelling.

Thus, a first qualification required is that the Greek rationalists' outlook was already anticipated in a *religious* form by early Greek, and in particular Homeric, poetry. For example, Homer frequently indicates that some individual who to sensuous representation appears to be a mere mortal is in fact—has as supersensible constitution, so to speak—a god, or that some sensuously perceptible event, such as the deflection of a spear from a warrior, in fact results from—has as supersensible causal principle, so to speak—the imperceptible action of a god. And Homer assumes that there is a mode of representation going beyond sensuous representation which gives men cognitive access to this realm of supersensible constitutions and causal principles, namely, divine inspiration (especially, though not exclusively, of poet by Muse). It is easy to recognize

---

32. Par. 143: here "the things of Perception . . . immediately and without rest turn into their opposite," " 'being' is . . . called *appearance,* for we call *being* that is directly and in its own self a *not-being* a surface show."
33. Par. 146: "The result is, of course, the same if a blind man is placed amid the wealth of the supersensible world . . . , and if one with sight is placed in pure darkness, or if you like, in pure light, just supposing the supersensible world to be this. The man with sight sees as little in that pure light as in pure darkness, and just as much as the blind man, in the abundant wealth which lies before him."
34. "Spirit is, in its simple truth [i.e., as Ethical World], Consciousness . . . It . . . exhibits in its own self the nature of Consciousness" (pars. 444–45; cf. 446).

in this Homeric pattern of thought the forerunner of Greek rationalism: Where Homer had the gods and their actions as supersensible constitutions and causal principles underlying sensible appearances, the Greek rationalists substituted Parmenidean Being, Platonic forms, Democritean atoms and their motions, and the like. And where Homer conceived divine inspiration as the mode of representation which went beyond the deliverances of the senses and gave men access to this underlying supersensible realm, the Greek rationalists substituted *nous*, reason. Now Hegel makes just this sort of qualification in the *Religion* chapter of the *Phenomenology*, where he correlates (Force and) the Understanding in one of its phases with early Greek religion and art (par. 706), and speaks of Greek epic poetry as representing a "dispersion of the whole into manifold and abstract forces, which appear hypostatized [i.e., as gods]" (par. 736), implying that the epic gods were the forerunners of the supersensuous forces described in the Force and the Understanding section.[35]

Hegel implies a second qualification in the *Religion* chapter as well—namely, that in its most primitive form the outlook of Force and the Understanding goes back even further than Homeric theology to the ancient oriental world, and in particular the religion of Pharaonic Egypt. For in the *Religion* chapter he explicitly associates (Force and) the Understanding in its most primitive form, "the abstract form of the Understanding," with the type of religion which he calls "The Artificer," and which he identifies with Pharaonic Egypt (pars. 692, 694). This type of religion too draws a distinction between outer appearances and inner essence or being (pars. 693, 696). Here the distinction mainly takes the form of interpreting outward monuments, "the crystals of pyramids and obelisks," as loci of the supersensible *ka* or soul of the dead, or of a supersensible god who makes an appearance in natural form, as Amun Ra appears as the sun, and thereby infuses these monuments with significance—"an alien, departed spirit that has forsaken its living saturation with reality and . . . takes up its abode in this lifeless crystal; or . . . Spirit as something

---

35. This qualification is made still clearer in the *Lectures on the Philosophy of World History*, where Hegel says with reference to a famous episode in the *Odyssey*, "When Ulysses among the Phaeacians has thrown his discus further than the rest and one of the Phaeacians shows a friendly disposition toward him, the poet recognizes in him Pallas Athena. Such an explanation denotes the perception of the inner meaning, the sense, the underlying truth; and the poets were in this way the teachers of the Greeks—especially Homer . . . Setting out from surmise and wonder, the Greek spirit advances to conceptions of the hidden meanings of nature" (*The Philosophy of History*, pp. 236–38).

which is itself there externally and not as Spirit [and to which the monuments are related] as to the dawning light, which casts its significance on them" (par. 692).

In sum, Hegel's considered conception of Force and the Understanding in the *Phenomenology* is that it is an outlook which has its earliest source in ancient Egyptian religion, develops further within Homeric religion, and then culminates in the perspective of the Greek rationalists.[36]

Hegel's considered view of the entire *Consciousness* chapter as a chronological history of consciousness is, then, that Sense-certainty emerges at the dawn of human prehistory, in ancient Persia, Perception in the next phase of human prehistory, in ancient India, and Force and the Understanding in the next phase of human prehistory, having its first beginnings in Pharaonic Egypt, developing further in Homeric Greece, and reaching its culmination in Greek rationalism.

Note, finally, in some confirmation of this interpretation, that such a conception of the beginnings of human history accords well both with the views of Hegel's most important forerunner in the philosophy of history, Herder, and with the views of the later Hegel himself. For, Herder had already argued that man's origins were in Asia, and that "the Greek [got his culture] from Asia and Egypt, Egypt from Asia."[37] And the later Hegel in the *Lectures on the Philosophy of World History* similarly conceives history to have begun in the ancient Orient, passed thence to ancient Egypt, and thence to ancient Greece.

* * *

The *Self-consciousness* chapter continues this chronological history of consciousness begun in the *Consciousness* chapter—again contrary to the conventional wisdom of the secondary literature.[38]

---

36. One of the most interesting features of this fuller account of how naive realism (Perception) gave way to a distinction between sensible appearances and an underlying supersensible reality is that it constitutes a sort of genealogy not only of Greek rationalism but also, and thereby, of *modern natural science*. For modern natural science has developed from and retains as a background assumption the general outlook of Greek rationalism. This is indeed part of the point of Hegel's constant allusions to Newtonian physics and its theory of *forces* in the section *Force and the Understanding*.

37. *Über den Ursprung der Sprache*, in *Herders Ausgewählte Werke* 3:688; cf. *Auch eine Philosophie der Geschichte zur Bildung der Menschheit*, ibid., 2:624–32. On man's origins in Asia specifically, see esp. *Ideen zur Philosophie der Geschichte der Menschheit*, pp. 303–13.

38. As already mentioned, Pöggeler, for example, argues in one essay that the *Self-consciousness* chapter makes a new historical beginning ("Zur Deutung der *Phänomenolo-*

The *Self-consciousness* chapter's shapes of consciousness are, in order: Life (and Desire), Lordship and Bondage, Stoicism, Skepticism, and Unhappy Consciousness. These shapes are collectively distinguished from those of the *Consciousness* chapter primarily by the fact that they assign ontological priority to the self over the object rather than vice versa, and moreover increasingly so as we proceed from each one to the next.[39] Along with this ontological ascendancy of the self over the object comes an increasing emphasis on *practical* as opposed to theoretical matters.[40] What, though, is the more specific character of these shapes, and what do they represent historically?[41]

The first of these shapes is Life (and Desire). What in general is distinctive of Life as a shape of consciousness is that it conceives as a *unity* items which other outlooks sharply distinguish from one another: Life is "the *unity* of what is distinguished" (par. 168). More specifically: (i) The deity is here conceived as present in, rather than as separate from, man and nature. Hegel implies this when he goes on to describe the Christian Unhappy Consciousness's introduction of the conception that God is *beyond* man and nature, symbolized in its claim that Christ has *died*, by saying that this "consciousness . . . can only find as a present reality the *grave*

---

gie des Geistes," pp. 268 ff.), and in a later essay that the chapter is not historical at all (*Hegels Idee einer Phänomenologie des Geistes*, pp. 248, 264).

39. Thus Hegel writes that "consciousness, as Self-consciousness, henceforth has a double object: one is the immediate object, that of Sense-certainty and Perception, which however *for Self-consciousness* has the character of a *negative;* and the second, viz. *itself*, which is the true *essence*, and is present in the first instance only as opposed to the first object. In this sphere, Self-consciousness exhibits itself as the movement in which this antithesis is removed, and the identity of itself with itself becomes explicit for it" (par. 167; cf. 166, 174).

40. Hegel also implies that there occurs in the *Self-consciousness* chapter a shift from the individual to society (par. 177), and some commentators have emphasized this as distinctive of the chapter (e.g., Findlay, *Hegel: A Re-examination*, pp. 96–97). This seems to me more problematic, however. For, although the *Lordship and Bondage* section conforms well enough to such a description, it is far from clear that the *Stoicism, Skepticism*, or *Unhappy Consciousness* sections do so. Another suggestion occasionally found in the literature is the superficially tempting one that the differentia of the shapes of the *Self-consciousness* chapter is self-consciousness, that is, consciousness of oneself as such. This is a mistake; as we saw earlier, consciousness of oneself as such is for Hegel an essential characteristic of *all* consciousness, and hence of the shapes of consciousness treated in the *Consciousness* and *Reason* chapters no less than of those treated in the *Self-consciousness* chapter.

41. Having done so for illustrative purposes in connection with the three shapes of the *Consciousness* chapter, I shall not henceforth undertake to characterize each shape of consciousness's distinctive conceptions/concepts of self, object, and representation *separately*.

of its Life" (par. 217). (ii) Natural objects in general are here conceived as *living selves,* there is no sharp distinction drawn between natural objects and living selves: "What self-consciousness distinguishes from itself as having *being* also has in it . . . not merely the character of Sense-certainty and Perception, but . . . the object . . . is a *living thing*"; "The object . . . is a living self-consciousness" (pars. 168, 176).[42] (iii) There is no awareness here of a sharp distinction between individual and community, since individuals have their community as their highest end and automatically judge in agreement with it. Hegel implies this feature of Life later in the text, writing that when the individual's "pleasure of enjoying his individuality . . . passes away in his own self-consciousness as a citizen of his nation," and he knows "that the law of his own heart is the law of all hearts," this is "universal Life" (par. 461). (iv) Thought and reality are here conceived as unified, they are not sharply distinguished from one another. (v) There is no sharp distinction drawn here between fact and volition. Hegel implies these two features of Life when he writes later in the text that "individuality qua acting should represent itself in a *living* manner or qua thinking should grasp the *living* world as a system of thought" (par. 200; emphasis added). (vi) There is no sharp distinction drawn here between duty and desire. Hegel implies this feature of Life later in the text when he writes that for "universal Life" "virtue" consists in the individual's "knowing that *the law of his own heart* is the law of all hearts" (par. 461; emphasis added). (vii) There is no sharp distinction here between virtue and happiness. Hegel implies this feature of Life when he writes at the same later point in the text that this law of all hearts "is virtue, which *enjoys* the fruits of its sacrifice, which brings about what it sets out to do . . . and its *enjoyment* is this universal Life" (par. 461; emphasis added). (viii) Minds or selves are here conceived as natural objects, there is here no dualism between mind or self and body: "A self-consciousness, in being an object, is just as much 'I' as 'object' "; "[Individuals] are for one another like ordinary objects, . . . individuals submerged in the being of *Life*" (pars. 177, 186). These eight unifying conceptions constitute together, in Hegel's view, a distinctive set of

---

42. The *Phenomenology* attributes conception (ii) to Life much more explicitly than conception (i). It is, however, crucial to recognize the attribution to Life of conception (i) if one is to make sense of the attribution to Life of conception (ii). For (i) *explains* (ii), which would otherwise be quite obscure; it is *because* Life identifies nature with personal gods that natural objects appear as selves to it.

conceptions and concepts of self, object, and representation—"a new shape of consciousness" (par. 164).

The account which has already been given in chapter 2 of Hegel's conception of man's early historical occupation of and subsequent fall from this sort of unified outlook should leave us in no doubt as to the historical reference intended here: an ideal early period of ancient Greek culture.[43] Confirmation of this historical reference is found in the extensive treatment of "Life" in Hegel's early essay *The Spirit of Christianity*.[44] As in the *Phenomenology*, "Life" in *The Spirit of Christianity* is a perspective characterized by unity, the absence of sharp distinctions and divisions.[45] And, as in the *Phenomenology*, "Life" there includes, more specifically, each of the unifying conceptions (i)–(viii) listed above.[46] Moreover, in *The Spirit of Christianity* the perspective of "Life" is explicitly identified in its historical aspect with the ideal culture of early ancient Greece. For instance, concerning (vi), the unity of duty and desire or inclination, Hegel there alludes to Aeschylus's *Oresteia* as exemplifying Life's commitment to such a conception.[47] And, as noted in chapter 2, concerning (viii), the unity of mind or self and body, Hegel there speaks of this as

---

43. Having collated the various unifying conceptions which Hegel ascribes to Life in the above manner, we can now see quite clearly that the *Self-consciousness* chapter is largely conceived as a systematic account of the crucial early stages of the historical fall from unified to dualistic conceptions which was discussed in chapter 2: The *Self-consciousness* chapter begins, in its treatment of Life, with the earlier ancient Greeks' unifying conceptions (i)–(viii). The chapter then charts and explains the collapse of all these unifying conceptions into corresponding dualistic ones in later periods of ancient Greek and Roman history, in the sections *Lordship and Bondage* (ancient oppression and slavery), *Stoicism* (ancient Stoicism), *Skepticism* (ancient Skepticism), and *Unhappy Consciousness* (early Christianity), in ways that were indicated in chapter 2.

44. This early essay is much more illuminating of the *historical* dimension of the *Phenomenology*'s conception of Life than are the treatments of "Life" found closer in time to the *Phenomenology* in the Jena Philosophy of Spirit.

45. See *Early Theological Writings*, pp. 229, 232, 247, 255, 260–61, 278.

46. Concerning (i), see ibid., pp. 262, 268, 300–301 (the unity of the deity with man), 262, 287–88, 292 (the unity of the deity with nature); concerning (ii), ibid., pp. 287–88; concerning (iii), ibid., pp. 223, 278, 284–85; concerning (iv), ibid., pp. 259, 297–98, 300; concerning (v), ibid., pp. 287–88; concerning (vi), ibid., pp. 212–13, 229–30; concerning (vii), ibid., pp. 215, 247, 317; concerning (viii), ibid., pp. 297–98.

47. Ibid., p. 229: "In the hostile power of fate, universal is not severed from particular in the way in which the law [of Judaism], as a universal, is opposed to man or his inclinations as the particular . . . For the man is alive, and before he acts there is no cleavage, no opposition, much less a mastery. Only through a departure from that united Life . . . is something alien produced . . . [Life] is immortal, and, if slain, it appears as its terrifying ghost which vindicates every branch of Life and lets loose its Eumenides."

"the *Greek* view that body and soul persist together in one *living* shape."⁴⁸ This identification of the *Phenomenology*'s shape of consciousness Life with the ideal culture of early ancient Greece is further confirmed by the recurrence of the word and concept Life each time Hegel comes to a discussion of the ideal culture of early ancient Greece in the text of the *Phenomenology*—specifically, in the *Reason* chapter (pars. 352–54); at the beginning of the *Spirit* chapter (pars. 442, 454, 461); and in the sections on Greek religion early in the *Religion* chapter (pars. 725, 742, 753; cf. the section title there "The *living* work of art").

Now, Hegel throughout his career placed the ideal early period of ancient Greek culture primarily in fifth-century Athens, especially during the age of Pericles.⁴⁹ We may therefore safely infer that he understands the shape of consciousness Life to belong primarily to that time and place.⁵⁰ This, then, is Hegel's conception of the shape of consciousness Life and its historical reference.⁵¹

---

48. Ibid., p. 298; emphasis added.
49. Concerning this position in the early theological writings, see Harris, *Hegel's Development*, pp. 120 n., 150–52. For the same position in the Jena writings, see especially *Natural Law*, where Hegel lists as examples of the flourishing of individuality within the "ethical organization" of the polis "Homer, Pindar, *Aeschylus, Sophocles*, Plato, *Aristophanes*" (emphasis added), noting that by contrast in extremes of individuality and of reactions against it exemplified by, and occurring at the time of, Socrates "inner vitality had . . . announced that it was going to extremes" and "proclaimed . . . the approaching death of this body [i.e., the ethical city] which bore the seeds" (p. 106). For the same position in the later Hegel, see *The Philosophy of History*, pp. 259–62 (Pericles' age as the zenith of Greek culture), 267–71 (Sophism and Socrates in the later fifth century as effecting the corruption of the polis).
50. It would be misguided to object—either to my interpretation or to Hegel—that chronological sequence is broken here because Plato has already been alluded to in the *Force and the Understanding* section. What matters to Hegel is that the historically *earliest* examples of the shapes occurring at earlier points in his text should have historically preceded the historically earliest examples of the shapes occurring at later points in his text, not that *all* of their examples should have done so. The transition from Force and the Understanding to Life (and Desire) as interpreted here easily meets that standard, since the earliest forms of Force and the Understanding—ancient Egyptian religion, Homeric Greek religion, and also the earlier forms of Greek rationalism—predate fifth-century Athens and the age of Pericles.
51. The above account affords the basis for a partial explanation of the *Self-consciousness* chapter's initially puzzling pairing of Life with *Desire*. As noted, *The Spirit of Christianity* and the *Phenomenology* attribute to the Life of ideal early Greek culture a unity between duty and desire. In doing so, they sharply contrast it with the Judeo-Christian tradition, for which desire is opposed and subjugated by duty. Putting this fact together with our historical interpretation of the *Consciousness* and *Self-consciousness* chapters, we get the following explanation of the prominence of Desire in the section on Life: In the

Turning next to Lordship and Bondage, this really comprises *two* shapes of consciousness rather than one.[52] First, there is a shape—initially belonging to people generally but later restricted to a subset of them, the lords—which is distinguished in its relations to objects and to other people by pure self-assertiveness, the regarding of them as wholly subject to its will.[53] This first shape is perhaps best understood as an extreme form of the preceding shape, Life and Desire, rather than as an entirely new shape.[54] Second, a new shape emerges from the conflicts which inevitably arise between individuals of this first sort, and the resulting submission of one such individual to another. This is the shape belonging to the bondsman. It is characterized by submissiveness toward other people and a recognition of the independence of objects, on which the bondsman labors for the lord.[55] Each of these shapes of consciousness has, in Hegel's

---

historical period covered by the immediately preceding *Consciousness* chapter, namely, the early Orient and Greece before the fifth century, sociopolitical subjugation by despots (the oriental despots and the Peisistratids thematized in the *Lectures on the Philosophy of World History*) restrained individual desire in an external manner. In the historical period covered by the following sections, *Lordship and Bondage* through *Unhappy Consciousness*, namely, from later Greek and Roman history down to medieval Europe, individual desire is again restrained, initially once again in an external manner by sociopolitical subjugation (the sociopolitical oppression represented in *Lordship and Bondage*), but later in an internal manner by moral subjugation (as in the Christianity of *Unhappy Consciousness*). The intervening period of ideal early Greek culture, Life, is by contrast a period in which desire becomes for a time uniquely dominant in the individual's experience, because restrained *neither* by external sociopolitical subjugation *nor* by internal moral subjugation.

52. "They exist as two opposed shapes of consciousness; one is the independent consciousness, whose essential nature is to be for itself, the other is the dependent consciousness, whose essential nature is simply to live or to be for another. The former is lord, the other is bondsman" (par. 189).

53. Thus Hegel writes: "Self-consciousness is, to begin with, simple being-for-self . . . For it, its essence and absolute object is 'I' . . . What is 'other' for it is an unessential, negatively characterized object. But the 'other' is also a self-consciousness; one individual is confronted by another individual. Appearing thus immediately on the scene, they are for one another like ordinary objects"; the lord's "essential nature is to exist only for himself; he is the sheer negative power for whom the thing is nothing" (pars. 186, 191).

54. Thus Hegel emphasizes that this first shape's conception of both objects and subjects is that of *Life:* these individuals "are for one another like ordinary objects, . . . individuals submerged in the being of *Life*—for the object in its immediacy is here determined as Life" (par. 186). And this shape's characteristic self-assertiveness or "being-for-self" can be understood as the dominance within it of *Desire*.

55. Thus Hegel describes this as "the dependent consciousness whose essential nature is simply to live or to be for another," and who is left "the aspect of [the thing's] independence" and "who works on it" (pars. 189–90).

view, distinctive conceptions and concepts of self, object, and representation.

What does the *Lordship and Bondage* section refer to historically? It refers to the demise of the ideal culture of fifth-century Athens (Life) through a twofold loss of freedom which Hegel believes to have occurred first in Athens beginning in the later fifth century and then subsequently, and in a similar way, in Rome during the period from the Second Punic War to the advent of the emperors: (i) a loss of political freedom by the mass of the citizenry, and (ii) a growth in the enslavement of noncitizens.[56]

That the section refers to ancient Greek and Roman history is readily seen from the fact that it immediately follows the presentations of Greek rationalism in the section *Force and the Understanding* and of the unified outlook of fifth-century Athens in the section *Life (and Desire)*, and immediately precedes the presentations of Hellenistic Greek and Roman Stoicism in the *Stoicism* section, Hellenistic Greek and Roman Skepticism in the *Skepticism* section, and the early Christianity of the Roman Empire in the *Unhappy Consciousness* section. This historical reference is confirmed by the *Encyclopaedia,* where, in a paragraph devoted to "the relation of Lordship and Bondage," Hegel writes that "so far as the historical aspect of this relation is concerned, it can be said here that the ancient peoples, the Greeks and Romans, had not yet raised themselves to the concept of absolute freedom, since they did not recognize that man as such . . . has a right to freedom."[57]

Let us consider the section's reference to *Greek* history first. Clearly, Lordship and Bondage represents for Hegel the first disruption of Life, the unified outlook of the ideal Greek culture which he conceives to have flourished in fifth-century Athens, particularly during the age of Pericles. One way to determine the precise period of Greek history to which Lordship and Bondage refers would therefore be to ask when Hegel understands the ideal Athenian culture of the fifth century to have begun its decline. Hegel gives roughly the same answer to this question in all periods of his career: the later fifth century. Thus, in the *Natural Law* essay

---

56. Pace, for example, Hyppolite who denies that the section makes any specific historical reference (*Genesis and Structure,* p. 35), and Solomon who takes it to be about a confrontation between individuals in the state of nature and "emphatically *pre*-social, *before* the formation of society" (*In the Spirit of Hegel,* p. 427).

57. *Encyclopaedia,* par. 433, addition.

of 1802–3 he identifies Socrates' age, with its excessive individualism, and the reaction against it, as the beginning of the end.[58] Similarly, in the *Spirit* chapter of the *Phenomenology* he associates the beginning of the end of the ideal Ethical World of Greece with Sophoclean tragedy. Similarly again, in the later *Lectures on the Philosophy of World History* he traces the decline of ideal Athenian culture back to the influence of Sophism and Socrates in the later fifth century.[59] Such a period for Lordship and Bondage would correspond well to its position in the text, where it follows Greek rationalism (Force and the Understanding) and the ideal Athenian culture of the fifth century culminating in the age of Pericles (Life), but precedes Stoicism and Skepticism, schools of philosophy which developed at Athens from the end of the fourth century on.

The *Lordship and Bondage* section in fact refers to two connected but distinct processes which occurred at Athens in this period. In the early theological writings Hegel had explained the decline from the ideal early culture of Athens (and Rome) toward the corruption of Stoicism and then Christianity in terms of a loss of sociopolitical freedom among the citizenry which, he claimed, had occurred in Athens (and Rome) when successful military campaigns had caused the ascent of a wealthy military aristocracy that came to wield power over the rest of the community, initially by (economic) influence, but eventually by force. Thus in *The Positivity of the Christian Religion* we read:

> Greek and Roman religion was only a religion for free peoples, and with the loss of freedom the sense for, the force of, this religion, its appropriateness for people, is inevitably lost as well . . . Fortunate wars, increase of wealth, and acquaintance with a number of life's comforts and with luxury produced in Athens and Rome an aristocracy of military glory and of wealth, and gave them a rule and influence over many people, who—enticed by the former's deeds, and still more by the use which they made of their riches—conceded to them gladly and of their own free will a superiority in power and a dominion in the state . . . Soon the superiority in power which had been freely conceded became maintained by force . . . In this

---

58. *Natural Law*, p. 106: "Both in the serious reaction against the ever more seriously developing individuality of Socrates, and still more in the regret and shame because of it, and in the pullulating abundance and high energy of the individualizations that were burgeoning at the same time, we must not fail to discern that inner vitality had thereby announced that it was going to extremes, that it proclaimed its strength in the maturity of these seeds but also the approaching death of this body which bore the seeds."
59. *The Philosophy of History*, pp. 265–71.

condition, without belief in anything permanent, in anything absolute, in this habit of obeying an alien will, an alien legislation ... a religion offered itself to people which ... fitted the needs of the age ... Reason could never give up finding the absolute, the independent, the practical, somewhere or other. It was no longer to be found in people's will. It now appeared to reason in the deity which the Christian religion offered it, beyond the sphere of our power, of our volition, but not of our pleading and asking.[60]

Similarly, a fragment from about the same period explains how "the collapse of Roman and Greek freedom" led to Stoicism's withdrawal from the world and Christianity's flight from the world to an imaginary invisible world.[61] Now the *Lordship and Bondage* section must surely in large part refer to this episode in Athenian history. For, the terminus a quo and the terminus ad quem are in both cases the same: ideal early Athenian culture (in the *Phenomenology*, "Life"), and ancient Stoicism and Christianity (in the *Phenomenology*, "Stoicism" and "Unhappy Consciousness"). And so too is the general character of the episode which explains the transition: one class of individuals in society attains coercive domination over another (in the *Phenomenology*, the "lords" over the "bondsmen"). We will therefore have discovered at least part of the specific historical reference of the *Lordship and Bondage* section to Athenian history if we can determine what episode in Athenian history Hegel had in mind in these earlier texts. Now, the reference just quoted to successful military campaigns leading to wealth and luxury in Athens can only be an allusion to Athens' success in the Persian Wars early in the fifth century and the great increase in her wealth which resulted from that success. And the reference to the emergence of an initially seductive but eventually coercive aristocratic domination must therefore be an allusion mainly to the rise to popular influence of the aristocrat Alcibiades and the subsequent oligarchic coups of the Four Hundred (411 B.C.) and the Thirty Tyrants (404 B.C.) at the end of the century. This historical reference is confirmed by another early fragment in which Hegel locates the damage caused to Athenian freedom by the rise of a disproportionately wealthy aristocracy at the conclusion of the age of Pericles.[62] This, then, is *one* development

---

60. In appendix I.
61. *Dokumente zu Hegels Entwicklung*, pp. 264–65.
62. Ibid., p. 269: "To what extent the disproportionate wealth of a few citizens is dangerous to even the freest form of constitution and is able to destroy freedom itself is shown by history in the example of Pericles in Athens." The parallel Roman example which follows this remark shows that Hegel mainly means that the *fate* of Periclean democracy illustrates the corrupting effects of a disproportionately wealthy aristocracy, rather than that Pericles'

in Athenian history in the later part of the fifth century to which the *Lordship and Bondage* section is referring (in highly abstract, stylized, and individualized terms, of course).

The section also refers, though, to a distinct, but roughly simultaneous and quite closely connected, development in Athenian history. The actual content of the section suggests even more strongly than a process of subjugation of citizens through political oppression a process of *enslavement*. And that Hegel does indeed have Greek (and Roman) slavery in mind in the section is confirmed by the *Encyclopaedia,* where he says concerning "the relation of Lordship and Bondage": "So far as the historical aspect of this relation is concerned, it can be said here that the ancient peoples, the Greeks and Romans, had not yet raised themselves to the concept of absolute freedom, since they did not recognize that man as such . . . has a right to freedom. With them, on the contrary, a person was only considered free when he was born a free man . . . Freedom thus still had, for them, the characteristic of naturalness. That is why there was slavery in their free states."[63] The key to understanding Hegel's historical conception here lies, I think, in recognizing a fact already indicated in chapter 4: that his conception of Lordship and Bondage is heavily indebted to J.F. Reitemeier's 1789 work *The History and Condition of Slavery and Bondage in Greece.* In this work Reitemeier had argued, quite cogently, that as a result of Athenian victory in the Persian Wars early in the fifth century, and the consequent expansion and change in the character of the Athenian economy (particularly from a rural and agrarian to an urban and manufacturing/trading emphasis), slavery had undergone a dramatic expansion and transformation for the worse in quality in fifth-century Athens.[64] I suggest that the *Lordship and Bondage* section refers in important part to this great increase in the quantity and severity of Athenian slavery during the fifth century, a development roughly contemporaneous with the political events mentioned in the previous paragraph and trace-

---

government *itself* does—though there is perhaps also a hint of the latter idea as well, a suggestion that Pericles himself already represented an unhealthy ascent in wealthy aristocratic power, an as yet benign example of the sort of seductive aristocratic domination that would later turn malignant in the case of his relative Alcibiades.

63. *Encyclopaedia,* par. 433, addition.

64. *Geschichte und Zustand der Sklaverei und Leibeigenschaft in Griechenland,* pp. 25 ff. Reitemeier's historical account has recently been praised as a landmark in its subject by the eminent ancient historian M.I. Finley in his *Ancient Slavery and Modern Ideology* (Harmondsworth: Penguin Books, 1983), pp. 35–38.

able to the same ultimate cause (Athenian success in the Persian Wars, and the resulting expansion of the Athenian economy).

Besides referring to these two developments in fifth-century *Greek* history, the *Lordship and Bondage* section also refers to a strikingly similar pair of developments which occurred later in *Roman* history. Thus, as we noted, the early theological writings explained the development from an ideal early culture to the corruption of Stoicism and Christianity in terms of "the collapse of *Roman* and Greek freedom." And more specifically, they explained it in terms of the emergence "in Athens *and Rome*," through successful wars and a resulting increase in prosperity, of a disproportionately wealthy military aristocracy which attained political domination at first by (economically) seducing the populace and then finally by coercion. In relation to Roman history, the early theological writings had in mind here Rome's success in the Second Punic War, the great increase in Roman prosperity to which this led, the monopolization of much of the new wealth by the aristocracy (despite the efforts of the Gracchae to prevent this), and the incremental destruction of the republic which resulted, as the mass of the citizenry initially fell into the habit of slavishly following a handful of economically and militarily powerful leaders, and then eventually Caesar put an end to the already corrupted republic altogether by making himself the first emperor. We can tell this mainly from two pieces of evidence: First, a fragment from the early theological writings shows clearly that this is at least the general period of Roman history that Hegel had in mind in connection with the collapse of freedom in the Roman world.[65] Second, later, in the *Lectures on the Philosophy of World History,* Hegel gives in some detail precisely the account of the sequence of developments in this period of Roman history just summarized above.[66] These developments in Roman history will therefore be one part of what the *Lordship and Bondage* section of the *Phenomenology* refers to within Roman history.

In addition to this loss of political freedom by the mass of citizens after and as a result of Rome's military success in the Second Punic War and the consequent great increase in Roman prosperity, the *Lordship and*

---

65. *Dokumente zu Hegels Entwicklung,* p. 269: "To what extent the disproportionate wealth of a few citizens is dangerous to even the freest form of constitution and is able to destroy freedom itself is shown by history in the example of a Pericles in Athens, [and] of the patricians in Rome, whose demise the imposing influence of the Gracchae and others in suggestions of agrarian laws vainly tried to stop."
66. *The Philosophy of History,* pp. 309–13; cf. *Philosophy of Right,* par. 357.

Bondage section also refers to the substantial growth in Roman *slavery* which occurred after and as a result of Rome's success in that war and the consequent great increase in Roman prosperity. Thus, as we recently noted, the actual contents of the section strongly suggest a reference to slavery, and the *Encyclopaedia* explicitly associates Lordship and Bondage with (Greek and) Roman slavery.[67] And it is generally recognized by historians that the prosperity which resulted from the military success of the Second Punic War led to a great growth in Roman slavery. This, then, will be a *second* development in Roman history to which the *Lordship and Bondage* section is referring.[68]

The historical references of the remaining shapes of consciousness treated in the *Self-consciousness* chapter are far less obscure and controversial than those of Life and Lordship and Bondage, and may therefore be dealt with more briefly. As Hegel characterizes it, Stoicism is distin-

---

67. At *Encyclopaedia,* par. 433, in the continuation of the passage recently quoted, Hegel indeed dwells especially on *Roman* slavery: "Freedom . . . still had, for [the Greeks and Romans] the characteristic of naturalness. That is why there was slavery in their free states and there arose among the Romans bloody wars in which the slaves tried to free themselves, to attain the recognition of their eternal human rights."

68. It deserves emphasis just how strikingly parallel the developments in Greek and Roman history referred to by the *Lordship and Bondage* section are on this interpretation: in each case a successful war led to economic expansion, and this situation in turn led to both (i) the rise of a military aristocracy possessed of disproportionate wealth, and its consequent ascent to domination over the rest of the people, at first by (economic) seduction, but finally by coercion, and (ii) a dramatic increase in slavery. Hegel was, I strongly suspect, inclined to see such a parallelism as extending beyond the *Lordship and Bondage* section to the other sections of the *Self-consciousness* chapter as well: Greek history proceeds from an early ideal culture (Life), through the development of political oppression and slavery in the manner just described (Lordship and Bondage), to Hellenistic Stoicism (Stoicism), Hellenistic Skepticism (Skepticism), and finally Christianity in the later Greek world (Unhappy Consciousness—for recall that Christianity spread in the Greek-speaking world before arriving at Rome, that the New Testament was written in Greek, etc.). Similarly, Roman history proceeds from an early ideal culture (Life—for as one sees from *The Positivity of the Christian Religion,* the young Hegel was inclined to regard the Romans as having enjoyed during the Republic a unified, free culture much like that of early Athens), through the development of political oppression and slavery in the manner just described (Lordship and Bondage), to the development under the Empire of Roman forms of Stoicism (Stoicism) and Skepticism (Skepticism) and eventually Christianity (Unhappy Consciousness). As we move along these parallel tracks in the *Self-consciousness* chapter, the emphasis shifts from the Greek track to the Roman: In the section *Life* we are almost exclusively concerned with the Greek case, by the *Unhappy Consciousness* section almost exclusively with the Roman (and its aftermath). In the intervening sections the emphasis is more even, with *Lordship and Bondage* probably somewhat emphasizing the Greek case, while *Stoicism* and *Skepticism* somewhat emphasize the Roman.

guished as a shape of consciousness mainly by the facts that the subject here (i) recognizes a sharp distinction between the conceptually articulated medium of its thought, on the one hand, and the reality which that thought is about, on the other, and (ii) seeks autonomy from reality through withdrawal into itself and its thought.[69] This shape of consciousness has, in Hegel's view, distinctive conceptions and concepts of self, object, and representation.

The historical reference here is obviously to Hellenistic Greek and Roman Stoicism. In particular, (i) is an allusion to the ancient Stoics' idea that incorporeal "sayables [*lekta*]" (that is, roughly, predicates and propositions) and also "impressions [*phantasiai*]" in the soul constitute a medium distinct from the existent (or strictly, in the case of impressions, the rest of the existent) through which cognition of the existent takes place.[70] And (ii) is an allusion to the ancient Stoics' attempt to find a criterion of truth in the subject's own "cataleptic" impressions, and to their practical ideal of autonomy. The emphasis in this section falls especially heavily on the *Roman* forms of Stoicism.[71]

The next shape of consciousness is Skepticism. Skepticism, as Hegel here interprets it, is distinguished mainly by the fact that it completes Stoicism's elevation of the self and its thought above independent reality by eliminating independent reality altogether.[72] Skepticism's conceptions

---

69. Thus Hegel writes of Stoicism: "We are in the presence of self-consciousness in a new shape, a consciousness which, as the infinitude of consciousness or as its own pure movement, is aware of itself as essential being, a being which *thinks* or is a free self-consciousness ... In *thinking*, the object does not present itself in picture-thoughts but in *concepts*, i.e., in a distinct *being-in-itself* or intrinsic being, consciousness being aware that this is not anything distinct from itself"; this consciousness's "aim is to be free, and to maintain that lifeless indifference which steadfastly withdraws from the bustle of existence ... into the simple essentiality of thought" (pars. 197, 199).

70. As noted in chapter 2, while the *Phenomenology* ascribes the genesis of outlook (i) to Platonism and especially to Stoicism, the later Hegel came—plausibly—to locate its genesis even earlier, namely, in Sophism, particularly as represented by Gorgias and his treatise *Concerning Nature or Concerning the Non-existent*.

71. Hence, for example, the *Spirit* chapter explicitly associates Stoicism with Legal Status, that is, the Roman Empire (par. 479; cf. 199); the *Stoicism* section clearly alludes to the Roman Stoics Marcus Aurelius (an emperor) and Epictetus (a slave) in the phrase "on the throne or in chains" (par. 199); and, as noted in chapter 2, the *Stoicism* section ascribes to Stoicism a dualistic conception of the relation between the mind or self and the body which is characteristic of Roman rather than of Hellenistic Greek Stoicism.

72. Thus Hegel writes that "in Skepticism ... the wholly unessential and non-independent character of [the] 'other' becomes explicit *for consciousness;* the thought becomes the concrete thinking which annihilates the being of the world in all its manifold determinateness ... It is *thinking*, or is in its own self infinite, and in this infinitude the inde-

and concepts of self, object, and representation are therefore, as Hegel interprets them, those of a sort of idealism.

The historical reference here is obviously to Hellenistic Greek and Roman Skepticism. Hegel is thinking in particular of the ancient skeptics' complete retreat from making claims about how things really are to making claims only about how things *appear* to them to be.[73] Thus he notes later on in the *Phenomenology* that "in Skepticism the reality . . . determined is called an illusory appearance and has only a negative value" (par. 480). As in the case of Stoicism, the reference falls especially heavily on the *Roman* forms of this philosophical movement.[74]

Finally, the Unhappy Consciousness is distinguished as a shape of consciousness largely by the characteristics that it (i) conceives reality as divided into two sharply separate realms, on the one hand, the realm of the changeable and unessential, in which it locates itself and everyday natural and social phenomena, and, on the other hand, the alien realm of an unchangeable and essential self (God), (ii) denies importance and value to the former realm in proportion as it exalts those of the latter, and (iii) regards its own activity and cognition as a gift passively received from the alien essential self (God).[75] This perspective constitutes, in Hegel's view, a new set of conceptions and concepts of self, object, and representation.

The historical reference here is in part to Neoplatonism, but mainly to

---

pendent things in their differences from one another are for it only vanishing magnitudes"; "What Skepticism causes to vanish is not only objective reality as such, but its own relationship to it, in which the 'other' is held to be objective and is established as such" (pars. 202, 204).

73. Sextus Empiricus opens the *Outlines of Pyrrhonism* "first premising that of none of our future statements do we positively affirm that the fact is exactly as we state it, but we simply record each fact, like a chronicler, as it appears to us at the moment" (bk. 1, chap. 1).

74. Hence, for example, the *Spirit* chapter explicitly associates Skepticism with Legal Status, that is, the Roman Empire (par. 480).

75. For example, Hegel writes: (i) "The Unhappy Consciousness . . . is the gazing of one self-consciousness into another . . . One of them, viz. the simple unchangeable, it takes to be the *essential* being; but the other, the protean changeable, it takes to be the *unessential*. The two are, for the Unhappy Consciousness, alien to one another; . . . it identifies itself with the changeable consciousness, and takes itself to be the unessential being"; (ii) the Unhappy Consciousness "is conscious that its essence is only its opposite, is conscious only of its own nothingness"; and (iii) in changing, or working on, the world, the Unhappy Consciousness "is also *in itself* or has intrinsic being; this aspect belongs to the unchangeable beyond and consists of faculties and powers, a gift from an alien source, which the unchangeable makes over to consciousness to make use of" (pars. 207–9, 220).

Christianity from its emergence in the Roman Empire down to medieval Europe. That the *Unhappy Consciousness* section does in part refer to Neoplatonism seems clear from the following circumstances: (a) There are strong resemblances both in terminology and in doctrine between the Unhappy Consciousness as depicted in this section and Neoplatonism as depicted by Hegel in the *Lectures on the History of Philosophy*.[76] And (b) in the *Lectures on the History of Philosophy* Neoplatonism arises immediately out of Skepticism, as the Unhappy Consciousness does here. That the section also, and above all, refers to Christianity (which Hegel in the *Lectures on the History of Philosophy* intimately associates with Neoplatonism), from its beginnings in the Roman Empire down to medieval Europe, is obvious and generally recognized.[77]

In sum, the *Self-consciousness* chapter continues the chronological history of consciousness begun in the *Consciousness* chapter, taking us from the ideal culture of fifth-century, and in particular Periclean, Athens (Life), to its decline through the development in later fifth-century Athens, and subsequently in Rome after the Second Punic War, of political oppression of citizens and systematic slavery (Lordship and Bondage), thence to Hellenistic Greek and Roman Stoicism (Stoicism), from there

---

76. For example, at the start of the *Unhappy Consciousness* section we are told that the Unhappy Consciousness takes God, "the simple unchangeable, ... to be the *essential* being," but itself and its world to be "the protean changeable, the *unessential*," to be afflicted with "nothingness," and that it takes the two to be "alien to one another," and God to be its own "opposite" (pars. 208–9). Compare these remarks both for terminology and for doctrine with Hegel's characterizations of the Neoplatonism of Philo and Plotinus in the *Lectures on the History of Philosophy:* for Philo, "the sensuous existent world stands in opposition to [the] ideal world ... As God is being, so the essence of matter is non-being"; for Plotinus, "the first, the absolute, the basis is ... , as with Philo, pure being, the unchangeable ... It is the unity which is likewise essence ... The true principle is not the multiplicity of present being, the ordinary substantiality of things" (2:393, 413). Again, Hegel proceeds in the *Unhappy Consciousness* section to say of this consciousness which is "an agonizing over [its] existence and activity" that, "raising itself out of this consciousness, it goes over into the unchangeable" (par. 209). This is most naturally read as an allusion to Plotinus's ideal of *ekstasis*, which Hegel discusses at length in the *Lectures on the History of Philosophy* (2:408 ff.).

77. Allusions to Christian doctrine are pervasive in the section. Concerning the section's reference to Christianity's beginnings in the Roman Empire specifically, see esp. pars. 482–83 in the *Spirit* chapter, where the Unhappy Consciousness is explicitly associated with the Roman Empire, and its conception of God and his relation to man indeed interpreted as a reflection of the Roman Emperor and his relation to his subjects. Concerning the section's reference to Christianity in medieval Europe specifically, note for example the allusions to the mediating functions of the Catholic priest and to the failure of the Catholic laity to understand the religion it practises due to the Church's use of Latin (pars. 227–29).

to Hellenistic Greek and Roman Skepticism (Skepticism), and finally to Neoplatonism and early to medieval Christianity (Unhappy Consciousness).

* * *

The *Reason* chapter continues, and indeed completes, the *Phenomenology*'s chronological history of the development of consciousness—again contrary to a number of popular readings.[78] The *Reason* chapter divides into a theoretically-oriented first half and a practically-oriented second half. In the *Lectures on the Philosophy of World History* Hegel makes it clear that he understands both halves to refer historically to post-Reformation Europe.[79] What, though, is his more specific conception of this chapter's contents and their historical references?

The first section of the chapter, *Observing Reason,* depicts the development of the modern natural scientific consciousness since the early seventeenth century. As Hegel represents it, this consciousness is distinguished mainly by an assumption of the implicitly rational or lawlike nature of reality—which Hegel interprets as, au fond, an idealist assumption that reality is one with the self—and by an active use of observation and experimentation as the means to discovering reality's laws.[80]

In three subsections Hegel distinguishes three temporally successive shapes of this modern natural scientific consciousness. The first subsection, *Observation of Nature,* represents its development in application to inorganic and then organic nature from the early seventeenth century

---

78. Pace Pöggeler, for example, who, as already mentioned, argues in one essay that, unlike the *Consciousness* and *Self-consciousness* chapters, the *Reason* chapter cannot be read as chronologically ordered ("Zur Deutung der *Phänomenologie des Geistes,*" p. 288).

79. *The Philosophy of History,* pp. 438–41: In this period "Protestantism has introduced the principle of subjectivity . . . Spirit perceives that Nature—the world—must also be an embodiment of Reason . . . An interest in the contemplation and comprehension of the present world became universal . . . Experimental science became the science of the world . . . Nor was thought less vigorously directed to the spiritual side of things: Right and morality came to be looked upon as having their foundation in the actual present will of man, whereas formerly it was referred only to the command of God enjoined ab extra."

80. Thus Hegel writes: "Previously, its perception and experience of various aspects of the thing were something that only *happened* to consciousness; but here, consciousness *makes its own* observations and experiments . . . Reason sets to work to *know* the truth, to find in the form of a concept that which, for 'meaning' [i.e., Sense-certainty] and 'perceiving' [i.e., Perception], is a thing; i.e., it seeks to possess in thinghood the consciousness only of itself. Reason now has, therefore a universal *interest* in the world, because it is certain of its presence in the world, or that the world present to it is rational" (par. 240).

onwards, especially by Bacon, Galileo, and the Accademia dei Lincei. Thus, the emphasis in this subsection on an implicitly idealist confidence in the rationality of nature is an allusion above all to Bacon—as can be seen from the fact that Bacon is depicted as the primary source of such an outlook in the *Lectures on the History of Philosophy*.[81] Likewise, the references in this subsection to criticisms of Scholasticism—specifically, to criticisms of Scholasticism's approach of merely collecting and describing empirical facts, and classifying them by genus, species, and differentiae (pars. 245–48)—and to the adoption, instead, of the modern natural scientific method—specifically, to the adoption, instead, of a new emphasis on the need to discover empirically grounded regularities or laws and to use experimentation (pars. 248, 251)—are references above all to Bacon. Accordingly, in the *Lectures on the History of Philosophy* Hegel portrays Bacon as the man who rejected Scholasticism and founded modern natural science's method.[82] Concerning Galileo, note in particular the subsection's clear allusion to his law of falling bodies (par. 250). Finally, when the subsection turns from the application of the modern natural scientific consciousness to inorganic nature toward its application to organic nature, the reference is mainly to the Accademia dei Lincei, which investigated organic nature in this manner during the first third of the seventeenth century (and of which Galileo was a member).[83]

The second subsection, *Logical and Psychological Laws*, depicts the subsequent application of this modern natural scientific consciousness to the sphere of human consciousness *itself*.[84] Hegel distinguishes two successive stages of this process: First, there occur developments in formal logic in which formal logical laws are discovered as though they were something given (pars. 299–300). Hegel is thinking here, I believe, of developments in formal logic which occurred in the mid-seventeenth century, such as Hobbes's *Computatio Sive Logica* of 1655 and the Port

---

81. Hegel, *Vorlesungen über die Geschichte der Philosophie* (Frankfurt am Main: Suhrkamp, 1971), 3:77: Bacon represents "Reason's faith in itself and in nature that if it turns in a thinking way to nature it will find truth in nature, because they are in themselves in harmony."

82. Ibid., pp. 74 ff.

83. Hence in *The Philosophy of History* Hegel notes that experimental science initially developed in application not only to "the moon and stars" but also to "plants and animals," "especially among the Italians" (p. 440).

84. Pars. 298–99: "Observation now turns in upon itself," it turns to "the concept which itself exists as concept, i.e., self-consciousness."

Royal Logic, *La Logique ou l'Art de penser*, of 1662.[85] Second, there occurs a subsequent development of an empirical psychology of an individualistic and dualistic cast (pars. 302–9). Hegel primarily has in mind here, I believe, the attempts made by Locke and Hume in the later seventeenth and earlier eighteenth centuries to apply natural scientific methods to the human mind within an individualistic and dualistic framework. Thus already in his 1802 essay *Faith and Knowledge* Hegel had credited Locke with having "transformed philosophy into empirical psychology,"[86] had emphasized the individualistic and dualistic character of Locke's empirical psychology,[87] and had noted Hume's close connection with Locke as a philosopher developing fundamentally similar principles.[88]

The third subsection, *Physiognomy and Phrenology*, depicts the further application of this modern natural scientific consciousness to the human body considered as an expression of human consciousness. Hegel has in mind here the pseudosciences of physiognomy and phrenology which developed in the second half of the eighteenth century. The key event in this process was the publication of Lavater's work *On Physiognomy* in 1772. Shortly afterwards Gall in particular went on to develop the pseudoscience of phrenology.

In the second section of the *Reason* chapter, *The Actualization of Rational Self-consciousness through its Own Activity*, we encounter a series of practically oriented shapes of consciousness which Hegel understands to have emerged in Germany in the 1770s and 1780s. These shapes of consciousness have (with one or another degree of explicitness) drawn from consciousness's success in discovering a rational order in nature by means of natural science the idealist moral that nature is at bottom simply one with consciousness.[89] In consequence they lose all theoretical interest

---

85. Hegel mentions the former work in the course of his treatment of Hobbes in the *Lectures on the History of Philosophy*, vol. 3.

86. *Faith and Knowledge*, p. 63. Cf. *Lectures on the History of Philosophy* 3:298–99: "The philosophy of Locke ... asserts ... that truth and knowledge rest upon experience and observation ... Here the matter in question is merely subjective and somewhat psychological, since Locke merely describes the methods of mind as it appears to us to be."

87. *Faith and Knowledge*, pp. 63, 137, 154 (individualism), 63, 78 (dualism).

88. Ibid., pp. 69, 99, 137, 154.

89. Par. 347: "Self-consciousness found the thing to be like itself, and itself to be like the thing, i.e., it is aware that it is *in itself* the objectively real world ... The *objectivity* of the immediate ... has only the value of something superficial, its inner being and essence being self-consciousness itself."

in nature as such, and instead focus on consciousness itself and its practical concerns.[90]

The first of these shapes of consciousness, Pleasure and Necessity, is purely egoistic and hedonistic.[91] Hegel sees this shape as typified by the Faust of Goethe's *Faust* fragment, as is shown by his direct quotation from and allusions to the play (pars. 360–61). Goethe's *Faust* fragment was first published in 1790, but was largely written a good deal earlier—the so-called *Urfaust* was already completed by 1775—and as a friend of Goethe's Hegel was well placed to know this.

The second of these shapes of consciousness, The Law of the Heart, is a type of moral individualism, an outlook which regards the self as an immediate source of moral law.[92] The historical reference here is primarily to the perspective of Karl Moor in Schiller's *The Robbers* from 1781.[93]

---

90. For consciousness, "the shadowy existence of science, laws, and principles . . . vanishes like a lifeless mist which cannot compare with the certainty of its own reality" (par. 361).

91. "It plunges . . . into life and indulges to the full the pure individuality in which it appears. It does not so much make its own happiness as straightway take it and enjoy it . . . It takes hold of life much as a ripe fruit is plucked" (par. 361; cf. 356–58).

92. Par. 367: "It knows that it has the universal of law *immediately* within itself, and because the law is *immediately* present in the being-for-*self* of consciousness, it is called the *law* of the *heart*."

93. Like the previous two, this is one of the less controversial historical identifications of shapes of consciousness in my account—agreeing, for example, with Royce, *Lectures on Modern Idealism*, p. 194, and Hyppolite, *Genesis and Structure*, p. 285. It may, though, be worth indicating a few of Hegel's many more specific allusions in this section to *Die Räuber* (Frankfurt and Leipzig: publisher unspecified, 1781) in order to show just how centrally he has this play in mind. (i) "It knows that it has the universal of law *immediately* within itself"; "What it realizes is itself the law . . . The law, on the other hand, which confronts the law of the heart is separated from the heart" (pars. 367, 370–71). Karl Moor says in *Die Räuber*, "I am my heaven and my hell," and that his aim is to "uphold the laws through lawlessness" (pp. 171, 219). (ii) "Its *being-for-self* has for it the character of necessity" (par. 367). Karl Moor says in *Die Räuber*, upon committing himself to the life of outlawry, that "an unbending fate rules over us" (p. 42). (iii) "This heart is confronted by a real world . . . This reality is . . . , on the one hand, a law by which the particular individuality is oppressed, a violent ordering of the world which contradicts the law of the heart, and, on the other hand, a humanity suffering under that ordering . . . This individuality therefore directs its energies to getting rid of this necessity which contradicts the law of the heart, and also the suffering caused by it" (pars. 369–70). Hegel fairly summarizes the plot of *Die Räuber* as follows in his *Aesthetics: Lectures on Fine Art*: "Karl Moor, injured by the existing order and by those who misused their authority in it, leaves the sphere of legality, and having the audacity to burst the bonds that constrain him, and so creating for and by himself a new heroic situation, he makes himself the restorer of right and the independent avenger of wrong, injury, and oppression" (p. 195). (iv) "It . . . speaks of the universal order as a perversion . . . invented by fanatical priests, gluttonous despots,

The third of these shapes of consciousness, Virtue, has the character of a reaction against the two preceding individualistic shapes. This shape is distinguished by its insistence that the law is independent of and prior to individual whims, its own identification with this law, and its demand that individuality must submit to this law: "This shape of consciousness, which, in the law, is aware of *itself,* which knows itself in what is *intrinsically* true and good, not as an individuality but only as it becomes an *essential* being; and which knows individuality to be perverted and the source of perversion, and therefore knows that it must sacrifice the individuality of consciousness—this shape of consciousness is Virtue . . . For the virtuous consciousness law is the essential moment and individuality the one to be nullified" (pars. 380–81). This is a depiction of the outlook championed both in philosophical theory and in political practice by Frederick the Great in the years before his death in 1786. Compare, for example, with the passage just quoted Hegel's description of Frederick the Great in the *Lectures on the Philosophy of World History:* "Frederick

---

and their minions, who compensate themselves for their own degradation by degrading and oppressing others" (par. 377). In *Die Räuber* Karl Moor boasts of his revenge against a priest, a count, and a government minister and treasurer, noting that the priest "had cried in public pulpit because the Inquisition fell into such decline," that the minister "had flattered his way up out of the mire of the people to be [the prince's] first favorite, his neighbor's fall was the footstool for his elevation—orphans' tears raised him," and similarly concerning the treasurer (p. 105). (v) "What the individual brings into being through the realization of his law, is not *his* law; . . . what he brings about is merely the entanglement of himself in the actual ordinance . . . Just as the individual at first finds only the rigid law, now he finds the hearts of men themselves, opposed to his excellent intentions and detestable" (pars. 373–74). In *Die Räuber* Karl Moor's attempt to save his companion Roller leads to his comrades destroying the city and committing atrocities against its inhabitants, resulting in the authorities moving against him militarily (pp. 90–101). (vi) "It reveals itself to be [the] inner perversion of itself, to be a deranged consciousness . . . It is the heart . . . or the individuality of consciousness that would be immediately universal, that is itself the source of . . . derangement and perversion, and the outcome of its action is merely that *its* consciousness becomes aware of this contradiction . . . The heart learns . . . that its self is not real, and that its reality is an unreality," while, on the other hand, it finds that the ordinance which it initially opposed "is really animated by the consciousness of all . . . it is the law of every heart . . . The universally valid order has . . . become for self-consciousness its own essential being and its own reality" (pars. 376–77, 374–75). At the end of *Die Räuber* Karl Moor recognizes the error of his ways, reproaching himself as a "fool, I who imagined that I would make the world better through atrocity, and that I would uphold the laws through lawlessness," lamenting that "two people like me would destroy the whole structure of the ethical world," and looking for a way "in which I can reconcile the offended laws, and make whole again the mistreated order" (pp. 219–20).

II may be mentioned as the ruler who inaugurated the new epoch in the sphere of practical life—that epoch in which practical political interest attains universality, and receives an absolute sanction. Frederick II merits special notice as . . . having been the first sovereign who kept the general interest of the state steadily in view, ceasing to pay any respect to particular interests when they stood in the way of the common weal. His immortal work is a domestic code—the Prussian municipal law."[94]

In the third and final section of the *Reason* chapter, *Individuality which takes Itself to be Real in and for Itself*, we encounter three further practically oriented shapes of consciousness from Germany toward the end of the eighteenth century. Hegel conceives these shapes as building on the idealist subordination of nature to the self and its practical concerns, and on the practical individualism, of the first two shapes of the previous section.[95] However, the shape Virtue, although it failed to crush the idealist practical individualism of those two shapes (par. 389), has now tempered it by adding to it an essential universal or *communal* dimension (par. 392). Consequently, "end and essence are for [self-consciousness] henceforth the spontaneous interfusion of the universal . . . and individuality" (par. 394). This gives us, in general terms, the recipe for the shapes of consciousness which follow, including in particular Hegel's own philosophical position, which we are now fast ap-

---

94. *The Philosophy of History*, p. 441; cf. *Lectures on the History of Philosophy* 2: 26. Some more specific allusions in this section to Frederick's viewpoint are worth noting in order to put the reference to him beyond doubt: (i) Hegel emphasizes that for Virtue individuality is to be nullified not only in others but also "in its own consciousness" and that "the good . . . presents itself as being for an *other*, as something that does not have a being of its own" (pars. 381, 384). These are both allusions to Frederick's well-known conception of himself as "the first servant of the state." (ii) Hegel emphasizes that Virtue conceives the law not merely as imposed on individuals from without but as their inner essence: "The absolute *order* is . . . a common moment, only one that is not present for consciousness as an *existent reality*, but as the *inner essence*" (par. 381). This is an allusion to Frederick's view, set forth in his *Essay on Self-love Envisaged as a Principle of Morality* (1770) for example, that self-interest can only be truly satisfied by virtue, and that the moralist's task is accordingly just one of making people realize that virtue lies in their own true self-interest.

95. Pars. 394–96: "Self-consciousness has now grasped . . . that in its certainty of itself it is all reality," it "holds fast to the simple unity of being and the self," it "has cast away all opposition and every condition affecting its action; it starts afresh from *itself*, and is occupied not with an *other*, but with itself . . . The element in which individuality sets forth its shape has the significance solely of putting on the shape of individuality."

proaching: a practically oriented idealism which synthesizes individualism with communalism.[96]

The first of these shapes is—to use the section's full title—The Spiritual Animalkingdom and Deception or The Matter Itself. This is one of the most important, and at the same time least understood, sections of the *Phenomenology*, and so it will be appropriate to treat it in some detail. The historical reference of this section is to the philosophy of Herder—particularly as expressed in *On the Cognition and Sensation of the Human Soul* (1778), *Ideas for the Philosophy of History of Mankind* (1784–91), and *Letters for the Advancement of Humanity* (1793–98). All of the key terms and concepts in the title of the section—"The Spiritual Animalkingdom [das geistige Tierreich]," "Deception [Betrug]," and "The Matter Itself [die Sache selbst]"—along with other central terms and concepts in the section, such as "honesty [Ehrlichkeit]" and "action [Tun]," come directly from Herder. So too do the various theses which together with them distinguish this shape of consciousness. Let us, therefore, run through the most prominent features of this shape of consciousness, as Hegel describes it, in order to identify their references to Herder's thought.

(i) We might usefully begin with the first words of the section's title, "The Spiritual Animalkingdom [das geistige Tierreich]." This phrase is an allusion to the conception of mankind which Herder sets forth in *Ideas for the Philosophy of History of Mankind*. There he considers "the animalkingdom [das Reich der Tiere]" in preparation for considering mankind, and argues that animals are "mankind's older brothers," and that man is basically animal in nature.[97] This idea that mankind is continuous with the animalkingdom is pervasive in Herder's work, and fundamental to his methodology for investigating mankind.[98] On the other hand,

---

96. Among the shapes which follow, exemplification of this recipe is clearest in the cases of the first, The Spiritual Animalkingdom (Herder's perspective), and the last, pars. 435-37 (Hegel's own perspective). However, Hegel would also include the intervening two shapes, Reason as Lawgiver (the commonsense philosophy of the *Popularphilosophen*) and Reason as Testing Laws (Kant's moral philosophy). And with a little effort one can see how they too might be interpreted in this mold.
97. *Ideen zur Philosophie der Geschichte der Menschheit*, pp. 53 (for the quoted expressions), 55–57, 154–55, 234 "Menschenherden" (for man being basically animal).
98. For instance, Herder likens the investigation of the different types of men to zoology (ibid., p. 194), and repeatedly explains human characteristics as derivative from and analogous to animal ones—e.g., men have learned most of their arts from the animals (p. 241), and given that men are basically animal one should expect the sorts of variations in species under varying conditions which one finds in the case of animals to occur in men too (pp. 55–57; cf. 398–99).

Herder also argues that mankind is distinguished from the rest of animal nature by the fact that mankind is "spiritual [geistig]," and he refers to mankind as "the spiritual kingdom [das geistige Reich]."[99] It is this Herderian conception of mankind as basically continuous with the animalkingdom but also distinguished from it by being spiritual which Hegel is attempting to capture, with obvious verbal echoes, in the expression "The Spiritual Animalkingdom [das geistige Tierreich]."

(ii) At paragraphs 402–3 Hegel attributes to this shape of consciousness the view that all human works are good insofar as they are expressions of individuality, and that one can only *compare* them descriptively, not evaluatively, since each individuality sets its own standard quite differently from the others, and meets it, so that there is no common standard which one could use as a basis for an evaluative comparison of one individuality with another:

> [Consciousness] can regard an individual whose work [Werke] is more wide-ranging as possessing greater energy of will or a richer nature, i.e., a nature whose original determinacy is less limited, and another, on the other hand, as a weaker and poorer nature. In contrast with this unessential *quantitative* difference, "good" and "bad" would express an absolute difference; but here this is not in place. Whether something is held to be good or bad, it is in either case an action and an activity in which an individuality [Individualität] exhibits and expresses itself, and for that reason it is all good. And it would actually be impossible to say what "badness" was supposed to be. What would be called a bad work is the individual life of a specific nature, which realizes itself therein. It would only be spoiled into a "bad" work through a comparing [vergleichenden] reflection, which however is empty, since it goes beyond the essential nature of the work, which is to be a self-expression of individuality, and in it looks for and demands something else, no one knows what . . . The things compared would be different works or individualities. But these have nothing to do with one another; each relates only to itself. The original nature is alone the *in-itself*, or what could be laid down as a standard [Maßstab] for judging the work . . . But both correspond to one another.

This refers, once again with echoes extending even to the very words chosen, to Herder's position concerning the evaluation of individuals,

---

Hegel reproduces this Herderian pattern of explanation at paragraph 398: "Here consciousness is a relation purely of itself to itself . . . Just as in the case of indeterminate animal life . . ."

99. *Ideen zur Philosophie der Geschichte der Menschheit*, p. 143; cf. 144 "Das Reich der Menschenorganisation ist ein System geistiger Kräfte," 144–48.

and in particular individual historical cultures, especially in *Another Philosophy of History for the Education of Mankind* and *Letters for the Advancement of Humanity*. Thus, for the Herder of these works the development of cultural individualities is something good in itself, but beyond this there can be no comparative evaluation of different cultural individualities:

> What would be the exact, the infallible standard [Maßstab]? . . . Nature has distributed her gifts in different directions; on different trunks/tribes [Stämme] . . . grow different fruits. Who could compare [vergliche] these with one another, or give the prize to a crab-apple before the grape? Rather, we should . . . rejoice that on the colorful meadow of the earth there are so many different kinds of flowers and peoples, that on this and that side of the alps such diverse blossoms bloom, so many different sorts of fruits ripen . . . The nature-investigator assumes no ranking among the creatures which he observes, all are equally dear and valuable to him. Likewise the nature-investigator of humanity.[100]

And for the Herder of these works the reason why there can be no meaningful comparative evaluation is because values vary fundamentally from culture to culture, each culture striving for, and attaining, something fundamentally different from the others, so that any comparative evaluation would involve importing a standard alien to (at least one of) the cultures comparatively evaluated:

> It is foolishness to extract even a single Egyptian virtue from its country and time . . . and to measure it with the *standard* [Maßstab] *of another time* . . . The best historian of ancient art, Winckelmann, obviously judged the works of art [Kunstwerke] of the Egyptians purely according to a Greek standard . . . But, my dear Greek, these statues were not at all supposed . . . to be exemplars of beautiful art *in accordance with your ideal*, full of charm, action, movement, about all of which the Egyptian knew nothing . . . They were supposed to be *mummies*, remembrances of dead parents or ancestors in accordance with all the precision of their facial traits, . . . in accordance with a hundred fixed rules . . . , and so of course precisely without charm, without action, without movement, precisely in this gravepose with hands and feet full of repose and death—eternal marble mummies. Behold, that is what they were supposed to be, and that is what they are too! . . . In a certain sense . . . every human perfection is national . . . and, most precisely viewed, individual [individuell] . . . The only person

---

100. *Briefe zu Beförderung der Humanität* 4:34; 10:73.

who will be astonished by the fact that a nation can on one side have virtues of the most sublime kind, but on another side defects . . . is he who brings with him an ideal outline of virtue from the compendium of his own century and is philosophical enough to want to find the whole earth on one spot of the earth, nobody else! . . . Even the conception of happiness varies with each condition and region (for what is this ever but the totality of satisfactions of wishes, attainments of purposes, and "gentle overcoming of needs," which, however, are all formed relative to country, time, and place?), and so all comparison [Vergleichung] becomes at bottom dangerous. Once the inner sense of happiness, the inclination, has changed . . . who can compare the different satisfaction of different senses [of it] in different worlds? . . . Each nation has its center of happiness within itself, as each sphere its center of gravity.[101]

(iii) At paragraphs 400–401 Hegel attributes to this shape of consciousness a very distinctive philosophy of mind and action. According to a familiar conception of these matters, Hegel notes, such mental dispositions as affective character and cognitive talent, and such associated but more occurrent mental items as purposes and beliefs about means to ends, are (a) sharply distinct from physical reality, belonging to a mind or consciousness sharply distinct from physical reality, and in particular (b) sharply distinct from any physical actions on the part of the person who has them to which they may give rise. Thus, concerning (a), Hegel notes that on a familiar view our "original nature [ursprüngliche Natur]"—which comprises in particular affective "character" and cognitive "talent" (par. 401)—makes its appearance "as an object which still belongs to *consciousness,* as a *purpose* . . . and thus opposed to present reality" (par. 400) and as a belief about "means" which likewise "falls within consciousness" so that the "whole" comprising "original nature . . . purpose . . . [belief about] means" which we call on to explain behavior "is one side of an opposition" (par. 401). And concerning (b), he notes, for example, that "to begin with . . . the original determinate nature

---

101. *Auch eine Philosophie der Geschichte zur Bildung der Menschheit,* in *Herders Ausgewählte Werke* 2:632–34, 642–45; cf. *Briefe zu Beförderung der Humanität,* in addition to the passages quoted above also 10:45, 77. (Note that in the *Ideen zur Philosophie der Geschichte der Menschheit* by contrast Herder tends to deviate from his usual position on these matters—downplaying value-divergences between cultures, setting up a single standard for measuring all, namely, "humanity" or "reason," and making highly differential comparative evaluations of different cultures, for example, very negative ones of ancient Rome and organized Christianity, in contrast with very positive ones of ancient Greece and modern Europe.)

of individuality, its immediate essence, is not yet posited as active [tuend] and thus is called *distinct* ability, talent, character, etc." (par. 401). Now the shape of consciousness The Spiritual Animalkingdom rejects this familiar conception of mind and action entirely. For this shape, there is *no* sharp distinction between the mind's dispositional or more occurrent states, on the one hand, and physical reality, on the other, and in particular there is *no* sharp distinction between those mental states and physical activity, since on the contrary physical activity *constitutes* those mental states:

> These various aspects are, however, according to the conception of this sphere, to be so understood that . . . no difference enters in, neither of individuality and being in general, nor of purpose . . . against given reality, and likewise not of the means against [given reality] . . . , nor of the effected reality [der bewirkten Wirklichkeit] against the purpose or the original nature or the means . . . The whole action . . . goes outside itself neither as the given conditions [which . . . are the original nature of the individual], nor as purpose or means, nor as work. (pars. 400–401)

In addition, and again in contradiction of familiar ideas, for this shape of consciousness, since affective character and the more occurrent purposes associated with it are constituted by the physical behavior characteristic of them, it is also the case that they can only be *known* from that physical behavior, even by the agent himself, and the same holds true of cognitive talent and the beliefs about means associated with it as well:

> In order that what [consciousness] is *in itself* [an sich] may be *for* it [für es], it must act, or action is simply the coming to be of spirit *as consciousness*. What it is *in itself* it thus knows from its active reality [aus seiner Wirklichkeit]. Therefore the individual cannot know what *it is* until it has brought itself to reality through action . . . [The individual] gets to know its original essence, which is perforce its purpose, *only from the deed* . . . The *how* or the *means* gets determined in and for itself in just the same way. *Talent* is likewise nothing but the determinate original nature considered as . . . *transition* of purpose into effected reality [Wirklichkeit]. (par. 401)[102]

This is all meant to be an expression of Herder's philosophy of mind and action, particularly as stated in *On the Cognition and Sensation of the*

---

102. In interpreting this passage it is important to keep in mind both of the senses of the distinction between *an sich* and *für sich* (or here *für es*) noted earlier: (a) being x potentially versus being x actually; (b) being x versus knowing that you are x.

Human Soul. For, in that work especially, Herder argues that the mind is intimately united with and essentially dependent on the physical body: our physical body is a "realm . . . which is in the most intimate union with the monarch which thinks and wills within us . . . Only through this realm, in this context, did she become and is she the human soul"; "In my modest opinion no *psychology* is possible which is not in every step a determinate *physiology*."[103] Moreover, Herder discusses specifically the two dispositional traits of "genius [Genie]" and "character [Charakter]," distinguishing the former as a more cognitive and the latter as a more affective aspect of the mind—these are Hegel's "talent [Talent]" and "character [Charakter]," respectively.[104] And Herder argues that these traits are constituted by the manner of a person's active existence, and that they can consequently only be known from his actions, even by the person himself: "Genius and character are only one's *living mode of human existence* [lebendige Menschenart], nothing more or less"; "Each pure mode of human existence sleeps, like all good seeds, in its inactive and silent seed [im stillen Keime]; it . . . does not recognize itself."[105] Similarly, concerning the more occurrent counterparts of these dispositions, he argues in the same essay that "cognition and feeling live only in *action* [Tat]."[106] And accordingly he writes (elsewhere) that quite generally "we know our soul only in a composite organism and only through its activities [Wirkungen]."[107] To give a more specific example, Herder implies that thought requires at least the action of speech: "May the pupil learn to *think with speech*. May the lock be removed from his lips which deprives him of a soul."[108] And accordingly, he implies that it is only from a person's speech that his thought can really be known, even by the person himself, quoting with approval Young's lines, "Speech

---

103. *Vom Erkennen und Empfinden der menschlichen Seele,* in *Herders Ausgewählte Werke* 3:719, 710; cf. *Ideen zur Philosophie der Geschichte der Menschheit,* p. 137.

104. *Vom Erkennen und Empfinden der menschlichen Seele,* in *Herders Ausgewählte Werke* 3:738 ff., esp. p. 741: "What is called *genius* in connection with the soul's powers is in connection with the will and feeling *character.*" Note that Hegel's preference for the word "talent" rather than "genius" is completely faithful to the *spirit* of Herder's position, for Herder deflates "genius" into something quite everyday and normal: "Every human being who has pure living powers is a genius in his place, in his work, for his calling" (ibid., p. 739).

105. Ibid., pp. 741–42.

106. Ibid., p. 734.

107. *Ideen zur Philosophie der Geschichte der Menschheit,* p. 131.

108. *Über die Fähigkeit zu sprechen und zu hören,* in *Herders Ausgewählte Werke* 3: 698; cf. *Vom Erkennen und Empfinden der menschlichen Seele,* ibid., pp. 734–35.

thought's canal, speech thought's criterion too. / Thought in the mine, may come forth gold or dross; / when coin'd in word, we know its real worth."[109]

(iv) This shape of consciousness, as Hegel describes it, also takes the distinctive view that the understanding of general concepts is essentially *communal*, so that mental life, which essentially requires such understanding for its articulation, and consequently also the individual self, are so too: "The universal [i.e., the general concept] . . . is an *existent* thing as [the] action of all and each"; "The category is *in itself* as the universal [i.e., the communal]"; "Simple individuality . . . , as this particular individuality, is no less immediately universal [i.e., employs general concepts and is communal] . . . The original *determinate* nature of the individual . . . is merely a superseded moment, and the individual is a *self* in the form of a universal [i.e., general-concept-using and communal] self" (pars. 418–19). This again reflects a prominent strand of Herder's thought. Thus, in *On the Origin of Language* Herder writes that "the

---

109. *Über die Fähigkeit zu sprechen und zu hören*, in *Herders Ausgewählte Werke* 3: 698. In connection with the above, the following further points also deserve notice: (a) In Herder's philosophy of mind the concept of mental "forces [Kräfte]" plays a very central role. Hegel too employs this concept, and in a Herderian manner, in the section *The Spiritual Animalkingdom* (see for example the expressions *anderer Kräfte* and *das Spiel seiner Kräfte* at pars. 405, 417). So we have here yet a further example of the section's allusion to Herder's philosophy of mind. (b) On the other hand, Hegel is sparing with this concept in his characterization of Herder's philosophy of mind in this section (e.g., it does not occur at all in pars. 400–401), and as a result he makes Herder's philosophy of mind sound somewhat more straightforwardly physicalistic and behavioristic than it really is. There are, I think, two main reasons/justifications for this. First, Hegel is no doubt in some measure simply yielding to a motive of charity in interpretation—an inclination to assimilate Herder's position as far as possible to the outright physicalism and behaviorism in which, as we saw in chapter 2, he himself believes. But second, and more interestingly, the measure of distortion of Herder's position which this involves must appear vanishingly modest to Hegel. For it follows from Hegel's (modified) antirealist analysis of the general concept of "force [Kraft]" (discussed in chapter 2) that if only one assigns to Herder the correct conception of "force" generally—that is, an antirealist conception which equates force with its expressions (rather than the realist conception to which, while strictly professing not to know what force is [*Herders Ausgewählte Werke* 3:708], he seems in fact to have inclined [see esp. the discussions of force in *Ideen zur Philosophie der Geschichte der Menschheit*])— then his theory that the mind is constituted by "forces" is *equivalent to* outright physicalism and behaviorism. It is, indeed, quite likely that it was just this modest revision of Herder's position that originally led Hegel to his own physicalism and behaviorism. Thus note that in the course of arguing against the realist and in favor of an antirealist conception of force generally in the 1804–5 *Logik, Metaphysik, und Naturphilosophie* Hegel explicitly includes as examples *mental* forces: "the imaginative force, the memory force [die Einbildungs-, Gedächtniskraft]" (p. 61; cf. *Encyclopaedia*, pars. 136–40, 445).

human being . . . is a creature of the herd, of society . . . No individual human being exists unto himself, 'he is woven into the totality of his kind, he is only single in relation to a continuing sequence' . . . The education of one's own soul is the sphere of thoughts belonging to the language of one's parents."[110] And similarly, in *On the Cognition and Sensation of the Human Soul,* having argued that language is the "medium of our . . . spiritual consciousness," that mental life of its nature depends on language and follows its lead,[111] Herder goes on to argue that the individual's language, and hence his mental life, which is essential to him, depend of their nature on a social source:

> Our cognition is . . . , though to be sure it is the deepest self within us, not so autonomous . . . as people think . . . The object must . . . come to us through *secret bonds,* through an *indication,* which *teaches* us to cognize. This teaching, this meaning belonging to someone else which makes an impression within us, gives our thought its entire form and direction . . . We would grope around in deep night and blindness, had not our early instruction thought *for us* and so to speak impressed in us ready-made thought-formulas . . . For a long time, and often for a lifetime, we proceed leaning on the sticks reached to us in earliest childhood, ourselves think, but only in forms in which others thought, cognize what the finger of such methods indicates to us; everything else is for us as though it did not exist at all. Typically this "birth of reason" seems so indecent to the wise men of our world that they wholly fail to recognize it . . . Obviously these wise men never wore infants' clothing, never learned to speak as their nurses spoke, or perhaps have absolutely . . . no mother- and human-tongue . . . Let them talk . . . ; they know not what they do.[112]

(v) Still more prominent in this shape of consciousness, as Hegel characterizes it, is a conception that it is the nature of reality or truth to be determined by social agreement—a form of social idealism. For example, Hegel writes that this shape of consciousness learns that the "matter itself [Sache selbst]" is not "something which stands opposed to action [Tun] in general, and to individual action," but "rather is its nature such that its *being* is the *action* of the *single* individual and of all individuals" (par. 418; cf. 398, 409–12). This prominent theme once again represents a striking feature of Herder's philosophy. Thus in *On the Cognition and Sensation of the Human Soul* we read: "Our cognition is only *human*

---

110. *Herders Ausgewählte Werke* 3:671–73; cf. 611–13.
111. Ibid., pp. 722–23.
112. Ibid., p. 723; cf. *Briefe zu Beförderung der Humanität* 5:59–62.

and must be so if it is to be *right* . . . Humanity is the nobler measure in accordance with which we cognize . . . *Love* is thus the noblest cognition, as it is the noblest feeling. The great impetus in one to enter into loving empathy with others and then to follow this sure pull—this is moral feeling, this is conscience. It stands in opposition only to empty speculation but not to cognition, for true cognition is *love,* is *feeling* in a human way"; "We live in a world which we ourselves create."[113]

(vi) In the course of expressing this shape of consciousness's conception of reality or truth as determined by social agreement, its social idealism, Hegel repeatedly uses the distinctive expression "the matter itself [die Sache selbst]" to characterize a reality so conceived (an expression which also appears prominently in the section's title). The passage just quoted from paragraph 418 is an example of this, as are the following passages in which Hegel first introduces the expression: for this shape of consciousness "reality is only a moment, i.e., something *for consciousness,* not something which exists in its own right; . . . reality . . . has for consciousness only the value of *being* as such whose universality is one with action. This unity . . . is the *matter itself*"; "The *matter itself* expresses . . . the *spiritual* essentiality" in which actions "only have validity qua universal"; "*The matter itself* expresses . . . idealism" (pars. 409, 410, 412). This distinctive use of the expression "the matter itself" to connote reality or truth *qua determined by social agreement* is once again inspired by Herder, who writes in the *Letters for the Advancement of Humanity,* "Is it not odd that in ages old and new the highest and most fruitful wisdom has ever come from the people . . . ? But why do I call this odd, for it is the nature of the matter itself [der Sache selbst]."[114]

(vii) Another striking feature of this shape of consciousness, as characterized by Hegel, is the pervasiveness of the concept of "action [Tun]," even in contexts where one might have expected to find concepts connoting *cognitive states,* such as the concept of belief, rather than *volition*

---

113. *Herders Ausgewählte Werke* 3:724–25; *Sämtliche Werke* 8:252 (an earlier version of the same essay). Cf. *Briefe zu Beförderung der Humanität* 5:52–53, 113: a "public," in the sense of "a universal judgment, or at least a majority of the voices in the sphere in which one speaks, writes, or acts" is "a reasonable, moral entity, which participates in our thoughts, our speech, our acts, and is able to assess their value or lack of it," and the "public" of all times and places is a "universal concilium . . . which alone . . . can be a judge of the true and the false" (cf. 1:7).

114. Ibid., 1:36; cf. 5:137, 139 "die gemeinschaftliche Sache," "der gemeinen Sache"; also 4:12–13 on national "Sachen."

and activity (for example, the passages quoted above from paragraphs 418 and 409). This *psychological* concept of "action" also has *ontological* counterparts in the concepts of *Wirklichkeit* and the *Sache selbst* used in this section to characterize reality generally.[115] For the concept of *Wirklichkeit* connotes here not only reality but also a resulting from volition and action.[116] And similarly, the concept of the *Sache selbst* carries here, in addition to the implication already mentioned of reality constituted by social agreement, implications of volition and activity.[117] This pervasiveness of connotations of volition and action in characterizing both the psychological and the ontological reflects several features of Herder's position. First, it reflects Herder's view, already described under (iii), that physical action is fundamental to all aspects of mental life (cognitive as well as affective, dispositional as well as occurrent). Second, it reflects a position which Herder expresses forcefully in *On the Cognition and Sensation of the Human Soul* that cognition is inseparable from affect and volition (not only when defective but also, and indeed especially, when at its best):

> Thought cannot arrive [in the head] unless feeling was already in its place. The extent to which we have sympathy with what surrounds us, the depth to which love and hate, disgust and loathing, dismay and pleasure drive their roots in us, this attunes the string-play of our thoughts . . . Cognition without volition is nothing . . . Precisely in the best cognition all [passions and feelings] can and must be effective, because the best cognition came to be, and only lives, in all of them. It is liars or exhausted people who boast of pure unalloyed principles and curse inclinations, from which alone true principles come to be. That would be to sail without wind and to fight without weapons. Stimulus is the motive force of our existence, and must remain so in the case of the noblest cognition also . . . True cognition is love, is feeling in a human way . . . True cognition and good volition are just one thing.[118]

Third, it reflects Herder's strong hints, already mentioned under (v), at a conception of truth as determined by social agreement, a social idealism.

---

115. Hegel writes that the individual's "action is . . . a *Wirklichkeit* or a *Sache*" (par. 415).
116. This connotation comes from the cognate verb *wirken*.
117. In idiomatic German *Sache* often connotes a "cause" which people will and act to realize.
118. *Herders Ausgewählte Werke* 3:710, 724–25. Here as elsewhere in this seminal essay Herder sounds a theme which will later reverberate loudly in Nietzsche.

This conception further effaces the distinction between a cognitive state like belief and volition or action, by eliminating as a differentia of the former the aim of fitting a reality independent of the state of belief itself rather than effecting a reality by means of it. Moreover, this social idealism licences an inference from the idea of the *psychological* fundamentalness of volition and action to the idea of their *ontological* fundamentalness as well. For, given this social idealism, the several Herderian reasons just mentioned for regarding volition and action as the basis of all psychological conditions are equally reasons for regarding them as the basis of all reality, since according to this social idealism reality is *constituted* by psychological conditions shared in common by members of society.

(viii) A further connotation which Hegel associates with the expression "the matter itself" in this section is that of an *impartial and disinterested concern for the truth:* "Consciousness is called honest" when it "possesses the truth . . . qua . . . formal universality; a consciousness which is concerned solely with the matter itself" (par. 412). This once again reflects a Herderian use of the expression. Thus in the *Letters for the Advancement of Humanity* Herder writes, "Is it not odd that in ages old and new the highest and most fruitful wisdom . . . has always been accompanied by serene impartiality of spirit . . . ? But why do I call this odd, for it is the nature of the matter itself [der Sache selbst]."[119]

Doctrines and concepts (i)–(viii) form the core of Hegel's *positive* characterization of the shape of consciousness The Spiritual Animalkingdom. These Herderian doctrines and concepts constitute together, in Hegel's view, a new set of conceptions and concepts of self, reality, and representation—a new shape of consciousness. We should now, though, conclude the interpretation of this section by turning to some of the more *critical* aspects of Hegel's characterization of this shape of consciousness. These will afford us still further evidence that and how the section refers to Herder's philosophy.

(ix) As a textual matter, Herder's ideal of an *impartial and disinterested* concern for truth presupposes or implies several distinct thoughts: (a) It presupposes the mind-independence of reality.[120] (b) It implies that

---

119. *Briefe zu Beförderung der Humanität* 1:36. For Herder's commitment to this ideal, cf. 1:34; 5:52 (second page numbering).

120. Ibid., 1:34: reality is something which we must "search for" and "find" (the words are Benjamin Franklin's, but quoted with approval by Herder).

History in the Chapters *Consciousness* through *Reason* 343

we must therefore, in order to attain cognition of reality, keep our cognitive assessments free from influence by our own affects and volitions.[121] (c) It implies the ideal of indifference to *who* discovers the truth, oneself or somebody else.[122] (d) It implies the ideal of indifference as to whether or not one's knowledge of the truth attains broader social endorsement.[123] Now Hegel's critique of Herder's outlook at paragraphs 412–18 consists fundamentally in charging, quite plausibly, that *these* (rather conventional) Herderian ideas, and implications of Herder's term "the matter itself," contradict the (much less conventional) Herderian ideas, and implications of that term, which we identified earlier under (v)–(vii), namely, those of reality's constitution by social agreement based on volition and action, or what one might for short call Herder's *activist social idealism*. Thus, at paragraphs 412–15 Hegel distinguishes these two sides of The Spiritual Animalkingdom's conception of "the matter itself," that "consciousness . . . is concerned solely with the matter itself" (i.e., the impartiality and disinterestedness side) and that it is "idealism which *the matter itself* expresses" (i.e., the activist social idealism side), and then charges that this shape of consciousness "does not bring together its *thoughts* about the matter in hand" and that they form a "contradiction [Gegensatz]." And Hegel then proceeds to show in more detail just how each of the aspects of Herder's ideal of impartiality and disinterestedness is in contradiction with his doctrine of activist social idealism. Thus, Hegel points out that the doctrine of activist social idealism contradicts (in its idealist and activist parts) thoughts (a) and (b): "*Reality* essentially exists only as *his* [the individual's] action and as *action in general* . . . While, therefore, it appears to him that he is concerned only with the *matter itself* or *abstract reality*, it also appears that he is concerned with it as his own action" (par. 415). Hegel implies further that the doctrine of activist social idealism contradicts (in its activist part) thought (c): "[An

---

121. Ibid., 1:34: we must search for the truth "without bias [unparteiisch]" (the words are again Benjamin Franklin's, but quoted with approval by Herder). Cf. 5:52 (second page numbering).

122. Ibid., 1:34: "Love truth for truth's own sake" (Benjamin Franklin, quoted with approval by Herder). Ibid., 5:52 (second page numbering): "[Truth's] champions may personally fall, but its victory is progressive and immortal."

123. Ibid., 5:123–24: the worthiest men of all times "did not consider that their name would be mentioned in the larger public. They were *their own* most critical and noble public; the encourager, witness, and judge of their deeds was a law that lived with them. The better for us when we are this public for ourselves; then we do not need the loud, often very unsure and impure voice of the larger world."

individuality] acts and in acting . . . seems to itself to be having to do with *reality*. The others therefore take its action for a sign of its interest in the matter itself as such, and its purpose to be the carrying-out of the matter *per se*, regardless of whether this is done by the first individuality or by them"; however "it is its *own* action and its *own* effort that constitute its interest in the matter itself" (par. 417; cf. 418).[124] And Hegel points out, additionally, that the doctrine of activist social idealism contradicts (in its social idealist aspect) thought (d):

> [Consciousness] is not concerned with the matter as *a separate matter of its own,* but as a *matter,* as something universal, which is for everyone . . . [Individuals] pretend that their action and efforts are something for themselves alone . . . However, in doing something, and thus bringing themselves out into the light of day, they directly contradict by their deed their pretence of wanting to exclude the glare of publicity and participation by all and sundry. Actualization is, on the contrary, a display of what is one's own in the element of universality whereby it becomes, and should become, the matter of everyone. (par. 417; cf. 418)

Hegel's own way of resolving this nest of contradictions within Herder's position is then sketched in the concluding paragraph of the section, paragraph 418. It is, in effect, to retain Herder's *activist social idealism* side while rejecting his incompatible *impartiality and disinterestedness* side in all of its components (a)–(d). Thus at paragraph 418 Hegel argues contrary to (a) and (b) that the "matter itself" is not in reality "merely something which stands opposed to action in general, and to individual action," contrary to (c) that the "individual . . . is concerned with the matter . . . as his *own,*" and contrary to (d) that, "instead of a *pure* action or an *individual* specific action, rather something has been opened up which is just as much *for other people,*" "rather is [the matter itself] something whose *being* is the *action* of the *single* individual and of all individuals."

(x) Finally, Hegel offers an additional criticism of the shape of consciousness The Spiritual Animalkingdom, in the course of which two further noteworthy words/concepts play a central role: "honesty [Ehrlichkeit]" and "deception [Betrug]" (the latter appearing prominently in the title of the section as well). Hegel indicates that this shape of consciousness purports to be "honest" in virtue of its impartial and disinter-

---

124. For the specific component of Herder's activism which appears to conflict with (c), see the second part of the Herderian evidence cited/quoted under (vii) above.

ested concern with the matter itself: "Consciousness is called *honest* [ehrlich]" when it "possesses the truth . . . qua . . . formal universality; a consciousness which is concerned solely with the matter itself" (par. 412). But he argues that this purported honesty is in fact a sham because (at least at some level) this shape of consciousness must be aware that the claim to impartiality and disinterestedness underpinning its claim to honesty is contradicted by its activist social idealism (par. 415), and moreover makes its claim to impartiality and disinterestedness only from a motive of perpetrating the "deception [Betrug]" on other people of thereby deceiving them into endorsing its own position in order that it may consequently enjoy the sort of self-realization, or translation of its own views into reality, for which, on the thesis of activist social idealism, such social endorsement is necessary and sufficient (pars. 416–18). The words/concepts *Ehrlichkeit* and *Betrug* employed in this further criticism are once again borrowed from Herder's own texts. Thus, in the *Letters for the Advancement of Humanity* Herder sympathetically reproduces a diatribe by a German nationalist against the excessive influence of French culture on Germany, in the course of which the contrary words/concepts "honest [ehrlich]" and "deception [Betrug]" (and cognates) play a central role, and which in particular contrasts respect for "truth's honor [der Wahrheit Ehre]" and "honest people [ehrliche Leute]" with the false "modesty" of Germany's enthusiasts for French culture, who are "pious hypocrites" driven by a "secret lust for domination," and argues that "this talk about modesty is a crude deception [Betrug] to which a person of integrity pays no attention. To call the deceiver [Betrüger] a deceiver is not only the part of integrity, but also of freedom; it is a necessary matter."[125] In his above criticism of Herder Hegel is in effect casting this same charge back in Herder's teeth, implying that Herder's professed commitment to the ideal of impartiality and disinterestedness, exemplified here in the remarks in support of "truth's honor" and of being "honest," is *itself* a "deception," a "pious[ly] hypocrit[ical]" show of "modesty" motivated by a "secret lust for domination."

In sum, the section *The Spiritual Animalkingdom and Deception or the Matter Itself* is concerned from beginning to end with Herder's philosophical standpoint, particularly as articulated in works from 1778 on.

This fact has been worth establishing in a little more detail than was strictly required for our main task here of determining the chronologically

---

125. *Briefe zu Beförderung der Humanität* 4:10–12.

historical character of the chapters *Consciousness* through *Reason*, because this section is of quite unique importance for understanding the *Phenomenology*, and indeed Hegel's philosophy generally, but has previously remained entirely undeciphered by the secondary literature.[126] Several aspects of the section's unique importance deserve brief mention before we proceed with our main task: First, with the exception of doctrine (viii), which, as we have seen, Hegel rejects, the positive doctrines which this section implicitly attributes to Herder form, with only modest modifications, *the core of Hegel's own philosophical position as well*—a sketch of which, at paragraphs 435–37, we are now rapidly approaching in the text.[127] Second, and connectedly, this section has unique impor-

126. It would be unkind to go into details concerning the many wild guesses at the significance of this section to be found in the secondary literature—ranging from academia to French monasteries to capitalism as envisaged by Adam Smith and beyond.

127. To indicate some of the more important common ground between Herder's position as characterized in this section and Hegel's own position: Like part (i) of Herder's position, Hegel's conception of man includes the ideas of man's continuity with animal nature and of man's *geistig* quality as his differentia from animal nature—both of which ideas are apparent, for example, in the Hegelian system's transition from animal nature at the culmination of the Philosophy of Nature to man in the Philosophy of *Geist*. (On the other hand, the continuity is less strong for Hegel than for Herder. For instance, Hegel would resist Herder's simple transference of investigative methods, and analogical reasoning, from the sphere of animal nature to that of mankind. The title of the section under discussion, *The Spiritual Animalkingdom*, implies a measure of ironic criticism of Herder on this score.)

Part (ii) of Herder's position finds two noteworthy echoes in Hegel's own position. First, Herder's setting of intrinsic value on *individuality*, especially in combination with the other more *collectivist* aspects of his thought, such as his views on meaning and truth (iv) and (v)—a combination on which Hegel focuses at paragraph 394—is echoed in Hegel's own position. For a satisfactory marrying of individualism with collectivism is one of the main goals of the philosophical position toward which Hegel is working in the *Phenomenology* as well (see for example pars. 351, 436). (On the other hand, Herder is primarily concerned to defend an individualism regarding *cultures*, though also committed to an individualism regarding *people within a culture* [concerning which see for example *Briefe zu Beförderung der Humanität* 5: 111 ff., 142–43], whereas the emphasis in Hegel's own individualism, at least in the *Phenomenology*, is distributed conversely. One symptom of this difference is that in Hegel's presentation of Herder's individualism at paragraphs 402–3 what was in Herder's formulation primarily a doctrine about the intrinsic worth of individuality in *cultures* is stated as though it were rather a doctrine about the intrinsic worth of individuality in particular *people*.) Second, Herder's argument in (ii) that there are fundamental differences between different peoples' evaluative standards, *Maßstäbe*, and that these fundamental differences place an immovable obstacle in the way of any comparative evaluation of different peoples' achievements, finds strong echoes in Hegel's position. For in the Preface Hegel too argues that the phenomenon of fundamental differences between different people's *Maßstäbe* puts an obstacle in the way of comparative evaluations of their positions (pars. 81, 83). (On the other hand, there are also significant differences between Herder and Hegel here. For one thing, Herder is mainly concerned with intercultural comparisons and with moral, prudential, and aesthetic value; Hegel, on the other

tance as the point in the *Phenomenology* where all three of the text's central and extended "skeptical paradox, skeptical solution" arguments which I have identified reach their conclusions: those for the identity of concept and object, the essential communality of meaning, and the enduring communal consensus theory of truth.[128] Third, the proper interpreta-

---

hand, is concerned just as much with comparisons of different positions *within* a culture, and with *cognitive* value. For another thing, unlike Herder, Hegel thinks that the comparison problem can be *solved*—namely, because it turns out that every position except one, Hegel's, contradicts its *own* standard [par. 84].)

As we saw in chapter 2, part (iii) of Herder's position, his conception of the mind as essentially realized in, and therefore only knowable from, physical activity, is central to Hegel's own position as well.

Concerning part (iv) of Herder's position, his view that linguistic meaning, and therefore also all thought, and therefore the individual mind as well, is of its essence *socially* constituted, we saw in chapter 4 that the first two parts of this are central to Hegel's own position, and in chapter 2 that the inference from them to the third part, the essential sociality of the individual mind, is so as well (for which specifically, see esp. pars. 349, 508).

Concerning parts (v)–(vi) of Herder's position, his conception that truth is constituted by social agreement, or his social idealism, we saw in chapter 4 that such a conception is central to Hegel's own position as well.

Concerning, finally, part (vii) of Herder's position, his conception of the mind as quite generally volitional and active, and of reality as so as well, Hegel not only ascribes this conception to Herder but also warmly embraces it himself. For example, concerning the mind, at paragraph 436 he explicitly replaces such cognitive concepts as belief with the concept of volition, and at paragraph 439 where one might have expected cognitive concepts he instead writes of the mind's "action [Tun]" and of the "*actual* [wirklichen] consciousness." And, concerning reality, at paragraph 439 he writes of the "objective *actual* [wirkliche] world." Moreover, Hegel's reasons for this activist psychology and ontology are essentially the same as those which he finds in Herder: namely, the constitution of all mental conditions by physical behavior (see above on [iii]), the fundamentalness of affect and volition even to cognition (in Hegel's case, especially the deep affect of "desire," or the impulse to decide the character of reality quite generally), and the constitution of truth or reality by communal agreement (see above on [v]–[vi]).

This is only a sketch of ways in which Hegel's own position is continuous with aspects of Herder's position that are prominent in the section *The Spiritual Animalkingdom*. In addition, there are many further distinctively Herderian ideas *not* prominent in this section which are emphatically echoed in Hegel's own position as well—a number of which either have been or will be noted elsewhere in this book.

128. The latter two conclusions are embodied, respectively, in parts (iv) and (v)–(vi) of the outlook ascribed to Herder by this section, whose genuine basis in Herder's texts has already been explained. As we saw in chapter 3, the first conclusion, that of concept/object identity, also figures prominently in this section (see esp. pars. 394–95, 418). Herder's general antidualism makes the attribution of such a conception to him very reasonable. However, it is somewhat less clear in this case what more specific textual basis for the attribution Hegel has in mind. His thought seems to be that since for Herder our shared communal practice constitutes our concepts ([iv]) and also constitutes the reality represented by those concepts ([v]–[vi]), at bottom our concepts and reality are for Herder the

tion of this section makes possible the settlement of an important dispute concerning the influences which formed Hegel's thought. Some scholars, notably Dilthey and especially Taylor, have suggested that Hegel's thought owes a fundamental debt to Herder.[129] This thesis has proved difficult to establish convincingly or in detail, however, because Hegel's texts contain hardly any explicit discussion of Herder.[130] And some commentators have consequently implied skepticism about it.[131] Once the section *The Spiritual Animalkingdom* is recognized as a treatment of Herder's philosophy, however, the dispute can be settled: This section now provides eloquent testimony that Herder *was indeed* a fundamental influence on Hegel's thought, and moreover a wealth of specific examples of just *how* he was so. For, not only does this section, as we have just noted, implicitly attribute to Herder a broad range of distinctive ideas which Hegel shares with him, and present Herder as the philosopher who first articulated the three conclusions of three "skeptical paradox, skeptical solution" arguments which are central to Hegel's own position, but it does so, moreover, as part of an explicit project of tracing the *etiology* of Hegel's own position, "the detailed history of the education of consciousness . . . to the standpoint of Science [i.e., to Hegel's standpoint]" (par. 78).

Continuing our investigation into chronology, the second shape of consciousness in this final section of the *Reason* chapter, Reason as Lawgiver, is distinguished mainly by its view that Reason is an immediate source of insight into moral truth: "Reason knows immediately what is right and good. Just as it knows the law immediately, so too the law is valid for it immediately, and it says directly: 'This is right and good' " (par. 422). This is the perspective of the German *Popularphilosophen* of

---

same. Thus at paragraph 418 Hegel writes: "The matter itself . . . is the universal [i.e., the general concept] which has being only as this action of all and each, and a *reality* in the fact that this particular consciousness knows it to be its own individual reality and the reality of all. The pure matter itself is . . . the category, being that is the 'I' or the 'I' that is being."

129. Dilthey, *Die Jugendgeschichte Hegels;* Taylor, *Hegel* and "Hegel and the Philosophy of Action."

130. Note, however, in this connection that Hegel *generally* tends to owe most to thinkers whom he explicitly mentions least. Besides Herder, Schiller, Hölderlin, and (to a lesser degree) Schelling are further examples.

131. For example, Shklar, *Freedom and Independence*, p. 142: "Hegel always spoke of Montesquieu's 'immortal work' from his earliest to his last years with utmost admiration . . . This is in contrast to the relatively apolitical theories of Herder which he never mentioned."

the last quarter or so of the eighteenth century—men like Feder and Garve, whose greatest intellectual debt was to the Scottish philosophy of common sense. Hegel's prominent attribution to this shape of consciousness of the concept "sound Reason [gesunde Vernunft]" helps to pin down this reference to the *Popularphilosophen* (pars. 422–24).[132] So too does the utterly conventional character of the moral principles which he associates with it: "Everyone ought to speak the truth"; "Love thy neighbor as thyself" (pars. 424–25).[133] Such, then, is the historical reference of Reason as Lawgiver.[134]

The third shape of consciousness in this final section, Reason as Testing Laws, is distinguished by the fact that instead of seeing Reason as the positive source of moral laws, it sees Reason merely as the source of a formal criterion for testing a maxim's capacity for becoming a law, namely, the criterion of self-consistency under universalization: "Since ... all idea of an absolute content must be given up, it can only claim a formal universality, or that it is not self-contradictory ... The ethical nature ... is ... only a standard for deciding whether a content is capable of being

---

132. Hegel explicitly employs the expression "sound Reason [gesunde Vernunft]" in connection with the *Popularphilosophen* and their inspirers among the Scottish philosophers of common sense, and gives a generally similar description of their position to that which he gives of the shape of consciousness Reason as Lawgiver, in the *Vorlesungen über die Geschichte der Philosophie* 3:283–86: "In general [these Scottish philosophers of common sense] amount to the same as what is accepted as the principle in Germany too ... They have set up as the ground of truth so-called sound Reason [gesunde Vernunft], the common human understanding ... This Scottish philosophy is now retailed as something new in Germany. Garve has translated several of their writings on morality ... It is popular philosophy [Popularphilosophie] which ... seek[s] the source of what should be valid for man in man, in his consciousness, the immanence of what should have value for him."

133. Note in addition that the *problem* which the *Phenomenology* detects in Reason as Lawgiver—roughly, the problem of the futility of attempting to encapsulate ethical judgments in such strictly universal principles—is explicitly charged against the philosophy of common sense at *Philosophy of Right*, par. 216.

134. Shklar (*Freedom and Independence*, p. 134) and Solomon (*In the Spirit of Hegel*, pp. 522 ff.) interpret Reason as Lawgiver as referring instead to Kant's moral philosophy. However, (i) as Solomon himself admits, the section would give "an unforgivably obscure rendition of Kant" (ibid., p. 524). And (ii) Shklar and Solomon fail to explain how this can be the intended historical reference, given that Kant's moral philosophy is quite clearly the subject of the *next* section, *Reason as Testing Laws* (as indeed they themselves acknowledge), and that moreover Reason as Lawgiver is there interpreted as a position *different from and incompatible with* Reason as Testing Laws: in Reason as Testing Laws, "laws are no longer given [i.e., by Reason], but *tested*" (par. 429). By contrast, the *Popularphilosophen* immediately preceded Kant's moral philosophy in time, and Kant's moral philosophy did react against them (see for example Kant, *The Moral Law*, pp. 73 ff.).

a law or not, i.e., whether it is or is not self-contradictory. Reason as the giver of laws is reduced to a Reason which merely *critically examines* them" (pars. 426–28; cf. 429). This is of course the perspective of Kant's moral philosophy, as developed mainly in the *Groundwork of the Metaphysics of Morals* (1785) and the *Critique of Practical Reason* (1788).

Finally, and very importantly, there is right at the end of the *Reason* chapter, in paragraphs 435–37, a characterization of one last perspective. This perspective is distinguished by several traits, among which the following are prominent: (i) It recognizes that communal consensus is sufficient and necessary for truth or reality.[135] (ii) Connectedly, it acknowledges the community as the final arbiter of judgment (on ethical matters), and abandons any claim to have (ethical) principles based in or justified to the individual as such.[136] (iii) On the other hand, it also recognizes that the community's final authority is not alien to the individual but is immediately the individual's own as well.[137] (iv) Connectedly again, it no longer, in its cognitive activity, engages, or conceives itself as engaging, in belief, which attitude presupposes a mind-independent object, but instead in a sort of creative volition.[138] This final perspective does not belong to the history of *past* consciousness, but is instead the perspective of Hegel's own philosophy and age—"the standpoint of Science" which the Introduction had advertised as the culminating goal of the *Phenomenology*'s history of past consciousness.

Granting perhaps a modicum of artificiality in the chronology of the last two sections of the *Reason* chapter, due to their attempt to cover a large number of outlooks very close together in time, it is clear, then, that the *Reason* chapter continues the chronological history of consciousness

---

135. Par. 436: "The absolute pure will of all . . . has the form of immediate being. It is not a commandment which only *ought* to be; it *is* . . . ; it is the universal 'I' . . . which is immediately a reality, and the world *is* only this reality."

136. Pars. 436–37: "The law is grounded not in the will of a particular individual, but . . . is the absolute *pure will of all* . . . If [the laws] are supposed to be validated by *my* insight, then I have already denied their unshakeable, intrinsic being . . . Ethical disposition consists just in sticking steadfastly to what is right, and abstaining from all attempts to move or shake it, or derive it."

137. Par. 436: "The obedience of self-consciousness is not the serving of a master whose commands were arbitrary, and in which it would not recognize itself. On the contrary, laws are the thoughts of its own absolute consciousness, thoughts which are immediately its own."

138. Par. 436: "It does not *believe* . . . for . . . belief . . . perceives [essential being] as something alien to itself"; "The law . . . is the absolute *pure will of all* which has the form of immediate being."

History in the Chapters *Consciousness* through *Reason*   351

begun in the preceding two chapters, and that it brings to completion the Introduction's plan of a history of consciousness culminating in the standpoint of Hegel's philosophy in the modern age, or a "detailed history of the formative education of consciousness itself to the standpoint of Science."[139]

The main steps in the *Phenomenology*'s chronological history of consciousness may now be summarized, briefly and approximately (see table 1).

Note, finally, in some further confirmation of this historical reading of the chapters *Consciousness* through *Reason*, one additional point. This reading attributes the following general model of historical development to these chapters: *Consciousness* = ancient Orient and Egypt (culminating in ancient Greece); *Self-consciousness* = ancient Greece and Rome (culminating in Christianity and its development through to medieval Europe); *Reason* = modern Europe. Now, such a general model of historical development is precisely what one would expect from Hegel at the time of the *Phenomenology* given the conception of history already espoused by his most important and influential forerunner in the discipline of philosophy of history, Herder, and the conception of history later espoused by Hegel himself in the *Lectures on the Philosophy of World History*. For in Herder, similarly, history begins in ancient Asia, passes thence to ancient Egypt, thence to ancient Greece, thence to ancient Rome—"The Roman got his culture from Greece, the Greek from Asia and Egypt, Egypt from Asia"—thence to Christianity and medieval Europe, and finally to modern Europe.[140] And in Hegel's *Lectures on the Philosophy of World History* too history begins with the ancient Orient, passes thence to ancient Egypt, thence to ancient Greece, thence to ancient Rome, thence to Christianity and medieval Europe, and finally to modern Europe.

This, then, is a positive case for reading the chapters *Consciousness* through *Reason* as a chronological history of the development of con-

---

139. Concerning the modicum of artificiality just mentioned, we shall see later that Hegel himself apparently came to recognize and feel dissatisfied with this in the course of writing the *Phenomenology*, since in the *Spirit* chapter he tried, in effect, to rewrite the last two sections of the *Reason* chapter, reidentifying their perspectives with different historical representatives, in such a way as to make their chronology less cramped and contrived.
140. Quotation from *Herders Ausgewählte Werke* 3:688. This whole pattern of historical development is especially clear in *Auch eine Philosophie der Geschichte zur Bildung der Menschheit*.

Table 1

Shape	Historical Reference
Sense-certainty	Early prehistory, first phase (Persia)
Perception	Early prehistory, second phase (India)
Force and Understanding	Prehistory, third phase (Pharaonic Egyptian religion, Homeric Greek religion, Greek rationalism)
Life (and Desire)	5th-century Athens, especially under Pericles (ideal Greek culture)
Lordship and Bondage	Late 5th-century Athens / Rome after 2nd Punic War (political oppression and slavery)
Stoicism	Hellenistic Greece / Roman Empire (Stoicism)
Skepticism	Hellenistic Greece / Roman Empire (Skepticism)
Unhappy Consciousness	Roman Empire to Medieval Europe (Neoplatonism and Christianity)
Observation of Nature	Early 17th century on (modern natural science, beginning with Bacon, Galileo, and the Accademia dei Lincei)
Observation of Self-consciousness . . . Logical and Psychological Laws	Mid-17th to earlier 18th century (formal logic of Hobbes / Port Royal; empirical psychology of Locke/ Hume)
Observation of Self-consciousness . . . Physiognomy and Phrenology	Early 1770s on (Lavater's physiognomy, Gall's phrenology)
Pleasure and Necessity	Mid-1770s on (Goethe's Faust)
The Law of the Heart	Early 1780s (Schiller's Karl Moor)
Virtue	1780s (Frederick the Great)
The Spiritual Animalkingdom	1780s (Herder)
Reason as Lawgiver	1780s (*Popularphilosophen*)
Reason as Testing Laws	Late 1780s (Kant's moral philosophy)
Concluding paragraphs 435–37	Early 19th century (Hegel's own outlook)

sciousness from ancient times up to the attainment of Hegel's philosophy in the modern age (no doubt among other things).

* * *

There do, however, remain certain objections which might still be raised against such a reading, and we should therefore now in conclusion briefly address these.

(i) It may seem to speak against a historical reading of the *Consciousness* chapter especially, and in only slightly lesser degree against such a reading of the *Self-consciousness* and *Reason* chapters as well, that the allusions to specific historical dates, individuals, works, and so forth in the *Consciousness* chapter, and to a great extent in the other chapters also, are at best extremely vague. If Hegel had really intended to give a chronological history here, would he not have made the allusions clearer, or included explicit references? In this spirit, Hyppolite, arguing that "history plays little more than the role of example" in the chapters *Consciousness* through *Reason,* notes that Hegel is there "generally stingy with historical detail and proceed[s] always by allusions."[141]

(ii) Relatedly, according to an influential, and at first sight somewhat plausible, interpretation of the *Phenomenology* due originally to Haym, the work starts out, in the Introduction and the *Consciousness* chapter, attempting to give an ahistorical psychology, and only later, in the chapters *Self-consciousness* and following, switches to giving a history. The work is therefore, in Haym's words, "a psychology thrown into confusion and disorder by history and a history disrupted by psychology."[142]

(iii) Perhaps most threateningly of all for a historical reading, it becomes apparent when one goes into the details of the various sections of

---

141. Hyppolite, *Genesis and Structure,* p. 35. Cf. Kelly, who similarly argues against "the temptation to read the *Phenomenology* as an enigmatic philosophy of history" and for the role of history in the work being merely "to illustrate forms of consciousness" on the ground that "Hegel's conscious avoidance of proper names is the best clue to his design" ("Notes," pp. 199–200).

142. Haym, *Hegel und seine Zeit,* pp. 232, 238, 243. The enduring influence of this interpretation is visible, for example, in Taylor's claim that the *Consciousness* chapter gives "ontological" dialectics or "transcendental argument" (*Hegel,* p. 131; "The Opening Arguments of the *Phenomenology,*" p. 151), whereas the chapters *Self-consciousness* and *Reason* contain "historical dialectics" and "from the dialectic of master and slave to the end of *Reason* the implicit references [have] a rough historical order" (*Hegel,* pp. 131, 171). Likewise, it is visible in Solomon's assertion that "the first chapters [i.e., the sections of *Consciousness*] . . . are written more or less without reference to history of any kind," but are followed by "historical chapters," beginning with the *Self-consciousness* chapter (*In the Spirit of Hegel,* p. 216).

the chapters *Consciousness* through *Reason* that many of the historical allusions which *are* found there occur *out of chronological sequence*. This might seem, at first blush, to be rather powerful evidence against the view that these chapters are designed to give a chronological history. Hence, for example, Harris has acutely observed that it seems to speak against such a view that "Chapter II [i.e., the *Perception* section] contains clear references to physical-chemical theories that are later than 1750; and Chapter III [i.e., the *Force and the Understanding* section] is firmly grounded in [Newton's] *Principia* of 1687."[143]

These objections do *not* in fact undermine our reading of the chapters *Consciousness* through *Reason* as a chronological history of consciousness's development, however. The key to seeing that they do not lies above all in recognizing a further very important principle of the general design of these chapters which should now be introduced: the sequence of shapes of consciousness presented in these chapters is supposed to be *not only* a chronological history of consciousness's development but *also and simultaneously a collection of the strata constitutive of the modern consciousness*.[144]

That the chapters have this further dimension is perhaps most readily seen by comparing them with the later versions of a "Phenomenology of Spirit" which Hegel went on to develop in the several editions of the Nuremberg *Doctrine of Consciousness* and the *Encyclopaedia*. For in these later versions of the discipline the same shapes of consciousness are presented, but clearly rather as a collection of the strata of (modern) consciousness than as a chronological history of consciousness's develop-

---

143. H.S. Harris, private correspondence. Cf. Solomon, *In the Spirit of Hegel*, p. 211: "The *Phenomenology* is not a book about history, and its structure is not historical, as even the most superficial scan of its contents will reveal . . . Locke, Leibniz, Newton, and Kant make their appearance in the first few chapters, along with Plato and Aristotle."

144. Lukács apparently failed to realize this, and consequently lacks the resources for answering the above objections.

I shall not here undertake actually to reread the chapters in question as a psychology of the modern consciousness, though it is of course implied by this interpretation that that could be done. Note that in order to do so one would often need to illuminate them by drawing on external evidence different from that which has been drawn on above in order to reveal their historical dimension. For example, whereas the first half of the *Self-consciousness* chapter on Life and Lordship and Bondage is illuminated in its historical dimension above all by the early theological writings, in its psychological dimension it is illuminated more by the Jena drafts of the Philosophy of Spirit.

ment.¹⁴⁵ Accordingly, when Hegel describes the *Phenomenology* of 1807 as a *Geschichte* of consciousness, he in fact means this in a twofold sense: on the one hand, in the idiomatic sense of a chronological *history* of consciousness, but, on the other hand, also in the less obvious sense of an ahistorical *collection of the strata* of the modern consciousness. This second sense is facilitated by a playful piece of pseudoetymology typical of Hegel: the word *Geschichte,* construed in a pseudoetymological fashion, can appear to mean a *collection of strata* or *Schichten*—the Ge- prefix connoting collectiveness, as, for example, in *Wolke* (cloud), *Gewölk* (clouds).¹⁴⁶ Hegel was not in fact the first person to use the word *Geschichte* to signify ahistorical psychology in this way; there was already a tradition of doing so reaching back at least as far as Platner's 1793 work *Philosophical Aphorisms.*¹⁴⁷ Indeed, the *double* sense of the word which occurs in the *Phenomenology* also had an earlier precedent, already being found in Schelling's *System of Transcendental Idealism* of 1800, a work from which Hegel drew much of his inspiration for the *Phenomenology*. Thus, like Hegel, Schelling describes his work as a "progressive *Geschichte* of self-consciousness."¹⁴⁸ And while for the most part his work reads like an account of the strata of (modern) consciousness rather than a chronological history of consciousness (in accordance with the tradition just mentioned),¹⁴⁹ he does also imply the possibility of reading it as a chronological history of consciousness.¹⁵⁰

145. Hence, for example, the 1809 ff. *Doctrine of Consciousness* says that in its own presentation the "three levels" Consciousness, Self-consciousness, and Reason "are not taken up empirically from outside, but are moments of consciousness itself" (*Nürnberger und Heidelberger Schriften,* p. 113).

146. Cf. the verbal adjective cognate with *Schicht, geschichtet,* meaning stratified. The real etymological background of the word *Geschichte* instead lies with the verb *geschehen,* meaning to happen.

147. On this see Hegel, *Phänomenologie des Geistes,* ed. J. Hoffmeister (Hamburg: Felix Meiner, 1952), pp. xix ff. Cf. Pöggeler, *Hegels Idee einer Phänomenologie des Geistes,* pp. 322–27, 353–55.

148. *System of Transcendental Idealism,* p. 2; cf. 50.

149. For example, ibid., p. 90: the work's "whole method consists in leading the self from one level of self-intuition to another, until it is posited with all determinations that are contained in the free and conscious act of self-consciousness."

150. Ibid., p. 201: because "no individual consciousness could be posited, with all the determinations it is posited with, and which necessarily belong to it, unless the whole of history had gone before," "historiography . . . could set out from the current situation and infer to past history."

How, though, can Hegel coherently intend the *Phenomenology*'s sequence of shapes of consciousness to be *both* of these things at once? He can do so because he believes the structure of the modern consciousness, and indeed the structure of any shape of consciousness later than Sense-certainty, to be the product of a preceding historical development of consciousness which has been *cumulative* in nature, a product of a sequence of earlier shapes of consciousness which *preserves each of those shapes within itself as part of its own essential constitution* (albeit in a modified form).[151] Thus he states that "the later moment retains within it the preceding one," and that "in a Spirit that is more advanced than another, the lower concrete existence has been reduced to an inconspicuous moment; what used to be the important thing is now . . . a trace; its pattern is shrouded to become a . . . shadowy outline" (pars. 679, 28).[152] Hence it is Hegel's idea that Sense-certainty is preserved within Perception (in a modified form), Perception in its turn within Force and the Understanding (in a modified form), and so forth, all of them eventually being preserved within the modern consciousness (in a modified form). Because of this cumulative nature of consciousness's development, the *Phenomenology*'s depiction of its series of shapes of consciousness can be read *both* as a representation of the history of the shapes which preceded and produced the structure of the modern consciousness *and* as a representation of the strata which make up the structure of the modern consciousness. (To give a rough analogy: due to the cumulative way in which a tree trunk develops, a picture of the series of rings in the cross-section of a tree trunk can be read both as a sort of history of the stages in the tree's development which preceded and produced the final structure of the tree trunk and as a representation of the strata which make up the final structure of the tree trunk.)

That the *Phenomenology*'s chapters *Consciousness* through *Reason*

---

151. As we have noted, the idea of preservation in a modified form plays a central role in Hegel's philosophy, being, for example, the force of his frequent use of the verb *aufheben* in a way combining its two contrary idiomatic senses "to preserve" and "to abolish."

152. Cf. *Lectures on the Philosophy of World History: Introduction*, pp. 150–51: "The present world and the present form and self-consciousness of the Spirit contain within them all the stages which appear to have occurred earlier in history . . . The Spirit has all the stages of the past still adhering to it . . . Those moments which the Spirit appears to have outgrown still belong to it in the depths of its present."

are designed to have this twofold character of being *not only* a chronological history of consciousness but *also and simultaneously a collection of the strata constitutive of the modern consciousness* helps greatly toward defusing the three indicated objections to reading these chapters as a chronological history of consciousness.

Thus, consider first objection (i), the objection that the *Consciousness* chapter especially, and to a great extent the subsequent chapters also, lack the sort of clear allusions or references to historical details that one would expect in a chronological history. We can now see that there are good reasons for this feature of the text quite consistent with its intention of providing a chronological history: (a) The depiction in these chapters of a series of shapes of consciousness is supposed to serve not *only* as a chronological history of consciousness, but also and simultaneously as an analysis of the strata of the modern consciousness. The intrusion of historical details, while it might have benefitted the former project, could have done so only at the serious cost of interfering with the latter. Hegel therefore decided to omit historical details as far as possible. (b) A further reason for the absence of historical details concerns the *Consciousness* chapter specifically, and explains the special degree of their absence from this chapter: As noted earlier, when Hegel actually wrote this chapter, he in all probability had no more precise idea of the historical reference of its first two sections, *Sense-certainty* and *Perception,* than that they depicted shapes of consciousness from the very beginnings of human pre-history.[153] He was therefore not even in a position to provide historical details in these sections when he wrote them.

Consider next the related objection (ii), Haym's somewhat plausible thesis that the *Consciousness* chapter gives an ahistorical psychology, and that Hegel only subsequently switches to giving a history, so that the work is "a psychology thrown into confusion and disorder by history and a history disrupted by psychology." We can now see that there is both enough truth in this thesis to explain its plausibility and enough error to prevent it from undermining our historical reading: In particular, it is true that the *Consciousness* chapter is especially light in clear allusions or references to historical details, but for the reasons just indicated

---

153. As I mentioned earlier, he has an epistemological theory of how one knows about past shapes of consciousness which makes this a perfectly sensible situation for him to have seen himself as in, and which will be discussed in the next chapter.

an error to infer from this fact that the chapter must therefore lack historical intentions. And it is true that the *Consciousness* chapter gives an ahistorical psychology of (modern) consciousness, but an error to infer from this fact that this is *all* that it gives, for it also and simultaneously gives a history of consciousness. (In addition, though less crucially for our present purposes, it is true that the chapters subsequent to *Consciousness* give a history of consciousness's development, but false that they give *only* this, for they also and simultaneously give an ahistorical psychology. And it is true that the work combines an ahistorical psychology of [modern] consciousness with a history of consciousness's development, but false that this is a symptom of "confusion and disorder," for it is instead a clear-headed intention of Hegel's founded on his conviction that such a combination is possible due to the cumulative nature of consciousness's development.)

Consider finally objection (iii), the objection that in the course of the *Phenomenology*'s treatment of consciousness in the chapters *Consciousness* through *Reason* many of the historical allusions which *do* occur do so out of chronological sequence. That this happens is beyond question. However, we can now see that that is quite consistent with the chapters' constitution of a chronological history. For, Hegel intends these chapters to provide not *only* a chronological history of consciousness but also and simultaneously, in exploitation of the putative circumstance that consciousness's development has been cumulative in nature, an analysis of the structure of the modern consciousness. Consequently, within any given section he will wish to allude, not only to examples of the shape of consciousness at issue from the period of its original emergence, but also to examples of its preservation in the modern consciousness. Additionally, he will no doubt wish to allude to examples of its preservation in historically intermediate types of consciousness as well, since the cumulative character of consciousness's development guarantees its preservation in these too. This helps to explain, for example, the copious allusions to Newtonian physics and its theory of forces in the section *Force and the Understanding*—a section which, as we have seen, is supposed in its historical aspect to depict ancient outlooks which culminated in Greek rationalism. For Greek rationalism's distinction between the sensible appearances of things recognized by the sensuous representation of the naive investigator and the underlying supersensible constitutions and causal principles of things recognized only through a more exalted mode of cognition is preserved as a fundamental background assumption within modern physics.[154]

154. Hegel is probably also concerned in the *Phenomenology* with the phenomenon of *atavism*, or of later perspectives which do not so much preserve an earlier perspective in a modified form within themselves as attempt to *return* to it—thereby exposing themselves to the same criticisms as it was vulnerable to. For example, it is plausible to interpret the *Sense-certainty* section as an attack, not only on the historically original form of the outlook which it describes, but also on later positions which Hegel regards as attempts to revert to that outlook, such as certain types of philosophical empiricism (see pars. 109, 558), and perhaps also Romantic ideas about immediate knowledge (see *Encyclopaedia*, par. 418, addition). If this is correct, then it provides a further reason, again consistent with an intention to provide a chronological history of consciousness in them, why the chapters *Consciousness* through *Reason* include allusions out of chronological sequence.

CHAPTER TEN

Intellectual Historicism in the Chapters *Consciousness* through *Reason*

Intimately bound up with the principle of the general design of the chapters *Consciousness* through *Reason* just explained, their provision of a chronological history of consciousness (and simultaneously an analysis of the modern consciousness), are a number of general intellectual historicist ideas which we should now consider. This further investigation should both contribute to a fuller understanding of the chapters and afford us an opportunity to pursue the ideas a little for their own sake. (The approach taken here will be less narrowly exegetical than in most of the rest of the present book.)

To begin with, now that we have established that the chapters *Consciousness* through *Reason* are conceived as a chronological history of consciousness, we can see clearly that they are deeply committed to expressing, and working out in historical detail, a version of the first and most basic intellectual historicist idea: the idea that human thought has changed in fundamental ways over the course of history, with respect to both concepts and beliefs.[1]

One can trace versions of this idea back to the very earliest periods of Hegel's thought.[2] However, it first assumes prominence in his systematic

---

1. As we saw in chapter 2, Hegel also believes, continuously with this view about the past, that human thought is about to change fundamentally again with respect to both concepts and beliefs, namely, through the advent of his own philosophy.
2. For example, already in 1788 Hegel argues that the ancients, in particular the ancient Greeks, had different concepts (and by implication also different beliefs) from us moderns: "They saw things in other relations [from us], and expressed these connections of one thing to another in their language, and so had concepts which we do [not] have, because we lack

thought in the revised beginning of *The Positivity of the Christian Religion* from 1800, where, as we noted in chapter 4, he argues on broadly empirical grounds for the fundamental diversity of human cognitive nature and against the Kantian view—to which he had previously found himself in some measure attracted—that in respect of cognitive nature all men share a large amount in common. The same idea remains central to Hegel's systematic thought in the *Phenomenology*. And it also persists to some extent in his later works (though there are complications here to which we shall turn in due course).

The greatest single influence on Hegel in connection with this idea was almost certainly Herder. Herder had written in the spirit of this idea in *On the Cognition and Sensation of the Human Soul,* for example: "Like individual human beings, . . . peoples are different from one another, only more so; according to the sphere of their mode of sensation varies their mode of thought too"; "I could tell you many a fairy tale here about the 'universal human understanding,' as for example of that clever man who believed all the ships in the harbor at Athens his, and was very happy about it . . . The 'universal human reason,' as people would like to understand the term, is a cover for our favorite fancies, idolatry, blindness, and laziness."[3] (Herder, and following him von Humboldt, had stressed, in addition to the phenomenon of fundamental changes in thought *over history,* also the companion phenomenon, less emphasized by Hegel, of fundamental variations in thought between cultures even within a *single* historical period, such as the modern for example.)[4]

The attribution of this first intellectual historicist idea to Hegel is likely to provoke a yawn from some readers—though for quite contrary rea-

---

the words for them . . . An essential advantage allowed by the learning of foreign languages is no doubt the enrichment of our conceptual resources brought about in this way" (*Dokumente zu Hegels Entwicklung*, p. 170).

3. *Herders Ausgewählte Werke* 3:729, 731–32. A forceful general working-out of this idea by Herder is *Auch eine Philosophie der Geschichte zur Bildung der Menschheit.* An especially impressive example of its application by him in analyzing specific conceptual changes over history can be found at *Fragmente*, in *Johann Gottfried Herder Werke* 1:319–22. As noted in chapter 4, it is probable that the latter of the two passages quoted above and its immediate context directly inspired Hegel's earliest systematic invocation of this first intellectual historicist idea (in criticism of Kant) in the revised beginning of *The Positivity of the Christian Religion.*

4. See esp. Herder, *Über den Ursprung der Sprache* and *Briefe zu Beförderung der Humanität* 10:70 ff.; W. von Humboldt, *Plan einer vergleichenden Anthropologie* and *Über die Kavi-Sprache auf der Insel Java*, both in *Gesammelte Schriften* (Berlin: B. Behr's Verlag, 1903–36).

sons depending on whether they come from the nonphilosophical human sciences or from philosophy. The former are likely to yawn because they regard this idea as a platitude, an obvious truth; the latter because they regard it as discredited or deflated, proven either false or only very qualifiedly true. It is appropriate that some observations be made to forestall each of these reactions in turn.

Concerning, first, the suggestion that this idea is a *platitude:* It is quite true that since Hegel's day the idea that human thought has changed in fundamental ways over the course of history has (together with its companion idea that human thought varies in fundamental ways between cultures even within a *single* historical period) become accepted, in one form or another, as virtually a given by most areas of the human sciences. However, it is important to recall that this was still a relatively new and revolutionary idea in Hegel's day, and that he himself deserves much of the credit for its subsequent wide currency. Just a few decades earlier, for example, Hume and Voltaire, both widely respected not only as philosophers but also as historians, had still been able to write, respectively, that "mankind are so much the same, in all times and places, that history informs us of nothing new or strange . . . Its chief use is only to discover the constant and universal principles of human nature," and that "man, generally speaking, was always what he now is."[5] Hegel sharply criticizes this received position in the *Lectures on the Philosophy of World History* on the ground that it falsifies the historical facts by overlooking the deep changes which have occurred over the course of history in the conceptual and propositional *content* of people's psychological attitudes:

> The expression "human nature" is usually taken to represent something fixed and constant. Descriptions of human nature are meant to apply to all men, past and present. The general pattern is capable of infinite modifications, but, however much it may vary, it nevertheless remains essentially the same. Reflective thought must disregard the differences and isolate the common factor which can be expected to behave in the same way and to

---

5. Hume, *Enquiry concerning Human Understanding* (1748), p. 83 (Hume is speaking here primarily of mankind's motives for action, but the passage also reflects his view of human mental life more generally); Voltaire, *Essai sur les Moeurs et l'Esprit des Nations* (1769), in *Ouevres completes de Voltaire* (Paris: L'imprimerie de la Société Littéraire-typographique, 1785), 16:39. There had been deep commitments to the same position in early German philosophy as well. For example, Leibniz, its most influential luminary, had held virtually as an axiom that all known languages expressed the same basic concepts (founding his project of formulating a universal language upon this assumption).

show itself in the same light in all circumstances. It is possible to detect the general type even in those examples which seem to diverge most widely from it . . . Those who look at history from this point of view will tend to emphasize that men are still the same as they always were . . . One might fittingly add with Solomon that there is nothing new under the sun . . . *It is obvious that this way of looking at history abstracts from the content and aims of human activity.* Such sovereign disregard of the objective situation is particularly common among French and English writers.[6]

Indeed, even more recently and closer to home Kant had still espoused a view of human cognitive nature similar to that of Hume and Voltaire—for which, as we have seen, Hegel in the revised beginning of *The Positivity of the Christian Religion* subjects him to similar criticism.[7]

---

6. *Lectures on the Philosophy of World History: Introduction*, pp. 44–45; emphasis added. In this criticism of writers such as Hume and Voltaire, Hegel again echoes Herder, who had written in *Auch eine Philosophie der Geschichte zur Bildung der Menschheit*: "Fair art of poetry . . . ! The art of poetry is also useful . . . But when the poet is a historian, a philosopher, as most of them pretend to be, and they then model all centuries after the one—often very small and weak—form belonging to their own age—Hume, Voltaire . . . , what are you in the light of truth?" (*Herders Ausgewählte Werke* 2:644).

7. Strictly speaking, Kant occupied an interesting half-way house between the Hume-Voltaire position and Hegel's own position. On his Hume-Voltaire side, Kant was very much wedded to the view that men had at all times and places been mentally committed to the single a priori framework of intuitions, concepts, and principles delineated by his philosophy: they had all possessed the same a priori intuitions of Euclidean space and of time, employed the same twelve a priori concepts of the Understanding (such as cause and effect), recognized the same a priori principles of Euclidean geometry and of arithmetic, thought in accordance with the same a priori principles of formal logic (such as the law of noncontradiction) and of transcendental logic (such as the causal principle), heard the same a priori moral call of the categorical imperative, and so forth. Hence, for example, concerning the categorical imperative, Kant writes in the *Groundwork of the Metaphysics of Morals* that "the ordinary Reason of mankind . . . always has [this] principle before its eyes" (*The Moral Law*, p. 67; cf. 69). On his more Hegelian side, however, Kant was well aware of such fairly obvious historical facts as that it had taken a Euclid to develop the principles of Euclidean geometry and an Aristotle to develop those of formal logic, and generally that the a priori framework, or "Reason," was something which had *developed* over the course of history—even to the point, indeed, of adopting the principle of the development of Reason as his key for the interpretation of history in the essay *Idea for a Universal History from a Cosmopolitan Point of View*. How did Kant reconcile these two seemingly irreconcilable sides of his thought? His solution was, in effect, to maintain that although the a priori framework was always and everywhere *implicitly* present within the human mind, it varied from epoch to epoch and individual to individual in its degree of *explicitness* within the mind. Hence, for example, in the *Critique of Pure Reason* he describes the philosopher's role in formulating the a priori principles of metaphysics as one of "following the suggestion of an idea lying hidden in our minds" and making it "possible for us to discern the idea in a clearer light" (A834–35). As Hegel implies in the revised beginning of *The Positivity of the Christian Religion,* the problem with this position is that when one mea-

In addition, the suggestion that Hegel is purveying a mere platitude in this first intellectual historicist idea of the *Phenomenology* deserves the response that the *Phenomenology* develops this idea in an unusually radical and interesting way. A claim that thought has changed in *fundamental* ways over the course of history with respect to concepts and beliefs could in fact mean a number of different things. It could mean, at a bare minimum, that there have been changes in *very important* concepts and beliefs; it could mean that there have been changes in *all*, or at least most, concepts and beliefs; it could mean that there have been changes in concepts and beliefs which were *foundational* with respect to all of the other concepts and beliefs of the people who possessed them, so that those changes automatically brought with them *global* changes in people's concepts and beliefs; it could mean in addition that the changes in concepts and beliefs which have occurred have been qualitatively *dramatic* rather than merely subtle ones. The *Phenomenology*'s version of the first intellectual historicist idea is unusually radical and interesting largely because it implies that changes have occurred in thought over the course of history which were fundamental in *all four* of these senses. Thus, the *Phenomenology* certainly implies that there have been changes in *very important* concepts and beliefs. Such a position is found in Hegel's other writings as well. For example, in the *Lectures on the History of Philosophy* he implies that our cherished concepts of cause and effect and of force—and therefore all the important beliefs which we articulate through them also—are time- and culture-bound.[8] However, the version of this position in the *Phenomenology* is still more radical. For, as we have seen, the work's core thesis that shapes of consciousness have changed over time implies that even such central and seemingly unchanging concepts as those of *reality, self,* and cognitive *representation* have changed over time.

---

sures it against the linguistic and textual evidence provided by history one finds that, while its proto-Hegelian concession of intellectual change at the explicit level is empirically well confirmed by that evidence, there proves to be *no* good empirical evidence for its neo-Humean/Voltairean insistence on constancy at an implicit level, which latter idea therefore appears to be, at best, an empirically groundless philosopher's dogma.

8. *On Art, Religion, Philosophy*, pp. 251, 262: "There are whole nations which have not this conception [of cause] at all; indeed it involves a great step forward in development . . . Difference in culture on the whole depends on difference in the thought determinations which are manifested . . . The forms of thought . . . which hold good in the sciences and constitute the ultimate support of all their matter . . . are common to the condition and culture of the time and of the people . . . In higher culture, such relations as those of cause and effect are involved, as also those of force and its manifestation."

In addition, the *Phenomenology* is committed to the positions that there have been changes over history in *all* concepts and beliefs; and that changes have occurred in concepts and beliefs which were *foundational* with respect to all of the other concepts and beliefs of the people who possessed them so that the changes in question automatically brought with them *global* changes in people's concepts and beliefs. For, as we saw in chapter 2, it is Hegel's view in the *Phenomenology* that all of a non-Hegelian individual's concepts and beliefs have to be articulated through some shape of consciousness—that is, some set of interdependent conceptions and concepts of reality, self, and representation—or another, that this shape enters into the very senses of all of his concepts and beliefs, and that the shapes which have played this role have changed over time. Finally, the *Phenomenology* is also committed to the view that the changes in conceptions and concepts of reality, self, and representation, and consequently in concepts and beliefs generally, which have occurred over the course of history have been fundamental in the sense that, in some cases at least, they have been qualitatively *dramatic* rather than merely subtle ones. In order to see this, it is especially important to have recognized the historical dimension of the *Consciousness* chapter. For this chapter contains some of Hegel's most extreme (and no doubt also most controversial) examples of how dramatically certain past shapes of consciousness have differed from our own. In particular, the *Consciousness* chapter implies that mankind once occupied shapes of consciousness as different from our own as the entirely sensuous shapes of Sense-certainty and Perception, and that it was only with the advent of a later intellectual movement culminating in the rationalist philosophies of ancient Greece, namely, Force and the Understanding, that those entirely sensuous shapes were superseded and the distinction between sensible appearances and supersensible reality which we moderns take so deeply for granted was introduced.

* * *

Let us next address the contrary, and in some ways more troubling, objection that this first intellectual historicist idea developed by the *Phenomenology* has now been *discredited or deflated*. Such an objection is especially likely to be raised by philosophers, because it has recently become very fashionable among philosophers to reject, or at least try to set severe limits to, the idea that thought has changed in fundamental ways over the course of history, and its companion idea that thought differs in fundamental ways across cultures even within a single historical period. This fashion seems to me misconceived, and I would accordingly like to offer here some observations toward a defense of the first intellectual historicist idea and its companion idea against it. I shall not attempt to make a *positive* case for the ideas in question—much of the existing literature in disciplines such as classical philology, anthropology, linguistics, and the history of science has already done that pretty effectively, it seems to me. Rather, my purpose will be the *negative* one of answering the sorts of objections that have been raised against these ideas by philosophers.

We might usefully begin with a little shifting of the burden of proof. In attacking these ideas, recent philosophers often imply that they are at bottom just pieces of a priori dogmatism. For example, Davidson characterizes the belief in different conceptual schemes as a way that "philosophers are prone to talk," a sort of "religion."[9] Since the questions at issue in these ideas appear to be largely empirical ones, concerned with relevant linguistic and textual evidence and how it should be interpreted, such an implication would be quite damaging if true. However, it is in fact far from true, and is indeed the very opposite of the truth. In this connection the following points deserve particular notice: (i) The individuals who were responsible for the original introduction and development of these ideas were the members of what Dilthey calls the "Historical School" of thought in later eighteenth- and nineteenth-century Germany—Herder, von Humboldt, Hegel, Schleiermacher, Böckh, and others. Now these were all people who possessed a broad and deep knowledge of ancient, and in some cases also modern but culturally distant, languages and texts, and who espoused the ideas in question on the basis of this knowledge.[10] (ii) Moreover, these ideas have continued to win emphatic support from

---

9. D. Davidson, "On the Very Idea of a Conceptual Scheme," in *Inquiries into Truth and Interpretation* (Oxford: Oxford University Press, 1991), p. 183. Ironically, as we shall see, the charge of a priori dogmatism would be much more aptly leveled against Davidson's *own* position on these matters.

10. It is noteworthy in this connection that these were the very same people who first developed the view—since fundamental to most modern philosophy of language—that thought is not merely contingently related to language but essentially dependent upon and bounded in scope by it (cf. chapter 4). That was no accident. For, absent such a view, it had been possible to dismiss variations in the linguistic and textual data from different times and places as, however striking, merely, so to speak, variations in the external clothing worn by fundamentally unchanging thoughts. With the advent of such a view, on the other hand, those variations instead came to be recognized as revelatory of corresponding variations in thought itself.

scholars in the human sciences—classical philologists, anthropologists, linguists, historians of science, etc.—who possess the most impressive expertise in actually interpreting ancient and modern but culturally distant languages and texts, and on the basis of their experience in doing so—for example, Eduard Fränkel and Evans-Pritchard, arguably the greatest classical philologist and the greatest anthropologist of this century, respectively.[11] (iii) Davidson's contrary impression arises from largely overlooking or neglecting this broad background of the ideas in question in later eighteenth- and nineteenth-century German thought and in the empirically informed interpretative disciplines of the human sciences, and instead focusing on their more recent representatives in the discipline of philosophy.[12] If there is a burden of proof to be borne in this dispute, then, it arguably rests on those who would contradict these ideas rather than on those who would defend them.

Within the recent philosophical literature which undertakes to contradict or set severe limits to these ideas, two broad approaches can be distinguished. A first is *a priorist* with respect to the relevant linguistic and textual evidence—paying no close heed to this at all, it attempts to generate arguments against the possibility of there being, or against the possibility of our having justification for believing in, radical differences in concepts and beliefs on the basis of very general considerations. These sometimes exclude, and sometimes include, a positive theory about the nature of meaning, understanding, and interpretation—and correspondingly, two subspecies of this first approach can be distinguished. The second approach is *a posteriorist* with respect to the relevant linguistic and textual evidence—it does pay heed to this, and argues from its specific character that the thesis of radical differences in concepts and beliefs is mistaken.

It seems to me that both of these approaches run into very grave diffi-

---

11. E. Fränkel, *Aeschylus: Agamemnon* (Oxford: Clarendon Press, 1950), 1:xi: "About the severe limitations of any translation, let alone a translation from Aeschylus into a modern language, there can be no disagreement among sensible people." E.E. Evans-Pritchard, *Social Anthropology* (London: Cohen and West, 1964), p. 61, describing the procedure of the anthropologist: "He learns to speak [the primitive people's] language, to think in their concepts, and to feel in their values. He then lives the experience over again critically and interpretatively in the conceptual categories and values of his own culture."

12. Thus the figures with whom Davidson mainly associates the belief in different conceptual schemes in "On the Very Idea of a Conceptual Scheme" are Bergson, Feyerabend, Putnam, Quine, and Smart (though, in fairness, he does also mention Sapir, Whorf, and Kuhn).

culties—that the *a priorist* approach is misconceived, not only in that its particular arguments fail, but also in principle, and that, while an *a posteriorist* approach is in principle the right approach to adopt, it yields the conclusion that radical differences in concepts and beliefs are illusory only through being faultily executed.

In order to illustrate these different approaches and the sorts of shortcomings to which they fall victim, I propose to consider an influential example of each. As an example of the *a priorist* approach (in both its subspecies) I shall consider the work of Davidson, especially his essay "On the Very Idea of a Conceptual Scheme."[13] As an example of the *a posteriorist* approach, I shall consider the work of the anthropologists Berlin and Kay, and following them the philosopher Hardin, on color conceptualization.[14]

Davidson argues, against the view that "we understand massive conceptual change or profound contrasts" and that "the beliefs, desires, hopes, and bits of knowledge that characterize one person have no true counterparts for the subscriber to another [conceptual] scheme," that "we could not be in a position to judge that others had concepts or beliefs radically different from our own."[15]

There is some ambiguity in the exact force of this denial that we could be justified in believing in radically different concepts or beliefs. Davidson concedes, as educated common sense would indeed seem to demand, that *some* significant differences in concepts and beliefs are found to occur.[16] What then does he mean to deny? *On the one hand,* his formulations of and arguments for this denial, in "On the Very Idea of a Conceptual Scheme" and elsewhere, standardly imply that it includes a denial that we

---

13. My characterization of Davidson's position as *a priorist* is already meant to suggest at least an internal criticism of it. Davidson, while certainly no *epistemological* empiricist (see *Inquiries into Truth and Interpretation*, pp. 4, 189–94), does evidently aspire to be a *methodological* empiricist (ibid., pp. 3, 25, 61–62). As we will see, however, his whole approach to the question of different conceptual schemes is deeply *at odds* with methodological empiricism.

14. B. Berlin and P. Kay, *Basic Color Terms: Their Universality and Evolution* (Berkeley: University of California Press, 1991); C.L. Hardin, *Color for Philosophers* (Indianapolis: Hackett, 1988), pp. 155–86. I have chosen this literature in part because the domain of color is likely at the outset to seem to most readers to be indeed a rather challenging case for the advocate of radical differences in conceptual schemes, more challenging for example than the domains of ethics or religion.

15. "On the Very Idea of a Conceptual Scheme," pp. 183, 197.

16. Ibid., pp. 183–84, 197. Cf. "The Myth of the Subjective," in *Relativism: Interpretation and Confrontation*, ed. M. Krausz (Notre Dame: University of Notre Dame Press, 1989), p. 160.

could be justified in believing in radicalness in the *quantity* of differences between someone else's concepts or beliefs and our own, no matter how slight we might find those differences to be in quality. For example, consider again closely Davidson's characterization of his opponents' view just quoted above. And note also that the conclusion of several of his specific arguments in "On the Very Idea of a Conceptual Scheme" and elsewhere in support of the denial in question (arguments which we are about to consider) is that interpreters must always find between themselves and those whom they interpret, not merely massive similarity, but massive *identity* in concepts and beliefs. *On the other hand*, certain of Davidson's formulations of his denial would permit the alternative reading that he means to deny only that we could be justified in believing in radicalness in the *quantity and quality* of differences (not in radicalness in the quantity of differences whatever their qualitative degree).[17] And indeed, sheer internal consistency seems to require that he move to this second position, because his first and standard position is inconsistent with his already-mentioned inevitable concession to educated common sense that we do at least find *some* significant variations in concepts *given his fundamental holism about meaning*.[18]

Davidson provides a priorist arguments for this denial of both the sorts recently distinguished, those which argue for the impossibility of (our hav-

---

17. See, for example, "On the Very Idea of a Conceptual Scheme," p. 184.
18. For this holism, see esp. *Inquiries into Truth and Interpretation,* p. 22. Leaving to one side for a moment our main question, to which we are about to turn, of the cogency or otherwise of his *arguments,* Davidson's first and standard position seems to me more clearly erroneous than this second position would be, although the latter too seems to me ultimately misguided. The reason for the difference in the relative defensibility of the two positions is that the notion of a high degree of qualitative difference between concepts or beliefs is intuitively *vaguer* and *less decidable in application* than that of a large quantity of differences between concepts and beliefs (of whatever qualitative degree), so that it is more difficult to refute the second position than the first by reference to clear counterexamples. However, this makes the relative invulnerability of the second position a very dubious virtue—deriving mainly from its vagueness and undecidability. Nor is such a complaint, as it might appear to be, a double-edged sword which cuts equally against the thesis of radicalness in the quantity and quality of differences in concepts and beliefs. For the sensible advocate of such a thesis will *make* the notion of radical qualitative difference clear and decidable in application by giving multiple concrete examples of what does and does not constitute radical qualitative difference (something which, note, lest concerns about a trivializing of the thesis arise, could perfectly well be done without yet looking beyond one's own system of thought). And it seems to me that his thesis is demonstrably true—and consequently the second Davidsonian position demonstrably false—in the sense that there are plausible and attractive ways of accomplishing that which leave the thesis demonstrably true.

ing justification for believing in) radical differences in concepts and beliefs *without* presupposing a positive theory of meaning, understanding, and interpretation, and those which argue for that impossibility *by* presupposing such a theory. Let us consider his arguments of each sort in turn.[19]

Davidson offers four main arguments of the former sort. The first of these, presented in "On the Very Idea of a Conceptual Scheme," undertakes, in effect, to force the believer in radical differences in concepts and beliefs onto the horns of a dilemma via the following reasoning: (i) In order to be justified in identifying a form of behavior as linguistic / expressive of concepts one must be able to interpret/translate its content in(to) one's *own* language.[20] However, (ii) if its content is interpretable/translatable in(to) one's *own* language, then it cannot be different in conceptual scheme from, but must be the same in conceptual scheme as, one's own language.[21] Therefore (iii), the implied dilemma: to the extent that one is justified in identifying a form of behavior as linguistic / expressive of concepts at all, it cannot represent a different conceptual scheme from, but must represent the same conceptual scheme as, one's own; or alternatively, to the extent that one cannot find such conceptual common ground with it, one cannot be justified in judging it to be linguistic / expressive of concepts at all.[22]

---

19. The readings of Davidson's arguments in what follows involve a good deal of reconstruction—which will though, I hope, be reasonably generous. Such reconstruction is unavoidable due to pervasive unclarities and ambiguities in Davidson's writings (reading Davidson on radical interpretation is often a bit like *doing* radical interpretation). I fear that these unclarities and ambiguities are in no small part responsible for the warmth with which his views have been received in some quarters.

20. Contrary to assertions of complete differences between conceptual schemes or complete failures of intertranslatability of languages, "nothing, it may be said, could count as evidence that some form of activity could not be interpreted in our language that was not at the same time evidence that that form of activity was not speech behavior. If this were right, we probably ought to hold that a form of activity that cannot be interpreted as language in our language is not speech behavior" (*Inquiries into Truth and Interpretation*, pp. 185–86).

21. Ibid., pp. 184–85, esp.: "We may identify conceptual schemes with . . . sets of intertranslatable languages." Cf. p. 190: "The failure of intertranslatability is a necessary condition for difference of conceptual schemes." Davidson accordingly finds it absurd that "Whorf, wanting to demonstrate that Hopi incorporates a metaphysics so alien to ours that Hopi and English cannot, as he puts it, 'be calibrated,' uses English to convey the contents of sample Hopi sentences. Kuhn is brilliant at saying what things were like before the revolution using—what else?—our post-revolutionary idiom" (p. 184).

22. This argument has a peculiar status in Davidson's essay. On the one hand, having formulated it near the beginning of the essay, he immediately distances himself from it as insufficient, in need of further support (ibid., pp. 185–86). And by the time it *becomes*

This argument has a superficial appearance of plausibility. But it quickly evaporates, I think, when one recalls a few fairly basic empirical facts and conceptual distinctions to which any close reflection on the practice of "interpretation"/"translation" should alert one. A first point to note is that premise (i) is far from being obviously true.[23] Moreover, the reason which makes it *appear* so is a bad one. Its appearance of obvious truth derives from the cooperation of two tempting assumptions: (a) Having justification for believing in the linguistic/conceptual character of someone's behavior requires being able to understand his language / grasp his concepts.[24] And (b) if his language and concepts are not *already* one's own, then one could achieve that only by mapping them onto language/concepts which one *does* already have.[25] However, assumption (a) is quite doubtful and assumption (b) is pretty clearly false. Assumption (a) would obviously not be true if it meant *able* to understand/grasp *on*

---

sufficient in the essay, it has in effect turned into a mere corollary of the elaborate argument based on a positive theory of meaning, understanding, and interpretation which we will be considering later. On the other hand, he clearly expects to win sympathy for the argument's conclusion in presenting it independently of his theory-based argument near the start of the essay. And it is indeed quite a seductive argument just by itself. So for these reasons it is appropriate for us to consider it here as an independent argument.

23. In fairness to Davidson, while he believes it true, he too wants to deny that it is *obviously* true (ibid., pp. 185–86). However, he does, I think, really find it so, and moreover for very much the same reason as others are likely to. (He would not be the first thinker to suppose that he was seeing deeper than received commonplaces while in truth rather repeating them.) Thus, he suggests and finds fault with the fact that its immediate acceptance amounts to deciding merely by "fiat" what is to count as a language (ibid., p. 186). But that does not, I think, well identify or dispose of the real source of its immediate appeal. And the *real* source of its immediate appeal, which I am about to describe, is a reason which Davidson *shares* with others who are likely to find it obviously true.

24. Davidson seems to take this more or less for granted in "On the Very Idea of a Conceptual Scheme." Consider for instance his discussion of the imaginary case of English, Saturnian, and Plutonian at p. 186.

25. Ibid., p. 184: "Different points of view make sense, but only if there is a common coordinate system on which to plot them" (now reading this ambiguous sentence in one of its two obvious senses, namely, that in which "different points of view make sense" means "different points of view can be understood" rather than "the hypothesis that there are different points of view is intelligible/defensible"). Davidson's constant reference to the task of achieving conceptual understanding in such cases as one of "interpretation" or "translation" implies or at least very strongly suggests the same assumption—for, unlike a more neutral expression like "achieving conceptual understanding," the term "interpretation" at least strongly suggests and the term "translation" outright implies some sort of mapping onto another representational medium (as one might indeed infer from the very etymologies of the Latin *interp*res, "one who mediates *between*," and *trans*lator, "one who carries *across*").

the spot, so to speak. For I am certainly justified in believing that, for example, the Chinese express language/concepts despite being unable to understand/grasp these on the spot. The assumption might have better prospects of being true (and could still serve its function in the argument) if it meant something more like *able* to understand/grasp *if one really works at it.* However, even on this construal it is far from clearly true. Suppose, for example, that a group of Martians were to come to earth performing all sorts of superior technological and organizational feats and chattering to each other all the while in ways which on the face of them appeared to us linguistic/conceptual but which, try as we might, we could not understand. Might we not, nevertheless, be justified in judging their chatterings to be indeed linguistic/conceptual (and in concluding that they were simply beings too intellectually different from and superior to us for us to be able to understand them)?[26] More importantly, assumption (b) is pretty clearly false.[27] For, while the acquisition of new language and new concepts certainly often does occur through such a mapping, it just as certainly often does *not*—a fact of which each of us has provided ample evidence in acquiring his *first* language and concepts as an infant and child.[28]

---

26. It is perhaps worth noting that the later Wittgenstein was much preoccupied with this question, and that he vacillated in his answer to it. Contrast, for example, his discussion at *Philosophical Investigations,* pars. 206–8, which implies that assumption (a) on the construal now in question is *true* with his parallel discussion at *Remarks on the Foundations of Mathematics,* pt. 6, par. 45, which implies rather that it is *false.* I have discussed Wittgenstein's views in this area in my "Wittgenstein's Later Philosophy: The Question of the 'Arbitrariness of Grammar' " (unpub.).

27. In addition to being false, it also exemplifies just the sort of a priori theorizing about language-learning that Davidson himself inveighs against, for example at *Inquiries into Truth and Interpretation,* pp. 3–7.

28. Two further points in some modest elaboration of this point: (α) There are some theorists who would question this counterexample on the ground that we are *born* with language/concepts—perhaps a "language of thought" "hard-wired" into us, for example. Such views seem to me highly implausible and a desperately uphill struggle to try to defend, however. (β) Someone might concede the counterexample, but claim that for all cases *other* than that of learning one's *first* language/concepts, that is, all cases in which a person *already* possesses language/concepts, assumption (b) holds good. Such a view does not seem plausible to me either, and certainly not plausible enough to pass without a substantial argument being provided in its support. Notice, for example, how Evans-Pritchard describes from first-hand experience the manner in which the field anthropologist learns a primitive people's language/concepts: "He goes to live among a primitive people and learns their way of life. He learns to speak their language, to think in their concepts, and to feel in their values. He *then* lives the experience over again critically and interpretatively in the conceptual categories and values of his own culture" (*Social Anthropology,* p. 61; emphasis added).

Second, premise (i) *may* nevertheless be true but for some *other* reason. However, if so, then there would remain a crucial question as to the *construal* on which it was so.[29] For the terms "interpret"/"translate" used there, and in the rest of the argument, could signify a wide range of very different processes—processes which remain crudely conflated and undistinguished in Davidson's argument and in his essay generally.[30] First, it perhaps deserves repetition, since this is a phenomenon which potentially falls under the term "interpretation," that it is quite possible to come to understand another's language/concepts without interpreting or translating them in(to) any of one's own at all—as the example of infants learning their first language/concepts reminds us. Second, though, and of more immediate relevance here, within the general category of interpretation/translation of the semantic content of a foreign language which *is* in(to) a home language there are (to all appearances at least) importantly different species that can and do occur. In particular, it is vital to mark the following distinctions, all completely disregarded in Davidson's presentation of his argument: (a) There is an important distinction between *interpretation* in and *translation* into a home language. Not all successful interpretations of foreign words in one's home language need employ, or even presuppose the possibility of, their translation into it (certainly not their *literal* translation into it *as it is already constituted*).[31] For instance, a classical philologist or anthropologist will often give an interpretation of an alien's word in English which succeeds admirably in conveying its sense—say, by describing the religious institutions, rituals, and general beliefs within which it has its home, the manner of its use, the family of cognate words to which it belongs, etc.—but without even attempting to give a translation of the word into English and without there being any apparent way to do so (certainly not a *literal* translation into English *as it is already constituted*). If this be found somehow paradoxical, it may help to recall that *non*-verbal means, for example acts of

---

29. The bad reason just considered, had it been compelling, would have required premise (i) to be construed in a certain way supportive of the conclusion of Davidson's argument. Once we abandon that bad reason, however, we are no longer constrained to that construal.

30. It is, frankly, baffling to me that someone who wrote a doctoral dissertation on the *Philebus* under W. Jaeger, as Davidson did, can write as though oblivious of these distinctions.

31. By "literal" translation I simply mean translation which expresses the meaning of the original without distortion. The significance of the qualification in parentheses will become clear in a moment.

ostension, can successfully convey the sense of a word without translating it, so that there should really be no great resistance to accepting the possibility that *verbal* means, such as nontranslating interpretations, might do so as well.[32] (b) There are important distinctions between *different types of translation*. In particular, not all translations of foreign words into a home language which in some measure succeed in conveying their sense need be *literal* translations into a home language *as it is already constituted*. Translations may fail of literalness in that they distort the sense of the language translated in one degree or another.[33] Moreover, but less obviously, they may achieve whatever degree of precision they do achieve by modifying the existing usages, and hence the existing meanings, of words in the language into which the translation is done.[34] Accordingly,

---

32. Davidson would probably object to the two scenarios which have just been distinguished within the general sphere of "interpretation"/"translation"—namely, coming to understand without any interpretation/translation in(to) a home language at all, and interpreting in a home language but without translation/translatability into it—that they raise the (indeed) dubious spectre of a *nonlinguistic form of understanding*. For he argues in "On the Very Idea of a Conceptual Scheme" that because of the close relation between language and the attribution of propositional attitudes "it seems unlikely that we can intelligibly attribute attitudes as complex as [those involved in such an assertion as, for example, that perseverance keeps honor bright] to a speaker unless we can translate his words into ours" (p. 186). However, there is a fallacy at work here. For to insist (very plausibly) that in order to attribute propositional attitudes to (or achieve understanding of) another, one's attribution (understanding) must be grounded in a linguistic competence that one has is not to say anything at all about *which* language that competence must be in, and in particular it is not to say that it must be in a language that one possesses prior to the interpretation in question or in one's first language. (A similar fallacy occurs as one strand of an ambiguous argument on p. 185: "Language we will not think of as separable from souls; speaking a language is not a trait a man can lose while retaining the power of thought. So there is no chance that someone can take up a vantage point for comparing conceptual schemes by temporarily shedding his own.") A Greek infant who came to understand a Greek word/concept without interpreting/translating it in(to) a home language, or an English philologist and his readership who came to understand a Greek word/concept but without being able to translate it into English, might therefore very well still possess their understanding in virtue of a linguistic competence—namely, a linguistic competence in (a part of) *Greek*.

33. The great translator of Plato, Schleiermacher, and the great translator of Aeschylus, Fränkel, both argue for the inevitability of such distortions at least when translating ancient texts into a modern language (see Schleiermacher, "On the Different Methods of Translation," in *German Romantic Criticism*, ed. A.L. Willson [New York: Continuum, 1982], pp. 14, 27; Fränkel, *Aeschylus: Agamemnon* 1:xi, the passage quoted in footnote 11 of this chapter).

34. It is one of Schleiermacher's greatest contributions to the theory of translation to have recognized this possibility, and to have argued that this is how good translations, particularly of ancient texts, in fact do and must proceed: the translator must "bend the language of the translation as far as possible toward that of the original in order to commu-

at least three types of translation need to be distinguished: literal translations into a home language as it is already constituted; nonliteral translations; and (partially overlapping with the previous type) translations which achieve whatever degree of success they achieve by modifying the existing usages and hence meanings of words in the home language. An important corollary of this is the following: Davidson states that "the failure of intertranslatability is a necessary condition for difference of conceptual schemes."[35] But when one distinguishes, in the way that I have just done, between the different types of translation which may occur, one can see that this statement (if read at face value anyway) contains at least as much falsehood as truth. It is true only of *literal* translatability into a language *as it is already constituted*. It is *not* true, however, of the other types of translatability just distinguished—nonliteral translatability and translatability into a language through modification of the existing usages and hence meanings of the language.

Now, once one distinguishes in these ways the various possible *sorts* of interpretation and translation of the semantic content of a foreign language in(to) one's home language which may occur, it surely seems plausible to say that premise (i), if true at all, is very likely to be so only on a construal of "interpret/translate" which embraces a good deal more than just *literal translation* into one's own language *as it is already constituted*. However, if premise (i) *is* thus broadly construed, then the expression "interpretable/translatable in(to) one's own language" in premise (ii) would have to be construed in the same broad manner if the dilemma (iii) were to follow. But if it is so, then premise (ii) will be *false*, and the dilemma will for this reason not follow.[36] If, alternatively, one insists on construing "interpretable/translatable in(to) one's own language" in premise (ii) to mean or imply "*translatable* and *literally* so and into one's own language *as it is already constituted*," then, while this will certainly ensure the truth of premise (ii), premise (i) would now have to be con-

---

nicate as far as possible an impression of the system of concepts developed in it" ("On the Different Methods of Translation," p. 25).

35. *Inquiries into Truth and Interpretation*, p. 190; cf. 184.

36. Unless, of course, Davidson just idiosyncratically *stipulatively defines* "different conceptual scheme" to imply something like: not interpretable/translatable *in any of these ways at all*. Certain of his remarks in "On the Very Idea of a Conceptual Scheme" do in fact suggest such a move (e.g., p. 184). However, this would improve the prospects of his argument only at the severe cost of drastically reducing the philosophical interest of its conclusion. For who has wanted to argue that there *are* different conceptual schemes in *that* sense? For example, who among Davidson's named opponents?

strued in the same narrow manner in order for the dilemma (iii) to follow. But if thus narrowly construed, premise (i) loses any real plausibility, so that once again the argument for the dilemma fails of cogency.

In sum, Davidson's first argument proves upon close examination to be really quite sophistical, depending for its air of plausibility on a failure to mark certain rather basic empirical facts and conceptual distinctions relating to "interpretation" and "translation."

Davidson sometimes suggests a simpler variant on this first argument which we might usefully distinguish as a second argument. In this variant, he flatly assumes that radically different conceptual schemes would have to be unintelligible to us. For example, in "The Myth of the Subjective" he identifies his target as "the idea that conceptual schemes and moral systems, or the languages associated with them, can differ massively—*to the extent of being mutually unintelligible*," or "the idea of a conceptual scheme *forever beyond our grasp*."[37] This assumption then permits a variant on the first argument. For if, by this assumption, we could not possibly understand radically different conceptual schemes, then what justification could we possibly have for believing them to exist? In this spirit, Davidson proceeds in "The Myth of the Subjective" to object to the idea in question that "this seems (absurdly) to ask us to take up a stance outside our own ways of thought."[38]

This way of arguing is again illegitimate, however. The argument's key assumption of the unintelligibility to us of radically different conceptual schemes is highly ambiguous, and the main problem with the argument

---

37. In *Relativism: Interpretation and Confrontation*, p. 160; emphasis added. Other Davidsonians are fond of making the same assumption, e.g., M. Root, "Davidson and Social Science," in *Truth and Interpretation: Perspectives on the Philosophy of Donald Davidson*, ed. E. Lepore (Oxford: Blackwell, 1989), pp. 275, 299, 300–301.

38. *Relativism: Interpretation and Confrontation*, p. 160. An argument of the same sort occurs in "On the Very Idea of a Conceptual Scheme," pp. 188–89: Concerning the suggestion by some philosophers "that we could improve our conceptual lot if we were to tune our language to an improved science," for example in relation to the mental, "the . . . question is . . . whether, if such changes were to take place, we could be justified in calling them alterations in the basic conceptual apparatus. The difficulty . . . is easy to appreciate. Suppose that in my office of Minister of Scientific Language I want the new man to stop using words that refer, say, to emotions, feelings, thoughts, and intentions, and to talk instead of the physiological states and happenings that are assumed to be more or less identical with the mental riff and raff. How do I tell whether my advice has been heeded if the new man speaks a new language? For all I know, the shiny new phrases, though stolen from the old language in which they refer to physiological stirrings, may in his mouth play the role of the messy old mental concepts. The key phrase is: for all I know."

can be put in the form of a trilemma corresponding to three possible ways of understanding it: *Either* this assumption is a substantive claim about radically different conceptual schemes—but in that case it begs, in the negative, a crucial question, namely, whether we could not come to understand radically different conceptual schemes by *acquiring quite new concepts* (as clearly happens when infants and children acquire their *first* concepts, for example). *Or* the assumption is trivially true because "unintelligible" here covertly means something like "unintelligible *as long as we have only our pregiven stock of concepts*"—but in that case the assumption does not entail that we could not come to understand radically different conceptual schemes, and the supposed problem about our being unable to arrive at any justification for believing them to exist therefore does not follow. *Or* the assumption just amounts to a stipulative definition of "radically different conceptual schemes"—in which case it may possibly guarantee their dubiousness in the way indicated by the argument (though that is doubtful in light of our Martian example and its like), but if so only at the severe cost of leaving all of the important philosophical questions entirely untouched, namely, those concerning radically different conceptual schemes *not* so stipulatively defined (but instead defined simply in terms of divergences in concepts and beliefs that are radical in quantity and quality).

Before proceeding further, we might tentatively express part of the thrust of the above criticisms of Davidson's first two arguments in the more positive form of what could be called (a little melodramatically) *the principle of the multiform cognitive accessibility of radically different conceptual schemes:* Provided that by "radically different conceptual schemes" we just mean sets of concepts and beliefs which differ from our own in quantitatively and qualitatively radical ways, then, some superficial appearances to the contrary notwithstanding, there is, it would seem, no problem in principle with the idea that we might come to understand radically different conceptual schemes (namely, by acquiring new concepts/language). Nor is there even a problem in principle with the idea that we might successfully interpret them in our own language (provided that the interpretation does not rely on literal translation into our own language as it is already constituted). Nor is there even a problem in principle with the idea that we might manage to translate them into our own language (provided that the translation either falls short of literalness or else achieves it by modifying the existing usages, and hence the existing meanings, of our own language).[39] The only idea that really *is* problematic in principle is the idea that we might *translate* them *literally* into our language *as our language is already constituted*.

Davidson also gives in "On the Very Idea of a Conceptual Scheme" a third argument independent of any positive theory of meaning, understanding, and interpretation: (i) He implies that the thesis of radically different conceptual schemes essentially rests on the assumption of one or another version of a sharp dualism between conceptual *scheme* and experiential or real *content*.[40] (ii) He then offers a number of reasons for thinking that each of the various possible versions of this sharp dualism is (a) intrinsically problematic and (b) in conflict with the thesis of radically different conceptual schemes.[41]

I shall bracket here the question of whether or not Davidson is correct in part (ii) of this argument. Instead, I would like to focus on and offer some criticisms of part (i), the implication that in order to believe in the thesis of radically different conceptual schemes one *must* accept some sharp form of scheme-content dualism. Depending, once again, on how

---

39. Hence when Davidson implies that Whorf's and Kuhn's attempts to interpret/translate alien conceptual schemes in(to) English are in principle absurd—"Whorf, wanting to demonstrate that Hopi incorporates a metaphysics so alien to ours that Hopi and English cannot, as he puts it, 'be calibrated,' uses English to convey the contents of sample Hopi sentences. Kuhn is brilliant at saying what things were like before the revolution using—what else?—our post-revolutionary idiom" ("On the Very Idea of a Conceptual Scheme," p. 184)—he is simply mistaken.

This is not necessarily to defend the specific *manner* of their attempts, of course. However, the prospects for doing so in fact look quite bright. Note, for example, that when Whorf undertakes to convey in English the Hopi metaphysics which he indeed says is "properly describable only in the Hopi language" he carefully stresses that this will be "by means of an *approximation* expressed in our own language, *somewhat inadequately* it is true, yet by availing ourselves of such concepts as we have *worked up* into *relative* consonance with the system underlying the Hopi view of the universe" (B.L. Whorf, *Language, Thought, and Reality* [Cambridge, Mass.: MIT Press, 1982], p. 58; emphasis added).

40. *Inquiries into Truth and Interpretation*, pp. 183, 189–92. Davidson is not entirely clear about the precise *sort* of dualism between these items that he has in mind. Since he presumably must and means to allow that *some* sort of distinction can legitimately be drawn between concepts on the one hand and corresponding experiences or realities on the other (even if only a conceptual distinction, or, in Aristotle's phrase, a distinction "in thought"), but rejects the dualism at issue here as illegitimate, he clearly does have in mind a dualism of a certain sort. To judge from his discussion of examples, what seems to be in question is a conviction in some form of *ontological distinctness* between concepts and their experiential or real content, of a character that would lend sense to the idea of the former "organizing" or "fitting" the latter (ibid., pp. 189–94; cf. 198). This, then, is what I mean here by a *sharp* dualism.

41. Ibid., pp. 189–95.

one resolves a serious ambiguity in Davidson's position, this implication seems to me either trivially true but irrelevant or relevant but quite implausible. One's initial reaction to this implication ought, it seems to me, to be somewhat as follows: "On the face of it, the thesis of radically different conceptual schemes essentially just amounts to a claim that there are people whose languages express meanings largely or entirely different from any expressible by our own language and who hold beliefs largely or entirely different from our own, and that the degree of the differences involved is often quite acute. How could *that* commit one to a sharp dualism of scheme and content?" Some of Davidson's remarks in "On the Very Idea of a Conceptual Scheme" suggest that he would respond to this rhetorical question by insisting that the implication at issue is true simply as a matter of stipulative definition, that is, by insisting that his concern with the thesis of radically different conceptual schemes is strictly a concern with the thesis of radically different conceptual *schemes* in a sense implying their sharp distinctness from *contents*. There is a severe cost to such a maneuver, however, namely, that his argument thereby ceases to address versions of the thesis of radically different conceptual schemes which are *not* thus committed to a sharply dualistic metaphysics of scheme and content, in particular claims simply that there are people whose conceptual resources and beliefs differ massively or entirely from our own and often in quite sharp degree. That seems clearly inconsistent with his intentions; and be that as it may, it would in any case render his argument irrelevant to our present concerns. This is the "trivially true but irrelevant" horn of the dilemma which he faces. As far as I can see, his only alternative response to our rhetorical question is a suggestion that because the believer in radically different conceptual schemes cannot in general regard himself as justified in his identification of other people's behavior as linguistic by his having mapped it onto his own language and concepts, since that would undercut his claim to have found radical conceptual differences in at least some cases, he must instead see himself as so justified by his having mapped it onto *something else* which he already has, such as his uninterpreted experiential "content."[42] But, of

---

42. Ibid., p. 190: "The common relation to experience or the evidence is what is supposed to help us make sense of the claim that it is languages or schemes that are under consideration when translation fails. It is essential to this idea that there be something neutral and common that lies outside all schemes. This common something cannot, of course, be the *subject matter* of contrasting languages, or translation would be possible" (cf. pp. 191–92).

course, to argue in this way is simply to foist on the believer in radically different conceptual schemes a thoroughly *Davidsonian* assumption which he need not, often does not, and in all probability should not share: namely, an assumption that acquiring new linguistic-conceptual understanding, and thereby evidence of the genuine linguisticness of behavior, must occur through a mapping onto something mentalistic that one already has. (Accordingly, while it is certainly true that *some* believers in radically different conceptual schemes have in addition been wedded to one or another sharp form of scheme-content dualism—Davidson mentions several examples—it is by no means true that they *all* have. Herder and Hegel are good counterexamples, for instance—both committed to the existence of a multiplicity of radically different conceptual schemes, but at the same time committed to *rejecting* any sharp form of scheme-content dualism.) This, then, is the "relevant but quite implausible" horn of the dilemma which Davidson faces.

Furthermore, it is even a mistake to imply, as Davidson does, that in all of the cases which he mentions of believers in radically different conceptual schemes who *do* happen to embrace some sharp form of scheme-content dualism, such as Sapir and Whorf for example, this dualism constitutes an essential part of *their* reason for believing in radically different conceptual schemes. Sapir's and Whorf's reason for this belief surely lies in what they have discovered, or believe themselves to have discovered, about the meanings and beliefs of the peoples whom they have studied through interpreting these peoples' languages and linguistic utterances, *not* in their metaphysical views about the nature of meaning and its relation to experience/reality. To attack their belief in radically different conceptual schemes by criticizing, not their interpretative findings, but their sharp scheme-content dualism and its alleged incompatibility with that belief would therefore be rather like attacking Gödel's belief in his famous theorem by criticizing, not his proof of it, but his Platonist metaphysics and some alleged incompatibility between that metaphysics and his belief.[43]

---

43. Another, less generous, but perhaps not less accurate, way of putting some of the above criticisms of Davidson's arguments against the thesis of radically different conceptual schemes in "On the Very Idea of a Conceptual Scheme" would be to say that these arguments conflate a number of really quite distinct questions, including: (a) the question of whether or not we have justification for believing that there are systems of concepts and beliefs which differ from our own in ways that are quantitatively and qualitatively radical (i.e., the question in which we are here interested); (b) a question of whether or not we

Davidson has a fourth and final argument independent of his positive theory of meaning, understanding, and interpretation. This argument is to the effect that it is a necessary condition of a person's talk or thought being *about* anything that he have a massive network of true beliefs relating to the subject matter in question, and a necessary condition of our identifying, as interpreters, what his talk or thought is *about* that we share with him such a massive network of true beliefs relating to the subject matter in question:

> Someone who can interpret an utterance of the English sentence "The gun is loaded" must have many beliefs, and these beliefs must be much like the beliefs someone must have if he entertains the thought that the gun is loaded. The interpreter must, we may suppose, believe that a gun is a weapon, and that it is a more or less enduring physical object. There is probably no definite list of things that must be believed by someone who understands the sentence "The gun is loaded," but it is necessary that there be endless interlocked beliefs . . . We can . . . take it as given that *most* beliefs are correct. The reason for this is that a belief is identified by its location in a pattern of beliefs; it is this pattern that determines the subject matter of the belief, what the belief is about. Before some object in, or aspect of, the world can become part of the subject matter of a belief (true or false) there must be endless true beliefs about the subject matter. False beliefs tend to undermine the identification of the subject matter; to undermine, therefore, the validity of a description of the belief as being about that subject. And so, in turn, false beliefs undermine the claim that a connected belief is false. To take an example, how clear are we that the ancients—some ancients—believed that the earth was flat? *This* earth? Well, this earth of ours is part of the solar system, a system partly identified by the fact that it is a gaggle of large, cool, solid bodies circling around a very large, hot star. If someone believes *none* of this about the earth, is it certain that it is the earth that he is thinking about? An answer is not called for. The point is made if this kind of consideration of related beliefs can shake one's confidence that the ancients believed the earth was flat. It isn't that any one false belief necessarily destroys our ability to identify further beliefs, but that the intelligibility of such identifications must depend on a background of largely unmentioned and unquestioned true beliefs . . . What makes interpretation possible, then, is the fact that we can dismiss a priori

---

have justification for believing that there are systems of concepts and beliefs which could not in any way be interpreted/translated by us in(to) our language; (c) a question of whether or not we have justification for believing that there are systems of concepts and beliefs which are unintelligible by us; and (d) a question of whether or not we have justification for believing that there are systems of concepts and beliefs which relate to experience or reality in a sharply dualistic manner of scheme to content.

the chance of massive error. A theory of interpretation cannot be correct that makes a man assent to very many false sentences: it must generally be the case that a sentence is true when a speaker holds it to be. So far as it goes, it is in favor of a method of interpretation that it counts a sentence true just when the speaker holds it to be true. But of course, the speaker may be wrong; and so may the interpreter. So in the end what must be counted in favor of a method of interpretation is that it puts the interpreter in general agreement with the speaker.[44]

It seems to me that this argument derives its plausibility largely from a rather crude equivocation on different senses in which talk or thought can be said to be *about something*. The central ambiguity here is between talk or thought being (i) about concepts (if the reader will excuse such a barbarism) and (ii) about things really in the world.[45] Davidson's argument systematically disregards and effaces this basic distinction—in particular, through only using examples in which the concepts involved happen also to refer to things really in the world (guns, the earth), and through such tendentious phrases as "Before some object in, or aspect of, the world can become part of the subject matter of a belief . . ." The seductiveness of the argument depends largely on befuddlement by this equivocation, as follows: The argument implies that in order for a person's talk or thought to be meaningful it must be about something, and that in order for others to interpret it they must determine what it is about. But this is half true and half false. It is true, and indeed trivially true, if it means *about something* in sense (i), that is, about concepts. However, it is far from trivially true, and is indeed clearly false, if it means *about something* in sense (ii), that is, about things really in the world. For example, the Greeks had no problem at all in meaning something by, and we can quite well interpret, their talk and thoughts about *Zeus* or *the gods*, even though there happen to be no such things really in the world. Now, *if* meaningfulness *did* require referring to, and interpretation reidentifying, things really in the world, then it would be at least somewhat plausible to infer that meaningfulness required possessing, and interpretation sharing, large amounts of true belief. But when we see that that is not so, that meaningfulness and interpretation can also occur in

---

44. "Thought and Talk," in *Inquiries into Truth and Interpretation*, pp. 158, 168; cf. 153, 156–58, 168–69, 200–201.
45. I intend this distinction in a theoretically unloaded sense which, I take it, just about anyone, including Davidson, would be bound to accept (*not* in a theoretically loaded sense that would fall under his proscription of scheme-content dualism).

cases of the *Zeus* and *the gods* type, then the inference to such a conclusion seems very far from obviously justified. After all, such a domain as Greek myth intuitively strikes us as a labyrinth of *false* beliefs which we *do not* share, rather than as a realm of true beliefs which we do.

It may, however, be possible to reconstruct Davidson's argument in ways which avoid reliance on the above crude fallacy of equivocation. One point which might be urged in this vein is that even in cases of the *Zeus* and *the gods* sort it seems that a person's possession of concepts requires that he have, and interpretation of him requires that the interpreter share, a substantial body of true beliefs, namely, ones of a more or less *analytic* sort—for instance, in the two cases just mentioned, respectively, the beliefs that "Zeus is a god" and that "gods are intelligent, immortal beings" (here in senses devoid of existential implications). Davidson's examples of the sorts of beliefs required in order to entertain thoughts about guns encourage such a reconstruction of the argument: one must "believe that a gun is a weapon, and that it is a more or less enduring physical object." Such a version of the argument seems quite plausible. However, it would not get Davidson to the sort of principle of the necessity of attributing shared beliefs when interpreting, or denial of justification for believing in radically different conceptual schemes, to which he aspires, and that for two reasons: (a) The beliefs here required to be true and shared would be nothing like "*most* beliefs," but rather only a modest subset of beliefs—and moreover one very restricted in subject matter, namely, to the realm of semantic rather than extrasemantic fact. Indeed, even that may be conceding too much, for it is at least somewhat doubtful that they are properly or best described as *beliefs* or as *true* at all. One reason which might be suggested for doubting this, for example, is that they are expressions of semantic rules rather than beliefs about realities. Moreover, (b) they are not such as to lend any support at all to Davidson's thought that interpreters must find the subjects whom they interpret agreeing with what they themselves *already* believe—being instead convictions of a sort that interpreters might very well acquire wholesale in the process of interpretation itself.

A second sort of reconstruction of the argument might be attempted instead (or as well). This would be to insist, in effect, that cases of the *Zeus* and *the gods* type are necessarily exceptions to the rule—that their meaningfulness essentially depends on the meaner's statements and thoughts being in other areas massively *about something* not only in sense (i) but also in sense (ii), and that interpreters, in order to interpret such exceptional cases, must reidentify the things really in the world which the meaner's statements and thoughts are in other areas about in sense (ii), and so likewise think about them in sense (ii). It might be urged in support of such a position, for example, that even if the Greeks' concept of *the gods* itself refers to nothing really in the world, still, there are concepts that have to be drawn on in order to give it its meaning which do so, and whose referents in the world we as interpreters are able to reidentify, such as the concept of *intelligence* [*mētis* or *nous*]. This is once again a plausible idea. In order to assess it and its usefulness to Davidson, however, we need to draw a further distinction between different senses in which talk or thought might be said to be *about something*, again a distinction disregarded and effaced by Davidson's statement of his argument, this time one between two more specific ways of understanding the expression *about something* in general sense (ii), the sense *about things really in the world*. A thought or statement can be about something really in the world, for example about the earth, either merely *de re* (i.e., not necessarily under that semantic description) or also *de dicto* (i.e., under that semantic description).[46] Once this distinction is noted, it becomes evident that any attempt to reconstruct Davidson's argument on the basis of the position indicated above will succumb to the following dilemma: That position seems plausible if it means *about something* (ii) merely in the *de re* sense. For example, it seems plausible to say that if the terms of Greek myth all failed to refer *in any way at all* to objects or kinds really in the world then Greek myth would not be meaningful, and that if Greek myth and we as its interpreters never co-referred to real objects or kinds *in any way at all* then we could not understand Greek myth. However, this will not get Davidson to his conclusion that a meaner's beliefs must be massively true and massively shared by interpreters. For, as McGinn has pointed out, reference that is successful merely de re is quite compatible with massively false beliefs about the objects or kinds referred to.[47] And moreover, agreement between a meaner and his interpreter merely in de re reference is quite compatible with their holding massively different beliefs about the objects or kinds to which they co-

---

46. "Semantic description" is different from "verbal description." A French-speaker can refer de dicto to the earth in the sense of de dicto reference in which we are here interested just as well as an English-speaker can.

47. C. McGinn, "Charity, Interpretation, and Belief," in *Journal of Philosophy* 74 (1977).

refer. If, on the other hand, the position in question is instead understood to mean *about something* (ii) in the sense of *de dicto* reference, then, while it would perhaps indeed in that case imply that meaners' beliefs had to be massively true and massively shared by their interpreters, the plausibility of the position itself is sacrificed. For instance, even considering our relatively favorable example, while it may indeed be plausible to say that the Greeks' concept of *intelligence* [*mētis* or *nous*] which constitutes an essential part of their concept of *the gods* refers de re to intelligence, and that they and we as their interpreters coincide in referring de re to intelligence, it is, as anyone familiar with philological work on the peculiarities of Greek psychological concepts can testify,[48] very far from clear that the Greeks' concept of *intelligence* [*mētis* or *nous*] refers de dicto to intelligence, or that they and we as their intepreters coincide here in reference de dicto (that certainly seems unlikely *before* we have interpreted, but note that even *after*, when we do at least possess their concept, any uses that we might happen to make of their term/concept in order to effect genuine reference might well be implicitly only "inverted commas" uses of one sort or another).[49] Either way, then, the suggested reconstruction of the argument fails.[50]

48. Two studies relevant to this particular example are M. Detienne and J.-P. Vernant, *Cunning Intelligence in Greek Culture and Society* (Chicago: The University of Chicago Press, 1991), and K. von Fritz, "*Nous, Noein,* and their Derivatives in Presocratic Philosophy (Excluding Anaxagoras)," in *The Presocratics,* ed. A.P.D. Mourelatos (Garden City, N.Y.: Anchor Press / Doubleday, 1974), pp. 23–85.

49. Accordingly, it seems to me that the sort of loss of a clear understanding of initially unproblematic-seeming referring terms under closer inspection that Davidson imagines in his "earth" example is exactly what often happens in such cases of interpreting cultural others—until one has done the often difficult philological work required in order to restore a clear, and establish a correct, understanding. (On the other hand, Davidson's own view of his "earth" example is ambiguous and puzzling. Unless he is to admit that it provides a blatant *counterexample* to his whole argument, he must believe either [a] that the ancients did indeed share with us beliefs such as the ones that he lists, i.e., that "this earth of ours is part of the solar system, a system partly identified by the fact that it is a gaggle of large, cool, solid bodies circling around a very large, hot star"—but such a view is surely highly implausible historically, and would moreover subvert the intended function of the example as an illustration that discrepancy in beliefs undermines our ability to understand; or [b] that we are unable to understand the ancients in their talk about the "earth"—but that is surely very implausible as well.)

50. Advocates of an austere version of the causal theory of reference for proper names, natural kind terms, and artefact terms, in the general spirit of Kripke's *Naming and Necessity* (Oxford: Blackwell, 1980), would contend that in the above discussion of Davidson's fourth argument I have accorded too much by way of connotation (as distinct from denotation) to such terms. I am not sympathetic to such a position. However, for present purposes

In sum, Davidson's four a priorist arguments against the thesis of radical differences in concepts and beliefs which operate *independently* of any positive theory of meaning, understanding, and interpretation all prove upon examination to be unconvincing, and indeed quite sophistical. It is, I think, reasonable to suspect that *any* a priori argument against the thesis that is of this type will in the end prove to have these flaws.

* * *

Davidson has, though, in addition, an a priorist argument against the thesis of radical differences in concepts and beliefs which is *based on* a positive theory of meaning, understanding, and interpretation.[51] The general structure of this argument is modus ponendo ponens: p, if p then q, therefore q. More specifically, Davidson (i) advances a positive theory about the nature of meaning, understanding, and interpretation, (ii) argues that if this theory is true then interpretation requires the discovery of massive agreement between interpreter and interpreted in both beliefs and concepts, and (iii) concludes that therefore interpretation does in fact require the discovery of such massive agreement.

To spell out the argument in a little detail: (i) *Meaning*, according to Davidson, is a property which words or sentences possess only in the context of a whole language.[52] Moreover, it is a requirement on any satisfactory account of meaning that it be able to explain a person's capacity to understand the infinite number of potential new sentences belonging to a language in which he is competent in terms of his grasp of a finite number of semantic rules.[53] In accordance with these two principles, the meanings of the words and sentences of a language are given by a finitely axiomatized theory yielding as theorems truth-conditional interpretations for all the infinitely many declarative sentence-types of the language, interpretations of the form " 's' is true-in-this-language iff p" (where " 's' " is a mention of a sentence-type and "p" a use of a sentence-token stating

---

it perhaps suffices to point out that such a position would be if anything even *less* friendly than mine toward Davidson's argument, because such a position just flatly denies that competent use of referring terms requires (any significant amount of) true belief and that shared competence in their use requires (any significant amount of) shared belief.

51. "On the Very Idea of a Conceptual Scheme," pp. 194–97. The exposition below appeals liberally to Davidson's other essays as well in order to flesh out his position.

52. *Inquiries into Truth and Interpretation*, p. 22.

53. Ibid., pp. xiii, 8–9. Cf. "A Nice Derangement of Epitaphs," in *Truth and Interpretation: Perspectives on the Philosophy of Donald Davidson*, p. 437.

the truth-conditions for that sentence-type).⁵⁴ To *understand* a language, or any part thereof, accordingly requires having knowledge of such a theory for the language.⁵⁵ *Interpretation* is in its fundamental nature one essential part of a broader commonsense theory of human physical behavior whose evidential support comes entirely from such behavior (a theory which also essentially includes the attribution of such psychological states as beliefs and desires).⁵⁶ Consequently, the fundamental case of interpretation is that in which an interpreter has as his evidential basis for interpreting a subject only the subject's physical behavior in its environmental context—"radical" interpretation, as Davidson calls it.⁵⁷ Among the behavioral facts ascertainable by observation prior to interpretation are a subject's holdings-true of certain sentence-tokens.⁵⁸ Accordingly, given what is required for understanding a language, the task of radical interpretation is one of reasoning from evidence consisting in an interpreted subject's holdings-true of certain sentence-tokens in certain environmental contexts to a finitely axiomatized theory of the sort described above, that is, one yielding truth-conditional interpretations for the sentence-types to which those tokens belong and for all the infinitely many other sentence-types of the interpreted subject's language.⁵⁹ (ii) Davidson argues that this conception of interpretation entails that interpretation could only be accomplished through "charity," that is, through the interpreter ascribing to the interpreted subject beliefs largely true by the interpreter's own lights⁶⁰—and, at least on later versions of Davidson's account, in addition nonaccidentally true, that is, true and believed by the interpreted subject in virtue of being caused by what makes them

---

54. *Inquiries into Truth and Interpretation*, pp. 22–24, 60–61.
55. Ibid., pp. 161, 174–75.
56. Ibid., pp. 158–63. Putting Davidson's position in this way leaves open the question of *behaviorism*. Davidson's commitment to the position is, I think, motivated by a form of behaviorism—very much in the tradition of Quine and through him Skinner. But it is a position which might well be found attractive independently of behaviorism (even, say, by a dualist or a mind-brain identity theorist).
57. Ibid., pp. 125 ff.
58. Ibid., pp. 133–35, 195–96. The above Davidsonian ideas about interpretation all have origins in W.V.O. Quine, *Word and Object* (Cambridge, Mass.: MIT Press, 1996), pp. 27–30.
59. *Inquiries into Truth and Interpretation*, pp. 24–27, 134–36, 167–68, 195–96.
60. Davidson's account is again indebted to Quine here. For Davidson's own description of the debt, see ibid., p. xvii; and "A Coherence Theory of Truth and Knowledge," in *Truth and Interpretation: Perspectives on the Philosophy of Donald Davidson*, pp. 315–16.

true[61]—and hence a large measure of commonality with himself in concepts also. The main reasons for this are, briefly: (a) Radical interpretation could only be accomplished if the radical interpreter was able to assume that the interpreted subject's beliefs were largely true of his environment as the radical interpreter believes it to be. For, *without* that assumption, the possibility that the interpreted subject's beliefs bore little or no relation to reality as conceived by the radical interpreter would thwart even the first step of radical interpretation, the inference from the evidence of the interpreted subject's having held tokens of "s" true when and only when p to the corresponding truth-conditional interpretation " 's' is true-in-this-language iff p"; *with* that assumption, on the other hand, this first step of radical interpretation, and thence the rest of the task, could in principle be accomplished.[62] (b) Since such commonality in beliefs also requires commonality in concepts, radical interpretation could only be accomplished if the radical interpreter was able to ascribe to the interpreted subject a large measure of commonality with himself in concepts as well.[63] (c) Since radical interpretation is fundamental to all interpretation,[64] this necessity of ascribing to the interpreted subject massive commonality with oneself in beliefs and concepts when undertaking *radical* interpretation is equally a necessity of doing so when undertaking *any* interpretation.[65] (iii) Hence, the conclusion: "Given the underlying methodology of interpretation, we could not be in a position to judge that others had concepts or beliefs radically different from our own."[66]

I want to suggest two lines of criticism of this argument. The first, perhaps predictably, is that premise (i), the claim that meaning, understanding, and interpretation have the character which Davidson ascribes to them, seems highly dubious. This is a large subject which it is not possible or desirable to treat at length here. But, briefly, the following are some of the aspects of this theory of meaning, understanding, and

---

61. Ibid., pp. 316–17; cf. "The Myth of the Subjective," *Relativism: Interpretation and Confrontation*, pp. 164–65. A version of this thought was in fact already part of Quine's original story (see *Word and Object*, p. 30).

62. *Inquiries into Truth and Interpretation*, pp. 27, 62, 134–37, 167–69, 196–97.

63. Ibid., p. 197.

64. Ibid., p. 125: "All understanding of the speech of another involves radical interpretation."

65. Ibid., pp. 195–97 (this step is implicit in Davidson's leap from talking about conditions for radical interpretation to talking about conditions for interpretation generally).

66. Ibid., p. 197.

interpretation which seem to me most problematic. Concerning, first, *meaning* and *understanding:* (a) Davidson's holism about meaning is deeply counterintuitive. He writes that "we can give the meaning of any sentence (or word) only by giving the meaning of every sentence (and word) in the language."[67] But can it really be the case that, for example, the meanings of my sentence "The cat sits on the mat" and my word "cat" necessarily change each time I add a new word/concept to, or lose one from, my language, no matter how remote in subject matter, for instance the word/concept "camcorder"? And can it really be the case that, for example, simply because my mother lacks the word/concept "camcorder" whereas I possess it, she and I, strictly speaking, *always* fail to communicate, even for instance when we are discussing "cats"?[68] (b) There are problems with Davidson's demand that any satisfactory account of meaning must be able to account for a person's capacity to understand the infinite number of potential new sentences of a language in which he is competent in terms of his grasp of a finite number of semantic rules. These problems are, roughly in order of increasing severity: First, it is not clear that our possession of this "infinite" capacity is the distinctive and mysterious phenomenon that Davidson makes it appear to be. For example, the skilled golfer too has an infinite capacity, in that he can make a potential infinity of different good shots in a potential infinity of different situations, and so indeed does the sharp knife, in that it can produce a potential infinity of different cuttings of a potential infinity of different materials and things. Second, it is not beyond dispute that such infinite capacities always require explanation in terms of finite mechanisms, rather than being in certain cases explanatorily fundamental. Third, and more seriously, assuming that such a view *is* correct (or that for some *other* reason the infinite capacity to understand new sentences cannot be explanatorily fundamental), it remains far from clear that an explanation of the infinite capacity to understand new sentences should be in terms of a finite *cognitive* mechanism, in terms of *knowing rules*. Just try, for example, transferring such an expectation to the case of the

---

67. Ibid., p. 22.
68. Davidson's account in "A Nice Derangement of Epitaphs," which ascribes to us largely transient and individual "passing theories" of meaning, suggests that he may well be happy to accept such counterintuitive consequences of his position as these. But that hardly diminishes the damage that they do to its credibility. (Note that *socializing* language would be of no real help to Davidson here—quite analogous, albeit slightly different, counterintuitive consequences would still follow from his holism.)

golfer, let alone to that of the knife. The appropriate explanation might very well instead be at a quite different level of description, for instance in terms of a physical mechanism in the brain. Fourth, and again seriously, one may reasonably doubt that appeal to a knowledge of semantic rules *could* constitute the sort of explanation in terms of a finite mechanism that Davidson is seeking. For it seems plausible to say that knowing semantic rules in essential part *consists in* possessing just the sort of infinite ability that Davidson is concerned to explain.[69] And if that is so, then it is doubtful that there would be a genuine *explanation* here, and certain that there would not be one in terms of a mechanism that was genuinely *finite*. (c) Prima facie at least, Davidson's idea that understanding one's language requires that one know a truth-conditional theory for it of the sort that he describes seems to fall victim to the following paradox. As we noted, knowing such a theory requires that one know for each sentence of the language a truth-conditional interpretation of the form " 's' is true-in-this-language iff p." But surely, knowing *that* would require having a means to represent it linguistically.[70] And this seems to lead to the para-

69. Think here, for instance, of Wittgenstein's and Kripke's well-known mathematical examples illustrating what is implied when we attribute to someone a grasp of a semantic rule. In doing so, part of what we are implicitly ascribing to him is a disposition to make an infinite set of appropriate responses in an infinite set of potential contexts for applying the rule—so that, if those responses prove not in fact to be forthcoming when the contexts in question actually arise, then this is treated as a sufficient ground for withdrawing the attribution.

70. This seems clear. However, Davidson's own position on the matter is deeply equivocal: (α) In "Radical Interpretation" and "Reply to Foster," where he takes up this issue directly, he vacillates. In "Radical Interpretation" (1973) he *affirms* what I have just said to be clear: "Any theory is in some language"; the "theory of interpretation for the object language" is "couched, of course, in familiar words" (*Inquiries into Truth and Interpretation*, pp. 129–30). Three years later in "Reply to Foster" (1976), on the other hand, he evidently *denies* it: "It cannot be said that on this view [i.e., his own], knowledge of a language reduces to knowing how to translate it into another. The interpreter does, indeed, know that his knowledge consists in what is stated by a T-theory, a T-theory that is translational (satisfies convention T). But there is no reason to suppose the interpreter can express his knowledge in any specific linguistic form, much less in any particular language. Perhaps we should insist that a theory is a sentence or a set of sentences of some language. But to know a theory it is neither necessary nor sufficient to know that these sentences are true. Not sufficient since this could be known by someone who had no idea what the sentences meant, and not necessary since it is enough to know the truths the sentences of the theory express, and this does not require knowledge of the language of the theory . . . It is clear, then, that my view does not make the ability to interpret a language depend on being able to translate that language into a familiar tongue" (ibid., pp. 174–75; cf. "The Second Person," in *Midwest Studies in Philosophy* 17 [1992], p. 257: "The speaker does not need to be able to put this knowledge into words"). However, one can see from equivocations in Davidson's formulation of this denial that he himself still feels the implausibility of the view

doxical dilemma that linguistic understanding requires either an infinite regress of metalanguages or logical inconsistency: *Either* the required linguistic representation is not included in the object language, in which case it itself requires a further theory of meaning in order to be understood, which again requires a means of linguistic representation, which is again not included in its object language, and so requires a further theory of meaning in order to be understood, and so on ad infinitum. *Or* at some finite level this regress comes to an end because the required means of linguistic representation is *part of* its object language—but in that case, notoriously, we run afoul of the semantic paradoxes.[71] (d) Prima facie again, there is a problem concerning the sense in which understanding is being said by Davidson to require "knowledge" of a "theory" of meaning of the sort described. If this meant what we usually mean when we speak of "knowledge" of a "theory," in which case it implies a conscious entertainment of and ability to state the theory's propositional contents, then we would have to conclude either that no one had ever had linguistic understanding (very unlikely) or that David-

---

to which it commits him. Note, for example, his desperate resort here to an illicit slide from formulating the question in the first sentence as one of whether his account implies that knowledge of a language *reduces* to knowing how to translate it into *another* language (an implication which it would indeed be implausible to ascribe to his account) to formulating it only at the very end as one of whether his account implies that knowledge of a language *depends on* knowing how to translate it into a *familiar* language (an implication which is much more plausibly ascribed to his account—provided only that the notion of translation is understood broadly enough to include such things as the not-strictly-translating sentences which a Davidsonian theory of meaning uses in order to state the truth-conditions for an object language's indexical-using sentences). Similarly, note the equivocation in his denial that on his account the interpreter must know his theory of meaning "in any specific linguistic form, . . . in any particular language." As the last sentence of the passage shows, what this must really mean is "in any linguistic form, . . . in any language" *simpliciter*. Why, then, does Davidson choose the more cumbersome formulation? Surely, because the denial which he really means is a highly implausible one and if clearly stated would instantly appear so to himself and to others, whereas the more cumbersome formulation buys it a superficial appearance of plausibility by suggesting that all that is being denied is, far more reasonably, that on his account the interpreter's knowledge must take some *specific* linguistic form, be in some *particular* language. (β) Similarly, concerning the more general question at issue here, in "Thought and Talk" (1975) Davidson argues formally that believing requires having linguistic competence (*Inquiries into Truth and Interpretation,* pp. 163–70), but not that one must be able to express linguistically whatever one believes (see esp. ibid., pp. 157–58). However, on the other hand, he avowedly remains strongly tempted to think that at least attributions of subtly definite thoughts require attributions of correspondingly definite language (ibid., pp. 163–64; cf. 184–85).

71. For a lucid sketch of how the paradoxes arise in such a case, see Quine, *Philosophy of Logic* (Englewood Cliffs, N.J.: Prentice Hall, 1970), chap. 3, esp. pp. 44–46.

son's account of what linguistic understanding consists in was false (much more likely). For it seems clear that, while consciousness of and an ability to state certain of the appropriate axioms and theorems might perhaps plausibly be ascribed to people whom we normally judge to understand a language, consciousness of and an ability to state most of the *rest* of a Davidsonian theory of meaning *cannot*. If, on the other hand, Davidson means something *other* in speaking of "knowledge" of a "theory" of meaning than what we usually mean by these words, then it is quite crucial that we be told *what* if we are either to attach any definite sense to his account or to know what would confirm or disconfirm it.[72] (e) Davidson seems not to have perceived problems (c) and (d) when he first developed his account. However, he did perceive them eventually, and developed a common solution (of sorts) to both of them. This solution was that his attribution to a person who understands a language of knowledge of a theory of meaning for that language should not, strictly, be construed as ascribing knowledge, or indeed anything else, to the person himself, but rather as saying that the person is such that in order satisfactorily to describe and explain his linguistic competence *others* need to invoke such a theory as a model of that competence. Thus, already in the early essay "Truth and Meaning" Davidson touches on the crux of problem (c) and hints at a solution of this sort.[73] And subsequently, in the essay "A Nice Derangement of Epitaphs," he perceives the crux of problem (d) as well,[74] and offers as his solution, similarly, but now more explicitly, that he does not wish to say that the person whose linguistic competence is in question,

---

72. Versions of this problem have been properly pressed by some of Davidson's Oxford critics, especially M. Dummett. For a helpful discussion, see M. Platts ed., *Reference, Truth, and Reality* (London: Routledge and Kegan Paul, 1980), editor's introduction.

73. *Inquiries into Truth and Interpretation,* pp. 28–29: "The semantic paradoxes arise when the range of the quantifiers in the object language is too generous in certain ways. But it is not really clear how unfair to Urdu or Wendish it would be to view the range of their quantifiers as insufficient to yield an explicit definition of 'true-in-Urdu' or 'true-in-Wendish.' Or, to put the matter in another, if not more serious way, there may in the nature of the case always be something we grasp in understanding the language of another (the concept of truth) that we cannot communicate to him."

74. "It is possible, of course, that most interpreters could be brought to acknowledge that they know some of the axioms of a theory of truth . . . And perhaps they also know theorems of the form 'An utterance of the sentence "There is life on Mars" is true if and only if there is life on Mars at the time of the utterance.' On the other hand, no one now has explicit knowledge of a fully satisfactory theory for interpreting the speakers of any natural language" (*Truth and Interpretation: Perspectives on the Philosophy of Donald Davidson,* p. 438).

the "interpreter,"[75] himself knows a Davidsonian theory of meaning, nor even that such a theory corresponds to inner workings in the person's brain, but instead that such a theory gives "a model of the interpreter's linguistic competence," "what must be said to give a satisfactory description of the competence of the interpreter," and in particular "to account for the [interpreter's] ability to interpret utterances of novel sentences."[76] This supposed solution to problems (c) and (d) is surely desperate, however. Note, to begin with, that it renders Davidson's original statements of his position at best extraordinarily misleading. For, obviously, the "knowledge" of a "theory" of meaning which he originally ascribed to the linguistically competent is now understood to be really no such thing. That does not at all inhibit Davidson from continuing to talk in the same way, though.[77] Such are the verbal contortions that result when a philosopher prefers to respond to serious objections to his theory by covertly reinterpreting it rather than acknowledging its refutation and going on to develop a new theory. (This is truly "charity" at work—and beginning at home.) Additionally, and more importantly, note that Davidson's talk in this putative solution of a "model" and "satisfactory description" of a person's linguistic competence is also highly misleading. It reassuringly suggests, at first hearing, that what is in question is some sort of approximate description of a person's linguistic mechanism—say, one that idealizes it and imagines its operation under ideal conditions. However, that is not at all what Davidson has in mind. Rather his "model" or "satisfactory description" is such that only a small part of it corresponds to *anything at all* in the person, even approximately—roughly, just a subset of the axioms and theorems. A less misleading term for *this* would surely be something more like "*fictional* description." Most importantly, once this

---

75. Davidson's shift in focus here from language-user to interpreter, while no doubt important in other connections, does not, I think, substantially affect the issues with which we are presently concerned.

76. Ibid., pp. 437-38: "To say that an explicit theory for interpreting a speaker is a model of the interpreter's linguistic competence is not to suggest that the interpreter knows any such theory . . . Claims about what would constitute a satisfactory theory are not . . . claims about the propositional knowledge of an interpreter, nor are they claims about the inner workings of some part of the brain. They are rather claims about what must be said to give a satisfactory description of the competence of the interpreter. *We* cannot describe what an interpreter can do except by appeal to a recursive theory of a certain sort." And describing satisfactorily an interpreter's linguistic competence requires in particular being able "to account for the [interpreter's] ability to interpret utterances of novel sentences."

77. See, for example, ibid., pp. 441–42.

is recognized, it is surely clear that we could not in fact be helped by such a theory to "give a satisfactory description of the competence of the interpreter" or "to account for the [interpreter's] ability to interpret utterances of novel sentences" (in any normal or interesting sense of these words). For how could it help us to "describe" or "account for" a person's linguistic competence to adduce an imagined inferential mechanism which corresponds to nothing (or next to nothing) in the person? Concerning next *interpretation,* in addition to the above problems: (f) Davidson's idea that holdings-true of sentences are purely behavioral matters determinable by observation prior to interpretation seems untenable. And to the extent that he retreats from this idea—as he sometimes clearly does[78]—then his notion that they can constitute evidential *starting-points* for radical interpretation becomes untenable. (g) It seems that Davidson's account cannot possibly be correct as an account of how radical interpretation, in the sense of coming to understand other people's linguistic behavior on the basis of exposure solely to their physical behavior in its environment, *must* occur. This is because infants learning their first language and concepts in fact achieve radical interpretation in that sense, but do not and could not do so in the manner described by Davidson. For how could a *languageless and conceptless* infant believe that a person was holding such and such sentence-tokens true, and that such and such was true of the environment, let alone, on the basis of this sort of information, infer propositions of the form " 's' is true-in-this-language iff p," or, thence, that a finitely axiomatized theory of the sort that Davidson describes was true? Surely—and this is indeed Davidson's *own* view[79]—the possession of such beliefs would require that one *already* have language and concepts. At least in the case of infants learning their first language and concepts, radical interpretation is and must be achieved through far less intellectual processes than Davidson describes.[80]

The above line of criticism of Davidson's theory-based a priorist argument against the thesis of radical differences in concepts and beliefs, while obviously important for assessing this particular argument, has only lim-

---

78. For an example of such a retreat, see *Inquiries into Truth and Interpretation,* pp. 161–63.
79. "Thought and Talk," ibid., pp. 163–70; cf. 185.
80. This objection is subject to some modest elaborations, in answer to potential replies appealing to innate language/concepts or to the possibility of reformulating Davidson's theory of interpretation so that it applies only to cases *other* than that of acquiring one's first language/concepts, similar to ones which I sketched in footnote 28.

ited *general* significance—merely illustrating the fairly obvious, though nonetheless important, point that one way in which a priorist arguments from theories of meaning, understanding, and interpretation to rejections of the thesis are likely to fail is in virtue of immediate weaknesses in the theories. The second line of criticism of Davidson's theory-based a priorist argument against the thesis which I wish to develop has more substantive general significance—illustrating more concretely a strategy of objection which could, I think, be successfully deployed against any such argument.

This second line of criticism is as follows. Unlike premise (i) of Davidson's argument, premise (ii), namely, his claim that *if* meaning, understanding, and interpretation have the character which he ascribes to them, then interpreters must impute to interpreted subjects massive commonality with themselves in both beliefs and concepts, seems quite plausible.[81] But, given so, it surely becomes attractive to turn the tables on Davidson's a priorist argument from his theory of meaning, understanding, and interpretation to the impossibility of discovering radical differences in beliefs and concepts—to accept the discovery of such differences as an established fact and to see in the incompatibility of this fact with Davidson's theory a further argument against the *theory*. In other words, indulging the old adage that one philosopher's modus ponendo ponens is another's

---

81. McGinn has questioned this, suggesting that the radical interpreter might in principle be able to get a Davidsonian theory of meaning off the ground by attributing consistently *false* beliefs to the interpreted subject: "We may equally provide a basis for deriving the meanings of sentences held true by *un*charitably imputing *false* beliefs to our speaker. We simply suppose, with or without good reason, that he has made a mistake and is expressing a false belief with a correspondingly false sentence" ("Charity, Interpretation, and Belief," p. 523). This seems incorrect to me. McGinn's counterpolicy, unlike Davidson's policy, would deny us all but the very slightest guidance from the interpreted subject's environment as to the content of his beliefs—if, knowing his environment, we assumed only that he believed something that was not true of his environment, then we would have advanced hardly at all toward determining the content of his belief, whereas if we assume that he believes something true of his environment, then we have advanced a good deal further, especially if, as on mature versions of Davidson's account, we in addition assume it to be nonaccidentally true, believed in virtue of a causal relation to what makes it true. McGinn's counterpolicy, unlike Davidson's policy, would thereby inevitably leave the content of the interpreted subject's beliefs too indeterminate to enable us to reach even the point of formulating truth-conditional interpretations for the interpreted subject's language. Davidson's policy of course seems preferable to McGinn's counterpolicy for other, more mundane, reasons as well—such as better coherence with the presumable fact of the interpreted subject's survival in his environment. (Note, however, that it would neither help Davidson's argument against the thesis of radical differences in concepts and beliefs nor undermine the *general* point which I am concerned to illustrate above if McGinn were right and I wrong about this whole matter.)

modus tollendo tollens, we convert Davidson's modus ponendo ponens argument (i)–(iii) into the following modus tollendo tollens argument casting further doubt on (i): (a) Interpretation does *not* generally require, because it in many cases does not permit, the discovery of massive agreement between interpreter and interpreted in beliefs and concepts. For, as the examples of Fränkel and Evans-Pritchard illustrate, those who have the greatest expertise and experience in actually interpreting historically and culturally remote peoples in relevant interpretative disciplines such as classical philology and anthropology firmly reject any claim of massive coincidence in beliefs and concepts between such peoples and themselves. And I would argue—though it would go far beyond the scope of the present discussion to try to show—that a careful retreading of the linguistic and textual evidence which leads them to this verdict would strongly support it. (b) If Davidson's theory of meaning, understanding, and interpretation were true, then interpretation *would* generally require the discovery of such massive agreement. (c) Therefore, Davidson's theory of meaning, understanding, and interpretation is not true.

There may be a temptation to reply to this line of criticism that the conflict to which it appeals between theories of meaning, understanding, and interpretation like Davidson's and the positions taken by such disciplines as classical philology and anthropology is not sufficiently deep to cause a serious problem for the former. The thought would be that it is only, so to speak, a conflict with the idle surface of these disciplines rather than with their busy depths, that is, a conflict with their more or less extracurricular and dispensable metacharacterizations of what they find in the course of their work rather than with that work itself—which is by contrast either quite neutral in the matter or even actually supportive of the theories in question.[82] Such a reply would be seriously mistaken, however; the conflict goes all the way down.

A first point to note in this connection is that there is a very intimate

---

82. I have encountered versions of the former idea of *neutrality* in discussions with several people. Davidson himself rather espouses the latter idea that the serious work of the disciplines in question actually *supports* a theory like his own; he recognizes that this work can conflict with a stance on the general issue of radical differences in concepts and beliefs, but sees it as conflicting, not with the stance implied by his own theory, but rather with its opposite. Consider, for example, his implication ("On the Very Idea of a Conceptual Scheme," p. 184) that Kuhn's sound interpretative/translational practice is inconsistent with his judgment that he is dealing with radically different conceptual schemes (an implication which we earlier saw good reason to reject).

relation indeed between these disciplines' thesis of radical differences in concepts and beliefs and their most fundamental work of all, namely, their work of making determinations, including comparative determinations, of the meanings and beliefs expressed by languages and texts. For their thesis of radical differences in concepts and beliefs is little more than a general summing up of what they have found in this fundamental work in particular cases. Hence to challenge their thesis of radical differences in concepts and beliefs is equally to challenge the particular findings which constitute their most fundamental work.

A second point to note is that the conflict also extends to these disciplines' work of interpreting and translating historically and culturally remote languages and texts in(to) their own home language. One way to put this point is to say that if a Davidsonian were actually to undertake the interpretation and translation of such languages and texts in(to) English in a manner which remained strictly consistent with his theory of meaning, understanding, and interpretation—that is, presupposing the necessity of finding, and therefore proceeding to insist on identifying, massive coincidence between those texts and himself in concepts and beliefs—then his interpretations and translations would be overall *bad* ones judged by the normal standards of the competent interpretative and translational disciplines. Or if, alternatively, they were overall *good* ones, then one could show that he had interpreted and translated in a manner that was inconsistent with the methodology required by his theory.[83] Thus, concerning to begin with *interpretation,* whereas the classical philologist or anthropologist typically finds himself unable to give more than very *approximate* translations of an ancient author's or native's words and sentences into existing English, and so regards the provision of lengthy nontranslating interpretations as essential in order to convey their meanings accurately to his readership, the consistent Davidsonian's principle of "charity" would require that he typically identify the concepts expressed by the ancient author or native with concepts of his own, and so treat the words and sentences in question as *literally* translatable into existing English (e.g., as literally translated by the translation which the

---

83. Davidson nowhere even considers the possibility that a conscientious commitment to his theory might have (detrimental) revisionist consequences for the practice of interpretation and translation in(to) one's home language. This is no doubt because he is convinced that interpretation and translation *necessarily* conform to the methodology prescribed by his theory. Once one sees the dubiousness of this alleged necessity, however, one can perceive the possibility in question.

philologist or anthropologist thinks merely approximate), therefore jettisoning the philologist's or anthropologist's lengthy interpretations as, strictly, superfluous for the purpose of conveying the ancient author's or native's meanings.[84] Again, whereas the classical philologist or anthropologist imputes to the subjects whom he interprets beliefs that are massively different from ours, the consistent Davidsonian would be compelled by his principle of "charity" to impute to them instead beliefs that are massively identical to ours. Less obviously perhaps, even *translation* would suffer in the hands of the consistent Davidsonian.[85] Thus, whereas the good translator of ancient texts will, following Schleiermacher, recognize that existing English typically fails to afford exact expression of the concepts of an ancient text, and therefore systematically modify existing English usage for the course of his translation, in order thereby to approximate more closely the expression of, and also flag by his strikingly unusual usage the peculiarity of, those concepts, the consistent Davidsonian would be motivated by his principle of "charity" to believe that existing English typically *already* expresses those concepts, so that such systematic modifications are unnecessary, and moreover to find such deviations from standard English usage unacceptable in the *absence* of appeal to such a strategy of modification, because in that case evidently expressive of bizarrely false beliefs.[86] Such is the conflict between a theory of

---

84. The consistent Davidsonian might in principle try to avoid this last consequence by offering the lengthy interpretations in question *as* his translations, of course. However, such an option would generally be too obviously absurd for him to choose it. Just try, for example, reading one of Fränkel's several-page philological analyses of a word in Aeschylus as a *translation* of the word!

85. I assume here that the first (though not of course only) duty of a translation is to *convey the meaning* of the text translated. This principle may seem self-evident, but is in fact surprisingly often disregarded or contradicted. For example, much of the bitter dispute in the last century between Newman and Arnold on the proper way to translate Homer comes down to a disagreement on just this point—Newman strictly representing the principle in question, whereas Arnold (and presumably with him the mass of commentators who have seen him as the outright victor in this dispute), while critical of some excesses in its disregard by predecessors such as Chapman, is often ready and eager to sacrifice communication of the meaning of the original text for more aesthetic advantages (e.g., when translating Homer's epithets).

86. Consider, for example, the epic Greek word *chlōros,* a word which the epic poets sometimes apply to objects which we would classify as green, such as green wood or healthy foliage, and at other times to objects which we would classify as yellow, such as honey. A good translator, working in the spirit of Schleiermacher, will recognize that existing English does not afford an exact expression of this concept, and that the best way to convey it in

meaning, understanding, and interpretation like Davidson's and the sound interpretative and translational practice of disciplines like classical philology and anthropology.[87]

The existence and seriousness of this sort of problem for Davidson's theory of meaning, understanding, and interpretation have been masked in large part by the fact that, having developed the theory, he makes no attempt whatever to go on and actually interpret or translate historically

---

English is therefore to modify existing English usage in a systematic way for the course of the translation in order thereby both to mimic Greek usage and hence meaning and to alert the reader of the translation by means of the odd usage to the fact that he is dealing with something conceptually unfamiliar. For instance, the translator might decide to use the single word "green" in all contexts, even those where *chlōros* is applied to objects which we would normally classify not as green but as yellow. (The success of this approach depends, of course, on certain favorable contingencies, such as that the word in question occurs a fair number of times in a reasonable variety of contexts within the text[s] translated—as indeed Schleiermacher himself implies.) A Davidsonian translator, by contrast, will be strongly motivated by his principle of "charity" to assume that the various occurrences of the word *chlōros* are conceptually identical to something expressible by existing English. He will therefore see no need for the sort of modification of existing English usage just described. Nor will he be able to find the suggested translations acceptable construed *other* than as such modifications, for if otherwise construed they will seem to him to attribute to the epic poet bizarrely false beliefs, such as that honey is green. Instead, a Davidsonian translator will be strongly motivated to opt for one or another alternative approach to translation—all of which, however, are markedly inferior. For example, he might conclude that in some contexts the best candidate for conceptual equivalence was the concept green and in others the concept yellow, and so translate the word *chlōros* as though it were homonymous, switching back and forth from "green" to "yellow" according to the context. This procedure, while no doubt more comfortable than Schleiermacher's for readers of the English translation, buys this slight virtue of comfort only at the price of the far more serious vice of distorting the sense to be conveyed to them by giving them the impression that the epic poet has two familiar concepts whereas he in fact has a single unfamiliar one. Alternatively, the Davidsonian translator might try giving the translation "green or yellow" in all contexts. But, besides obvious stylistic infelicity, this has the more serious vices that it both again imputes to the epic poet possession of the two familiar concepts of green and yellow whereas he in fact has only the single unfamiliar concept of *chlōros* and also imputes to him a disjunctive concept whereas he in fact has a nondisjunctive one. Further approaches to the translation of *chlōros* consistent with Davidsonian expectations are imaginable as well, but they will in each case face serious objections similar to these.

87. It bears repeating that this conflict could only be expected to show up *overall*, that is, over the whole course of a reasonably extensive amount of interpretation and translation by the Davidsonian. No *individual* case could prove decisive—if only because, as was mentioned earlier, Davidson is prepared to allow that there is a *modicum* of variation in concepts and beliefs, so that he could always retain sound interpretative and translational practice in any *individual* case consistently with his theory by assigning the case to this modest class of exceptions.

or culturally remote texts in(to) his own language in a manner consistent with the theory.[88] It may therefore be instructive to compare his position briefly with that of a philosopher whose theory of meaning, understanding, and interpretation is in relevant respects quite similar (and certainly not less plausible) but who by contrast *does* proceed actually to interpret texts of the sort in question in a manner consistent with his theory—namely, Aristotle.[89]

According to Aristotle's theory of *meaning* and *understanding*: (i) Descriptive concepts are in their very nature forms acquired by the mind through sense-perception from extra-semantic reality (or at least compounded from forms so acquired).[90] Consequently, a mind can only possess descriptive concepts to the extent that there exist, and it has perceived, instances of them in reality (or at least of their component concepts). (ii) Moreover, possession of a descriptive concept requires, not only a cognitive relation to a real kind through sense-perception, but also a substantial body of true beliefs about that real kind. For, according to Aristotle, it requires signification of the kind's definable real essence, and that can only be accomplished in one of two ways: *either* one signifies the real essence by knowing its definition, in which case one possesses the substantial body of true beliefs constitutive of an Aristotelian definition, *or* one does not actually know the definition, but instead signifies the real essence by associating with a term beliefs which, though falling short of a definition, are nevertheless true of the real essence.[91] Either

---

88. This is no doubt mainly, once again, because of his conviction that the interpretative methodology prescribed by the theory is *necessary*. If one is convinced of the *necessity* of employing a certain methodology which one advocates, one is unlikely to see any very pressing need to show that it works well in practice.

89. References to Aristotle's works in what follows are according to the Aristotle volumes of the Loeb Classical Library (line numberings in particular are intended to reflect these volumes). Translations are my own.

90. *De Anima*, 431b30–432a8; *Posterior Analytics*, 99b35–100b4. The qualification in parentheses is required due to Aristotle's concession of descriptive meaning to such a term as "goatstag" (ibid., 92b7–8). There are no goatstags in reality. However, there *are* both goats and stags, and the mind can therefore abstract the forms of goathood and staghood from these through sense-perception, and then compound them to produce the concept of a goatstag. For a helpful discussion of this and similar cases, see D. Charles, "Aristotle on Names and Their Signification," in *Ancient Thought 3*, ed. S. Everson (Cambridge: Cambridge University Press, 1994), pp. 49–52.

91. For a helpful discussion of the latter sort of case, see T. Irwin, "Aristotle's Concept of Signification," in *Language and Logos*, eds. M. Nussbaum and M. Schofield (Cambridge: Cambridge University Press, 1982), pp. 248–50.

way, one must be in possession of a substantial body of true beliefs. (iii) Furthermore, (i) and (ii) together in effect imply that the possession of descriptive concepts requires one's beliefs to be *largely* true of reality. For (i) implies that all of one's beliefs about which general kinds exist must be true (or at least rest on beliefs in the existence of component kinds which are true) and that one's remaining beliefs will at least not prove false because the descriptive concepts which they employ lack any instances in reality (even in respect of component concepts); while in addition (ii) states that the possession of descriptive concepts requires that one have substantial bodies of true beliefs about relevant real kinds. This, I take it, is a major reason why Aristotle writes in the *Metaphysics* concerning the study of the truth that "each person states something about nature" and "matters seem to stand in accordance with our proverb, 'Who could miss a door?' "[92] This whole theory of meaning and understanding implies a view of *interpretation* that is quite similar to Davidson's. In particular, it similarly implies that an interpreter must in large measure assimilate the concepts and beliefs of anyone whom he interprets with his own. Thus, concerning concepts: Part (i) of the theory implies that an interpreter could only even possess descriptive concepts in terms of which to interpret another person to the extent that he had himself already acquired them by discovering instances of them in reality (or at least of their component concepts), and could only be justified in ascribing them to the person to the extent that he had reason to believe that the person had discovered instances of them in reality also (or at least of their component concepts). Consequently, the theory implies a view of the interpreter's situation with respect to concepts that is very much like Davidson's view of the interpreter's situation with respect to beliefs: the interpreter must in large measure find anyone whom he interprets to possess descriptive concepts which he himself already uses, which moreover have application to reality, and which in addition are used by the person

---

92. *Metaphysics*, 993a30–b5; cf. *Nicomachean Ethics*, 1098b27–30. Aristotle's method of *dialectic*, that is, roughly, his method of seeking truth, and in particular true definitional first principles, by collecting and as far as possible reconciling people's actual beliefs, exploits this conclusion and the line of thought that has just been shown to support it (see *Nicomachean Ethics*, 1098b27–30, 1145b2–8; *Topics*, 100a30–b24, 101a37–b5).

Aristotle certainly also has *other* reasons for thinking people's beliefs largely true of reality in addition to those just explained—for example, his faith in the general reliability of the senses.

in question in virtue of being caused in him by real instances.[93] Note especially that Aristotle's theory, like Davidson's, implies that an interpreter must find anyone whom he interprets to possess concepts which are largely identical to ones already used by himself.[94] Moreover, concerning beliefs: Part (iii) of Aristotle's theory implies, like Davidson's theory, that an interpreter must find anyone whom he interprets to hold beliefs that are largely true of reality and therefore largely identical to his own.[95] Finally, note that this whole Aristotelian theory of meaning, understanding, and interpretation, like Davidson's, is established in a manner that is entirely a priorist relative to the practice and results of interpreting historically and culturally remote texts.[96]

Now, unlike Davidson, Aristotle goes on actually to interpret historically distant texts in a manner that remains consistent with his theory of meaning, understanding, and interpretation—that is, presupposing the necessity of finding, and therefore insisting on identifying, massive agreement between those texts and himself in both concepts and beliefs. And the point to note is that precisely because he *does* thus remain faithful

---

93. One could say that in a sense Aristotle and Davidson are committed to the same model of interpretation, only Aristotle within the context of a more word-/concept-based and Davidson within the context of a more sentence-/belief-based theory of meaning.

94. Indeed, given a few natural and plausible additional assumptions, such as that all people's environments and sensory capacities are basically similar, part (i) of Aristotle's theory implies the still stronger view that there must be a large amount of sameness in the descriptive concepts possessed by all people. That this is in fact Aristotle's position can be seen from the following remark at *De Interpretatione*, 16a6–9: "Just as all men do not share the same writing, so they do not share the same speech, but *the experiences of the soul which these directly signify are the same for all, as are already the things of which these experiences are likenesses*" (emphasis added, of course).

95. Note, however, that for Aristotle the process of assimilating the beliefs of people whom one interprets with one's own will not be simply a matter of fixing one's own beliefs independently of theirs and then assimilating theirs as much as possible to one's own, as it basically is for Davidson. Rather, for Aristotle the process of assimilation will involve at least a measure of accommodation in the other direction as well. For his method of *dialectic* implies a measure of moving toward sameness of belief with people whom one interprets through modifying one's own beliefs in order to bring one's own beliefs into line with theirs (a process which clearly has limits, though, since, for one thing, the beliefs of the different people whom one interprets are often mutually inconsistent). This significant difference in positions entails that if Aristotle's interpretative methodology forces bad interpretations, then those forced by Davidson's methodology can reasonably be expected to be even worse.

96. There might be a temptation to respond that this point is true only in a trivial sense, namely, for want of the very existence of such a practice in Aristotle's day. However, this response would be mistaken. History of ideas of relevant sorts was already in existence in Aristotle's time, and indeed Aristotle was himself a historian of ideas after a fashion (as we shall observe shortly). Moreover, anthropological investigations of alien cultures were already part of the intellectual landscape as well, most notably in the works of Herodotus.

to his theory he gives interpretations of the texts in question which are generally *bad* ones—interpretations which, precisely because they insist on representing the concepts and beliefs expressed by the texts as identical with his own, systematically misinterpret the texts. For example, as Jaeger points out,[97] according to the interpretation which Aristotle gives in the *Metaphysics* of the ancient popular religion of the Greeks that religion originally and fundamentally expressed his own conception that the heavenly bodies were gods enclosing all of nature, and only later and superficially added the further assertion at odds with his own beliefs that they had human or animal form.[98] But of course that is an outrageous interpretative claim. Again, as Cherniss has shown in quite convincing detail, Aristotle's interpretations of the presocratic philosophers in the *Metaphysics* and elsewhere systematically misrepresent their views by assimilating their concepts and beliefs to his own.[99] Again, Aristotle's interpretation of Socrates' philosophy involves, I would argue, a similar self-assimilating misinterpretation of Socrates' views.[100] Again, as we noted in passing in chapter 2, Aristotle falsely ascribes to the Greek tragedians an understanding of their tragedies as *fiction*, and thereby misinterprets them on a grand scale—once again, I would suggest, through striving to assimilate their belief system to his own.[101] Indeed, Aristotle himself often

---

97. W. Jaeger, *Early Christianity and Greek Paideia* (Cambridge, Mass.: Harvard University Press, 1961), p. 47.

98. *Metaphysics,* 1074a39–b14; this further assertion was merely "added subsequently in a mythical fashion with a view to the persuasion of the masses and to usefulness for the laws and expediency." Cf. *De Caelo,* 270a24–b24.

99. H. Cherniss, *Aristotle's Criticism of Presocratic Philosophy* (Baltimore: The Johns Hopkins Press, 1935), and "The Characteristics and Effects of Presocratic Philosophy," *Journal of the History of Ideas* 12 (1951).

100. In the *Metaphysics* Aristotle says that Socrates was the first thinker to seek a general definition of the moral virtues and that "it was natural that he should be seeking 'what a thing is,' for he was seeking to syllogize and 'what a thing is' is the starting-point of syllogisms" (1078b18–25). As I argue in "The Socratic Demand for Definitions" (unpub.), this account involves a self-assimilating misinterpretation of the historical Socrates' philosophical standpoint (which was far more skeptical in character than Aristotle suggests). It does so especially in implying that Socrates shared an Aristotelian conception of science and that he really aspired to achieve ethical knowledge (so that he was demanding ethical definitions in the hope of attaining demonstrative knowledge in ethics by syllogizing from these definitions as first principles, as happens in an Aristotelian science).

101. The tragedians' representations, for example concerning the gods, were of course profoundly at odds with Aristotle's own conception of the world. His large-scale misinterpretation of their representations as deliberate fiction was, I suggest, motivated mainly—as in the case of his misreadings of traditional religion and earlier philosophy—by the aim of maximally assimilating his predecessors' beliefs to his own.

seems to notice the strains involved in forcing such readings as these upon the reluctant texts, invoking in an attempt to explain away the evident discrepancies the hypothesis that his predecessors shared his own views only *unclearly* or *confusedly*.[102] Similarly, when Aristotle finds himself quite *unable* to assimilate a text's concepts and beliefs to his own, his characteristic response is to deny that it is meaningful at all, even though sounder interpretation would accord it a perfectly clear meaning. Examples of this are his implication that the Eleatics' denial of the reality of change and motion, and even the arguments of those who take this denial seriously enough to undertake a proof of their reality, are "necessarily about mere words" and "mean nothing," and his dismissal of the Platonic theory of self-subsistent forms as, likewise, meaningless sound.[103] The point deserves emphasis: the inadequacies of all these interpretations do not result from mere interpretative naivety or carelessness on Aristotle's part,[104] but rather from his having interpreted precisely as his a priorist theory of meaning, understanding, and interpretation implies that he must.[105] The fact that the theory forces such failures of interpretation shows, I suggest, that there is something deeply wrong with it.[106] Likewise, the fact that Davidson's similar theory would force similar failures of interpretation shows that there is something deeply wrong with *it*.[107]

* * *

102. For example, in the *Metaphysics* he says that "on all subjects the earliest philosophy resembles one who speaks inarticulately" (993a15–16) and that his predecessors grasped two of his own concepts of cause but "vaguely, however, and not at all clearly," and in such a way that they "do not seem to know what they say" (985a11–17).

103. *Physics*, 193a3–10; *Posterior Analytics*, 83a34–35.

104. A contrast-case here would be Herodotus in whom rather similar failures of interpretation *do* result from mere interpretative naivety.

105. This, surely, is the proper answer to Guthrie's objection to Cherniss that it is incredible to suppose that a philosopher as "clear-headed and methodical, sane and cautious" as Aristotle is in *other* areas should, when he comes to the assessment of his predecessors' views be "so blinded by the problems and presuppositions of his own thought that he loses all common sense and even any idea of the proper way to handle evidence" (W.K.C. Guthrie, "Aristotle as a Historian of Philosophy: Some Preliminaries," *Journal of Hellenic Studies*, 1957, p. 36).

106. I do not mean to suggest that this is the only, or even the most serious, problem faced by Aristotle's theory. Like Davidson's, it no doubt faces other, more direct, problems as well.

107. It seems to me that philosophers' theories of meaning, understanding, and interpretation quite often run into difficulties of this sort—that is, forcing bad interpretations/translations of historically/culturally remote texts. For example, an austere version of the causal theory of reference, in the manner of Kripke (but not Putnam), seems likely to succumb to such difficulties.

A final point which I wish to urge against a priorist attacks such as Davidson's on the thesis of radical differences in concepts and beliefs—whether the attacks be of the nontheoretical or of the theoretical sort—is that they err, not only in that their specific arguments fail, but also in their very a priorism.

Such attacks are, after all, attempts to settle what should and should not be said about the meanings and beliefs expressed by a broad range of historically and culturally distant languages and texts, in contradiction of disciplines such as classical philology and anthropology whose very raison d'être is the interpretation of those languages and texts, and without paying the slightest heed to the actual linguistic and textual evidence (or for that matter, the theoretical and methodological considerations) which motivate the contrary views taken by these disciplines. That ought surely to strike one as quite extraordinary intellectual hubris.

This hubris is, moreover, all the more anomalous because completely at odds with the dominant—and, in my view, much more enlightened—approach found in other areas of contemporary philosophy, such as the philosophy of science. There was, to be sure, a time, indeed not so very long ago, when philosophers of science, especially those wedded to an "ordinary language" approach to the subject, similarly imagined that they could, for example, establish conclusions about space and time which carried serious revisionary implications for physics, the discipline whose very raison d'être lies in the investigation of such phenomena, and without paying any close heed to the empirical evidence (or for that matter, the theoretical and methodological considerations) operative in physics and motivating its contrary positions. However, this sort of approach to the philosophy of science is generally considered disreputable these days.

Moreover, the rejection of such approaches seems to be clearly right. For what could possibly justify them? Brute commonsense intuitions concerning the phenomena in question? But the unreliability of *those* is surely clear. The sovereignty of principles of formal logic? But it really seems quite unlikely that philosophers will prove to have a significantly better grasp of, or more scrupulous respect for, *those* than the community of physicists or the community of philologists and anthropologists. Conceptual truths? This is apparently what Davidson has in mind. Thus he writes at one point in "The Myth of the Subjective" that "the meaninglessness of the idea of a conceptual scheme forever beyond our grasp is due not to our inability to understand such a scheme or to our other human limitations; *it is due simply to what we mean by a system of concepts.*¹⁰⁸ However, the notion that conceptual truths can provide a royal road to weighty insights apart from relevant empirical considerations is outmoded and (more important) philosophically dubious.

In many contemporary philosophers, of course, skepticism about this notion derives from a denial in the spirit of Quine of the very existence of an analytic/synthetic distinction.¹⁰⁹—Indeed, Davidson's explicit reflections on the analytic/synthetic distinction show that he shares Quine's skepticism about its existence.¹¹⁰ So there at least seems to be an internal inconsistency in his implicit appeal to the distinction in the one case of theorizing about meaning.¹¹¹—The denial of the very existence of an analytic/synthetic distinction in fact seems quite implausible to me.¹¹² However, disbelief in this distinction is by no means the only reason that one might have for skepticism about the notion that conceptual truths can provide a royal road to important insights apart from relevant empirical considerations. For one might very well acknowledge the validity of the distinction and yet still remain skeptical about this notion for the quite different, and in my view much better, reason that in any domain of inquiry the concepts employed and their sets of constitutive analytic principles will always face competition from multiple *alternative* concepts and sets of constitutive analytic principles which could be employed in their stead, so that there will always be questions about which of various alternative concepts we should employ and which of various alternative sets of analytic principles we should allow really to matter to us, *questions which are only sensibly decidable in the light of relevant empirical considerations.*

If this is correct, then the philosopher of science concerned with space

---

108. *Relativism: Interpretation and Confrontation*, p. 160; emphasis added.
109. The classic statement of Quine's position is "Two Dogmas of Empiricism," in Quine, *From a Logical Point of View* (Cambridge, Mass.: Harvard University Press, 1953).
110. *Inquiries into Truth and Interpretation*, pp. 187–89. Cf. *Truth and Interpretation: Perspectives on the Philosophy of Donald Davidson*, pp. 312–13: on the matter of the analytic/synthetic distinction Davidson is, he says, "Quine's faithful student."
111. It is almost as though Davidson thinks that the general ban on truths exclusively in virtue of meaning is somehow magically suspended where the subject matter in question is *meaning itself.*
112. I am unconvinced by both Quine's arguments and his conclusion—in part for reasons of the sort given by H.P. Grice and P.F. Strawson in their classic response, "In Defense of a Dogma," *Philosophical Review* 65 (1956). The matter is complicated, though, and I do not propose to go into it here.

and time cannot reasonably hope to settle substantive questions about space and time on purely conceptual grounds in blissful disregard of the physicists' empirical evidence about space and time, because this empirical evidence is an important part of the empirical evidence with a view to which the concepts of space and time must be fixed. Similarly, the philosopher concerned with the phenomenon of meaning cannot reasonably hope to settle substantive questions about meaning on purely conceptual grounds in blissful disregard of the philologists' and anthropologists' empirical evidence concerning languages and texts across different historical periods and cultures, because this empirical evidence is an important part of the empirical evidence in the light of which the concept of meaning must be fixed. For what more relevant source of empirical pressures on the concept of meaning than this could one imagine?

To put the point in another way: Even if the philosopher were to succeed in determining that such and such a principle dear to his heart was a conceptual truth, still that would not in itself settle anything of much philosophical importance. An early Greek would have been on pretty firm ground had he claimed that it was a conceptual truth that the sun was intelligent—that is, that it was part of the very concept of Helios that he was a god, and part of the very concept of gods that they were intelligent. But of course that does not in any important sense settle in the affirmative the question of whether or not the sun is intelligent. For, given good empirical evidence for denying that the object in question is intelligent, it instead merely becomes a good reason for avoiding or revising the early Greek's concept of the sun. Similarly, even if it were to turn out that our pregiven concept of meaning made it an analytic truth that there could be no such thing as radical differences in concepts and beliefs—and we have seen no reason to think that it in fact does, although, especially given the parochial context in which the concept of meaning must presumably have first arisen, that no doubt *could* have turned out to be the case—still that would not in any important sense settle the philosophical question of whether or not there are radical differences in concepts and beliefs. For, given good empirical evidence for saying that there are, it would instead merely become a good reason to revise our pregiven concept of meaning.[113]

---

113. Quine has argued (*Word and Object*, pp. 57–60; *Philosophy of Logic*, chap. 7), and Davidson agrees with his case (*Inquiries into Truth and Interpretation*, p. 136; "A Coherence Theory of Truth and Knowledge," p. 316), that we must at least find other

In sum, Davidson's a priorist arguments against the thesis of radical differences in concepts and beliefs all fail, it seems to me. Those *independent of* his positive theory of meaning, understanding, and interpretation

people believing the *logical laws* of the sentential calculus, such as the law of noncontradiction. Do these not indeed constitute exceptions to the general anti-a priorist moral for which I have just been arguing? This is a complicated question which really requires separate treatment. However, a few provisional observations may be in order which suggest that the answer is no. Quine's main argument is that one's understanding of the truth functions of the sentential calculus, such as negation, conjunction, and disjunction, is constituted by patterns of assent/dissent to sentences of a sort that would be subverted by any failure to accept / attempt to deny a law of the sentential calculus, so that this could not in fact constitute a disagreement about the law in question, but only a failure to understand, or an assignment of different meanings to, the truth functions. Two points about this: First, while the general idea that certain patterns of assent/dissent are essential to an understanding of the truth functions is very plausible, it seems far more questionable whether the patterns in question include as much as Quine's argument implies and whether, as it also implies, they must take the form of sincere conviction (rather than merely competent performance upon demand). It is far from clear, for instance, that Engels's notorious attempts to deny the law of noncontradiction or Brouwer's to question the law of excluded middle should cause us to construe all of their uses of such words as "not," "and," and "or" as either meaningless or bearing nonstandard senses. Second, even if Quine were right about all that, his argument would only show (i) that people cannot be found denying the laws of the sentential calculus, *not* (ii) that they must be found believing them. For all that the argument could show, a person might quite well fail to accept them and instead recognize some set of deviant logical principles with a correspondingly deviant construal of the truth functions. (Quine and Davidson both tend to slide illicitly from [i] to [ii], though Quine in his more considered remarks certainly acknowledges the possibility just indicated.) Quine also argues that (a) in interpretation we must attribute to others an acknowledgement of "obvious" claims and (b) the laws of the sentential calculus are "obvious," in order thereby to arrive at the conclusion that in interpretation we must find those whom we interpret to recognize these laws (*Philosophy of Logic*, pp. 82–83; cf. *Word and Object*, p. 59, where, though, the version of [a] invoked is weaker, only proscribing attributions of obvious falsehoods, and would consequently not generate the desired conclusion). However, if "obvious" here means obvious *to us* then (a) would seem to be a sadly misguided principle of interpretation, while if it means obvious *to us and those whom we interpret* then (b) simply begs the crucial question. Finally, one further line of argument from a quite different source may also be worth mentioning here. There is a long tradition in philosophy of arguing that the classical laws of logic are essentially constitutive of thought itself. Aristotle initiated this tradition, arguing in the *Metaphysics*, with the law of noncontradiction as his example, that (α) it is impossible to believe a contradiction true (1005b22–35) and (β) in order to mean/understand anything by words, and hence in order to engage in thought, one must believe the truth of the law of noncontradiction (1005b13–20, 1006a10–1007a1). Two remarks about this: First, (α) and (β) are by no means obviously true (think of Engels again, for example), and indeed the complexities of Aristotle's arguments in their support suggest that even he did not think them obviously true; nor are his arguments, when examined, likely to persuade many people today. Second, and more importantly, even if (α) and (β) *could* be established, that would by no means settle the question of whether everyone must be interpreted as conforming to / believing in classical laws of logic. For even if such conformity/belief are essentially constitutive of *thought*, might there not

prove uncompelling to the point of sophistry. Those *dependent on* that theory fail both because of the immediate dubiousness of the theory and because it is much more reasonable to take the theory's incompatibility with the well-established claim that radical differences in concepts and beliefs have been discovered as a further reason to reject the theory than as a reason to reject this claim. Moreover, it turns out, on reflection, that the very attempt to settle the question of the existence or otherwise of radical differences in concepts and beliefs in an a priorist fashion is misconceived.

* * *

The second approach commonly taken in attacking the thesis of radical differences in concepts and beliefs is the *a posteriorist* approach—the approach of actually examining putative expressions of radically different concepts and beliefs with a view to showing that they are in truth nothing of the sort. As should already be evident from the preceding discussion, the a posteriorism of this approach seems to me a virtue—the issue is at least here addressed in the right general way. However, I want to suggest that the a posteriorist approach can only be made to yield the conclusion that radical differences in concepts and beliefs are a myth through being faultily executed, through misinterpretation of the evidence.

A good example of this approach, and of the faults in execution on which its conclusion essentially depends, is the work of the anthropologists Berlin and Kay, and following them the philosopher Hardin, on color conceptualization. Berlin and Kay present their work as a refutation of denials by "anthropologists and linguists" of "the existence of semantic universals," by which they evidently mean (through a curiously Hegelian ambiguity) general concepts shared by all people. Contrary to such denials, Berlin and Kay claim that "the research reported here [i.e., in their book] strongly indicates that semantic universals do exist in the domain of color vocabulary."[114]

In order to establish this conclusion (and others), Berlin and Kay appeal to linguistic data, and, where possible, tests performed on native

---

be some similar (and perhaps even superior) activity which people either do or could engage in, and need to be interpreted as engaging in, of which they are *not* (say, *schmthinking*)? (This, in essence, was the later Wittgenstein's position on the matter.) In sum, it is far from clear that any exception to the above general moral that a priorist denials of radical differences in concepts and beliefs are misconceived needs to be conceded in the special case of logic.

114. *Basic Color Terms*, p. 1; cf. Hardin, *Color for Philosophers*, pp. 155–56.

subjects, to determine such matters as the "foci" (i.e., the paradigm examples) and the "boundaries" (i.e., the extensions) of the color concepts which people use.[115]

This research suffers from deep conceptual flaws and essentially depends on them for arrival at its conclusion. For, granting, as we indeed may, the substantial correctness of Berlin and Kay's empirical findings, those findings do not *support*, but instead *persuasively contradict*, their conclusion that "semantic universals do exist in the domain of color vocabulary." Their belief that their empirical findings do support this conclusion is a product of conceptual confusion.

The specific empirical finding which Berlin and Kay adduce in support of this conclusion is the putative, and if true interesting, fact that, although different peoples vary greatly in the richness of their color vocabularies, one finds striking agreement across all peoples who do have terms relating to a particular color concept on the "focus" (i.e., the paradigm examples) of the color in question.[116]

Now, assuming that this empirical finding is correct, the problem remains that it does not establish, and moreover Berlin and Kay's other empirical findings persuasively contradict, their conclusion that there are "*semantic universals* . . . in the domain of color vocabulary," uniform color concepts across all peoples.

First, the finding *does not establish* this claim. For, (i) agreement across *all peoples who have terms relating to a particular color concept* is not the same as *universal* agreement, agreement across *all peoples*. There are in fact, according to Berlin and Kay, only two color concepts in relation to which all peoples have terms, namely, black and white. Hence the empirical finding in question could only show *universal* agreement on "foci" and thence on semantics for these two cases at best. Furthermore, (ii) it does not show even that. For sameness in the "foci," the paradigm examples, associated with a set of terms is by no means sufficient to establish sameness in the terms' meanings, their *semantic* sameness. For instance, it might quite well be that someone's paradigm examples for the terms *dog* and *animal* were in both cases large dogs, but that would not in the least entail that he meant the same by the terms *dog* and *animal*. (iii) Nor should it be thought that the empirical finding in question establishes the uniformity of color concepts across all peoples by establishing

---

115. *Basic Color Terms*, pp. 5–14.
116. Ibid., pp. 5–12.

the uniformity of all peoples' color *perception*. The finding may indeed suggest an interesting measure of uniformity in color perception across all peoples—though it could only *show* a very modest measure, because, for one thing, given that the only color concepts in relation to which all peoples have terms are white and black, these are the only "foci" which it could show to be common to all peoples. But even if complete uniformity across all peoples in color perception were actually established, that would still not establish uniformity across all peoples in color *conceptualization*, "the existence of *semantic* universals . . . in the domain of color vocabulary." For, as Berlin and Kay themselves rightly stress at one point, questions about color *conceptualization* need to be clearly distinguished from questions about color *perception;* and in particular, it could in principle quite well be the case that there were marked differences in color *conceptualization* across different peoples even though their color *perception* was uniform.[117]

Second, Berlin and Kay's other empirical findings *persuasively contradict* their claim that there are "semantic universals . . . in the domain of color vocabulary," uniform color concepts across all peoples. For, (a) most obviously, their other empirical findings show that different peoples vary tremendously in the number of basic color concepts which they possess—some, such as a New Guinean tribe the Jalé, having as few as two, approximating to our white and black, while others, such as ourselves, have as many as eleven, and yet others fall at one or another point between these numerical extremes.[118] Moreover, (b) Berlin and Kay's other empirical findings show that the "boundaries" or extensions of the color concepts which different peoples share (in a very loose sense of "share," as it turns out) do *not* exhibit the sort of uniformity across the different peoples who (in the same very loose sense) share them that is found in connection with their "foci."[119] This is true of *all* color concepts, including white and black—as indeed one might expect given (a), for if a tribe such as the Jalé has only two color concepts to cover *everything,* one for darker things and one for lighter, what likelihood is there that these concepts will coincide in their extensions with our concepts white and black?

---

117. See ibid., pp. 139–45, where Berlin and Kay discuss sympathetically the work of Magnus, who was the first person to emphasize this possibility, and who argued, moreover, on the basis of empirical evidence, that it represented reality.
118. Ibid., pp. 23–36.
119. Ibid., p. 13.

Thus, to give a specific example, in epic Greek the closest equivalent to our term *white*, namely, *leukos*, is applied not only to things which we would classify as white, but also to things which are otherwise bright or transparent, such as a cloudless, radiant sky or clear water.[120] Similarly, the closest equivalent to our term *black*, namely, *melas*, is applied not only to things which we would classify as black, but also to things which are otherwise dark, such as an oak tree, wine, and the sea.[121] Now the problem which this fact poses for the claim that there are "*semantic* universals . . . in the domain of color vocabulary" should be obvious: if color concepts vary thus markedly in their *extensions* between different peoples, then they must do so in their *intensions*, their *meanings*, as well. Hence, even in connection with the only hopeful candidates, white and black, let alone in other cases, it in fact proves false to say that there are color concepts which all peoples share, "semantic universals . . . in the domain of color vocabulary." Finally, (c) as Berlin and Kay themselves note, words for colors often in addition "encode a great deal of non-colorometric information."[122] In epic Greek, for example, the word *chlōros* implies, in addition to a color, the idea of moistness, and the word *porphureos*, which in later Greek connotes purple but in Homer probably dark color more generally, implies also qualities of motion such as surging or swelling.[123] This poses yet a further serious problem for the claim that there are "*semantic* universals . . . in the domain of color." For these

---

120. See for example *Odyssey*, bk. 6, l. 45; bk. 5, l. 70. In connection with transparency, note also the Greeks' classification of winds as *leukos*—for a discussion of which, see E. Irwin, *Colour Terms in Greek Poetry* (Toronto: Hakkert, 1974), pp. 168–73.

121. See for example *Odyssey*, bk. 14, l. 12; bk. 5, l. 265; *Iliad*, bk. 24, l. 79. I do not mean to imply here, and it should not be thought, that establishing from such differences in the *application of terms* the presence of corresponding differences in the *extension of concepts* is a straightforward or simple matter. In particular, such alternative explanations of the former as homonymy, metaphor, and sheer error have to be excluded. However, there are methods that can decide among these various possible explanations with a fair degree of certainty in most cases—especially (though not exclusively) *philological* methods. And at the end of the interpretative day corresponding differences in the extension of concepts there are here.

122. *Basic Color Terms*, p. 1.

123. On *chlōros* see Irwin, *Colour Terms in Greek Poetry,* chap. 2. Irwin indeed goes as far as to assert that moistness was the original and primary sense of the word in epic poetry *to the exclusion* of ideas of color, such as the green-yellow-pale which it has traditionally been taken to connote there. But in this she goes too far. Thus, a careful review of the evidence which she collects from Indo-European, Homer, the Homeric Hymns, and Sappho rather confirms than disconfirms the traditional view that the color range in question was part of the word's original connotation. Nor do applications of the word to blood and red wine by Sophocles and Euripides give any serious cause to doubt that—both because of the lateness of this evidence and because the tragedians have a general proclivity

non-colorometric connotations are integral aspects of the *meanings* of the terms with which they are associated, and yet clearly there is not uniformity in these connotations across all peoples but instead great variation.[124]

In sum, it seems to me that the current widespread skepticism among philosophers concerning the ideas that there occur radical differences in concepts and beliefs over the course of history, and between cultures within single historical periods, is ill-grounded. Whether derived from a priorist arguments or from a posteriorist ones, this skepticism proves when scrutinized to rest upon a foundation of errors. Hegel's first intellectual historicist idea, and its companion idea, have little to fear from contemporary philosophy.

* * *

Resting on (and in turn in a certain way supporting) this first intellectual historicist idea that human thought has changed in fundamental ways over the course of history with respect to concepts and beliefs is a second intellectual historicist idea at work in the *Phenomenology*'s chapters *Consciousness* through *Reason:* the idea that it is a major and difficult task to understand and represent past thought "from the inside," so to speak, that is, without distorting it by reading in one's own alien concepts and beliefs.[125] Hegel focuses on this point briefly in the Introduction,

---

for modifying epic usage in peculiar ways (e.g., calling swords "spears"). Concerning *porphureos*, note that a cognate verb, *porphurō*, means to boil up or surge up, and that accordingly we find the adjective applied to such objects as a surging sea and a swollen river (*Iliad,* bk. 1, l. 482; bk. 21, l. 326).

124. There may be a temptation to respond to this point somewhat as follows: "These non-colorometric connotations relate to the concepts in which they are involved as component concepts to compound concepts, so that if we abstract them from their compounds we find their users in possession of purely colorometric concepts which do perhaps prove to be common to all peoples after all." Such a response would be misguided, however. Unless one is prepared to divorce concept-possession from linguistic competence in a very dubious way, one cannot, for example, judge that the epic poet's concept of *chlōros* is a compound of the non-colorometric concept of moistness and the colorometric concept of green/yellow, because *he has no concept of green/yellow,* but only our old friend the concept of *chlōros.* Abstracting the non-colorometric connotation in such a case leaves, not the shining residue of a purely colorometric concept, but rather no concept at all.

125. "Difficult" note, *not* "impossible." Hegel, like most of his contemporaries who are interested in the phenomenon of deep differences in conceptual schemes, but unlike some more recent philosophers, is innocent of the seductive but confused view that to understand or even literally translate an alien conceptual scheme is an incoherent ambition. The aim of *understanding* an alien conceptual scheme is not incoherent, because coming to understand an alien conceptual scheme need not take the incoherent form of identifying *alien*

when he comments in connection with the work's projected history of consciousness: "We do not need to import standards [Maßstäbe], or to make use of our own bright ideas and thoughts during the course of the inquiry; it is precisely when we leave these aside that we succeed in contemplating the matter in hand as it is *in and for itself*" (par. 84).[126] The chapters *Consciousness* through *Reason* contain Hegel's attempt to do justice to this task. (We shall see shortly how he hopes to surmount some of the difficulties which it would seem to involve.)

This idea that because thought has changed in fundamental ways over the course of history it is a major and problematic task to understand

---

concepts with concepts which one *already possesses,* but may instead take the quite coherent form of acquiring *new* concepts (something which, note, happens all the time to infants and children). Even the aim of *literally translating* an alien conceptual scheme can be seen to be quite coherent once we recognize, with Schleiermacher, that although our language may be incapable of articulating somebody else's concepts with its *existing* linguistic usages and hence concepts, so that his conceptual scheme is in this good sense alien to us, we may nonetheless be able to *modify* the existing linguistic usages and hence concepts of our language in such a way as to enable it to express his concepts.

126. For this theme, cf. Hegel's later *Rezension der Schrift "Über die unter dem Namen Bhagavad-Gita bekannte Episode des Mahabharata. Von Wilhelm von Humboldt."* Two points to observe in this connection: (i) Hegel's concern in the passage quoted above is not *only* with the hermeneutical task of understanding and representing other viewpoints accurately, but also—as we saw earlier—with the epistemological task of assessing them properly for correctness or incorrectness. (ii) We have already noted the probable influence of Herder on the passage's *epistemological* concern that alien *Maßstäbe* not be employed in the assessment of other viewpoints for correctness or incorrectness because this would vitiate the assessment. We may now note Herder's probable influence also on the passage's *hermeneutical* concern that alien *Maßstäbe* not be imposed in understanding and representing other viewpoints because this would render the understanding and representation of them inaccurate. For this too is an important part of Herder's concern when he warns against the imposition of alien *Maßstäbe:* "What foolishness to tear even a single Egyptian virtue out of the land, time, and boyhood of the human spirit and measure it with the standard [Maßstabe] of another time . . . The best historian of ancient art, Winckelmann, has obviously passed judgment on the works of art of the Egyptians wholly according to a Greek standard, and thus depicted it so little according to its own nature and type that in almost every one of his sentences in this essential respect the obvious one-sidedness and sidewards-glancing aspect shows forth. Similarly Webb, when he contrasts their literature with the Greeks'; similarly a number of others who have written about Egyptian ethics and form of government even with a [modern] European spirit"; it is a "shame that we are slow to transpose ourselves to the time [of the Greek philosophers] and prefer to accommodate them to our own mode of thought. Each nation has in general concepts its own way of seeing" (*Auch eine Philosophie der Geschichte zur Bildung der Menschheit,* in *Herders Ausgewählte Werke* 2:632–33; *Ideen zur Philosophie der Geschichte der Menschheit,* p. 431; cf. *Fragmente,* in *Johann Gottfried Herder Werke* 1:319–22, where Herder undertakes an impressive development of the latter passage's point in relation to specific value concepts).

and depict past thought "from the inside" is the basis of much of what has been most valuable in German thought since the *Phenomenology:* It is the basis of Schleiermacher's attempts, begun at around the same time as the *Phenomenology,* to develop adequate theories of understanding ("hermeneutics") and translation, and to practise the interpretation and translation of ancient texts in a manner informed by and faithful to such theories. For these attempts grew out of Schleiermacher's recognition that when we try to understand or translate historically remote texts, such as those of the ancient Greeks on which he was an expert, their distance from ourselves in concepts and beliefs is so great that "misunderstanding arises naturally, and . . . understanding must be intended and sought at each point."[127] The same idea underlies Dilthey's insight that it is the primary task of the human sciences, and a task which simultaneously distinguishes them from the natural sciences and warrants their being accorded the status of sciences in common with the natural sciences, to *understand* other people's thoughts from their linguistic and other expressions. For it is only because Dilthey recognizes that thought has changed in fundamental ways over the course of history and that the task of understanding past thought is therefore a major and difficult one that he can see the task of understanding as one *substantial* enough to constitute the main goal of the human sciences, and to warrant, if successfully performed, their being accorded the status of sciences alongside the natural sciences.[128] The same idea also underlies as an indispensable foundation the unprecedentedly sensitive interpretative *practice* in several areas of the human sciences which we owe—either directly or indirectly—to later eighteenth- and nineteenth-century Germany. The remarkably advanced quality of modern classical scholarship is the most striking example of a direct debt, while the development of modern anthropology is a good example of an indirect debt.[129]

* * *

127. F.D.E. Schleiermacher, *Hermeneutik* (Heidelberg: Carl Winter Verlag, 1959), p. 86. For corresponding statements in connection with translation, see "On the Different Methods of Translation."

128. Note in this connection that Dilthey's early work *Introduction to the Human Sciences* (Princeton, N.J.: Princeton University Press, 1989) was explicitly motivated by the aim of providing a methodology for the "Historical School," the modern movement comprising Winckelmann, Herder, the Romantics, Niebuhr, Jakob Grimm, Savigny, Böckh, and others which "considered spiritual life as historical through and through" (p. 48).

129. For the influence of this and other ideas from the German tradition on the development of modern anthropology—especially through such figures as Müller, Maine, Tylor,

We must now, however, pause to consider an exegetical paradox concerning the two intellectual historicist ideas of the *Phenomenology* just discussed. This paradox lies in the fact that these two ideas at work in the chapters *Consciousness* through *Reason* seem to be contradicted by views which Hegel expresses elsewhere concerning the history of thought and the appropriate method for interpreting it. Thus, in seeming contradiction with the first idea that thought has changed in fundamental ways over the course of history, a prominent strand in Hegel's treatments of the histories of art, religion, and philosophy asserts, not fundamental change, but instead fundamental *continuity* in these areas of thought over the course of history.[130] Hegel's later lecture series on art, religion, and philosophy exemplify this alternative strand of interpretation—indeed in systematic application to all of these areas of thought over the whole course of history.[131] Still more strikingly, the apparent contradiction in

---

and Boas—see G.W. Stocking, *Victorian Anthropology* (New York: Free Press, 1987), pp. 20–25, 118–19, 157–58, 287, 305–10. In addition to the channels of influence traced by Stocking note also the following: (i) One already finds in Herder and von Humboldt the development of a serious interest in the comparative linguistics and ethnography of contemporary cultures (see esp. Herder's *Über den Ursprung der Sprache* and *Ideen zur Philosophie der Geschichte der Menschheit*, and von Humboldt's *Über die Kavi-Sprache auf der Insel Java*), and the development in conception of a discipline recognizable as our comparative anthropology, indeed under just that name (see Herder's *Briefe zu Beförderung der Humanität* 10:70 ff., and von Humboldt's *Plan einer vergleichenden Anthropologie*). (ii) The classical educations of several of modern anthropology's nineteenth-century founders, for example, de Coulanges, Lane, and Frazer, establishes an immediate link with German classical scholarship, and thereby with its theoretical and methodological presuppositions, for German classical scholarship dominated nineteenth-century classical scholarship throughout Europe (as a glance at the works of Grote or Jebb, for instance, can quickly illustrate).

130. A. MacIntyre has acutely noted this tension in Hegel's thought in *A Short History of Ethics* (New York: Macmillan, 1966), pp. 199–200. However, MacIntyre's way of attempting to resolve it, namely, by suggesting that the parts of Hegel which emphasize continuity are not really meant seriously, does not seem satisfactory.

131. Thus, for example, in the *Lectures on the Philosophy of Religion* Hegel writes concerning the history of religious thought: "These definite religions . . . are included in ours as essential . . . moments, which cannot miss having in them absolute truth. Therefore in them we have not to do with what is foreign to us, but with what is our own . . . The thought of incarnation, for example, pervades every religion" (*On Art, Religion, Philosophy*, pp. 198–99). Even Hegel's 1826 *Rezension der Schrift "Über die unter dem Namen Bhagavad-Gita bekannte Episode des Mahabharata. Von Wilhelm von Humboldt,"* the late work of Hegel's which perhaps goes furthest in the direction of a commitment to the first intellectual historicist idea, in the end stresses that there is a core of intellectual common ground shared by all peoples, namely, their highest concepts, those expounded by Hegel in his Logic (see esp. pp. 75–76, 115–16, 130–31).

question arises within the *Phenomenology* itself, where, after having emphasized fundamental intellectual change over the course of history in the chapters *Consciousness* through *Reason,* Hegel later, in the *Religion* chapter, instead affirms fundamental intellectual continuity. To give a specific example of this, in the *Unhappy Consciousness* section, as we have seen, Hegel argues that Christianity does not, like his own philosophy, recognize God to be identical with human beings: "The Unhappy Consciousness itself *is* the gazing of one self-consciousness into another, and itself *is* both, and the unity of both is also its essential nature. But it is not as yet explicitly aware that this is its essential nature, or that it is the unity of both" (par. 207). In the *Revealed Religion* section, by contrast, Hegel argues that Christianity *does,* just like his own philosophy, recognize God to be identical with human beings: in Christianity, "God is sensuously and directly beheld as a self, as an actual individual man . . . [Consciousness's] object now is the self, but the self is nothing alien; on the contrary, it is the indissoluble unity with itself . . . The divine nature is the same as the human, and it is this unity that is beheld" (pars. 758–59).[132] Correspondingly, in seeming contradiction with the second intellectual historicist idea, Hegel's insistence on the importance and difficulty of avoiding reading in aspects of one's own viewpoint when interpreting and representing historically distant viewpoints, there is a prominent strand in Hegel's writings about the histories of art, religion, and philosophy which maintains that the appropriate method for interpreting and representing past art, religion, and philosophy is rather to assume Hegelian philosophical truth and then interpret and represent them in such a way as to maximize its attribution to them. This is Hegel's dominant interpretative approach in his later lecture series on art, religion, and philosophy.[133] Still more strikingly, as the contrasting passages from the *Unhappy Consciousness* and *Revealed Religion* sections of the *Phe-*

---

132. Note that the continuity-emphasizing strand of interpretation had already been prominent in Hegel's early thought. Good examples are his Kantian interpretation of the gospels in *The Life of Jesus,* and his Jena essays in the *Critical Journal of Philosophy* such as *Faith and Knowledge* in which he interprets the views of previous philosophers as attempts (albeit imperfect ones) to express his own philosophical position.

133. Thus, for example, Hegel states in the *Lectures on the Philosophy of Religion* that in interpreting the definite religions we must "recognize the meaning, the truth . . . ; in short get to know what is *rational* in them . . . We must do them this justice, for what is human, rational in them, is *our own,* too, although it exists in our higher consciousness as a moment only . . . We look at these definite religions in accordance with the Concept [i.e., the principle of Hegelian philosophy]" (*On Art, Religion, Philosophy,* p. 200; cf. *Ency-*

nomenology just quoted illustrate, this seemingly incompatible interpretative approach co-resides with the first approach within the *Phenomenology* itself, taking over from it in the later parts of the work.[134]

Does this paradox not represent an outright inconsistency in Hegel's thought? I do not think so. Concerning the second half of the paradox, to begin with this, it seems plausible to argue that *Hegel applies the two different interpretative approaches in question in different theoretical contexts governed by different theoretical purposes* and that *each is appropriate to its own theoretical context and purpose*. In the *Phenomenology*'s chapters *Consciousness* through *Reason* Hegel is undertaking an assessment of both his own philosophical viewpoint and all non-Hegelian viewpoints for truth or falsehood. Such a theoretical context and purpose make it (i) inappropriate for him to presuppose the truth of his own philosophical viewpoint as a basis for interpretation, and (ii) appropriate for him to adopt a highly sensitive interpretative approach to non-Hegelian viewpoints in order to avoid the charge of having read problems or other implications *into* them. This theoretical context and purpose therefore speak against using the interpretative method found in later parts of the *Phenomenology* and in the later lecture series, and for instead using the interpretative method actually found in the chapters *Consciousness* through *Reason*. However, these chapters, working with this interpretative method, eventually demonstrate, Hegel believes, that his own philosophical viewpoint is true and all non-Hegelian viewpoints false and indeed self-contradictory. This dramatically changes the theoretical context and purpose of interpretation, and consequently the relative appropriateness of alternative interpretative methods, for subsequent investigations, such as those undertaken in later parts of the *Phenomenology* and in the later lecture series. In particular, the assessment of positions for truth or falsehood is no longer at issue, so that arguments (i) and (ii) against employing the interpretative method of assuming Hegelian philosophy's truth as the basis for interpretation and assimilating all viewpoints to this

---

clopaedia, par. 562). Once again, even Hegel's 1826 review of von Humboldt, perhaps the most sympathetic among his later works to the second intellectual historicist idea, in the end effectively endorses this alternative interpretative approach, at least where mankind's most fundamental concepts are concerned.

134. Once again, note that the alternative interpretative approach in question here had already been prominent in Hegel's early thought, being for example the official interpretative method of the essays in the *Critical Journal of Philosophy*, as one can see most clearly from Hegel's explicit account of this method in *On the Nature of Philosophical Critique* (see appendix VII).

one as far as possible, and for instead using the alternative method, no longer apply. Moreover, since the truth of Hegelian philosophy, and the falsehood and indeed self-contradictoriness of all non-Hegelian viewpoints, are now established, it seems plausible to suppose that the former is now indeed a more reasonable interpretative method to adopt than the latter.

This still leaves the first half of the paradox, though. What are we to say about the apparent conflict between the claim implied by the *Phenomenology*'s chapters *Consciousness* through *Reason* that thought has undergone fundamental changes over the course of history and the claim implied later in the *Phenomenology* and in subsequent works such as the later lecture series that there has rather been fundamental continuity? And more specifically, what are we to say about such apparent conflicts between particular interpretative judgments as that between the *Unhappy Consciousness* section's verdict that Christianity, unlike Hegelian philosophy, fails to assert the identity of God and man and the *Revealed Religion* section's verdict that Christianity, like Hegelian philosophy, does assert their identity? Surely, someone might say, there must at least be a real inconsistency *here*.[135] I want to suggest that, on the contrary, it is not at all clear that there really *is* an inconsistency here. The two alternative interpretative approaches which we have been considering involve, after all, the adoption of significantly different criteria of meaning-identity, and it would therefore be plausible to say—particularly given Hegel's general position on the internality of much "theory" to concepts—that they employ *different concepts of meaning*. Consequently, Hegel could plausibly say that when his first interpretative approach judges the meanings of the various views developed over the course of history to be fundamentally different and his second interpretative approach then turns around and judges them to be not fundamentally different but fundamentally continuous, or when his first interpretative approach judges Christianity to mean, unlike Hegelian philosophy, that God is nonidentical with man and his second interpretative approach then turns around and judges it to mean, like Hegelian philosophy, that God is identical with man, *the contradictions are strictly speaking only apparent, not real.*[136]

* * *

---

135. Solomon, for one, implies so (*In the Spirit of Hegel*, pp. 168–69).

136. To pursue further a suggestion begun in footnote 88 to chapter 4, having effected this shift in his criteria and concept of meaning, Hegel is driven to a corresponding shift in his criteria and concept of truth. For having made the former shift, he now inevitably

A third intellectual historicist idea at work in the chapters *Consciousness* through *Reason* is the idea which we earlier found underpinning the double project in these chapters of providing simultaneously a history of consciousness's development and an analysis of the strata of the modern consciousness: consciousness's historical development has been *cumulative* in character, earlier shapes of consciousness always being preserved within later ones as part of their essential constitution (albeit in a modified form).[137]

This would not be a good *general* model of how intellectual change has occurred over the course of history. For example, it would leave no room for the historically discernible phenomena of concepts simply fall-

---

finds a good deal of agreement in concepts and beliefs among all men, whereas formerly he had found very little, and he hence loses this one serious obstacle which had prevented him from equating truth with agreement among all men in some fashion rather than merely with enduring agreement within a communal tradition. Doing so at the culmination of his discrediting of conceptions/concepts of truth as correspondence to independent fact need no longer entail that the class of the true would be virtually empty. And the shared linguistic behavior constitutive of meaning can now include, and hence confer a truth-determining authority on, mankind at large, rather than just a community or communal tradition. Hence Hegel's tendency in later parts of the *Phenomenology*, such as paragraphs 70–71, and in later writings, such as *Encyclopaedia*, paragraph 22, addition, to equate truth in a certain way not just with enduring agreement within a communal tradition, but with agreement among all of humanity—or more specifically, with both the explicit enduring agreement of a communal tradition and the implicit agreement of all humanity. (Note that this move parallels, in the domain of epistemology and metaphysics, the later Hegel's integration, in the practical domain, of an element of cosmopolitan concern into his patriotism, in the manner of *Philosophy of Right*, paragraph 209, as discussed in the notes of chapter 2.)

137. Schelling had already strongly hinted at such a view in his *System of Transcendental Idealism*: "We . . . maintain that no individual consciousness could be posited, with all the determinations it is posited with, and which necessarily belong to it, unless the whole of history had gone before" (p. 201). It is also plausible to see Herder as an influence on Hegel here. For in *Auch eine Philosophie der Geschichte zur Bildung der Menschheit* Herder had argued, similarly, that history's succession of cultures had been *cumulative* in its development, each building on the attainments of the one before: "Do you see how this stream runs on, how it sprang from a small source, grows . . . ever meanders and pushes on wider and deeper . . . What if it were thus with the human species? Or do you see that growing tree, that developing human being. It must go through various periods of life, all clearly in a progressive manner—a striving from one to another in continuity . . . No one is alone in his period of life, he builds on the preceding one . . . Clearly it is thus with the human species! The Egyptian could not exist without the Oriental; the Greek built on the Egyptian; the Roman raised himself onto the back of the whole world—truly progress, advancing development"; "There is the [ancient] East, the cradle of the human species . . . Even if religion should be despised and extinguished in the whole cold world . . . the childhood of the species will have its effect on the childhood of every individual: the last young person still born in the first East!" (*Herders Ausgewählte Werke* 2:647, 680). Cf. *Phenomenology*, pars. 28–29.

ing out of earnest use altogether at a certain point in history, such as the Greek concept of *miasma* for instance, or, like the concept of an atom, falling into earnest disuse for a long time and then returning to earnest use much later on. It is therefore important to emphasize that Hegel offers this model in the *Phenomenology* only as a model of how a certain sort of very fundamental intellectual change has occurred through history, namely, changes in people's shapes of consciousness, or their interdependent conceptions and concepts of self, reality, and representation.

So understood, this idea has significant appeal, at least in certain of its applications by the *Phenomenology*. For example, it seems quite plausible to suppose, as Hegel does, that men must at some point in the very distant past have occupied an immediate sensory perspective somewhat like that of Sense-certainty, that this was later preserved in a modified form within a naive realist perspective somewhat like that of Perception, that this in turn was then preserved in a modified form within a perspective somewhat like that of Force and the Understanding (namely, as its perspective on *sensible appearances,* as distinguished from supersensible reality), and that all of these perspectives are now preserved in a modified form within the perspective of the modern consciousness (so that we can, if we choose, so to speak, peel off accreted layers of sophistication from our modern perspective and find ourselves occupying, albeit only imaginatively and temporarily, something like those earlier perspectives once again).

On the other hand, some of the *Phenomenology*'s applications of this idea go beyond the bounds of plausibility. For example, how plausible is it to suggest that the distinctive perspectives of the eighteenth-century physiognomist and phrenologist lurk within the modern consciousness as essential constitutive elements? Arguably, though, the fault in these cases lies not with Hegel's idea that all shapes of consciousness change in a cumulative fashion, but rather with his classification of such outlooks as those of the physiognomist and phrenologist as distinct *shapes of consciousness.* For, whatever novelties in *mere conceptions* of self, reality, and representation the physiognomist and phrenologist may have introduced, it seems quite doubtful that these were of such a fundamental kind as to constitute new *concepts* of self, reality, and representation.

* * *

A fourth intellectual historicist idea at work in the history of consciousness of the chapters *Consciousness* through *Reason* is Hegel's *an-*

swer to the question of how the major and difficult task of understanding past thought "from the inside" can and should be accomplished. This answer rests on the preceding intellectual historicist idea, the idea that thought has developed in a cumulative fashion, so that earlier types of thought are preserved within later ones (albeit in a modified form). Thus Hegel indicates in the Preface that it after all proves somewhat easier than one might have feared for the modern individual to achieve an understanding of past types of thought, because the modern individual's consciousness has preserved them and contains them within itself as strata of its own essential structure, so that *all that he has to do is to isolate these strata of his own consciousness in imagination*. This is the force of the following passage:

> The individual whose substance is the more advanced Spirit runs through [the] past just as one who takes up a higher science goes through the preparatory studies he has long since internalized [längst innehat] . . . [He has] less trouble, since [his historical education] has already been implicitly accomplished, the content is already the actuality reduced to a possibility, its immediacy overcome, and the shape reduced to an abbreviation of itself, to a simple determination of thought. The task is . . . only to turn the . . . already recollected/inwardized [erinnerte] in-itself into the form of being-for-itself. (pars. 28–29)[138]

This would not be very helpful as a suggestion for solving the hermeneutical problem *in general*. It would not, for example, help as an explanation of how we can understand, or as a method for understanding, concepts from the past within our own cultural tradition which have fallen into disuse without leaving any active trace. Nor would it help as an explanation of how we can understand, or as a method for understanding, concepts within cultural traditions *other* than our own. It is important, therefore, to emphasize that Hegel advances this idea in the *Phenomenology* with a more restricted aim in view, namely, to give an explanation of how we can understand, and a method for understanding, *shapes of consciousness*, or sets of interdependent conceptions and con-

---

138. Schelling had already strongly hinted at a similar position in the *System of Transcendental Idealism*, where he had argued: "We . . . maintain that no individual consciousness could be posited, with all the determinations it is posited with, and which necessarily belong to it, unless the whole of history had gone before . . . Historiography . . . could thus . . . set out from the current situation and infer to past history, and it would be no uninteresting endeavor to see how the whole of the past could be derived from this" (p. 201).

cepts of self, reality, and representation, which all fall within *our own cultural tradition*. In this more restricted application the idea has somewhat more plausibility.[139]

Hegel in fact seems to give this idea two rather different sorts of such application within the *Phenomenology*—one less radical and controversial, the other much more so. First, and least radically, he applies it as an explanation of how we can understand, and as a method for understanding, past perspectives different from our own *for which we have independent historical evidence,* in particular texts. This is the nature of its application in the sections *Force and the Understanding* and following, where Hegel is dealing with types of thought which fall unequivocally within textually recorded history. So applied, Hegel's idea has considerable plausibility, at least as a significant *part* of the explanation and method appropriate to such cases. For example, our ability to understand the general outlook common to Homeric theology and its successor Greek rationalism when we encounter this in written sources surely *is* in large part explained by, and surely *will* be advanced if we allow ourselves to exploit, our preservation of a modified version of their distinction between sensible appearances and supersensible reality within our modern natural scientific perspective, which distinction we can therefore abstract from this modern perspective of ours and use as a basis for interpretation. (Imagine, by contrast, the difficulties that a naive realist, someone with a perspective like Hegel's Perception, would have in understanding the general outlook of Homer or the Greek rationalists upon encountering it in a text for the first time.)

On the other hand, Hegel in the *Phenomenology* apparently gives this idea a decidedly more radical and controversial application as well. He apparently believes that this sort of imaginative abstraction from our modern perspective can not only explain how we are able, and enable us, to understand past perspectives for which we have independent historical evidence, but also *explain how we are able, and enable us, to establish the past existence of and to understand perspectives for which we have no independent historical evidence to speak of at all, because they oc-*

---

139. The *Phenomenology* is not the place to look for a *general* solution to the hermeneutical problem. Much more significant strides in *that* direction were beginning to be taken at around the same time by Hegel's contemporary Schleiermacher in his lectures on hermeneutics.

curred before textually recorded history. For, as we noted in the previous chapter, Hegel apparently—at least when he first writes about them—conceives some of the perspectives represented in the *Phenomenology* to belong to periods of the very distant past about which he has no independent historical evidence at all, in particular Sense-certainty and Perception.[140]

Though Hegel does not go into the matter explicitly, the crux of his idea here would seem to be the rather interesting one that, having, so to speak, peeled off successive layers of our modern consciousness and correlated what is left each time with independent historical evidence (texts) leading further and further back in time, we eventually find ourselves left with these two least complex layers, Perception and Sense-certainty, and, although we no longer have any independent historical evidence to correlate these with, since we have now run out of that, we have now nevertheless built up a sort of inductive justification for assigning them as perspectives to still earlier periods of time. (One might look here, for an analogy, to the sorts of inferences that archaeologists draw when they dig beyond the historically identifiable strata on a site into still deeper strata.)

* * *

140. The passage quoted from Schelling's *System of Transcendental Idealism* in the note before last strongly suggests that Schelling had already envisaged such a radical possibility. Note also that Herder had implied, similarly, that an investigation of language as it was found within later periods of history was capable of establishing both the existence and the character of forms of mental life in earlier periods of history for which there was no independent historical evidence. For example, in *Über den Ursprung der Sprache* he argues that we can infer from the preserved fully developed structure of the oldest oriental languages the existence and character of man's thought, and of its development, in the earliest periods of history, and specifically that we can infer from the *onomatopoeic* and *verbal* character of the roots in these (Semitic) languages that concepts of *audible actions* had primacy in man's earliest thought: "Resounding verbs are the first ruling elements of the oldest languages. Resounding verbs? Actions, and still nothing which acts there? Predicates and still no subject? The divine genius may find this alien to himself but not the sensuous human creature. For what stirred the latter . . . , precisely, more intimately than these resounding actions? And what, therefore, is the whole structure of language but a mode of development of his mind, a history of his discoveries? The first dictionary was collected from the *sounds* of the world. From each resounding being its name rang forth. The human soul formed its image after it, thought of them as indicators. How then could it be otherwise than that these resounding interjections became the first ruling words of the language? And thus it is that, for example, the oriental languages are full of verbs as basic roots of the language. The thought of the thing itself still hovered between the agent and the action . . . In a 'philosophical dictionary of the Orient' each root-word with its family, if properly laid out and soundly developed, would be a chart of the course of the human mind, a history of its development" (*Herders Ausgewählte Werke* 3:639–40).

A fifth intellectual historicist idea at work in the chapters *Consciousness* to *Reason* concerns the *mechanism* through which major conceptual changes of the sort that these chapters describe have taken place over the course of history: the history of thought has been a process in which genuine self-contradictions have been discovered in prevailing thought from time to time and these have then operated as motors driving men to escape them by developing their conceptual resources in appropriate ways.

This would not be plausible as an explanation of how *all* major conceptual change has occurred over the course of history. It is therefore of some importance to emphasize that the *Phenomenology* only makes the more limited claim that changes from one *shape of consciousness* to the next—one set of interdependent conceptions and concepts of self, reality, and representation to the next—have always occurred in this way. Even this claim may well be more than could really be defended; it is at least not obvious to me that Hegel succeeds in the *Phenomenology* in showing that all, or even any, of the intellectual transitions which he describes there really conform to this model. Nevertheless, this fifth intellectual historicist idea still seems to me to be an important and valuable one. For it is, I think, true that major conceptual changes of the sort that Hegel is interested in have at least *sometimes* occurred in this way.

In order to illustrate this claim, we might consider a major conceptual development which especially interests Hegel both in the *Phenomenology* and in later works: the development of a sharp distinction between the medium of *thought*, on the one hand, and the *reality* that thought is about, on the other (a development which, as we have noted, the *Phenomenology* attributes mainly to Stoicism, but Hegel later credits in its earliest form to Sophism, and in particular Gorgias's treatise *Concerning Nature or Concerning the Non-existent*). For it seems to me that, although Hegel nowhere quite tells it, the true account of how this distinction developed conforms extremely closely to the model of his fifth intellectual historicist idea.

The main impulse, or at least *a* main impulse, behind the original development of this distinction was the emergence in the fifth century of Parmenides' argument for the incoherence of the notion of not-being. Parmenides gives the crux of this argument several times in the extant fragments of his poem: "For you could not know what is not—that cannot be done—nor indicate it"; "For to be thought and to be are the same"; "What is said and thought must have being; for it is so as to be, but nothing is not"; "For that it is not cannot be said or thought"; "For thought and that because of which thought exists are the same. For you will not find thinking without what is."[141] Interpretation of this argument is a difficult and much disputed matter. Passing over several complicated issues,[142] the point of the argument seems to me to be somewhat as follows: "Saying" and "thinking" are—like "seeing" and "beating," but unlike "sleeping" and "flying," for example—essentially *relational* activities, they have to be performed *on something*. There can no more be an act of saying or thinking which is not an act of saying or thinking *something* than there can be an act of seeing or beating which is not an act of seeing or beating *something*. Now, when people speak or think of existent objects or states of affairs, and say or think that they exist, this seems unproblematic; they speak or think of *the object* or *the state of affairs,* this is the required relatum. What though of cases in which people either (i) say or think that an object or state of affairs exists when in fact it does not or (ii) say or think that an object or state of affairs does not exist? In case (i), it looks as though there is no relatum, and hence after all no act of speaking or thinking either. In case (ii) it seems that if (per impossibile, as it turns out) the act of speaking or thinking were true, then again it would lack a relatum, and so again not really be an act of speaking or thinking after all; at best it could only be an act of speaking or thinking if it were false. In consequence, all of the central uses which we make of the notion of not-being turn out to be incoherent in one way or another: If I claim that somebody asserts or thinks that some object or state of affairs exists but that it does not, or that somebody truly asserts or thinks that some object or state of affairs does not exist, then I am guilty of an implicit self-contradiction. And if I simply say or think that some object or state of affairs does not exist, then I am still guilty of a sort of pragmatic self-contradiction.[143]

---

141. G.S. Kirk, J.E. Raven, M. Schofield, *The Presocratic Philosophers* (Cambridge: Cambridge University Press, 1983), pp. 245, 246, 247, 249, 252.

142. I address some of these in a longer version of the present discussion, "Parmenides' Paradox" (unpub.).

143. The pragmatic self-contradiction is between my statement or thought that such and such an object or state of affairs does not exist, on the one hand, and my belief that I say or think that, on the other. The self-contradiction is only *pragmatic* because, although possession of the latter belief is a necessary condition of engaging in the former statement or thought—for, quite generally, in order to say or think that p, one must believe that one says or thinks that p—its content is not strictly implied by the content of what is stated

Now there is a strong temptation for us to respond to this argument of Parmenides' by saying that it rests on a straightforward mistake.[144] This is because the solution to the alleged paradox seems obvious to us: it is *thoughts* (or propositions, or concepts, etc.) which constitute the missing relata in each case. However, if the story were that simple, then it would be quite puzzling that Parmenides' paradox managed to impress, exercise, and in most cases baffle the best Greek philosophical minds for several generations. The problem with the response just indicated, I suggest, is that it is insensitive to certain key facts about the conceptual context within which the paradox arose. In particular, (a) there was not yet at the time of its emergence any concept of thoughts as items *distinct from* acts of thinking, and consequently (b) when someone used a concept like "thinking" and thereby implied the existence of a relatum, he implied that there was something *more* than a mere thought, something which, unlike a mere thought, could *be* a relatum for the act of thinking. If the suggested solution had actually been offered to Parmenides or his contemporaries, therefore, they would have had to dismiss it as no more than a piece of linguistic sophistry: "To be sure," one can imagine them saying, "we can speak of 'thinking a thought,' just as we can speak of, for example, 'fighting a fight' (indeed even more naturally in our ancient Greek than in your English). But the thought here, like the fight, is merely a cognate accusative, not a genuine relatum.[145] If a skeptical Ariadne had raised a doubt about whether there had really been anything in the labyrinth for Theseus to fight, and whether therefore he had really fought, a response from him that, despite the absence of animate opponents, he had been able to fight a fight would hardly have impressed her. Why should we be any more impressed by the suggestion that thinkers, lacking relata of other kinds, may yet think thoughts?" I suggest, in other words, that at the time when Parmenides advanced his paradox, people really

---

or thought: "Object / state of affairs X does not exist" does not imply "I say/think that object / state of affairs X does not exist."

144. In this spirit, G.E.L. Owen writes: "What is mistaken is his claim that we cannot talk of the non-existent. We can, of course: mermaids, for instance" ("Eleatic Questions," in *Classical Quarterly* 10 [1960], p. 94). Similarly, D.J. Furley writes: "Parmenides' premise (and his fundamental fallacy) was . . . that 'what is not' is absolutely unthinkable and unknowable" (*Encyclopaedia of Philosophy*, ed. P. Edwards [New York: Macmillan, 1972], 6:50).

145. On cognate accusatives in Greek, where they are much commoner than their equivalents in English, see for example H.W. Smyth, *Greek Grammar* (Cambridge, Mass.: Harvard University Press, 1984), pp. 355–57.

were guilty, in using the notion of not-being, of just the sorts of implicit self-contradictions and pragmatic self-contradictions to which he was attempting to draw their attention.

Eventually, however, a way was found of *escaping* such self-contradictions. How was this accomplished? In effect, I suggest, by changing the two features of the prevailing conceptual situation, (a) and (b), just mentioned: by (a') developing an ontologically weightier concept of thoughts as items *distinct from* acts of thinking, and consequently (b') coming, when using a concept like "thinking" which implies the existence of a relatum, to imply no more than that there are *thoughts* as relata. It was a consequence of this conceptual change that (c') whereas previously thinking and thought had been in a sense bound by conceptual necessity to the existence of their objects or states of affairs, the existence of the latter to serve as relata being implied by the very application of the concept of thinking or thought, now thinking and thought came to be conceived as in principle quite independent of the existence of those objects or states of affairs. In other words, there began to emerge for the first time the sort of sharp distinction between thinking and thought, on the one hand, and reality, on the other, in which Hegel is so interested.

This sort of solution to the Parmenidean paradox is first found, albeit in a rather crude and confused form, in the Sophist Gorgias, specifically in the second and third parts of his treatise *Concerning Nature or Concerning the Non-existent.* In this work Gorgias responds to the Parmenidean paradox by, in effect, making exactly the two conceptual adjustments just described, (a') and (b'), and embracing their consequence, (c'), the independence in principle of thinking from existence.[146] Here are the relevant parts of Gorgias's text as summarized by Sextus Empiricus, with the moves in question indicated as they occur:

> If, says Gorgias, the things thought are not existent [i.e., if Parmenides is wrong, if one *can and does* think what is not], the existent is not thought [i.e., at least, (b'), thinking does not have the existent as its essential relatum, so that (c'), thinking is in principle independent of existence][147] . . . But the things thought . . . are not existent, as we shall establish; therefore the existent is not thought . . . For if someone thinks of a man flying or of a chariot running over the sea, it does not follow at once that a man is

---

146. Gorgias's ultimate aim in the treatise is in fact to exploit this consequence for skeptical ends.
147. I say "at least" because Gorgias in fact means more than this as well.

flying or a chariot running over the sea. So that the things thought are not existent . . . Scylla and Chimaera and many non-existent things are thought. Therefore the existent is not thought. And just as the things seen are called visible because of the fact that they are seen, and audible because of the fact that they are heard, and we do not reject the visible things because they are not heard, nor dismiss the audible things because they are not seen . . . so also the things thought will exist, even if they should not be viewed by the sight nor heard by the hearing, because they are perceived by their own proper criterion.[148] [This last sentence shows (a'), the development of a concept of thoughts as items distinct from acts of thinking, as genuine relata for such acts; note in particular how the relation of an act of thinking to its thought is here conceived on the model of the relation of an act of sense-perception to its object.][149]

A much more sophisticated version of the same moves occurs later in Stoicism. The Stoics hypothesized a realm of incorporeal, merely subsistent "sayables [*lekta*]" (i.e., roughly what we would call propositions and predicates) and fictional entities, distinct from corporeal, existent things, and serving as the primary and essential relata for the acts of thinking and speaking performed by the corporeal soul.[150] The Stoics developed this theory largely as a solution to Parmenides' paradox of not-being, as is shown, for example, by Seneca's explanation of why they posited a genus "something" including under it not only the existent corporeal but also the subsistent incorporeal: "Some Stoics consider 'something' the first genus, and I shall add the reason why they do. In nature, they say, some things exist, some do not exist. But nature includes even those which do not exist—things which enter the mind, such as centaurs, giants, and whatever else falsely formed by thought takes on some image despite lacking substance."[151] The theory effects its solution by making (even more

---

148. Sextus Empiricus, *Against the Logicians,* bk. 1, secs. 77–82.
149. In this connection, cf. Gorgias's observation at ibid., bk. 1, sec. 86: "Even if *logos* subsists, yet it differs from the rest of subsisting things, and the visible bodies differ very greatly from *logoi;* for the visible object is perceptible by one organ and *logos* by another."
150. For this Stoic theory see Long and Sedley, *The Hellenistic Philosophers,* vol. 1, esp. pp. 162–65, 195–202. My short description of the Stoic position here disagrees with Long and Sedley in one respect, namely, in interpreting fictional entities as incorporeals, like *lekta*. The grounds for this interpretation are, briefly: (i) One piece of evidence from a careful source seems to require it, namely, Alexander of Aphrodisias's observation that the Stoics' highest genus " 'something' is said only of bodies and incorporeals" (ibid., pp. 179–80). (ii) No evidence speaks against it. (iii) This seems the most natural position for the Stoics to take.
151. Ibid., p. 162.

clearly than Gorgias) the three moves mentioned above, (a′)–(c′): (a′) It introduces an ontologically weighty concept of thoughts as items distinct from acts of thinking (i.e., the incorporeal *lekta* and fictional entitities distinct from the corporeal soul and its acts). (b′) It consequently uses concepts like "thinking" in a way which implies no more than the existence of thoughts as relata (i.e., the *lekta* or fictional entities which are conceived as the only essential relata for acts of thinking). And (c′) it therefore conceives of thinking as in principle quite independent of the existence of the objects or states of affairs which the thinking is about (a conception reflected in the sharp metaphysical contrast between the incorporeal and merely subsistent character of thinking's only *essential* relata, the *lekta* and fictional entities, and the corporeal, existent character of the objects and states of affairs normally thought about).

It is, I suggest, thanks, and only thanks, to these conceptual innovations due originally to the Sophists and the Stoics that we today are no longer caught in the trammels of Parmenides' paradox, but instead find a solution to it along the general lines of the one sketched earlier so obvious and satisfactory.

This, then, is a fifth intellectual historicist idea deserving of note in the chapters *Consciousness* to *Reason*: the mechanism through which major conceptual changes have occurred over the course of history has—in at least some important cases—been that genuine self-contradictions were discovered in prevailing thought and these then acted as motors driving men to escape them by inventing new conceptual resources which would enable them to do so.[152]

* * *

A sixth intellectual historicist idea at work in the chapters *Consciousness* through *Reason* is the idea that we can come, and can only come, to a proper knowledge or comprehension of our *own* thought by becoming conscious of the historical development in thought which preceded and produced our own thought.[153] Since Hegel's time, this idea has formed

---

152. This model for understanding the historical emergence and solution of such paradoxes as Parmenides' should be clearly distinguished from the much commoner conception that such paradoxes uncover *merely apparent* self-contradictions (rather than *genuine* ones) which are subsequently *seen to be illusory* (rather than *escaped*) through the *recognition* of relevant conceptual distinctions (rather than their *invention*).

153. This idea was already at work in the young Hegel's investigations in the early theological writings into the historical origins of modernity's dualistic worldview, and so was no doubt in some measure implicit in the *Phenomenology* from the start. However, to judge from the *Phenomenology*'s virtual silence about it in the Introduction but great

the foundation of several of the most interesting and fruitful attempts by philosophers to throw light on aspects of modern thought and culture. One thinks, for example, of Nietzsche's enterprise of a "genealogy of morals" and Foucault's of an "archaeology of knowledge"—both of which, other differences with Hegel and between themselves notwithstanding, rest squarely on this Hegelian idea.

Hegel acknowledges, certainly, that our own thought is in *some* sense intimately familiar to us before we trace its historical genesis—for example, we understand the meanings involved in it (semantic understanding), and find their employment quite natural. However, in Hegel's view this intimate familiarity with our own thought fails to ensure, and is even in large measure hostile to, our full and proper knowledge of it. Thus he writes in the Preface that "the representation that has arisen" has "familiarity," but that "the familiar . . . is not, just because it is *familiar* [bekannt], *known* [erkannt]" (pars. 30–31).[154]

According to Hegel, the modern individual's retrieval, by means of the *Phenomenology*, of the historical development in thought which preceded and produced his own cultural milieu and conception of the world effects his first full comprehension of this milieu and conception, and without it such comprehension would be impossible:

> [We] will recognize in the pedagogical development [of the *Phenomenology*] the history of the formative education of the world as though traced out in silhouette. This past existence is the already acquired property of the universal Spirit, which constitutes the substance of the individual and, appearing as external to him, constitutes his unorganic nature. In this respect, the formative education, considered from the standpoint of the individual, consists in this, that he acquires this already present content, digests his unorganic nature, and takes possession of it . . . The individual certainly cannot in the nature of the case comprehend his substance in an easier fashion. (pars. 28–29)[155]

---

emphasis on it in the Preface (pars. 28–31), it was not initially central to Hegel's conception of the work's tasks but only became so as the work was written.

154. The ambiguity of the latter sentence—it could mean either "familiarity is not a sufficient condition of being known" or "familiarity inhibits being known"—is in the German. I believe that Hegel intends *both* senses.

155. A point of clarification is in order here. This idea might sound like the simple converse of the fourth intellectual historicist idea, the idea that we can and should come to an understanding of past thought by using our own modern thought as a basis. And that might give rise to an impression of vicious circularity: How can one use one's present thought to understand past thought (the fourth idea) if proper comprehension of one's present thought requires that one already have understood and traced the development of

Hegel's choice in paragraphs 30–31 of the terms *bekannt* and *erkannt* is, I believe, meant to suggest that there is an analogy between our cognitive situation with respect to our own thoughts and our cognitive situation with respect to *people* of our acquaintance. For in idiomatic German the term *bekannt* is often used to connote familiarity or acquaintance with a person, and the verb *erkennen* is often used to connote recognition or correct identification of a person.[156] This implicit analogy of Hegel's seems to me both carefully chosen and fruitful. Accordingly, in what follows I shall attempt to throw light on his sixth intellectual historicist idea by taking it somewhat seriously.[157]

A first question which we should ask concerning this idea is what exactly Hegel means when he indicates at paragraphs 30–31 that familiarity with our own representations is both consistent with and conducive to a failure really to know them? In order to answer this question, let us take Hegel's analogy seriously, and consider to begin with our cognitive situation with respect to people of our acquaintance. Person A may achieve familiarity, even intimate familiarity, with person B, and yet still lack real knowledge of him. In an extreme form such a situation might

---

past thought (the sixth idea), and how can one attain proper comprehension of one's present thought by understanding and tracing the development of past thought (the sixth idea) if understanding past thought requires that one use as a basis, and therefore already understand, one's present thought (the fourth idea)? The answer to this objection is that the converseness is not exact, because the sort of "comprehension" of one's own thought at stake in the sixth idea is something richer than the mere semantic understanding of it presupposed by the fourth idea. The vicious circularity is therefore illusory; we may very well already semantically understand our own thought, and so be in a position to use it as a basis for understanding past thought in the manner of the fourth idea, despite still lacking the full "comprehension" of our own thought at stake in the sixth idea. Indeed, Hegel's characterization of our own thought as already "familiar" to us even though not yet "comprehended" by us implies that we are generally in just this situation.

156. It is significant in this connection that when, as he does, Nietzsche repeats Hegel's claim from paragraphs 30–31 in *The Gay Science,* trans. W. Kaufmann (New York: Vintage Books, 1974)—"What is familiar [bekannt] is what we are used to; and what we are used to is most difficult to 'know' [erkennen]" (p. 301)—he makes the analogy between our cognitive situation with respect to our own thoughts and our cognitive situation with respect to people explicit: "I take this explanation from the street. I heard one of the common people say, 'He knew me right away [er hat mich erkannt].' Then I asked myself: What is it that the common people take for knowledge? What do they want when they want 'knowledge'? Nothing more than this: Something strange is to be reduced to something *familiar* [etwas Bekanntes]" (p. 300).

157. Note that the analogy in question is also *more* than that for Hegel, since for him familiarity with / knowledge of our own thoughts is also *literally* familiarity with / knowledge of another person, namely, Absolute Spirit.

look like this: A has lived with B for some time and has achieved, through observing and interacting with B, an acute sensitivity to B's current physical and psychological traits of the sort needed for, and manifested through adeptness in, practical dealings with B. Nevertheless, A still falls short of really knowing B in the following two sets of respects. (i) A's sensitivity is not, or at least not generally, reflective in the sense of including an ability to describe those traits of B's to which he is sensitive in propositional terms. Moreover, it does not include any developed awareness that B is an exemplar of various *kinds* to which he belongs, or of which traits B shares with and which distinguish him from the other members of these kinds (and in this connection it is plausible to suggest that real knowledge of someone requires such awareness concerning not only very general kinds to which he belongs, such as the kind "human being" or "man," but also rather specific kinds—for example, if he happens to be a Zulu man, then the kind "Zulu men," or if a painter, then the kind "painters"). Connectedly, A's sensitivity does not include an awareness of many of B's traits which are implicitly traits *relative* to the other members of his kinds, and which could therefore only be discovered by comparing him with them (for example, his tallness, which is a trait implicitly relative to other men, or his being a skilled painter, which is a trait implicitly relative to other painters). (ii) A's sensitivity includes no real awareness that B has become what he now is as the result of an extended process of development or change. And it includes no real awareness of what that process of development or change has been.[158]

Furthermore, intimate familiarity with someone of the sort which A possesses is not only *consistent* with ignorance of that person in respects (i) and (ii); it may actually tend to *promote* this. For example, the fact that A already has a sensitivity to B's current physical and psychological traits which is acutely developed and adequate for practical dealings with him may tend to make explicit propositional articulation of these traits, comparison of them with the traits of other individuals, and the tracing of their genesis through time seem to A both theoretically uninteresting and practically unnecessary. And the very intimacy of A's contact with

---

158. In such an extreme form the condition of being intimately familiar with someone while lacking real knowledge of him is no doubt very unusual. (Shakespeare depicts the sort of situation in which it might arise in *The Tempest*, where Miranda has grown up from early childhood on a remote island in intimate contact with her old father Prospero, but without meeting any other human beings, and in ignorance of his biography.) However, less extreme forms of this condition are common enough in everyday life.

B may, if driven to an extreme, stand in the way of A's acquiring the sort of acquaintance with other individuals which is necessary if a classification and comparison of B with them is to occur.

Now Hegel's thought at paragraphs 30–31 is, I suggest, that in quite analogous ways it is possible—and in this case not only possible, but also very common—for a person to have intimate familiarity with his own thoughts, and yet still lack real knowledge of them, and indeed for the latter condition not only to coexist with the former but actually to be promoted by it: A person may be familiar with his own thoughts in the sense of understanding the meanings involved in them and finding the use of these meanings natural, yet still fall short of really knowing his own thoughts in the following two sets of respects. (i′) This person's facility with the meanings involved is not reflective in the sense that it would allow him to describe them at all fully in propositional terms. Contrast, for example, the unreflective manner in which an ancient Greek typically understood the meanings of the words of his language with the further ability possessed by the classical philologist to give a propositional description of the linguistic rules constitutive of those meanings.[159] Thus in a speech from 1809 on the importance of classical education Hegel argues that "since the categories of the Understanding . . . *are in us* and we understand them immediately, the beginning of education consists in *having* them, i.e., in having made them an object of consciousness and being able to distinguish them by means of characteristic marks."[160] Moreover, this person's facility does not include any developed awareness that the meanings involved are but single exemplars of various kinds to which they belong, or of which characteristics they share with and which distinguish them from the other members of these kinds (and, as in the case of knowing persons, it seems plausible to argue that real knowledge of one's thoughts and meanings requires this sort of awareness concerning not only very general kinds, such as the kind "meanings," but also more specific kinds—for example, if the meaning in question is our concept of the self, then the kind "concepts of the self"). Connectedly, this person's facility does not include an awareness of many implicitly relative charac-

---

159. It was with this sort of contrast in mind that Schleiermacher, and following him Böckh, described the aim of the philologist as one of coming to understand an author better than the author had understood himself.

160. *Nürnberger und Heidelberger Schriften*, p. 323.

teristics of the meanings involved, characteristics which could only be discovered by comparing them with the other members of the kinds to which they belong (for example, his concept of the self's characteristic of being *atomistic,* a characteristic which is implicitly relative to concepts of the self in which the self is conceived as essentially penetrated by a larger context in some way—for instance, a divine context, as in Homer, who interprets sudden mental states, such as Achilles' sudden inhibition against attacking Agamemnon at the beginning of the *Iliad,* as intervention by gods, in this case Athena; or a social context, as in Hegel's own conception of the individual's language, thought, and self as essentially socially constituted). I take it that this first set of omissions is a large part of what Hegel has in mind when he says that representations which are only familiar to us but not known by us have the character of "uncomprehended immediacy" (par. 30). (ii') This person's facility does not include any clear awareness that the meanings involved have resulted from an extended process of historical development or change (perhaps the question of their past has simply never occurred to him, or perhaps they appear to him to have been unchanging throughout history, or, in exceptional cases, to have sprung forth fully-formed from the mind of some great thinker ex nihilo). Nor does his facility include an awareness of what this process of historical development or change has been.[161] I take it that this second set of omissions is a large part of what Hegel has in mind when he speaks at paragraphs 30–31 of merely familiar representations not being *erkannt.* For among the common idiomatic implications of saying that people or things are not *erkannt* is the implication that they are not recognized as identical or continuous with earlier phases of themselves.

Furthermore, as in the personal analogue, intimate familiarity with one's own thoughts of the sort described is not only consistent with ignorance of sorts (i') and (ii'), but may actually promote it. For example, the very fact that one understands the meanings involved in one's own thoughts and finds their use entirely natural may tend to make explicit propositional descriptions of them, comparisons of them with other meanings, and the tracing of their genesis through time seem both theoret-

---

161. As Kierkegaard would later remark in this connection, explicitly invoking the analogy with people, "Concepts, like individuals, have their histories" (*The Concept of Irony,* trans. L.M. Chapel [Bloomington: Indiana University Press, 1968], p. 47).

ically uninteresting and practically unnecessary. And the very intimacy of one's relation to them may preclude the sort of acquaintance with other meanings from the kinds to which they belong which is required if classification and comparison of them with these other meanings is to occur.

These, I suggest, are some of the more specific points that Hegel has in mind when he argues at paragraphs 30–31 that our familiarity with our own representations is both consistent with and conducive to a failure really to know them.

The next question which we should ask is why Hegel maintains at paragraphs 28–29 that the indispensable key to getting beyond mere familiarity with our own thoughts and achieving a real knowledge or comprehension of them lies in acquiring insight into the history of their genesis? In order to answer this question, consider once again, to begin with, the personal analogue. Suppose that person A has familiarity with person B but is lacking in respects (i) and (ii), and so lacks proper knowledge or comprehension of B. Obviously, the only way for A fully to overcome omission (ii) is to achieve biographical knowledge about B, knowledge that and how B has developed or changed over time to become the person he now is. As for omission (i), the most obvious way for A to overcome this omission would be to get to know other individuals from the various kinds to which B belongs. For such knowledge would, by contrasting B with those other individuals, help to make A reflectively aware of, able to describe, the traits of B's of which he had previously been aware only in an unreflective, inarticulate way; is essential, moreover, for coming to know that B is a member of those kinds, and determining which characteristics he shares with and which distinguish him from the other members of those kinds; and is also essential, consequently, for discovering traits of B's which are implicitly relative to the other members of those kinds. Still, here too biographical knowledge of B could be a significant help. For it could afford A an acquaintance with B's "earlier selves," so to speak, and this could go some significant way toward serving the same functions as acquaintance with other individuals from the kinds to which B belongs.

Somewhat similarly where knowing one's own thoughts is concerned: Suppose that one has familiarity with a thought but is lacking in respects (i′) and (ii′) and so lacks proper knowledge or comprehension of it. Obviously, the only way fully to overcome omission (ii′) is to achieve a knowledge of the "biographies" of the meanings involved in the thought, a knowledge that and how they came to be as they now are through a process of development or change.[162] One way of overcoming omission (i′) would be to gain acquaintance with meanings from the kinds to which the meanings involved in the thought belong but not related to these as genealogical antecedents (for example, if the meanings involved in the thought included our concept of the self, we might look at concepts of the self in languages and cultures contemporary with and unrelated to our own). For this would help, by affording contrasts with our own meanings, to bring us to reflective awareness of, an ability to describe, features of our own meanings of which we had previously been only unreflectively, inarticulately, aware; is essential, moreover, for enabling us to recognize that our meanings are members of the various kinds to which they belong, and what their similarities and differences from the other members of those kinds are; and is also essential, consequently, for enabling us to discover characteristics of our own meanings which are implicitly relative to the other members of those kinds. Hegel does not greatly stress the possibility of overcoming omission (i′) in this manner. But he does occasionally acknowledge it. For example, in the *Lectures on the History of Philosophy* he writes: "The natural man . . . lives quite unconsciously in his own particular way, in conformity with the morality of his town, without ever having reflected on the fact that he practises this morality. If he then comes into a foreign land, he is much surprised, for through encountering the opposite he for the first time experiences the fact that he has these customs."[163] As in the personal analogue, however, it is plausible to think that another way of overcoming omission (i′) would be to discover the "biographies" of our own meanings. And here, *unlike* in the personal analogue, it is plausible to think that this would be *no less* useful and indispensable for overcoming omission (i′)—for, typically, the items which make up the "biography" of a concept will be in a more literal sense distinct concepts belonging to the same kinds as the resulting concept, not merely "earlier selves" of that concept in the

162. For the analogy between a history of conceptual development and personal biography, consider paragraphs 28–29 in the Preface, where Hegel characterizes the *Phenomenology*'s history of conceptual development as a sort of biography. Note, though, that the analogy is not *merely* an analogy. For Hegel is also envisaging the work's history of conceptual development as *literally* the biography of a person, namely, of Absolute Spirit.

163. Lectures on the History of Philosophy 2:355.

metaphorical sense involved in the personal analogue.[164] It is this second way of overcoming omission (i′) which especially interests Hegel. Thus, the 1809 speech on the importance of classical education mentioned earlier, like the passage just quoted from the *Lectures on the History of Philosophy,* implies that, in order to achieve genuine knowledge of one's own intellectual standpoint one must become acquainted, and contrast it, with alien intellectual standpoints.[165] But the 1809 speech looks to our own intellectual forebears—in particular the ancient Greeks and Romans—to provide the alien intellectual standpoints required: we must "offer the soul itself the separation which it seeks from its natural being and condition and implant a remote, alien world into the young spirit . . . But the dividing wall by means of which this separation . . . is effected for education is the world and language of the ancients."[166] And it is this second method for overcoming omission (i′) which is the method actively pursued in the *Phenomenology* as well.

It is, I suggest, mainly for reasons of this sort that Hegel indicates in paragraphs 28–29 that the indispensable key to proceeding beyond mere familiarity with our own thoughts to a proper knowledge or comprehension of them lies in acquiring insight into the history of their genesis.

Before we proceed further, it may be helpful to illustrate the above points with an example based on some details from the *Phenomenology*'s history of consciousness. A modern individual who occupies the perspective of modern natural science might be intimately familiar with this perspective of his, in the sense of having a good semantic understanding of its concepts, finding their use quite natural, and being generally proficient in modern natural science by all the usual criteria, and yet still fall short of really knowing or comprehending this perspective in the following respects: (i″) There is a principle partly constitutive of this perspective's concept of reality, namely, the principle of a distinction between the way things appear to our senses, on the one hand, and their supersensible constitutions and causal principles, on the other, which, while he in *some* sense takes it deeply for granted, he never entertains reflectively and would be at a loss to articulate in propositional terms. Detailed questions

---

164. For this reason there is some ground for preferring Nietzsche's metaphor of "genealogy" over the metaphor of "biography" in connection with the history of concepts.

165. *Nürnberger und Heidelberger Schriften,* p. 321: "In order to become an *object,* the substance of . . . spirit must have received the form of something alien," and what is required for this is "to occupy oneself with something non-immediate, something alien."

166. Ibid., p. 321.

concerning the specific *character* of the constitutions and causal principles in question he reflects on constantly and can articulate propositionally at the drop of a hat, but of the background assumption—the forest about the trees, so to speak—he has only an implicit awareness. Moreover, he has only a very limited awareness that his concept of reality belongs to larger kinds, and of what it shares with and what distinguishes it from the other members of these kinds. For example, while he certainly recognizes that it belongs to a larger kind "concepts," he does not recognize that it is but one member of a larger kind "concepts of reality," which includes also such concepts of reality as that of the naive realist perspective which Hegel calls Perception, nor that it is but one member of a larger kind "concepts of reality incorporating a distinction between sensible appearances and supersensible constitutions and causal principles," which includes also such concepts of reality as those belonging to Homeric theology and Greek rationalism. Consequently, he also fails to recognize which characteristics his own concept of reality shares with and which distinguish it from the other members of these larger kinds. Consequently again, he has no awareness of many implicitly relative characteristics belonging to his concept of reality, characteristics of it which are implicitly relative to the members of these larger kinds, and which he could therefore only discover by comparing it with them—for example, its *complexity* (relative to such concepts of reality as those of Sense-certainty and Perception). (ii″) He lacks any clear awareness that his concept of reality, with its essential component assumption of a distinction between sensible appearances and supersensible constitutions and causal principles, is the result of a long process of conceptual development or change (perhaps the question of its history has simply never occurred to him, or perhaps he imagines that people have always possessed it, or that it emerged fully formed ex nihilo in the minds of certain recent thinkers, for example the scientific thinkers of the seventeenth century). And he also lacks, therefore, any clear idea of what this process of development or change has been. Furthermore, for reasons of a sort indicated earlier, his intimate familiarity with his modern natural scientific perspective not only thus consistently co-resides in him with this failure really to comprehend or know the perspective in respects (i″) and (ii″), but actually tends to promote this failure.

Now, as we have seen, Hegel in the *Phenomenology* traces modern natural science's concept of reality, with its essential component distinction between sensible appearances and supersensible constitutions and causal principles, back historically to a Greek rationalist forerunner, thence to an earlier forerunner in Homeric theology, thence to a still earlier forerunner in the religion of ancient Egypt, thence to an even earlier naive realist concept of reality which lacked the distinction in question and which Hegel calls Perception, and so forth. If correct, this historical account will enable the modern natural scientific individual whom we are considering to overcome shortcomings (i″) and (ii″), and thereby achieve a fuller knowledge or comprehension of his modern natural scientific perspective. For, to begin with, this is obviously just the sort of account that he needs in order to overcome shortcoming (ii″). Moreover, it provides him with a key for remedying shortcoming (i″) as well. For, to take up the several parts of this shortcoming in turn: The contrast which this account displays between, on the one hand, his modern natural scientific perspective and its preforms (Greek rationalism, Homeric theology, and ancient Egyptian religion) and, on the other hand, the naive realism of Perception will bring him to reflective awareness of, an ability to describe, the distinction between sensible appearances and supersensible constitutions and causal principles which is essential to the former perspectives but absent from the latter. The account will, furthermore, advance his awareness that his modern natural scientific perspective's concept of reality is a member of larger kinds to which it belongs—in particular, the larger kinds "concepts of reality" and "concepts of reality incorporating a distinction between sensible appearances and supersensible constitutions and causal principles"—and of its similarities to and differences from the other members of these kinds. And the account will also, thereby, enable him to recognize characteristics of his modern natural scientific perspective's concept of reality which are implicitly relative to the other members of these kinds, such as for example its complexity (relative to such concepts of reality as Perception's).

Let us now pursue more closely the question of how exactly overcoming omissions (i′) and (ii′), through attaining knowledge of the history of our concepts, represents an increment in our knowledge or comprehension of our own thought. Enough has perhaps already been said to make the answer to this question clear in the case of overcoming omission (i′). However, more still needs to be said in connection with overcoming omission (ii′)—the most direct contribution of a history of our concepts.

How, then, does overcoming omission (ii′)—or coming to recognize that our concepts are the products of an extended process of development or change over time, and what this process has been—represent an increment in our knowledge or comprehension of our own thought? *Part* of the answer to this question seems fairly obvious. Thus, consider the corresponding question concerning persons: How does coming to recognize that a person is the product of an extended process of development or change over time, and what this process has been—the most direct contribution of biography—represent an increment in knowledge or comprehension of him? There are certain immediate and obvious ways in which it does so. First, it makes clear that he is the sort of entity that *has* a biography, the sort of entity that has become what it now is as the result of a process of development or change over time, and not, for example, through having existed in its present form forever or through having sprung into existence fully formed ex nihilo. Second, since the story of his development or change over time is the story of *his* development or change over time, this biographical information, whatever its specific details may turn out to be, represents an increment in knowledge of *him*—namely, of him in earlier phases of his existence. Analogously, discovering that a concept is the product of an extended process of development or change over time, and what this process has been, contributes to our knowledge or comprehension of it in two immediate and obvious ways. First, it makes clear that this is the sort of entity that came to be what it now is as the result of a process of development or change over time, and not, for example, through having existed thus forever or for as long as human thought has been around, or through having sprung into existence at a certain point fully formed ex nihilo in the mind of some thinker. Second, since the account of its development or change over time is an account of *its* development or change over time, this account, whatever the specific details may turn out to be, represents an increment in knowledge of *it*—namely, of it in earlier phases of its existence.[167]

The *rest* of the answer to the question is considerably less obvious, however. What I want to suggest here is that the *Phenomenology* offers an explicit further answer to it which is very specific, and which just for that reason could not plausibly be generalized, but that the work's im-

---

167. In the case of concepts, unlike that of people, these two claims require a measure of qualification, though. For, as noted earlier, in giving the history of a concept one is typically in a more literal sense identifying other members of the kinds to which it belongs than is the case in personal biography, where to describe the account as one about a person's "earlier selves" is more metaphorical. And consequently, of course, to describe the history of a concept as a treatment of earlier phases of *its* existence is typically more metaphorical than the corresponding description of personal biography, which is more literal.

plicit running analogy between our knowledge or comprehension of our own thoughts and of persons points to a further answer which is more flexible, and which thereby has a more plausible claim to generality.

The *explicit* further answer offered by the *Phenomenology* is roughly as follows: By determining the past history of our present perspective we will discover that this perspective is an organic composition of a number of conceptual elements each of which originally arose in a cruder and simpler form at some point in the past history of man as (in every case except the very first) a rational solution to, and the only possible rational solution to, an intellectual problem then confronting man—namely, a self-contradiction in his current perspective—and thereafter underwent successive steps of improving enrichment in rational response to, and each time as the only possible rational response to, further intellectual problems which subsequently emerged—further self-contradictions—until eventually reaching its most satisfactory and richest form yet in us. Thus, the Preface notes a kinship between Hegel's way of illuminating our modern perspective in the *Phenomenology* and the Kantian procedure of conceptual analysis, in that both of them consist in "dissecting a representation into its original [i.e., for Hegel, though not for Kant, both constitutively *and temporally* original] elements" in order to achieve "the overcoming of the form in which it is familiar" (par. 32). And the Preface implies that the *Phenomenology*'s demonstration of the rational *necessity* of each of the steps by which the emergence and development of these elements over the course of history took place is also an essential aspect of the work's contribution to our full comprehension of our own perspective: "The length of this path has to be endured [i.e., by the modern individual instructed through the *Phenomenology*], because, for one thing, each moment is necessary . . . Since [the World Spirit] . . . could not have attained consciousness of itself by any lesser effort, the individual certainly cannot in the nature of the case comprehend his substance in an easier fashion" (par. 29).

Our discussion earlier in this chapter of the Parmenidean paradox, and the conceptual developments which it occasioned, and which we have ourselves inherited, suggests that something very much like this model for explaining features of our modern thought *is* in fact applicable *in certain cases* (no small victory for Hegel). However, it seems unlikely that this model will prove applicable to all, or even to very many, features of our modern thought. And in this sense it could not plausibly be generalized.

If, on the other hand, we follow Hegel's implicit analogy between knowledge of one's own thoughts and knowledge of persons, then a much more flexible and more plausibly generalized model emerges. Consider once again to begin with the situation concerning knowledge of persons. In addition to the two *obvious* ways mentioned earlier in which coming to know a person's biography contributes to knowledge or comprehension of him, there are any number of further and less obvious ways in which it may do so as well. For example, one might discover that some present character trait of his—say, his cautious approach to strangers—originally emerged at some point in the past in a simpler and cruder form as a rational response to a problem which he then confronted—say, being taken advantage of by strangers—and thereafter remained with him as a rational mechanism for dealing with that problem, subsequently however undergoing steps of qualifying refinement in rational response to further problems which he encountered later on—say, the problem of excluding strangers too indiscriminately and irrevocably, and so ending up lonely—until it eventually reached its present most qualified and optimal form. Or one might discover that some current activity of his which initially seemed quite normal and even praiseworthy—say, his work for Palestinian rights—originated in a dubious impulse—say, his desire for revenge on the Jewish girl who broke his heart in school—which impulse, one then recognizes, still somehow underlies it. And one can of course imagine many other possibilities as well. It seems plausible to say that one can be fairly confident in advance of learning the specific details of a particular person's biography that in doing so one will discover *something* which will enrich one's comprehension of him in ways going beyond the two obvious ones mentioned earlier, but that the exact nature of the facts in question and the exact way in which they will enrich one's comprehension of him may in principle, and will in practice, vary greatly from case to case.

Now, analogously, concerning knowledge of our own thoughts, it seems that, in addition to the two obvious ways mentioned earlier in which discovering the histories of our own thoughts contributes to our knowledge or comprehension of them, there are in principle any number of further ways in which it may do so. The *Phenomenology*'s explicit model of tracing the conceptual elements of our thoughts back to their original emergence and finding this, and subsequent refinements in them, to be rationally necessary solutions to intellectual problems—specifically, to self-contradictions—indicates *one* way in which it might do so. And, as we have noted, there do in fact seem to be real examples very much like this—in particular, that of our intellectual debt to the Parmenidean paradox and the early responses to it. (This model is roughly analogous to the first, "caution with strangers," type of explanation in the context of personal biography.) However, one can well imagine other ways over and above the obvious ones in which discovering the histories of our thoughts might contribute to our knowledge or comprehension of them instead. For example, it might do so by revealing that some currently employed concept which at first sight seemed normal and appropriate originally developed from a dubious or pathological motive, which can then be seen to underlie it still—as, for example, in Nietzsche's thesis that the historical origin and enduring basis of Christian value concepts and judgments lies in the motive of social *ressentiment*. (This would be roughly analogous to the second, "Palestinian-sympathizer," type of explanation in the context of personal biography.) And one can certainly imagine many further possibilities as well. As in the case of personal biography, it seems plausible to say that we can be fairly confident in advance of looking at the specific details of the history of any particular thought that by doing so we will turn up *something* which will contribute to our knowledge or comprehension of it in ways going beyond the two obvious ones, but that the exact nature of these facts and the exact way in which they will make this contribution may in principle, and probably will in practice, vary considerably from case to case.

Understanding the *Phenomenology*'s sixth intellectual historicist idea in the manner sketched above enables us to see beyond an objection to it which might at first sight seem to pose a serious threat to it, namely, the objection that because Hegel's explicit model of explaining our modern thought in terms of the rational necessity of its development out of past thought proves to be inapplicable, or of only very limited applicability, his whole project of explaining our modern thought through its history is thereby discredited. We can now see that, even if the antecedent assumption here is granted, the inference to the conclusion is fallacious, and this for several reasons. First, it overlooks the contribution which a history of our modern thought can make to remedying shortcomings of sort (i′) and in *this* way enhancing our comprehension of our modern thought. Second, it overlooks the contribution which a history of our modern thought can make to remedying shortcomings of sort (ii′) and thereby enhancing our comprehension of our modern thought in the two *obvious* ways mentioned earlier. Third, it overlooks the fact that in all probability a history of our modern thought can, by remedying shortcomings of sort (ii'), also enhance our comprehension of our modern thought in further, *non*obvious ways, *whether or not these turn out to be as Hegel's explicit model envisages them*.[168]

Finally, it may be appropriate to append a few words in defense of Hegel's sixth intellectual historicist idea against a further somewhat tempting objection, namely, the objection that in seeking to enhance our comprehension of our modern thought by tracing its history Hegel commits the "genetic fallacy" of believing that one can infer from the character of a thought's historical origins (or sustaining causes) to its truth-value.[169] Such a charge is groundless. First, none of the ways indicated above in which Hegel envisages an acquaintance with the past history of our modern thought enabling us better to comprehend our modern thought envisages it doing so via an inference from the character of our modern thought's past history to its *truth-value*.[170] Second, one can see that Hegel is innocent of inferring from the character of a thought's historical origins to its truth-value from the fact that his conception of the historical development of thought as unilinear and cumulative implies that his own true thought and all past false thought share the *same* historical origins. Hegel is quite innocent of the "genetic fallacy."[171]

---

168. Note that an analogous objection might be raised against Nietzsche's commitment to this sixth intellectual historicist idea, and that the appropriate response to it would be analogous as well.

169. One commonly hears such a charge leveled against Hegel and other nineteenth-century German philosophers. For an example, where Marx is the main target, see H.B. Acton, *The Illusion of the Epoch* (London: Cohen and West, 1955), chap. 1.

170. As we saw in chapters 2 and especially 3, Hegel has a set of quite different techniques for establishing the truth-values of the various types of thought that occur, including his own.

171. There is perhaps a *little* more excuse for charging Nietzsche and Marx with this fallacy, because, unlike Hegel, they do at least prominently call on the pernicious origins and sustaining causes of certain beliefs in order to discredit them—for example, on the origins and sustaining causes of Christian religious beliefs in pernicious *ressentiment* (Nietzsche) or pernicious ruling-class interests (Marx). However, like Hegel, Nietzsche and Marx prove on closer inspection to be fundamentally innocent of the charge—and for interestingly similar reasons in each case. Crucial points to note in this connection are the following.

(i) For both Nietzsche and Marx the *falsehood* of Christian religious beliefs is essentially a *given*, something already established by earlier generations of atheistic criticism, and largely on *empiricist* grounds. Thus Nietzsche writes in connection with religion of "we children of the Enlightenment," and states that "today we possess science precisely to the extent to which we have decided to *accept* the testimony of the senses . . . The rest is miscarriage and not-yet-science—in other words, metaphysics, theology" (*Human, All Too*

This concludes our investigation of the sixth intellectual historicist idea at work in the chapters *Consciousness* through *Reason,* and therewith our investigation of the intellectual historicist ideas of these chapters generally.

Human, trans. R.J. Hollingdale [Cambridge: Cambridge University Press, 1990], p. 41; *Twilight of the Idols,* in *The Portable Nietzsche,* trans. W. Kaufmann [New York: Penguin, 1987], p. 481). And similarly, Marx already in 1843–44 writes that "for Germany the criticism of religion has been essentially completed," and in continuity with the empiricism of his atheistic predecessor and inspirer Feuerbach invokes "an entirely empirical analysis" (*Marx: Selections,* pp. 23, 41; cf. 218–19).

(ii) The question which Nietzsche and Marx *actively* pursue is rather the further question which becomes pressing given the established falsehood of the beliefs concerned, namely, why then they are so pervasive and deeply-rooted? Nietzsche, for example, writes at one point: "In former times one sought to prove that there is no god—today one indicates how the belief that there is a god could *arise* and how this belief acquired its weight and importance" (*Daybreak,* trans. R.J. Hollingdale [Cambridge: Cambridge University Press, 1989], p. 54). And a similar stance can be found in the fourth of Marx's *Theses on Feuerbach.*

(iii) Nietzsche and Marx do indeed understand their answers to this further question to add to the discrediting of the beliefs concerned. Nietzsche, for example, implies that without answering it the atheist cannot "make a clean sweep," but that by answering it he can achieve a "definitive refutation" of religion (*Daybreak,* p. 54; cf. *Human, All Too Human,* p. 72). However, this is *not* because the answers which they give in terms of certain pernicious origins and sustaining causes make possible inferences from the perniciousness of the origins and sustaining causes to the falsehood of the beliefs, in commission of the genetic fallacy. Rather, it is in two quite different and more legitimate ways: First, and least obviously, providing a plausible causal explanation of the beliefs' pervasiveness and deep-rootedness complements and reinforces the assumed empiricist case for their falsehood by precluding the counterargument that, in the absence of such an explanation, the beliefs' very pervasiveness and deep-rootedness itself creates a presumption of their truth. (The idea that a direct refutation of pervasive and deeply-rooted beliefs requires such a complement and reinforcement in fact has a long and distinguished history in philosophy, going back at least as far as Aristotle, who in *On Sophistical Refutations* argues that a proper refutation of common fallacies requires not only a direct demonstration of their fallaciousness but also an explanation of why people are nevertheless inclined to think them valid.) Second, and more obviously, since the particular explanations which Nietzsche and Marx provide explain the beliefs as serving functions which are pernicious by their own and their anticipated readers' lights (namely, the expression of *ressentiment,* or the reinforcement of ruling-class interests), the explanations additionally discredit the beliefs by showing that, besides being false, they also serve such pernicious functions.

Far from succumbing to the genetic fallacy, then, Nietzsche and Marx in fact share a sophisticated and powerful strategy for discrediting beliefs. In short, it seems to me that *none* of the major nineteenth-century German philosophers against whom the charge of the genetic fallacy is commonly leveled is really guilty of it.

CHAPTER ELEVEN

History in the Chapters
Spirit through
Absolute Knowing

As was indicated in chapter 9, the historical design of the remaining chapters of the *Phenomenology*, those after the chapters *Consciousness* through *Reason*, is fundamentally as follows: The *Spirit* chapter offers a second chronological treatment of the whole course of history, this time focusing on the series of "Spirits" or social contexts within which the shapes of consciousness dealt with in the earlier chapters occurred. The chapters *Religion* and *Absolute Knowing* then offer a third chronological treatment of the whole course of history, this time focusing on the attempts associated with those shapes of consciousness and social contexts to express the nature of God or the Absolute, through art and religion (the *Religion* chapter), and eventually Hegel's own philosophy (the *Absolute Knowing* chapter). A case for this reading should now be sketched.[1]

Let us begin with the *Spirit* chapter. That this chapter contains a chro-

---

1. I shall be briefer in discussing these remaining chapters. This is for several reasons, the counterparts of those indicated earlier for treating the chapters *Consciousness* through *Reason* at greater length: First, the historical and historicist dimensions of these remaining chapters, unlike those of the preceding chapters, are strictly speaking superfluous for the official project of the *Phenomenology* described in parts 1 and 2. Second, and connectedly, as we shall see in part 4, these remaining chapters were only included in the book as an afterthought, in contrast to the earlier chapters, which constitute the book as originally planned, so that in this sense too these remaining chapters are less central to the book. Third, the claim that these remaining chapters have a chronologically historical design of the sort described above is better argued for by Lukács and much less controversial than the corresponding claim about the chapters *Consciousness* through *Reason*. Fourth, these remaining chapters are not as rich in new intellectual historicist ideas as the earlier chapters, and are therefore less crucial for understanding the *Phenomenology*'s intellectual historicism.

447

nological history is widely recognized, not only by Lukács.[2] That its history is intended to be a history of *social contexts* is a little more controversial, but can readily be seen from two circumstances: First, this is implied by Hegel's opening characterization of the chapter's subject matter as "the universal work produced by the action of all and each as their unity and identity," and as, in contrast to "shapes merely of consciousness," "real Spirits" which "are shapes of a world" (pars. 439, 441). Second, it is confirmed by the emphatically social focus of most sections of the chapter, especially the early sections *Ethical World, Ethical Action, Legal Status,* and *Culture.* The subject matter of the chapter is roughly what Hegel in the *Lectures on the Philosophy of World History* calls "National Spirits," but considered in the social dimension which the *Encyclopaedia* calls "Objective Spirit."

That this chapter is designed to give a chronological history focusing on the sequence of "Spirits" or social contexts *from which the shapes of consciousness in the chapters Consciousness through Reason were abstracted* is less obvious. However, this is shown by two sorts of evidence. First, such a plan is implied by Hegel's general remarks at the start of the *Spirit* chapter: "All previous shapes of consciousness are abstract forms of [Spirit] . . . [The] isolating of those moments *presupposes* Spirit itself and subsists therein, the isolation exists only in Spirit which is a concrete existence"; the coming shapes "are distinguished from the previous ones by the fact that they are real Spirits . . . ; and instead of being shapes merely of consciousness, are shapes of a world" (pars. 440–41). Second, this plan is confirmed by the fact that Hegel indicates through fairly explicit remarks in the main body of the chapter that each of the "Spirits" or social contexts dealt with there is associated historically with a shape of consciousness from a corresponding point in the chapters *Consciousness* through *Reason* (with a qualification to be entered later).

Let us run through the earlier parts of the *Spirit* chapter in order to illustrate this latter claim. As we noted previously, Hegel explicitly associates the first social context of the *Spirit* chapter, the Ethical World of early ancient Greece, with contents from the *Consciousness* chapter. Thus

---

2. In addition to Lukács, see for example Hyppolite, *Genesis and Structure,* p. 38. Even Solomon is forced to concede the chapter's historical design, though very grudgingly: the *Spirit* chapter "is ostensibly historical," though "by no means a complete outline of Western history" and "hardly history at all" (*In the Spirit of Hegel,* p. 483). Lukács gives a fairly accurate account of the main historical steps covered in the chapter (*The Young Hegel,* pp. 485–507).

he writes that "Spirit is, in its simple truth [i.e., as the Ethical World], Consciousness . . . It . . . exhibits in its own self the nature of Consciousness" (pars. 444–45; cf. 446). The association envisaged is mainly with the culminating shape of Consciousness, Force and the Understanding.[3] Hegel also associates the Ethical World in a later phase with the first shape of consciousness from the *Self-consciousness* chapter, Life. Thus he refers to the Ethical World as "the *living* ethical world" and describes its content as "universal *Life*" (pars. 442, 461; emphasis added; cf. 454). The next social context in the *Spirit* chapter, Ethical Action, represents the corruption of the Ethical World, as reflected in the Greek tragedy of the fifth century. This corresponds to subsequent contents from the *Self-consciousness* chapter—hence Hegel writes that "what is active in this movement . . . is Self-consciousness" (par. 465). More specifically, it corresponds to the contents of the *Lordship and Bondage* section.[4] The next social context in the *Spirit* chapter, Legal Status, represents the Roman Empire and its abstract laws. Hegel associates this with the next and final contents of the *Self-consciousness* chapter: Stoicism, Skepticism, and the (early) Unhappy Consciousness. Thus he writes in the *Legal Status* section, successively, that "Stoicism is nothing else but the consciousness which reduces to its abstract form the principle of Legal Status" (par. 479; cf. 199); that, "like Skepticism, the formalism of legal right [i.e., Legal Status] is . . . by its very nature without a peculiar content of its own; it finds before it a manifold existence in the form of 'possession' and, as Skepticism did, stamps it with the same abstract universality,

---

3. This can be inferred from the following circumstances: (i) The *Spirit* chapter implies that the Ethical World already subsumes Sense-certainty and Perception within itself (par. 446). (ii) The *Religion* chapter represents Sense-certainty and Perception as already developed in association with *pre*-Greek oriental cultures' forms of religion (pars. 686, 689), and even a primitive phase of Force and the Understanding itself as already developed in association with *pre*-Greek Pharaonic Egypt's form of religion (par. 692). (iii) The *Religion* chapter then associates a mature phase of Force and the Understanding with Greek culture's form of religion, Religion in the Form of Art (par. 706), which it in turn identifies with the Ethical World (par. 700).

4. This is implied by several things: (i) Ethical Action and Lordship and Bondage are both conceived by Hegel as principles of the corruption of ideal Greek culture (Ethical World, Life). (ii) The place and date of Ethical Action, as fixed by the Greek tragedy dealt with in the section, namely, Athens in the later fifth century, coincide with those which we earlier saw Hegel to have principally in mind for Lordship and Bondage. (iii) At paragraph 475 Hegel identifes war, physical strength, and the bravery of youth as principles of corruption within Ethical Action—ingredients central to the process depicted in the Lordship and Bondage section as well.

whereby it is called 'property' " (par. 480); and that in Legal Status "the actual truth of [Unhappy Consciousness] has become apparent" (par. 483). Furthermore, Hegel explicitly correlates the next social context in the *Spirit* chapter, the Spirit divided between the realms of Culture and Faith, with a later phase of the Unhappy Consciousness. Thus he writes of "religion . . . in the form in which it appears here as the Faith belonging to the world of Culture" that "we have already seen it in other characteristic forms, viz. as the Unhappy Consciousness, as a shape of the insubstantial process of consciousness itself " (par. 528). Finally, it is clear that Hegel understands the next social context in the *Spirit* chapter, the Pure Insight which becomes disseminated to all by the Enlightenment (par. 539), to correspond to the next shape of consciousness from the chapters *Consciousness* through *Reason*, Observing Reason from the start of the *Reason* chapter. Thus, he explicitly associates Pure Insight with Reason: "Pure Insight is . . . the certainty of self-conscious Reason that it is all truth"; its slogan is, "Be for yourselves what you all are in yourselves—reasonable" (pars. 536–37). And he characterizes Pure Insight as serving precisely the same intellectual function which we earlier saw him to associate with Observing Reason, namely, that of recognizing the objective world to be implicitly one with the subject: "In Pure Insight, . . . objectivity has the significance of a merely negative content, a content which is reduced to a moment and returns into the self; that is to say, only the self is really the object of the self, or the object only has truth so far as it has the form of the self " (par. 529; cf. 536–37). These correlations may now be summarized (see table 2).

It is, then, pretty clear that the officially intended design of the *Spirit* chapter is that it should give a second chronological treatment of history focusing on the sequence of "Spirits" or social contexts associated with the shapes of consciousness whose chronological history has already been told in the chapters *Consciousness* through *Reason*.

* * *

This reading of the *Spirit* chapter requires a major qualification, however (a point which Lukács fails to note). For, as Hegel actually wrote the chapter, it falls a considerable way short of fully realizing this officially intended design.[5] The chapter conforms to this design well enough in its

---

5. Not for nothing did Hegel complain to Schelling of "the major deformity of the later parts [of the *Phenomenology*]" (appendix XII).

Table 2

Consciousness to Reason	Spirit
Consciousness:	
Sense-certainty	
Perception	
Force and Understanding	Ethical World (early)
Life	Ethical World (late)
Lordship and Bondage	Ethical Action
Stoicism	Legal Status (early)
Skepticism	Legal Status (later)
Unhappy Consciousness (early)	Legal Status (latest)
Unhappy Consciousness (late)	Culture and Faith
Observing Reason	Pure Insight
.	.
.	.
.	.

earlier stages—Ethical World, Ethical Action, Legal Status, and Culture. Thereafter, however, it deviates from this design in two major respects. First, it lapses from its official intention of depicting contents *historically associated* with contents treated in corresponding sections of the chapters *Consciousness* through *Reason*. This is readily seen from the fact that, whereas the second half of the *Reason* chapter is, as we observed, exclusively concerned with modern *German* developments, the corresponding sections of the *Spirit* chapter instead focus over a long stretch on modern *French* developments. This shift to France already begins in later parts of the *Culture* section, where we encounter characterizations of the French ancien régime (pars. 511 ff.) and of Diderot's critique thereof in his *Rameau's Nephew* (pars. 520 ff.). The section *The Enlightenment* continues this French focus, having as its main topic the French Encyclopaedists. So too, thereafter, does the section *Absolute Freedom and Terror,* which is concerned with Rousseau and the French Revolution. Second, from the section *Faith and Pure Insight* onwards—with a partial exception in the treatment of the French Revolution in the section *Absolute Freedom and Terror*—the chapter ceases to depict *social contexts,* instead focusing once again, like the earlier chapters, on very general perspectives or "shapes of consciousness," this contrary to the official policy stated at the beginning of the chapter that we have now left behind "shapes of consciousness" for "shapes of a world" (par. 441). Thus, for example, Hegel's treatment of Pure Insight reads much more like an abbreviated redescription of the shape of consciousness Observing Reason than a description of a social context for that shape. And it is also symptomatic of this change that later parts of the chapter actually begin to characterize its contents as "shapes of consciousness" once again (pars. 499, 559, 582).[6]

The later parts of the *Spirit* chapter deviate from its officially intended design in these ways because they in effect *abandon* that design in order to undertake a sort of *rewriting of the later parts of the Reason chapter*, a rewriting of them identifying a different series of historical representatives for a similar series of developments in thought.[7] To illustrate this rewriting project: It will be recalled that the *Pleasure and Necessity* section of the *Reason* chapter depicted a development in thought which consisted in consciousness responding to modern natural science's implicit idealism by turning away from a theoretical concern with the objective world and instead toward the subject and its own hedonistic interests, and that it identified Goethe's *Faust* fragment as the main historical representative of this development. Now, by contrast, the *Spirit* chapter's section *The Enlightenment* reidentifies basically the same development in thought with the Enlightenment and its principle of Utility or the Useful: "Things are simply *useful* and to be considered only from the standpoint of utility. The *cultivated* self-consciousness which has traversed the world of self-alienated Spirit has . . . produced the thing as its own self; therefore it still retains its own self in it and knows that the thing lacks self-

---

6. It is an important example of this second lapse from the chapter's officially intended design that, as Taylor points out, whereas the official conception of the chapter leads one to expect it to culminate, like the later *Lectures on the Philosophy of World History,* in a description of "the law-state of modern times," in fact "we pass into the new moral consciousness of contemporary German philosophy as a prelude to a new philosophically interpreted religious consciousness" (*Hegel,* p. 172). This particular feature of the text has tempted several interpreters into ideas about Hegel's philosophical position at the time of the *Phenomenology* which are, I think, seriously mistaken—such as that, in sharp contrast to both his earlier and his later positions, he had at this time temporarily demoted the state in importance for modernity (F. Rosenzweig, *Hegel und der Staat* [Munich/Berlin: Verlag von R. Oldenbourg, 1920], 1:206–20; 2:3–4), or even that, so far from envisaging history as culminating in a modern law-state, he now envisaged it as culminating in the *abolition* of the state (Westphal, *History and Truth,* pp. 176–78, 183, 222).

7. It is possible, and indeed likely, that this rewriting project was inconsistently copresent in Hegel's mind with the more official project of furnishing the social contexts for the preceding shapes of consciousness *from the start of his work on the chapter.* The fact that the whole course of the chapter as it was eventually written is already sketched at paragraphs 442 and 486 suggests that this probably was the case.

subsistence, that it is *essentially* only a *being-for-an-other*"; "The useful is the object insofar as self-consciousness penetrates it and has in it the *certainty* of its *individual self*, its enjoyment" (pars. 791, 581). Similarly, the developments in thought which the sections of the *Reason* chapter following *Pleasure and Necessity*—namely, *The Law of the Heart, Virtue and the Way of the World,* and *The Spiritual Animalkingdom*—had identified with a sequence of German representatives are now all reassigned by the next section of the *Spirit* chapter, *Absolute Freedom and Terror,* to various aspects of the French Revolution. Thus, as we saw, the section *The Law of the Heart* associated a development in thought consisting in the emergence of a faith in the self as an immediate source of moral law in defiance of existing society, and the demise of this faith in disaster resulting from its practical realization, with Karl Moor in Schiller's *The Robbers*. But now the section *Absolute Freedom and Terror* associates the very same development in thought with the French Revolution, and in particular Robespierre, instead: the "*single, individual* will to which universal law and work stand opposed," but which at the same time is "directly conscious of itself as universal will; . . . is aware that its object is a law," and whose attainment of control and action results in "merely the *fury* of destruction" (pars. 587, 589). Again, as we saw, the *Reason* chapter's sections *Virtue and the Way of the World* and *The Spiritual Animalkingdom* ascribed developments in thought consisting in the disciplining of individualism so as to restore respect for the community, and the resulting emergence of a more communal attitude, to the governmental discipline of Frederick the Great, and the outlook of Herder, respectively. But now the section *Absolute Freedom and Terror* reassigns the same developments to the Jacobin Terror of 1793, which is similarly described as disciplining unbridled individualism and restoring individuals to deference toward their community and its functional roles: "These individuals who have felt the fear of death, of their absolute master, again submit to negation and distinctions, arrange themselves in the various spheres, and return to an apportioned and limited task, but thereby to their substantial reality . . . Absolute freedom has thus removed the antithesis between the universal and the individual will" (pars. 593–95).[8]

8. From this point on the *Spirit* chapter returns us from French to German soil, as in the second half of the *Reason* chapter. In the section *The Moral View of the World* we focus, as in the section of the *Reason* chapter *Reason as Testing Laws*, on Kant's moral philosophy—though this time, in order to keep chronological sequence after the treatment of the Jacobin Terror of 1793 in the section *Absolute Freedom and Terror*, on Kant's moral

That the later parts of the *Spirit* chapter develop into a sort of rewriting of the later parts of the *Reason* chapter in this way is also reflected in some of the things that Hegel says when he looks back over the whole work's contents from the vantage point of the *Absolute Knowing* chapter. Thus, reviewing there the work's sequence of shapes of consciousness, he begins with shapes from the chapters *Consciousness* through *Reason*, but goes only as far as Observing Reason, and then completes the sequence by switching to The Enlightenment and its principle of Utility and the rest of the later sections of the *Spirit* chapter (pars. 789–92, 803). And in the *Absolute Knowing* chapter he distinguishes only *two* routes toward the ultimate perspective of Absolute Knowing where one might have expected him to distinguish three: he distinguishes the route of the *Religion* chapter, but then runs together the two routes of the chapters *Consciousness* through *Reason* and the *Spirit* chapter, counting these as but a single route (pars. 794, 796; cf. 680).

How are we to explain this deviation in the second half of the *Spirit* chapter from the chapter's officially intended design, its development instead into a sort of rewriting of the later sections of the *Reason* chapter? Four factors help to explain this, the first two as mere causes, the second two as positive reasons: First, as has been mentioned, and will be demonstrated in part 4, Hegel did not when he began writing the *Phenomenology* plan to include a *Spirit* chapter at all. That the chapter was thus conceived at the last moment, rather than having been carefully planned in advance, must have made it very vulnerable to the sort of deviation from its officially intended design that occurred. Second, the chapter seems from the start to have been officially conceived as a treatment of the social contexts for shapes of consciousness *as they appeared to those shapes of consciousness themselves.* Thus, for example, the early part of the chapter represents Greek society *through the plays of Sophocles,* and in the *Doctrine of Consciousness* from 1808–9 Hegel describes the con-

---

philosophy as stated in *Religion within the Bounds of Reason Alone* from 1793, rather than as stated in the works of the 1780s. After that we pass on to some still more recent German developments not included in the *Reason* chapter at all: in particular, Fichte's *Wissenschaftslehre* of 1794, and then, in the section on The Beautiful Soul, the Romantics Novalis, the Schlegels, et al. Finally, in the concluding paragraphs of the chapter (670–71) we arrive at Hegel's own standpoint. Note that this new culmination of the history of thought—Kant, then Fichte, then the Romantics, then Hegel's own standpoint—was henceforth canonical for Hegel, being retained almost unaltered as the culmination of the history of philosophy in the *Lectures on the History of Philosophy*.

tents of the *Spirit* chapter generally as "*the consciousness of* the world of finite Spirit."[9] This role for consciousness officially present in the chapter from the start made the chapter's slide from treating social contexts into treating mere shapes of consciousness once again a very easy one to fall into.[10] Third, and more positively, as we noted previously, the later sections of the *Reason* chapter were somewhat chronologically cramped and artificial. This gave Hegel an incentive to develop a less chronologically cramped and artificial version of this part of his account, just such as we find in the later parts of the *Spirit* chapter. Fourth, and again positively, the later sections of the *Reason* chapter were, in their exclusively German focus, dubiously parochial, particularly in allowing no role in the recent history of thought to the French. Moreover, as Hegel actually wrote the *Phenomenology*, Napoleon and the French army advanced through Germany, and Hegel became increasingly optimistic that a Napoleonic conquest was about to transform the sociopolitical face of Germany decisively for the better.[11] Together these circumstances gave Hegel a strong reason to develop a less parochial, more French-oriented, revision of the later parts of the *Reason* chapter, of just the sort that we find toward the end of the *Spirit* chapter. Thus the French ancien régime, Enlightenment, and Revolution now receive their due, and—as Lukács points out—history is now written to conclude in a way reflecting Hegel's utopian vision of a Napoleonic Germany.[12] At the same time, the ongoing flux of military events made it impossible for Hegel to be confident about the sociopolitical details of such a vision for the future, and his position on the German side of the lines also made it dangerous for him to be at all explicit about them (an invitation to charges of treason). And so he rather strictly steered his account, especially toward its later end, away from sociopolitical matters and toward the less predictively problematic and personally hazardous *intellectual* aspects of French influence and the resulting new Germany. This fourth reason is probably the most important of all.[13]

9. *Nürnberger und Heidelberger Schriften*, p. 72; emphasis added. This feature of the *Spirit* chapter seems to be motivated largely by a concern to minimize the discontinuity between the added project of this chapter and the original project of the preceding chapters.
10. Cf. Taylor's explanation of why the chapter ends not with the modern law-state but with certain contemporary forms of consciousness (*Hegel*, pp. 172, 187).
11. On this see chapter 12 below.
12. Lukács, *The Young Hegel*, pp. 503–4.
13. The above explanation is not meant to exclude additional, more philosophical reasons (or perhaps rationalizations?) for the drift from social phenomena to shapes of con-

Still, this one major qualification should not be allowed to obscure the more important point that it *was* the officially intended design of the *Spirit* chapter, and a design to which Hegel at least adhered in the earlier half of the chapter, that it should contain a second chronological treatment of history focusing on the "Spirits" or social contexts associated with the shapes of consciousness whose history had already been told in the chapters *Consciousness* through *Reason*.

* * *

We may now turn to the *Religion* and *Absolute Knowing* chapters. That these chapters are designed to give a chronological history of men's representations of God or the Absolute in art and religion (the *Religion* chapter) and eventually Hegel's own philosophy (the *Absolute Knowing* chapter) is relatively obvious and uncontroversial.[14]

That this chronological history of representations of God or the Absolute is, in addition, intended to be a chronological history of those *associated with the shapes of consciousness and the "Spirits" or social contexts whose histories were told in the preceding chapters* is less obvious. However, two things show this to be so: First, Hegel's general remarks at the start of the *Religion* chapter imply such a plan. He writes there that in the development of religion, the religious Spirit "assumes *specific* shapes . . . ; at the same time, the specific religion has likewise a *specific actual* Spirit . . . The specific shapes which were specially developed within Consciousness, Self-consciousness, Reason, and Spirit belong to the specific shapes of self-knowing Spirit [i.e., to the specific shapes of religion] . . . From [those] shapes . . . the *specific* shape of religion picks out the one appropriate to it for its actual Spirit" (par. 680). Second, that this is Hegel's plan is confirmed by the fact that he indicates through a series of fairly explicit remarks in the text that the forms of religion in the *Religion* chapter are in each case historically associated with shapes of conscious-

---

sciousness toward the end of the chapter, such as for example a greater inwardness which Hegel attributes to modern German culture as compared to French.

14. Thus, besides Lukács, Hyppolite too asserts the chronologically historical character of the *Religion* chapter (*Genesis and Structure,* p. 38). And even Solomon comes close to grudgingly acknowledging it: despite an (alleged) official aim to "avoid 'temporalizing' or 'historicizing' " the sequence of the chapter, Hegel proceeds there in such a way that he can "put in historical order first the Greeks and then medieval philosophy and Christianity" (*In the Spirit of Hegel,* pp. 600, 605).

ness and "Spirits" or social contexts found at corresponding points in the two preceding treatments of history.

Let us go through the earlier parts of the *Religion* chapter in order to illustrate this latter claim. As has already been noted, the first forms of religion in the chapter, the forms of Natural Religion, are all associated with the ancient oriental and Egyptian world, the first of them, God as Light, representing mainly the Zoroastrian tradition of ancient Persia, the second, Plant and Animal, mainly the pantheism of ancient India, and the third, The Artificer, mainly the monumental religion of Pharaonic Egypt. Now Natural Religion corresponds to the contents of the *Consciousness* chapter: in Natural Religion "Spirit in general is in the form of Consciousness" (par. 683). More specifically, Hegel explicitly associates each of the forms of Natural Religion in turn with a shape of consciousness from a corresponding position in the *Consciousness* chapter: God as Light with Sense-certainty (par. 686), Plant and Animal with Perception (par. 689), and The Artificer with Force and the Understanding (par. 692), or more precisely with a primitive form of Force and the Understanding, "the abstract form of the Understanding" (pars. 692, 694). The social correlates of these forms of religion would be oriental and Egyptian forerunners of the Ethical World of early ancient Greece with which the *Spirit* chapter begins.[15] The next form of religion in the *Religion* chapter, Religion in the Form of Art, refers to the religious and artistic institutions of ancient Greece. It is associated with five consecutive stages from each of the two preceding treatments of history: first, the culmination of *Consciousness* in a more mature form of Force and the Understanding = the Ethical World; second, Life = the Ethical World; third,

---

15 The oriental and Egyptian beginnings of history with which the *Religion* chapter opens were clearly not yet (at least, not in any focused way) a part of Hegel's conception of the beginnings of history when he wrote the two preceding treatments of history in the chapters *Consciousness* through *Reason* and in the *Spirit* chapter, which only become geographically and culturally definite with the ancient Greeks. In thus pushing Hegel's geographically and culturally definite conception of the beginnings of history back to the ancient Orient and Egypt, the *Religion* chapter implies some modest revisions at the start of each of the two preceding treatments of history: specifically, the shapes of consciousness in the *Consciousness* chapter prior to the mature form of Force and the Understanding, which had previously been thought of as only vaguely prehistorical, now become identified more definitely with the ancient Orient and Egypt (in the manner described above); and it is also implied that at the start of the *Spirit* chapter there should strictly be treatments of ancient oriental and Egyptian social forms preceding the treatment of the Greeks' Ethical World.

Lordship and Bondage = Ethical Action; fourth, Stoicism = Legal Status; fifth, Skepticism = Legal Status.[16] Thus, to go through these associations in turn: First, Hegel indicates that in its initial form Religion in the Form of Art is still associated with (Force and the) Understanding, and also with the Ethical World: here "the ensoulment of the organic is taken up into . . . the Understanding and, at the same time, its essential nature—incommensurability—is preserved for the Understanding"; "If we ask, which is the *actual* Spirit which has the consciousness of its absolute essence in the religion of art, we find that it is the *ethical* or the *true* Spirit" (pars. 706, 700). Second, Hegel implies the association of the next stage of Religion in the Form of Art with Life, for he entitles it "b. The *Living Work of Art*" (cf. the references to Life at pars. 725, 742, 753). And since, as we have already seen, Life is associated with a phase of the Ethical World, this implies that this stage of Religion in the Form of Art is associated not only with Life but also, again, with the Ethical World. Third, Hegel indicates that Religion in the Form of Art reaches its zenith, the "absolute art" of Greek tragedy, with the emergence of Self-consciousness and the break-up of the Ethical World (pars. 701–2). Since Hegel equates the emergence of Self-consciousness with Lordship and Bondage—"the immediate existence of Self-consciousness" (par. 479; cf. 686)—this implies an association of the "absolute" form of Religion in the Form of Art with Lordship and Bondage. Moreover, since he equates the break-up of the Ethical World with Ethical Action (in the *Spirit* chapter), it implies the association of the "absolute" form of Religion in the Form of Art with Ethical Action as well. And indeed he indicates explicitly that when Religion in the Form of Art reaches its "absolute" expression in Greek tragedy we are in the period of Ethical Action (pars. 736 ff.)—a social form which, it will be recalled, was also associated with Greek tragedy in the *Spirit* chapter. Fourth and fifth, Hegel indicates that Religion in the Form of Art's last phase, ancient comedy, is associated with Legal Status, and with Stoicism and Skepticism. Thus, concerning the association with Legal Status, he writes generally that "the Religion of Art belongs to the Ethical Spirit which we earlier saw perish in the *condition of right* or law [i.e., in Legal Status]," and more specifically that the final form of Religion in the Form of Art, ancient comedy, is associated with Legal Status, that "in the condition of right or law [i.e.,

---

16. The indicated equalities, and those which follow below, were demonstrated in our earlier discussion of the *Spirit* chapter.

Legal Status] . . . the ethical world and the religion of that world are lost in the comic consciousness" (pars. 750, 753).[17] And since, as we have seen, Legal Status = Stoicism and Skepticism primarily—a point which the section on Religion in the Form of Art reiterates (par. 751)—this association of the final form of Religion in the Form of Art, ancient comedy, with Legal Status implies its association with Stoicism and Skepticism as well. Turning now to the next form of religion in the Religion chapter, Revealed Religion, Hegel associates this in an early phase with the Unhappy Consciousness = Legal Status / Culture and Faith. Thus he writes that "the content which we have to consider [in Revealed Religion] has partly been met with already as the idea of the Unhappy Consciousness and the consciousness with Faith" (par. 768; cf. 750–54). A later phase of Revealed Religion is associated with Observing Reason = Pure Insight, as one can see from Hegel's strikingly similar description of it as, like them, recognizing the universal or self-like character of the natural world: "Abstract essence is alienated from itself, it has natural existence . . . ; this its otherness, or its sensuous presence, is taken back again . . . and posited as superseded, as *universal*. The essence has thereby come to be its own self in its sensuous presence; the immediate existence of actuality has ceased to be something alien and external . . . , since that existence is superseded, is *universal*" (par. 779; cf. 781, 783).[18] These correlations may now be summarized (see table 3).

* * *

What is the guiding principle behind this grand threefold treatment of history developed by the *Phenomenology,* in which each treatment in turn focuses on a different aspect of social totalities—first their shapes of consciousness, then their social contexts, then their conceptions of God

17. It is part of Hegel's idea here that just as Legal Status elevates the individual person, in it "the self as such . . . is absolute being" (par. 750), so comedy elevates the "individual self" as well (par. 747).

18. At this point, the two preceding treatments of history in the chapters *Consciousness* through *Reason* and the *Spirit* chapter diverge due to the rewriting project described earlier. As one might expect, the *Religion* chapter henceforth attempts to remain correlated with the latter revising treatment rather than the former revised treatment. Hence, for example, one can see from the following passage late in the *Revealed Religion* section that a still later phase of Revealed Religion is correlated with Absolute Freedom and Terror: "We see self-consciousness at its last turning-point become *inward* to itself and attain to a *knowledge* of its inwardness; we see it divest itself of its natural existence and acquire pure negativity" (par. 787). For the references here to self-consciousness becoming "inward" and attaining "a knowledge of itself as inward" and acquiring "pure negativity" are clear allusions to developments in the *Absolute Freedom and Terror* section (cf. pars. 589–90 in that section).

Table 3

Consciousness through Reason	Spirit	Religion and Absolute Knowing
Sense-certainty	[Oriental forerunner of] Ethical World	Natural Religion: God as Light
Perception	[Oriental forerunner of] Ethical World	Natural Religion: Plant and Animal
Force and Understanding (early)	[Egyptian forerunner of] Ethical World	Natural Religion: The Artificer
Force and Understanding (late)	Ethical World	Religion of Art (first phase)
Life	Ethical World	Religion of Art (second phase)
Lordship and Bondage	Ethical Action	Religion of Art (third phase)
Stoicism	Legal Status (early)	Religion of Art (fourth phase)
Skepticism	Legal Status (later)	Religion of Art (fifth phase)
Unhappy Consciousness (early)	Legal Status (latest)	Revealed Religion (first phase)
Unhappy Consciousness (late)	Culture and Faith	Revealed Religion (second phase)
Observing Reason	Pure Insight	Revealed Religion (third phase)
.	.	.
.	.	.
.	.	.

or the Absolute? The—or at least *a*—guiding principle is that these different aspects of social totalities are unequal in their levels of fundamentalness for the explanation of social totalities and their historical development, and that one should proceed from giving the history of the less explanatorily fundamental aspect to giving the history of the more explanatorily fundamental aspect. Shapes of consciousness are understood to be least explanatorily fundamental and so are treated first, social contexts are conceived to be more explanatorily fundamental and so are treated next, conceptions of God or the Absolute are considered to be most explanatorily fundamental of all and so are treated last.

It is illuminating in this connection to consider the *Phenomenology* in the light of Hegel's earlier and later works. It had been very characteristic of Hegel's *pre*phenomenological writings from the mid-1790s on to treat the types of thought that had arisen over the course of history as explicable in terms of the specific socio-economico-political contexts within which they had arisen. One example of this is *The Spirit of Christianity*'s explanation of Judaism's "positive" or divine-command conception of moral obligation, and commitment to moral prescriptions which opposed rather than expressing human desires, in terms of the socio-economico-political fact of the Jews' *enslavement* in the ancient world, beginning with their enslavement by the Egyptians. A second, related, example is *The Positivity of the Christian Religion*'s explanation of the decline of polytheism and the rise of Christianity in the later ancient Greek and Roman world in terms of the socio-economico-political process of a collapse of sociopolitical freedom in Athens and Rome resulting from the ascent through successful wars of a socio-economico-political elite which came to oppress the rest of the citizenry. A third example is Hegel's socio-economico-political explanation of the Reformation in *The German Constitution*, according to which the economic development of the cities of the Holy Roman Empire during the Middle Ages led to the rise of the bourgeoisie, whose individualist spirit then developed Protestantism as its legitimating ideology.[19] Hegel's *post*phenomenological writings, on the other hand, tend to reverse the order of explanation: social contexts are explained in terms of the types of—artistic, religious, and philosophical—thought which develop within them, and more specifically in terms of their appropriateness to these, rather than the other way around. Hence, for example, in the *Lectures on the Philosophy of World History* we read that "the highest point in the development of a nation is reached when it has understood its life and condition by means of thought . . .

---

19. *The German Constitution*, in Hegel, *Political Writings*, trans. T.M. Knox (Oxford: Oxford University Press, 1964), pp. 189–90. The later Hegel, by contrast, while never abandoning it altogether, tends to de-emphasize the theme of the socio-economico-political causation of ideas. For example, whereas the fundamental explanans of the corruption of Greek culture in *The Positivity of the Christian Religion* is the socio-economico-political process mentioned above, in the *Lectures on the Philosophy of World History* it is instead an intellectual process, namely, the corrupting influence of Sophistic and Socratic ideas.

The aim of its endeavours is for it to have itself as its own object . . . Thus, if we wish to know what Greece really was, we find the answer in Sophocles and Aristophanes, Thucydides and Plato."[20] (To put the point facetiously, one could say that Hegel began his career a Marxist and later became a Hegelian.)

The *Phenomenology*'s threefold treatment of history constitutes an interesting compromise between, or synthesis of, the earlier and the later positions. On the one hand, and I think most deserving of emphasis, the *Phenomenology* retains a version of the earlier position, in that it treats the very general forms of thought, or "shapes of consciousness," depicted in the chapters *Consciousness* through *Reason* as belonging to and explicable in terms of the social contexts, or "Spirits," depicted in the *Spirit* chapter. Thus, as noted, when Hegel makes the transition from the former to the latter he writes that "all previous shapes of consciousness are abstract forms of [Spirit] . . . [Their isolation] *presupposes* Spirit itself and subsists therein; in other words, the isolation exists only in Spirit which is a concrete existence" (par. 440). And, as we will see in some detail in chapter 12, he then proceeds in the *Spirit* chapter to offer a series of explanations of the shapes of consciousness already encountered in terms of their social contexts. On the other hand, the *Phenomenology* anticipates Hegel's later position as well, in that it treats these social contexts as, in their turn, belonging to, and explicable in terms of their appropriateness to, the types of artistic, religious, or philosophical thought associated with them. Thus when Hegel turns from the *Spirit* chapter's history of social contexts to the *Religion* chapter's history of the forms of artistic and religious thought associated with them, he writes: "The specific religion has . . . a *specific actual* Spirit . . . The specific shapes which were specially developed within . . . Spirit belong to the specific shapes of self-knowing Spirit [i.e., to the specific shapes of religion] . . . From [these] shapes . . . the *specific* shape of religion picks out the one appropriate to it for its actual Spirit. The one distinctive feature which characterizes the religion penetrates every aspect of its actual existence and stamps them with its common character" (par. 680).[21]

---

20. *Lectures on the Philosophy of World History: Introduction*, p. 146. The Hegel of the early theological writings, by contrast, still fundamentally lacked the later Hegel's idea of explaining social contexts and their histories in terms of ideas as final causes.

21. Someone might be moved to object that this compromise or synthesis in the *Phenomenology* between Hegel's earlier and later positions is inconsistent in implying that (i) thought is to be explained in terms of its social context (in the *Spirit* chapter) and vice

versa (in the *Religion* and *Absolute Knowing* chapters), and (ii) the explanans is in each case more explanatorily fundamental than the explanandum. Note, to begin with, that there would clearly be no inconsistency in (i) *per se,* for causation and hence explanation could quite well be *reciprocal* between thought and social context. Hegel does in fact prefer reciprocal over unidirectional causal explanations in such cases (concerning which, see for example *Encyclopaedia,* par. 156, addition). It might, though, more plausibly seem that (i) *conjoined with (ii)* was inconsistent. Such an objection would still be ill grounded, however, and this for at least two reasons: First, the thoughts which serve first as explanandum (in the *Spirit* chapter) and then subsequently as explanans (in the *Religion* and *Absolute Knowing* chapters) are, officially at least, not the same; the former are very general forms of thought, or "shapes of consciousness," the latter rather specific contents of thought, specific artistic, religious, and philosophical ideas. Second, the types of causation and explanation involved in the two cases are different; when thought appears as explanandum (in the *Spirit* chapter) what is at issue is basically the *efficient* causal explanation of thought by social context, whereas when thought appears as explanans (in the *Religion* and *Absolute Knowing* chapters) what is in question is rather the *final* causal explanation of social context by thought. Consequently, even if the thoughts figuring first as explanandum and then as explanans *were* the same, (i) and (ii) would not produce inconsistency. For it could consistently be, and in part is, Hegel's position that social contexts are more explanatorily fundamental than thoughts *in terms of efficient causation,* but thoughts more explanatorily fundamental than social contexts *in terms of final causation* (and that, additionally, final causal explanation is a more fundamental form of explanation than efficient causal explanation [concerning which, see again for example *Encyclopaedia,* par. 156, addition]).

CHAPTER TWELVE

Further Intellectual
Historicism in the
Phenomenology

The former of the two ideas guiding the design of the second half of the *Phenomenology* mentioned at the end of the previous chapter—the idea, continuous with the position in Hegel's earlier writings, that the general types of thought which have arisen during the course of history belong to and are explicable in terms of their specific social contexts—deserves special emphasis. For, (i) this is an idea which proves, on close inspection, to play a very pervasive and fundamental role within the *Phenomenology*—not only guiding the official project of the *Spirit* chapter in the way indicated in the last chapter, but also dominating the historical account of the *Self-consciousness* chapter, and in addition the work's conception, expressed cryptically in the Preface, of the relation of Hegel's *own* intellectual outlook to its social context. Yet (ii) this is an idea which easily can be, and usually is, overlooked in the *Phenomenology*, and in Hegel generally. For, it is an idea which is in various ways obscured within the *Phenomenology*—for example, by the *Spirit* chapter's methodological policy of treating the social contexts for shapes of consciousness *as they appeared to consciousness itself,* and by the chapter's midstream switch from its official project of considering the social contexts for shapes of consciousness to an unofficial project of rewriting the later parts of the *Reason* chapter's history of shapes of consciousness and so considering only shapes of consciousness once again.[1] And it is an idea which

---

1. These two features of the *Spirit* chapter encouraged the Marx of the *Economic and Philosophic Manuscripts*, for example, to think the differences between the *Phenomenology*'s position and his own much greater than they really are. The chapter's *methodological*

belongs mainly to Hegel's earlier thought, up to and including the *Phenomenology*, but is not significantly sustained in his later writings.[2] Moreover, (iii) this is an idea of great originality and intrinsic interest, which has, in one form or another, gone on to play a major role in much of the most interesting philosophy and social science since Hegel.[3] This, therefore, is a seventh intellectual historicist idea of the *Phenomenology* which deserves our close attention.

The *Phenomenology* is in fact committed to two distinguishable forms of this idea. First, it is committed to the possibility of giving social explanations of the *origination* of types of thought. This is a major function of the *Self-consciousness* chapter, where Hegel gives social explanations of the origination of the dualistic types of thought which have, in his view, dominated Western culture from later ancient times until his own day. Second, the *Phenomenology* is also committed to the possibility of

---

policy of treating social contexts for shapes of consciousness as they appeared to consciousness itself was misinterpreted by Marx as a commitment to the *ontological reducibility* of social facts to consciousness (*Marx: Selections*, p. 66). It thereby encouraged him to take the generally mistaken view that for the Hegel of the *Phenomenology*, unlike himself, the fragmentation of consciousness does not reflect social fragmentation, but instead conversely: "The alienation of self-consciousness is not taken to be an expression of the *actual* alienation of human nature reflected in knowledge and thought. *Actual* alienation . . . is rather in its *innermost* and concealed character . . . only the *appearance* of the alienation of actual human nature, of *self-consciousness*" (ibid., p. 68). Similarly, the *Spirit* chapter's midstream switch in project from considering social contexts for shapes of consciousness to considering only shapes of consciousness once again, and more specifically its displacement, after considering alienating social contexts, of an expected culmination in the modern reconciling law-state by a culmination in certain mere forms of consciousness, was misread by Marx as reflective of quite deliberate philosophical design. It thereby encouraged him in the generally mistaken conception that for the Hegel of the *Phenomenology*, unlike himself, overcoming social alienation is solely a matter of changing how we *think*: "The appropriation of man's essential capacities . . . is only an *appropriation* taking place in *consciousness*, in *pure thought* . . . It is the appropriation of . . . objects as *thoughts* and thought processes" (ibid., p. 66). (One qualification of this criticism of Marx's criticisms will be entered later.)

2. In the later writings not only do ideas become more explanatorily fundamental than social contexts as *final* causes (as noted in the previous chapter) but they tend to do so also as *efficient* causes. Thus, whereas, as we have seen, the earlier writings explained the development of Judaic moral conceptions, the displacement of polytheistic ideas by Christian ideas in the later ancient world, and the ideology of the Reformation in terms of socioeconomico-political efficient causes, the *Lectures on the Philosophy of World History* explains the social corruption of the later ancient world in terms of the efficient causality of Sophistic and Socratic ideas, and the French Revolution's social transformation in terms of the efficient causality of the ideas of the French *philosophes*.

3. One thinks, for example, of Marx, Durkheim and Mauss, Mannheim, Bloor's "strong program" in the philosophy of science, and Foucault.

providing social explanations of the subsequent *survival and growth* of types of thought. This is a major function of the *Spirit* chapter, where Hegel gives social explanations of the subsequent survival and growth of the dualistic types of thought whose origination has been explained socially in the *Self-consciousness* chapter.[4] (This division of labor between the two chapters is not rigid, though, but rather a matter of emphasis.)

Let us consider, as prime examples of this twofold social explanation of types of thought in the *Phenomenology,* the work's social explanations, mainly in the *Self-consciousness* chapter, of the origination, and, mainly in the *Spirit* chapter, of the subsequent survival and growth of the dualistic outlooks of Stoicism and Christianity.

To begin with the *Self-consciousness* chapter's social explanation of the origination of Stoicism's outlook: Already in a fragment from the late 1790s Hegel had explained the origination of Stoicism's outlook in the later ancient world in terms of the development of sociopolitical oppression in later periods of Greek and Roman history, arguing that Stoicism's distinctive epistemological and practical retreat from the external world to the subject's own mind was an attempt at a theoretical level to escape from that sociopolitical oppression, to establish a surrogate sphere of freedom internally: "After the demise of Roman and Greek freedom, when men had been deprived of the rule of their ideas over objects . . . the spirit of the Stoics . . . said: you [objects] are foreign to my nature, which knows nothing about you; I rule over you in my idea; you can be as you wish, that is a matter of indifference to me, you are too contemptible in my eyes for me to want to touch you."[5] The *Self-consciousness* chapter of the *Phenomenology* implies a similar explanation of the origination of Stoicism in its direct transition from Lordship and Bondage to Stoicism (for, as we have seen, Lordship and Bondage again represents the development of sociopolitical oppression in later periods of Greek and Roman history). Thus we read in the *Stoicism* section that "Stoicism could only appear on the scene in a time of universal fear and bondage," and that the Stoic consciousness's (epistemological and practical) "withdraw[al] from existence only into itself" was aimed at a sort of restoration of the freedom which it had lost in the objective and social sphere,

---

4. Norman, in *Hegel's Phenomenology,* well recognizes and describes the *Spirit* chapter's role in this (pp. 86–97). But he fails to recognize, and even denies, the *Self-consciousness* chapter's role (p. 55).

5. *Dokumente zu Hegels Entwicklung,* p. 264.

at the goal that "in thinking, I *am free*, because I am not in an *other* [object or person], but remain simply and solely in communion with myself" (pars. 198, 201, 197). As one can see from these passages, Hegel also understands this explanation to account more broadly for Stoicism's development of each of the several dualisms which he associates with it in the *Phenomenology:* its sharp division of the individual from his community (with respect to both ultimate ends and cognitive authority); its sharp division of the individual's thought from reality; its sharp division of the individual's volition from fact; and its sharp division of the individual's mind or self from his body. The ultimate motive behind each of these sharp theoretical divisions, in Hegel's view, is an impulse arising from the development of sociopolitical oppression in the objective and social sphere to restore the individual to the freedom thereby lost by theoretically detaching him from the now oppressive objective and social sphere.

Hegel in the *Self-consciousness* chapter also offers a further explanation of Stoicism's development of the last three of the four dualisms just mentioned in terms of the emergence of socio-economico-political oppression in the later ancient world and its psychological impact on the oppressed. The crux of this further explanation is as follows. The social deference which the oppressed, the "bondsman," must now show to his oppressor, the "lord," and the intellectual deference which he must now show to the objects on which he is forced to labor for the lord, are—in contrast to the self-assertiveness characteristic of the lord in his relations to both men and things—conducive, respectively, to introspection and the recognition of objectivity. And these two outcomes together generate Stoicism's characteristic perception of sharp distinctions between the subject's thought and objective reality, volition and objective fact, and mind/self and objective body. Thus Hegel writes that, unlike for the lord, "the thing is independent vis-à-vis the bondsman" who "works on it," and the bondsman "as a consciousness forced back into itself . . . will withdraw into itself and be transformed into a truly independent consciousness," so that consequently "for the subservient consciousness [i.e., the bondsman] . . . , these two moments—itself as an independent object, and this object as a mode of consciousness and hence its own essential nature—fall apart" (pars. 190, 193, 197).[6]

---

6. In this whole social explanation of the origination of Stoicism Hegel appears to have in mind especially the examples of the early Stoic Cleanthes, who was extremely poor and

The above social explanations of the *origination* of Stoicism's outlook also serve in part as social explanations of the outlook's subsequent *survival and growth* within the Roman Empire. For the socio-economico-political oppression in question of course persists there. However, the *Spirit* chapter's section *Legal Status* also adds a further social explanation of the outlook's subsequent survival and growth within the Roman Empire (for, as we have seen, the *Legal Status* section explicitly associates Stoicism with the social context Legal Status, that is, the Roman Empire). This explanation is that Stoicism's sharp theoretical divisions of the subject from objective and social reality found widespread acceptance within the Roman Empire in part because they reflected in an abstract theoretical way the *concrete social and legal atomism* experienced by the citizens of the Roman Empire:

> Stoicism is nothing else but the consciousness which reduces to its abstract form the principle of Legal Status . . . By its flight from the actual world [Stoicism] attained only to the *thought* of independence; it is absolutely for *itself,* in that it does not attach its being to anything that exists, but claims to give up everything that exists and places its essence solely in the essence of pure thought. In the same way, the right of a person [in Legal Status] is not tied to a richer or more powerful existence of the individual as such, nor again to a universal living Spirit, but rather to the pure One of its abstract actuality. (par. 479)[7]

Such, then, in sum, are the *Phenomenology*'s social explanations of the origination and subsequent survival and growth of Stoicism's outlook.[8]

* * *

---

supported himself in Athens by menial labor, and the later Stoic Epictetus, who was actually a slave in the Roman Empire. (For a clear allusion to the latter, see paragraph 199.)

7. This explanation in the *Legal Status* section has to be read primarily as an explanation of Stoicism's *survival and growth* rather than *origination* because the section is exclusively concerned with the Roman Empire, whereas Hegel is of course well aware that Stoicism *predated* the Roman Empire, having its origins in Hellenistic Greece. On the other hand, as we have seen, Hegel certainly envisages the condition of social atomism described here as commencing earlier among the Greeks—a theme in the section *Ethical Action*—and so it would be at least in the general spirit of his position to understand this explanation as part of his explanation of Stoicism's origination as well.

8. The *Phenomenology* gives very similar social explanations of the origination and the subsequent survival and growth of ancient Skepticism's outlook, once again mainly in the *Self-consciousness* chapter and the *Legal Status* section of the *Spirit* chapter (par. 480) respectively.

Let us turn next to the *Phenomenology*'s social explanations of Christianity's outlook, beginning with its social explanations of the *origination* of this outlook. As we have seen, the early theological writings had explained the origination of Christianity's outlook, like Stoicism's, in terms of the development of sociopolitical oppression in the later ancient world, particularly in this case the Roman Empire. According to the fullest version of this explanation, given in *The Positivity of the Christian Religion*, the experience of this sociopolitical oppression in the Roman Empire had favored the development of Christianity's outlook in two main ways: (i) It had made irresistibly attractive Christianity's escapist thesis of a perfect divine realm separate from the real world with its misery, and of the Christian soul's eventual attainment of that realm and therein of happiness.[9] (ii) It had developed in people habits of slavish obedience, which made natural their acceptance of Christianity's "positive" or divine-command conception of moral obligation, and their acceptance of the desire-thwarting content of Christianity's moral prescriptions.[10] This social explanation had yielded, more specifically, social explanations of the origination of the several dualisms characteristic of Christianity's outlook. Thus, (i) had explained the original appeal of Christianity's sharp division of God from the realm of man and nature, and hence also the original appeal of Christianity's sharp division between man and nature, since this was entailed thereby; moreover, it had explained the original appeal of Christianity's sharp division between the mind or self and the body, since this served as a convenient mechanism facilitating the advancement of expired Christians to heaven. In addition, the ancient community's oppressiveness itself, together with (ii), had explained Christianity's sharp division between the individual and the community, the Christian individual's ceasing to regard the community as his highest end, and to defer automatically to the community's judgments, especially on moral matters, but coming instead to defer to God's commands; and

---

9. "The despotism of the Roman emperors had chased the human spirit from the face of the earth, its robbery of freedom had forced the human spirit to carry off its eternal aspect, its absolute aspect, to safety in the deity, the misery which it spread abroad had forced the human spirit to seek and expect happiness in heaven" (appendix I).

10. There had now developed a "habit of obeying an alien will, an alien legislation . . . But reason could never give up finding . . . the practical, somewhere or other. It was no longer to be found in people's will. It now appeared to reason in the deity which the Christian religion offered it, beyond the sphere of our power, of our volition . . . The right of legislation [was] conceded to God exclusively" (appendix I).

(ii) had also explained Christianity's characteristic sharp oppositions between duty and desire, and, relatedly, between virtue and happiness. The *Self-consciousness* chapter of the *Phenomenology,* in deriving the Unhappy Consciousness of Christianity from Lordship and Bondage, implies basically the same social explanation of the origination of Christianity's outlook. (For some further details, see chapter 2 above.)

Besides this, the *Spirit* chapter's section *Legal Status* explains the origination of further aspects of Christianity's outlook in terms of concrete sociopolitical conditions which prevailed within the Roman Empire. Specifically, it adds the interesting suggestion that Christianity's characteristic conceptions of God and his relation to men reflect the concrete sociopolitical nature of the Roman emperor and his relation to the inhabitants of the Roman Empire: The Roman emperor was (a) a person, a "self"; (b) an authority whose power and interest extended to (virtually) all regions and men, "the universal power of the actual world"; (c) an absolute power, one with "complete supremacy"; and moreover (d) one whose relation to the inhabitants of the Roman Empire was characterized by alienness—"They exist . . . in a merely negative relationship . . . to him who is their bond of connection and continuity . . . He is . . . a content alien to them, and a hostile being" (par. 482). These concrete sociopolitical features of the Roman emperor and his relation to the people of the Roman Empire are reflected in the Christian Unhappy Consciousness's characteristic conceptions of a God who is (a') a self; (b') the God of all regions and men (not merely a local or national deity); (c') an absolute power; and moreover (d') alien to men. Thus Hegel writes that "if [the Unhappy Consciousness] appeared . . . merely as the one-sided view of consciousness as consciousness, here [i.e., in these concrete sociopolitical features of the Roman emperor and his relation to the people of the Roman Empire] the *actual* truth of that view has become apparent. This truth consists in the fact that this *universally acknowledged authority* of self-consciousness is the reality from which it is alienated" (par. 482).

The *Spirit* chapter complements the above social explanations of the *origination* of Christianity's outlook with a social explanation of the outlook's subsequent *survival and growth* in the medieval to modern period: The *Culture* section of the *Spirit* chapter gives an account of the socio-economico-political development of Europe, and in particular France, from medieval times to the eighteenth century—an account focusing on the institutions of state power and wealth (or what Hegel later calls "civil society"), and on individuals' relations to these institutions, in their connected evolution.[11] This account identifies three features as more or less constant throughout the evolution: (i) State power and wealth have for the individuals who make up society the appearance of objective powers independent of themselves (pars. 486, 490, 493–95). (ii) In addition, state power and wealth are experienced by individuals as oppressing themselves.[12] (iii) Moreover, they appear to individuals as powers opposed to each other as well (pars. 486, 491).[13] Now, according to Hegel, the otherworldly Christian outlook which thrives during this whole period, Faith, is to be explained as a reflection and result of the three socio-economico-political conditions just mentioned: "The world of this Spirit breaks up into two. The first is the world of reality or of its self-alienation; but the other is that which Spirit, rising above the first, constructs for itself in the aether of pure consciousness. This second world, standing in antithesis to that alienation, is for that very reason not free from it; on the contrary, it is really only the other form of that alienation" (par. 487). Hegel conceives it as such a reflection and result in several specific ways (in each case ways analogous to those in which he conceived *early* Christianity as reflecting and resulting from the socio-economico-political realities of the Roman Empire): First, conditions (i)–(iii) make the socio-economico-political world as experienced by individuals during this period alien and oppressive, so that Christianity's "beyond" of God, heaven, and happy afterlife becomes an irresistibly seductive escape:

---

11. The section begins with feudalism (pars. 500 ff.), then proceeds to absolute monarchy, in particular that of the Bourbons, especially Louis XIV (pars. 511 ff.), then to the corruption of absolute monarchy with the ascent of nobles' ambitions and the power of wealth, in particular under the later Bourbons (pars. 512 ff.), then finally to the Enlightenment's intellectual penetration of this corrupt system, particularly as expressed in Diderot's *Rameau's Nephew* (pars. 520 ff.).

12. For example, to the commoner under feudalism state power appears as "a fetter" (par. 501), and much later, when absolute monarchy has suffered corruption, wealth "is the power over the self, the power that knows itself to be *independent* and *arbitrary*" (par. 519).

13. The last part of the section interprets the Enlightenment, and in particular Diderot in *Rameau's Nephew*, as eventually seeing through these several appearances as illusions (pars. 520 ff.). In thus implying that the alienating social phenomena dealt with in this section are mere illusions, and that the task of overcoming them is therefore merely one of unmasking them as such, Hegel *in this specific context* provides some reason for Marx's observation and complaint that he in the *Phenomenology* ontologically reduces actual social alienation to alienation in consciousness and conceives the overcoming of social alienation as solely a matter of changing how we think. However, one could plausibly argue, I think, that Hegel is deviating from rather than reflecting his considered position here. (This is the qualification of my criticism of Marx's criticisms mentioned in the first footnote of the present chapter.)

Christian "Faith ... is a *flight* from the real world" (par. 487; cf. 527, 529). (This explanation is of course closely analogous to Hegel's explanation of the same "beyond" in *early* Christianity as an escapist flight from the socio-economico-political oppression of the Roman Empire.) Second, Hegel argues that the central conceptions of Christian theology in this period mirror the components and relations of the socio-economico-political sphere: "Since [this consciousness] is the flight from this world and therefore has the character of an *antithesis* to it, it bears this world within itself"; "Faith ... is nothing else but the actual world raised into the universality of pure consciousness. The articulation of this world, therefore, constitutes the organization of the world of Faith" (pars. 529, 531). Specifically, Hegel interprets the doctrine of the Trinity as in part an imaginary reflection of state power (reflected as God the Father) and wealth (reflected as God the Son)—together with their envisaged unification (reflected as God the Holy Spirit) (pars. 512, 532). (This is analogous to Hegel's explanation of aspects of *early* Christianity's conceptions of God and his relation to men as mirroring characteristics of the Roman emperor and his relation to his subjects.) Third, Hegel implies that this imaginary reflection of elements of the fragmented and oppressive social world includes also an imaginary overcoming of their fragmentation and oppression, an imaginary replacement of this with unity and harmony: "The articulation of this world ... constitutes the organization of the world of Faith, except that in the latter the parts do not alienate themselves in their spiritualization," their "being lies in thinking the unity which they constitute," a unity which, specifically, unites state power (God the Father) and wealth (God the Son) together (as God the Holy Spirit), and moreover renders them no longer "alien to self-consciousness" (pars. 531–33). That Christianity thus provides an imaginary otherworldly solution for real social problems constitutes a further part of its seductive appeal.[14] (This is analogous—though not quite as closely this time—to Hegel's explanation of *early* Christianity's otherworldism in terms of its provision of an imaginary solution to the real problem of social oppression.)

* * *

14. Note that, in contrast with this *imaginary otherworldly* solution, it is one of the central aims of Hegel's political philosophy, for example in the *Philosophy of Right*, to discover a *genuine this-worldly* solution to the same problems, that is, a set of relations between the components of modern society in question here—state power, wealth or "civil society," and the individual—which overcomes each of the forms of opposition and oppression (i)–(iii).

This much of Hegel's position regarding the socio-economico-political origins and underpinnings of types of thought is stated explicitly in the *Phenomenology*. It is natural, however, to want to know, in addition, what Hegel's views are at the time of the *Phenomenology* concerning the socio-economico-political origins and underpinnings of certain important later types of thought, in particular, the dualistic outlooks of modern Germany, and the unifying outlook of his own philosophy. If he had fully realized the official project of the *Spirit* chapter, instead of changing its project in midstream in the manner recently described, we would have received much of the answer to this question in the second half of the *Spirit* chapter: accounts of the socio-economico-political underpinnings of the modern German dualistic outlooks already covered in the second half of the *Reason* chapter and of the unifying Hegelian outlook with which the *Reason* chapter culminated. The midstream change in the *Spirit* chapter's project deprived us of these accounts. However, all is not thereby lost, for there is, fortunately, sufficient evidence to enable us to reconstruct Hegel's accounts with a considerable degree of confidence, and this we should therefore now attempt to do.

Concerning, to begin with, the dualistic outlooks of modern Germany, an answer to the question of their socio-economico-political *origins* is in fact to a great extent given by the *Phenomenology*. For the *Self-consciousness* chapter's socio-economico-political explanations of the origination, and the *Spirit* chapter's socio-economico-political explanations of the subsequent survival and growth, of the outlooks of Stoicism and Christianity and their eight dualisms *are,* implicitly, at least the core of an account of the socio-economico-political origins of the dualistic outlooks of modern Germany (and written largely for just this reason).

What, though, is Hegel's conception of the socio-economico-political *underpinnings* of these dualistic outlooks within modern Germany itself? The change in the project of the *Spirit* chapter deprived us of any statement of this in the *Phenomenology*. Fortunately, however, we are well-placed to make good the loss. For only a few years before writing the *Phenomenology* Hegel had written a long essay addressing precisely this question. As we have seen, the early theological writings from the mid-1790s to the turn of the century had developed a strong interest in the phenomenon of dualisms in modern, and in particular modern German, culture, and they had also developed a keen appreciation of the socio-economico-political origins and underpinnings of dualistic types of thought (especially Judaism and Christianity within an ancient context).

474   History and Historicism in the *Phenomenology*

Given this combination of positions, it was inevitable that Hegel would sooner rather than later feel the need to complement his investigation of the dualisms of modern Germany with a systematic investigation of their socio-economico-political underpinnings within German society. And that is precisely what he had set out to accomplish at the end of this period in *The German Constitution* of 1799–1803.[15]

The socio-economico-political underpinning of the dualistic outlooks, or intellectual fragmentation, of modern Germany which *The German Constitution* identifies is *the fragmentation of modern Germany as a sociopolitical entity:* "Germany is a state no longer . . . Every center of life has gone its own way and established itself on its own; the whole has fallen apart. The state exists no longer."[16] Hegel is here mainly referring to, and his essay goes on to give a detailed description of, (i) the de facto disintegration of the Holy Roman Empire into a multiplicity of political entities which are autonomous and mutually opposed with respect to political authority, legal right, foreign policy, military power, finances, etc., and (ii) the religious division of the Holy Roman Empire between Catholics and Protestants, each confession intolerant of the other, which both exacerbates the distintegration into separate and opposed political entities, and creates similar disintegration *within* each of these political enti-

---

15. In order to recognize this fundamental project of *The German Constitution*, one has to read the work against the background of such immediately preceding and contemporary works as *The Positivity of the Christian Religion* and *The Spirit of Christianity*. The work does not *by itself* clearly reveal this project—and nor, for that matter, do either of the latter works (at least in their published forms). This is mainly due to the very strict way in which Hegel divides between these works the two tasks of investigating modern Germany's intellectual dualisms (a task of the latter works) and investigating modern Germany's socio-economico-political constitution (a task of the former work). The most explicit evidence that *The German Constitution* does pursue the project in question perhaps lies in a canceled heading at the start of the revised draft of *The Positivity of the Christian Religion* which Dilthey reports on and interprets as follows: "[Hegel] intended to set ahead of the introduction about the concept of positive religion a comparison of the process in which living religion degenerates and becomes positive under new conditions of spiritual life with the degeneration of the constitution of the state, in which the same process takes place only in another domain, and refers in this connection to a sketch on this subject" (*Die Jugendgeschichte Hegels*, pp. 126–27).

16. *Political Writings*, pp. 143–46. The theme of modern Germany's sociopolitical fragmentation had already been developed forcefully years earlier by Herder in his essay *Haben wir noch das Publikum und Vaterland der Alten?*, with specific reference to regional, class, linguistic, cultural, political factional, and religious divisions (*Briefe zu Beförderung der Humanität*, vol. 5, esp. pp. 62–66, 70–79, 86–87, 120–22, 144–46).

ties.¹⁷ Hegel offers an explanation of this fragmentation of modern Germany in terms of two main factors: (a) He attributes to the Germans a longstanding native "drive for freedom," or "stubborn insistence on independence."[18] (b) More interestingly, he gives a socioeconomic explanation of how that longstanding tendency toward particularism developed into the modern political fragmentation of (i) and religious fragmentation of (ii): the growth in the later Middle Ages of the cities of the Holy Roman Empire as industrial and trading centers brought about the rise of the bourgeoisie, whose characteristic individualism caused the political fragmentation of the Holy Roman Empire and, in the process, developed as its legitimating ideology the religious individualism of Protestantism, thereby producing the religious fragmentation of the Holy Roman Empire as well.[19] The modern political and religious fragmentation of the Holy Roman Empire which resulted constitutes the sociopolitical underpinning of the dualistic or fragmented intellectual outlooks of modern Germany.[20]

It is reasonable to infer that this is the *Phenomenology*'s implicit un-

---

17. Factor (i) is the subject of the bulk of the essay; for factor (ii) see especially *Political Writings*, pp. 189–95.

18. Ibid., pp. 147, 196.

19. Ibid., pp. 189–90: "When religion was uniform, and when the still embryonic bourgeoisie had not introduced a great heterogeneity into the whole, princes, dukes, and lords could regard one another more easily as a whole ... But when, through the growth of the imperial cities, the bourgeois sense, which cares only for an individual and not self-subsistent end and has no regard for the whole, began to become a power, this individualization of dispositions would have demanded a more general and positive bond. When, through the advance of culture and industry, Germany was now pushed into the dilemma of deciding whether to obey a universal power or break the tie for ever, the original German character swung it preponderantly toward insistence on the free will of the individual and on resistance to subjection to a universal, and it thus determined Germany's fate in accordance with its old nature. In the course of time a number of great states had been built up along with the dominance of trade and commercial wealth ... The bourgeois spirit that was gaining countenance and political importance needed a kind of inner and outer legitimation. The German character betook itself to man's inmost heart, to his religion and conscience, and based dispersal on that foundation, so that separation in externals, i.e., into states, appeared as a mere consequence of this."

20. Ironically, this thesis, though absolutely fundamental to the point of *The German Constitution*, is not stated explicitly in the text, where Hegel essentially brackets out the whole question of modern Germany's *intellectual* fragmentation. It is stated a little more explicitly in the roughly contemporary *Natural Law* essay, however, where Hegel, after again describing the sociopolitical fragmentation of modern Germany, observes that "this inmost lack of truth of the whole results ... in there being little truth in the science of philosophy in general, in ethical life, and in religion too" (p. 131).

derstanding of the socio-economico-political underpinning of modern Germany's dualistic outlooks as well.[21]

* * *

21. The above sorts of sociopolitical fragmentation which Hegel sees as responsible for modern Germany's dualistic outlooks should be distinguished from certain others which he does not, or at least not to the same degree.

(α) Both Herder and Schiller had identified modern *division of labor* and *class divisions* as sources of modern dualistic outlooks, and accordingly as in some measure pathological (see esp. *On the Cognition and Sensation of the Human Soul* and *On the Aesthetic Education of Man*). Hegel, by contrast, does not consider these social phenomena to be sources of dualistic outlooks or in any degree pathological. Concerning modern division of labor, note for example how in the following passage he represents this as compatible with a unified outlook and as essential for a healthy modern state: "Labor, production, legal system, administration, and the military—each develops itself completely, in accordance with its one-sided principle. The organic whole has complete inner parts which develop themselves in their abstraction. Not every individual is a manufacturer, a farmer, a manual worker, a soldier, a judge, etc., but these roles are divided, each person belongs to an abstraction, and he is a whole for himself in his thought" (*Jenaer Realphilosophie*, p. 252). Similarly concerning modern class divisions, note how in the following passage Hegel represents these too as quite compatible with a healthy sociopolitical whole, and by implication therefore with a healthy unified outlook: "The fact that a state counts amongst its subjects villeins, burghers, free noblemen, and princes with subjects of their own in turn . . . is as little a hindrance to the formation of a multitude into a state as the fact that the particular geographical members of the state constitute provinces variously related to the internal constitutional law" (*The German Constitution,* p. 155; cf. 156–57). Recall in this whole connection also Hegel's emphasis in the *Phenomenology*'s section *Absolute Freedom and Terror* on the *need* for a restoration of division of labor and class divisions after the French Revolution (par. 593).

(β) In a 1788 essay, *Über einige charakteristische Unterschiede der alten Dichter* (in *Dokumente zu Hegels Entwicklung,* pp. 48–49), and again in *The Positivity of the Christian Religion* (*Early Theological Writings,* pp. 147–48), Hegel points to sharp differences between the classes of modern German society in language and culture—in contrast, for example, to the relative linguistic and cultural homogeneity among the classes of ancient Athens, where all could understand and appreciate the tragedies—as a factor destructive of genuine modern community. And this might seem to imply that he understands such sharp differences to be part of the social basis of modern dualistic outlooks as well. That is not straightforwardly wrong. However, Hegel is ambiguous on the question of whether or not linguistic and cultural heterogeneity is destructive of genuine modern community, and hence productive of dualistic outlooks. Thus, by the time of writing *The German Constitution* he has changed his mind from the position of the earlier essays just mentioned, now seeing sharp linguistic and cultural differences between the classes as compatible with and even essential to a genuine modern community: "In our day the tie between members of a state in respect of manners, education, language may be rather loose or even non-existent. Identity in these matters, once the foundation of a people's union, is now to be reckoned amongst the accidents whose character does not hinder a mass from constituting a public authority . . . Dissimilarity in culture and manners is a necessary product as well as a necessary condition of the stability of modern states" (p. 158). And this vacillation persists beyond the early writings as well, the *Phenomenology* once again implying that a substantial measure of linguistic and cultural common ground between the classes is essential for a genuine modern

Further Intellectual Historicism in the *Phenomenology* 477

What, finally, is Hegel's conception of the sociopolitical origins and underpinnings of his own emergent unifying philosophy (for, as we are about to see, he does understand his own emerging *true* philosophy to be no less susceptible to sociopolitical causation and explanation than the *false* outlooks of the present and the past)?[22] This question is in fact addressed within the *Phenomenology,* but only in the most brief and allusive way, and so we must once again turn mainly to external evidence from the period immediately preceding the *Phenomenology* in order to understand its position.

The German Constitution shows that Hegel does indeed consider his own unifying philosophy to stand in need of sociopolitical origins and underpinnings no less than other intellectual outlooks. Specifically, concerning *underpinnings*, just as this text implicitly identifies as the sociopolitical underpinning of the dualistic or fragmented outlooks of modern Germany which Hegel had already investigated in the early theological writings the sociopolitical fragmentation of modern Germany, so *it projects to serve as the sociopolitical underpinning of the philosophical outlook incorporating difference within unity which Hegel had already begun to develop in the early theological writings a future German state incorporating sociopolitical differences within a strong sociopolitical unity; differentiated monism in philosophy is to be underpinned by differentiated monism in the sociopolitical sphere.*[23] In particular, the text en-

---

community (par. 13), while the later writings retreat from this position once again (as we shall see in part 5). We may reasonably conclude that the absence of linguistic and cultural common ground between the classes is for Hegel at least a less certain and fundamental cause of modern communal fragmentation and hence intellectual dualism than the sorts of political and religious divisions emphasized in *The German Constitution.*

These two points have deserved mention in part because one of the very few works to have perceived clearly the intimate connection for Hegel between intellectual fragmentation and social fragmentation, Plant's *Hegel: An Introduction,* mistakenly equates Hegel's position to Herder's and Schiller's in respect of division of labor and class divisions, and misleadingly represents sharp linguistic and cultural differences between the classes as for Hegel no less certain and fundamental causes of intellectual fragmentation than the other forms of social fragmentation (pp. 18–29).

22. Hegel is in complete agreement with the principle of "symmetry," or the principle that it is possible to explain true beliefs as well as false ones in terms of social causes, argued for quite forcefully by D. Bloor in *Knowledge and Social Imagery* (Chicago: The University of Chicago Press, 1991), chap. 1.

23. As in the case of the corresponding conception concerning modern dualistic outlooks, the conception that there is such a link between the sociopolitical differentiated monism which Hegel explicitly sketches in *The German Constitution* and the intellectual differentiated monism of his own philosophy, although absolutely fundamental to the point of

visages the current political and religious fragmentation of the Holy Roman Empire being incorporated into a strong sociopolitical unity, in the following ways: (i) Political divisions are to be incorporated into a strong unified state by establishing a unified Germany with a strong central government under a single monarch, and accommodating political differences through a representative legislature.[24] (ii) In addition, religious divisions are to be made compatible with a strong unified state by instituting the separation of church and state, together with religious toleration.[25]

Furthermore, *The German Constitution* offers an account of how this sociopolitical transformation of modern Germany must be brought about—an account, in effect, of the sociopolitical *origins* of Hegel's emergent unifying philosophy. This can only be accomplished, Hegel argues, through the force of a conqueror, a new "Theseus": "If all parts of Germany were to succeed by these means [i.e., the unifying constitutional reforms which Hegel has just explained] in making Germany into one state, an event of that sort has never been the fruit of deliberation, but only of force . . . The common people in Germany, together with their Estates Assemblies, who know nothing at all of anything but the division of the German people, would have to be collected together into one mass by the power of a conqueror; they would have to be compelled to treat themselves as belonging to Germany."[26] It is disputed whom Hegel has

---

The German Constitution, is not explicitly stated in the work. It has, once again, to be inferred from reading the work against the background of the immediately preceding and contemporary early theological writings.

24. *Political Writings*, pp. 202–3, 237; cf. *Jenaer Realphilosophie*, pp. 250–51. In *The German Constitution* Hegel argues that this constitutional principle was originally invented by Germanic peoples, and is the principle of modern European constitutions generally, but that it is not yet realized in modern Germany itself (pp. 202–3, 206). He argues that it should be realized in modern Germany for the future, however, and offers a series of very specific proposals for transforming the existing constitution of Germany in order to accomplish this (pp. 239–41).

25. Ibid., pp. 159, 193–94 (separation of church and state), 192 (toleration).

26. Ibid., p. 241. In thus looking to a strong leader to reverse Germany's sociopolitical disintegration, and casting himself in the role of adviser to such a leader, Hegel has certain historical precedents explicitly in view. He mentions as strong leaders who have actually accomplished such a reversal of sociopolitical fragmentation or disintegration in their states, besides Theseus, also Cardinal Richelieu (ibid., pp. 216–17). And as a precedent for his own advisory function, he interprets Machiavelli—in an interpretation which had its origins in Herder (*Briefe zu Beförderung der Humanität*, vol. 5, letters 58, 59) and became popular in nineteenth-century Germany (recurring in von Ranke, for example)—as an author who in the *Prince* similarly encouraged strong political leadership from a motive of reversing the sociopolitical disintegration of Italy and restoring a unified state, praising him for his "belief that the fate of a people which hastens to its political downfall can be averted by

in mind in *The German Constitution* as his new "Theseus."²⁷ However, thanks to his private correspondence from the period of the *Phenomenology*'s composition and publication, there can be no doubt whom he saw as his new "Theseus" by *this* time: *Napoleon*, who was now conquering Germany with his army, indeed in Hegel's immediate vicinity, and, as Hegel interpreted events, thereby fulfilling the task assigned to the new "Theseus" in *The German Constitution*. Thus, in a letter from October 1806 Hegel famously enthuses about Napoleon: "I saw the emperor—this worldsoul—ride out through the city for reconnaissance. It is truly a wonderful feeling to see such an individual who, concentrated here in one point, sitting on a horse, extends his reach over the world and rules it . . . As I did earlier, now everybody wishes the French army good fortune."²⁸ And in a letter from August 1807 he specifically assigns to Napoleon two of the key functions which he had assigned to the new "Theseus" in *The German Constitution*, namely, those of unifying Germany's many fragmented political entities and ensuring that monarchy in Germany is combined with a representative legislature:

> The large number of small princes who remain in northern Germany by itself makes a firmer bond necessary. The German professors of constitutional law are not slow to write a mass of works on the subject of the concept of sovereignty and the meaning of the nation's laws. The great professor of constitutional law has his chair in Paris [i.e., Napoleon].— From the provinces of the kingdom of Westphalia deputies of all classes have been summoned to Paris. In Berg the diet still exists. When the diet was abolished in Württemberg Napoleon said angrily to the Minister of Württemberg: "I have made your master a sovereign, not a despot!"—The German princes have still not grasped the concept of a free monarchy, nor attempted to realize it—Napoleon will have to organize all this.²⁹

---

genius" (*Political Writings*, pp. 219–23). (At *Jenaer Realphilosophie*, pp. 216–18 Hegel again reflects in connection with the sociopolitical disintegration of Germany on the need for the "force" of a "great man" to establish a unified state, and on the merits of Machiavelli's position. But he now significantly—and somewhat reassuringly—qualifies his endorsement of Machiavelli, implying that the disintegration of modern Germany has gone so far that the sort of *ruthless tyranny* which Machiavelli envisaged would not there be necessary in order to restore unity.)

27. Rosenzweig argues for Archduke Charles of Austria (*Hegel und der Staat* 1:125–27); Dilthey suggests Napoleon (already) (*Die Jugendgeschichte Hegels*, pp. 136–37).

28. *Briefe von und an Hegel* 1:120–21.

29. Ibid., p. 185; cf. 218–19. As Plant points out, Hegel had some good evidence supporting his optimistic expectation that a conquering Napoleon would institute such reforms in a conquered Germany, namely, the fact that he had already instituted such reforms—

In the light of these views developed at length and fairly explicitly in *The German Constitution* and in Hegel's private correspondence we are now in a position to interpret the following brief and allusive passage in the Preface of the *Phenomenology:*

> It is not difficult to see that ours is a birth-time and a period of transition to a new era. Spirit has broken with the world of its existence and representation up to this point, and is of a mind to submerge it in the past, and in the labor of its own transformation. Spirit is indeed never at rest but always engaged in moving forward. But just as the first breath drawn by a child after its long, quiet nourishment breaks the gradualness of merely quantitative growth—there is a qualitative leap, and the child is born—so likewise the Spirit in its formation matures quietly and slowly into its new shape, dissolving bit by bit the structure of its previous world, whose tottering state is only hinted at by isolated symptoms. The frivolity and boredom which unsettle the established order, the vague foreboding of something unknown, these are the heralds of approaching change. The gradual crumbling that left unaltered the face of the whole is cut short by a sunburst which, in one flash, illuminates the features of the new world. But this new world is no more a complete actuality than is a newborn child; it is essential to bear this in mind. It comes on the scene for the first time in its immediacy or its concept. Just as little as a building is finished when its foundation has been laid, so little is the achieved concept of the whole the whole itself. When we wish to see an oak with its massive trunk and spreading branches and foliage, we are not content to be shown an acorn instead. So too, Science, the crown of a world of Spirit, is not complete in its beginnings. (pars. 11–12)

This passage expresses, albeit obscurely, Hegel's conception of the sociopolitical underpinnings and origins of his own emergent unifying philosophy, or Science. First, the passage implies that, like the outlooks which are being left behind, Hegel's new Science will be underpinned by a specific sociopolitical context: Spirit has now broken "with the world of its *existence and representation* up to this point" (emphasis added), and "Science" too will be "the crown of a world of Spirit." Thanks to our reading of *The German Constitution* we know what this means more precisely: The old "world of . . . representation" was the dualistic, fragmented outlooks of modern Germany, and the corresponding "world of . . . existence" the political and religious fragmentation of modern Ger-

---

in particular, a measure of representation for the various estates—in Italy after conquering her (*Hegel: An Introduction*, pp. 119–20).

many which formed the sociopolitical underpinning of those dualistic outlooks. "Science," on the other hand, is Hegelian philosophy's differentiated monism, and the "world of Spirit" of which it will be the "crown" the sociopolitically unified but also differentiated Germany that is required to serve as its sociopolitical underpinning—more specifically, a Germany unified under a strong central monarchy (unity), together with a representative legislature, and in religion separation of church and state plus toleration (differentiation). Second, when Hegel refers here to the present day as "a birth-time and a period of transition to a new era," of a "qualitative leap," of "a sunburst which, in one flash, illuminates the features of the new world," this is an allusion to the sociopolitical origins of his own emergent unifying philosophy. For he is thinking in these remarks primarily of Napoleon's current invasion of Germany which, in his view, is effecting the transition from Germany's sociopolitical fragmentation, and hence the dualistic outlooks which this supports, to Germany's sociopolitical unity incorporating differentiation, and hence the unifying Hegelian philosophy which this will underpin.[30] Third, in addition to these ideas already familiar to us, the passage also implies that there are importantly different phases to be distinguished within the process of sociopolitical and intellectual transition in question: The "new [sociopolitical] world is no more a complete actuality than is a newborn child"—that is, the transition in Germany from sociopolitical fragmentation to sociopolitical unity incorporating differentiation, which Napoleon is currently effecting, is underway but not immediately completed. "So too, Science, the crown of a world of Spirit, is not complete in its beginnings"—that is, correspondingly, in the present early phase of the sociopolitical transition we have only proto-Science, and Science proper will emerge only with the completion of the sociopolitical transition. Hegel clarifies this point in the next paragraph, indicating that in the present

---

30. This of course helps to explain the *allusiveness* of the whole passage, as of Hegel's only other *public* treatment of the same matters in this period, his closely related remarks delivered at the end of a lecture course on the *Phenomenology* in September 1806 (*Hegels Leben*, pp. 214–15; also in appendix X); Hegel is pinning all of his hopes for Germany's sociopolitical and intellectual future on *the leader of a foreign power currently invading German soil*—hardly a position which it would be prudent to broadcast too explicitly! (As noted in the previous chapter, this awkward situation is also an important reason for the absence of the expected explicit treatment of a modern German reconciling law-state at the end of the *Spirit* chapter; much more prudent, under the immediate circumstances, to focus on progress made in recent German intellectual history—Kant, Fichte, and the Romantics—than to herald the advent of a new Napoleonic sociopolitical order in Germany.)

early phase of the sociopolitical transition only Science's general principle, and the *Phenomenology*'s preform of and path toward Science, are available: Science is initially without "the articulation of forms whereby distinctions are securely defined, and stand arrayed in their fixed relations," "it is as yet present only in its concept or in its inwardness"; we have only "the Understanding's form of Science," "the way to Science open and equally accessible to everyone" (par. 13). Hegel conceives these different phases of the process of sociopolitical and intellectual transition in the following more specific way, I suggest: In the present early phase, there are still aspects of sociopolitical fragmentation combined with the emerging sociopolitical unity incorporating differentiation; and just so, at an intellectual level, the *Phenomenology* still combines aspects of intellectual fragmentation or dualism (such as the subject-object opposition of consciousness) with its expression of Science's differentiated monism.[31] At the end of the transition, there will be only sociopolitical unity incorporating differentiation; and just so, at an intellectual level, Science proper will express only differentiated monism. This, in sum, is the *Phenomenology*'s conception of the sociopolitical underpinnings and origins of Hegel's own emergent unifying philosophy.

* * *

Finally, Hegel never, I think, fundamentally contradicted or changed this position of the *Phenomenology*'s in later years. (i) He did not fundamentally contradict or change the *Phenomenology*'s conception here of the sociopolitical underpinnings and origins of his own unifying philosophy (except for coming to believe them actually *realized*). Thus, concerning underpinnings, a sociopolitical unity incorporating differentiation—and indeed more specifically, a strong central government under a single monarch, together with a representative legislature, and in religion the separation of church and state plus religious toleration—remains Hegel's conception of the proper principle of the modern state in the *Philosophy of Right*. And concerning origins, authors such as Rosenzweig and Lukács who have argued that Hegel was later disappointed in Napoleon as a source of sociopolitical reform in Germany are, it seems to me, mis-

---

31. The latter, intellectual, combination is part of the force of Hegel's characterization of the *Phenomenology* as the "appearance" of Science (cf. chapter 5 above). It therefore supports this reading that Hegel's 1806 lecture on the *Phenomenology* speaks of the current sociopolitical context as likewise the "appearance" of a new stage of Spirit (*Hegels Leben*, pp. 214–15; also in appendix X).

taken.³² It is true, of course, that by the time of Hegel's later works Napoleon had lost power in Germany (and generally). But Hegel had already in the 1805–6 Philosophy of Spirit conceived the authoritarian role required of the "great man" as merely temporary, and his power as to be overthrown by the people once he had played it.³³ And he had also already anticipated at the time of the *Phenomenology* that history's initiative was passing from France to Germany.³⁴ And so it was far from disingenuous of him to claim at the time of Napoleon's defeat and fall at the hands of the German forces of liberation, as he did, that he had already foreseen this course of events at the time of the *Phenomenology*.³⁵ Moreover, after Napoleon's defeat and fall Hegel continued to see Germany's sociopolitical institutions as fundamentally Napoleonic in their origin and inspiration. Thus, in an 1816 letter he characterizes the forces of reaction as, for all their noise, effecting only the most superficial changes in Napoleon's legacy,³⁶ in an 1821 letter he credits Bavaria's progressive constitution to the impact of Napoleon,³⁷ and in the *Lectures on the Philosophy of World History* he can still say that Napoleon "subjected all Europe, and diffused his liberal institutions in every quarter," and that, while in France, Italy, and Spain they were strangled by Roman Catholicism, "one of the leading features in the political condition of Germany is that code of rights which was certainly occasioned by French oppression, since this was the especial means of bringing to light the deficiencies of the old system," with the result that the states of modern Germany now have the right sort of sociopolitical constitution.³⁸ (The only significant qualification that needs to

---

32. Rosenzweig, *Hegel und der Staat* 2:27–30; Lukács, *The Young Hegel*, pp. 453, 457.

33. *Jenaer Realphilosophie*, pp. 247–48.

34. Thus the *Spirit* chapter of the *Phenomenology* makes the transition from France and the aftermath of the French Revolution to Germany and recent German thought beginning with Kant commenting: "Absolute freedom leave[s] its self-destroying reality and pass[es] over into another land of self-conscious Spirit where . . . freedom has the value of truth" (par. 595). Cf. a letter from January 1807 in which Hegel predicts that the Germans "perhaps . . . will eventually excel their teachers [the French]" (*Briefe von und an Hegel* 1:138).

35. Hegel makes this claim in a letter from April 1814, specifically quoting *Phenomenology*, par. 595 as supporting evidence (*Hegel: The Letters*, p. 307).

36. Ibid., p. 325.

37. Ibid., p. 469.

38. *The Philosophy of History*, pp. 451–56. A good, if perhaps somewhat overstated, general antidote to the general Rosenzweig-Lukács myth of Hegel's later retreat from regarding the French Revolution and its aftermath as a crucial turning point in modern history is J. Ritter, *Hegel und die französische Revolution* (Frankfurt am Main: Suhrkamp, 1965).

be entered to this thesis that the later Hegel's position was continuous with, and satisfied with respect to the expectations of, the *Phenomenology*'s is that he later gave up his conception from the period of the *Phenomenology* that his sociopolitical ideal would be realized in Germany in the form of a united and reinvigorated Holy Roman Empire, instead reconceiving its realization as occurring in the sovereign states to which the Holy Roman Empire had by this time irrevocably given way, especially Prussia. Thus in the *Lectures on the Philosophy of World History* he states that "the fiction of an Empire has utterly vanished. It is broken up into sovereign states," and he depicts the latter as the loci of the realization of his sociopolitical ideal.[39] However, *philosophically* speaking, this is a fairly modest revision of his earlier conception. For, philosophically speaking, what was really essential to that conception was the character of his sociopolitical ideal, and the expectation that it would be realized in Germany through the intervention of a strong leader such as Napoleon; the exact scale, place, and number of its realization[s] was a rather secondary matter.)

(ii) Nor, I think, did Hegel later contradict or change the general conception of his philosophy's relation to its age which we find here in the *Phenomenology*. His conception of the *Phenomenology* itself in these paragraphs from the Preface is that it emerges in an early phase of a process of sociopolitical transformation and looks to the future. Later, in the *Philosophy of Right*, by contrast, he famously expresses the view that philosophy emerges at the *end* of a process of sociopolitical transformation, reflecting and comprehending fully developed sociopolitical institutions, and so looks to the *present and past* only: "Philosophy always comes on the scene too late to give [instruction as to what the world ought to be]. As the thought of the world, it appears only when actuality is there cut and dried after its process of formation has been completed . . . It is only when actuality is mature that the ideal first appears over against the real . . . and the ideal apprehends this same real world in its substance and builds it up for itself into the shape of an intellectual realm. When philosophy paints its grey in grey, then has a shape of life grown old."[40] Lukács for one has argued that these two positions are flatly inconsistent with each other and that they represent a fundamental change of mind on Hegel's part (in particular, a displacement of the decisive

39. *The Philosophy of History*, p. 456.
40. *Philosophy of Right*, pp. 12–13.

turning-point of modern history back several hundred years from Hegel's own age to the Reformation).[41] However, this is a mistake; the two positions are in fact perfectly consistent and represent no change of mind at all. Thus note the following points: (a) The *Philosophy of Right* in speaking here of "philosophy" means (in relation to modern times) Hegelian Science *proper* (it in fact has in mind primarily a particular part of Hegelian Science proper, namely, *itself*). But concerning Hegelian Science *proper* the *Phenomenology* implies just the same position as the *Philosophy of Right*. For the *Phenomenology*'s Preface uses the image of Science proper being the "*crown* of a world of Spirit"—surely an echo of the New Testament image of a "crown of life," meaning the reward of a life of righteous struggle which comes at its *conclusion*.[42] And the Preface also implies in another way that Science proper will emerge only with the *completion* of the sociopolitical transformation currently underway: "But this new world is no more a complete actuality than is a newborn child . . . So, too, Science . . . is not complete in its beginnings . . ." In short, the Preface implies precisely the *Philosophy of Right*'s position that Science proper emerges at the end of a process of sociopolitical transformation, reflecting and comprehending fully developed sociopolitical institutions, and therefore looking to the present and the past rather than to the future. (b) The *Phenomenology*'s conception of *itself*, on the other hand, is indeed strikingly different, in that it locates itself in an early phase of a process of sociopolitical transformation and understands itself as looking to the future. But since this is a conception not of Science *proper*, but instead of "the Understanding's form of Science," "the way to Science," the "appearance" of Science, it is perfectly consistent with the *Philosophy of Right*'s position.[43] (c) There does, of course, remain the difference between the two works that Hegel in the *Phenomenology*

---

41. Lukács, *The Young Hegel*, pp. 454, 456.
42. For the New Testament image of a "crown of life," see *Revelation* 2:10, and *Jacob* 1:12; cf. *Timothy* 4:8, and *Peter* I 5:4.
43. It might still seem that the *Phenomenology*'s self-understanding conflicts with the *Philosophy of Right*'s apparently more general strictures against thought "transcend[ing] its contemporary world" and constructing "a state as it ought to be" instead of "comprehend[ing] what is" (p. 11). However, this is not so. For the *Phenomenology* (α) does not prescribe how the state ought to be, and (β) to the extent that it looks to the future of the state does so precisely *by* reflecting "what is" in the "contemporary world," namely, the current sociopolitical mixture and transition. That is quite different from what the *Philosophy of Right* is concerned to ban, namely, a prescription of a state for the future, and one not anchored in but detached from reflection of what currently is.

sees himself as actually standing in an early phase of a process of sociopolitical transition and looking to the sociopolitical future, whereas in the *Philosophy of Right* he sees himself as actually standing at the end of a process of sociopolitical transition and looking to the present and the past. But this is simply a function of the fact that the sort of sociopolitical transformation to which the *Phenomenology* looks forward *had indeed occurred* by the time of the *Philosophy of Right* in Hegel's view (as we just noted under [i]).

* * *

Turning now to a further but closely related subject, as can already be seen from the preceding, the Hegel of the *Phenomenology* draws from his seventh intellectual historicist idea, his general recognition that sociopolitical contexts are key causal determinants of the emergence and subsequent survival and growth of ideas, important consequences concerning his own philosophy specifically: He recognizes that, because sociopolitical context plays such a decisive role in determining whether or not ideas achieve broad dissemination and acceptance, if his own philosophy is to attain that broad dissemination and acceptance on which—for reasons indicated in part 1—its success, and even its very existence, depend, then certain sociopolitical changes must occur as well. In particular, the current sociopolitical fragmentation of Germany, which causes the broad dissemination and acceptance of fragmenting, dualistic ideas, must be replaced by a German sociopolitical unity incorporating differentiation, which will cause the broad dissemination and acceptance of his own philosophy's differentiated monism. Moreover, he is also deeply concerned with the inevitable further question of the *means* by which this sociopolitical change is to be brought about, and of his own relation to this means—specifically, looking to the reforming authoritarianism which Napoleon is currently bringing to bear on Germany as the means for accomplishing it. Marx is therefore mistaken when he complains in the *Economic and Philosophic Manuscripts* that for the Hegel of the *Phenomenology* both the ills of modern man and their cure lie solely in the domain of thought *rather than of society*.[44] On the contrary, Hegel's position is in fact strikingly close to Marx's own, for example in the *Theses on Feuerbach*, that modern man's harmful illusions are produced by social causes, and that their successful elimination therefore requires the philosopher not only to see through them but also to understand their social

44. Marx: Selections, pp. 66, 68–69, 75–76.

causes and find a way of removing these.⁴⁵ This whole stance of Hegel's concerning his own philosophy is an eighth intellectual historicist idea in the *Phenomenology* deserving of note.

In order to understand the *Phenomenology*'s position on these matters more precisely, it is necessary to see its place in the evolution of Hegel's thought on the question of philosophy's relation to the sociopolitical sphere. Until the mid-1790s Hegel was committed to a faith that the philosopher's true and right ideas, once made public, would more or less automatically disseminate themselves in an undistorted fashion, and thereby bring about whatever changes in the sociopolitical sphere they deemed appropriate (we might call this, for short, a faith in the *pure activism* of true and right ideas). Hence, for example, in a letter to Schelling from 1795 Hegel writes: "I expect from the Kantian system and its highest completion a revolution in Germany . . . The philosophers prove [the dignity of man], the people will learn to feel it, and not ask for their rights which lie humiliated in the dust, but themselves assume them again—make them their own . . . With the spread of the new ideas about how things *should* be, the indolence of sedate people which makes them forever accept things as they are will disappear. This enlivening power of ideas . . . will elevate spirits, and they will learn to make sacrifices for them."⁴⁶ Hegel's commitment to such a faith in this period is wholly unsurprising given that it, first, was a commonplace of the Enlightenment, and moreover, second, seemed recently to have received striking empirical confirmation in the dissemination of the Enlightenment's ideals and their translation into the sociopolitical changes of the French Revolution (a historical paradigm which is clearly in Hegel's mind in the passage just quoted, for example).

In the late 1790s Hegel lost this faith in the pure activism of true and right ideas. He came to believe, instead, that even true and right ideas, when made public, could be and often were denied undistorted dissemination—suffering either outright extinction or serious distortion—and

---

45. Ibid., p. 81: "Feuerbach starts out from the fact of religious self-estrangement, of the duplication of the world into a religious world and a secular one. His work consists in resolving the religious world into its secular basis. But that the secular basis lifts off from itself and establishes itself as an independent realm in the clouds can only be explained by the inner strife and intrinsic contradictoriness of this secular basis. The latter must, therefore, itself be both understood in its contradiction and revolutionized in practice" (thesis 4; cf. 7, 11).
46. *Briefe von und an Hegel* 1:23–24.

thereby also sociopolitical effectiveness, through the influence of existing sociopolitical forces. Two sorts of empirical evidence appear to have brought him to this realization. First, his investigations during this period into the history of religion and morals led him to such conclusions as that the superior religious and moral conceptions of the early ancient Greeks and Romans had been extinguished in favor of the inferior religious and moral conceptions of organized Christianity through the influence of sociopolitical oppression in the later ancient world; and that Jesus's superior message of a purely rational morality had been distorted into the "positivity" and otherworldism of organized Christianity first by the nature of Jewish society and culture and then further by the sociopolitical oppression prevalent in the Roman Empire.[47] Second, the course of recent events forced Hegel to revise his earlier assessment of them sharply: the Jacobin Terror of 1793 revealed to him that the ideals of the Enlightenment had not, after all, undergone the sort of undistorted dissemination and translation into sociopolitical practice which the French Revolution had initially seemed to bespeak; and he also came to realize that the sort of general dissemination and sociopolitical efficacy of similar (Kantian) ideals in Germany which he had anticipated in his letter to Schelling of 1795 was not in fact occurring.[48]

This new insight brought Hegel to a realization that merely responding to the illusory and harmful dualistic ideas currently accepted by expounding his own philosophy's true and practically beneficial differentiated monism would not in itself be sufficient, that he needed to supplement this with (i) a determination of the sociopolitical basis of the illusory and harmful dualistic outlooks currently accepted and of the sociopolitical basis required for an undistorted dissemination of his own philoso-

---

47. *The Positivity of the Christian Religion*, pp. 151–65, 68–86. (The theme of a distortion of Jesus's ideas by Jewish society and culture reappears in *The Spirit of Christianity*, though with significant differences in the details.)

48. Hegel in fact already expresses a sense of disillusionment with the course of the French Revolution in a letter from December 1794 (*Briefe von und an Hegel* 1:12); a few years later in *The German Constitution* he writes of "extremely dangerous experiments" in France and of "French libertarian madness" (pp. 207, 220). Disillusionment with the condition and trajectory of contemporary Germany is of course the central theme of *The German Constitution*. Note in addition that disillusionment with the courses of contemporary French and German events can be seen as a sort of subtext (possibly an unconscious one) in the accounts which Hegel gives during this period in *The Positivity of the Christian Religion* and *The Spirit of Christianity* of the fates suffered by the ideas of the early Greeks and Romans and of Jesus in antiquity.

phy's true and practically beneficial differentiated monism, together with (ii) a discovery of means for effecting a change from the former sociopolitical conditions to the latter. Hegel's first and fullest response to these tasks was *The German Constitution* of 1799–1803.

As we have already seen, Hegel's answer to task (i) in *The German Constitution* is the determination that the sociopolitical basis of the illusory and harmful dualistic outlooks currently accepted is the current political and religious fragmentation of Germany, and that the sociopolitical basis required for an undistorted dissemination of his own philosophy's true and practically beneficial differentiated monism is a German state unified under a monarch but also incorporating differentiation in the form of a representative legislature together with the separation of church and state plus religious toleration. This answer to task (i) henceforth remained fundamentally unchanged in Hegel, and in particular, as we have seen, is implicitly part of the *Phenomenology*'s position.

Hegel's solution to task (ii) was, by contrast, much less settled over time. In particular, two quite strikingly different solutions which he developed at different periods need to be distinguished. The first of these is found in *The German Constitution* and in the roughly contemporary *Logic and Metaphysics* of 1801–2. This solution—which has not been at all well perceived or understood by the secondary literature—might be described as a conviction in the *qualified activism* of true and right ideas: philosophy can *itself* bring about the changes in the sociopolitical sphere which will remove the sociopolitical causes of harmful dualistic illusions and provide the sociopolitical basis necessary for the undistorted dissemination of its own true and practically beneficial monistic ideas, *but only through being targeted at a particularly potent instrument of sociopolitical change, a "great man."*[49] Thus in the 1801–2 *Logic and*

---

49. Two points to note here: (a) This position is interesting, among other reasons, because it brings Hegel's thought on the relation of philosophy to the sociopolitical sphere into *very* close proximity to Marx's for a time—with only the quite modest residual difference that the potent instrument which Hegel expects to influence philosophically in order to bring about the required sociopolitical change is a "great man," whereas for Marx it is the labor movement. (b) Someone might object to Hegel that his continued, albeit now qualified, belief here in thought's *activism* in the sociopolitical sphere contradicts his belief at this period that thought can be explained in terms of sociopolitical causes. The contradiction is illusory, however. It would only be genuine if Hegel thought, or had to think, that the explicability of thought in terms of sociopolitical causes implied that the causality was unidirectional, that thought was merely an epiphenomenon caused by but without causal influence upon sociopolitical conditions. But that is not the case, either as a matter of exege-

Metaphysics Hegel argues as follows. Although the philosopher has a conception of the world as "something harmonious," a "unity," the world itself may be sociopolitically and intellectually in a state of fragmentation—"the external world may itself be separated and in a state of hostility"; "itself it does not recognize this unity." Nevertheless, the world's fragmented self-conception can be overcome: "It is possible, however, even for this external unity to be brought from unconscious to conscious identity." The means for accomplishing this are "great men," who "grasp with vigor and truth the ideal of the level which the ethical nature of man can now reach," who "say the word and the nations will follow them." In order to serve this function, a great man must have been educated by philosophy to its vision of sociopolitical and intellectual unity, so that he then implements this vision in the sociopolitical sphere: "He must have recognized the whole and hence have purified himself of all limitation . . . In other words, he must be educated in the school of philosophy. From within the school of philosophy he can raise the still slumbering form of a new ethical world to consciousness and boldly join battle with the old forms of the World Spirit, . . . confident that the form which he can destroy is an obsolete form and that the new form is a new divine revelation . . . which he now reveals to the light of day and brings to determinate existence." Hegel's historical paradigm for this scenario of philosophy replacing sociopolitical disunity with sociopolitical unity, and thereby effecting the sociopolitical basis for undistorted dissemination of its own unified vision, through implanting its vision of sociopolitical and intellectual unity in a great man, who then brings this about, is Aristotle's influence on Alexander the Great and the latter's subsequent unifying conquests: "In this way . . . did Alexander the Macedonian leave the school of Aristotle to conquer the world." Clearly, however, Hegel is also, and indeed especially, thinking of himself and his own philosophy in relation to the modern world.[50] Accordingly, in *The German Constitu-*

---

sis or normatively. A similar point applies to Marx, against whom a similar objection might be raised. For, when, in his theory of ideology, Marx explains thought in terms of its causation by socioeconomic factors, he allows the causal influence of the former on the latter as well (for example, in *The German Ideology*, ed. C.J. Arthur [London: Lawrence and Wishart, 1978], he writes of "the *reciprocal* action of these various sides on one another" [p. 58; emphasis added]), and indeed *requires* this, since his explanations are in terms of ideologies being caused by their socioeconomic bases because of their reinforcing *effects* on these socioeconomic bases.

50. For the full text of the above account in the 1801–2 *Logic and Metaphysics*, see appendix V.

tion he explicitly applies the same model to himself and his own philosophy in relation to modern Germany, interpreting his own role as a philosopher in relation to the sociopolitical fragmentation of modern Germany as like that of Machiavelli giving philosophical advice to Lorenzo de'Medici to inspire him to reunify a sociopolitically fragmented Italy, and hence concluding the essay with an appeal for a new "Theseus" to bring about a similar unifying transformation of modern Germany by implementing through force a set of concrete sociopolitical reforms which he outlines.[51] This, in sum, was Hegel's solution to task (ii) during the early Jena period.[52]

---

51. *Political Writings*, pp. 219–23, 239–42. Rosenzweig claims that in *The German Constitution* Hegel cherishes no hope of influencing the new "Theseus" but instead displays "a hard feelingless renunciation of will before the inexorable course of things" (*Hegel und der Staat* 1:129). This is sufficiently disproved by such features of the text as Hegel's invocation of Machiavelli as a model and the detailed character of his own prescriptions of sociopolitical reforms for Germany. It is also incompatible with the model of philosophy's relation to "great men" in the contemporary 1801–2 *Logic and Metaphysics* as this has been explained above.

52. This position of Hegel's in the early Jena period has been more or less completely overlooked by the relevant secondary literature—in particular, Rosenzweig, Taylor, Plant, and Hyppolite—which has instead mistakenly assimilated Hegel's position at this time to the very different one which he held later in the *Philosophy of Right*, according to which philosophy's proper function is the reconciling comprehension of the sociopolitical sphere as it is, not the transformation of it into something different (Rosenzweig, *Hegel und der Staat* 1:129–30; Taylor, *Hegel*, pp. 73–74; Plant, *Hegel: An Introduction*, pp. 75 ff., 130; Hyppolite, "The Significance of the French Revolution in Hegel's *Phenomenology*," pp. 41–42). The following points should be noted in this connection.

First, one can see immediately that this orthodox reading is mistaken from the fact that the overwhelming bulk of relevant textual evidence in the 1801–2 *Logic and Metaphysics* and *The German Constitution*, as just quoted and cited, clearly shows Hegel at this period believing that philosophy can and must produce a sociopolitical transformation. (Note in this connection also the prescriptive character of the Jena political writings more generally—as noticed, but mistakenly interpreted as contradictory of Hegel's considered position at this time, by Plant, *Hegel: An Introduction*, pp. 96, 112, 152.)

Second, as far as I can see, there is only one piece of evidence which even really *seems* to speak *for* the orthodox reading. This is a well-known passage from near the start of *The German Constitution* which appears at first sight to anticipate the position of the *Philosophy of Right*. Hegel writes in this passage: "The thoughts contained in this essay can have no other aim or effect, when published, save that of promoting the understanding of what is, and therefore a calmer outlook and a moderately tolerant attitude alike in words and in actual contact. For it is not what is that makes us irascible and resentful, but the fact that it is not as it ought to be. But if we recognize that it is as it must be, i.e., that it is not arbitrariness and chance that make what it is, then we also recognize that it is as it ought to be" (*Political Writings*, p. 145). This seems at first sight very similar to the *Philosophy of Right*'s assertions that the task of philosophy is not to "construct a state as it ought to be," but instead "to comprehend what is," and to produce a reconciliation with what is

In sharp contrast to this early solution to task (ii) is the solution which Hegel offers later in the *Philosophy of Right*. This later solution is wholly *non-activist* concerning philosophy: philosophy emerges only *after* the

through the recognition of its necessity or rationality, in such a manner that "to recognize reason as the rose in the cross of the present and thereby to enjoy the present, this is the rational insight which reconciles us to the actual, the reconciliation which philosophy affords" (*Philosophy of Right,* pp. 11–12). Accordingly, Rosenzweig, Plant, and Hyppolite all explicitly appeal to the passage in question in support of their orthodox reading, while Taylor evidently follows Rosenzweig and thereby implicitly appeals to it as well (Rosenzweig, *Hegel und der Staat* 1:129; Plant, *Hegel: An Introduction,* p. 130; Hyppolite, "The Significance of the French Revolution," p. 42).

Read carefully in its context, however, the passage in question can be seen *not* in fact to be expressing the same position as the *Philosophy of Right* at all. It does, no doubt, represent the beginning in Hegel of a train of thought which will eventually *become* the *Philosophy of Right*'s position. However, it does not yet express that position itself, but instead something entirely different. In this connection, the following points are crucial: (a) As we have noted, Hegel himself goes on in *The German Constitution* to prescribe in detail a set of sociopolitical reforms for Germany—and indeed the main point of the essay is to convey the pressing need for these reforms. This is completely inconsistent with the essay's adoption of a position like the *Philosophy of Right*'s. (b) Read more closely, the critical passage reveals certain important differences from the corresponding passages in the *Philosophy of Right*. One difference is that the passage claims that "what is" will, by being seen to be necessary, be recognized to be "as it ought to be," whereas the *Philosophy of Right* on the contrary *disavows* any aim of "teaching the state what it ought to be" (*Philosophy of Right,* p. 11). Another difference concerns the nature of the "necessity" which is ascribed by the passage to what currently "is" in Germany. In *The German Constitution* this necessity is conceived as in reality thoroughly *conditional and surmountable*. It is *conditional* in that it amounts only to efficient causal necessity *given the current sociopolitical disintegration of Germany*. Thus just before the critical passage Hegel had explained that the essay was concerned with "the inner causes, the spirit" of Germany's recent misfortunes, "in what way the results are only the external and necessary appearances of that spirit," meaning by the "inner causes" or "spirit" in question Germany's current sociopolitical disintegration (*Political Writings,* p. 144). Moreover, the "necessity" is *surmountable,* in that what is "necessary" in this sense could quite well not have been, and could quite well not be in the future, namely, if only the "inner causes," German sociopolitical disintegration, were removed. Indeed, Hegel goes on in the essay to argue forcefully that such a removal can and should occur, that by means of the sort of political "genius" which Machiavelli envisaged for Italy, and Richelieu actually realized in France, German sociopolitical disintegration can and should be overcome in favor of sociopolitical unity. (Similar points apply to the equivalent concept of the "fate" of contemporary Germany which Hegel employs in the essay. The same is true, mutatis mutandis, of the concept of the "fate" of Christianity which he uses at around the same time in *The Spirit of Christianity*—in which connection, observe his emphasis on the conditional and surmountable character of this "fate" at *Early Theological Writings,* pp. 230–39. It is important to recall here that the Greek tradition from which Hegel is borrowing his conception of "fate" prominently included ideas of the escapability of fate—as, for example, in Homer's ubiquitous notion of escaping a *kēr* and in the popular tale of Apollo's tricking of the *moirai* on behalf of Admetus.) Now such a merely conditional and surmountable "necessity" is quite differ-

full development of the sociopolitical conditions to which it corresponds—reflecting and comprehending them, and, by displaying their rationality, reconciling people to them—and so can have *no* efficient causal

---

ent from the sort of necessity or rationality postulated by the *Philosophy of Right*, which is above all *unconditional and insurmountable*. (c) Connectedly, there are some quite striking peculiarities concerning the relation between the critical passage and the rest of *The German Constitution*. Not only is the passage's talk of "what is" being recognized, through being seen to be necessary, to be "as it ought to be" at odds with the *Philosophy of Right*'s renunciation of "teaching the state what it ought to be." It also jars with Hegel's indication in later passages of *The German Constitution* itself that there is a standpoint higher than that of legal/moral "oughts," namely, the standpoint of the (Machiavellian) philosopher and the political leader through whom he saves the unity of the state (*Political Writings*, pp. 221–23; cf. *Jenaer Realphilosophie*, pp. 246–47). And while, as just noted, *The German Constitution* as a whole understands the "necessity" of which it speaks to be in truth merely conditional and surmountable, the critical passage in particular does rather describe it as being recognized as though unconditional and insurmountable. Thus the passage speaks of a recognition that what is "is as it must be" *simpliciter* (suggesting unconditionality), and implies that the necessity is of such a kind as to absolve in the eyes of those who recognize it people who are subject to it from moral responsibility, so that what is "is as it ought to be" (suggesting insurmountability). (d) Points (a)–(c) invite the hypothesis that the moral which Hegel presents in the critical passage, *far from showing that he is already anticipating the Philosophy of Right's position, does not even express his own philosophical view at all, but instead the implications of his argument for a more limited viewpoint*, a viewpoint which, unlike his own and that of his new "Theseus," does see matters in terms of legal/moral oughts, and for which, unlike for his own viewpoint and that of his new "Theseus," the sort of merely conditional and surmountable necessity which he describes is, so to speak, as good as an unconditional and insurmountable necessity (both because the viewpoint in question can only see as far as the "inner causes," without being able really to grasp the possibility of their removal, and because from its perspective of legal/moral oughts "inner causes" which only political "genius" could remove would in any case exculpate agents subject to them as effectively as an unconditional and insurmountable necessity would). This hypothesis is confirmed by the context of the critical passage: Hegel is here opening an essay which postulates the complete sociopolitical disintegration of contemporary Germany, dwells on Germany's recent disasters, especially in the military sphere, as symptoms of this disintegration, and develops in response a program of radical sociopolitical reforms. Obviously, this is a message which is likely to seem inflammatory of the masses, and which is hence likely to incur the displeasure of Germany's leaders, including perhaps particularly the new "Theseus" whom Hegel especially hopes to influence by the essay. Accordingly, Hegel is at pains here at the start of the essay to forestall any such appearance of inflammatoriness by showing that his diagnosis of Germany's present condition, so far from inciting the masses to resentment and revolt against their leaders, in fact implies for the viewpoint of the masses, with its limited causal horizons and conception of legal/moral oughts, the *exculpation* of their leaders, due to the necessitation of the latter's disasters by "inner causes," namely, German sociopolitical disintegration, and so the appropriateness of an attitude of *resignation*. Thus, in the paragraph immediately preceding the critical passage Hegel had argued that while "those who so act in the midst of these great affairs that they could themselves direct them [such as Hegel's new "Theseus"] are few, . . . others have to wait on events with understanding and insight into their necessity," and that the person

influence on their development, which must therefore, to the extent that it results from efficient causes, result from efficient causes of other kinds. Thus the *Philosophy of Right* famously states:

> To comprehend what is, this is the task of philosophy . . . To recognize reason as the rose in the cross of the present and thereby to enjoy the present, this is the rational insight which reconciles us to the actual, the reconciliation which philosophy affords . . . Philosophy . . . always comes on the scene too late to give [instruction as to what the world ought to be]. As the thought of the world, it appears only when actuality is already there cut and dried after its process of formation has been completed . . . It is only when actuality is mature that the ideal first appears over against the real and that the ideal apprehends this same real world in its substance and builds it up for itself into the shape of an intellectual realm. When philosophy paints its grey in grey then has a shape of life grown old.[53]

Having noted this development in Hegel's thought concerning task (ii) between the early Jena period and his later works, we are now in a position to understand the *Phenomenology*'s stance on this task. The *Phe-*

---

who recognizes Germany's recent military disasters to be only the "necessary appearances" of "inner causes," namely, German sociopolitical disintegration, "differentiates himself from those who see only arbitrariness and chance because their own folly convinces them that they would have managed everything more wisely and more fortunately" (*Political Writings,* p. 144). And the continuation of the critical passage makes it still clearer that the passage's message concerns specifically the potentially critical and unruly masses, with their limited causal insight and their legal/moral oughts: "Yet it is hard for the ordinary run of men to rise to the habit of trying to recognize necessity and to think it. Between events and the free interpretation of them they insert a mass of concepts and aims and require what happens to correspond to them . . . Whether they suffer under events or merely find them contradicting their concepts, they find in their assertion of their concepts the right to complain bitterly about what has happened" (ibid., p. 145). We should therefore understand the opening words of the critical passage—"The thoughts contained in this essay can have no other aim or effect, when published . . ."—not as meaning that what Hegel then goes on to specify is the real and sole point of the essay, but instead as addressing an implied objection that the content of his essay will rouse the German masses against their leaders, and as meaning in effect: "*You may worry that my reflections are going to have an incendiary effect on the masses, but on the contrary* the thoughts contained in this essay can have no other aim or effect *in relation to them,* when published . . ." In sum, the critical passage, so far from showing that Hegel already in *The German Constitution* espouses the position of the *Philosophy of Right,* does not even express Hegel's own position at all, but instead merely the consequences of his argument for the limited viewpoint of the masses.

We may safely conclude, then, that the orthodox reading of Hegel's position in the early Jena period is mistaken, and that Hegel's solution to task (ii) in this period was as described in the main text above.

53. *Philosophy of Right,* pp. 11–13.

nomenology's solution to task (ii) *combines* features of the qualified activism of the early Jena period and the non-activism of the *Philosophy of Right*. On the one hand, the Preface's metaphor of Science proper being "the *crown* of a world of Spirit" and implication that Science proper will emerge only with the full development of its "world of Spirit" imply the same position as the *Philosophy of Right* concerning *Science proper*: Science proper emerges only *after* the full development of the sociopolitical institutions to which it corresponds, and so can have *no* efficient causal influence on their development, which, to the extent that it results from efficient causes, must therefore result from efficient causes of other kinds. On the other hand, the *Phenomenology* retains a measure of continuity with the early Jena position as well, in that it espouses a form of qualified activism concerning *itself,* that is, not Science proper, but "the Understanding's form of Science," "the way to Science," the "appearance" of Science: the *Phenomenology* itself *does* play a role in causally effecting both the process of sociopolitical transformation which is its own sociopolitical underpinning and the resulting sociopolitical world which will be the sociopolitical underpinning of Science proper—though no longer, as in the early Jena writings, *through* the actions of a "great man," but rather *in conjunction with* them. Thus, note that in a letter from 1808, the year following the *Phenomenology*'s publication, Hegel can still write in an emphatically activist spirit: "Theoretical work, I become daily more convinced, brings about more in the world than practical. If the realm of representations is only revolutionized, actuality cannot hold out."[54] And observe also that the Preface, read carefully, seems to imply that the *Phenomenology,* "the Understanding's form of Science" and "the way to Science open and equally accessible to everyone," serves as a means to the full realization, not only of Science, but also of *the new sociopolitical "world" of Spirit that is emerging to support Science:*

> But this new world is no more a complete actuality than is a newborn child . . . So too, Science, the crown of a world of Spirit, is not complete in its beginnings . . . While the initial appearance of the new world is, to begin with, only the whole veiled in its *simplicity,* or the general foundation of the whole, the wealth of previous existence is still present to consciousness in memory. Consciousness misses in the newly emerging shape its former range and specificity of content, and even more the articulation of form . . . Without such articulation, Science lacks universal intelligibility . . . The

---

54. *Briefe von und an Hegel* 1:253.

Understanding's form of Science is the way to Science open and equally accessible to everyone. (pars. 12–13)

What this conception of the *Phenomenology*'s function signifies more specifically can readily be inferred: As we have noted, the Preface certainly envisages Napoleon as the *main* cause of the incipient sociopolitical transformation of Germany from sociopolitical fragmentation to sociopolitical unity incorporating differentiation. But the *Phenomenology* is propagating among the Germans an outlook which will surely *aid* Napoleon in his task of sociopolitically unifying Germany—for instance, by providing its arguments for the virtual ontological identity of the individual with his community, and for the realization of the individual's deepest aspirations and hence the very core of his happiness consisting in solidarity with his community, and thereby overcoming individual-community division, or restoring individuals to a regard for their community as their highest end and an automatic deference to it in their judgments (in the manner described in chapter 2). The *Phenomenology* thus *reinforces* the causal influence of Napoleon in his direction of Germany away from sociopolitical fragmentation toward sociopolitical unity incorporating differentiation.[55] On the other hand, Hegel can certainly have had no illusions that the *Phenomenology* would actually *inspire* Napoleon to his sociopolitical reforms. Hence in his 1806 lecture on the *Phenomenology* he acknowledges that the incipient development of Spirit is for the most part beyond the philosopher's control: "A new progression of Spirit is in the making. Philosophy primarily [vornehmlich] has the task of greeting its appearance and acknowledging it."[56] And we must therefore understand the *Phenomenology* to revise the position of the early Jena writings that Hegel's own role was one of causing sociopolitical change *through* a political leader to the more modest position that it was one of doing so *in conjunction with* a political leader.[57]

* * *

55. Note in this connection that it had been a central claim of Schiller's *On the Aesthetic Education of Man,* a work whose strong influence on Hegel and the *Phenomenology* we have already seen, that, in order for the establishment of the sort of unified but diversified political community which Schiller, like Hegel, aimed for to occur, mere political revolution alone would not suffice, but an education of individual minds from division to unity was also essential (pp. 17, 19–23, 45–47, 215).

56. *Hegels Leben*, pp. 214–15; also in appendix X.

57. This, together with the fact that it is no longer Science proper but only "the Understanding's form of Science," "the way to Science," the "appearance" of Science which is

Further Intellectual Historicism in the *Phenomenology*   497

This qualified activism in the *Phenomenology*'s self-conception is not contradicted or revised by Hegel's later non-activist view of philosophy in the *Philosophy of Right*. For, the *Philosophy of Right*'s non-activism concerns philosophy or Science *proper,* and, as we have seen, on that subject the *Phenomenology* implies the same non-activist view; whereas the *Phenomenology*'s qualified activism concerns only "the Understanding's form of Science," "the way to Science," the "appearance" of Science, a subject on which the *Philosophy of Right* simply expresses no opinion. Nor does the *Philosophy of Right*'s non-activism concerning philosophy proper spring from any *general* skepticism about the capacity of thought to operate as an efficient cause of sociopolitical change. On the contrary, the later Hegel is if anything *more* committed than the early Hegel to the view that it can do so—arguing, for example, in the *Lectures on the Philosophy of World History* that the collapse of the ideal form of Greek society was caused in this way (specifically, by the thought of the Sophists and Socrates) and the French Revolution likewise (specifically, by the thought of the *philosophes*).

I would suggest, indeed, that, so far from seeing the *Philosophy of Right*'s position as contradicting and revising the *Phenomenology*'s, we should rather see the *Phenomenology* as filling out what is in fact an incomplete statement in the *Philosophy of Right* of Hegel's conception of his own thought's relation to the sociopolitical sphere: although Hegelian Science proper has no role in efficiently causing the "cut and dried" sociopolitical world which underpins it, the *Phenomenology,* "the Understanding's form of Science," "the way to Science," the "appearance" of Science, *does* (or, from the *Philosophy of Right*'s temporal standpoint, *did*).[58] If this is correct, then the standard reading of the mature Hegel as a philosopher whose position "rules out the possibility of a revolutionary praxis founded on reason" and maintains that "revolutions are only understood and justified by reason ex post facto" stands in need of substantial revision.[59]

---

understood to effect the sociopolitical transformation, are the two main *dis*continuities between the *Phenomenology*'s qualified activism and that of the early Jena writings.

58. The plausibility of this suggestion depends in part on that of a more general claim for which I shall argue in part 5, namely, that the later Hegel never lost faith in, or fundamentally revised his conception of, the *Phenomenology.*

59. These quotations are from Taylor, *Hegel,* p. 425; cf. 425–26.

PART FOUR

Phenomenology and Ur-*Phenomenology;*
Phenomenology and Logic

CHAPTER THIRTEEN

The Issues

In this part of the book we shall pursue two further questions concerning the structural design of the *Phenomenology* which have been much debated in the secondary literature: first, the question of whether or not Hegel changed his plan of the structure and scope of the work during the process of composition, and if so with what results, and second, the question of the character of the work's underpinning by Hegel's Logic.

Over the years several commentators have suggested that Hegel's plan of the structure and scope of the *Phenomenology* underwent a radical revision as he actually wrote the work, that he added large amounts of new material, perhaps even whole new chapters, to what he had originally intended to include; behind or within the *Phenomenology* there lies an Ur-*Phenomenology* of more modest scope. For example, Haym suggests that Hegel, having begun with the ambition of providing a transcendental-psychological proof of his own philosophy found in the *Consciousness* chapter, subsequently superimposed the historical proof of it found in the following chapters, and that "the *Phenomenology* thus becomes a palimpsest: over and between the first text we discover a second."[1] Again, Haering argues that Hegel originally intended the *Phenomenology* to extend only as far as the *Logical and Psychological Laws* section half way through the *Reason* chapter, whence he would have made a direct transition to the Logic; and that the rest of the *Reason* chapter, and the chapters *Spirit, Religion,* and *Absolute Knowing* were added as

---

1. Haym, *Hegel und seine Zeit*, pp. 235–38. It is not entirely clear how literally Haym intends this suggestion to be taken.

an afterthought.² More recently, and less dramatically, Pöggeler has suggested that, although Hegel did not add whole new chapters to the work, the work's conception and division changed and its scale got out of hand during the process of composition, so that "from the planned brief introduction grew a disproportioned, voluminous work."³

Associated with such hypotheses of a shift from an Ur-*Phenomenology* to the published *Phenomenology* has generally been an implication that the work which resulted from the shift inevitably lacked whatever coherence in design its original plan might have lent it. Thus, as we noted in part 3, Haym sees the resulting work as "a psychology thrown into confusion and disorder by history and a history disrupted by psychology." Similarly, Haering writes that "the *Phenomenology* did not grow in Hegel and from his previous development organically and in accordance with a carefully considered and long cherished plan, but . . . as a manuscript which demonstrably first came about piece by piece for the press, in the course of which the basic intuition and intention by no means always remained the same."⁴ And Pöggeler argues that "Hegel was only too correct when he wrote to Schelling that the 'work on the details' had harmed his 'overview of the whole' . . . We can have no doubt that already soon after the publication of the *Phenomenology* the structure of the work had no final validity any more."⁵

Concerning these matters, I shall argue in this part of the book for three main claims. First, I shall argue that the general hypothesis that Hegel shifted in the course of writing the *Phenomenology* from an originally planned Ur-*Phenomenology* of more modest scope to the enlarged *Phenomenology* which he eventually published is quite correct. Second, though, I shall argue that none of the authors mentioned above has correctly identified the nature of this shift. What in fact happened, I shall argue, is that Hegel originally intended to include in the work only and all of the materials in the chapters *Consciousness* through to the very end

---

2. Haering, "Die Entstehungsgeschichte der *Phänomenologie des Geistes*," and *Hegel sein Wollen und sein Werk* 2:479–86. In basic agreement with Haering, though less inclined to see an open break in the published text of the *Phenomenology*, are Hoffmeister, in Hegel, *Phänomenologie des Geistes*, ed. Hoffmeister, editor's introduction; and Hyppolite, *Genesis and Structure*, pp. 55–56.
3. Pöggeler, "Die Komposition der *Phänomenologie des Geistes*," pp. 48, 64; "Zur Deutung der *Phänomenologie des Geistes*," pp. 280–88.
4. "Die Entstehungsgeschichte der *Phänomenologie des Geistes*," p. 119.
5. "Die Komposition der *Phänomenologie des Geistes*," p. 64.

of *Reason,* and to make a direct transition from there to the Logic, and only later decided to add the chapters *Spirit, Religion,* and *Absolute Knowing.* (Of the authors mentioned above, Haering comes *closest* to recognizing this.) Third, I shall argue, in still sharper contrast to the authors mentioned above, that this very dramatic shift in the plan of the *Phenomenology* did not in fact, as one might certainly have expected, bring any fundamental confusion into the work's design, that the work was fundamentally coherent in design before the change and remained equally so afterwards as well.

In order fully to address this issue of an Ur-*Phenomenology,* we shall have to address a second issue also: that of the logical underpinning of the *Phenomenology.* Both in the Introduction, the part of the work which Hegel wrote first, and in a paragraph near the end of the work, written near the time of the work's completion, the *Phenomenology* appears to advertise some sort of one-to-one correspondence between its contents and the categories of the Logic, and indeed even to suggest that its contents somehow just *are* the Logic's categories, seen through a glass darkly, so to speak (pars. 89, 805).[6] This has prompted a number of recent commentators, in particular Fulda and Heinrichs, to investigate the work's underlying logical framework. And the results of their investigations have seemed, both to themselves and to others, to conflict with the hypothesis that the *Phenomenology* developed out of a radically smaller Ur-*Phenomenology.* Our interest in the question of the *Phenomenology*'s underlying Logic arises in the first instance from this bearing which it has on the question of an Ur-*Phenomenology.* It is, though, also a question of some independent importance for understanding the *Phenomenology*'s structure, and interpreting its particular parts.[7]

---

6. That the Logic is at issue in both of these passages—rather than, for example, the system as a whole—is not entirely obvious from their wording, but has been convincingly argued by Fulda in *Das Problem einer Einleitung,* pp. 140 ff., and "Zur Logik der *Phänomenologie* von 1807," *Hegel Studien,* Beiheft 3 (1966), pp. 78 ff.

7. In the latter connection, I would caution, however, that there are serious limits to the power of a discovery of the *Phenomenology*'s logical design to provide a key for interpreting the work, limits to which the existing secondary literature on the work's logical design—not only that by Fulda and Heinrichs, but also, and indeed especially, that by earlier authors on the subject, such as Purpus and Schmitz—seems to me insufficiently sensitive. In particular, (i) as we saw in part 2, Hegel's official and considered intention is that the argument of the *Phenomenology* should be fully intelligible and compelling even for someone who lacks any understanding of or conviction in Hegelian Science proper, including specifically the Logic. And (ii) attempts to throw philosophical light on the *Phenom-*

Concerning this question of the *Phenomenology*'s underlying Logic, I shall argue that Fulda's and Heinrichs's approaches have been fundamentally flawed, that the logical design of the work is quite different from any that they have envisaged, and especially that, properly understood, this design does not in fact conflict with but instead strongly *supports* my hypothesis of the *Phenomenology*'s development out of a radically smaller Ur-*Phenomenology*.

Our order of business will, then, be as follows. Chapter 14 will construct a basic case for the hypothesis of a shift in the design of the *Phenomenology* during its composition from an Ur-*Phenomenology* comprising only and all of the chapters *Consciousness* through to the end of *Reason* to the published *Phenomenology* which added the chapters *Spirit*, *Religion*, and *Absolute Knowing*. Chapter 15 will then answer certain possible objections to this hypothesis, especially objections stemming from Fulda's and Heinrichs's investigations into the logical underpinning of the *Phenomenology*. Chapter 16 will then show that and how the work remained fundamentally coherent in design despite this dramatic shift. Finally, chapter 17 will briefly address the question of Hegel's motives for this shift.

―――

enology by determining its underpinning in the Logic run very serious risks of explaining obscurum per obscurius, due to the philosophical opacity of the Logic itself.

CHAPTER FOURTEEN

The Basic Case for a Shift in Plan

The basic case for the hypothesis that the original plan of the *Phenomenology* foresaw only and all of the chapters *Consciousness* through to the end of *Reason,* and that the remaining chapters were added as an afterthought, consists of five pieces of evidence. In this chapter I shall present each of these pieces of evidence in turn, beginning with the more important and proceeding to the less.

First, the Introduction, the part of the work which was written first, characterizes the *Phenomenology* as an exposition just of a series of *shapes of consciousness,* concluding in "true knowledge" or Hegelian Science proper: the work is "the path of the natural consciousness which presses forward to true knowledge," and "the moments of the whole are *shapes of consciousness*" (pars. 77, 89). The Introduction knows nothing of any "real Spirits" or "shapes of a world" (the subject matter of the *Spirit* chapter), nor of any "shapes of religion" (the subject matter of the *Religion* chapter). In accordance with this fact, the original title of the work was *Science of the Experience of Consciousness,* a title which reflects the Introduction's project of expounding just a series of shapes of consciousness (cf. pars. 86–88). The title *Phenomenology of Spirit* was substituted only later.[1] Now the exposition of *shapes of consciousness* in the *Phenomenology* covers, officially at least, only and all of the chapters

---

1. This title first appears in a lecture announcement of Hegel's for winter 1806–7, the composition of the *Phenomenology* having begun some time in 1805 or possibly early 1806.

Consciousness through to the end of *Reason*.² For, as we have already seen, when Hegel comes to the end of the *Reason* chapter, and begins the *Spirit* chapter, he writes that what follows will no longer be shapes of consciousness, as hitherto, but instead "real Spirits" or "shapes of a world": "These shapes . . . are distinguished from the previous ones by the fact that they are real Spirits . . . and, instead of being shapes merely of consciousness, are shapes of a world" (par. 441). And subsequently, at the beginning of the *Religion* chapter, he further distinguishes the contents of the *Religion* chapter from both "shapes of consciousness" and "real Spirits" or "shapes of a world" as "shapes of religion" (par. 680). This evidence would surely, just by itself, warrant at least a strong suspicion that Hegel originally planned to write only and all of the chapters *Consciousness* through to the end of *Reason*, and to pass thence to Hegelian Science proper, and that he added the subsequent chapters only as an afterthought.

Second and connectedly, the Introduction, the part of the work which was written first, implies that the *Phenomenology* will contain just a single treatment of history, a history of shapes of consciousness culminating in the standpoint of Hegelian Science in the modern age: "the detailed history of the education of consciousness . . . to the standpoint of Science" (par. 78). The Introduction neither plans nor indeed leaves room for any further treatment(s) of history, or any treatment(s) of history dealing with items other than shapes of consciousness. Now, as we saw in part 3, the chapters *Consciousness* through to the end of *Reason* contain precisely: a single treatment of history, a history of shapes of consciousness culminating in the standpoint of Hegelian Science in the modern age. By contrast, the *Spirit* chapter contains a second treatment of history, dealing not with shapes of consciousness but with "real Spirits" or "shapes of a world," and the chapters *Religion* and *Absolute Knowing* contain yet a third treatment of history, dealing not with shapes of consciousness but with "shapes of religion" and then Hegel's own philosophy. Once again, it is surely natural to infer from these facts that Hegel originally intended to write no more than the chapters *Consciousness* through to the end of *Reason*, and that the subsequent chapters were only included as an afterthought. Additionally, in light of our reading of the chapters *Con-*

---

2. I say "officially at least" due to a—here negligible—exception noted and explained in part 3: the fact that later parts of the *Spirit* chapter deviate from Hegel's official intentions for the chapter by slipping into depicting shapes of consciousness once again.

sciousness through to the end of *Reason* in part 3, we can see that Hegel's original plan must have included more or less the *whole* of these chapters. He cannot, at least, have intended to stop at some point in them short of the end of the *Reason* chapter (e.g., at the section *Logical and Psychological Laws,* as Haering suggested). For had he done so he would have fallen short, both in terms of intellectual standpoint and temporally, of the *goal* of "the history of the education of consciousness . . . to the standpoint of Science" projected by the Introduction, since it is only at the very end of the *Reason* chapter that Hegelian Science and its age are reached (pars. 435–37). Here once again, then, we have good evidence that the original plan of the *Phenomenology* encompassed only and all of the chapters *Consciousness* through to the end of *Reason*, and that the remaining chapters of the book were only added later as an afterthought.

A third piece of evidence supporting this hypothesis is a passage from the *Encyclopaedia* in which Hegel writes of the demonstration of his philosophical Science undertaken in the *Phenomenology* of 1807:

> It was not possible . . . to remain at the formal aspect of mere consciousness; for the standpoint of philosophical knowing is at the same time within itself the most contentful and concrete standpoint, so that in being produced as a result it presupposed also the concrete shapes of consciousness, for example those of morality, ethical life, art, and religion. The development of the *substantial content,* of the objects of particular parts of philosophical Science, therefore also falls within that development of consciousness . . . even though that development initially seemed to be limited to the formal aspect only. The presentation thereby becomes more complicated, and what belongs to the concrete parts to some extent already falls within this introduction along with the rest. (par. 25)[3]

I suggest that the most plausible interpretation of this passage is as follows: Hegel is stating that, and explaining why, in composing the *Phenomenology* he was forced to abandon an original plan of including in the work only "the formal aspect of mere consciousness." By this he means the "shapes of consciousness" which *Phenomenology,* paragraph 441 identifies as the subject matter of just the chapters *Consciousness* through to the end of *Reason*. And he is stating that, and explaining why, he was forced to include in addition "the concrete shapes of consciousness." By this he means the "shapes of a world" which *Phenomenology,*

---

3. This is translated in full in appendix XVII.

paragraph 441 identifies as the subject matter of the *Spirit* chapter, and the "shapes of religion" which *Phenomenology*, paragraph 680 identifies as the subject matter of the *Religion* chapter. Hence he specifies exclusively contents from the *Spirit* and *Religion* chapters in order to illustrate what he means by "the concrete shapes of consciousness" as contrasted with "the formality of mere consciousness": "morality, ethical life, art, and religion." So here once again we have strong evidence that Hegel changed his plan for the work from an original plan envisaging only the chapters *Consciousness* through to the end of *Reason* to a plan which added the subsequent chapters.

Finally, we may add two pieces of evidence originally adduced by Haering, and in the meantime too lightly dismissed by others, in particular Pöggeler: A fourth piece of evidence concerns the several later versions of the *Phenomenology* found in the various editions of the Nuremberg *Doctrine of Consciousness* and the *Encyclopaedia*. It is a striking fact that almost immediately after publishing the *Phenomenology* of 1807, and forever thereafter, Hegel in these later versions of the discipline scaled back its scope to include just the contents of the chapters *Consciousness* through to the end of *Reason*, and moreover in the earliest of these later versions, the Nuremberg *Doctrine of Consciousness* of 1808–9, made a direct transition from the conclusion of *Reason* to the Logic. It is true that—as Pöggeler objects to Haering—when Hegel *began* writing the version of the *Phenomenology* in the 1808–9 *Doctrine of Consciousness* he intended it to have the full scope of the *Phenomenology* of 1807 and to proceed directly to a Psychology rather than to the Logic.[4] But the fact remains that when he *executed* this version he wrote just the chapters *Consciousness, Self-consciousness,* and *Reason*, and made thence a direct transition to the Logic of the 1808–9 *Logic*. Moreover, the first paragraphs of the 1808–9 *Logic* make it quite clear that, pace Pöggeler, Hegel in the end conceived this transition from *Reason* to the Logic as a genuine transition, not merely a cutting short of one discipline and turning to another.[5] The restriction of the discipline of a "Phenomenology of Spirit" to the chapters *Consciousness, Self-consciousness,* and *Reason* was henceforth canonical for Hegel, being observed again in the *Doctrine of Consciousness* of 1809 ff., and in all editions of the *Encyclopaedia*, in-

---

4. Pöggeler, "Zur Deutung der *Phänomenologie des Geistes*," pp. 274–76.
5. Pace Pöggeler, ibid., p. 276. The paragraphs of the 1808–9 *Logic* in question are pars. 1/33, 2/34, 4/36 (*Nürnberger und Heidelberger Schriften*, pp. 86–87).

cluding the unpublished edition of 1808 ff. and the published editions of 1817, 1827, and 1830.⁶ Now it is surely very plausible—and indeed, in the light of the other evidence already cited becomes virtually unavoidable—to conclude from these facts that these later versions of the *Phenomenology* are reverting to an original conception of the work, that they all return to an original plan of having the work include just the chapters *Consciousness* through to the end of *Reason,* and that the 1808–9 *Doctrine of Consciousness* and *Logic* in addition return to an original plan of having the culmination of the *Reason* chapter make a direct transition to the Logic.

A fifth piece of evidence—again pointed to by Haering, but with inaccuracies noted by Pöggeler and corrected in what follows—consists in the peculiar division of the *Phenomenology* found in its table of contents.⁷ During the process of composition Hegel numbered parts of the work, beginning with *Sense-certainty* and ending with *Absolute Knowing,* with the Roman numerals I–VIII. However, when he came to draw up the table of contents he superimposed the following very odd division: A. Consciousness; B. Self-consciousness; C. (AA) Reason, (BB) Spirit, (CC) Religion, (DD) Absolute Knowing. Now—particularly when seen in the light of the other evidence already cited—this odd division surely invites the following explanation: Hegel had initially begun with a threefold division of the work in mind: A. Consciousness, B. Self-consciousness, C. Reason.⁸ In the process of composition, he went beyond these originally planned contents by adding the chapters *Spirit, Religion,* and *Absolute Knowing.* However, for some reason or other he felt a need to maintain a threefold division (perhaps he had led his publisher to expect such a division, or perhaps his well-known liking for threefold divisions simply proved irresistible).⁹ He therefore decided to effect a compromise with his original threefold schema, by making *Reason* merely the first

---

6. That even the version of a "Phenomenology of Spirit" envisaged in the unpublished first edition of the *Encyclopaedia* from 1808 ff. excluded the chapters *Spirit, Religion,* and *Absolute Knowing* can be seen from *Nürnberger und Heidelberger Schriften,* p. 42, pars. 128–29.

7. Pöggeler notes the relevant inaccuracies in Haering's account at "Zur Deutung der Phänomenologie des Geistes," pp. 272–73.

8. Thus in the 1808–9 *Doctrine of Consciousness* we find the division: I. Consciousness, II. Self-consciousness, III. Reason (*Nürnberger und Heidelberger Schriften,* p. 74).

9. Thus, as Pöggeler points out, there is evidence within the text that Hegel struggled to maintain a threefold division of the *Phenomenology* during its composition ("Die Komposition der *Phänomenologie des Geistes,*" pp. 49–50).

part of C instead of the whole of it, and accommodating *Spirit, Religion,* and *Absolute Knowing* as further parts of C.

Taken together, these five pieces of evidence yield a strong prima facie case for the hypothesized shift in Hegel's plan of the *Phenomenology.* However, certain potential objections are waiting in the wings, and in the next chapter we must confront these.

CHAPTER FIFTEEN

The Underlying Logic of
the *Phenomenology*

Despite the considerable strength of the prima facie case developed in the last chapter for the hypothesis of a shift in the plan of the *Phenomenology* from the inclusion of only and all of the chapters *Consciousness* through to the end of *Reason* to the addition of the remaining chapters, this hypothesis is bound to provoke certain objections. Especially imposing ones might seem to arise from a consideration of the logical design of the *Phenomenology*. As has been mentioned, both in a paragraph of the Introduction, the part of the work which was written first, and in a paragraph near the conclusion of the work, written toward the end of the work's composition, Hegel appears to advertise some sort of one-to-one correspondence between the work's contents and the categories of the Logic (pars. 89, 805). This fact has led certain commentators to question hypotheses of a fundamental shift in the plan of the work such as that which I have advanced, and this in two main ways. First, and most straightforwardly, Fulda has asked rhetorically how Hegel could possibly have added whole new chapters to the work, given that we can see from these two paragraphs that his conception of a one-to-one correspondence between its contents and the categories of the Logic remained constant from the beginning until the end of its composition (assuming that no fundamental change occurred in the Logic itself during the process of composition).[1] Second, Fulda, and subsequently Heinrichs, taking their cue from these two paragraphs, have attempted to work out the intended one-to-one correspondence between the *Phenomenology* and its underly-

1. Fulda, *Das Problem einer Einleitung,* p. 130.

ing Logic in detail, and purport to have shown that this correspondence includes and requires the contents of all chapters of the *Phenomenology*—so that in this way too it would be shown that the logical design of the *Phenomenology* required all of the work's chapters from the start.[2]

Now, I agree with these commentators that the question of the *Phenomenology*'s relation to its underlying Logic is highly relevant to deciding whether or not Hegel's plan for the work underwent a fundamental shift. However, I disagree with their view that reflection on that relation tells *against* such a fundamental shift as that which I have hypothesized. On the contrary, I believe, and shall attempt to show, that *when correctly understood* the relation between the *Phenomenology* and its Logic provides further strong evidence *for* the shift which I have hypothesized.

Fulda and Heinrichs make a first and fatal error, it seems to me, in their interpretation of the two key passages from the Introduction and the end of the *Phenomenology* in which Hegel announces the one-to-one correspondence between contents of the *Phenomenology* and logical categories. Fulda, and following him Heinrichs, believe that in both passages Hegel is announcing a one-to-one correspondence between *all contents* of the *Phenomenology* and logical categories (and consequently they set out to try to demonstrate such a correspondence in detail).[3] However, this is a mistake. We need to distinguish between the claims (i) that all of the work's *contents* are correlated one-to-one with logical categories and (ii) that all of the work's *shapes of consciousness* are so correlated. When we do so, we find the following. The passage from the Introduction implies both (i) and (ii). Thus Hegel writes in this passage: "The way to Science . . . is the Science of the *experience of consciousness* [i.e., the *Phenomenology*]. The experience of itself which consciousness goes through can . . . comprehend nothing less than the entire system of consciousness, or the entire realm of the truth of Spirit [i.e., the entire contents of the Logic]. For this reason, the moments of this truth are exhibited in their own proper determinateness, viz. as being not abstract moments, but as they are for consciousness, or as consciousness stands forth in its relation to them. Thus the moments of the whole are *shapes*

---

2. Fulda, ibid., pp. 140 ff., and "Zur Logik der *Phänomenologie* von 1807"; Heinrichs, *Die Logik der Phänomenologie des Geistes,* esp. pp. 102–3.

3. That Heinrichs follows Fulda in this belief is evident especially from his criticisms of Puntel (ibid., p. 94).

of consciousness" (pars. 88–89). So if restricted to *this* passage Fulda's and Heinrichs's belief is justified. However, the passage near the end of the work implies *only (ii), not (i)*. Thus Hegel writes there just that "in [Science], the moments of [Spirit's] movement no longer exhibit themselves as specific *shapes of consciousness,* but . . . as specific concepts . . . Conversely to each abstract moment of Science corresponds a shape of manifest Spirit [i.e., a shape of consciousness] as such," and that in the *Phenomenology* we "know the pure concepts of Science in [the] form of shapes of consciousness" (par. 805). Indeed, since by the time Hegel writes this passage he has carefully distinguished the *Phenomenology*'s "shapes of consciousness" from other contents of the work which are "shapes of a world" and yet others which are "shapes of religion" (pars. 441, 680), his claim here of a one-to-one correspondence between shapes of consciousness and logical categories can quite properly be said to imply a *denial* of (i). In short, the two passages disagree on the question of whether or not there is a one-to-one correlation between all *contents* of the *Phenomenology* and logical categories—the Introduction implying yes, the later passage implying no. And the only claim in which they agree is that there is a one-to-one correlation between all of the work's *shapes of consciousness* and logical categories.

This enables us to answer immediately Fulda's first objection to the hypothesis of a major shift in the plan of the work. Fulda asks how—assuming constancy in the content of the Logic during the course of the *Phenomenology*'s composition—Hegel could possibly have made a massive addition of new content to the *Phenomenology* such as that which I have hypothesized, given that he both begins and ends the work advertising a one-to-one correlation between its contents and the categories of the Logic. The answer to this rhetorical question is that Hegel does *not* both begin and end the work advertising a one-to-one correlation between *all contents* of the work and the categories of the Logic, as Fulda's argument implies and requires. Hegel advertises *that* only at the beginning of the work, but not at the end, where on the contrary he implicitly denies it. Instead, Hegel only begins and ends the work advertising a one-to-one correlation between *all shapes of consciousness* in the work and the categories of the Logic. But this, even assuming an unchanged Logic, is perfectly consistent with our hypothesis that he at the beginning intended to include just the contents of the chapters *Consciousness* through to the end of *Reason,* that is, all of the work's shapes of consciousness, and later added the remaining chapters, which deal only with such different sorts of items as "shapes of a world" and "shapes of religion."[4]

Furthermore, turning to the question of the detailed correspondence between the *Phenomenology* and the Logic, let us consider what expectation about this these two passages from the Introduction and the end of the work license. Since Fulda and Heinrichs read both passages as advertising a one-to-one correspondence between *all contents* of the *Phenomenology* and logical categories, they expect and proceed to try to find such a correspondence—thereby generating their second argument against such hypotheses of a fundamental shift in the plan of the work as that which I have advanced. However, as we have just seen, that reading is mistaken; the two passages implicitly *disagree* on the question of whether or not *all contents* of the work correspond one-to-one with logical categories—the Introduction implying yes, the later passage no. And so taken together they justify no such expectation. On the other hand, the two passages *do* agree that there is a one-to-one correspondence between all of the work's *shapes of consciousness* and logical categories. And this, I suggest, justifies a very different expectation from Fulda's and Heinrichs's: Since Hegel tells us explicitly that the work's shapes of consciousness are confined just to the chapters *Consciousness* through to the end of *Reason* (par. 441), it justifies an expectation that there is a one-to-one correspondence between *just the contents of the chapters Consciousness through to the end of Reason* and logical categories.[5] If this expectation proves correct, then—especially given that when Hegel wrote the passage in the Introduction, though no longer when he wrote the later passage, he understood this correspondence to exhaust all of the contents of the *Phenomenology*—this provides strong new evidence that Hegel's original plan of the work foresaw only the chapters *Consciousness* through to the end of *Reason*, that is, strong new evidence *for* my hypothesis.

---

4. Strictly speaking, as we noted in part 3, Hegel did introduce *some* new shapes of consciousness after the chapters *Consciousness* through *Reason*, namely, those in later parts of the *Spirit* chapter. However, these were not *additions* to those in the chapters *Consciousness* through *Reason*, but rather *substitutes* for an equal number of the latter, introduced in the course of an attempt to rewrite the later parts of the *Reason* chapter. They would not, therefore, in Hegel's eyes, have disrupted the one-to-one correlation between an unchanged Logic and the work's shapes of consciousness.

5. Or alternatively: between the rewritten version of these chapters identifed in part 3—comprising *Consciousness, Self-consciousness, Reason* up to the section *Observing Reason*, and then the later parts of the *Spirit* chapter—and logical categories. This, strictly speaking, would be what Hegel had in mind in the passage at par. 805.

Is this expectation correct, though? *Does* a detailed examination of the *Phenomenology* and the Logic confirm that there is a one-to-one correspondence between just the shapes of consciousness of the chapters *Consciousness* through to the end of *Reason* and logical categories (thus confirming the last paragraph's new argument for my hypothesis)? Or does it not rather, as Fulda and Heinrichs believe, reveal a one-to-one correspondence between all of the work's contents and logical categories (thus calling into question the last paragraph's new argument for my hypothesis, and leaving an obstacle in the way of my hypothesis)? This is the question to which we must now turn.

* * *

The task of determining the details of the correspondence between the *Phenomenology* and its underlying Logic is a double one: First we need to identify the contents and sequence of this Logic (for Hegel unfortunately nowhere tells us how he envisaged the Logic at the time when he wrote the *Phenomenology*). Then we need to see how these map onto the *Phenomenology*. Fulda and Heinrichs have, between them, offered three different identifications of the Logic in question and three different mappings—all of which mappings share, though, the key characteristic that they correlate the contents of the Logic in a one-to-one fashion with *all contents* of the *Phenomenology*. Fortunately for my hypothesis, however, none of these identifications or mappings stands up to scrutiny. And when we *do* correctly identify the underlying Logic and correctly map it onto the *Phenomenology*, we find that, sure enough, it corresponds one-to-one, not with all of the contents of the *Phenomenology*, but instead with just the shapes of consciousness of the chapters *Consciousness* through to the end of *Reason*.

In order to see this, let us begin by briefly going through each of Fulda's and Heinrichs's suggestions in turn. To start with the later of two suggestions offered by Fulda, in his essay "Zur Logik der *Phänomenologie* von 1807" Fulda chose the very brief sketch of "Speculative Philosophy" found near the end of the 1805–6 Philosophy of Spirit as his basis for identifying the Logic of the *Phenomenology*. This sketch reads as follows: "Speculative Philosophy: absolute Being, which becomes Other (Relation) to itself, Life, and Cognition; and Knowing Knowing, Spirit, Spirit's Knowledge of Itself."[6] Now Fulda believes that the *Phenomenology* is

---

6. *Jenaer Realphilosophie*, p. 272.

correlated one-to-one with the contents of the Logic, and he believes that we have here a sketch of the Logic. But is this right? No, we in fact have here a sketch of Logic *and Metaphysics,* that pair of disciplines which *together* bore the title "Speculative Philosophy" throughout the Jena period (until at about the time of the *Phenomenology*'s composition Hegel fused them together into a single discipline called Logic). How can one tell that this is a sketch of *both* disciplines? Well, note the semicolon after "Cognition." Hegel clearly has a division of "Speculative Philosophy" in mind: a division between, on the one hand, "absolute Being, which becomes Other (Relation) to itself, Life, and Cognition," and, on the other hand, "Knowing Knowing, Spirit, Spirit's Knowledge of itself." Now this division corresponds quite exactly to the division between Logic and Metaphysics in the only slightly earlier 1804–5 *Logic, Metaphysics, and Philosophy of Nature.* Thus in this earlier text the Logic proceeds through "Relation" to culminate in "Cognition," and then we arrive at a Metaphysics, whose threefold division into "Cognition as a System of Axioms," "Metaphysics of Objectivity" (culminating in "The Highest Being"), and "Metaphysics of Subjectivity" (culminating in "The Absolute Spirit") clearly corresponds to the 1805–6 sketch's "Knowing Knowing, Spirit, Spirit's Knowledge of Itself."

Someone might reply, however, that this is little more than an ad hominem objection to Fulda's identification of the form of the discipline underlying the *Phenomenology:* "Fulda was wrong, indeed, to insist that the *Phenomenology* is correlated one-to-one with the Logic only, for it is actually correlated one-to-one with the early Logic and Metaphysics; but the 1805–6 sketch really does give us the form in which these disciplines underlie the *Phenomenology.*" This is in effect the position adopted by Pöggeler.[7] So modified, Fulda's suggestion would also closely resemble Heinrichs's suggestion in *Die Logik der Phänomenologie des Geistes* that the early Logic and Metaphysics *both* underlie the *Phenomenology,* and that we should take the version of these disciplines found in the 1804–5 *Logic, Metaphysics, and Philosophy of Nature* as our basis for estimating the form in which they do so.[8] Let us, therefore, consider the modified version of Fulda's suggestion and Heinrichs's suggestion together.

The first question which we need to ask about these suggestions is

---

7. Pöggeler, "Hegels Phänomenologie des Selbstbewußtseins," in *Hegels Idee einer Phänomenologie des Geistes,* esp. pp. 261, 269–70.

8. Heinrichs, *Die Logik der Phänomenologie des Geistes,* esp. pp. 102–3.

The Underlying Logic of the *Phenomenology* 517

whether it really is the case, as they imply, that both the early Logic and the early Metaphysics underlie the *Phenomenology*, or whether it is not rather, after all, the Logic alone that does so. We know that at around the time of the *Phenomenology*'s composition Hegel's ideas about Logic and Metaphysics underwent a dramatic change. In particular, (i) he fused these disciplines together into a single discipline which he called Logic, and (ii) whereas he had conceived the earlier Logic as merely a sort of introduction to his system proper, he made the resulting later Logic the first and fundamental discipline within his system proper. So the question which we need to ask is where Hegel was in relation to this change when he came to write the *Phenomenology*. The suggestions which we are evaluating presuppose that he had not yet effected it. Is this correct, or was the transition to the later Logic instead already essentially completed?

Now there is, admittedly, *some* evidence which might seem at first sight to speak for the former answer. For example, Rosenkranz reports that the *Phenomenology* developed out of Hegel's introductions to Logic and Metaphysics, from 1804 on.[9] And in his lecture announcement for winter 1806–7 Hegel could still write of his "Phenomenology of Spirit" as an introduction to "Logic and Metaphysics or Speculative Philosophy."[10] On the whole, however, the evidence speaks much more strongly for Hegel's having essentially completed the transition to the later Logic by the time he came to write the *Phenomenology*.[11] Thus, an even earlier lecture announcement, for summer 1806, speaks of "Speculative Philosophy *or Logic*" only.[12] Moreover, nowhere in the *Phenomenology*, not even in its Introduction, is there any hint of a division between Logic and Metaphysics, or of a Logic which is merely introductory in character. On the contrary, the Preface clearly identifies Logic alone as the discipline to which the work leads, referring to this as "Logic or Speculative Philosophy" (par. 37; cf. 48, 56), and clearly assumes Hegel's later conception of Logic as the fundamental discipline of the system proper. Again, in his 1807 Announcement of the *Phenomenology* Hegel describes the work as introducing the later Logic alone (followed immediately by the Philosophies of Nature and Spirit), as he does forever thereafter (e.g., in the pref-

---

9. *Hegels Leben*, p. 202.
10. Hegel, *Phänomenologie des Geistes*, ed. E. Moldenhauer and K.M. Michel (Frankfurt am Main: Suhrkamp, 1970), p. 595.
11. As Fulda himself holds ("Zur Logik der *Phänomenologie* von 1807," p. 80).
12. In Haering, "Die Entstehungsgeschichte der *Phänomenologie des Geistes*," p. 123; emphasis added.

ace of the *Science of Logic* from 1812). Also, the Nuremberg writings, which immediately followed the *Phenomenology* in time, know only of the later Logic, not of Metaphysics. And so forth. Furthermore, the seemingly contrary evidence mentioned at the beginning of this paragraph is not, on closer inspection, nearly as persuasive as it might appear to be at first sight. To say, as Rosenkranz does, that the *Phenomenology* developed out of Hegel's introductions to Logic and Metaphysics is not at all the same as saying that the *Phenomenology* which was actually written was an introduction to both of these disciplines. And the fact that Hegel's lecture announcement for winter 1806–7 still speaks of "Logic and Metaphysics or Speculative Philosophy" is no safe basis for inferring that Hegel still really divided Speculative Philosophy in this way at all. For even in his *Berlin* (!) lecture announcements Hegel still used this traditional title, that is, long after he had decisively fused Logic and Metaphysics into the single discipline of the later Logic. So, on balance, the evidence tells pretty clearly that it is the later Logic, not the early Logic and Metaphysics, which lies behind the *Phenomenology*.[13]

Furthermore, the thesis that it must be not Hegel's early Logic and Metaphysics but his later Logic which underlies the *Phenomenology* is reinforced when we examine Fulda's and Heinrichs's attempts actually to map the early Logic and Metaphysics onto the *Phenomenology*. These mappings, particularly Heinrichs's, have some plausibility as long as they are dealing with the early Logic, which is what one would expect if the later Logic underlay the *Phenomenology,* since the contents and order of the later Logic have much in common with those of the early Logic. But when these mappings try to correlate the Metaphysics with the *Phenomenology* all plausibility vanishes. Thus, in order to make the metaphysical parts of the 1805–6 sketch—"Knowing Knowing, Spirit, Spirit's Knowledge of Itself"—look as though they map onto the *Phenomenology,* Fulda has to resort to the desperate ad hoc move of transferring "Knowing Knowing" from the beginning of this sequence to the end.[14] And Hein-

---

13. We shall in due course see this confirmed by a closer examination of the later Logic and its relation to the text of the *Phenomenology*.

14. "Zur Logik der *Phänomenologie* von 1807," pp. 97–99. Pöggeler's variant on Fulda's interpretation might seem more attractive at this point. Pöggeler leaves the order of the 1805–6 sketch—"absolute Being, which becomes Other (Relation) to itself, Life, and Cognition; and Knowing Knowing, Spirit, Spirit's Knowledge of Itself"—unchanged, associating "Life, and Cognition" with the *Self-consciousness* chapter, "Knowing Knowing" with the *Reason* chapter, "Spirit" with the *Spirit* chapter, and "Spirit's Knowledge of Itself" with the *Religion* and *Absolute Knowing* chapters ("Hegels Phänomenologie des Selbstbe-

richs, after implausibly trying to map the first section of the 1804–5 Metaphysics, "Cognition as a System of Axioms," onto the *Spirit* chapter of the *Phenomenology,* effectively capitulates at the second section, "Metaphysics of Objectivity," which by his hypothesis should have mapped onto the *Religion* chapter, excusing himself with the lame ad hoc hypothesis that this section was moved back to correspond to material in the *Reason* chapter and that "in the structural place of the Metaphysics of Objectivity [Hegel] develops in the *Religion* chapter a logic of Appearance which still is not to be found in the [1804–5 *Logic, Metaphysics, and Philosophy of Nature*]."[15]

These difficulties facing the modified-Fulda and Heinrichs readings strongly suggest that we should explore the alternative hypothesis that it is the later Logic that underlies the *Phenomenology*. In this case, we will need to look for the earliest version of the later Logic that we can find, to serve as our source of information about the contents and sequence of the discipline as it underlies the *Phenomenology*. This, in essence, was Fulda's approach—both in his essay "Zur Logik der *Phänomenologie des*

---

wußtseins," pp. 269–70). This might look appealing at first sight. However, Fulda's avoidance of such an obvious solution, while not explained by him explicitly, was well motivated. For, (i) there is no plausible textual evidence that "Cognition" corresponds to material in the *Self-consciousness* chapter (and Pöggeler offers none). Moreover, (ii) there is compelling evidence that the chapter instead corresponds to the quite different logical categories designated by the 1804–5 Logic as those of Relation: Substance, Cause, Interaction, Concept, Judgment, Syllogism (as Fulda notes—"Zur Logik der *Phänomenologie* von 1807," p. 98— and Heinrichs agrees). Furthermore, (iii) there is compelling evidence that the category of "Cognition" corresponds instead to material late in the *Reason* chapter (again as Fulda notes—ibid., pp. 98–99—and Heinrichs agrees; though their *precise* location of the material in question seems to me inexact, namely, slightly later in the *Reason* chapter than is warranted). Consequently, Fulda's avoidance of Pöggeler's easy-looking solution, and resort instead to his desperate ad hoc move, was well motivated given his general position; the desperate ad hoc move cannot plausibly be avoided along Pöggeler's lines, at least.

To pursue this matter a little further, one might just possibly, particularly in light of the slightly earlier correlation of "Cognition" with material late in the *Reason* chapter which I just mentioned and will argue for in due course, propose as an alternative way of saving Fulda's general hypothesis of the 1805–6 sketch's correspondence to the *Phenomenology* without resorting to his desperate ad hoc move that after "Cognition" correlates with the material in the *Reason* chapter in question "Knowing Knowing" then correlates with the very end of the *Reason* chapter (the subsequent correspondences proceeding as in Pöggeler's account). However, one would then have to explain how it can be that the vast stretch of the *Phenomenology* from the very beginning of the *Self-consciousness* chapter (="Life") up to the material late in the *Reason* chapter which corresponds to "Cognition" is left without any correspondences in the 1805–6 sketch, while the end of the *Reason* chapter receives no fewer than two such correspondences. So this proposal does not seem attractive.

15. Heinrichs, *Die Logik der Phänomenologie des Geistes,* pp. 406–7, 462.

Geistes" and earlier in his book *Das Problem einer Einleitung in Hegels Wissenschaft der Logik*. We have seen that it misfires in his essay through a failure there to focus on a version of the later Logic at all. So let us now instead consider how it fares in his book. In his book Fulda looks to the Nuremberg *Logic* of 1808–9 for the information in question. However, this choice is again flawed, for two reasons: First, as Fulda is himself well aware, this version of the Logic is incomplete, breaking off abruptly about two-thirds of the way through at the treatment of the category Judgment, so that it is an unsatisfactory guide to the underlying Logic of the *Phenomenology* (one which Fulda has to supplement by copious appeals to a later sketch of the Logic). But second, and more importantly, Fulda has failed to notice that there is a version of the later Logic which is both *complete* and in all probability *earlier* than that in the 1808–9 *Logic*, and hence immediately proximate in date to the composition of the *Phenomenology*. This is the version of the later Logic found in the Nuremberg *Encyclopaedia* of 1808 ff. That this version is earlier than the one in the 1808–9 *Logic*, and must therefore have been composed either at the time of or immediately after the *Phenomenology*, can be most readily seen by focusing on the single major respect in which these two versions differ from one another (besides the 1808–9 *Logic*'s incompleteness): the Logic of the 1808 ff. *Encyclopaedia* makes a direct transition from the categories Substance, Cause, and Interaction to the categories Concept, Judgment, and Syllogism, whereas the 1808–9 *Logic* instead inserts between these two groups of categories a section on the Faculty of Judgment and one on Reason and the dialectic thereof. Here the Logic of the 1808 ff. *Encyclopaedia* follows the example of the earlier Logic of the 1804–5 *Logic, Metaphysics, and Philosophy of Nature*, which also makes the transition in question in a direct way. The 1808–9 *Logic*, on the other hand, deviates from that earlier example and instead anticipates the later Nuremberg *Logic* of 1810–11, which similarly inserts a section on the antinomies of Reason between Substance, Cause, and Interaction, on the one hand, and Concept, Judgment, and Syllogism, on the other.[16] If we wish to estimate the nature of the Logic underlying

---

16. H.S. Harris has indicated a further piece of evidence for the earliness of the Logic of the 1808 ff. *Encyclopaedia*, namely, its close correspondence to the *Realphilosophie* of 1805–6 (*Hegel's Development: Night Thoughts* [Oxford: Oxford University Press, 1983], pp. 418 ff.). Heinrichs agrees that this is the earliest of the Nuremberg Logics (*Die Logik der Phänomenologie des Geistes*, p. 97).

the *Phenomenology*, therefore, we should consider, not the version of the discipline found in the 1808–9 *Logic*, but the version of it found in the 1808 ff. *Encyclopaedia*.[17]

* * *

We have, then, seen good reasons for rejecting each of Fulda's and Heinrichs's proposed sources of information about the content and sequence of the discipline (early Logic and Metaphysics or later Logic alone) which underlies the *Phenomenology*. And we have arrived instead at a more promising candidate: the Logic of the 1808 ff. *Encyclopaedia*.

Is there any way, before we actually try to map it onto the *Phenomenology*, to reassure ourselves that this 1808 ff. Logic really does give us accurate information about the Logic behind the *Phenomenology*? One way of accomplishing this would be to show that the content and sequence of this 1808 ff. Logic agreed in important respects with those of the early Logic which immediately preceded the *Phenomenology* in time. For it is very unlikely that Hegel would have given the Logic a certain content and sequence immediately before writing the *Phenomenology*, changed these during the composition of the *Phenomenology*, and then changed them back again immediately after writing the *Phenomenology*. Let us, therefore, set alongside a summary of the content and sequence of the 1808 ff. Logic summaries of the content and sequence of the Logic of the 1804–5 *Logic, Metaphysics, and Philosophy of Nature* and of the Logic sketched in the 1805–6 Philosophy of Spirit (for, although the sketch in the 1805–6 Philosophy of Spirit is extremely brief, it is important due to its addition of two new categories to those of the 1804–5 Logic: Being and Life). See table 4.

Comparison of these summaries reveals a very substantial amount of agreement between the content and sequence of the Logic as Hegel envisaged them just before he composed the *Phenomenology* and as he envisaged them just afterwards in the 1808 ff. Logic. The 1808 ff. Logic is virtually identical with the sum of its earlier counterparts from its beginning—as in the 1805–6 Logic, Being—up to the category of Infinity. And after the categories of Essence it is once again virtually identical with the sum of its earlier counterparts all the way up to and including the category Idea of Cognition. We can therefore be reasonably confident that this vast bulk of the 1808 ff. Logic faithfully reflects the content and sequence of the Logic underlying the *Phenomenology*.

17. The Logic of the 1808 ff. *Encyclopaedia* is translated in full in appendix XIV.

Table 4

1804–5	1805–6	1808 ff.
		1. Ontological Logic
	Being	I Being
I Unity (?)		
Quality (Negation, Boundary)		Quality (Being, *Dasein*, Change)
Quantity (Numerical One, Manyness of Numerical Ones, Totality)		Quantity (Being-for-self [Numerical One, Manyness . . .],
Quantum (?)		Quantum,
Infinity		Infinity)
		II Essence
		Essence
		Proposition
		Ground and Grounded (Whole and Parts, Force and its Expression, Inner and Outer)
II Relation	Otherness/	III Actuality
Relation of Being (Substance,	Relation	Substance
Cause,		Cause
Interaction)		Interaction
		2. Subjective Logic
Relation of Thought (Concept,		Concept
Judgment,		Judgment
Syllogism)		Syllogism
		3. Doctrine of the Idea
	Life	Idea of Life (Organic Parts, Sensibility, Irritability, Reproduction . . . , Inorganic Condition, Preservation of the Genus)
III Proportion		
Definition		
Division		
Cognition	Cognition	Idea of Cognition
		Absolute Idea/
		Absolute Knowing/
		Knowing

There are just two major respects in which the 1808 ff. Logic differs from the sum of its earlier counterparts. First, the 1808 ff. Logic adds after the category of Cognition a culminating category which Hegel variously calls Absolute Idea, Absolute Knowing [das absolute Wissen], or Knowing.[18] This change is very important, systematically speaking, for it is here that the fusion of the early Metaphysics into the Logic has taken place: Hegel has in effect turned the whole of the early Metaphysics into this single culminating category of the Logic.[19] Now we can see that Hegel had already effected this change, that he was already presupposing a Logic culminating in this category, by the time he began composing the *Phenomenology* from some remarks in the final paragraph of the Introduction, the part of the work which he wrote first. In this paragraph he explains that the contents of the *Phenomenology*, its shapes of consciousness, correspond to and are indeed implicitly identical with the categories of the Logic, and he then goes on to say that in the course of the *Phenomenology* consciousness will eventually arrive "at a point where appearance becomes identical with essence [i.e., with the categories of the Logic, often referred to by Hegel as "essences," e.g., at *Phenomenology*, par. 34] . . . And finally, when consciousness itself grasps this its own essence, it will signify the nature of Absolute Knowing [des absoluten Wissens] itself" (par. 89). One can scarcely doubt that Hegel means here by "Absolute Knowing" the final category which we find in the 1808 ff. Logic. The facts that he here mentions it in connection with the Logic, represents it as a sort of culmination in logical essence, and uses the very same (in his texts, quite rare) name for it as he uses for the final category of the 1808 ff. Logic should be enough to establish this. But if further proof be required, one need only consider the striking similarity between the structure which he ascribes to Absolute Knowing in this passage from the Introduction and the structure which he ascribes to it in the 1808 ff. Logic. Here in the Introduction it is said to signify an achieved self-

---

18. Cf. the conclusion of the 1809–10 *Doctrine of the Concept*, in appendix XIV.

19. Hence this category, like the content of the early Metaphysics, is conceived by Hegel as a self-awareness of the contents of the Logic as they really are, namely, as moments of a unitary totality—concerning which, compare the characterization of this category at the end of the Logics of the 1808 ff. *Encyclopaedia* and the 1809–10 *Doctrine of the Concept* (in appendix XIV) with the characterization of the early Metaphysics at *Logik, Metaphysik, und Naturphilosophie*, pp. 131, 134–36. The fundamental *idea* of the early Metaphysics thus lives on in this culminating category of the Logic even after the discipline itself has disappeared.

consciousness in logical essence: "And finally, when consciousness grasps . . . its own essence, it will signify the nature of Absolute Knowing." In the 1808 ff. Logic, similarly, it is characterized as that which has "nothing external or in any way given as its object but only itself. It is the Concept [i.e., the content of the Logic] which exists as Concept."[20]

The second major respect in which the 1808 ff. Logic differs from the sum of its earlier counterparts is that it inserts between Infinity, on the one hand, and Substance, Cause, and Interaction, on the other, the categories of Essence. This is the only part of the 1808 ff. Logic concerning which, prior to actually examining the course of the *Phenomenology*, we cannot say with confidence that it belongs to the Logic underlying the *Phenomenology*.

Even before actually examining the course of the *Phenomenology*, then, we can be reasonably confident that the content and sequence of the 1808 ff. Logic are identical with those of the Logic underlying the *Phenomenology* in all major respects—with the sole exception of the categories of Essence, about which we do not yet know.

* * *

We should now turn to the question of how this 1808 ff. Logic actually maps onto the *Phenomenology*. Taking the contents of the 1808 ff. Logic in order, the main outlines of the mapping are as follows.[21]

The categories of Quality correspond to Sense-certainty. Thus the *Sense-certainty* section makes it clear that the category Being is associated with Sense-certainty (pars. 90 ff.). For example, Hegel writes there that "the thing *is*, and it *is*, merely because it *is*. It *is*; this is the essential point for sense-knowledge, and this pure *being*, or this simple immediacy, constitutes its *truth*" (par. 91).[22] And the section reveals that the category *Dasein* is associated with Sense-certainty as well (pars. 107–8). Thus, the 1808 ff. Logic defines *Dasein* paradoxically as a being which (i) includes "relation to another, or *being-for-another*," but also (ii) is "not relation

---

20. Appendix XIV.
21. The following mapping agrees in many points—though by no means all—with Heinrichs's mapping of the Logic of the 1804–5 *Logic, Metaphysics, and Philosophy of Nature* onto the *Phenomenology*. This should be no surprise, but is rather what one would expect, given the substantial similarities just noted between the 1804–5 Logic and the 1808 ff. Logic.
22. Cf. par. 789: the category of "immediate being" corresponds to "immediate consciousness."

to another, but *in itself*."²³ And in the *Sense-certainty* section Hegel writes, reflecting that definition: "*This* is posited; but it is rather an *other* that is posited, . . . and this *otherness*, or the setting aside of the first, is *in turn set aside*, and so has returned into the first" (par. 107).

The categories of Quantity correspond to Perception. In particular, one can see that the categories Numerical One, Being-for-self, and Manyness do so from the emphasis in the *Perception* section on "the one" which is "for itself" and the "many properties" (pars. 112 ff.).²⁴

The categories of Essence correspond to Force and the Understanding. Thus, in his remarks in the *Absolute Knowing* chapter on the work's logical correlations, Hegel explicitly says that "Essence . . . corresponds to the Understanding" (par. 789). And we encounter in the *Force and the Understanding* section copious references to the category of Essence itself (pars. 132 ff.), as well as to the categories of Ground and Grounded, especially Force and its Expression (pars. 136 ff.). (Thus our only remaining question about the reliability of the 1808 ff. Logic as a guide to the Logic underlying the *Phenomenology*—the question of whether or not the 1808 ff. Logic's categories of Essence belong to the Logic underlying the *Phenomenology*—is now answered in the affirmative. We can now say with confidence that, possible differences of detail aside, the 1808 ff. Logic simply *is* the Logic of the *Phenomenology*.)

Turning to the categories of Actuality, the first of these, Substance, corresponds to Life at the beginning of the *Self-consciousness* chapter. Thus, for example, the *Life* section refers to "the simple *substance* of Life" (par. 171; emphasis added). The next two categories of Actuality, namely, Cause and Interaction, correspond to phases of Lordship and Bondage—as one can see, for example, from Hegel's statements in the *Lordship and Bondage* section that the movement of self-consciousness there is initially "represented as the action of *one* self-consciousness" but that "this action of the one has itself the double significance of being both its own action and the action of the other as well . . . Each . . . does what it does only insofar as the other does the same" (par. 182).

Turning to the categories of the Subjective Logic, the first of these, Concept [Begriff], corresponds to Stoicism in the *Self-consciousness* chapter. Thus Hegel tells us that in the *Self-consciousness* chapter "we have before us the Concept of Spirit. It is in Self-consciousness, in the Concept

---

23. Appendix XIV.
24. Cf. par. 789: the category of "being-for-self" corresponds to "Perception."

of Spirit, that consciousness first finds its turning-point," and he goes on to say more specifically that it is in Stoicism that "the Concept is for me straightway *my* Concept" (pars. 177, 197; cf. 200, 203). The next category of the Subjective Logic, Judgment [Urteil], corresponds to Skepticism. Thus Hegel always understands this logical category in the etymological sense of an "original division" [Ur-teilen], namely, an original division of the Concept. And in the *Skepticism* section he tells us, accordingly, that in Skepticism the simple freedom of Self-consciousness "*itself* becomes two . . . and is now a duality . . . The doubling of Self-consciousness in itself, which is essential in the Concept of Spirit, is here present" (par. 206). The next category of the Subjective Logic, Syllogism, corresponds to the Unhappy Consciousness. Thus Hegel writes of the Unhappy Consciousness that "this mediated relation is . . . a syllogism in which the individuality, initially fixed in its antithesis to the in-itself, is united with this other extreme only through a third term" (par. 227; cf. 230–31).

Turning finally to the categories of the Doctrine of the Idea, the first of these is the category Idea of Life (Organic Parts, Sensibility, Irritability, Reproduction . . . , Inorganic Condition, Preservation of the Genus). This corresponds to the first section of the *Reason* chapter, *Observing Reason; a. Observation of Nature*. One can see this immediately from the summary of this section's subject matter in the *Phenomenology*'s table of contents: "Observation of Nature . . . Observation of the Organic . . . Sensibility, Irritability, and Reproduction . . . The Organic Idea Transposed into the Inorganic, Genus . . ."

What of the next category of the Doctrine of the Idea, the category Idea of Cognition? The contents of this category are not specified in any detail by the 1808 ff. Logic itself, but in the 1809–10 *Doctrine of the Concept* we find it—under the heading "The Idea of Cognition and the Good"—subdivided into two parts, the first theoretical and the second practical.[25] The theoretical part—"1. Cognition"—contains primarily the categories of Definition and Division. Now Definition corresponds to the section of the *Reason* chapter *Observing Reason; b. Observation of Self-consciousness . . . Logical and Psychological Laws*. One can see this by comparing the account of Definition given in the 1809–10 *Doctrine of the Concept* with the opening paragraph of this section. Hegel describes Definition as follows in the 1809–10 *Doctrine of the Concept*: "*Defini-*

---

25. Appendix XIV.

tion expresses of an object . . . its *genus* [Gattung] as its *universal* essence, and the particular determinacy of this universal through which it is this object."[26] In the opening paragraph of the section *Observing Reason; b. Observation of Self-consciousness . . . Logical and Psychological Laws* the transition to this section is made in a way which clearly reflects that conception of Definition: Hegel writes that in the content of the preceding section (organic Nature) "the essence is not the genus [Gattung] . . . Observation finds this free concept, whose universality contains just as absolutely within it developed individuality, only in . . . self-consciousness [i.e., the content of the present section]" (par. 298). The next theoretical category, Division, corresponds to the section of the *Reason* chapter *Observing Reason; c. Observation of Self-consciousness . . . Physiognomy and Phrenology*. This is best seen by comparing the definition of Division in the 1804–5 Logic with the opening paragraph of this section. The 1804–5 Logic defines Division as follows: "In that the universal in its immediate unity with determinacy is itself a determinate, unity of both is a determinate unity, and a particular; this particular . . . becomes rather a universal . . . ; this universal is the equality of both opposites, that to which they return and in which the one is what the other is."[27] In the opening paragraph of the section of the *Reason* chapter in question Hegel writes in a way reflecting this definition of Division that, having previously found self-consciousness (read: the universal) opposed to actuality or the world (read: determinacy), consciousness is now "forced to fall back on the *peculiar determinateness* of real individuality which exists *in and for itself*, or contains the opposition of being *for itself* and being *in itself* effaced within its own absolute mediation" (par. 309). The second, practical, part of "The Idea of Cognition and the Good," called "2. Should or the Good," Hegel describes as follows in the 1809–10 *Doctrine of the Concept*: it concerns "the purpose [Zweck] existing in itself which *should* be realized in actuality [Wirklichkeit]," "the good" "as absolute purpose," "the determination that *in itself* actuality *agrees* with the good, or the belief in a moral world order [Weltordnung]."[28] This corresponds to the next section of the *Reason* chapter, *The Actualization* [Verwirklichung] *of Rational Self-consciousness through its Own Activity*. For, this section turns to practical matters, and each of

26. Ibid.
27. *Logik, Metaphysik, und Naturphilosophie*, pp. 113–14.
28. Appendix XIV.

the logical themes just mentioned plays a prominent role within it: the subject matter here is "the purpose [Zweck] which self-consciousness proceeds to actualize [verwirklichen]" (par. 368); Virtue's "purpose . . . is the conquest of the actuality of the way of the world [Weltlauf]" which effects "the existence of the good" (par. 383); the way of the world proves not to be "something opposed to the good" (par. 386); and so forth.

This leaves just the last category of the Doctrine of the Idea, the culminating category of the 1808 ff. Logic: the Absolute Idea, Absolute Knowing, or Knowing. This corresponds to the last section of the *Reason* chapter, *Individuality which takes Itself to be Real in and for Itself*. One can see this by comparing the definition of this culminating logical category in the 1809–10 *Doctrine of the Concept* with the opening paragraphs of the section. Hegel defines the category as follows in the 1809–10 *Doctrine of the Concept:* "Absolute Knowing is the Concept which has itself as its object and content, and so is its own reality"; there occurs "here the return of the conceptual moments which have passed over into difference back into unity."[29] Correspondingly, he opens the section of the *Reason* chapter in question with observations which clearly reflect that definition: "Self-consciousness has now grasped the Concept of itself . . . , viz. that in its certainty of itself it is all reality . . . The individual moments . . . have coalesced [into unity] . . . With this Concept of itself . . . self-consciousness has returned into itself out of [the] opposed determinations . . . It has for itself the pure category itself, or it is the category which has become aware of itself" (pars. 394–95). A further point of comparison is that the Logic characterizes this culminating category as essentially involving a *two-phase process* which we can identify in the section of the *Reason* chapter in question. The two-phase process is described as follows in the 1808 ff. Logic: (i) "The Concept constructs itself out of itself by existing as becoming and representing the opposition contained within it in the form of different independent real determinations or determinations of the Understanding." (ii) "Their dialectic represents them . . . as passing over into their unity. From this their negative movement results their positive unity, which constitutes the Concept in its real totality."[30] Now we find just such a two-phase process over the course of the section of the *Reason* chapter in question. Thus, corresponding to (i), as we approach this section's first subsection, *The Spiritual Animalkingdom*

29. Ibid.
30. Ibid.

(Herder's standpoint), Hegel writes that here "[the moments] still fall apart within . . . consciousness as a *movement* of distinct moments, a movement which has not yet brought them together into their substantial unity" (par. 395).[31] And, corresponding to (ii), when we reach the section's last subsection, paragraphs 435–37 (Hegel's own standpoint), Hegel writes that here, "since [the moments] have been superseded, consciousness has returned into the universal and [the] antitheses have vanished. Spiritual being is actual substance through these modes being valid, not in isolation, but only as superseded [moments]; and the unity in which they are merely moments is the self of consciousness" (par. 435).

Commentators should indeed have been alerted to the likelihood of the correspondence just demonstrated between the categories of the concluding section of the Logic, Doctrine of the Idea, and the contents of the *Reason* chapter of the *Phenomenology* by the fact that in the *Encyclopaedia* Hegel explicitly correlates the content of the concluding *Reason* chapter of the *Encyclopaedia*'s version of a "Phenomenology of Spirit" with the Idea in the Logic, that is, with exactly the same section of the Logic.[32]

We may now summarize the details of this one-to-one correspondence between the 1808 ff. Logic and contents from the *Phenomenology* (see table 5).

* * *

A detailed examination of the one-to-one correspondence between the Logic and the *Phenomenology* therefore shows that this correspondence, far from taking in the *whole* of the *Phenomenology*, as Fulda and Heinrichs argued, in fact takes in just the contents of the chapters *Consciousness* through to the end of *Reason*. Hence my earlier claim that paragraphs 89 and 805, instead of contradicting, actually support my hypothesis that Hegel did not originally intend to go beyond the end of the *Reason* chapter is fully confirmed by an examination of the details of the correspondence between the Logic and the *Phenomenology*. So far from refuting hypotheses like this one of a dramatic shift in the plan of the *Phenomenology*, as Fulda thought, those two paragraphs, together

---

31. Note that in thus making Herder's standpoint the first correlate of the culminating category of his own Logic Hegel once again shows the unique importance which he attaches to Herder's standpoint.

32. Thus at *Encyclopaedia*, par. 437 Hegel writes of "Reason as the Idea (par. 213)," thereby correlating Reason with the Idea and referring back to the specific paragraph of the *Encyclopaedia*'s Logic which commences the exposition of the Idea.

Table 5

1808 ff. Logic	Phenomenology

1. Ontological Logic
   I Being
        Quality (Being, *Dasein*, Change) ------ Sense-certainty
        Quantity (Being-for-self ------------- Perception
           [Numerical one, Manyness . . .],
           Quantum, Infinity)
   II Essence --------------------------- Force and Understanding
        Essence
        Proposition
        Ground and Grounded (Whole and
           Parts, Force and its Expression,
           Inner and Outer)
   III Actuality
        Substance --------------------------- Life
        Cause [and] ------------------------ Lordship and Bondage
        Interaction

2. Subjective Logic
        Concept ----------------------------- Stoicism
        Judgment ---------------------------- Skepticism
        Syllogism --------------------------- Unhappy Consciousness

3. Doctrine of the Idea
        Idea of Life (Organic ------------- Observing Reason;
           Parts, Sensibility, Irritability,   a. Observation of Nature
           Reproduction . . . , Inorganic
           Condition, Preservation of the Genus)
        Idea of Cognition
           [Cognition:
              Definition ------------------- b. Logical and Psychological
                                               Laws
              Division] ---------------------- c. Physiognomy and
                                               Phrenology
            [Should or the Good] ------------- The Actualization of Rational
                                               Self-consciousness through its
                                             Own Activity (Pleasure and
                                             Necessity, The Law of the
                                             Heart, Virtue)
        Absolute Idea/Absolute Knowing/ -------- Individuality which takes Itself
        Knowing   to be Real in and for Itself
                                             (Spiritual Animalkingdom, Rea-
                                             son as Lawgiver, Reason as
                                             Testing Laws, pars. 435–37)

with the true details of the correspondence, provide strong new evidence *in support of* the hypothesis that Hegel did not originally intend to go beyond the end of the *Reason* chapter.

Moreover, we can now see some further reasons, over and above those indicated in the previous chapter, for the part of my hypothesis which maintains that Hegel *did originally intend to go as far as the end of the Reason chapter* (that he did not intend to stop somewhere short of the end of the *Reason* chapter, as Haering for example suggested). For, to modify Fulda's two arguments in the light of our recent discoveries: (i) Assuming constancy in the Logic during the composition of the *Phenomenology*— and we have now effectively *demonstrated* such constancy (with a possible, but in any case modest, exception concerning the categories of Essence)—and given that Hegel both *began* the *Phenomenology* advertising a one-to-one correspondence between all of its shapes of consciousness and the Logic's categories (par. 89) and also *ended* the book doing so (par. 805), in a context where "all shapes of consciousness" now clearly implied all of the shapes in the chapters *Consciousness* through to the end of *Reason*, one must infer that Hegel originally intended to include all of the shapes in the chapters *Consciousness* through to the end of *Reason*.[33] Moreover, (ii) we have now seen by examining in detail the Logic underlying the *Phenomenology* and its correspondence with contents of the *Phenomenology* that this Logic did indeed require all of the shapes of consciousness in the chapters *Consciousness* through to the end of *Reason* in order to be fully mapped one-to-one onto shapes of consciousness from the *Phenomenology* as the Introduction planned at the start of the work's composition—so that in this way too it can be seen that all of these shapes of consciousness were intended from the start.[34]

In sum, far from speaking *against* a dramatic shift in the plan of the *Phenomenology* such as I have hypothesized, scrutiny of the logical de-

---

33. A perfectly strict statement of this argument would of course take into account the rewriting of the later parts of the *Reason* chapter which occurred in the later parts of the *Spirit* chapter, and Hegel's attitude to this at paragraph 805.
34. These two arguments for Hegel's having originally intended to go as far as the end of the *Reason* chapter, and those which I gave in the previous chapter likewise, of course leave open the possibility that changes may have occurred in some of the *details* of the chapters *Consciousness* through *Reason* during the process of composition—including perhaps even such important details as the exact identities and characters of some of the shapes of consciousness covered.

sign of the work provides strong new evidence *in support of* the hypothesis that Hegel originally intended to write only and all of the chapters *Consciousness* through to the end of *Reason*, and that the rest of the book was an afterthought.

* * *

We may now, in conclusion, address more briefly certain further possible objections to this hypothesis. One such objection is the following. As we have seen, the Introduction of the *Phenomenology*, the part of the work which Hegel wrote first, advertises that the work will culminate in "Absolute Knowing": "In pressing forward to its true existence [i.e., to the "moments" of "the entire realm of the truth of Spirit," the categories of the Logic], consciousness will arrive at a point at which it gets rid of its semblance of being burdened with something alien, with what is only for it, and some sort of other, or where appearance becomes identical with essence [i.e., with the contents of the Logic], so that its exposition will coincide with just this point of the authentic Science of Spirit. And finally, when consciousness itself grasps this its own essence, it will signify the nature of Absolute Knowing itself" (par. 89). There is obviously a rather strong temptation to read this as a prediction of the *Absolute Knowing* chapter of the published *Phenomenology*, which would conflict with my hypothesis that, along with the *Spirit* and *Religion* chapters, this chapter was only added later as an afterthought.

However, we are now in a position to give this passage from the Introduction a more plausible reading consistent with the hypothesis. As we noted earlier, the "Absolute Knowing" referred to in this passage is almost certainly the culminating category of the same name found in the 1808 ff. Logic. Moreover, as we saw recently, this category corresponds to the last section of the *Reason* chapter, *Individuality which takes Itself to be Real in and for Itself*. It is therefore plausible to suggest that when the Introduction predicts the culmination of the *Phenomenology* in "Absolute Knowing," what Hegel has in mind is not the *Absolute Knowing* chapter of the published *Phenomenology* but this concluding section of the *Reason* chapter. This suggestion receives strong support from a fragment of an early draft of the *Phenomenology* dated to the early summer of 1805 or so, and known as "A Sheet on the *Phenomenology*." For in this fragment Hegel actually says that "Absolute Knowing [das absolute Wissen] first emerges as Lawgiving Reason [gesetzgebende Vernunft]," that is, as one of the subsections of the final section of the *Reason* chapter,

Individuality which takes Itself to be Real in and for Itself.[35] Moreover, this suggestion is also strongly supported by a closer comparison of the predictions in the Introduction with the contents of the section *Individuality which takes Itself to be Real in and for Itself*. The passage from the Introduction predicts a process of culmination comprising two steps: (i) Consciousness arrives at "a point at which it gets rid of its semblance of being burdened with something alien, with what is only for it, and some sort of other, or where appearance becomes identical with essence [i.e., with the contents of the Logic]," at which point the work coincides "with just this point of the authentic Science of Spirit," that is, with the point where Hegelian Science begins dealing with logical essence, namely, the Logic. (ii) Consciousness comes itself to "grasp this its own essence," at which point it will "signify the nature of Absolute Knowing itself." Now these two predicted steps correspond, I suggest, to two steps discernible in the section *Individuality which takes Itself to be Real in and for Itself* (roughly, the two steps in the process of Absolute Knowing which we distinguished there earlier). Thus, corresponding to (i), Hegel tells us at the start of this section that "self-consciousness has now grasped . . . that in its certainty of itself it is all reality . . . Consciousness has cast away all opposition . . . ; it starts afresh from *itself,* and is not occupied with an *other*, but with *itself*" (pars. 394–96), and a little later in the section that consciousness's "object . . . divides itself into masses or spheres which are the *determinate laws* of the absolute essence" (pars. 420–21), the fact that these "masses" or "laws of the absolute essence" are barely disguised logical categories giving us here a sort of coincidence with the Logic. And corresponding to (ii), at the very end of the section, in paragraphs 435–37, Hegel speaks of the self of consciousness now making "spiritual being . . . self-conscious," of a "unity of essence and self-consciousness"; and since, as we noted earlier, the content of these paragraphs corresponds to the full realization of the Logic's category Absolute Knowing, in reaching it consciousness could, moreover, very well be said to "signify the nature of Absolute Knowing itself."[36]

---

35. Appendix XI.
36. Haering (*Hegel sein Wollen und sein Werk* 2:485–86) was therefore right to deny that the passage from the Introduction was a prediction of the *Absolute Knowing* chapter. But he oversimplified when he interpreted its prediction of a coincidence with the "authentic Science of Spirit" and culmination in "Absolute Knowing" to mean simply a concluding transition to Hegel's system proper, beginning with the Logic. Rather, it meant that the *Phenomenology* would conclude with an anticipation within itself of the categories of

Finally, we may deal with two remaining potential objections to my hypothesis consisting in suggestions by certain authors that two fragments of Hegel's which significantly antedate the completed *Phenomenology* show that Hegel already early on intended to include in the work some or all of the material in the chapters *Spirit, Religion,* and *Absolute Knowing,* contrary to my hypothesis. First, Pöggeler points to a report of Michelet's that in a lecture from the winter semester 1805–6 Hegel said that Spirit achieved Science via Nature (?), State, and Art (Religion?). And Pöggeler infers from this evidence that Hegel already at this early date planned to include in the *Phenomenology* the contents of the *Spirit* and *Religion* chapters.[37] This inference is unjustified, however, because in all probability Hegel is not here describing the contents of the *Phenomenology* at all, but instead the course of his system proper. For, as developed in the 1805–6 *Realphilosophie,* contemporary with the lecture on which Michelet reports, Hegel's system proper, after treating Nature in the Philosophy of Nature, in the Philosophy of Spirit treated the constitution of the State and then culminated in Art, Religion, and finally Science.[38]

Second, Heinrichs and Pöggeler argue that the fragment "A Sheet on the *Phenomenology*" from early summer 1805 or so shows Hegel already at this early date engaged in (Heinrichs) or about to begin (Pöggeler) the development of the work's *Spirit* chapter.[39] In this fragment Hegel speaks of Lawgiving Reason—familiar to us as one of the contents of the later part of the *Reason* chapter—and appears to be attributing to it a role in the historical diremption of "ethical substance," and to be beginning to describe this historical diremption.[40] Now this theme of the historical diremption of "ethical substance" is indeed highly reminiscent of the contents of the *Spirit* chapter. But one cannot therefore infer that Hegel is here already within or about to begin the *Spirit* chapter. The illegitimacy of such an inference can be seen from the fact that almost identical reflections on the historical diremption of "ethical substance" can be found,

---

the Logic and their culmination in the unifying self-consciousness of Absolute Knowing or the Absolute Idea—a manifestation of these through its own concluding contents. Only *then* would they realize themselves in a pure form as the Logic itself.

37. "Zur Deutung der *Phänomenologie des Geistes*," pp. 281–82.
38. *Jenaer Realphilosophie.*
39. Heinrichs, *Die Logik der Phänomenologie des Geistes*, pp. 502–3; Pöggeler, "Zur Deutung der *Phänomenologie des Geistes*," p. 281.
40. Appendix XI.

indeed developed at considerable length, early in the *Reason* chapter of the published *Phenomenology,* where they furnish a sort of historical contextualizing for the development of Reason which is there in progress (pars. 349–58). Nor can one infer from Hegel's fragment, or from these passages early in the *Reason* chapter, that Hegel had already formed an intention to go on and write a *Spirit* chapter. Hoffmeister, in his discussion of the passages early in the *Reason* chapter, suggests, in effect, that they do not show Hegel at that time already possessed of an intention to write a *Spirit* chapter, but instead merely preoccupied with themes which—induced by this preoccupation with them to do so—he would *eventually* decide to develop at length in a *Spirit* chapter.[41] That is very plausible. After all, if Hegel had already decided to write the *Spirit* chapter when he wrote these passages, why did he bother to develop its themes in them at such length, and why do they not refer forward to the still fuller development of the same themes in the *Spirit* chapter? I suggest that we should probably give a similar explanation of the anticipation of the *Spirit* chapter's themes in the fragment "A Sheet on the *Phenomenology.*"

This concludes my case for saying that within the *Phenomenology* there is an Ur-*Phenomenology* comprising just the chapters *Consciousness* through to the end of *Reason,* to which Hegel added the remaining chapters of the work only as an afterthought.

41. As Hoffmeister puts it: "The tendency to Objective Spirit was . . . already so strong that in the stream of the presentation there was, so to speak, no stopping before the 'shapes of a world' [of the *Spirit* chapter]" (Hegel, *Phänomenologie des Geistes,* ed. Hoffmeister, p. xxxv).

CHAPTER SIXTEEN

The Effects of the Shift in
Plan on the Design of
the *Phenomenology*

As noted in chapter 13, commentators who have hypothesized a major shift in the plan of the *Phenomenology* have as a rule implied that the work which resulted inevitably lacked whatever coherence in design its original plan might have afforded it. It is certainly somewhat natural to suppose that such a major shift in the plan of the work as that which I have hypothesized would inevitably have had this consequence. However, this in fact turns out not to have been the case; not only the Ur-*Phenomenology*, comprising the chapters *Consciousness* through to the end of *Reason*, but also the published *Phenomenology*, with its additional chapters *Spirit*, *Religion*, and *Absolute Knowing*, have fundamentally coherent designs.[1]

Let us consider in particular the historical and logical designs of the work. As we have already seen in parts 3 and 4, Hegel began writing the *Phenomenology* with the perfectly coherent plan of offering in the chapters *Consciousness* through to the end of *Reason* a chronological history of the development of consciousness from ancient times up to the attain-

---

1. This is not to say that the *execution* of either of these designs is without flaws. For example, concerning the Ur-*Phenomenology*, we noted earlier a measure of chronological cramping and artificiality toward the end of the *Reason* chapter. Again, concerning the expanded *Phenomenology*, Hegel himself remarked in a letter to Schelling that his "work on the details" had "harmed the overview of the whole," complaining in particular of "the major deformity of the later parts" (appendix XII); and we saw earlier an example of this in the abandonment by the later parts of the *Spirit* chapter of the chapter's official project of giving a history of social contexts for shapes of consciousness, and development instead into a sort of rewriting of the end of the *Reason* chapter.

536

ment of his own standpoint in the modern age, and having the contents of this history correspond one-to-one with the categories of the underlying Logic.

Now one might have thought that the addition of the chapters *Spirit*, *Religion*, and *Absolute Knowing* would inevitably have thrown this pleasing historical and logical design into incoherence. But in fact this was not so. Thus, to begin with the historical design, we can see from part 3 that these new chapters did not add further historical material in a way which deprived the work of historical coherence, but instead quite carefully grafted onto the original chronological history of shapes of consciousness a second chronological history dealing with the social contexts of those shapes of consciousness (the *Spirit* chapter) and then a third chronological history dealing with the conceptions of God or the Absolute associated with those shapes of consciousness and social contexts (the *Religion* and *Absolute Knowing* chapters).

The logical design of the work likewise remained as coherent after as before the addition of the new chapters. This is in part because, as we have seen, the originally planned one-to-one correspondence between the shapes of consciousness of the chapters *Consciousness* through *Reason* and the categories of the Logic remains firmly in place within the expanded work. But that is not a sufficient reason, for someone might concede it and yet still complain that incoherence had intruded in the sense that a work which was originally supposed to be logically underpinned in its entirety now seems to have whole new chapters—*Spirit, Religion, and Absolute Knowing*—which lack any logical underpinning. The further point which needs to be noted, in response to this residual complaint, is that these added chapters do *not* in fact lack a logical underpinning, because Hegel utilizes the logical underpinning of the chapters *Consciousness* through *Reason* to underpin these additional chapters as well. His plan, simply put, is the architectonically pleasing one that the logical category which corresponds to and underpins a given shape of consciousness in the chapters *Consciousness* through *Reason* also corresponds to and underpins the social context for that shape of consciousness in the *Spirit* chapter and the conception of God or the Absolute associated with that shape of consciousness and its social context in the *Religion* or *Absolute Knowing* chapter.

In order to illustrate that the expanded *Phenomenology* has this pleasing logical design, let us consider as examples the first and last categories of the Logic behind the work: Being and Absolute Knowing or Knowing.

As we saw in the previous chapter, in the history of shapes of consciousness developed by the chapters *Consciousness* through *Reason* Being corresponds to and underpins Sense-certainty. Now, as was noted in part 3, the social context provided for Sense-certainty within the *Spirit* chapter is Ethical World. And that Being corresponds to and underpins not only Sense-certainty but also Ethical World can be seen from such passages in the *Ethical World* section as this: "As the consciousness of abstract, sensuous being [i.e., Sense-certainty] passes over into Perception, so likewise the immediate certainty of real ethical being" (par. 446). Again, as was noted in part 3, the conception of God correlated with Sense-certainty and its social context in the *Religion* chapter is God as Light. And that Being also corresponds to and underpins God as Light we can see, for example, from Hegel's remark that in this form of religion "[Spirit] beholds itself in the form of *being*" (par. 686).

Turning to the category of Absolute Knowing [Absolutes Wissen] or Knowing [Wissen], as we saw in the previous chapter, in the history of shapes of consciousness developed by the chapters *Consciousness* through *Reason* this category corresponds to Hegel's own viewpoint presented in paragraphs 435–37 at the very end of the *Reason* chapter. Now if we go to the very end of the *Spirit* chapter, where Hegel meant to depict the social context for this viewpoint, we again find clear evidence of a correspondence with Absolute Knowing or Knowing: here determinations "constitute *pure knowing* [Wissen], which through . . . opposition is posited as *consciousness*," here we find "God appearing among those who know themselves as pure knowing" (par. 671). Again, if we go to the place in the chapters *Religion* and *Absolute Knowing* where Hegel depicts the conception of God or the Absolute corresponding to the viewpoint of paragraphs 435–37 and its social context, namely, the culminating *Absolute Knowing* chapter itself, we find there clear evidence that this conception of God or the Absolute corresponds to the logical category of Absolute Knowing or Knowing as well. This is shown most strikingly, of course, by the very title of the chapter in question: "Absolute Knowing."[2]

We can therefore schematically represent the logical underpinning of the expanded *Phenomenology* as in table 6.

It is fair to say, then, that the dramatic shift in the plan of the *Phenome-*

---

2. It is also shown by the structure of the chapter's content, as this is explained at paragraph 798 for example, which precisely matches the structure which we have seen to belong to the logical category of Absolute Knowing.

Effects of the Shift in Plan on the Design of the *Phenomenology*

Table 6

Logic	*Consciousness* to *Reason*	*Spirit*	*Religion / Absolute Knowing*
Being	Sense-certainty	Ethical World	God as Light
.	.	.	.
.	.	.	.
.	.	.	.
Absolute Knowing	Last shape of *Reason* (pars. 435–37)	Last shape of *Spirit* (par. 671)	Absolute Knowing

nology which we have discovered left the work with a design quite as coherent in fundamentals as that which it had had at the outset. There is, no doubt, in this shift good reason for Hegel's complaint to Schelling of the "wretched confusion . . . which in part governed . . . the composition [of the *Phenomenology*] itself."[3] But we ought not to infer that the work which resulted was therefore itself a fundamentally confused work.

3. Appendix XII.

CHAPTER SEVENTEEN

Hegel's Reasons for the Shift in Plan

In this chapter we should briefly address the question *why* Hegel expanded the Ur-*Phenomenology* into the *Phenomenology* which he eventually published. Haering argues that the work grew beyond its original modest proportions during the process of composition because Hegel, in his anxiety to make his existing system known to a wider circle at long last, increasingly tried to include in the work as much as possible of the material from this system, and especially from its Philosophy of Spirit.[1] Hoffmeister suggests that Hegel's increasingly strong preoccupation with Objective Spirit, already evident in the section of the *Reason* chapter *The Actualization of Rational Self-consciousness through its Own Activity*, impelled him to go on to develop the *Spirit* chapter.[2] I suspect that there is much truth in both of these explanations. However, they do not yet provide any real *philosophical* reason for the shift in plan, and by themselves they therefore remain unsatisfying.[3]

Hegel does in fact in one place offer a fairly explicit statement of his philosophical reasons for the shift in plan—specifically, indicating a philosophical reason rooted in the *Phenomenology*'s original, official project of serving as an introduction to the system. Thus in a passage from the

---

1. "Die Entstehungsgeschichte der *Phänomenologie des Geistes*," pp. 119–20.
2. Hegel, *Phänomenologie des Geistes*, ed. Hoffmeister, p. xxv.
3. Analogously, an explanation of Rembrandt's unusual choice of subject matter in *The Anatomy Lesson of Dr. Tulp* in terms of his desire to please a patron interested in anatomy or his having recently read and been interested by van den Spiegel's work on anatomy might contain much truth, but alone it would remain unsatisfying because it as yet provides no *artistic* reason.

Encyclopaedia which we have already encountered he states that in the *Phenomenology*

> It was not possible . . . to remain at the formal aspect of mere consciousness [i.e., at the shapes of consciousness of the Ur-*Phenomenology*]; for the standpoint of philosophical knowing is at the same time within itself the most contentful and concrete standpoint, so that in being produced as a result it presupposed also the concrete shapes of consciousness, for example those of morality, ethical life, art, and religion [i.e., the contents of the *Spirit* and *Religion* chapters]. The development of the *substantial content,* of the objects of particular parts of philosophical Science, therefore also falls within that development of consciousness . . . even though that development initially seemed to be limited to the formal aspect only. (par. 25)[4]

The explanation offered here, to unpack it a little, is this: Hegel was of, or came to, the view that in order to be a satisfactory introduction to his system, the *Phenomenology* would have to give a provisional presentation of virtually *all contents* of the system (recall our earlier discussion of pedagogical task [3] in part 1). But this required that it go beyond the originally planned chapters *Consciousness* through *Reason* dealing with shapes of consciousness. For, although these chapters contained a sort of provisional presentation of the Logic (whose categories underlay, and manifested themselves as, the shapes of consciousness of these chapters), the Philosophy of Nature (in the *Observing Reason* section of the *Reason* chapter), and one part of the Philosophy of Spirit (that concerned with consciousness, and which Hegel in the *Encyclopaedia* calls "Phenomenology of Spirit"), they contained *no* provisional presentation of other parts of the Philosophy of Spirit, in particular the parts dealing with morality and ethical life (roughly, what Hegel in the *Encyclopaedia* calls "Objective Spirit"), and with art, religion, and philosophy (what Hegel in the *Encyclopaedia* calls "Absolute Spirit"). In order to make good this deficit Hegel had to add the remaining chapters of the *Phenomenology*, where these parts of the Philosophy of Spirit do now receive a sort of provisional presentation.

Hegel, however, clearly went on to develop very serious doubts about whether this reason rooted in the work's original, official project of serving as an introduction to the system was sufficient to warrant the expansion of the Ur-*Phenomenology* into the published *Phenomenology*. He apparently came to believe that, from the viewpoint of that project, the

---

4. In appendix XVII.

fairly modest advantage of having a provisional presentation of *all* contents of the system was outweighed by the disadvantage of the added complexities, materials strictly extraneous to an introduction, and no doubt also further imperfections imported by the chapters *Spirit* through *Absolute Knowing*. Thus, immediately after giving the above explanation in the *Encyclopaedia* he remarks that with the addition of the contents of these chapters "the presentation thereby becomes more complicated, and what belongs to the concrete parts [of philosophical Science] to some extent already falls within this introduction along with the rest" (par. 25).[5] And already in 1807 he had complained to Schelling more generally of "the major deformity of the later parts" of the *Phenomenology*.[6]

Hegel might have added a further motive rooted in the original, official project of the *Phenomenology* as an introduction to the system which drew him to expand the work beyond the *Reason* chapter as well, namely, the prospect which this opened up of revising the second half of that chapter in the manner of the *Spirit* chapter's rewriting project, to the positive ends of eliminating chronological cramping and doing justice to the French (as discussed in chapter 11). For it is very possible that this was already in his mind at the point when he took the step beyond the *Reason* chapter. And if it was not, it did at least *become* a motive for the added material.

However, this was only in a very limited sense a reason for including the added parts of the work. For (i) it motivated only the modest stretch of the *Spirit* chapter in question, and moreover (ii) it in no way motivated the added *project* of that chapter (let alone of the subsequent chapters), since the modest stretch in question rather constitutes a *lapse* from that project (as we saw in chapter 11).

In short, the expansion of the Ur-*Phenomenology* into the published *Phenomenology* appears to have had only very tenuous justification in the original, official project of the work as an introduction to the system. It is accordingly not surprising that (as we have already seen) Hegel evidently decided almost immediately after the work's publication and forever thereafter to prune the discipline back to its original scope in the Nuremberg *Doctrine of Consciousness* and the various editions of the *Encyclopaedia*.

It seems unlikely, however, that the philosophical reason for the expansion of the Ur-*Phenomenology* into the published *Phenomenology*

5. Ibid.
6. Appendix XII.

stated by the *Encyclopaedia* (or, for that matter, the further philosophical reason just discussed) was really Hegel's main philosophical motive for changing the plan of the work in this way. Hegel no doubt emphasizes it because it is rooted in the *Phenomenology*'s original, official project of serving as an introduction to the system. His strongest philosophical motive, by contrast, was probably one without real roots in that project: In the course of developing, in the chapters *Consciousness* through *Reason*, the chronological history of consciousness from ancient times up to his own age and standpoint which the *Phenomenology*'s original, official project had required, and which he had originally intended to write, Hegel developed a strong *intrinsic*, as opposed to merely instrumental, interest in the historical and historicist aspects of the account. He saw the potential for developing these into the sort of broader historical and historicist project which emerges with the addition of the new chapters.[7] And he therefore grasped the opportunity to do so.

Hegel later went on to develop the added parts of this historical and historicist project—the contents of the chapters *Spirit, Religion,* and *Absolute Knowing*—much more fully and carefully in his later lecture series: the *Lectures on the Philosophy of World History* (corresponding to the *Spirit* chapter), the *Aesthetics* and *Lectures on the Philosophy of Religion* (corresponding to the *Religion* chapter), and the *Lectures on the History of Philosophy* (corresponding to the *Absolute Knowing* chapter). Hence, in addition to executing its original, official project, the *Phenomenology* is also in large measure the birthplace of the historical and historicist accounts of these later lecture series.[8]

To a great extent, therefore, the Ur-*Phenomenology* and the added chapters of the published *Phenomenology* address different projects: The Ur-*Phenomenology* mainly addresses the work's original, official project of providing an introduction to Hegel's system. The added chapters, by contrast, are only very tenuously anchored in that project, and instead primarily address an unofficial historical and historicist project which Hegel subsequently went on to develop further in his later lecture series.

---

7. Important aspects of this broader historical and historicist project were explained in part 3. A fuller account would need to say more especially about the work's "law and purpose" historicism.

8. This claim requires a qualification where the *Lectures on the History of Philosophy* are concerned. For Hegel was already lecturing on the history of philosophy by the time he wrote the *Phenomenology*, having begun doing so in 1805. It would consequently be as true to say that these particular lectures were the birthplace of the *Phenomenology* as vice versa.

PART FIVE

Hegel's Later Attitude toward
the *Phenomenology*

CHAPTER EIGHTEEN

A Fundamental
Reinterpretation
or Devaluation?

The *Phenomenology* certainly is not, and was not perceived by Hegel to be, a flawless work. On the contrary, both during and after the work's composition Hegel came to perceive numerous weaknesses in its execution, and provided or suggested means of repair for these. Thus, as we have noted: During the work's composition he came to perceive, and acted to meet, a need to expand the Ur-*Phenomenology* comprising the chapters *Consciousness* through *Reason* which he had originally planned to write into the much larger *Phenomenology* containing in addition the chapters *Spirit* through *Absolute Knowing* which he eventually published (chapters 13 to 17). Moreover, he came to see shortcomings in the later parts of the *Reason* chapter, and consequently curtailed the official project of the added *Spirit* chapter in order to substitute toward its end a revised version of the later parts of the *Reason* chapter, thereby acknowledging and attempting to repair one set of weaknesses, in the *Reason* chapter, while at the same time manifestly creating another, in the *Spirit* chapter (chapter 11). Moreover, by the time he added the *Religion* chapter he saw a need to push the work's concrete historical focus back to the ancient Orient and ancient Egypt, which implied significant revisions of the beginnings of the two preceding treatments of history already developed in the chapters *Consciousness* through *Reason* and in the *Spirit* chapter—specifically, revisions of the former's conception of the historical significance of Sense-certainty, Perception, and Force and the Understanding, and an implication of oriental and Egyptian forerunners to the latter's Ethical World of ancient Greece (chapters 9 and 11). After the work's composition, he developed serious misgivings about, and a strong inclination to retract, the expansion of the Ur-*Phenomenology* into the published *Phenomenology* (chapter 17). In addition, he came to recognize that the work's dialectic had at points illicitly relied on the Logic, and accordingly attempted to revise its dialectic in order to make it immanent at these points (chapter 6). Moreover, he made further revisions in the historical conceptions of the work, for example coming to perceive that the breach between thought and reality whose invention the work had attributed to Platonism and Stoicism had in fact already been accomplished earlier by Sophism (chapters 2 and 9). And one could certainly add to this list of Hegel's perceptions of and attempts to repair flaws in the work. For example, later on, in the *Encyclopaedia*, he criticized the *Phenomenology* for its inclusion of "Here" and "Now" in its characterization of Sense-certainty, arguing that they did not really belong there.[1]

In keeping with this pattern of recognizing and attempting to rectify weaknesses in the *Phenomenology*, Hegel immediately after the work's completion in 1807, and forever thereafter, acknowledged to correspondents that there were significant flaws in the work and stressed the need for a revised edition. Thus, already in 1807, he wrote to Schelling of the "wretched confusion . . . which in part governed . . . the composition [of the *Phenomenology*] itself," noting that the "work on the details" had "harmed the overview of the whole," and that there was "major deformity" in "the later parts" of the work; and to Niethammer, of his experience in reading over the manuscript of the *Phenomenology* again for printer's errors, "I admittedly often had the wish that I might yet clear the ship here and there of ballast and make it swifter. With a second edition to follow soon—if it please the gods?!—everything should be improved, that is my consolation to myself and to others."[2] And in 1829 he was still writing in this vein, remarking in a letter to von Meyer concerning a proposed second edition of the *Phenomenology*, "I regard revision of the work to be necessary."[3]

There should, however, be no temptation to see in the above facts evidence that the later Hegel subjected the *Phenomenology* to a fundamental reinterpretation or devaluation. Rather than speaking for a later fundamental reinterpretation of the work, they seem to show merely that Hegel later saw room for improving, and wished to improve, the work's

---

1. *Encyclopaedia*, par. 418.
2. Appendix XII.
3. *Hegel: The Letters*, p. 121.

execution of its original project. Nor do they speak for a later fundamental devaluation of, or loss of faith in, the work. That it would be an error to suppose that they did can readily be seen from the fact that a few years after the unusually harsh criticisms of the work quoted above from the letters of 1807 Hegel nevertheless went on to endorse the work as a whole with the utmost enthusiasm in the *Science of Logic*.[4] Indeed, one could much more plausibly argue that all this evidence of Hegel's later preoccupation with, and concern to revise, particular weak points in the work on the contrary speaks *against* any fundamental loss of faith in the work.

Nonetheless, it has been widely argued in the secondary literature that Hegel did in fact fundamentally change his mind about the *Phenomenology* later in his career, subjecting it to a fundamental reinterpretation or devaluation (or both). We have already encountered, and found erroneous, one such argument, namely, Lukács's thesis that Hegel later retracted the *Phenomenology*'s fundamental conceptions that Napoleon would effect the realization of Hegel's sociopolitical ideal in Germany and that the *Phenomenology* stood at the beginning of a process of sociopolitical transformation (chapter 12). We should now consider three further influential examples of such an argument, advanced by Haering, Fulda, and Pöggeler.

According to Haering, Hegel's original understanding of the *Phenomenology* was hopelessly inconsistent: originally conceived as an introduction to his system, the work thereby fell into conflict with his long and deeply cherished objections to introductory philosophizing, or to "grounding" a philosophical viewpoint. In a desperate attempt to paper over this embarrassing contradiction, he initially reinterpreted the work to be the first part of his system, and then eventually gave it up altogether, instead treating its subject matter in the different and unproblematic context of the system's Philosophy of Spirit in the *Encyclopaedia*.[5] According to Fulda, Hegel originally conceived the *Phenomenology* as an introduction to Hegelian Science of a kind serving as both the "coming-to-be" of Hegelian Science and its first part, and therefore as preceding and involving no presupposition of Hegelian Science. However, from the start it did in practice surreptitiously rely on such a presupposition, thereby falling into internal inconsistency. Later on, Hegel reinterpreted the work so that it ceased to be the "coming-to-be" and first part of Hegelian Science, and

---

4. Appendix XV.
5. Haering, "Die Entstehungsgeschichte der *Phänomenologie des Geistes*."

became instead an introduction to Hegelian Science unequivocally based on a presupposition of Hegelian Science.[6] Finally, Pöggeler too sees Hegel's original conception of the relation between the *Phenomenology* and the system as thoroughly ambiguous and problematic, and argues that the later Hegel accordingly distanced himself from the work, transferring its contents to the Philosophy of Spirit of the *Encyclopaedia*, and its guiding idea, its function as an introduction to or justification of the system, to the *Lectures on the History of Philosophy*.[7]

Like Lukács's argument, these arguments that Hegel later subjected the *Phenomenology* to a fundamental reinterpretation or devaluation are, I believe, mistaken. The remainder of this chapter will be devoted to showing the extreme weakness of the main evidence appealed to by these readings. In the next chapter I shall deal with one remaining piece of evidence, and shall show what Hegel's later attitude to the *Phenomenology* was *really*.

An important part of the evidential motivation for these readings lies in their putative discoveries of fundamental inconsistencies in Hegel's original conception of the *Phenomenology*. This evidential motivation has already been invalidated by part 2. Thus, as we saw in chapter 7, the inconsistency alleged by Haering, and apparently by Pöggeler also, between the original introductory function of the *Phenomenology* and Hegel's ban on introductory philosophizing, or on the "grounding" of philosophical viewpoints, proves upon inspection to be illusory. And, as we noted in chapter 6, although Fulda is correct to say that within the *Phenomenology* there was a reliance on the Logic which conflicted with the work's original project, this reliance was not fundamental and did not cause a reinterpretation of the work's project in the direction of making it official, as Fulda implies, but was instead quickly recognized by Hegel as a flaw and subjected to elimination, in the Nuremberg *Doctrine of Consciousness* and subsequent writings.[8]

In this chapter we may therefore focus on the *other* part of the evidential motivation behind these readings: certain pieces of evidence from Hegel's later works to which they appeal. It seems to me that, on inspec-

---

6. Fulda, *Das Problem einer Einleitung*, pp. 79–115. In basic agreement with Fulda are Habermas, *Knowledge and Human Interests*, chap. 1; and Rosen, *Hegel*, esp. pp. 123–24.

7. Pöggeler, "Zur Deutung der *Phänomenologie des Geistes*," pp. 290–92.

8. It was also noted in chapter 6 that seemingly still more fundamental forms of this original inconsistency asserted by Habermas are illusory.

A Fundamental Reinterpretation or Devaluation? 551

tion, this evidence quite fails to support the claim that Hegel fundamentally reinterpreted or devalued the *Phenomenology* in later years. In this chapter I shall consider and defuse each main piece of this evidence in turn (leaving just one last piece for treatment in the next chapter).

First, all three authors mentioned appeal in support of their readings to the fact that in the *Encyclopaedia* Hegel's system, instead of being introduced by the *Phenomenology,* begins with the Logic. Thus, Haering notes in support of his reading that "in all versions of the complete system, i.e., in the *Encyclopaedia,* the *Phenomenology* is silently no longer mentioned as introduction. The system always begins with the Logic."[9] Similarly, Fulda argues in support of his reading that it is impossible to reconcile the *Phenomenology*'s position that philosophy commences with the *Phenomenology* itself with the *Encyclopaedia*'s position that philosophy commences with the Logic (and is determined to do so by the structure of the Idea, which dictates the division of the system).[10] Similarly, Pöggeler argues in support of his reading that in the *Encyclopaedia* a beginning Logic "closed together with Philosophies of Nature and Spirit to form a syllogism of syllogisms in which the *Phenomenology* as a first part of the system could no longer have a place."[11]

Contrary to these claims, however, this characteristic of the *Encyclopaedia* is entirely consistent with the originally intended relation between the *Phenomenology* and the system, as this was explained in part 2. For, as we saw in part 2, the *Phenomenology* was from the start conceived as merely an "appearance" of Hegelian Science, not "the Science of the true in its true shape," and accordingly as destined to undergo an *Aufhebung* to Hegelian Science, which implied, on its negative side, *an abolition leaving only Hegelian Science itself.* Hence the absence of the *Phenomenology* at the start of the *Encyclopaedia* and the latter's commencement of the system with the Logic instead in no way suggest that Hegel has changed his interpretation or evaluation of the *Phenomenology.*

Second, all three authors mentioned appeal in support of their readings to the fact that the system of the *Encyclopaedia* includes in its Philosophy of Spirit its own version of a "Phenomenology of Spirit," containing a re-treatment of the *Phenomenology*'s principal subject matter, conscious-

---

9. "Die Entstehungsgeschichte der *Phänomenologie des Geistes,*" p. 135.
10. *Das Problem einer Einleitung,* pp. 106–7.
11. "Die Komposition der *Phänomenologie des Geistes,*" p. 62; cf. "Zur Deutung der *Phänomenologie des Geistes,*" p. 290.

ness. Thus, Haering argues that "Hegel in the *Encyclopaedia* retracted and corrected the original idea of a 'Phenomenology' . . . explicitly: namely, by using the name of the *Phenomenology* in a quite different and more correct way."[12] Similarly, Fulda appeals to the same fact in support of his view that Hegel later expelled the *Phenomenology* from the system: "Since one cannot accept that the system must contain one and the same discipline in two forms, and also one finds nothing of the sort in the *Encyclopaedia*, one must consider the *Phenomenology*, so far as it is an introduction, to be no longer a limb of the system. This perhaps explains why Hegel now uses the title that he had first used for the first part of the system for the middle part of Subjective Spirit. In that the justification of the system is expelled from the system, its systematic title becomes free."[13] Similarly, Pöggeler argues in support of his reading: "People have rightly been very surprised at the strange fact that Hegel in his Nuremberg period built the phenomenological development from Sense-certainty to Reason into the philosophy of Subjective Spirit . . . The question why the *Phenomenology*, which initially appeared as an introduction to the system, could also appear as a part of the philosophy of Subjective Spirit must immediately impress itself on one."[14]

Once again, contrary to these claims, the explanation given in part 2 of the originally intended relation between the *Phenomenology* and Hegelian Science shows this occurrence of a "Phenomenology of Spirit" within Hegelian Science's Philosophy of Spirit to be entirely consistent with, and indeed required by, the *Phenomenology*'s original self-conception. As we saw in part 2, Hegel originally understood the *Phenomenology* to be subject to an *Aufhebung* to the higher level of Hegelian Science, which implied, on its positive side, that the work's contents would be re-treated at the higher level of Hegelian Science. Moreover, the *Phenomenology* indicated toward its end, more specifically, that there would be a scientific re-treatment of its principal subject matter, consciousness, within Hegelian Science's Philosophy of Spirit (pars. 806–7). Even the entitling of this scientific re-treatment of consciousness as a "Phenomenology of Spirit" was probably part of Hegel's original

---

12. "Die Entstehungsgeschichte der *Phänomenologie des Geistes*," p. 135.
13. *Das Problem einer Einleitung*, p. 109.
14. "Die Komposition der *Phänomenologie des Geistes*," p. 61; cf. "Zur Deutung der *Phänomenologie des Geistes*," p. 292. Another example of this line of argument can be found in Solomon, *In the Spirit of Hegel*, pp. 4–5.

plan, for we already find a section of the Philosophy of Spirit with this title projected by the 1808 ff. *Encyclopaedia*.[15] The existence of the *Encyclopaedia*'s "Phenomenology of Spirit" is thus entirely consistent with, and indeed required by, Hegel's original conception of the *Phenomenology*. It therefore in no way constitutes evidence that Hegel later changed his interpretation or evaluation of the *Phenomenology*.

Third, all three authors mentioned claim support for their readings from a series of later remarks of Hegel's concerning the status of the *Phenomenology*. The *Phenomenology* had originally proclaimed on its title page and at paragraph 35 that it was "the first part of the System of Science." Later on Hegel made the following observations concerning this status: (i) In the Heidelberg *Encyclopaedia* he wrote, "I earlier treated the *Phenomenology of Spirit*, the scientific history of consciousness, as the first part of philosophy in the sense that it should precede pure Science, since it is the production of pure Science's Concept. But at the same time consciousness and its history, like every other philosophical science, is not an absolute beginning, but a link in the circle of philosophy" (par. 36). (ii) In the Berlin *Encyclopaedia* he wrote, "In my *Phenomenology of Spirit*, which for this reason was called the first part of the System of Science at the time of its publication, the procedure is followed of beginning from the first, simplest appearance of Spirit, *the immediate consciousness*, and developing its dialectic up to the standpoint of philosophical Science, the necessity of which is demonstrated through this progression" (par. 25). (iii) Finally, in a note added in 1831 to the first-edition preface of the *Science of Logic* he wrote that "the second edition [of the *Phenomenology*], which will be published next Easter, will no longer bear this title ['first part of the System of Science']."[16] Haering, with passages (i) and (ii) in mind, argues in support of his hypothesis of the *Phenomenology*'s eventual abandonment: "When [Hegel in the *Encyclopaedia*] does come to speak of the earlier *Phenomenology* for once, one notices clearly the systematic uneasiness and the convolutedness of his explanations."[17] Similarly, Fulda appeals to (i) in support of his claim that Hegel later reinterpreted the *Phenomenology*, reading this passage as an "objection against the sense . . . in which the *Phenome-*

---

15. *Nürnberger und Heidelberger Schriften*, p. 42, pars. 128–29.
16. The above three passages can be read in context in appendices XVI, XVII, and XV, respectively.
17. "Die Entstehungsgeschichte der *Phänomenologie des Geistes*," p. 135.

nology was earlier treated as the first part of philosophy."[18] Similarly, Pöggeler appeals to (i) and (iii) as evidence that Hegel changed his mind about the role of the *Phenomenology* from regarding it as an absolute beginning and the first part of the system to seeing it as merely "an anticipation of the system."[19]

These readings all, it seems to me, miss the point of the passages in question entirely. Hegel's explanations in (i) and (ii) of what he had meant by calling the *Phenomenology* "the first part of the System of Science," and his eventual retraction of this title in (iii), reflect no change from his original conception of the work at all, but are instead just what they purport to be: attempts to make clearer and to prevent misunderstandings of his original intentions. As we saw in part 2, Hegel from the start understood the *Phenomenology* to be not part of Science proper, "the Science of the true in its true shape," but instead merely an "appearance" of Science. It was only in this very qualified sense, therefore, that the work purported to be "the first part of the System of Science." However, this title tempted misunderstandings, since it naturally suggested to all but the most attentive readers that the *Phenomenology* was itself part of Science proper. Passages (i)–(iii) simply represent Hegel's later efforts to make clear that this was not what he had meant. Hence in (i) he emphasizes that the *Phenomenology* was only "the first part of the System of Science" in the sense that it should "precede pure Science" as "the production of pure Science's Concept," that is, *not* in the sense that it was itself part of pure Science.[20] In (ii) he emphasizes that the *Phenomenology* was only "the first part of the System of Science" in the sense that its dialectic developed "up to the standpoint of philosophical Science" and demonstrated the latter's necessity, that is, once again, *not* in the sense that it was itself part of Science proper. And in (iii) he finally decides that the title "the first part of the System of Science" is simply too misleading to be worth retaining, and so dispenses with it altogether. It is highly ironic that these innocent attempts of Hegel's to clarify his original meaning,

---

18. *Das Problem einer Einleitung*, pp. 112–13.

19. "Zur Deutung der *Phänomenologie des Geistes*," p. 290. Cf. Rosen, *Hegel*, pp. 123–24.

20. The reference in (i) to consciousness and its history being "at the same time . . . a link in the circle of philosophy" is simply an allusion to the fact that in addition to the *Phenomenology*'s treatment of consciousness there is a re-treatment of consciousness within Science proper—in perfect accordance with Hegel's original intentions, as has already been shown.

to prevent misunderstandings caused by a slightly unfortunate choice of words in his original entitling of the work, should have so exacerbated the misunderstanding of his position in the hands of interpreters such as Haering, Fulda, and Pöggeler.

Like their putative diagnoses of deep incoherences in Hegel's original conception of the *Phenomenology*, therefore, the main evidence from Hegel's later works to which Haering, Fulda, and Pöggeler appeal in order to support their hypotheses of a fundamental reinterpretation or devaluation of the *Phenomenology* after its publication entirely fails to support such hypotheses.

CHAPTER NINETEEN

The Historical Relativity of
the *Phenomenology*

In arguing for Hegel's eventual abandonment of the *Phenomenology*, Haering does, though, point to one last piece of evidence in addition to those already considered which might still give us some pause: the simple fact that the Berlin *Encyclopaedia* of 1827 and 1830 does not positively affirm the *Phenomenology*'s role as an introduction to Hegelian Science, and instead employs in that function its own very different treatment of the "Attitudes of Thought to Objectivity."[1] The force of this evidence is somewhat diminished upon closer scrutiny for the following reasons: (i) If the Berlin *Encyclopaedia* does not *affirm* the *Phenomenology*'s role as an introduction to Hegelian Science, nor does it *deny* it. (ii) Also, when the Berlin *Encyclopaedia* begins its treatment of the "Attitudes of Thought to Objectivity," it compares this *unfavorably* as an introduction to Hegelian Science with the *Phenomenology*—for it states that, although the *Phenomenology* has the weakness of including some material properly belonging to Hegelian Science itself, this treatment "has the *still greater* shortcoming of being able to operate only historically and in a rationalizing manner [nur historisch und räsonierend]," by which Hegel means without the necessity of the *Phenomenology*'s dialectic (par. 25; emphasis added). (iii) Moreover, Hegel had already in the 1812 *Science of Logic* indicated the possibility of a merely *historisch* and *räsonierend*

---

1. Haering, "Die Entstehungsgeschichte der *Phänomenologie des Geistes*," p. 135. Solomon, in a similar vein, refers to the lack of positive enthusiasm for the *Phenomenology* in Hegel's later writings in support of a hypothesis of the work's later abandonment (*In the Spirit of Hegel*, p. 4).

introduction to Science, while nonetheless simultaneously stressing the *Phenomenology*'s indispensability as Science's only proof.² Still, the Berlin *Encyclopaedia*'s failure to endorse the *Phenomenology* explicitly, and its decision actually to employ in place of the *Phenomenology* a merely *historisch* and *räsonierend* introduction to Science, remain disturbing. Must we not, after all, infer from this evidence a thesis of the general sort advanced by Haering, that is, that Hegel eventually lost faith in the *Phenomenology*?

There are very strong reasons against doing so. For one thing, if Hegel had simply lost faith in the *Phenomenology* by the time of publishing the Berlin *Encyclopaedia* in 1827 and 1830, then why did he in the substantially revised second edition of the *Science of Logic* of 1831 retain virtually unaltered, and quite undiminished, the passages from the first edition's preface and introduction which praise the *Phenomenology* as his Science's indispensable and sole proof? And especially, why did he *rewrite* the section "With What Must Science Begin?" in a way *reaffirming* the importance of the *Phenomenology*?³ Moreover, if he had simply lost faith in the *Phenomenology* by the time of the Berlin *Encyclopaedia* of 1827 and 1830, then why did he shortly before his death decide to publish a second edition of the *Phenomenology* and begin the task of revising the work for this second edition?⁴

I want to suggest a very different explanation of Hegel's diminished enthusiasm for the *Phenomenology* in the Berlin *Encyclopaedia* and other late texts, one which seems to me both truer to the evidence and more of a credit to Hegel and the *Phenomenology*: The *Phenomenology* was from the start conceived as a work most of whose central tasks were in various ways *relative to the historical context in which it was written*,

---

2. Appendix XV.
3. Appendices XV, XVIII.
4. In light of this evidence it becomes attractive to read a little more enthusiasm for the *Phenomenology* out of the Berlin *Encyclopaedia* than would otherwise have been justified. The description which Hegel gives at Berlin *Encyclopaedia*, paragraph 25 of the *Phenomenology*'s function now looks like an endorsement of the work in that function. And we may see a similar significance in the strong resemblance, pointed out in part 2, between the path by which Hegel at Berlin *Encyclopaedia*, paragraphs 12 and 50 envisages thought ascending to the absolute standpoint and the *Phenomenology*.

On the other hand, one *cannot*, I think, here appeal to the supportive discussion of a "Phenomenology of Spirit" found in the Berlin *Lectures on the Philosophy of Religion* (*Sämtliche Werke* 15:124–26). For this is evidently concerned with the *systematic* version of the discipline rather than the version of 1807.

and whose success in performing those tasks would change that historical context in ways which would relieve it of the need to perform them any longer, thereby making it largely redundant. Hegel's later diminished enthusiasm for the work stemmed from a recognition that the historical context for its performance of those tasks was past, and this precisely because it had succeeded in performing them. On this explanation, therefore, Hegel's diminished enthusiasm for the *Phenomenology* in the Berlin *Encyclopaedia* and other late texts is a symptom, not of a loss of confidence in the *Phenomenology,* but—paradoxical as this may sound—of a belief that the work has been *successful.*

A first indication that Hegel did indeed from the start conceive the *Phenomenology* and its function as relative to the historical context of its composition and as destined to be superseded with the passage of that historical context can be seen in the remarks from the Preface which we considered in chapter 12. For in those remarks Hegel implies that the work is a proto-Science—"the Understanding's form of Science"—and "way to Science" belonging to the current historical context of incipient sociopolitical and intellectual transformation, and destined to be superseded, at the completion of this transformation, by Science itself, "the crown of a world of Spirit" (pars. 11–13). When, a few years later, Hegel actually comes to publish Science itself in the 1812 *Science of Logic,* he accordingly implies that that period of sociopolitical and intellectual transformation is now over, and the transformed sociopolitical and intellectual world now a reality: "The period of fermentation with which a new creation begins appears over," "the substantial form of Spirit has transformed itself," a "new Spirit . . . has arisen for Science no less than for actuality."[5] Accordingly, in subsequent writings he implies that the *Phenomenology* and its function now belong to a past historical context. For example, describing the work and its function in the Heidelberg *Encyclopaedia,* he now consigns them to the past: "I *earlier* treated the *Phenomenology of Spirit* . . . as the first part of philosophy in the sense that it should precede pure Science, since it is the production through witnessing of pure Science's Concept" (par. 36; emphasis added). And this later relativizing of the *Phenomenology* and its function to a historical context now past is even more explicit in Hegel's notes from 1831 concerning a projected second edition of the work: the *Phenomenology* is

---

5. *Science of Logic,* pp. 26–27.

"distinctive early work" and "relative to the former time of its composition," a time when "the *abstract Absolute* held sway."[6]

Certain aspects of these conceptions of the *Phenomenology* and its function as relative to the historical context of its composition, destined to supersession with the passage of that context, and eventually in fact superseded with the passage of that context, have already been sufficiently explained in chapter 12. In particular, we saw there that Hegel from the start conceived the work as belonging to a current period of transition in Germany from sociopolitical and intellectual fragmentation toward sociopolitical unity incorporating differentiation and the corresponding intellectual unity incorporating differentiation of his own Science, and as having the function (together with Napoleon) of effecting this transition.

Moreover, concerning the *sociopolitical* side of this conception, we noted in chapter 12, and can see again from the remarks just quoted from the 1812 *Science of Logic,* that the later Hegel came to perceive the transition in Germany from sociopolitical fragmentation to sociopolitical unity incorporating differentiation as now essentially accomplished—implying that the sociopolitical aspect of the *Phenomenology*'s historical context and function had disappeared, thus rendering the work to this extent past and redundant, though presumably at least in part because the work had *successfully played* its original sociopolitical role.

Concerning the *intellectual* side of the above conception, it is clear from the very fact of Hegel's publication of the *Science of Logic* in 1812, and from his recently quoted remarks in doing so, that he by this time also believed the transition in Germany from intellectual fragmentation to the intellectual unity incorporating differentiation of his own Science to have been accomplished—so that the *Phenomenology* had also lost the intellectual aspect of its historical context and function, and was now past and redundant in this as well as in its sociopolitical aspect, though presumably once again at least in part because it had *successfully played* its original intellectual role. In order to penetrate this key intellectual side of Hegel's conception more deeply, however, we should reconsider the original tasks of the *Phenomenology* which were identified in part 1, this time, for the sake of convenience, taking them more or less in reverse order: metaphysical tasks first, epistemological tasks next, pedagogical tasks last.

* * *

6. Appendix XIX.

Consider, to begin with, the three main metaphysical tasks: (7) the task of raising human consciousness to the level of Hegelian Science in order to accomplish Absolute Spirit's essential self-knowledge and thereby its full realization, (9) the task of establishing a community-wide Hegelian usage of terms so as to constitute the concepts of Hegelian Science, and (11) the task of establishing an enduring communal consensus in favor of Hegelian Science so as to make possible and actual its truth.[7] These tasks were, obviously enough, relative to a historical context in which human consciousness had *not* reached the level of Hegelian Science, there was *no* community-wide Hegelian usage of terms, and there was *no* enduring communal consensus in favor of Hegelian Science. If the *Phenomenology* were once to succeed in performing these tasks, it would eliminate that historical context, and therewith the need to perform them any longer.[8]

Now one must, I think, infer from the fact of Hegel's publication of the *Science of Logic* and the *Encyclopaedia* several years after publishing the *Phenomenology,* that by this time Hegel *did indeed* believe that the

---

7. From the perspective of the later Hegel's altered ideas about meaning, intellectual continuity, and truth, as sketched in chapter 10, these tasks will look somewhat different than they did from the perspective of the *Phenomenology,* but they will not have been invalidated. It might seem that task (11) would be invalidated by the later Hegel's reconception of truth as a matter of agreement among all men rather than merely enduring agreement within a communal tradition. For on this new conception what need would there be to do anything special for Hegelian philosophy in Hegel's modern community in order to ensure its truth, and if something did need to be done, then how could that ensure its truth, given that the past and other modern communities would in that case presumably stand in equal need but not thereby be helped? However, this is to overlook the particular version of a reconception of truth as agreement among all men which the later Hegel embraces, namely, that truth consists in the *explicit* agreement of an enduring communal consensus plus the *implicit* agreement of mankind at large (*Encyclopaedia,* par. 22, addition). For, on this version, there *is* a special need for Hegel's modern community to be brought to an acceptance of his philosophy (namely, in order to meet the former condition), but *not* therefore a like requirement that the same would have to be done for the past and for other modern communities (namely, in order to meet the latter condition). An analogous situation holds in relation to task (9), which is similarly reconceived but not invalidated. And task (7), similarly, is now reconceived as a task of accomplishing Absolute Spirit's essential *explicit* self-knowledge and thereby full realization, rather than its essential self-knowledge *simpliciter* and thereby full realization.

8. Someone might object that the *Phenomenology* would still be needed to *sustain* human knowledge of Hegelian Science, a communal Hegelian usage of terms, and a communal consensus in favor of Hegelian Science. However, this would be to forget Hegel's dramatic conception that upon the performance of these tasks time itself in some sense comes to an end.

The Historical Relativity of the *Phenomenology* 561

Phenomenology had successfully performed these tasks. For the *Science of Logic* and the *Encyclopaedia* imply that Absolute Spirit is a reality (so that task [7] must have been accomplished), that the concepts of Hegelian Science are available (so that task [9] must have been accomplished), and that Hegelian Science is true (so that task [11] must have been accomplished).[9] Consequently, Hegel must now indeed have believed that the *Phenomenology* had eliminated the historical context within which it needed to perform these tasks, and that its performance of them had become a thing of the past.[10]

This explains the relativizing of these tasks to the past implied by the Heidelberg *Encyclopaedia,* where, encapsulated in the expression "the production through witnessing of pure Science's Concept," they are spoken of as something which the *Phenomenology* had to do *earlier*.[11] It also explains Hegel's comment in 1831 that the *Phenomenology* was "relative to the former time of its composition," a time when "the *abstract Absolute* held sway." For by this Hegel means a time when Absolute Spirit still lacked full realization, and its philosophical expression conceptual clarity and truth—or, in other words, a time when metaphysical tasks (7), (9), and (11) had not yet been accomplished.

Now someone might object—either to this interpretation or, granting it, to Hegel—that when one reflects on the implications of a belief that the *Phenomenology* had successfully performed tasks (7), (9), and (11), and in particular the implications that Hegelian linguistic usage / concepts and doctrines had now achieved community-wide acceptance, it is clear that for Hegel to have held such a belief by the time of his later

---

9. Or at least that these things are *on the verge* of being so. A few passages appear to qualify the implications in question in this direction—for example, the remarks in the prefaces of the 1817 Heidelberg and 1827 Berlin editions of the *Encyclopaedia* that it is "an *introduction or contribution* to the satisfaction [of the interest in cognition of the truth]," and that Hegel is here "*working toward* . . . the philosophical cognition of the truth" (*Enzyklopädie der philosophischen Wissenschaften* 1:13, 14; emphasis added).

10. Or at least, with due regard to the qualification in the preceding note, that these things were *on the verge* of being so.

11. The expression "the production through witnessing of pure Science's Concept" refers most obviously to metaphysical task (9) (as was noted in chapter 4). However, it can also be understood to refer to the other two metaphysical tasks mentioned. Thus, because "the Concept" is in Hegel more or less a synonym for "Absolute Spirit," the expression can very well also refer to metaphysical task (7), the task of realizing Absolute Spirit by raising human consciousness to knowledge of it. And the expression could also be construed, for similar reasons, as equivalent to "the production through witnessing of pure Science's *truth*," and hence as referring to metaphysical task (11).

writings would have required a quite fantastic measure of self-delusion on his part. In response to this objection, two points deserve notice.

First, the impact of Hegel's concepts and doctrines on the German public by the time of his later writings should not be underestimated. The influence of the *Phenomenology* on the public prior to the first edition of the *Science of Logic* was indeed fairly modest. But by the time of the first edition of the *Encyclopaedia* in 1817 Hegel could point to the more impressive combined impact of the *Phenomenology* and the *Science of Logic*, and also to the recognition of his thought implied by appointment to a professorship at the University of Heidelberg. And by the time of the second and third editions of the *Encyclopaedia* in 1827 and 1830 the public influence of his various works was still greater, and he had in addition achieved the recognition implied by appointment to the prestigious University of Berlin, an influential network of followers, a journal dedicated to the propagation of his own philosophy, namely, the *Yearbooks for Scientific Criticism,* and the status of something very much like national philosopher of Prussia.

Second, by the time of Hegel's later works an important revision had taken place in his thought about how his concepts and doctrines were to achieve general dissemination, a revision rendering a belief that this had now in fact been accomplished significantly less implausible. At the time of writing the *Phenomenology* he had envisaged this occurring through the *Phenomenology* making his philosophy understood and accepted by the mass of his contemporaries in a perfectly *direct* manner.[12] After writing the *Phenomenology* he was evidently realistic enough to recognize that the work which he had produced could not reasonably hope to accomplish this.[13] And, no doubt largely in response to this recognition, he now revised his position in order to allow that the great majority of men should receive the concepts and doctrines of his philosophy only *indirectly*, namely, in the form of *religion*. Hence, in his later years he indi-

---

12. Pars. 13, 26: "The Understanding's form of Science is the way to Science open and equally accessible to everyone, and consciousness as it approaches Science justly demands that it be able to attain to rational knowledge by way of the ordinary Understanding"; "Science . . . requires that self-consciousness should have raised itself . . . in order to be able to live—and [actually] to live—with Science and in Science. Conversely, the individual has the right to demand that Science should at least provide him with the ladder to this standpoint." Cf. Hegel's 1805 letter to Voss, *Briefe von und an Hegel* 1:100–101.

13. See, for example, his expression of regret in an 1807 letter to Knebel that the *Phenomenology* had not achieved greater "intelligibility and clarity" and had not been better able to satisfy "men of insight and taste" (ibid., p. 200).

cates that philosophy itself "is destined only for the few."[14] But he clearly still aspires to have it accepted by the masses in *some* manner.[15] And accordingly in the second edition of the *Encyclopaedia* he presents his new solution: "Religion is the mode of consciousness in which truth exists for all men, for men of all levels of education. The scientific cognition of truth, on the other hand, is a special form of their consciousness, to whose labor not all but rather only a few subject themselves. *The content is the same,* but . . . there are two languages for that content, the one the language of feeling, of picture-thinking, and of the thought of the Understanding which lives in finite categories and one-sided abstractions, the other the language of the concrete Concept."[16] Hegel's new idea was not simply that religion *as it preexisted* his philosophy should serve as a vehicle of "truth . . . for all men" (though he certainly believed that it could do so in some degree), but rather that the advent of his philosophy would *reinterpret* religion in a way which enabled it to serve this function. Thus he goes on to say in the *Encyclopaedia* that "mere faith" "only becomes *truth* through" the "spiritual, completely thinking, and scientific expansion" of the "doctrine which is the foundation of the faith belonging to the Christian church."[17] Accordingly, while for the later Hegel, as for the Hegel of the *Phenomenology,* philosophy continues to depend essentially—for the full realization of its subject matter Absolute Spirit, for conceptual articulability, and for truth—on the general acceptance of its concepts and doctrines, this is now to be achieved with the aid of religion, namely, qua reinterpreted by philosophy in a manner enabling it to serve as a vehicle for philosophy's popular dissemination: "Homer says of some celestial bodies that they bear certain names among the immortal gods, and other names among mortal men. So the language of picture-thought [i.e., religion] differs from that of the Concept . . . Science must not only

---

14. From an 1830 letter to Göschel (*Hegel: The Letters,* p. 544). Cf. *Lectures on the Philosophy of Religion* 3:151: "Philosophy forms . . . a sanctuary apart, and those who serve in it constitute an isolated order of priests, who must not mix with the world." Cf. also Hegel's choice in 1831 of the following quotation from Cicero as a motto for the new edition of his *Science of Logic:* "For philosophy is content with few judges. With fixed purpose it avoids, for its part, the multitude, which in turn views it as an object of suspicion and dislike" (*Hegel: The Letters,* p. 551).
15. Thus, for example, in an 1831 poem he expresses the hope that his followers "may bear it to the people and put it to work" (ibid., p. 680).
16. *Enzyklopädie der philosophischen Wissenschaften* 1:24. Cf. par. 573: "Religion is the truth *for all men.*"
17. Ibid., pp. 35–36.

inscribe its ideas in the realms of abstraction . . . , but must authenticate and specify their concrete embodiment. This, the immediate existential form which they receive in actual life, is the picture-thought."[18]

It might seem, at first sight, as though there was something incoherent about this new approach, that if religion required a philosophical reinterpretation in order to become an acceptable vehicle for philosophical ideas, then a person would have to understand philosophy *directly* in order to grasp religion in a way that acceptably represented philosophical ideas to him, so that religion would inevitably be either ineffective or else redundant as a means to his acceptable grasp of philosophical ideas.[19] However, Hegel's idea appears to be that the required philosophical reinterpretation of religion need only be undertaken in any detail by the intellectual stratum of society, and that the remaining strata of society need only receive its general principles, specifically through deferring for the interpretation of their religion to the intellectual stratum as an authority.[20] Consequently, the requirement that religion must be philosophically reinterpreted before it can properly serve as philosophy for the masses does *not* entail that it must be either ineffective or else redundant in that function; even after the required philosophical reinterpretation of religion has occurred, there will still be many aspects of philosophy which the masses have not grasped directly, and for which they will therefore still need counterparts in religion if they are to grasp them at all.

This whole new conception embraced by the later Hegel of the form which the broad dissemination of his philosophy's concepts and doctrines

---

18. Hegel, *Berliner Schriften* (Hamburg: Felix Meiner, 1956), pp. 318–19.

19. In this spirit, Plant objects to Hegel: "Religion can only be socially benign when grasped philosophically, but once grasped in this way it is difficult to see the point of religion within the community" (*Hegel: An Introduction,* p. 198).

20. Thus, on the one hand, Hegel's many detailed philosophical reinterpretations of religion in his later works are directly addressed almost exclusively to intellectuals. But on the other hand, the later Hegel is also very much concerned that these reinterpretations should achieve an impact on the broader public through himself and his followers communicating their general principles to the broader public from a position of authority. This was a major purpose, for example, of the *Yearbooks for Scientific Criticism* which he and his followers published during the period 1826–31. By means of this journal he intended, as he wrote, "to increase knowledge and spread concepts among the public," not so much through original scientific works from which "anyway only relatively few can ever draw profit," but rather through critical reviews which suit the needs of the many "who need to be informed by others of the *general* state of scientific advances, and to receive a judgment . . . from competent judges" delivered by a publication which "appears as an *authority*" (*Sämtliche Werke* 20:37–39; cf. *Hegel: The Letters,* p. 514).

can and should take renders a judgment by him in his later years that (thanks in important part to the influence of the *Phenomenology,* especially on the more educated public) such broad dissemination had actually been achieved far less clearly self-deluding than it would have been had he retained his earlier conception that such broad dissemination needed to be perfectly *direct*.[21]

Consider, next, the two epistemological tasks of (4) defending Hegelian Science against the skeptical equipollence problem by showing all nonscientific viewpoints to be self-contradictory, and (5) defending Hegelian Science against the skeptical concept-instantiation problem by refuting the skeptic's assumption of a distinction between Hegelian Science's concept and its instantiation in reality and also discrediting all competing concepts as self-contradictory.

Once again, I think, Hegel from the start conceived the need for the *Phenomenology* to perform these tasks as relative to the historical context of the work's composition, and the work's success as bound to change that context in a way that would make its performance of them redundant. This is because, as was suggested in part 2, he from the start expected tasks (4) and (5) to be performed not only by the *Phenomenology* but also, and independently, by the later Logic. In the historical context of the *Phenomenology*'s composition the Logic's performance of these tasks was not available; it would become so only once the *Phenomenology* had performed its metaphysical tasks and thereby made Hegelian Science, including the Logic, conceptually articulable and true. Hence in the historical context of its composition the *Phenomenology* was necessary for the performance of tasks (4) and (5) if they were to be performed at all. Once the *Phenomenology* had successfully performed its metaphys-

---

21. Note that the explanation just given of the new function which religion assumes for the later Hegel casts light on the later Hegel's increased preoccupation with religion and its relation to philosophy. This increased preoccupation resulted not so much from the later Hegel's having somehow mysteriously become more conventionally religious—as many commentators have thought—but rather from his having come to believe that religion was required as a means for the essential broad dissemination of his philosophy, and that in order to play this role it had to be reinterpreted philosophically. For example, the *Encyclopaedia*'s arguments for the ultimate jurisdiction of philosophy in the interpretation of religion (*Enzyklopädie der philosophischen Wissenschaften* 1:31), polemics against contemporary theological positions at odds with Hegelian philosophy (ibid., pp. 24 ff.), and attacks on interpretations of Hegelian philosophy as fundamentally at odds with Christianity, and in particular as atheistic or pantheistic (ibid., pars. 50, 573), can all be understood in these terms.

ical tasks, however, and the Logic had thereby become available, the *Phenomenology*'s performance of tasks (4) and (5) was bound to be superfluous. This was not only because its performance of them would then reduplicate that in the Logic, but also because, given such a reduplication, Hegel was bound to prefer the Logic's performance of them over the *Phenomenology*'s, for the reason that, as we saw in part 2, whereas he conceived the Logic to be properly scientific and true, he undertood the *Phenomenology* to be merely an "appearance" of Science and less than true.

Accordingly, by the time of Hegel's later writings, when he actually believed that the *Phenomenology* had accomplished its metaphysical tasks, and the Logic had thereby become available, his discussions of epistemological tasks (4) and (5) focused exclusively on the Logic as the locus of their solution, to the complete neglect of the *Phenomenology*—for example, in the *Encyclopaedia* (pars. 1, 78), and in the last of the late *Lectures on the Proofs of God's Existence*.[22]

A similar situation obtains, I suggest, in connection with metaphysical tasks (8) and (10), the tasks, respectively, of demonstrating Hegel's social theories of meaning and of truth. The *Phenomenology*'s versions of these demonstrations consist, it will be recalled, in its serial critiques of individualistic conceptions of meaning and of conceptions of truth as correspondence between representations and independent objects—or in other words, in its serial critique of "shapes of consciousness." Once the Logic becomes available, these demonstrations are reproduced in a truer form by Hegelian Science itself. They are so, specifically, as the serial critique of the same "shapes of consciousness" found within the Philosophy of Spirit's version of a "Phenomenology of Spirit," which is performed now in light of a grasp of the underlying logical categories and their self-contradictions. Hence, concerning task (8), the *Encyclopaedia*'s version of a "Phenomenology of Spirit" begins by stressing the individualism of consciousness's self-conception (par. 413), but concludes with the result that "the truth in and for itself which reason is is the simple identity of the subjectivity of the concept and its . . . universality" (par. 438). And concerning task (10), it begins by stressing consciousness's commitment to the idea of independent objects standing over against representations and truth consisting in their correspondence (par. 416), but concludes

---

22. For an account of the Logic's performance of epistemological tasks (4) and (5) as envisaged in these texts, see my *Hegel and Skepticism*, chap. 8.

with the result that "the self-consciousness which is certain that its determinations are just as much objective . . . as its own thoughts is reason" which is "truth as knowing" and has "certainty of oneself as infinite universality" or as "Spirit" (par. 439).

Consider, finally, the pedagogical tasks (1), (2), and (3): the project of teaching modern individuals to understand and accept Hegelian Science by discrediting nonscientific viewpoints, including those which they currently occupy, providing them with a compelling path to Hegelian Science, and, along the way, giving them a provisional presentation of Hegelian Science.

Here, once again, it seems plausible to suggest that Hegel from the start regarded the need to have the *Phenomenology* perform these tasks as relative to the historical context of the work's composition, and as destined to be eliminated by the success of the work, which would change that context in crucial ways. Thus, note, to begin with, that Hegel nowhere in the *Phenomenology* says that the very elaborate and rigorous method of teaching his Science embodied in tasks (1), (2), and (3), and executed by the *Phenomenology,* would be required, or even most appropriate, for teaching his Science *in all contexts*. On the other hand, he *does* say that learning a body of information becomes dramatically easier as history progresses—with the presumable implication that less arduous methods for teaching it become appropriate as well: "As far as factual information is concerned, we find that what in former ages engaged the attention of men of mature mind has been reduced to the level of facts, exercises, and even games for children" (par. 28).[23] And it is therefore plausible to infer that he believes that the elaborate and rigorous method of teaching his Science embodied in tasks (1), (2), and (3), and executed by the *Phenomenology,* while required for teaching his Science in the historical context of the *Phenomenology*'s composition, in which his Science's acquisition is still difficult, will be dispensable in favor of less arduous methods of teaching it in a new historical context in which its acquisition is easier. If this *is* Hegel's view, then we may understand his conception more specifically as follows. Hegel indicates in the *Phenome-*

---

23. A nice illustration of Hegel's general point here is found in the area of arithmetic. In Plato's *Lesser Hippias,* 366c–d Socrates, evidently for once without irony, treats as a suitable test of Hippias's great skill in arithmetic his ability to multiply three times seven hundred—a calculation which nowadays most seven-year-olds could perform in a flash. (This change is no great mystery, of course, but a result of developments in mathematical notation.)

nology that the historical context of its own composition is one in which his Science still lacks detailed articulation and widespread familiarity and acceptance, but that the work aims to change this context by lending his Science more detailed articulation and making it more widely known (par. 13). It is reasonable to infer that he regards the current historical context of Science's lack of detailed articulation and widespread familiarity and acceptance as one unfavorable to the learning of his Science, and consequently as demanding the sort of elaborate and rigorous method for teaching it embodied in tasks (1), (2), and (3), and executed by the *Phenomenology*. And it is reasonable to infer further that he foresees the new historical context which the *Phenomenology* aims to bring about, a context in which his Science has achieved more detailed articulation and more widespread familiarity and acceptance, as by contrast one more favorable to the learning of his Science, and hence demanding only some less elaborate and rigorous method for teaching it. In this way, it is attractive to see Hegel as already at least implicitly committed in the *Phenomenology* to the position that the need for the work to perform pedagogical tasks (1), (2), and (3) is relative to the historical context of its composition and destined to be eliminated by its own success, which will change that context in crucial ways.

This, I suggest, explains why in the *Encyclopaedia* Hegel sets aside the *Phenomenology*'s elaborate and rigorous method of teaching his Science in favor of the less elaborate and rigorous—"only historical and rationalizing"—introduction provided by the "Attitudes of Thought to Objectivity" (together, it should be noted, with a presentation of Science itself which is more pedagogically oriented than that envisaged at the time of the *Phenomenology* and partially realized in the *Science of Logic*). For by the time of the *Encyclopaedia*'s publication the historical context has indeed changed in the ways foreseen and intended by the *Phenomenology*: thanks largely to the role of the *Phenomenology* itself, Hegelian Science has now indeed received more detailed articulation and become familiar to and accepted by a broader public.

In sum, I suggest that Hegel from the start conceived most of the central tasks of the *Phenomenology* as relative to the historical context of its composition, and this historical context as one which the success of the work would change in ways which would relieve the work of the need to perform them any longer, thereby rendering the work largely redundant. Hegel's later diminished enthusiasm for the work in places such as the Berlin *Encyclopaedia* may therefore be understood as symptomatic, not of a loss of faith in it, but, on the contrary, of a conviction that it had been *successful*.[24]

* * *

This interpretation of Hegel's later attitude to the *Phenomenology* requires qualification, however. The reader will have noticed that not quite all of the eleven major tasks of the work which we originally distinguished have yet been mentioned in this chapter. In particular, epistemological task (6), the task of justifying Hegelian Science by providing a proof of it for all nonscientific viewpoints purely on the basis of their own initial

---

24. It is an interesting further question, and one much debated in the literature, whether Hegel may not have conceived Hegelian Science *itself* as, similarly, merely relative to the historical context of its composition and destined to be superseded in the course of subsequent history.

As I read the texts, his official position is rather emphatically opposed to such a view, and this in a number of ways. For example, it seems precluded by (i) his conception that history is the striving of Absolute Spirit to achieve perfect self-knowledge, and that this is achieved in Hegelian Science; (ii) his conception of history as the realization of "Reason," or of the categories expounded by his Logic, which categories reach a definite conclusion in the all-encompassing category of the Absolute Idea, corresponding to Hegelian Science; (iii) his conception of history as a progression from freedom for one, to freedom for some, to freedom for all, and of Hegelian Science and its age as the perfect realization of freedom for all; and (iv) his doctrine in the *Phenomenology* that with the attainment of Hegelian Science time itself somehow comes to an end. Indeed, he explicitly states in the *Lectures on the Philosophy of World History* that historical "progress . . . is not an indeterminate advance ad infinitum, for it has a definite aim—namely, that of returning upon itself" or "mak[ing] itself its own object," as it does with the emergence of Hegelian Science (*Lectures on the Philosophy of World History: Introduction*, p. 149).

However, that said, there does remain enough evidence strongly suggesting the heretical view in question to show that Hegel at least found it very tempting. For example, in the preface of the *Philosophy of Right* he argues, famously, with his own philosophy in mind, that just as "every individual is a child of his time; so philosophy too is its own time apprehended in thoughts," that it is "absurd to fancy that a philosophy can transcend its contemporary world," and that with the arrival of philosophy "then has a shape of life grown old" (pp. 11–13). Again, in an 1829 letter to Hegel one of his followers, Weisse, writes, "You yourself, honored teacher, intimated orally to me one day that you were entirely convinced of the necessity of new progress and new forms of the universal Spirit even beyond the form of Science achieved by you, without, however, being able to give me any more precise account of these forms . . . With you, however, this conviction finds itself in flat contradiction with your systematic teachings, which, far from demanding such a progress of the World Spirit, on the contrary definitely exclude it" (*Hegel: The Letters*, p. 540). And finally, in a similar and closely connected vein, Hegel speculates (rather prophetically) in the *Lectures on the Philosophy of World History* that America is "the country of the future" and will "abandon the ground on which world history has hitherto been enacted," and in an 1821 letter to von Üxküll that Russia may look forward to such a future role as well (*Lectures on the Philosophy of World History: Introduction*, pp. 170–71; *Hegel: The Letters*, p. 569).

views and criteria, has not. This task *cannot,* I think, plausibly be seen as relative to the historical context of the *Phenomenology*'s composition in any of the ways in which the other tasks can. In particular, the *Phenomenology*'s performance of this task, unlike its performance of epistemological tasks (4) and (5) and metaphysical tasks (8) and (10), was never fully reduplicated within Hegelian Science proper and in this way superseded by Hegelian Science proper. It is therefore probably significant that in a few late remarks on the *Phenomenology*, including some of his very latest, Hegel ascribes a function to the work *without* implying, in the manner of some of the other late passages recently quoted, that it belongs only to the past, and that in these remarks he has in view epistemological task (6) specifically. Thus, in the introductions of not only the 1812 but also the 1831 edition of the *Science of Logic* he states: "In the *Phenomenology of Spirit* . . . I have represented consciousness in its advance from the first immediate opposition of itself and the object up to absolute knowing. This path goes through all forms of the relation of consciousness to the object and has the Concept of Science as its result. This Concept therefore needs . . . no justification here, because it has received it in that work. And it admits of no other justification than just this bringing forth of it through consciousness, whose own shapes all dissolve into the Concept as the truth."[25] Similarly, in both editions of the *Science of Logic,* and *especially* as rewritten in the 1831 edition, the section "With What Must Science Begin?" represents task (6) as a task for whose performance the *Phenomenology* must still be relied on.[26] And the same is true, on reflection, of a passage in the last editions of the *Encyclopaedia* from 1827 and 1830.[27] It was perhaps above all his sense of the enduring indispensability of the *Phenomenology* for the performance of this task that motivated Hegel to begin preparing a second edition of the work shortly before his death.

25. Appendix XV.
26. See appendices XV and esp. XVIII.
27. Par. 25, in appendix XVII: "In my *Phenomenology of Spirit* . . . the procedure is followed of beginning from the first, simplest appearance of Spirit, the immediate consciousness, and developing its dialectic up to the standpoint of philosophical Science, the necessity of which is demonstrated through this progression."

Appendices

The following appendices contain some of Hegel's writings from before, during, and after the *Phenomenology*'s composition which are most illuminating for interpretation of the work's idea. Their order here is basically chronological, with a few minor exceptions. Allowing the exceptions permitted the following approximate thematic order as well: Appendices I–X contain texts from before the completion of the *Phenomenology* which throw light, in turn, on the pedagogical, epistemological, and metaphysical tasks of the work explained in part 1. Appendices X–XI contain texts from the time of, and tied to, the *Phenomenology*'s composition which bear on specific aspects of the work. Appendices XII–XIII contain texts from immediately after the *Phenomenology*'s composition in which Hegel reflects on the work as a whole. Appendix XIV contains the version of the Logic from 1808 ff. which was found in part 4 to underlie the *Phenomenology*. Appendices XV–XIX contain Hegel's most important later reflections on the *Phenomenology*. In these translations I have aimed at literalness rather than literariness (a quality in fairly short supply in Hegel's originals).

    I: *The Positivity of the Christian Religion* (1795–1800)—Extract   572–581
   II: *Fragment of a System* (1800)—Extract   581–582
  III: *Letter to Schelling* (1800)—Extract   582–583
  IV: *The Need for Philosophy* (1801)   583–586
   V: *Logic and Metaphysics* (1801–2)   586–590

VI: *The Relation of Skepticism to Philosophy* (1802)—Extract 590–605
VII: *On the Nature of Philosophical Critique* (1802)—Extract 605–607
VIII: Philosophy of Spirit (1803–4)—Extract 607–608
IX: Aphorism, "Science . . ." (1805–6?) 608–609
X: Lecture Fragment, "The Absolute . . ." (1806) 609–611
XI: A Sheet on the *Phenomenology* (1805) 611
XII: Letters to Niethammer and Schelling (1807)—Extracts 611–612
XIII: Hegel's Announcement of the *Phenomenology* (1807) 612–613
XIV: *Logic* (1808 ff.) 613–629
XV: *Science of Logic,* First Edition (1812)—Extracts 629–635
XVI: Heidelberg *Encyclopaedia* (1817)—Extracts 635–636
XVII: Berlin *Encyclopaedia* (1830)—Extracts 636–641
XVIII: *Science of Logic,* Second Edition (1831)—Extract 641–646
XIX: Note for the Second Edition of the *Phenomenology* (1831) 646

Appendix I: *The Positivity of the Christian Religion* (1795–1800)—Extract

[This extract from *The Positivity of the Christian Religion* is illuminating for the *Phenomenology* in many ways, including in particular the following. First, it illustrates Hegel's early thought concerning one of the dualisms which remain of central concern for the *Phenomenology,* namely, Christianity's sharp division of God from man and nature (see chapter 2). Second, and connectedly, it throws considerable light on the *Self-consciousness* chapter of the *Phenomenology,* especially on the historical significance of the *Lordship and Bondage* section and its transition to the treatment of Christianity in the *Unhappy Consciousness* section (see chapters 2 and 9). Third, it provides a striking, and particularly interesting, example of the early Hegel's attempts to explain intellectual developments in terms of socio-economico-political ones (see chapters 2 and 12).—Text translated from H. Nohl, *Hegels theologische Jugendschriften* (Tübingen: J.C.B. Mohr, 1907).]

It is one of the pleasantest feelings of the Christians to compare their happiness and their science with the unhappiness and darkness of the heathen, and one of the commonplaces whither the spiritual shepherds most like to lead their sheep to the pasture of self-satisfaction and proud humility to bring this happiness before their eyes in a right lively manner—in which process the blind heathen usually then come off very badly. They get particularly [pitied] for the comfortlessness of their religion, which promises them no forgiveness of sins, and especially leaves them without the belief in a providence directing their fates in accordance with wise and beneficent purposes. But we can soon see that we may save our pity, for the reason that we do not find in the Greeks the needs which our modern practical reason has—on which people are in the habit of imposing an altogether very great burden indeed.

The displacement of the heathen religion by the Christian religion is one of those astonishing revolutions the search for whose causes must occupy the thoughtful historian. The great conspicuous revolutions must have been preceded in advance by a silent, hidden revolution in the spirit of the age, not visible to every eye, least observable for contemporaries, and equally difficult to represent in words as to understand. Lack of acquaintance with these revolutions in the spiritual world causes a consequent amazement at the result. A revolution of such a kind that a native, ancient religion gets displaced by a foreign one, such a revolution occurring immediately in the spiritual realm must all the more immediately have its causes in the spirit of the age itself.

How was it possible for a religion to be displaced which had rooted itself in the states for centuries, which was connected with a state's constitution in the most intimate way? How could there end the belief in gods to whom the cities and realms ascribed their origin, to whom the peoples sacrificed every day, on whose blessing they called at every undertaking, under whose banner alone the armies had been victorious, whom they had thanked for their victories, to whom gaiety devoted its songs and seriousness its prayers, whose temples, altars, treasures, and statues were the pride of the peoples, the glory of the arts, whose worship and festivals were only occasions for universal joy? How could the belief in the gods, which was entwined with a thousand threads into the fabric of human life, be torn loose from this context? To a bodily habit the will of the spirit and other bodily forces can be opposed, to a habit belonging to a single force of the soul (except for the firm will) other forces of the soul. But to a habit of the soul which is not isolated as religion frequently is now, but which permeates all aspects of human forces and is most intimately interwoven with the most self-active force itself, how strong must the counterweight be which overcomes that power?

"Acquaintance with Christianity had the negative effect that the peoples were alerted to the inadequacy and comfortlessness of their religion, that their understanding recognized the incongruousness and ridiculousness of their mythology's fables and was no longer satisfied with this, the positive effect that they adopted Christianity, this religion which, so adequate to all the needs of the human spirit and heart, answers so satisfactorily all the questions of human reason, and which in addition verified its divine origin by means of miracles as well." This is the usual answer to that question, and the expressions "enlightenment of the understanding," "new insight," and suchlike which get used in the process are so familiar to us that we imagine that we are thinking great things here and that we have hereby explained everything. And we imagine that operation so easy and the effect so natural because of course it is so easy for us to make any child understand how incongruous it is to believe that up there in heaven such a pack of gods as the heathen believed wander around, eat and drink, brawl about, and do other things too of which every decent person among us is ashamed.

But whoever has only made the simple observation that those heathen on the contrary had understanding too, that they are moreover still so much our examples in everything that is great, beautiful, noble, and free that we can only wonder at these people as a kind foreign to us—whoever knows that religion, especially a religion of the imagination, does not get torn from the heart, let alone from the heart and the whole life, of the people by cold syllogisms which somebody works out for himself there in his study—whoever, furthermore, knows that in the spreading of the Christian religion rather anything but reason and understanding was applied—whoever, instead of finding the acceptance of Christianity explicable through miracles, has rather already raised in his mind the question: how must the age have been constituted that miracles, and particularly such miracles as history tells us of, became possible within it?—whoever has already made these observations will find the question raised above not yet satisfactorily answered by the response mentioned.

Free Rome, which had subjugated to itself a mass of states which had—in Asia earlier, in the West later—lost their freedom, and had destroyed a few that were still free—for these would not have allowed themselves to be subjugated—for this conqueror of the world there remained only the honor of being at least the last to lose its freedom. Greek and Roman religion was only a religion for free peoples, and with the loss of freedom the sense for, the force of, this religion, its appropriateness for people, is inevitably lost as well. What good are cannons to an army which has used up its ammunition? It must look for other weapons. What good are nets to a fisherman, when the stream has dried up?

As free people they obeyed laws which they had given themselves, they obeyed people whom they had themselves made their leaders, they conducted wars on which they had themselves decided, they gave up their property, their passions, they sacrificed thousands of lives for a cause which was their own, they did not teach and learn but rather practised in actions maxims of virtue which they could call completely their own, in public life as in private and domestic life each was a free man, each lived in accordance with his own laws. The idea of his fatherland, of his state, was the invisible thing, the higher thing, for which he worked, which motivated him, this was the final purpose of the world for him, or the final purpose of his world, which he found represented in reality, or himself helped to represent and to preserve. Before this idea his individuality vanished, he demanded preservation, life, and endurance only for it, and could effect this himself. To demand, or beg for, endurance or eternal life for himself as an individual could not occur to him, or if so then only that,[1] he could feel a little more strongly a wish that concerned merely himself only in moments of inactivity, of indolence. Cato only turned to Plato's *Phaedo* when that which had previously been for him the highest order of things, his world, when his republic was destroyed; then he took flight to a still higher order.

Their gods ruled in the realm of nature over everything which can cause men to suffer or to be happy. Lofty passions were their work, just as great talents in wisdom, speaking, and counsel were their gift. They were asked for advice concerning the happy or unhappy outcome of an undertaking, and begged for their blessing, they were thanked for their gifts of every kind. A person could oppose

---

1. Nohl's unnecessary *selten* omitted.

himself, his freedom, even to these rulers of nature, this power, when he came into collision with them. People's will was free, obeyed its own laws, they knew no divine commandments, or when they did call the moral law a divine commandment then it was not given to them anywhere, or in any letter of the alphabet, it governed them invisibly (Antigone). Moreover, they recognized the right of each person to have his own will, be it good or bad. Good people recognized the duty of being good for themselves, but at the same time they honored the freedom of another person to be able not to be so as well, so that they set up neither a divine morality nor one made by or abstracted from themselves which they expected others to follow.

Fortunate wars, increase of wealth, and acquaintance with a number of life's comforts and with luxury produced in Athens and Rome an aristocracy of military glory and of wealth, and gave them a rule and influence over many people, who—enticed by the former's deeds, and still more by the use which they made of their riches—conceded to them gladly and of their own free will a superiority in power and a dominion in the state, which they were conscious that they had given them themselves and could take away from them again at the first onset of a dissatisfied mood. But gradually they ceased to deserve a reproach which has so often been leveled against them, namely, that of being ungrateful toward their leaders and of, when faced with the choice between this injustice and [the loss of] freedom, preferring the former—of being able to curse a man's virtues when these were causing the destruction of their fatherland.[2] Soon the superiority in power which had been freely conceded became maintained by force, and the very possibility of this presupposes the loss of that feeling, of that consciousness, which Montesquieu makes, under the name of "virtue," the principle of republics, and which is the ability and readiness to sacrifice the individual for an idea, one realized for republicans in their fatherland.

The image of the state as a product of his activity disappeared from the soul of the citizen. The care for, the oversight of, the whole rested in the soul of a single person, or of a few. Each person had his own place—prescribed for him, more or less limited, different from the next person's. The government of the state-machine was entrusted to a small number of citizens, and these served merely as individual cogs, which only achieve their value in combination with others—the part of the dismembered whole which was entrusted to each of them was, in relation to this whole, so insignificant that the individual did not need to know this relation or have it in view. Utility in the state was the great purpose which the state prescribed for its subjects, and the purpose which they prescribed here for themselves was earning a living and subsistence, and perhaps also vanity. All activity, all purposes related now to what was individual, there was no longer any activity for a whole, for an idea—each person either worked for himself or, through compulsion, for another individual. The freedom to obey self-given laws, to follow in peace governing authorities and [in war] generals elected by oneself,

---

2. The last part of this sentence probably alludes in particular to Pericles' treatment by the Athenians during the Pelopponesian War.

to execute plans which one had oneself had a role in deciding, fell away. All political freedom fell away. The right of the citizen gave him only a right to security of property—which now made up the whole content of his world. The phenomenon which tore down for him the whole fabric of his purposes, the activity of his whole life, namely, death, was inevitably something terrible for him, for nothing survived him. The republican was survived by the republic, and the thought hovered before his mind that the republic, his very soul, was something eternal.

But when in this way all of a person's purposes, all of his activity, took aim at something individual, when he no longer found for them any universal idea for which he might live and die, he then found no refuge among his gods either, for they too were individual, incomplete beings who could not satisfy the requirements of an idea. Greeks and Romans were satisfied with gods so poorly equipped, with gods possessing the weaknesses of human beings, because they had the eternal, the independent, in their own breast. They could bear to see the mockery of the gods on the stage because it was not the holy that could be mocked in them. It was all right for a slave in Plautus to say: *si summus Jupiter hoc facit, ego homuncio idem non facerem*[3]—an inference which his audience inevitably found strange and ridiculous, because the principle that what a human being ought to do is to be discovered among the gods was quite foreign to them, but which a Christian on the other hand would have to judge correct. In this condition, without belief in anything permanent, in anything absolute, in this habit of obeying an alien will, an alien legislation, without a fatherland, in a state to which no joy could adhere, and whose pressure the citizen felt alone, with a form of religious worship to whose celebration, to whose festivals, they could not bring along the gaiety which had flown from their lives, in a condition where the slave, who was already very often superior to his master in natural abilities and in education, could no longer see in him the advantage of freedom and independence—in this condition, a religion offered itself to people which either already fitted the needs of the age, for it had arisen among a people in a similar state of corruption and with a similar (merely differently nuanced) emptiness and inadequacy,[4] or from which people could form that to depend on which their need demanded.

But reason could never give up finding the absolute, the independent, the practical, somewhere or other. It was no longer to be found in people's will. It now appeared to reason in the deity which the Christian religion offered it, beyond the sphere of our power, of our volition, but not of our pleading and asking. Thus the realization of a moral idea could now only be wished for (for what one can wish for one cannot accomplish oneself, one expects to receive it without our cooperation), no longer willed. The first disseminators of the Christian religion roused hopes of just such a revolution, to be brought about by a divine being while human beings behaved quite passively, and when these hopes finally disap-

---

3. "If Jupiter the highest does this, why should I, a manikin, not do likewise?" (Terence [in fact], *Eunuchus,* iii, 5. 42).
4. That is, the Jews.

peared people rested satisfied with awaiting that revolution in the whole at the end of the world. As soon as the realization of an idea has once been projected beyond the bounds of human power—and the people of that time felt themselves capable of little any more—it is a matter of indifference how far the object of hope gets exaggerated beyond measure, and this object was therefore able to absorb into itself—not for the imagination, but in the awaiting of actuality—everything with which an oriental power of fantasy in its rapture had decked it out.— As long as the Jewish state found within itself the courage and strength to preserve its independence, we find [the Jews], too, seldom—or, as many claim, never— taking refuge in awaiting a Messiah. Only once subjugated by foreign nations, in the feeling of their impotence and weakness, do we see them digging for this sort of comfort in their holy books. At that time, when a Messiah offered himself to them who did not fulfil their political hopes the people thought it worth the trouble to keep their state still a state—a people to which this is a matter of indifference will soon cease to be a people—and a short time later it threw aside its lazy hopes of a Messiah, took up arms, and after [it] had done everything which the most fanatical courage can achieve, and had borne the most awful human misery, it buried itself and its state under the ruins of its city. And it would stand in history, in the opinion of the nations, beside the Carthaginians and the Saguntines, and higher than the Greeks and Romans, whose cities outlived their state, if the sense for what a people can do for its independence were not too foreign to us, and if we had not the impudence to presume to prescribe to a people that it should not have made its own cause its cause, but rather our opinions, and should have lived and died for these—opinions for whose maintenance we lift not a finger. The dispersed remainder of the Jews has not indeed abandoned the idea of its state, but has never again returned with it to the banner of its own courage, but instead once again only to the emblem of a lazy hope for a Messiah.—The followers of the heathen religion too felt this want of practical ideas. That these should be found among human beings was the sense of a Lucian, a Longinus, and the sad experience which they made in this connection vented itself in bitter complaints. Others, in contrast, for example Porphyry and Iamblichus, tried to equip their gods with a wealth which was no longer the property of human beings, and then to receive a part of it back again from them as a gift by means of conjury. Aside from earlier attempts, it has been reserved especially for our age to vindicate the treasures which have been squandered on heaven as at least in theory—the property of human beings. But which epoch will have the strength to enforce this right, and to take possession?

   It was inevitable that in the womb of this corrupted humanity, which had to despise itself from the moral point of view, but otherwise esteemed itself as a favorite of the deity, the doctrine of the corruption of human nature was begotten and gladly accepted. It accorded, on the one hand, with experience, while on the other hand it satisfied pride's interest in freeing oneself of blame and giving oneself a ground for pride in the feeling of wretchedness itself. It brought into honor what is shameful, it sanctified and immortalized their incapacity, by making into a sin even the ability to believe in the possibility of possessing a power. The domain of the rule exercised by the heathen gods, who had previously conducted their business only in nature, became extended, like that of the Christian God, to cover the free world of the spirit. Not only was the right of legislation conceded to God exclusively, but every good motive, every better intention and decision, came to be expected of him as his work—not in the sense in which the Stoics ascribed everything good to the deity, namely, by conceiving their souls as of one kind with the deity, as a spark of the deity, but in the sense of being the work of a being which is outside us, of whom we are no part, which is remote from us, with whom we have nothing in common. Likewise, moreover, even the capacity of behaving passively in relation to those influences of God's became weakened through the constant machinations and cunning of an evil being, who made constant intrusions into the other's domain both in the natural and in the spirit realm. And when the Manichaeans seemed to concede to the evil principle undivided rule in the realm of nature, the orthodox church justly vindicated, against this assertion dishonoring God's majesty, the largest share of that rule for the majesty of God, but the evil principle had been sufficiently compensated by the orthodox church for this loss by the concession to it of a power in the realm of freedom.

It was with an honest heart and a well-meaning zeal that the powerless race fled to the altar, on which it found independence and morality and made prayer to them. But when Christianity penetrated the more corrupt upper class, when great differences between high and low arose within Christianity itself, when despotism further poisoned all the sources of life and being, then the age made plain the complete insignificance of its nature through the turn taken by its concepts of the divinity of God and its quarrels about these. And it revealed its nakedness all the more plainly in putting around it the nimbus of holiness, and lauding it as the highest honor of humankind.

For from the ideal of perfection too, from the only place where the holy was preserved, the moral disappeared, or was at least consigned to oblivion. Instead of the moral, the truly divine—from the contemplation of which warming rays would still yet have been reflected back into the heart—the mirror revealed nothing more than the image of its age: nature, directed at whatever purpose the pride and passion of human beings chose to lend it. "Nature," because we see all the interest of cognition and faith turned toward the metaphysical or transcendental side of the idea of the deity. We see [people] occupied less with dynamical concepts of the Understanding, which theoretical Reason is able to extend to the infinite, than with, rather, applying numerical concepts, Reflection's concepts of "difference" and suchlike, indeed even mere perceptual representations of "arising," "creating," and "producing," to their infinite object, and deriving its properties from events in its nature. These determinations and subtleties did not remain, as formerly, locked up in the studies of the theologians. Their public was the whole of Christendom—all classes, all ages, both sexes were equally engaged with them, and difference in such opinions provoked the deadliest hatred, the bloodiest persecutions, often a complete destruction of all moral bonds and of the holiest relationships. Such an inversion of nature could not but take its revenge in the most awful way.

Concerning the purpose which they gave to this infinite nature, it was, far from being a moral final purpose of the world, limited not merely to the spreading of the Christian religion, but to purposes which a particular community, particular people (especially priests), adopted for themselves, who infused it with every manner of conceit, pride, overweening ambition, envy, hate, and other passions.[5] However, it was not yet time for our age's prettily-depicted consoling theory of providence, which constitutes the key-stone of our doctrine of eudaemonism. The situation of the Christians was for the most part too unhappy for them to have expected much happiness on earth, the universal concept of a church too deep in their souls for the individual to have expected or demanded this much for himself. But so much the stronger were the demands which a person made as soon as he could connect his interest together with the interest of this church. They despised the joys of the world and the goods of the earth which they had to forgo, and found their generous compensation in heaven. A fatherland, a free state, had been replaced by the idea of the church, which differed from the former in that—over and above the fact that in it there was no room for freedom—whereas the former existed complete on earth the latter stood in the most intimate connection with heaven, which was so close to the Christians' system of feeling that the yielding up of all joys and goods can appear as no sacrifice, and had to seem extraordinary only to those witnesses of the death of the martyrs who were unacquainted with that feeling of the proximity of heaven.

In this way the despotism of the Roman emperors had chased the human spirit from the face of the earth, its robbery of freedom had forced the human spirit to carry off its eternal aspect, its absolute aspect, to safety in the deity, the misery which it spread abroad had forced the human spirit to seek and expect happiness in heaven. The objectivity of the deity developed in pace with the corruption and enslavement of mankind, and the former is in fact merely a revelation, merely a manifestation, of this spirit of the times. In this way, through its objective God, this spirit gave a revelation of itself when people began to know such an astonishingly large amount about God, when so many secrets of his nature, in so many formulas, were shouted out everywhere—not, as formerly with secrets, [whispered] by one neighbor into the ear of another—and children knew them by heart. The spirit of the age gave a revelation of itself in the objectivity of its God when he was projected—not quantitatively forth to infinity, but—into a world foreign to us in whose domain we [have] no share, where we cannot settle through our own deeds, but into which we can at most beg or conjure our way, when man himself was a not-self and his deity another not-self. The spirit of the age revealed itself most clearly in the mass of miracles which it produced, which, in connection with deciding and attaining conviction, took the place of a person's own reason. But the spirit of the age revealed itself most monstrously when people fought, murdered, slandered, burned, stole, lied, and cheated for this God. In such a period the deity had to have completely ceased to be something subjective, to have instead become entirely object, and that perversion of moral maxims was then quite easily and consistently justified through theory. The Christians know

---

5. Possible alternative translation: "but to purposes . . . , which every manner of conceit, pride, overweening ambition, envy, hate, and other passions inspired in the individual."

through God's own revelation that he is the all high, lord of heaven, lord over the whole earth, over lifeless living nature,[6] and also lord of the world of spirit. To deny this king his due reverence in the manner which he has himself commanded is necessarily ingratitude and crime. This is the system of every church, and they only diverge in the maxims which they follow on the question of who should be the judge, the punisher, of this crime. One church administers this office of judge itself, another damns in its system but does not move a finger to execute this judgment already on earth, and is instead assured that the deity itself will execute it. And the zeal for [intervening] by means of teaching lessons or other modest means of bribery or oppression (which had only to stop short of death) seems to be cooling down gradually, and a feeling of sympathy seems to be taking the place of hatred, a feeling of impotence which, however much its ground is a conceit which convinces itself that it is in possession of the truth, is still preferable to that hatred. The free man was as little capable of that zeal as of this sympathy, for as a free man living among free men he would not concede to anyone else the right to presume to make improvements and changes in him and interfere in his maxims, nor himself presume to dispute other people's right to be as they are and as they wish, be it good or bad. Piety and sin are two concepts which, in this sense, the Greeks lacked. The former is for us a disposition which acts from respect for God as lawgiver, the latter an action which transgresses commandments in so far as they are divine. *hagion, anagion, pietas,* and *impietas* express holy feelings of humanity, and dispositions or actions which accord with or contradict them. At the same time they [the Greeks] also call them divine commandments, but not in the positive sense, and if it had been possible for the question to occur to one of them by what means he proposed to prove the divinity of a command or prohibition, he could have cited no historical fact, but only the feeling of his heart and the agreement of all good men.

It belongs to the situation of a people that, when after the destruction of all political freedom all interest in a state has disappeared (for we can only take interest in something for which we can be active), and when the purpose of life is limited only to earning one's daily bread together with more or less comfort or luxury, and all interest in the state only to the hope that its preservation will grant or preserve this for us, and is therefore completely selfish, then among the traits which we see in the spirit of the age aversion to military service must inevitably be found as well. For military service entails the opposite of what is universally wanted—a peaceful, uniform enjoyment—namely, troubles, and even the loss of the possibility of enjoying anything any more, death. Or whoever resorts to this as the last means[7] for preserving himself and satisfying his desires which his indolence or dissoluteness or boredom leaves him, will be merely cowardly when confronted by the enemy. In this condition of oppression, of political inactivity, we see among the Romans a large number of men who escaped military service

---

6. Nohl's *und* omitted; Hegel's paradoxical formulation is probably intentional.
7. Reading: *dieses als letztes Mittel.*

through desertion, through bribery, through mutilation of their limbs. And to a people in this mood a religion was inevitably welcome which qualified the ruling spirit of the times, moral impotence, the dishonor of being trampled upon, as honor and the highest virtue under the name of "passive or suffering obedience," through which operation people saw in happy amazement the contempt of others and their own feeling of their shame transformed into glory and pride—a religion which preached to them that it was a sin to spill human blood. Thus it is that we now see St. Ambrosius or St. Antony with his many people, when their city was approached by a horde of barbarians, instead of rushing to the ramparts to defend it, kneeling down in the churches and the streets and begging the deity to avert the disaster threatening them. And for what reason, then, could it have been their will to die fighting? The preservation of the city could have importance for each of them only in order to preserve his property and the enjoyment of it. If he had exposed himself to the danger of dying fighting he would have done something ridiculous, for the means, death, would immediately have done away with the purpose, property and enjoyment. The feeling that in defending one's property one maintains through one's death not so much this property itself but the right to it (for whoever dies in defense of a right has maintained it)—this feeling was foreign to an oppressed people which was satisfied to possess its property through mercy alone.

Appendix II: *Fragment of a System* (1800)—Extract

[In this fragment from 1800, somewhat misleading entitled by editors the *Fragment of a System*, Hegel reflects on some of the deep dualisms distinctive of modern culture which preoccupied him in writings before the *Phenomenology*, and on the intimate connections between their presence and unhappiness, and their absence and happiness. These themes are of central importance for understanding the pedagogical project of the *Phenomenology* as this was explained in chapter 2. Note that Hegel has not yet in this fragment arrived at the view that the solution to the problem of dualisms lies in a *philosophical system*, instead still looking to religion to provide it. This is the main reason why the conventional title of the fragment is misleading.—Text translated from Hegel, *Frühe Schriften* (Frankfurt am Main: Suhrkamp, 1979).]

This more complete unification in religion—such an elevation of finite life to infinite life that as little as possible that is finite, limited, i.e., purely objective or subjective, remains, and each opposition, even those which have arisen in this elevation and completing, is again brought to completion—is not absolutely necessary. Religion is *any* elevation of the finite to the infinite, as a posited life, and such an elevation is necessary because the finite has the infinite as its condition, but the level of opposition and unification at which the particular nature of a race of men may stop is a contingent matter in view of indeterminate nature. The most perfect completeness is possible for peoples whose life is torn and separated apart as little as possible, i.e., for happy peoples. Unhappier peoples cannot attain that level, but they *have to* give themselves pains [sich bekümmern] in the separation to preserve one limb of the separation, pains on behalf of independence [Selbständigkeit]. They may not attempt to lose this independence, their greatest pride must be to keep the separation fast and to preserve the one part [das Eine]. Now one can consider this part from the side of subjectivity as independent existence of the self [Selbständigkeit] or from the other side as alien, removed, unattainable object. Both seem to be compatible alongside one another, although necessarily the stronger the separation is, then the purer the I is and at the same time the further above and removed from man the object is; the more developed and detached the inner is, then the more developed and detached the outer is and, if the outer is posited as the independent part, the more subjugated man must seem. But it is precisely this subjugation by an excessive object that is the constant aspect of the relationship [ist es, was als Beziehung festgehalten wird]. It is a contingent matter which side man's consciousness turns to, that of fearing a God who is infinitely exalted above the heaven of all heavens, above belonging to any connection, and who, hovering above all nature, has overwhelming power, or that of setting oneself as pure I over the ruins of this body and the shining suns, over the million heavenly bodies and the new solar systems as many in number as all of you together, you shining suns. If the separation is infinite, then the holding fast of the subjective or the objective part is an indifferent matter, but the opposition remains, an absolutely finite in opposition to an absolutely infinite. The elevation of finite life to infinite life could only be an elevation *above* finite life. The infinite attains its highest level of completeness [under these conditions] through being set in opposition to totality, i.e., to the infinitude of the finite—not through this opposition being sublated [aufgehoben] in a beautiful unification, but through unification being sublated and the opposition being a hovering of the I *above* all nature or the dependence upon—or more accurately, relation to—a being above all nature. This religion can be sublime and terribly sublime, but not beautiful and humane [schön menschlich]. And so the bliss in which the I has everything—everything having been posited in opposition to it—beneath its feet is a phenomenon of the age, signifying at bottom the same as the bliss of depending upon an absolutely alien being which cannot become man, or which, if it had become man (and consequently, within time), would remain, even in this unification, an absolutely particular, merely an absolute singularity [ein absolutes Eins]—the most venerable and noble thing, if the unification with time were ignoble and base.

Appendix III: Letter to Schelling (1800)—Extract

[In this extract from a letter which he wrote to Schelling in 1800 Hegel announces that his aim of meeting the needs of modern men—by which, as we can infer from the *Fragment of a System* for example, he primarily means overcoming the pervasive dualisms which destroy their happiness—has led him to develop a philosophical system. However, he implies that a problem remains in that this philosophical system's standpoint is distant from the viewpoints of the modern men whom it is designed to help, and who must accept it if it is to achieve its purpose, and he wonders how this gap is to be bridged. This defines one of the most fundamental tasks of the early Logic, and subsequently of its successor discipline the *Phenomenology,* as we saw in our discussion of their pedagogical project in chapter

2.—Text translated from *Briefe von und an Hegel,* ed. J. Hoffmeister (Hamburg: Felix Meiner, 1969), vol. 1.]

In my scientific education, which began from men's less exalted needs, I was inevitably driven to Science, and the ideal of youth inevitably modified itself into the form of Reflection and into a system. I wonder now, while I am still occupied with it, what return is to be found to an impact on the life of men.

Appendix IV: *The Need for Philosophy* (1801)

[In this section from his first publication, *The Difference between the Fichtean and Schellingian Systems of Philosophy* of 1801, Hegel gives further details about the dualisms which he sees pervading modern culture, condemning it to unhappiness, and about how his philosophy is supposed to remove, or rather to mitigate, these. He goes on in subsequent sections to sketch his solution to the problem which he had raised in his 1800 letter to Schelling (appendix III) of how to bridge the gap between his philosophy and the viewpoints of ordinary men: namely, the early Logic. However, a much fuller presentation of this solution is found in the roughly contemporary *Logic and Metaphysics* of 1801–2, and we shall therefore focus on this presentation of it instead (appendix V).—Text translated from Hegel, *Jenaer Schriften* (Frankfurt am Main: Suhrkamp, 1977).]

If we take a closer look at the particular form which a philosophy bears we see that it arises, on the one hand, from the living originality of the mind [Geist] which has produced through itself and formed by its own action the dirempted harmony in it and, on the other hand, from the particular form borne by the division [Entzweiung] which occasions the system. Division is the source *of the need for philosophy,* and as the culture of the age the unfree and given side of philosophy's form. In culture that which is the appearance of the Absolute has isolated itself from the Absolute and become fixed as something independent. At the same time, though, the appearance cannot deny its origin and inevitably strives to constitute the manifoldness of its limitations into a whole. The power of limitation, the Understanding, attaches to its construction, which it places between men and the Absolute, everything that is valuable and sacred to men, makes it fast through all the powers of nature and talent, and extends it to infinity. The whole totality of limitations is to be found within it, only the Absolute itself is not. Lost in the parts, the Absolute drives the Understanding to its infinite development of manifoldness, and the Understanding, by attempting to develop itself to the Absolute but endlessly producing only itself, makes a mockery of itself. Reason attains the Absolute only by leaving behind this manifold partial structure [aus diesem mannigfaltigen Teilwesen heraustritt]. The firmer and more impressive the Understanding's construction is, the more restless becomes the striving of life, which is caught in this construction as a part, to release itself from this construction into freedom. By life's drawing away into the distance as Reason, the totality of limitations is at the same time destroyed, in this destruction connected with the Absolute, and hereby at the same time understood and posited as mere appearance. The division between the Absolute and the totality of limitations has disappeared.

The Understanding imitates Reason in its absolute positing and gives *itself* the illusory appearance of Reason by means of this form, although the matters posited are implicitly posited in opposition and therefore finite. The Understanding does this all the more illusorily when it turns rational negating into a product and holds it fast. The infinite, insofar as it is opposed to the finite, is just such a rational content posited by the Understanding—in itself as a rational content it expresses only the negation of the finite. The Understanding, by holding it fixed, posits it in absolute opposition to the finite, and Reflection, which had raised itself to Reason in sublating the finite [indem sie das Endliche aufhob], has once again degraded itself to the level of the Understanding by fixing Reason's deed fast in opposition. On top of that, Reflection now indulges in the pretention that even in this relapse it is rational. Such opposed contents, which were supposed to be valid as products of Reason and as absolutes, have been set up by the culture of various times in various forms and been the object of the Understanding's labors. The oppositions, which formerly had significance and bore the whole weight of human interests in the form of mind and matter, soul and body, faith and understanding, freedom and necessity, etc., and in more limited areas in many further forms, have in the course of culture's progress passed over into the form of the oppositions of reason and sensuousness, intelligence and nature, and, to give the general encapsulating expression, absolute subjectivity and absolute objectivity.

The sublation of such frozen oppositions [Solche festgewordene Gegensätze aufzuheben] is the sole interest of Reason. This interest of Reason is not to be understood as though Reason set itself against opposition and limitation without qualification, for the necessary division is *one* factor in life, which develops itself by eternally setting up oppositions, and totality is only possible in its highest degree of liveliness through reestablishment from the highest degrees of separation. Rather, Reason sets itself against the Understanding's absolute fixing of division, and especially when the contents absolutely opposed are themselves products of Reason.

When the power of unifying disappears from men's lives and the oppositions have lost their living connection and interaction and attain independence, the need for philosophy arises. To this extent it is something contingent, but given the division it is the necessary attempt to sublate the opposition of subjectivity and objectivity in their fixedness and to understand the already-become character of the intellectual and the real worlds as a becoming, their existence in the form of products as an act of producing. In the infinite activity of becoming and producing Reason has united what was separated and has demoted the absolute division to a merely relative division which is conditioned by the original identity. It is a contingent matter when and where and in what form such self-reproductions of Reason emerge as philosophies. This contingency must be understood in terms of the fact that the Absolute posits itself as an objective totality. To the extent that the Absolute's objectivity is seen as a progression in time, the contingency is a contingency in time. But to the extent that the Absolute's objectivity makes its appearance as something extended in space, the division is subject to climate. In the form of fixed Reflection, as a world of thinking substance and substance thought about, in contrast to a world of actuality [Wirklichkeit], this division falls within the western part of the North.

The further the development of culture thrives and the more diverse the development of life's expressions into which division can entwine itself becomes, the greater becomes division's power, the firmer its climatically conditioned sacredness, the more alien to the whole of culture and the more meaningless the efforts of life to be reborn into harmony. Such—in relation to the whole, few—attempts against the more recent culture as have taken place and the more significant beautiful depictions of the past or of foreign parts have only been able to awaken such attention as remains possible once the deeper, serious reference [Beziehung] of living art cannot be understood. With the separation of the whole system of the conditions and relations of everyday life [Lebensverhältnisse] from that reference the concept of their all-embracing and connecting context [ihres allumfassenden Zusammenhangs] is lost and has turned into the concept either of superstition or of an entertaining play. The highest aesthetic perfection—as it develops within a particular religion in which man raises himself above all division and sees the freedom of the subject and the necessity of the object disappear in the realm of grace—was only capable of vibrance up to a particular stage of culture and in conditions of general barbarism or the barbarism of the rabble. The culture has in its development become divided from this aesthetic perfection and has set it *beside* itself or itself *beside* it, and because the Understanding has become sure of itself, both have developed to the point of a certain peaceful coexistence beside one another by separating off from one another into quite disconnected domains, each of which treats as entirely without meaning what happens in the other.

But the Understanding can also be attacked immediately in its own domain by Reason, and the attempts to destroy division and thereby the Understanding's absoluteness by Reflection itself can be more readily understood. That is why division, which felt itself under attack, has turned itself with hatred and fury against Reason until the realm of the Understanding has raised itself to such a power that in this power it can keep itself safe from Reason. But just as people say of virtue that the best witness to its reality is the illusory appearance which hypocrisy borrows from it, so likewise the Understanding too cannot defend itself against Reason and it tries to preserve itself against the feeling of inner contentlessness and the secret fear by which limitation is tormented by means of an illusory appearance of Reason with which it varnishes over its separated elements [Besonderheiten]. The contempt for Reason is most clearly revealed not by the fact that Reason is openly despised and derided but by the fact that limitation gloats of the mastery of philosophy and of friendship with philosophy. Philosophy must refuse all friendship with such spurious attempts, which dishonestly boast of destroying what is separated, begin from limitation, and, in order to save and preserve such limitations, use philosophy as a means.

In the battle between the Understanding and Reason the former attains strength only to the degree that the latter exercises self-denial. Hence success in the battle depends on Reason itself and on the genuineness of the need for the reestablishment of totality from which Reason arises.

The need for philosophy can be called philosophy's *presupposition* [Voraussetzung] if a sort of forecourt [Vorhof] is to be made for philosophy, which begins with itself, and in our times much has been said about an absolute presupposition. What people call the presupposition of philosophy is nothing but the need for philosophy given expression. Because the need for philosophy is thereby posited for Reflection, there must be two presuppositions.

The one presupposition is the Absolute itself. It is the goal which is striven for. It is already present—how else could it be striven for? Reason produces it only in the sense that it frees consciousness from limitations. This sublation [Aufheben] of limitations has as its precondition the presupposed limitlessness.

The other presupposition would be the fact that consciousness has come forth from and left behind the totality [das Herausgetretensein des Bewußtseins aus der Totalität]—or the division into being and non-being, into concept and being, into finitude and infinitude. For the standpoint of division the absolute synthesis is a beyond—the indeterminate and formless which stands in opposition to its own determinacies. The Absolute is the night and the light is younger than it, and the difference between the two is, like the light's coming forth from and leaving behind the night, an absolute difference—the first being the nothing from which all being, all manifoldness of the finite, has arisen. But the task of philosophy consists in unifying these presuppositions, in setting being into non-being—or division into the Absolute, as becoming—as its appearance, the finite into the infinite—as life.

But it is artless to express the need for philosophy as a presupposition of philosophy, for in this way the need for philosophy receives one of Reflection's forms. This form of Reflection appears as contradictory propositions, about which more will be said below. It can be demanded of propositions that they justify themselves. The justification of these propositions as presuppositions is supposed to be not yet philosophy itself. And consequently the giving of grounds and establishing by grounds [das Ergründen und Begründen] begins and comes undone [geht los] before and outside of philosophy.

Appendix V: *Logic and Metaphysics* (1801–2)

[This text contains one of Hegel's first and most illuminating sketches of his early Logic. As shown in chapters 2 and 3, the early Logic was his initial solution to the pedagogical task which has emerged in the preceding texts, and also to certain epistemological, and in particular skeptical, problems which he came to perceive facing his philosophical system (for which see especially appendices VI and VII), in both of which functions it was eventually superseded by the *Phenomenology*. This text is also interesting because of its expression of the qualified activist conception of philosophy which we in chapter 12 saw Hegel to embrace during the early Jena period.—Unpublished ms.; partially published in K. Rosenkranz, *Georg Wilhelm Friedrich Hegels Leben* (Darmstadt: Wissenschaftliche Buchgesellschaft, 1977); full version forthcoming in Hegel, *Gesammelte Werke* (Hamburg: Felix Meiner), vol. 5.]

That philosophy unlocks man's inner world for him and allows him to bear the limitation of actuality [Wirklichkeit], though not to find satisfaction in it, does not preclude that this inner world can at the same time become a determinate ethical world [eine bestimmte sittliche]. The external world and man's inner world of philosophy are not, to be sure, separate worlds, but the external world may itself be separated and in a state of hostility [mag getrennt und in Feindschaft begriffen sein]. Certainly, this world's disharmony resolves itself into harmony for the philosopher, but not for itself. Reason, to be sure, perceives herself in this world, but this self-moving world lacks consciousness of the harmony. This world is something harmonious only in the mind of the philosopher, but itself it does not recognize this unity. It is possible, however, even for this external disunity to be brought from unconscious to conscious identity. The examples of Solon and others who established identity in their world were cited recently. Long periods[8] of time may elapse before an old ethical form can be fully conquered by the new one. The epochs of philosophy fall within these periods of transition. Among smaller nations the budding new ethical life [Sittlichkeit] has permeated the whole mass of the nation more quickly than among larger nations, particularly the national colossi of recent times. But when the new ethical life has once developed to this maturity in the spirit of the nation and the shadowy need for it has permeated all men's hearts, the mass of men, while certainly feeling ill at heart, knows neither what oppresses it nor what it wants instead. The developing ethical nature [of the nation] has been able to cultivate its new formation under the bark of the old to such a point that it will only require a gentle push to break through the old bark and win space and light for the unfolding of the new. It is the great men who understand the ethical nature in this; they grasp with vigor and truth the ideal of the level which the ethical nature of man can now reach. These more reflective types do nothing more than say the word, and the nations will follow them. The great minds who are able to do this must, in order to be able to do so, be purified of all the distinctive features of the preceding form. If they want to complete the task in its totality, they must have grasped it and the ethical nature in their whole totality. They may perhaps grasp only one end of the task and advance it, but then because the strength of their mind grasped only one end of it while the ethical nature wants the whole, the ethical nature topples them from the position of power which they took for themselves and puts other men there, and if these too are one-sided, then a sequence of individuals, until the whole task is completed. But if it is supposed to have been the deed of a single man, then he must have recognized the whole and hence have purified himself of all limitation. The terrors of the objective world, and all the fetters of ethical actuality, and hence also all alien supports of continued existence in this world and all trust in a secure bond within it, must have fallen from him—in other words, he must be educated in the school of philosophy. From within the school of philosophy he can raise the still slumbering form of a new ethical world to consciousness and boldly join battle with the old forms of the World Spirit [des Weltgeistes], like Isaac struggled with God, confident that the form which he can destroy is an obsolete form and that the new form is a new divine revelation which appeared to him in a dream as an ideal and which he now reveals to the

---

8. Reading: *Perioden*.

light of day and brings to determinate existence [Dasein]. He can regard the whole presently available mass of humanity as a material which he takes possession of and from which his great individuality fashions its own body—a material which, itself living [lebendig], constitutes the more sluggish or more lively [lebendigeren] organs of this great form. In this way—to cite the greatest example of a man who wove his individuality into destiny and gave it a new freedom—did Alexander the Macedonian leave the school of Aristotle to conquer the world.

In the lecture course on Logic and Metaphysics which I am offering to present to you this winter, I shall both give this propaedeutic consideration to this characteristic of philosophizing—that it in general proceeds from finite beginnings—and begin from what is finite in philosophizing in order to proceed from this, namely, insofar as it is first destroyed, to the infinite.

The presentation of philosophy formerly had the form of a Logic and Metaphysics. I follow this form in my presentation not so much because this form has had a long authority as because it is suitable in the following respect.

That is, philosophy as the Science of truth has infinite cognition [Erkennen] or the cognition of the Absolute as its subject matter. But standing in contrast to this infinite cognition or to Speculation is finite cognition or Reflection [die Reflexion]. Not that one should think that the two are absolutely opposed to one another; finite cognition or Reflection only abstracts from the absolute identity of what in rational cognition is related to one another [aufeinander bezogen] or equated with one another, and only through this abstraction does it become a finite cognition. In rational cognition or philosophy the matter is certainly this finite cognition, and its forms are certainly also posited as finite forms, but at the same time their finitude is also destroyed due to the fact that in Speculation they are related to one another. For what they are they are merely through opposition, so that when their opposition is sublated [aufgehoben], when they are posited as identical, their finitude is simultaneously sublated as well. But mere Reflection has cognition of them only in opposition and hence possesses them only in the form of their finitude.

Now the forms of speculative thought are taken up in Logic as such forms of finitude. As people are usually in the habit of saying, in Logic one abstracts from all the content of thought and considers only the subjective aspect of thought.

At the same time, the Understanding or Reflection, the faculty of finite thinking, is secretly driven by Reason to reach an identity. The Understanding in its finitude imitates Reason by striving to bring its forms to a unity. But the unity which the Understanding is able to produce is only a formal unity or a unity which is itself finite, because the Understanding is founded on absolute opposition, on finitude.

The subject matter of a true Logic will therefore be this:

I. To set up the forms of finitude—not, indeed, collected together in an empirical fashion, but rather as they proceed forth from Reason, appearing however only in their finitude because robbed of their rational aspect by the Understanding.

II. To depict the striving of the Understanding as it imitates Reason in a production of identity but is only able to bring forth a formal identity. However, in order to recognize the Understanding as imitative we must at the same time hold constantly before us the original model [das Urbild] which the Understanding copies, the expression of Reason itself.

III. We must finally sublate [aufheben] the forms of the Understanding themselves through Reason, we must show what meaning and what content these finite forms of cognition have for Reason. Insofar as it belongs to Logic, therefore, the cognition of Reason will only be a negative cognition of Reason.

I believe that only Logic can serve as an introduction to philosophy and only from this speculative side [daß von dieser spekulativen Seite allein die Logik als Einleitung in die Philosophie dienen kann]—insofar as it determines the finite forms as such; by completely knowing Reflection and clearing it out of the way, so that Reflection sets no obstacles in the way of Speculation; and by at the same time constantly holding forth the image [Bild] of the Absolute in a reflection [Widerschein], so to speak, and making people familiar with it.

After this general overview of the Logic I shall proceed in the following order, the necessity of which will be shown in the science itself:

I. I shall represent the universal forms or laws of finitude, both in objective and in subjective respects, or in abstraction from whether these forms are subjective or objective—in the process constantly representing their finitude and representing them as a reflection [Reflex] of the Absolute.

II. I shall consider the subjective forms of finitude, or finite thought—the Understanding. Because the Understanding exists only as belonging to the organization of the human mind, we shall briefly construct this organization in accordance with just these aspects [i.e., the subjective forms of finitude], considering the mind in its progression through concepts, judgments, and syllogisms [Schlüsse]. With regard to syllogisms it should be noted that even though the rational form reveals itself more clearly in them so that they are indeed usually ascribed to Reason as rational thought, we show that to the extent that they are a merely formal inferring [Schließen] they belong to the Understanding, and that that in them which belongs to Reason is merely an imitation of Reason by the Understanding.

III. Third, the sublation of this finite cognition through Reason will be demonstrated. This will be the place in part to investigate the speculative meaning of syllogisms, in part to demonstrate the sublation of the forms of the Understanding or laws of finitude presented in the preceding, in part generally to indicate the foundations of a scientific cognition—the actual laws of Reason so far as they belong in the Logic, i.e., the negative side of Speculation.

It is customary to append to this pure Logic an applied Logic. But in part cognition will find what is actually scientific from this applied Logic in the third section, and in part what is customarily treated here is too general and trivial to be worthy of any attention.

The transition to actual philosophy or to Metaphysics will be made from this third section of the Logic, i.e., from the negative or destructive side of Reason. Here our task is above all to construct for ourselves the principle of all philosophy completely and to make it clear according to its diverse moments. The true knowledge of this principle will lead to the conviction that at all times there has been only one and the same philosophy. I am therefore not only not promising you to produce something new in my philosophical strivings, I am promising to produce what is actually the oldest of the old—and to clean it of the misunderstanding [Mißverstand] in which our modern times of unphilosophy [Unphilosophie] have buried it. It is not long since the mere concept of philosophy was reinvented in Germany, but its invention is only a novelty for our times. It must, as one might put it, be considered a touchstone of genuine philosophy whether it recognizes itself in the true philosophy.

Starting from this highest principle of philosophy we shall be able to construct for ourselves the possible systems of philosophy. We shall perceive in the various systems, if only they are philosophy, the attempt to represent one and the same fundamental principle [Grundsatz]. One system will simply make one factor of the totality stand out more, and another another. In particular we shall expose to the light of day and perceive in its nakedness the ghost of skepticism with which people have tried to frighten philosophy and which in modern times some still wish to bring to bear as a terrible opponent of philosophy. After that I shall continue with the presentation of those systems, i.e.,[9] the Kantian and the Fichtean, which more intimately concern our culture, and of which particularly the Kantian, even though it no longer has any significant followers, nevertheless still runs rampant in other sciences.

Appendix VI: *The Relation of Skepticism to Philosophy* (1802)—Extract (Plus Related Materials)

[The core of what follows is a long extract from Hegel's 1802 essay *The Relation of Skepticism to Philosophy*. This extract contains many of the ideas which are of greatest importance for understanding the epistemological dimension of the early Logic and its successor discipline the *Phenomenology,* as this was explained in chapter 3. In two noteworthy respects Hegel modified or clarified his position in this extract by the time of writing the sections on the New Academy and Pyrrhonism in the *Lectures on the History of Philosophy*

---

9. Reading: *also.*

(probably largely during the later Jena period, that is, still before the completion of the *Phenomenology*): (i) In this extract he tends to treat the (alleged) fact that the Pyrrhonists' Ten Tropes of Aenesidemus were directed solely against the Understanding and not at all against genuine philosophy, whereas their Five Tropes of Agrippa were directed against *both*, as a mark of the superiority of the former over the latter. In the *Lectures on the History of Philosophy*, by contrast, he tends to reverse this estimation of their relative values, arguing that the Five Tropes of Agrippa are superior to the Ten Tropes of Aenesidemus because of their greater effectiveness against the more sophisticated forms of the Understanding and their own greater scientificness. (ii) Whereas in this extract Hegel assigns what I have been calling the skeptical problem of "concept-instantiation" to modern skepticism, in the *Lectures on the History of Philosophy* he makes it clear that he also believes ancient skepticism to have deployed a version of this problem, especially in the case of the Academic skeptic Arcesilaus. In order to illustrate these two modifications or clarifications, I have appended to the extract from the essay of 1802 two short extracts from the *Lectures on the History of Philosophy*. It is arguable, I think, that both of these later developments in fact have the character more of clarifications than of modifications. Thus, concerning (i), Hegel's apparent shift in his relative evaluation of the two sets of tropes probably represents less a real change of view than a shift in focus from one of two desiderata which he accepts (not attacking genuine philosophy) to another (being effective against even the more sophisticated forms of the Understanding and being scientific). He is, at any rate, already prepared in at least one passage of our extract from the essay of 1802 to praise the Five Tropes of Agrippa on the ground that "there exist no more effective weapons against the dogmatism of the finite." Similarly, concerning (ii), Hegel already hints in the essay of 1802, probably with ancient skepticism in mind, that there was a form of the concept-instantiation problem even before modern skepticism—remarking in our extract that the invention of the opposition between thought and reality at the root of this problem is "older than the newest skepticism."—Texts translated from Hegel, *Jenaer Schriften* (Frankfurt am Main: Suhrkamp, 1977); and *Vorlesungen über die Geschichte der Philosophie* (Frankfurt am Main: Suhrkamp, 1982), vol. 2.]

The representation and assessment of this newest skepticism [i.e., Schulze's] requires that we go into the question of the relation of this skepticism and of skepticism generally to philosophy. On the basis of this relation, the various modifications of skepticism will automatically define themselves, and the relation of this newest skepticism itself—which imagines that it has raised itself onto the shoulders of ancient skepticism and that it both sees further and doubts more rationally—to ancient skepticism will at the same time become clear. A treatment of the relation of skepticism to philosophy, and a resulting knowledge of skepticism itself, seems not without merit also for the reason that the ideas about skepticism in common circulation are extremely formal and the noble nature which skepticism possesses when in its true form is habitually perverted into a general hidingplace and excuse for unphilosophy in the most recent times . . .

This speculative philosophy which [as conceived by Schulze] attempts to know things that are supposed to *exist* and *outside* our consciousness has standing in opposition to it the positive side of this [Schulzean] skepticism. For this skepticism has not only the negative side which occupies itself with the destruction of the dogmatists' fantasies and efforts to attain knowledge of the *existence of hyperphysical* things.

The *positive side* of this skepticism consists, namely, in the fact that it is in general described as a *philosophy* which goes *no further than consciousness*, and indeed (p. 51) "the existence of what is given in the sphere of our consciousness has *undeniable certainty;* for since it is present in consciousness we can doubt its certainty as little as conciousness itself; but to wish to doubt consciousness is absolutely impossible, for such a doubt, since it cannot occur without consciousness, would destroy itself and so be nothing. What is given in and with consciousness is called a *fact of consciousness,* and consequently facts of consciousness are the undeniable actual, to which all philosophical speculations must refer and which is to be explained or made intelligible through these speculations."[10] . . .

Mr. Schulze himself senses that a skepticism which accords an undeniable certainty to the facts of consciousness scarcely agrees with the concept of skepticism which the ancient skeptics give us. We must first hear Mr. Schulze's own opinion about this difference. He explains his view about it in the introduction and the first section of the third part. To begin with, he reminds us that "it has of course often been the case that the man who first found a thought on the path of truth *understood much less* of its content, grounds, and consequences *than others* who after him carefully investigated its origin and meaning. Hitherto the true intention of skepticism has for the most part gone unrecognized," etc. For the *skepticism* which Mr. Schulze regards as the *true* skepticism and a more perfect skepticism than that of the ancients "*refers* to those judgments which are *distinctive* of philosophy, i.e., those which," as Mr. Schulze expresses the final purpose of this science, "determine the absolute or rather supersensuous grounds, i.e., the grounds present outside the sphere of consciousness, of the something which according to the testimony of our consciousness is conditionally present." But "the judgments which only belong *to* philosophy are no object of this skepticism; for they either express so-called facts of consciousness or are based on [gründen sich auf] analytic thought; their truth can therefore be established [ergründet] and recognized according to skepticism also." On the other hand, this skepticism asserts against theoretical philosophy that, "of the grounds of the being of things that are present outside the scope of our consciousness," or as the author also puts it, "not given in consciousness as to *their existence,* or of things which exist outside existing things, nothing at all can be *known.*" Mr. Schulze himself raises the objection to this concept of skepticism that according to it "*nothing* of what *experience teaches* us, and in particular *not* the *aggregate of outer sensations,*

---

10. G.E. Schulze, *Kritik der theoretischen Philosophie* (Hamburg: Born, 1801), vol. 1. All of Hegel's subsequent quotations and citations of Schulze in this extract concern this work as well. Following Harris's helpful practice in *Between Kant and Hegel,* I have here and subsequently put Hegel's verbatim or nearly-verbatim quotations from Schulze into quotation marks even where they are not actually so put by Hegel himself.

and *of all the sciences only philosophy* (because no other science is concerned with the knowledge of things outside the scope of consciousness), can be an *object of skeptical* doubts," whereas ancient skepticism extended to both, and the very oldest at least to the former. Mr. Schulze appeals in this connection especially to the circumstance that "the beginning and development of skepticism has always determined itself in accordance with the presumptions of the dogmatists"; the ancient skeptics "confess that there is a knowledge through the senses and a conviction thereby in the existence and in certain properties of independently existing things, in accordance with which every rational human being must orient himself *in active life.*"—It follows immediately from this fact—that such a conviction was aimed merely at active life—that it had nothing to do with philosophy, that it and the limited, fact-filled conciousness were not at all set up as the principle of an undeniable certainty in opposition to Reason and to philosophy, least of all in a self-righteously insistent manner [pochend], but were only the tribute instituted as meagerly as possible which was paid to the necessity of an objective determining; we would, say the skeptics, *not* choose this or avoid that when it concerns things which are in our power, however those which are not in our power but by necessity we cannot avoid, like being hungry, thirsty, freezing cold, for these cannot be removed through Reason. But the ancient skeptic was far from elevating the consciousness connected with these necessary needs to the rank of a knowledge that is an objective assertion; we live, says Sextus, paying attention to what appears, in accordance with the common understanding of life, because we cannot be entirely inactive, without thereby advancing any opinion or assertion.[11] But there is no question in this skepticism of a conviction in *things* and their properties; the criterion of skepticism, states Sextus, is what appears (*phainomenon*), which in fact means his appearance (*phantasian autou*), i.e., the subjective; for because it lies in conviction (*peisei,* but not about a *thing*) and an involuntary affectedness, no investigation occurs; it is *azētētos* (the German expression *Zweifel* [doubt] is always distorting and unsuitable in application to skepticism). But Mr. Schulze explains the facts that the skeptics, instead of ascribing undeniable certainty to perception, declared all perception to be mere appearance and asserted that one had just as much to say the opposite of what one had said of the object in accordance with its appearance, just as much that the honey was bitter as that it was sweet, and that—as Mr. Schulze himself notes—the ten first and genuine tropes of the skeptics concerned this uncertainty of sense-perception alone in terms of the following reason: that already in the earliest periods of speculative philosophy sensations had been declared by the dogmatists to be an *appearance,* of which, however, something quite different was the underlying ground, and the appearance itself had been ascribed an agreement with what is supposed to be *present behind* it as an *actual thing,* and indeed knowledge through sensations had even often been championed by the dogmatists as a science of the *object lying hidden behind* sensation. It was for *this* reason that the skeptics attacked these doctrines of the dogmatists of the certainty of sense-

---

11. *Outlines of Pyrrhonism,* bk. 1, chap. 11.

knowledge and denied that anything could be known with reliability by means of the object in sensation about what is supposed to be present *behind* this object as a true, actual, independently existing *thing*.—We see here reproduced with reference to the ancient philosophers precisely the same utterly crass conception which Mr. Schulze has of rational knowledge; but the interpretation that skepticism did not attack sense-perceptions themselves but only the things placed behind and beneath them by the dogmatists is entirely baseless; when the skeptic said that the honey was just as much bitter as sweet and just as little bitter as sweet he did not mean by this a thing placed behind the honey.—"The fact that for the skeptics of Greece in addition *the propositions of all doctrines* which make claims to validity for every human Understanding were an object of doubt bespeaks a lack of acquaintance on their part with the true grounds of their doubts," and *moreover,* at that time, unlike *today,* the specific sources of the cognitions of each science and the degrees of the conviction possible within it had not yet been investigated; "many doctrines, *which now defy any rational urge to doubt, like for example physics and astronomy,* were at that time still only an aggregate of indemonstrable opinions and groundless hypotheses."—This trait completes the character of this new skepticism and its difference from ancient skepticism. Besides the facts of consciousness, the physics and astronomy of recent times would, then, also in addition be sciences which defied any rational skepticism, these doctrines which—excluding their purely mathematical part, which does not belong to their distinctive character—consist of a narration of sense-perceptions and an amalgamation of these with the Understanding's concepts of forces, matters, etc. in a cognition which without qualification claims objectivity and yet is purely formal—a cognition whose one part, the narration of perceptions, has nothing at all to do with a scientific cognition, and therefore certainly also falls outside of skepticism, to the extent that in the expression of the perception nothing is supposed to be expressed except its subjectivity; but whose other part is the highest summit of a dogmatizing Understanding. What would the ancient skeptics have said about such a mongrel-bastard skepticism, which can even go so far as to harmonize with the glaring dogmatism of these sciences? . . .

In the absence of the determination of the true relation of skepticism to philosophy, and without the insight that skepticism itself is most intimately one with each true philosophy, and that there is therefore a philosophy which is neither skepticism nor dogmatism and so is both at the same time, all the histories and accounts and new editions of skepticism can lead to nothing . . . Those whom Diogenes [Laertius] follows recognized that a true philosophy necessarily itself has at the same time a negative side which is turned against everything limited and thereby against the heap of facts of consciousness and their undeniable certainty and against the narrow-minded concepts used in those wonderful doctrines which Mr. Schulze believes to be unassailable by reasonable skepticism—against this whole field of finitude upon which this newer skepticism has its essence and its truth—and which is infinitely more skeptical than this skepticism. What more complete and self-standing document and system of genuine skepticism could we find than the *Parmenides* in the Platonic philosophy, which encompasses the whole sphere of that cognition through concepts of the Understanding and destroys it? This Platonic skepticism does not aim at a *doubting* of these truths of the Understanding—which knows things as manifold, as wholes consisting in parts, as a coming-to-be and a passing away, as a multiplicity, similarity, etc., and makes assertions of that kind—but at a complete negation of any truth in such a cognition. This skepticism is not a system unto itself, but is itself the negative side of the cognition of the Absolute and immediately presupposes Reason as the positive side . . .

This skepticism which in its pure and *explicit* form makes its appearance in [Plato's] *Parmenides* is, though, *implicitly* present in each genuine philosophical system, for it is the free side of each philosophy . . .

But, not to be unjust to Mr. Schulze, it should be pointed out that he has certainly been alerted by Sextus to a relation between the Academy and skepticism. How, though, does Mr. Schulze understand this relation and what Sextus says about it? In the note where Mr. Schulze deals with the matter (vol. 1, p. 608), he says that "through the teaching" of Arcesilaus (the founder of the Middle Academy) *to be sure* "the doubting of the truth of the doctrines of dogmatism was turned into a business *stripped of all application of reason,* because it cancels itself again, and thereby no longer hears the voice of reason at all." Then Mr. Schulze recounts that "Sextus (*Outlines of Pyrrhonism,* bk. 1, chap. 33) *was concerned that* the teaching of Arcesilaus *be distinguished* from *skepticism for the reason*" that according to the teaching of Arcesilaus and Carneades "*even this too, that everything is uncertain, must in turn be declared uncertain*"; such a business of doubting, Mr. Schulze adds on his own account, is stripped of all reason.

Concerning first the historical side, one cannot believe one's eyes when one reads such a ground attributed to Sextus for excluding the teaching of Arcesilaus from skepticism. It is of course the skeptics themselves who declare in the most emphatic manner—as Mr. Schulze himself points out at the beginning of his note—that their usual *phōnai*—"Everything is false," "Nothing is true," "One [proposition] just as little as the other," etc.—also include themselves in turn, *sumperigraphein* (*Outlines of Pyrrhonism,* bk. 1, chap. 7), and cancel themselves in turn, *huph' heautōn autas anaireisthai emperigraphomenas ekeinois peri hōn legetai* (bk. 1, sec. 206)—a doctrine which, besides lying in the nature of skepticism itself, was also absolutely necessary externally against the dogmatists, who objected to the skeptics that they did after all have a dogma, "Determine nothing," or "No [proposition] is truer," and also for distinguishing them from other philosophers, e.g., the Democriteans (chap. 30), to whom the skeptical expression "One [proposition] just as little as the other"—e.g., "The honey is just as little sweet as bitter"—belonged. The skeptics distinguished themselves by saying that there was a dogma here, namely, that the honey was neither; while they on the other hand show through this expression "One [proposition] as little as the other" that they do not know whether the appearance is both or neither. This is also how Sextus (chap. 33) distinguishes the skeptics from the New Academy of Carneades, whose fundamental principle is that everything is unintelligible; perhaps indeed, he says, the New Academy is only different [from skepticism] in that it expresses just this unintelligibility in the manner of an assertion. What Mr. Schulze says concerning the restriction of those skeptical expressions—namely, that "Sextus no doubt only meant to teach that the skeptic determined nothing concerning the transcendental constitution of things" either positively or negatively—yields no visible contrast at all [of these positions] with that claim of the skeptics and Arcesilaus that a skeptical expression includes itself in its own scope and cancels itself. And what then is the *transcendental constitution of things* supposed to mean? Does the transcendental not consist precisely in there being neither things nor a constitution of things? Sextus was therefore definitely through and through entirely far from distinguishing the teaching of Arcesilaus from skepticism for the reason which Mr. Schulze gives, for this teaching was literally that of skepticism itself. Sextus himself says that this teaching seems to him to agree so much with the Pyrrhonian *logois* that it is almost one and the same *agōgē* [12] as the skeptical, unless one wants to say that Arcesilaus *declares* that *epochēn* is *good and according to nature,* but *assent evil,* which is an assertion, since the skeptics by contrast even about this say nothing in the manner of an assertion. The distinction which Sextus thinks it still possible to make therefore has precisely the opposite ground: according to Mr. Schulze this Academy was declared by Sextus to be *too* skeptical; but Sextus finds it, as we have seen, *not sufficiently* skeptical . . .

But besides the skepticism which is one with philosophy, the skepticism which is separated from philosophy can be of two kinds, in being either not directed against Reason or directed against it. From the form in which Sextus gives us the skepticism which is separated from and turned against philosophy, it is easy to abstract the old genuine skepticism which to be sure did not like philosophy have a positive side, maintaining rather a pure negativity in relation to knowledge, but was just as little directed *against* philosophy. Likewise separated from philosophy is skepticism's later added hostile directedness in part against philosophy and in part against dogmatism. Its turn against philosophy, like philosophy's own development into dogmatism, shows how skepticism kept pace with the general deterioration of philosophy and of the world in general, until finally in the most recent times it sinks so far down in its association with dogmatism that now for both the facts of consciousness have undeniable certainty and for both truth lies in the temporal sphere [in der Zeitlichkeit], so that, since the extremes come to touch each other, from them we get once again in these happy times the attainment of the great goal that dogmatism and skepticism coincide *in their decline* and both reach out to each other the hand of warmest friendship and brotherhood. Schulze's skepticism unites with itself the crudest dogmatism, and Krug's dogmatism at the same time carries that skepticism within itself.

Sextus represents the maxims of skepticism for us in seventeen tropes, whose diversity indicates for us precisely the difference of his skepticism from the old skepticism, which indeed stood independently, without philosophical knowledge,

---

12. Hegel's own note: "For this is how skepticism preferred to call itself rather than a *hairesis.* Sextus explains that skepticism can only be called a school, a sect, in the sense of a *logōi tini kata to phainomenon, akolouthousēs agōgēs* (bk. 1, sec. 17)."

but at the same time falls entirely within philosophy, and is especially completely identical with the old philosophy which had less to do with subjectivity.

To the old skepticism belong the first ten of the seventeen tropes, to which only the much later skeptics—Sextus says simply the more recent; Diogenes names Agrippa, who lived about five hundred years after Pyrrho—added five more. The two tropes which were added on top of these appear still later; Diogenes does not mention them at all, Sextus too separates them, and they are insignificant.

These ten tropes, now, to which the old skepticism restricted itself are, like all philosophy generally, directed against the dogmatism of the common conciousness itself. They ground uncertainty concerning the finite matters in which it is unconsciously enmeshed and this indifference of mind before which everything that appearance or the Understanding provides is made to totter—in which tottering of everything finite, according to the skeptics, *ataraxia* enters earned through Reason, just as the shadow follows the body . . .

From a brief mention of the ten points which ground the *epochēn* of skepticism, their direction against the certainty of things and of the facts of consciousness will immediately become apparent. The uncertainty of all things and the necessity of *epochēs* is expounded, namely, (1) from the diversity of animals, (2) of human beings, (3) of the organization of the senses, (4) of circumstances, (5) of positions, distances, and places, (6) from mixtures (because of which nothing presents itself purely to sense), (7) the different sizes and constitutions of things, (8) relation (that is, the fact that everything is only in relation to an other), (9) more frequent or infrequent occurrence, (10) the diversity of education, customs, laws, mythical belief, and prejudices . . .

One sees that they are gathered together in a contingent manner, and presuppose an undeveloped Reflection, or rather a lack of intention on Reflection's part to have a doctrine of its own, and a lack of skill which would not be present if skepticism had already been engaged in the criticism of the sciences.

But the content of these tropes demonstrates still more how far removed they are from a tendency against philosophy, and how they aim quite exclusively against the dogmatism of the common human Understanding. Not one of them concerns Reason and its knowledge, but all quite exclusively the finite and the cognition of the finite, the Understanding. Their content is in part empirical, and to this extent it of its very nature does not at all concern speculation; in part it concerns relation in general, or the fact that everything actual is conditioned by an other, and to this extent it expresses a principle of Reason. This skepticism is thus not at all directed against philosophy, and is turned against the common human Understanding or the common consciousness—which holds fast the given, the fact, the finite (whether this finite be called appearance or concept), and sticks to it as something certain, secure, eternal—in a manner which is precisely not philosophical but popular. Those skeptical tropes show the common consciousness the instability of such certainties in a manner which is likewise close to the common consciousness. This skepticism, that is to say, likewise calls to its aid the appearances and finite matters, and from their diversity together with the equal right of all to attain validity, from the antinomy recognizable in the finite itself, it recognizes the untruth of this finite. This skepticism can therefore be seen as the first step to philosophy, for the beginning of philosophy must, of course, be the elevation above the truth which the common consciousness gives, and the presentiment of a higher truth. The newest skepticism with its certainty of the facts of consciousness ought therefore to be referred before all else to this ancient skepticism and to this first step of philosophy . . .

It is an accident of time if later the various philosophical systems completely separated from one another, and now apathy became in the eyes of ataraxia, the dogmatists of the Stoa (Sextus, *Outlines of Pyrrhonism,* bk. 1, sec. 65) in the eyes of the skeptics, their most opposed enemies. To this complete separation of the philosophies and the complete ossification of their dogmas and distinctions, as well as to the direction of skepticism henceforth in part against dogmatism and in part against philosophy itself, relate the skeptics' *later five tropes* alone. These later five tropes constitute the real arsenal of the skeptics' weapons against philosophical knowledge, which we will now briefly present in order to bring our presentation to a justified conclusion [rechtfertigen]. The first among these *tropes* of epoche is the trope of *diversity,* that is, no longer the diversity of animals or human beings as in the first ten tropes, but of common opinions and philosophers' doctrines, both in opposition to each other and in opposition among themselves. This is a trope about which the skeptics always go on at great length, everywhere detecting and introducing diversity where they would better see identity. The second trope is that which drives one *to infinity.* Sextus uses this as frequently as it has appeared in more recent times in the form of the tendency to establish by grounds [Begründungstendenz]. It is the familiar idea that for that which grounds a new grounding is demanded, for this again a new one, and so forth ad infinitum. The third trope was already among the first ten, namely, the trope of relation. The fourth trope concerns *presuppositions* [Voraussetzungen]—[and is] against the dogmatists who in order to avoid being driven into an infinite regress posit something as simply first and unproven, and whom the skeptics immediately imitate by positing the opposite of that presupposition without proof with just the same right. The fifth trope is [that of] the *circularity* when what is supposed to serve for the proof of another itself needs for its own proof that which is supposed to be proved through it . . .

One sees both from the repetition of several of the first ten tropes, namely, the partial repetition of what among the five tropes are the first and third, and also from their whole content, that the intention of these five tropes is quite different from the tendency of the first ten and that they alone relate to skepticism's later turn against philosophy. There exist no more effective weapons against the dogmatism of the finite, but they are completely useless against philosophy. Since they contain purely concepts of Reflection, they have a quite opposite significance depending on which of these two different sides they are turned toward: turned against dogmatism they appear under the aspect of belonging to Reason, which puts beside the one part of the necessary antinomy, the part asserted by dogmatism, the other part; turned against philosophy, on the other hand, they appear under the aspect of belonging to Reflection. Against dogmatism, therefore, they must be victorious, but in the face of philosophy they must collapse internally or be themselves dogmatic. Since the essence of dogmatism consists in its positing something finite and afflicted with an opposition—e.g., pure subject or pure object, or in dualism duality in the face of identity—as the absolute, Reason shows of this absolute that it has a relation to what it excludes and exists only through and in this relation to an other and so is not absolute—in accordance with the *third trope* of relation. If this other is supposed to have its ground in the first and the first its ground in the other, then this is a circle and falls under the *fifth* trope, the trope of diallelus. If circularity is to be avoided by having this other as the ground of the first be grounded in itself and making it into an ungrounded presupposition, then since it is something which grounds it has an opposite and this its opposite can be presupposed as something unproven or ungrounded with just the same right, since this time the grounding has been taken into account in accordance with the *fourth trope* of presuppositions. Or if instead this other as ground is supposed to be in turn grounded in an other, then what is here grounded is driven ad infinitum to Reflection's infinity of finite conditions and is again without ground, in accordance with the *second trope*. Finally, that finite absolute of dogmatism ought also to be a universal, but this universality will necessarily fail to be discovered because that finite absolute is something limited, and here belongs the *first* trope of diversity.—Sextus used these tropes, which dogmatism cannot overcome, with great success against dogmatism, especially against physics, a science which like applied mathematics is the true warehouse and trading center [Stapelplatz] of Reflection, limited concepts, and the finite, but which to be sure is regarded by the most recent skeptic as a science which defies all reasonable skepticism. It can on the contrary be said that the older physics was more scientific than the new and therefore less generous in exposing points of vulnerability to skepticism.

Against dogmatism these tropes are rational because they introduce against dogmatism's finite element [das Endliche des Dogmatismus] the opposite from which dogmatism abstracted it and so produce antinomy. Turned against Reason, on the other hand, they retain as their distinctive trait the pure difference by which they are affected; their rational side is already a part of Reason. Concerning the *first trope* of diversity, the Rational is eternally and everywhere like itself; there is pure unlikeness only for the Understanding and everything unlike is posited as one by Reason. To be sure, this unity, like that unlikeness, must not be understood in the, as Plato says, common and puerile fashion that an ox, or what have you, is posited as the one, of which it would be claimed that it was at the same time many oxen. It cannot be shown of the Rational *in accordance with the third* trope that it exists only in relation [Verhältnis], in a necessary relation [Beziehung] to an other, for it itself is nothing other than relation. Because the Rational is relation itself [die Beziehung selbst ist], those elements standing in relation which when posited by the Understanding ought to ground one another no doubt will, but the Rational itself will not, fall into circularity or *under the fifth* trope, the trope of diallelus. For in relation [itself] there is nothing which can be grounded reciprocally by something else. Likewise, the Rational is not un unproven presupposition in accordance with the *fourth* trope, against which the opposite could be presupposed without proof with just the same right. For the Rational has no opposite—

it contains the finite elements, of which one is the opposite of the other, both within itself. The two preceding tropes contain the concept of a ground and a consequence, according to which one other would be grounded by means of another. Since for Reason there is no other standing in opposition to another, both these tropes and the demand for a ground which is made on the assumption of oppositions and reiterated ad infinitum, or the *second* trope which presses toward infinity, fall away—neither the demand nor the infinity is any concern of Reason's.

Since, then, these tropes all contain and depend upon the concept of something finite, it is an immediate consequence of their application to the Rational that they pervert it into something finite, that in order to be able to scratch the Rational they give it the itch of limitation. In and of themselves they do not oppose rational thought, but when they do oppose it, as they do in Sextus's use of them, they immediately alter the Rational. It is possible to understand from this standpoint all the charges leveled by skepticism against the Rational. We saw an example earlier, where skepticism calls into question Reason's cognition from out of itself by turning Reason either into something absolutely subjective or into something absolutely objective and either into a whole or into a part. Both alternatives were first added to Reason by skepticism itself. Thus when skepticism takes the field against Reason one must immediately reject the concepts which it brings with it and cast aside its weapons, which are bad and unsuitable for an attack.

What the newest skepticism always brings with it is, as we saw earlier, the concept *of a thing* which lies *behind* and *under* the appearance-things. When ancient skepticism uses the expressions *hupokeimenon, huparchon, adēlon,* and so forth, it in this way signifies the objectivity avoidance of the expression of which constitutes its own essence. This skepticism for its own part stops at the subjectivity of appearance. But this appearance is not for it a sensuous *thing,* behind which dogmatism and philosophy would claim there to be yet other things, namely, the supersensuous things. Since this skepticism altogether refrains from expressing a certainty and a being, it certainly for its part has no thing, no conditioned something, about which it would have knowledge, and it has no need to read into philosophy either this certain thing or another thing which would lie behind it, in order to discredit philosophy.

Through skepticism's turning against knowledge in general, because it here opposes one thought to another and fights against the "is" of philosophical thought, it is driven to eliminate likewise the "is" of its own thought, and so to keep itself in the pure negativity which is through itself a pure subjectivity. How particular the skeptics were in this regard we saw earlier from the example of the New Academy which claimed that everything was uncertain and that this proposition [Satz] included itself as well. But even this is not skeptical enough for Sextus. He distinguishes the New Academy from skepticism on the ground that just by doing this the New Academy sets up a proposition and dogmatizes. However, this proposition expresses the highest skepticism to such a degree that the distinction proves to be something quite empty. Likewise, it inevitably befell even Pyrrho that someone claimed him to be a dogmatist. Again, it is with this formal illusion of making an assertion that the skeptics are habitually baited, in that the reply is made to them that if they doubt everything yet this "I doubt," "It seems to me," and so forth is certain—or in other words, in that the reality and objectivity of the activity of thought is pointed out to them in reply—when they in each case of positing [Setzen] through thought hold fast to the form of positing and in this way declare each expressed activity to be something dogmatic.

In this extreme of the highest self-consistency, namely, the negativity or subjectivity which no longer limited itself to the subjectivity of character which is at the same time objectivity, but became a subjectivity of knowledge which directed itself against knowledge, skepticism inevitably became inconsistent, for the extreme cannot preserve itself without its opposed opposite [sein Entgegengesetztes]. The pure negativity or subjectivity is therefore either nothing at all, in that it destroys itself in its extreme, or it would have to become at the same time supremely objective. It is the consciousness of this situation which readily suggests itself and which the opponents pressed. Just for this reason, the skeptics declared, as was mentioned earlier, that their *phōnai*—"Everything is false," "Nothing true," "None more than the other"—include themselves and that the skeptic, in expressing these formulas, says only how things appear to him, and thereby expresses his affect, not an opinion or assertion about an objective being. See Sextus, *Outlines of Pyrrhonism*, bk. 1, chap. 7 and elsewhere, especially chap. 24 where Sextus indicates that in connection with what the skeptic says—just as the man who states *peripatō* in reality says "I go"—one must always understand in addition "according to us" or "as far as I am concerned" or "as it seems to me." This purely negative stance which wishes to remain mere subjectivity and appearance ceases precisely thereby to be anything for knowledge. Whoever clings fast to the vanity that it appears so *to him*, that *he* thinks it so [er es so meine], and wants his utterances to be interpreted as no objective assertion of thought [kein Objektives des Denkens] and judgment whatever, such a man must be left to his position. His subjectivity concerns no other person, still less does it concern philosophy or does philosophy concern it at all.

From this consideration of the various sides of ancient skepticism, then, emerges, to encapsulate it briefly, the distinctive character and essence of the newest skepticism.

This newest skepticism lacks, to begin with, skepticism's noblest side, the direction against the dogmatism of the common consciousness which is found in all three of skepticism's variants exhibited above, i.e., whether it is identical with philosophy and only philosophy's negative side, or separated from philosophy but not turned against it, or turned against it. For the newest skepticism the common consciousness with its whole sphere of infinitely numerous facts rather has an undeniable certainty. A rationalizing concerning these fact of consciousness, a reflecting and classifying of them, constitutes for this skepticism the occupation of Reason and gives as the science of this skepticism in part an empirical psychology and in part, through analytical thought applied to the facts, many other sciences exalted beyond all reasonable doubt.

Neither the earlier skepticism, nor any materialism, nor even the commonest human Understanding, unless it be quite animal, has made itself guilty of this barbarism of placing undeniable certainty and truth in the facts of consciousness. This barbarism is quite unheard of in philosophy until the most recent times.

In addition, according to this newest skepticism our physics and astronomy and analytic thought defy any reasonable impulse to doubt, and consequently it lacks also the noble side of the later ancient skepticism, namely, the side which turns against limited cognition, against finite knowledge.

What, then, now remains of skepticism for this newest skepticism which sets its truth and certainty in the crudest limitation of both empirical intuition and the empirical knowledge which turns empirical intuition into Reflection and imagines that it only analyzes it but adds nothing to it? Necessarily nothing but the denial of the truth of Reason and, to this end, the alteration of the Rational into Reflection, the alteration of the cognition of the Absolute into finite cognition. The all-pervasive and basic form of this alteration consists, though, in the fact that the opposite of the first definition of Spinoza discussed earlier, which explains a *causa sui* to be that whose essence at the same time includes existence, is made into a principle and is asserted as an absolute axiom: *what is thought,* because it is something thought, does not at the same time include within it a *being.* This separation of the Rational, in which thought and being are one, into the opposed aspects thought and being, and the absolute holding fast of this opposition, or in other words the Understanding made absolute, constitutes the infinitely repeated and everywhere applied basis of this dogmatic skepticism. This opposition, considered in itself, has the merit that in it difference is expressed in its highest abstraction and in its truest form. The essence of knowledge consists in the identity of the universal and the particular or of what is posited under the forms of thought and of being, and Science is in its content an embodiment of that rational identity and, on its formal side, a constant repetition of it. Non-identity, the principle of the common consciousness and of the opposite of knowledge, expresses itself most emphatically [aufs Bestimmteste] in that form of the opposition. Admittedly though, this form loses a part of its merit again through the fact that it is understood only as the opposition of a thinking subject to an existing object. But if we consider the merit of this opposition in relation to the newest skepticism then it falls away entirely, for the invention of this opposition is in itself anyway older than the newest skepticism. But furthermore this newest skepticism also lacks any merit for introducing this opposition to the culture of more recent times, for as is well known it is the Kantian philosophy which, though to be sure in that limited area in which it is idealism—in its deduction of the categories—it sublates this opposition, otherwise is inconsistent enough to raise this opposition to the highest principle of speculation. The holding fast of this opposition comes up most emphatically and with infinite self-satisfaction against the so-called ontological proof of God's existence and, as the reflecting faculty of judgment, against nature, and particularly in the form of a refutation of the ontological proof this opposition has caused a general and widespread delight. Mr. Schulze has accepted this form as adapted to his purposes and has not only used it in general but has also repeated Kant's words verbatim (see [vol. 1], p. 71 and elsewhere) . . .

This skepticism has for its game absolutely only a single move and only one turn, and even this is not its own, but it has taken it from Kantianism. This character of the newest skepticism will display itself most clearly in what it calls its grounds, and in an example of their application.

This character of the newest skepticism already reveals itself sufficiently in the manner in which it has construed its object, namely, the interest of speculative Reason, that is, as the task of *explaining* the *origin* of human cognitions of things, of spying out for the conditionally existent the unconditionally existent. Here, first of all, things get opposed to cognition within Reason, and second, an explanation of their origin and thereby the causal relation gets imported [into Reason]. Now cognition's ground is an other than cognition's grounded, the former the concept, the latter the thing, and after this fundamentally false picture of rational thought is once presupposed then there remains nothing to do now but to repeat constantly that ground and grounded, concept and thing, are different in kind, that all rational cognition aims—as it is put with words which are likewise Kantian—*to pick out* a being from thought, existence from concepts.

According to this newest skepticism the human faculty of cognition is a thing which has concepts, and because it has nothing more than concepts it cannot go out to the things which are outside it. It cannot *find out about* or *explore* them—for the two things are (vol. 1, p. 69) "different *in kind*. No rational man will imagine that in the *possession* of the *representation* of something he at the same time *possesses* this something itself."

We nowhere see this skepticism being consistent enough to show that no reasonable man would imagine himself to be in *possession of a representation* of something either. Since of course the representation is a something as well, a reasonable man can imagine himself to possess only the representation of the representation, not the representation itself, and again not the representation of the representation either, since this representation to the second power is a something too, but only the representation of the representation of the representation, and so on ad infinitum. Or since the situation is here so represented that there are two different pockets, of which one is the something which contains representations, and the other the something which contains things,[13] one cannot see why the former should remain the full one and the latter the eternally empty one.

The reason why the former *is* full, and why we only imagine the latter to be full, could only be that the former is the shirt of the subject, the latter his jacket, that the representation-pocket lies closer to him, but the thing-pocket further away from him. But in this way the proof would be conducted by means of a presupposition of what should be proved. For the question precisely concerns the advantage in reality between the subjective and the objective.

What is said concerning the undeniable certainty of the facts of consciousness indeed accords ill with this skeptical fundamental position [Grundwesen], that one should only reflect that the representation is not the thing which is represented, and not that both are identical. For according to Mr. Schulze (vol. 1, p. 68), "the representations are true, real, and constitute a cognition to the extent

---

13. Reading: *welche Dinge enthalte [sei]*.

that they *completely agree* with that to which they refer and which is represented through them, or *present nothing other to consciousness than what exists in what is represented*," and (p. 70) "in *daily* life we constantly presuppose such an *agreement* as certain without concerning ourselves in the slightest about its possibility" as the new metaphysics does.—So on what else then does Mr. Schulze base the undeniable certainty of the facts of consciousness but the absolute identity of thought and being, concept and thing—he who then again in the same breath declares the subjective, the representation, and the objective, the thing, to be different in kind? In daily life, says Mr. Schulze, we pre*suppose* that identity; that it is *presupposed* in daily life means that it is not present in the common consciousness. *The new metaphysics attempts to ground the possibility of this identity*—but there is of course not a word of truth in the claim that the new philosophy attempts to ground the possibility of the identity *presupposed* in common life, for it does nothing but express and recognize that presupposed identity. Precisely because in daily life that identity is a presupposed one, the common consciousness always posits the object as something different from the subject, and again the objective among itself and the subjective likewise as an infinite manifoldness of matters absolutely different from one another. Metaphysics brings this identity which is for the common consciousness only presupposed and unconscious to consciousness, it is metaphysics' absolute and sole principle.

Lectures on the History of Philosophy—Two Extracts

(1) The skeptics themselves (Sextus) distinguish among these forms [i.e., the tropes] older and newer ones: ten in number which belong to the older skeptics, and five (or seven) which belong to the newer. It will become clear from their statements that those older forms are directed against the common consciousness in general and belong to a thought of little culture, to a consciousness which begins with the sensuously existent before it. They attack what we call the common belief in the immediate truth of things and refute this truth in an equally immediate manner, not through the concept but through the opposed being. They exhibit this lack of concept in their enumeration as well. The five later forms, though, are of more interest. They make attack against Reflection, aiming at a consciousness which relates to the developed Understanding [den ausgebildeten Verstand], against scientific categories—against the intellectualization of the sensuous [das Gedachtsein des Sinnlichen], against the determination of the sensuous through concepts. For example, the former forms attack an *is*—"This *is* a rectangular thing"; the latter attack "This thing is *one*." Now, even if the majority of the former forms may appear to us quite trivial, still we must certainly put up with them, for they are historically conditioned [geschichtlich] and so essentially directed against the form "it is." But it is without doubt a high form of abstract consciousness that takes for its object this abstract form "it is" and combats it. These tropes appear very trivial and common, but still more trivial and common is the reality of so-called external objects, the immediate knowledge "Blue exists, this is yellow." One should not be at all willing to call it philosophizing when such a claim is asserted in a spirit of curiosity. Skepticism was by nature far removed [wesentlich davon entfernt] from considering the things of immediate certainty to

be true. In more recent times Schulze in Göttingen has forced himself on people's attention with his skepticism. He has even written an *Aenesidemus* and in other works as well has expounded skepticism in opposition to Leibniz and Kant. In this modern skepticism it is assumed that what is in our immediate consciousness, everything sensuous, is something true. The skeptics accepted that one must guide oneself by this, but it did not occur to them to present it as something true. The newer skepticism is directed only against thoughts, Concept, and Idea, i.e., against the higher subject matter of philosophy. It thus leaves the reality of things standing in place quite undoubted and claims only that nothing can be inferred from this for thought. However, that is not even a peasant's philosophy, for [even] peasants know that all earthly things are transitory, and therefore that they just as much are as they are not. In contrast, the ancient skepticism which we are now considering takes its aim precisely against the reality of things.

(2) So Arcesilaus ... draws the same famous distinction which has again appeared with such an air of importance [mit so großer Wichtigkeit] in more recent times as the opposition between thought and being, ideality and reality, the subjective and the objective. The things are something different from myself. How can I reach the things? Thought is the self-active determination of a content qua a universal, but a given content is something particular, one cannot assent to such a thing. The one is here, the other beyond—the subjective and the objective, which cannot reach each other. The whole culture of modern philosophy has revolved around this point for some time. It is important to be conscious of this distinction and to bring this consciousness to bear against the principle of the Stoics. It was concerning this unity of thought and reality that the Stoics ought to have justified themselves—something which they did not do, and which quite generally failed to happen in antiquity. For the Stoics did not show that the subjectivity of thought and the objective in their difference essentially have it as their nature to pass into one another, to posit themselves as identical.

Appendix VII: *On the Nature of Philosophical Critique* (1802)—Extract

[This essay from 1802 is particularly interesting in connection with the *Phenomenology*'s epistemological side, for two main reasons. First, the method of philosophical critique which is sketched here, and actually executed in such roughly contemporary essays as *Faith and Knowledge*, namely, a method of, in effect, assuming the truth of Hegelian philosophy and then seeking to interpret competing viewpoints as anticipations of this true philosophy as a means to their and its assessment, is explicitly criticized and rejected as an epistemological approach by the *Phenomenology*. This is the force of the remark in the *Phenomenology*'s Introduction: "Still less can Science appeal to whatever intimations of something better it may detect in the cognition that is without truth, to signs which point in the direction of Science. For one thing, it would only be appealing again to what merely *is;* and for another, it would only be appealing to itself, and to itself in the mode in which it exists in the cognition that is without truth" (par. 76). Second, and more importantly, this essay sketches in addition to the method of philosophical critique a supplementary technique for dealing with any residual skeptical "equipollence" problems arising from viewpoints which appear to remain in confrontation with Hegelian philosophy, namely, a technique of discrediting these apparently competing viewpoints by showing them to be "nothing." At the time of this essay, the discipline in which Hegel envisaged accomplishing this was his early Logic. Later on, when the *Phenomenology* superseded the early Logic, it inherited this task. These matters are discussed in more detail in chapter 3.—Text translated from Hegel, *Jenaer Schriften* (Frankfurt am Main: Suhrkamp, 1977).]

Critique, in whichever area of art or science it is practised, demands a standard which, equally independent of the person judging and of what he judges, is derived not from the individual appearance or the distinctive particularity of the subject, but from the eternal and immutable original model [Urbild] of the matter itself [der Sache selbst]. Just as the idea of fine art is not first created or invented by art criticism but is simply presupposed by it, similarly in philosophical critique the idea of philosophy is itself the condition and presupposition without which critique would for all eternity have to set forth only subjectivities against subjectivities, never the Absolute against the conditioned [das Bedingte].

Philosophical critique differs from art criticism not through its judgment of the capacity for objectivity which finds expression in a work, but only through the object or the idea itself which underlies this capacity and which can be none other than the idea of philosophy itself. Therefore, since in regard to its judgment of the capacity for objectivity philosophical critique has claims to universal validity equal to those of art criticism, anyone who nevertheless wished to deny philosophical critique objectivity of judgment would have to assert not the possibility merely of different forms of one and the same idea, but the possibility of essentially different and nevertheless equally true philosophies—a thought which, however consoling it may be, is not in fact worthy of any consideration. That philosophy is and can only be *one* rests on the fact that Reason is only *one*. And no more than there can be different Reasons can there arise a wall between Reason and its self-cognition [Selbsterkennen] through which this self-cognition could become an essential diversity of appearance. For Reason, considered absolutely, and insofar as it becomes its own object in self-cognition, i.e., becomes philosophy, is again just one and the same and hence completely identical.

Thus the basis of a diversity in philosophy itself cannot lie in its own essence, which is simply *one,* and also not in the inequality of the capacity to form the idea of philosophy objectively, since considered philosophically the idea itself is everything, but the capacity to represent the idea, which is additional to the possession of it, only gives philosophy another side not essentially its own. For this reason one could only generate a potential for infinitely many and diverse reflections [Reflexe], each of which, posited as essentially different from the others, would have an equal right to maintain itself against the others, by—while understanding philosophy to be a cognition of the Absolute—thinking of this Absolute, whether it be conceived as God or in some other way as nature, as in immovable and absolute opposition to cognition qua something subjective.

But even given this view, the diversity would have to sublate [aufheben] and reform itself. For in being imagined to be something formal, cognition is thought of as completely passive in its relation to the object, and it will be demanded of the subject who is supposed to be capable of this reception of God or of the pure objective intuition of nature that he quite generally close himself off against any other relation to any limitation and refrain from any activity of his own, since this would cloud the purity of the reception. Through this passivity of the reception and the sameness of the object, that which is envisaged as the result, the cognition of the Absolute, and a philosophy proceeding therefrom would certainly once again have to be just one and everywhere the same.

Critique is only possible as objective judgment because the truth of Reason, like beauty, is only *one,* and it is an immediate consequence of this that critique only has sense for those in whom the idea of the one and selfsame philosophy is present, and likewise can only concern those works in which this idea can be recognized as more or less clearly articulated. The business of critique is completely lost on such people and works as should lack that idea. This lack of the idea is what causes critique the greatest difficulty, for if all critique is subsumption under the idea then all critique necessarily comes to an end where this idea is absent, and the only immediate stance that critique can adopt is that of dismissal [Verwerfung]. In this dismissal, however, critique completely breaks off any relation between that in which the idea of philosophy is lacking and that in whose service critique stands. Because reciprocal recognition is hereby eliminated, there appear just two subjectivities opposed to one another. Positions which have nothing in common come forth for just that reason with equal right, and critique, because it has declared the position subject to judgment to be anything but philosophy and thereby—since this position aims, on the other contrary, to be nothing but philosophy—to be nothing at all, has put itself into the position of something subjective and its verdict appears as a one-sided assertion of authority [Machtspruch]—a position which, since critique's action is supposed to be objective, immediately contradicts critique's essence. Critique's judgment is an appeal to the idea of philosophy, which idea, however, because it is not recognized by the adversary, is for the adversary an alien court of appeal. To oppose this relation involved in critique, which separates off unphilosophy [Unphilosophie] from philosophy, by standing on one side and having unphilosophy on the opposite side is obviously no solution. Because unphilosophy stands in a negative relation to philosophy so that there can be no question of philosophy [here], the only thing that can be done is to recount how this negative side expresses itself and confesses its nothingness—which, insofar as it has an appearance, is sheer banality. And since it cannot fail to happen that what is nothing in the beginning appears in its development ever more and more as nothing, so that it can be pretty universally recognized as such, critique again reconciles through this construction which proceeds from the first nullity even the incompetence which could see nothing but high-handedness [Eigenmächtigkeit] and arbitrariness in the initial verdict.

Where, on the other hand, the idea of philosophy is really present, it is the job of critique to make clear the manner and the degree in which this idea is freely and clearly manifested, and also the extent to which it has developed itself into a scientific system of philosophy.

Appendix VIII: Philosophy of Spirit (1803–4)—Extract

[This extract from Hegel's Philosophy of Spirit of 1803–4 contains an early expression of his theses that thought is essentially linguistic and language essentially communal. It is especially helpful, consequently, for recognizing and understanding metaphysical tasks (8) and (9) of the *Phenomenology,* the tasks of demonstrating the essential communality of linguistic meanings or concepts, and of establishing a community-wide Hegelian usage of linguistic terms in order to constitute the concepts of Hegelian Science. It also, for the same reason, helps to throw light on the argument of the *Sense-certainty* section of the *Phenomenology.* For more detailed discussion of these matters, see chapter 4.—Text translated from Hegel, *Jenenser Realphilosophie* (Leipzig: Felix Meiner, 1931–32), vol. 1.]

The preceding powers are in general ideal, they are first existent in a people. *Language* [Sprache] *only exists as the language of a people, and Understanding and Reason,* likewise. Only as the work of a people is language the ideal existence of the Spirit, in which Spirit expresses itself [sich ausspricht], [saying] what it is in its essence and in its being. Language is something universal [ein Allgemeines], something acknowledged in itself, something resounding in the same way in the consciousness of all; every speaking consciousness [jedes sprechende Bewußtsein] immediately comes to be another consciousness in it. In respect of its content too, language for the first time comes to be true language, to express what each person means [meint], in a people. Barbarians do not know how to say what they mean; they only half say it, or say the exact opposite of what they want to say. Only in a people is that present—already *posited* as *sublated,* present as *ideal, universal consciousness*—which memory, the becoming of language, to begin with just makes ideal. Language is, of its essence, present for itself, nature posited as ideal, and it is so to speak mere form. It is a mere *speaking* [Sprechen], an outward expression [Äußerlichkeit]. It is not a producing but the mere form of making outward [Äußerlichmachens] what is already produced, as it must be spoken [wie es gesprochen werden muß].

The cultural development of the world for speaking [zum Sprechen] is present in itself. Like the becoming of the Understanding and of Reason it falls within education. The world is present for the consciousness which is coming to be *as an ideal world,* as consciousness's inorganic nature, and consciousness must not tear itself away from nature in this way but must *find the reality for nature's ideality,* must seek for language that meaning which lies in being. This being likewise exists for consciousness. There remains, so to speak, only the formal activity of the relating of the two, which are already present, to each other.

Hence language gets reconstructed in a people in this way: as the ideal destruction of what is outward it is itself *something outward* which must be destroyed, sublated in order to become meaningful language, or in order to become what it is in itself or is according to its concept. Hence it exists in the people as something totally other than itself and becomes a totality by being sublated as something outward and becoming its own concept.

Appendix IX: Aphorism, "Science . . ." (1805–6?)

[This aphorism from the later Jena period is particularly important as evidence of Hegel's commitment at that time to what has been called in this book an "enduring communal consensus theory of truth." As was shown in chapter 4, the establishment of such a theory of truth constitutes a central task of the *Phenomenology,* metaphysical task (10), and such a theory of truth also underpins the work's metaphysical task (11), the task of establishing an enduring communal consensus in favor of Hegelian Science in order to make Hegelian Science true. I have tentatively dated this aphorism to 1805–6, primarily on the ground of its prediction of the imminent demise of Schelling's philosophy.—Text translated from K. Rosenkranz, *Georg Wilhelm Friedrich Hegels Leben* (Darmstadt: Wissenschaftliche Buchgesellschaft, 1977).]

Science. Whether the individual possesses it is something he can make assurances to himself and others about. Whether that is true is something which his immediate context decides, his contemporaries [die Mitwelt] and then posterity [die Nachwelt] after his contemporaries have already indicated their approval. However, consciousness has advanced so far in culture [Bildung], the barbaric viscosity of comprehension has become so much more fluid and rapid, that it only takes a few years to bring about posterity already. Kantian philosophy was condemned to death a long time ago, while Wolffian philosophy lasted fifty years or more. The fateful determination [Bestimmen] of its standpoint sped close more quickly for Fichte's philosophy. What Schelling's philosophy is in its essence the near future will reveal. The court which is to pass judgment on it stands at the door, so to speak, for many people understand it already. Yet these philosophies succumbed less to proof than to the empirical experience of how far one can proceed with them. Their devotees develop them blindly, but the fabric becomes ever thinner until finally the devotees find themselves startled by its cobweb-like transparency. It has melted like ice for them and run through their fingers like mercury without them knowing how this happened to them. They simply have it no longer and anyone who looks into the hand with which they purveyed their wisdom sees only the empty hand and leaves with derision. While the former, sensitive of the cold, still advertise that this wisdom is something, the latter imagine that they have got to the bottom of the matter, for they see only its nothingness, not what it was. Both sides are mistaken. Meanwhile the truth is that it is this disappeared thing itself that has brought them to this position. The words of scripture are fulfilled: when we are silent, the stones cry out.

Appendix X: Lecture Fragment, "The Absolute . ." (1806)

[This lecture fragment comes from Hegel's 1806 lectures on Phenomenology of Spirit and Logic. The first part of the fragment is of interest, among other reasons, because it helps to throw light on the metaphysical tasks of the *Phenomenology*—concerning which see chapter 4 above. The second part, Hegel's comment at the conclusion of the lectures, is closely connected with his reflections at *Phenomenology,* paragraphs 11–13 on his thought's relation to its immediate sociopolitical context—concerning which see chapter 12 above.—Text translated from K. Rosenkranz, *Georg Wilhelm Friedrich Hegels Leben* (Darmstadt: Wissenschaftliche Buchgesellschaft, 1977).]

The Absolute is itself the element of this consciousness. Hence, in this consciousness the concepts are neither empty abstractions and thoughts in self-movement beyond being, for they have filled themselves with the actual consciousness; nor are they alien essentialities and an objective in-itself or a being that is non-conceptual, for actuality has revealed itself to this consciousness as this consciousness's own Spirit. On account of this certainty of itself in being, or because self-consciousness has formed [gebildet] itself into the element and substance of Science, *a special reflection of self-consciousness into itself is not necessary.* Such a reflection would mean that self-consciousness did not immediately possess itself in the Concept but had first to make a point of recalling [erinnern] the Concept and producing itself within the Concept, as is for example the case with representation [Vorstellung] when self-consciousness recalls some "this" as its representation. Self-consciousness therefore freely entrusts itself to the nature and necessity of the Concept, certain of its own immediate presence therein, conscious that it does not stand under an alien power, and therefore confident of not being kidnapped by the Concept and losing itself in an unfamiliar land.

Self-consciousness therefore also need not give the Concept the form of self-consciousness immediately, calling it *I* for example, and reminding itself constantly of itself in the object of its knowing [seines Wissens]. The nature of the Concept would thereby receive the distorted appearance and the false meaning of only belonging to self-consciousness to the extent that self-consciousness stands opposed to the objective mode, and the Concept would thereby at the same time lose the immediate significance of being and universality. But for knowing, as the unity of the universal and the individual self-consciousness, just this its element and essence is itself the object and content of its Science and must therefore be expressed in an objective mode. Hence this object and content is *being.* In being, as the simple absolute Concept, knowing knows itself immediately as self-consciousness, so that it does not even occur to knowing that it might have expressed in this being something opposed to self-consciousness and that it might be entering into a conflict with it which would decide for the first time whether knowing or this being was the loser—nor does it even occur to it that it might through the recognition of this being give rise to a misunderstanding or perhaps even a danger for its own independence. Knowing has in its truth the certainty of itself and hence it is with confidence of this certainty that it observes the free self-movement in which being, which appears *immediate,* develops its essence, which is to be Spirit, and presents itself as what it is in itself. To the extent that self-consciousness mixes and threads itself as such into the movement of the object which it has in Science, it is at a level where it has not yet grasped either itself or its object as Spirit, and has not yet attained that peace in relation to its object which it has only achieved once it can bear the object's freedom and independence because it is knowing Spirit.

If, then, the consciousness that comes to Science for the first time takes exception to what turns out to be Science's content—being, non-being, unity, etc.— as though these essential forms of the content were empty and without substance, as though these terms referred to alien essences of no concern to this living self-consciousness, then the consciousness that has been educated through Science and has returned to it from experience of the world distinguishes itself from this view by being *knowing.* That is to say: it possesses in those abstractions the meaning of their universality and they are not abstract moments for it in the sense of being removed from reality and conducting their business far away from reality, but in the sense that they are universal essences in which reality in being sublated [aufgehoben] is just as much preserved; and furthermore it comprehends [begreift] these essences, their course of development, and their totality, or possesses its own self in them immediately and is at home in them . . .

This, my gentlemen, is Speculative Philosophy, to the extent that I have advanced in developing it. Consider it a beginning of philosophizing which you are to continue further. We find ourselves in an important epoch, a fermentation, in which Spirit has made a move, has developed beyond its preceding shape, and wins a new shape. The whole mass of previous representations, concepts, the bonds of the world, are dissolved and collapse inwardly like a dream image. A new progression of Spirit is in the making. Philosophy primarily has the task of greeting its appearance and acknowledging it, while others, resisting it powerlessly, stick to what is past, and most constitute unconsciously the substance of its appearance. But philosophy must recognize it as the eternal and render it its due honor. Commending myself to your kind memories, I wish you pleasant holidays.

Appendix XI: A Sheet on the *Phenomenology* (1805)

[This sheet from an early draft of the *Phenomenology*, dated to early summer of 1805 or thereabouts, is important in connection with the question of an Ur-*Phenomenology* discussed in part 4.—Text translated from *Dokumente zu Hegels Entwicklung*, ed. J. Hoffmeister (Stuttgart: Fr. Frommanns Verlag, 1936).]

Thus Absolute Knowing [Das Absolute Wissen] first emerges as Lawgiving Reason [gesetzgebende Vernunft]. In the concept of the ethical substance itself there is no distinction of consciousness from being-in-itself [des Ansichseins], for the pure thought of pure thought [das reine Denken des reinen Denkens] is in itself or is self-identical substance and equally it is consciousness. But with the emergence of a determinacy in this substance—and it turns out that the first determinacy is that laws are given—the distinction between consciousness and the in-itself appears as well. This in-itself, however, is the ethical substance itself or the absolute consciousness.

a) Divine right of consciousness; as ethical essence an immediate relation to duty; actuality is no reality in itself [die Wirklichkeit ist keine Realität an sich]; it is only ethical reality; ambiguity of actuality, the devil's deception, inward essence.

b) Diremption present: departed Spirit and [Text breaks off.]

Appendix XII: Letters to Niethammer and Schelling (1807)—Extracts

[These two extracts from letters which Hegel wrote in 1807 shortly after completing the *Phenomenology* already contain some interesting criticisms by him of the work.—Texts translated from *Briefe von und an Hegel*, ed. J. Hoffmeister (Hamburg: Felix Meiner, 1969), vol. 1.]

[To Niethammer, January 1807.] Soon, but not yet, I can wish the child [i.e., the *Phenomenology*] a happy trip. During the final read-through for printer's errors I admittedly often had the wish that I might yet clear the ship here and there of ballast and make it swifter. With a second edition to follow soon—if it please the gods?!—everything should be improved, that is my consolation to myself and to others.

[To Schelling, May 1807.] My work [i.e., the *Phenomenology*] is finally finished; but in the distribution of copies to my friends there arises again the same wretched confusion which governed the whole book-selling and printing process, and which in part governed also the composition itself. This is why you still have no copy from me in your hands, but I hope that I will eventually manage to get to the point that you do actually receive one soon. I am curious to know what you will say about the idea of this first part, which is actually the introduction—for I have not yet got beyond the introducing stage into the heart of the matter. The work on the details has, I think, harmed the overview of the whole. This, though, is itself by its very nature such an intertwining back-and-forth that even if it were better articulated it would cost me much time to make it clearer and more finished. Needless to say, in addition individual parts would still require diverse work on the details in order to get the better of them. You will find this to be only too true for yourself. Concerning the major deformity of the later parts, may your leniency attribute this also to the fact that I actually finished the work in the middle of the night before the Battle of Jena. In the preface you will not find that I have been too rough on the insipidness which engages in so much nonsense particularly with your formulas and degrades your Science into a barren formalism. In addition, I need not tell you that if you give your approval to a few pages of the whole this will mean more to me than if others are satisfied or unsatisfied with the whole—just as I know of no one by whom I could rather wish this work to be introduced to the public and a judgment to be passed on it for myself.

Appendix XIII: Hegel's Announcement of the *Phenomenology* (1807)

[This is Hegel's own Announcement of the *Phenomenology* from the year of its publication, in which he describes the work and its relation to his whole system.—Text translated from Hegel, *Phänomenologie des Geistes* (Frankfurt am Main: Suhrkamp, 1980).]

G.W.F. Hegel's *System of Science,* volume one, containing *The Phenomenology of Spirit,* has been published by the press of the bookstores of Josef Anton Goebhardt at Bamberg and Würzburg and distributed to all good bookstores.

This first volume represents *knowledge in its becoming.* The Phenomenology of Spirit should replace psychological explanations and more abstract discussions concerning the grounding of knowledge. It considers the *preparation* for Science from a standpoint which makes it a new, interesting science and the first science in philosophy. It contains within itself the various *shapes of Spirit* as stations along the path by which Spirit becomes pure knowledge or absolute Spirit. Therefore, Consciousness, Self-consciousness, observing and acting Reason, and Spirit itself in the forms of ethical, cultured, and moral Spirit, and finally as religious Spirit in its various forms are considered in the main divisions of this science, which in turn divide up into several further ones. The wealth of appearances of Spirit which seems at first sight to be chaotic is brought into a scientific order which represents them in accordance with their necessity, by which those that are incomplete dissolve themselves and pass into higher ones which are their immediate truth. The final truth they find first of all in Religion and then in Science as the result of the whole.

In the preface the author explains his views concerning what seem to him to be the needs of philosophy at its present standpoint, and in addition concerning the presumption and nonsense of philosophical formulas which currently injures the dignity of philosophy, and generally concerning what is essential in philosophy and its study.

A *second volume* will contain the system comprising *Logic,* as Speculative Philosophy, and the two remaining parts of philosophy, the *Sciences* of *Nature* and of *Spirit.*

Appendix XIV: *Logic* (1808 ff.) (Plus Related Materials)

[The main text translated here is the version of the later Logic from the 1808 ff. *Encyclopaedia.* In chapter 15 this was shown to be the version of the later Logic which underlies the *Phenomenology.* In addition, I have appended the version of the final part of the later Logic, the Doctrine of the Idea, which is found in the slightly later *Doctrine of the Concept* of 1809–10, since this version is significantly more detailed than that in the 1808 ff. *Encyclopaedia.*—Texts translated from Hegel, *Nürnberger und Heidelberger Schriften* (Frankfurt am Main: Suhrkamp, 1979).]

Logic (1808 ff.)

Par. 12

Logic is the science of the pure Understanding and of pure Reason, of their characteristic determinations and laws. The logical accordingly has three sides: 1. the abstract side or the side belonging to the Understanding, 2. the dialectical or negatively rational side, 3. the speculative or positively rational side. What *belongs to the Understanding* remains at the level of concepts in their fixed determinacy and distinction from other concepts. What is *dialectical* exhibits them in their transition and dissolution. What is *speculative* or *rational* grasps their unity in their opposition or the positive in the dissolution and transition.

Par. 13

The Understanding and Reason are usually in Logic understood in the subjective sense of belonging as thought to a self-consciousness, and Logic is consequently a merely *formal* science, which first needs another content, an external matter, if something really true is to come about.

Par. 14

As its content Logic considers the Understanding and Reason in and for themselves and the absolute concepts as the in and for itself true ground of everything, or in other words the content of the Understanding and of Reason to the extent that it is not merely a conceptualization in consciousness. The Logic is therefore in itself Speculative Philosophy, for the speculative manner of considering things is nothing but the consideration of that essence of things which is just as much the pure concept belonging to Reason as it is the nature and law of things.

Par. 15
Logic divides into three parts: 1. into *Ontological* Logic, 2. into *Subjective* Logic, 3. into the *Doctrine of the Idea*. The first of these is the system of the pure concepts of the existent [des Seienden], the second is the system of the pure concepts of the universal, the third contains the Concept [den Begriff] of Science.

FIRST PART—Ontological Logic
I. Being [Sein]
A. Quality
a. Being

Par. 16
1. The beginning of Science is the immediate, indeterminate concept of *being*. 2. This concept is, in its lack of content, equivalent to *nothing* [das Nichts]. Nothing, as a thought of that emptiness, is therefore, conversely, itself a being and because of its purity the same as being is. 3. So there is no distinction between the two, but what is is thereby only the positing of them as distinguished and the vanishing of each in its opposite, or it is pure *becoming* [Werden].

b. Determinate Being [Dasein]

Par. 17
But because in becoming those previously posited [concepts] only vanish, becoming is their coincidence and collapse [ihr Zusammenfallen] into a still simplicity in which they are not nothing but also no longer each exist independently [für sich] but rather as sublated factors [als aufgehobene] or moments. This unity is *determinate being*.

Par. 18
Determinate being is 1. a being in whose concept also lies its non-being as relation to another, or *being-for-another*; 2. but in accordance with its moment of being it has the side of being not relation to another, but *in itself*. As the concept which combines these two determinations within itself, it is reality [Realität].

Par. 19
The *real* [das Reelle] or the *something* [Etwas] is in its difference [als verschieden] from another real initially indifferent [gleichgültig] toward it, in that in its otherness it is at the same time in itself. The difference from another real lies initially in the boundary [Grenze], as the middle between them in which they just as much are as are not.

Par. 20
They are 1. different from the boundary or from their difference, which is their middle outside which they are something. But 2. the boundary belongs to them themselves, because it is *their boundary*.

Par. 21
The difference is therefore 1. the real's own difference or its *determinacy* [Bestimmtheit]. But this determinacy which exists in itself [Diese an sich seiende Be-

stimmtheit] is also 2. external determinate being or *constitution* [Beschaffenheit]. The determinacy which is both something external and something internal constitutes *quality*.

c. Change [Veränderung]

Par. 22
Constitution or external determinate being both belongs to the something and is alien to it or is its otherness, and so its non-being. It is therefore the something's inequality with itself, through which *change* is posited.

Par. 23
In that change is the negation of the negative which the something has in it, *being-for-self* [das Fürsichsein] has arisen. Or determinacy, as the internal difference which the something has in itself, is the relation of the something, in its distinction, only to itself, or the something is for itself.

B. Quantity
a. Being-for-self (Ideality)

Par. 24
Being-for-self is 1. distinction, but only from self, or relation not to another but to self. 2. But to the extent that distinction contains otherness in itself and the relation to it is negative, another is *for* it, but qua excluded.

Par. 25
What has being-for-self is numerical *one* [das numerische Eins]. It is simple, related only to itself, and the other is excluded from it. Its otherness is *manyness* [Vielheit].

Par. 26
The many [die Vielen] are each identical. They are therefore one. But the one is no less manyness. For its exclusion is the positing of its opposite, or it thereby posits itself as manyness. The former process of becoming is *attraction*, the latter *repulsion*.

Par. 27
In that each process of becoming is posited just as much as the other, their truth is the rest [die Ruhe] which is just as much the being-outside-itself of the one or its positing of itself as manyness, *discreteness*, as it is the self-equal relation of the many, or their *continuity*: pure *quantity*.

b. Quantum

Par. 28
Quantity has in itself the negativity of the one only as a sublated negativity, or because in the self-equality of being-for-self otherness is immediately nothing other than an external boundary, or a boundary which is no boundary. Quantity with this indifferent boundary is *quantum*.

Par. 29
Quantum is *extensive quantum* to the extent that the boundary is related to the moment of the manyness of quantity, or *intensive quantum* to the extent that it is related to the moment of self-equality or exists in the determination of self-equality.

Par. 30
Since negativity exists in quantum as the indifferent boundary, being-for-self or absolute determination is a *beyond* for quantum. It is possible to go beyond each quantum and posit another boundary which is likewise no immanent boundary. In this way there arises the *progress ad infinitum* or the *bad infinity*.

Par. 31
But the absolute determination which was posited as a beyond is qua being-for-self one of quantity's own moments. Or the boundary which is none is nothing other than the otherness which is sublated within being-for-self. It is the determinacy whose positing is self-determination: *qualitative magnitude*.

C. Infinity

Par. 32
Qualitative magnitude is to begin with, as simple determination, *specific* magnitude, but as self-differentiating self-determination a specification of magnitudes which are at the same time determinate magnitudes in contrast to one another and have a qualitative relation to one another, or whose quotient is their relations' number [ihre Verhältniszahl] and is a quotient of items whose reciprocal relations are qualitative. Since the magnitudes are here not only sublated qua finite magnitudes, but their sublatedness is itself even posited as their qualitative law, this is their true and present infinity.

II. Essence
A. Concept of Essence

Par. 33
The simple interpenetration of quantitative or external determination and of inner self-determination is essence. As the interpenetration of self-determination and of indifferent determinacy essence has in itself the moments of *essentiality* and *inessentiality*. The essential is what belongs to self-determination, but the inessential is the moment of indifferent determinate being.

Par. 34
Becoming, as the becoming of essence, is to begin with action [das Tun], a transition of essence into the freedom of determinate being, which transition is however a remaining-within-self [ein Insichbleiben].

Par. 35
To the extent that action is an internal distinguishing of essence from itself [ein Unterschied des Wesens von sich selbst] and determinate being or determinacy is produced by it, action is positing [Setzen].

B. Proposition [Satz]

Par. 36
The proposition contains the moments of remaining-within-self or self-equality and of pure distinguishing. The former would be the pure *matter*, the latter the pure *form*. But the pure form is the action which remains within itself and so the same self-equality which was called pure matter, just as the latter, conversely, is distinctionless externality to one another [das unterschiedslose Außereinander] and is not distinguished [nicht unterschieden ist] from pure form.

Par. 37
But distinction must equally be posited, and the unity of form and self-equality stands in opposition to being-within-self [das Insichsein], or what in the form of external determinate being is usually called *matter*. To the extent that this matter exists in the form of inner being, it is *content* [Inhalt], but the form is each of these determinations of difference.

Par. 38
a) The simple proposition is the *proposition of identity*, $a = a$. It is indifferent toward its matter. Its content [Inhalt] has no determination, or it has no substance [Gehalt], and the form is therefore distinctionless self-equality.

Par. 39
b) The *proposition of indifferent difference* [der gleichgültigen Verschiedenheit] posits indeterminate distinction in general and states that there are no two things which are completely like each other.

Par. 40
c) The *proposition of opposition* [Satz der Entgegensetzung] reads: a is either b or -b, *positivity* and *negativity*. Of opposed predicates things have only one, and there is no third between them.

Par. 41
d) The *proposition of* [causal] *ground* [Satz des Grundes] expresses the return of what has been posited [des Gesetzten] into itself or it expresses positing [das Setzen] itself as the third in which the opposed determinations [die entgegengesetzten Bestimmungen] are sublated and which, as the simple, is the determination opposed to what is grounded [dem Begründeten] qua manifold determinate being.

C. Ground and Grounded
1. Whole and Parts

Par. 42
Essence as the ground of its determinate being, without which essence itself does not exist, is to begin with *whole* and *parts*. The whole is the positing of its parts and, conversely, consists in them. Both sides constitute one and the same thing [machen ein und dasselbe aus]. The whole is equal to the parts only qua the parts together, i.e., qua the whole, and the parts are equal to the whole qua parted

whole [als Geteiltem], i.e., qua parts. Or both sides are indifferent toward each other and the activity of the whole as the form has the matter as its condition.

2. Force and its Expression [Kraft und ihre Äußerung]

Par. 43
The parts are, however, only parts qua posited through the whole. This their relation is their determinedness [Bestimmtheit] through the unity of the ground. Or the quality of determinate being is posited through the activity of the ground, as form, and the matter of appearance is ground's own content. Ground is therefore *force* which expresses itself.

Par. 44
Force is the self-positing of its determinate being qua determinate quality. In the respect that determinate being is still being-for-another or externality, force is at the same time free of determinate being and does not come to an end through the fact that this its appearance vanishes. In this respect force to be sure no longer has as its condition the matter which is force's content and to which force immanently belongs, but force still has as its condition an activity which solicits it.

Par. 45
The soliciting activity is itself force and in order to be something solicited must become solicited [by something]. In that the relation of both activities to each other is this reciprocal exchange of their determinations, each is the ground of the activity or the expression of the other. Thus the concept has arisen of the ground which is the ground of its own activity and of the other activity which stimulates its own activity.

3. Inner and Outer

Par. 46
Essence is the ground of its determinate being qua self-stimulating activity, and there is in its determinate being nothing alien or nothing but what is posited through the ground itself. Essence and its determinate being [Dasein] are therefore the same. Essence relates as inner to itself as outer, the latter being only the presentation [Darstellung] of the inner.

Par. 47
Ground is qua this relation the unconditioned, the inner, the unity of matter as self-equality at rest and of form as unity of opposition. It presents itself in its determinate being as matter whose forces are at rest in it and as the opposition and play of the forces which stimulate and act against one another. Essence has hereby become *actuality* [Wirklichkeit].

III. Actuality

Par. 48
Actuality is independent relation. It has the moments both of its appearance or its determinate being, which is relation to itself, and of its possibility, as the being-

Appendix XIV

in-itself or essence of its determinate being. The actual is itself the unity of its possibility and its determinate being.

1. Substance [Substanz]

Par. 49
The actual is *substance*. It is essence which contains the determinations of its determinate being [die Bestimmungen seines Daseins] as simple attributes and laws within itself and posits the same as a determinately existent play [als daseienendes Spiel] or as its own accidents, whose sublation is not a vanishing of substance but its return into itself.

Par. 50
Substance is the necessity of its accidents. In their free determinate being these accidents have the relation of their nature to an other as a relation which is inner and hidden in them and they seem to lose their independence through external contingency and an alien power. However, this is in truth only the reestablishment of the whole taking back into itself again the separating-off [Absonderung] which has taken place in them.

2. Cause

Par. 51
Substance enters into the relation of causality to the extent that it presents itself in necessity's opposition [in dem Gegensatz der Notwendigkeit]. The freely effecting absolute cause is substance qua the source of motion which not only has its activity's beginning within itself but also has within itself the whole content which this activity produces and which receives determinate being as effect.

Par. 52
This activity is therefore according to [the standpoint of] the opposition of activity and effect transition into the opposite [Übergehen in das Entgegengesetzte], but according to its content an identical transition.

3. Interaction [Wechselwirkung]

Par. 53
Substance is therefore as cause only active upon and in itself and stands in interaction only with itself, or it is the universal [das Allgemeine].

SECOND PART—Subjective Logic
I. Concept [Begriff]

Par. 54
The *Concept* is the whole of the determinations brought together [zusammengefaßt] into their simple unity.

Par. 55
The Concept has the moments of universality, particularity [Besonderheit], and individuality [Einzelheit].

Par. 56
Universality is the Concept's unity within itself in the determination. Particularity is the negative as the simple determination which is permeated by universality, or it is the mark [Merkmal]. Individuality is the negative as pure self-relating negativity.

Par. 57
Individuality, as self-relating determinationless negativity, has the determination in itself as its property in the form of indifferent, though not independent, but rather sublated determinate being, and is *subject*.

II. Judgment [Urteil]

Par. 58
Judgment is the separation of the subject from its determination or particularity and the relation of the subject to this, which is the subject's predicate. Subject and predicate relate to one another as individuals and particulars or universals or as particulars and universals.

Par. 59
Judgment at the same time both extends the subject to universality and posits the subject's limitations. The predicate thereby at the same time both goes beyond the subject and is contained in the subject, or the predicate is at the same time both particular and universal.

a. Quality of Judgment or Determination of the Predicate

Par. 60
In that the judgment is the relation of the predicate to the subject, 1. the judgment's content and expression is to begin with this: the individual is universal—*positive* judgment. 2. But the individual is not universal—*negative* judgment—but something particular. 3. The individual is not something particular—*infinite* judgment—whereby all determination and also the universal sphere, and so the predicate in general, is sublated.

b. Quantity of Judgment or Determination of the Subject

Par. 61
The infinite judgment contains the individual as individual or as *this* and there arises 1. the judgment "This is constituted so"—*singular* judgment. 2. Since the predicate also at the same time asserts something universal of the subject, the judgment must be "*Some things* are constituted so"—*particular* judgment, in which lies immediately the opposite judgment "Some things are not constituted so." 3. This indeterminacy sublates itself through the judgment "*Everything* is constituted so"—*universal* judgment.

c. Relation of Judgment or Determination of Relation

Par. 62
Through qualitative and quantitative judgment both subject and predicate have

been posited in all the determinations of the Concept, and the Concept is hereby present *in itself,* and the judgment now contains a relation of the determinately existent [des Daseienden] to the Concept. This real judgment is 1. *categorical.* But because that relation of the Concept to determinate being is to begin with only an inner connection the categorical judgment is at the same time only *assertoric.*

Par. 63
2. The *hypothetical* judgment, "If a is then b is," explicitly expresses the connection as such, namely, without assurance or assertion of determinate being, whereby it is *problematic.*

Par. 64
3. The *disjunctive* judgment, "a is either b or c or d," contains in the predicate both universality and the particularization [Besonderung] of universality. It is just as much the case that the subject is related to these determinations as to something universal as that these determinations also exclude one another and only one of them can belong to the subject. The judgment is *apodictic.*

III. Syllogism [Schluß]

Par. 65
The syllogism is the presentation of the Concept in its moments. Individuality, particularity, and universality are therein both distinguished as moments and the extremes are bound together [zusammengeschlossen] by the middle which is their unity.

Par. 66
The syllogism is 1. to begin with the binding together of individuality and universality through *particularity* as the middle. The meaning of this syllogism is a) the individual is through its determinacy a universal or has determinate being in general, b) the individual has through its immediate determinacy yet another determinacy which encloses the former within it [welche jene in sich schließt].

Par. 67
The form of this syllogism, I[ndividual]—P[articular]—U[niversal], is the universal *rule of subsumption* of a determinate content under a universal determination. If, as in identical propositions, this determination is in its content no more universal than the determination of which it is immediately predicated, yet still it has as predicate the form of universality in contrast to the other determination as subject.

Par. 68
In quantitative determinations the moments of the syllogism have no formal relation to one another, but the relation of equality. The *mathematical* syllogism therefore reads: Things which are equal to a third thing are equal to each other.

Par. 69
Syllogisms can, whatever position the moments contained in them may have, be

traced back to the form indicated above, which is the universal rule of all syllogisms.

Par. 70
In the syllogism, considered according to its determinate moments, the middle is particularity, a determinacy whose multiplicity contains the individual as something concrete within itself, which individual can accordingly also be bound together with other universal determinations which can reciprocally limit and even sublate each other.—Likewise the particular is itself relatable to other universal determinations. Conversely, the universal embraces within itself other determinations and hence also other individualities. Consequently, here the individual and the universal bound together are a contingent content for each other.

Par. 71
Concerning the relation of the moments, there are in the syllogism two immediate relations or judgments, namely, the relation of the individual to the particular and the relation of the particular to the universal, and a mediated relation: the conclusion [der Schlußsatz]. Because only the mediated relation contains the unity of what is bound together [der Zusammengeschlossenen] and hence in its form the necessity of their relation, the two immediate relations must likewise be presented as mediations. But if this happens through the same kind of syllogism then the progression into the bad infinite arises, in that each such interposed syllogism stands in the same need.

Par. 72
The immediate relations of the individual to the particular and of the particular to the universal must therefore first be mediated in accordance with the universal form of syllogism in general but through a different determination of the middle. 2. The second universal syllogism is therefore that the particular is bound together with the universal through *individuality*.—But the individual as determinately existent must, in order to be middle, be *totality* [Allheit]: syllogism through *induction*. Because the determinately existent individual belongs to free contingency, induction cannot become complete, and this syllogism therefore remains to that extent incomplete and imperfect [unvollkommen], just as it also contains no inner necessity.

Par. 73
But individuality qua middle, to the extent that it is a *universal* moment of the Concept, binds the particular and the universal together in a true manner. It is the negative unity in which, as becoming and activity, particularity, as distinguished manifoldness and the condition of determinate being, has been bound together into one and raised to simple universal unity—or conversely, in which the universal is individualized and has passed into the manifoldness of determinate being.

Par. 74
3. Finally, the relation of individuality to particularity must be mediated, for which the universal is available: syllogism of *analogy*. In this syllogism the middle has in contrast to the extreme of particularity the determination of individuality

and falls apart into *individual and universal,* for what applies only to an individual is taken universally. This syllogism therefore actually contains four determinations (*quaternio terminorum*) and is therefore imperfect.

Par. 75
But *universality* as true middle is inner nature and the whole Concept, in which negative unity, subjectivity and also objectivity, the content and the particularity of determinate being interpenetrate, and which is the absolute ground and connection of being-within-self and determinate being.

Par. 76
The first syllogism, I—P—U, which mediates individuality and universality through particularity, *presupposes* the two following ones through which both its immediate relations are mediated. But conversely, these two reciprocally presuppose one another and presuppose likewise the first. The immediate demands mediation and only arises from it, just as conversely mediation arises from the immediate. Those syllogisms constitute a circle of reciprocal presupposition which binds itself together as a whole and encapsulates itself in the simple mediation which is no less immediate as its center.

Par. 77
This whole of mutually presupposing mediations, which precisely therein are simple immediacy, produces a determinate being which has that cause and its activity as its[14] presupposition, though conversely what is produced is just as much ground of the activity and the production itself. This *mediation* is therefore neither a *transition* like the becoming of being in general, in which what makes the transition gets lost in its opposite [in seinem Entgegengesetzten]; nor is it a *production* like the *appearance* of the ground, which is only immediate, or the *expression* of force, whose activity is conditioned; nor is it an *effecting* like that of the cause, whose activity vanishes in the effect.

Par. 78
A. The *purpose,* considered more closely, is the real and self-realizing Concept, both as a whole and in its parts, the whole syllogism. It is to begin with, as the subjective, the whole syllogism, namely, 1. the immediate universal existing within itself which 2. determines or particularizes itself and 3. drives itself to externalization, to determinate being.

Par. 79
B. The *realization* of the purpose is likewise the whole syllogism. This mediation is 1. active purpose as effecting cause, but 2. through a means which, on the one hand, belongs to the subjective, and which is brought into connection with the purpose by the activity, and, on the other hand, belongs to determinate being or objectivity and is brought into connection with this objectivity by the activity. 3. The activity has its effect upon immediate determinate being and gives itself a mediated, produced objectivity through the sublation of determinate being.

14. Reading: *seiner.*

Par. 80
C. This objectivity, the *fulfilled* purpose, represents mediation through the universal [stellt die Vermittlung durch das Allgemeine dar]. It is something external which is, on the one hand, product and, on the other hand, ground of the production. Therefore, in it what effects has equally come out of itself and passed over into its opposite [in sein Entgegengesetztes] and also returned into itself from the mediating activity and in its otherness found only itself.

Par. 81
To the extent that the purpose, as active cause, lets means and product fall apart in existence [in der Existenz], so that the means does not have the purpose in itself and the product does not have the activity in itself, suitedness to purpose [die Zweckmäßigkeit] is merely *external,* and it is in general *relative* to the extent that the purpose itself has a subordinate content and what is the means for achieving it has this relation to it only on one side or another.

Par. 82
The purpose of the existent is what the existent is in itself and in truth or what its concept is. Hence relative suitedness to purpose, which has regard to only one or another determination of the existent, does not exhaust its concept.

Par. 83
Inner suitedness to purpose is this, that something is in itself reciprocally just as much purpose as means, that it is its own product and this product the producer itself. Such a thing is a *purpose in itself* [Selbstzweck].

THIRD PART—Doctrine of the Idea

Par. 84
The Idea is the adequate Concept in which objectivity and subjectivity are the same or determinate being corresponds to the Concept as such. The Idea contains true self-life within itself. The Idea is in part Life, in part Cognition [Erkennen], in part Science [Wissenschaft].

I. Idea of Life

Par. 85
Life is the Idea in the element of determinate being. Through the unity of the Concept and objectivity the living is the kind of whole in which the parts are nothing for themselves but only through and in the whole, *organic parts* in which matter and form are an inseparable unity.

Par. 86
Life has in it the universal moments, which constitute just as many universal organic systems: 1. its universal, simple being-within-self in its externality, *sensibility;* 2. its excitability from outside and immediate reaction against it, *irritability;* 3. the return of this action outward into itself, *reproduction.*

Par. 87
As self-realizing self-movement, life is the threefold process: 1. the *shaping* of the individual in itself, 2. the individual's *self-preservation* against its inorganic nature, 3. the preservation of the *genus*.

Par. 88
The process of *shaping* is the relation of the organic to itself and consists in the fact that all organic parts continually produce each other reciprocally and the preservation of the one depends on the preservation of the rest. This production is, on the one hand, only the evolution of the organization which is in itself present but, on the other hand, the continual change of this organization. But the former mere *growth* or quantitative change is a process of increase through *accepting into oneself* [Intussuszeption], not through juxtaposition, i.e., it is not a mechanical increase.

Par. 89
The process of organic *change* is just as little a chemical process. In chemism the matters standing in relation to one another [die sich zueinander verhaltenden Materien] are, to be sure, referred [bezogen] to one another through their concept—chemical relatedness [Verwandtschaft]—and so contain *in themselves* their product, which is not already produced through what was previously present and like it. But its production is no self-preservation. It is therefore only a neutral product, i.e., one in which the activity, which only belongs to the separated matters, is extinguished, not self-productive and separable again into the product's components qualitatively and quantitatively.

Par. 90
The organic *process of nourishment* is, on the other hand, a perfect determination of material increase through the inner, preexisting form, which as the subjective or as the simple form of all parts relates itself to itself—or each part relates to the remaining parts as to something objective—and is only with itself in the process.

Par. 91
The *process of the self-preservation* of the organic against its inorganic nature.— Life's free opposition [Entgegensetzung] into the subjective and the objective presents itself as organic and inorganic nature. The latter is life without subjective individuality [Individualität], in which the individual thing [das Einzelne] exists for itself, has its concept only as a law of natural necessity, not in a subjective form in itself, and its significance falls only within the whole. This whole, as subject, is the organic, to which inorganic nature is essentially related, constituting its condition.

Par. 92
The inorganic *condition* relates to the organic not as cause or as chemical moment, but rather what is posited in the organic through the effect of the inorganic is essentially determined through the organic itself and has its effect only qua *stimulating*. The organic is the double movement of the continual fight which, on the one side, prevents the development of elements [das elementarische Wer-

den] and the transition into what is opposed, sublates the organic's condition, and gives subjective individuality to objective universality [die objektive Allgemeinheit individualisiert], but, on the other side, dissolves the individual or subjective aspect from out of itself and demotes it to inorganic determinate being.

Par. 93
The process of the *preservation of the genus* is a) in general the realization of the genus, which as universal life makes the transition to actuality in the individual, or to individuality, through the particularization [Besonderung] of the kind, b) the relation of the organic to the organic which is like it, through which it produces itself as another individual of the same genus, which genus presents itself in this exchange of individuals and return of individuality to universality.

II. Idea of Cognition [des Erkennens]

Par. 94
Cognition is the representation of an object in accordance with its determinately existing determinations [nach seinen daseienden Bestimmungen] as they are contained in the unity of its Concept and follow from this or, conversely, to the extent that the Concept's own effective activity generates its determinations for itself. These determinations, posited as contained in the Concept, are cognition or the Idea which realizes itself in the element of thought.

III. The Absolute Idea or Knowing

Par. 95
Absolute Knowing [Das absolute Wissen] has 1. nothing external or in any way given as its object but only itself. It is the Concept which exists as Concept. 2. The Concept constructs itself out of itself by existing as becoming and representing the opposition contained within it in the form of different independent real determinations or determinations of the Understanding. 3. In that the real determinations initially become in their reflection determinations of the Understanding, their dialectic represents them not only as essentially relating to one another but also as passing over into their unity. From this their negative movement results their positive unity, which constitutes the Concept in its real totality.

The Doctrine of the Idea—As Restated in the 1809–10 Doctrine of the Concept

Doctrine of the Idea

Par. 66
The *Idea* is the objectively True or the adequate Concept in which determinate being is determined through its own inner Concept and existence is, as self-producing product, in outward unity with its purpose. The Idea is that actuality which corresponds not to just any old representation or concept found outside itself but to its own Concept, and which is consequently as it is supposed to be in and for itself and as it itself contains this its Concept.—The *ideal* is the Idea considered according to the side of *existence,* but as an existence which is ade-

quate to the Concept. It is therefore the actual in its highest truth.—In distinction from the expression "ideal" one calls Idea rather the True considered according to the side of the *Concept*.

Par. 67

There are three Ideas: 1. the Idea of Life, 2. the Idea of Cognition and the Good, and 3. the Idea of Science or of Truth itself.

I. Idea of Life

Par. 68

Life is the Idea in its immediate determinate being, whereby the Idea passes over into the sphere of appearance or of changeable, manifoldly and externally self-determining being and an inorganic nature.

Par. 69

Life is, as the immediate unity of the Concept and determinate being, the sort of whole in which the parts are nothing for themselves but exist through and in the whole and the whole equally exists through the parts. It is an *organic system*.

II. Idea of Cognition and the Good

Par. 70

In this Idea the Concept and actuality separate from one another. The Concept, on the one hand, by itself empty, should receive its determination and its fulfillment [Erfüllung] from actuality. On the other hand, actuality should receive its determination from the Concept's independent determination.

1. Cognition

Par. 71

Cognition is the relation of the Concept and actuality. The thought which is in itself filled only with itself [Das an sich nur mit sich erfüllte . . . Denken] and *to that extent* empty thereby gets filled with particular content, which gets raised from out of determinate being [Dasein] to universal representation [zu allgemeiner Darstellung].

Par. 72

Definition expresses of an object, which plays the role in it of an individual or a particular, its *genus* as its *universal* essence, and the particular determinacy of this universal through which it is this object.

Par. 73

Division expresses of a genus or a universal in general, a species, an order, etc. the *particularizations* in which it exists as a multiplicity of *kinds*. These particularizations, which are contained in a unity, must flow from a common principle of division.

Par. 74

Cognition is partly analytic, partly synthetic.

Par. 75

Analytic cognition begins from a concept or a concrete determination and develops only the multiplicity of the immediate, or identically therein contained, simple determinations.

Par. 76

Synthetic cognition, by contrast, develops the determinations of a whole which are not immediately contained therein nor flow out of one another in an identical manner but have the form of difference over against each other, and it shows the necessity of their determinate relation to one another.

Par. 77

This happens through *construction* and *proof*. Construction in part represents the concept or proposition in its real determinations, in part it represents this reality belonging to the concept or proposition in its division and dissolution for the purposes of proof, whereby this reality's transition into the Concept begins.

Par. 78

Proof gathers together the dissolved parts and through the comparison of their relations to each other produces that combination of them which is the relation of the whole expressed in the theorem. Or proof shows of the real determinations how they are moments of the Concept and how their combined relation represents the Concept in its totality.

Par. 79

In this cognition, which in its strictest form is geometrical cognition, 1. the construction does not proceed from the Concept but is an invented contrivance, which shows itself to be suited to purpose only in relation to the proof, or in other cases even an empirical description. 2. In proof, already familiar or discovered synthetic propositions are pulled into service from elsewhere for the analytic determinations, and what lies at hand gets subsumed and combined under them. Proof thereby receives the semblance of contingency, because it presents for scrutiny only a necessity but not the immanent course and inner necessity of the object itself.

2. Should or the Good

Par. 80

In the Idea of Cognition the Concept is sought and should be appropriate to the object. In the Idea of the Good, conversely, the Concept has the standing of being the first and of being the purpose existing in itself which *should* be realized in actuality.

Par. 81

The good in itself, since it first needs to be realized, stands in opposition to a world which does not correspond to it and a nature which has its own laws of necessity and is *indifferent* toward the laws of freedom.

Par. 82

On the one hand, as absolute purpose the good ought in itself to be brought to fulfillment without any regard to the consequences, in being entrusted to an actuality which is independent of it and which *can pervert* it.

Par. 83
At the same time, though, there lies therein the determination that *in itself* actuality *agrees* with the good, or the belief in a moral world order.

III. Idea of Knowing or of the Truth

Par. 84
Absolute Knowing is the Concept which has itself as its object and content, and so is its own reality.

Par. 85
The course or the *method* of Absolute Knowing is just as much analytic as synthetic. The development of what is contained in the Concept, analysis, is the emergence of different determinations which are contained in the Concept but are not immediately given as such, and is therefore at the same time synthetic. The presentation of the Concept in its real determinations here proceeds from the Concept itself, and what in ordinary cognition constitutes proof is here the return of the conceptual moments which have passed over into difference back into unity, which is thereby *totality*, the Concept which is fulfilled and has become its own content.

Par. 86
This mediation of the Concept with itself is not only a *course of subjective cognition* but equally *the immanent movement of the matter* [Sache] *itself*. In absolute cognition the Concept just as much makes the beginning as it is also the result.

Par. 87
The transition to further concepts or to a new sphere is likewise guided and necessary through the preceding sphere. The Concept which became reality is at the same time again a unity which must represent in itself the movement of realization. However, the development of the opposition contained in this unity is not a mere dissolution into the moments from which this unity came to be, but these moments now have another form in virtue of the fact that they have proceeded through the unity. In the new development they are now posited as what they are through their relation [Beziehung] to each other. Thus they have received a new determination.

Appendix XV: *Science of Logic,* First Edition (1812)—Extracts

[In this and the remaining appendices we turn to Hegel's most important later reflections on the *Phenomenology*. This appendix contains those in the first edition of the *Science of Logic* from 1812. The passages translated from the preface and the introduction were subsequently reprinted in the second edition of 1831 almost without alteration (changes of any significance at all are indicated here in footnotes). On the other hand, the passage translated from the section "With What Must Science Begin?" underwent substantial rewriting in the 1831 edition, and I have therefore included the rewritten version of it separately, as appendix XVIII.—Text translated from Hegel, *Gesammelte Werke* (Hamburg: Felix Meiner, 1978), vol. 11.]

From the Preface

The *Understanding determines* and holds fast the determinations. *Reason* is negative and *dialectical* because it dissolves the determinations of the Understanding into nothing; it is *positive* because it produces the *universal* and comprehends [begreift] the particular within it. Just as the Understanding is usually taken to be something separate from Reason in general, similarly dialectical Reason is usually taken to be something separate from positive Reason. But in its truth Reason is *Spirit*, which is higher than either—it is understanding Reason or rational Understanding. Spirit is the negative, that which constitutes the quality both of dialectical Reason and of the Understanding; it negates the simple, and in this way posits the determinate difference of the Understanding; it just as much dissolves this determinate difference, and in this way is dialectical. Spirit does not, however, remain in the nothingness of this result, but is just as much positive within it, and so has produced thereby the first simple, but as something universal which is concrete within itself. It is not the case that a *given* particular [ein gegebenes Besonderes] gets subsumed under this universal—rather, in the above-mentioned process of determination and the dissolution of determination the particular has already determined itself as well. This spiritual movement—which in its simplicity gives itself its determinacy and in its determinacy its equality with itself, and which is thus the immanent development of the Concept—is the absolute method of cognition and simultaneously the immanent soul of the content itself.—Only along this self-constructing path, I claim, can philosophy be objective, demonstrated science.—It is in this way that I have attempted to represent *consciousness* in the *Phenomenology of Spirit*. Consciousness is Spirit in the form of knowing which is concrete or caught up in externality; but this object's advance [die Fortbewegung dieses Gegenstandes] rests solely, like the development of all natural and spiritual life, on the nature of the *pure essentialities* which constitute the content of Logic. Consciousness, as the appearing Spirit which frees itself along its path of its immediacy and external concretion, becomes the pure knowing which gives itself as object those pure essentialities themselves as they are in and for themselves. They are the pure thoughts, the Spirit which thinks its own essence. Their self-movement is their spiritual life and is that by means of which Science constitutes itself and of which Science is the presentation.

This has indicated the connection of the science which I call *Phenomenology of Spirit* to Logic.—Concerning their external relation, it was planned that the first part of the *System of Science*[15] which contains the Phenomenology would be followed by a second part which would contain the Logic and the two real

---

15. Hegel's own note, added in the 1831 edition: "(Bamberg and Würzburg, from Goebhardt, 1807.) The second edition, which will be published next Easter, will no longer bear this title.—In place of the plan mentioned in what follows of a second part which would contain all the other philosophical sciences, I have since published the *Encyclopaedia of the Philosophical Sciences*, last year in its third edition."

sciences of philosophy, the Philosophy of Nature and the Philosophy of Spirit, and which would have concluded the System of Science. But the necessary expansion which the Logic required on its own account has prompted me to present it to the public separately. It therefore constitutes on an expanded plan the first sequel to the Phenomenology of Spirit. Later I shall add the treatment of the two mentioned real sciences of philosophy.—This first volume of the Logic, though, contains as its first book the *Doctrine of Being;* the second book, the *Doctrine of Essence,* as the second part of the first volume, is already in the press; on the other hand, the second volume will contain the *Subjective Logic* or the *Doctrine of the Concept.*[16]

Nuremberg, March 22, 1812

From the Introduction

In the *Phenomenology of Spirit* (Bamberg and Würzburg, 1807) I have represented consciousness in its advance from the first immediate opposition [Gegensatz] of itself and the object up to absolute knowing [das absolute Wissen].[17] This path goes through all forms of the relation of consciousness to the object and has the *Concept* [Begriff] *of Science* as its result. This Concept therefore needs—disregarding the fact that it emerges within the Logic itself—no justification here, because it has received it in that work. And it admits of no other justification than just this bringing forth [dieser Hervorbringung] of it through consciousness, whose own shapes [Gestalten] all dissolve into the Concept as the truth.—A rationalizing [räsonierende] grounding or explanation of Science's Concept can at most effect that the Concept is brought before the faculty of representation [Vorstellung] and a historically conditioned [historisch] cognition of it produced. But a definition of Science or more precisely of Logic has its proof solely in the necessity of its coming forth [ihres Hervorgangs] just mentioned. A definition with which some science or other makes an absolute beginning can only contain the determinate proper expression of what people imagine *in a generally conceded and familiar way* to be the object and purpose of the science. That the object and purpose of the science is imagined to be just this is a historically conditioned assurance [eine historische Versicherung] in connection with which one can only appeal to this or that generally acknowledged circumstance, or rather can only adduce the plea that this or that circumstance might be treated as generally acknowledged. There is no end to the process of one person adducing a case and an authority from one source and then another person from another according to which there is still something more and different to be understood by this or that expression so that a more precise or more general determination still has to be included in its definition and the science too has to be set up accordingly.—In this process, moreover, it depends on rationalization [Räsonement] just what is to be included or excluded, and to what limit and extent. But for rationalization itself the most multifarious and diverse opinions are possible, concerning which

---

16. The words "is already in the press" are omitted in the 1831 edition.
17. The words "(Bamberg and Würzburg, 1807)" are omitted in the 1831 edition.

in the end only arbitrariness can arrive at a firm decision. In this process of beginning a science with its definition, however, there cannot even be any question of demonstrating the *necessity* of the science's object and thereby of the science itself.[18]

The Concept of pure Science and the deduction of this Concept is therefore presupposed here to the extent that the Phenomenology of Spirit is nothing other than its deduction. Absolute knowing is the truth of all forms of consciousness because, as the course of consciousness's development produced absolute knowing in the Phenomenology, it is only in absolute knowing that the separation of the object from self-certainty [Gewißheit seiner selbst] has dissolved itself completely and the truth has become equal to this certainty and this certainty to the truth.

Pure Science hence presupposes the liberation from the opposition of consciousness [von dem Gegensatze des Bewußtseins]. It contains *thought insofar as it is equally the matter in itself* or the matter in itself insofar as it is equally pure thought. Or the Concept of Science is that the truth is pure self-consciousness and has the self-like shape that *what is in itself is the Concept* and *the Concept is what is in itself*.[19]

This objective thought is, then, the *content* of pure Science. This Science is therefore so little formal, it so little lacks the matter necessary for an actual and true cognition, that its content is rather alone the absolutely true or, if one still wished to use the word "matter," the true matter—a matter, however, for which the form is not something external, since this matter is rather pure thought and hence the absolute form itself. Accordingly, the Logic should be understood as the system of pure Reason, as the realm of pure thought. This realm is the truth itself as it is in and for itself without a covering. One can therefore say that this content is the representation of God as he is in his eternal essence before the creation of nature and a finite spirit.

Anaxagoras is praised as the man who first expressed the idea that *nous, thought* is the principle of the world, that the essence of the world should be identified as thought. He thereby laid the foundation for an intellectual perspective on the universe whose pure form must be *Logic*. In Logic we are not concerned with a thought about something which would constitute an independent basis outside thought, with forms which would supply mere marks [Merkmale] of the truth. Rather, thought's necessary forms and its own determinations are the highest truth themselves.[20]

---

18. The 1831 edition substitutes for "In this . . . science itself": "In this process of beginning a science with its definition the need to demonstrate the *necessity* of the science's *object* and thereby of the science itself is never addressed."

19. The 1831 edition substitutes for "Or . . . *the Concept is what is in itself*": "As *Science* the truth is the pure self-developing self-consciousness and has the self-like shape that *what is in and for itself is the known Concept, but the Concept as such is what is in and for itself*."

20. The 1831 edition expands "are the highest truth themselves" to: "are the content and the highest truth themselves."

From "With What Must Science Begin?"

It is presupposed from the Phenomenology of Spirit, or the science of consciousness as appearing Spirit, that *pure knowing* [das reine Wissen] emerges as consciousness's last, absolute truth. The *Logic* is the *pure Science* [die reine Wissenschaft], pure knowing in its full scope and extension. Pure knowing is the certainty which has become truth, or the certainty which no longer stands in opposition to the object but has made the object internal, knows the object as itself, and which equally, on the other hand, has given up the knowledge of itself as something which is in opposition to and only the destroyer of the objective, has externalized itself and is a unity with its externalization.

Pure knowing, compacted into this unity, has sublated all relation to an other and has sublated mediation and *is simple immediacy*.

"Simple immediacy" is itself an expression of Reflection, and refers to the distinction from what is mediated. Truly expressed this simple immediacy is *pure being*, or *being* in general—*being*, nothing more, without any further determination or content.

This look back at the concept of pure knowing is the *ground* from which *being* emerges in order to constitute the *beginning* of absolute Science.

Or second and contrarily, the *beginning of absolute Science* must itself be an *absolute beginning*, it may *presuppose nothing*. It must therefore be mediated by nothing, and must have no ground. It should rather itself be the ground of the whole Science. It must therefore simply be an immediate, or rather the immediate itself. Just as it cannot have a determination in contrast to an other, it also cannot contain a determination within itself, it can contain no content, for that sort of thing would likewise be a distinguishing and a relating of different things to one another, and hence a mediation. The beginning is therefore *pure being*.

Especially in recent times it has been seen as a problem to find a beginning in philosophy, and the source of this problem and the possibility of solving it have been much discussed. The beginning of philosophy must be either something mediated or something immediate, and it is easy to show that it can be neither the one nor the other. Hence both ways of beginning find their refutation.

In the first representation just given of being as the beginning, the concept of knowing is presupposed. Hence this beginning is not absolute but proceeds from the preceding movement of consciousness. In this case the science of this movement from which knowing results would have to have the absolute beginning. This science makes that beginning with the *immediate consciousness*, the knowledge that something *is*.—So being makes the beginning here likewise, but as the determination of a concrete shape of consciousness. Only pure knowing, the Spirit which has freed itself from its appearance as consciousness, also has free pure being as its beginning.—But the former beginning, the immediate consciousness, contains the I as related to something simply other, and conversely the object as related to the I, and hence a mediation.—To be sure, consciousness contains both the mediating factors—which are, again, also the mediated factors—itself, and hence does not point beyond itself and is closed within itself. But since the mediation is reciprocal, each mediating factor is also mediated, and hence there is no true immediacy present.—But conversely, if such a true immediacy were present, then it is, because not grounded, something arbitrary and contingent.

The insight that the absolutely true must be a result, and conversely that a result presupposes something first and true, which, however, because it is a first, is, considered objectively, not necessary, and, on the subjective side, not known—has in recent times given rise to the thought that philosophy can only begin with a hypothetical and problematic truth and that philosophizing can hence to begin with be only a search.

On this view, the advance forward in philosophy is rather a movement backward and a grounding through which it first emerges that what the beginning was made with is not merely something arbitrarily assumed but in fact, on the one hand, the true and, on the other hand, the first true.

It must be admitted that it is an essential observation—which will emerge more precisely within the Logic itself—that the advance forward is a *return* into the *ground* and to what is *original,* on which that with which the beginning was made depends.—In this way consciousness, on its path from the immediacy with which it begins, gets led back to absolute knowing as its truth. This last thing, the ground, is, then, also that from which the first thing comes forth, though the latter initially made its appearance as something immediate.—In this way Spirit will also at the *end* of the development of pure knowing freely externalize itself and release itself into the shape of an *immediate* consciousness as a consciousness of a being which stands over against it as an other. What is essential is actually not that something purely immediate be the beginning, but that the whole is a circular course within itself in which the first thing becomes also the last and the last thing also the first.

Therefore, on the other side, it is just as necessary to consider that into which the movement returns, as into the first's *ground,* as a *result.* From this point of view, the first is just as much the ground and the last is something deduced. For, in that the beginning is made from the first and the last is arrived at as the ground through correct inferences, this ground is in fact a result. Moreover, the advance from what makes the beginning is only a *further determination* of it, so that it remains as the basis of everything that follows and does not vanish from it. The advance does not consist in a deduction of something *other* or in a transition to something which is truly other—and to the extent that this transition does happen, it just as much sublates itself again [so hebt es sich ebensosehr wieder auf]. Hence the beginning of philosophy is the foundation which is present and preserves itself in all the developments which follow, the Concept which is entirely immanent to its further determinations.

Through this advance in which the beginning further determines itself, the beginning loses the one-sidedness which it has in this determination of being an immediate, it becomes something mediated and in just this way makes the line of the scientific advance into a circle.—At the same time, what makes the beginning, since in its beginning it is what is still undeveloped and contentless, is still not truly known, for that is how it is in the beginning, i.e., still before Science. Only Science for the first time, and indeed Science in its whole development, is the complete, contentful, and for the first time truly grounded cognition of it.

But because the result also constitutes the absolute ground, the advance of this cognition is not something provisional, nor something problematic and hypothetical, but it is determined by the nature of the matter [Sache] and the content itself. Nor is that beginning something arbitrary and only provisionally assumed, nor something which appears arbitrary and is presupposed only through special pleading [noch ein als willkürlich erscheinendes und bittweise vorausgesetztes], of which it would however turn out in what follows that one was right to make it the beginning—in the way that, concerning geometrical constructions, it does in fact only emerge afterwards in the proofs that one did right to draw precisely these lines, or even in the proofs themselves it only emerges afterwards that it was good to begin with the comparison of these lines or angles; this is not intelligible independently from this line-drawing or comparing itself.

Appendix XVI: Heidelberg *Encyclopaedia* (1817)—Extracts

[The following are two paragraphs from the first edition of the *Encyclopaedia* published at Heidelberg in 1817 which concern the *Phenomenology*.—Text translated from Hegel, *Enzyklopädie der philosophischen Wissenschaften* (Heidelberg: August Oswalds Universitätsbuchhandlung, 1817).]

Par. 35
Now in order to raise oneself to the standpoint of Science one must give up the presuppositions [Voraussetzungen] which are contained in the already mentioned subjective and finite modes of philosophical cognition: (1) the presupposition of the firm *validity* of limited and opposed *determinations of the Understanding* in general, (2) the presupposition of a *given*, represented, *already complete substratum*, which is supposed to be a standard for determining whether one of those thought-determinations is adequate to it or not, (3) the presupposition of cognition as a mere *relating* of such ready and fixed predicates to some substratum or other, (4) the presupposition of the opposition between the cognizing subject and its object, which cannot be united with it—each side of which opposition is supposed once again, as in the case of the opposition just mentioned, to be independently [für sich] something fixed and true.

Par. 36
It cannot yet really be demanded that these presuppositions be given up on the ground that they are false, for Science, in which the above-mentioned determinations must come forth, has itself first to demonstrate this by examining them themselves [denn dies hat die Wissenschaft . . . an ihnen selbst erst zu zeigen]. Rather, it is demanded that they be given up on the ground that they belong to *representation* and to immediate thinking, i.e., thinking caught up in *what is given*, to *opinion*, and in general because they are *givens* and *presuppositions*, whereas Science presupposes nothing except that it wills to be pure thought.

I earlier treated the *Phenomenology of Spirit*, the scientific history of *consciousness*, as the first part of philosophy in the sense that it should precede [vorausgehen] pure Science, since it is the production [Erzeugung] of pure Science's Concept. But at the same time consciousness and its history, like every other philosophical science, is not an absolute beginning, but a link in the circle of philosophy. *Skepticism,* as a negative science applied to all the forms of finite cognition, would likewise be available as such an introduction. However, it would not only be a joyless path but also something superfluous, because the dialectical is itself an essential moment of positive Science, as was said above. And in addition it would have to discover the finite forms in a merely empirical and unscientific fashion and to take them up as given. The demand for such a completed skepticism is the same as the demand that Science should be preceded by *the doubting of everything* [das Zweifeln an Allem], or rather *the despair of everything* [die Verzweiflung an Allem], i.e., perfect *presuppositionlessness* with respect to everything. This is actually realized in the resolve *to will pure thought,* through the freedom which abstracts from everything, and grasps its pure abstraction, the simplicity of thought.—The demand which has become customary through the Kantian philosophy, that before actual cognition the *cognitive faculty be subjected to critical investigation,* appears plausible at first sight. However, this investigation is itself a cognition; that it should be performed without cognition is senseless. Moreover, even the assumption of a *cognitive faculty* before actual cognition is a presupposition both of the unjustified category or determination of *faculty* or *power* and of a *subjective cognition* (a presupposition of a piece with what was just mentioned). In addition, it is also the case that the Logic is that demanded investigation, but in a truer manner than the critical process, which ought to have investigated its own immediate presuppositions and the nature of its own activity before anything else.

Appendix XVII: Berlin *Encyclopaedia* (1830)—Extracts

[The second and third editions of the *Encyclopaedia,* published at Berlin in 1827 and 1830, contain an explicit discussion of the *Phenomenology* at paragraph 25—where Hegel is concerned to contrast the *Phenomenology* with the introductory treatment of "Attitudes of Thought to Objectivity" which prefaces the *Encyclopaedia*'s Logic. This is the most important material on the *Phenomenology* in these editions of the *Encyclopaedia,* and I therefore begin with it here. However, these editions of the *Encyclopaedia* also contain, at paragraphs 12 and 50, some significant general observations concerning thought's ascent to the absolute standpoint. These observations are particularly interesting for their emphasis on the negative character and the eventual sublation of that which provides the "mediation" to the absolute standpoint. Although these observations do not explicitly identify the mediation in question with the *Phenomenology,* the description and vocabulary in the first few sentences of paragraph 12, and also the last sentence of paragraph 50, suggest that this is what Hegel has in mind. For these reasons, paragraphs 12 and 50 are included here as well. Since the differences between the formulations of these three paragraphs in the 1827 and 1830 editions are minor and without substantive implications, consisting mainly in orthographic, grammatic, and stylistic improvements in the 1830 edition, I here translate from the 1830 edition only.—Text translated from Hegel, *Enzyklopädie der philosophischen Wissenschaften* (Frankfurt am Main: Suhrkamp, 1981), vol. 1.]

Par. 25
The expression *objective thoughts* signifies the *truth* which should be the absolute *object* of philosophy, not merely its *goal.* But this expression in itself immediately

reveals an opposition—namely, that opposition around whose determination, fate, and validity [um dessen Bestimmung und Gültigkeit] revolves the interest of the contemporary philosophical standpoint and the question of the *truth* and its cognition. If thought-determinations are afflicted with a fixed opposition, i.e., if they are only *finite* in nature, then they are inadequate to the truth, which is absolutely in- and for-itself, and the truth cannot enter into thought. Thought which only produces and moves in *finite* determinations is called *Understanding* (in the more exact sense of the word). The *finitude* of the thought-determinations is to be understood more precisely in two ways: first, that they are *only subjective* and have their persistent opposite in the objective; second, that being of *limited content* in general they remain in opposition both to one another and still more to the Absolute. The *attitudes to objectivity available for thought* should now be considered as a more precise introduction, in order to explain and inculcate the meaning and the standpoint here accorded to Logic.

In my *Phenomenology of Spirit*, which for this reason was called the first part of the System of Science at the time of its publication, the procedure is followed of beginning from the first, simplest appearance of Spirit, *the immediate consciousness*, and developing its dialectic up to the standpoint of philosophical Science, the necessity of which is demonstrated through this progress. But for this purpose it was not possible to remain at the formal aspect of mere consciousness; for the standpoint of philosophical knowing is at the same time within itself the most contentful and concrete standpoint, so that in being produced as a result it presupposed also the concrete shapes of consciousness, for example those of morality, ethical life, art, and religion. The development of the *substantial content* [des Gehalts], of the objects of particular parts of philosophical Science, therefore also falls within that development of consciousness—behind whose back, so to speak, that development must proceed, insofar as the content relates as the *in-itself* to consciousness—even though that development initially seemed to be limited to the formal aspect only. The presentation thereby becomes more complicated, and what belongs to the concrete parts to some extent already falls within this introduction along with the rest.—The examination to be undertaken here has the still greater shortcoming of being able to operate only historically and in a rationalizing manner [nur historisch und räsonierend]. But it is supposed primarily to contribute to the realization that the questions about the nature of *cognition*, about *belief*, and so forth which one has before one's mind and which one regards as quite *concrete* in fact rest on *simple* thought-determinations, which however are only for the first time truly disposed of in the Logic.

Par. 12
The *emergence* of philosophy which results from the need [for philosophy] mentioned above has *experience* [Erfahrung], the immediate and rationalizing consciousness, as its *starting-point*. Aroused by this need as a stimulus, thought's behavior is essentially to *elevate* itself above the natural, sensuous, and rationalizing consciousness into its own pure element and in this way to adopt initially a withdrawing, *negative relation* to that beginning. In this way thought initially finds its satisfaction in itself, in the idea of the *universal* essence of these appear-

ances [Erscheinungen]; this idea (the Absolute, God) can be more or less abstract. On the other hand, the experiential sciences bring with them the stimulus to conquer *the form* in which the wealth of their content is offered as a multiplicity merely immediate and discovered and lying *next to each other,* therefore in general as something *contingent,* and to raise this content to necessity. This stimulus tears thought out of that universality and the satisfaction which has been made possible *in itself* [an sich] and drives it to *develop out of itself.* This self-development is, on the one hand, just a taking up of the content and of the content's given determinations, and at the same time, on the other hand, it gives this content the form of emerging freely in accordance with the necessity of the matter [Sache] itself alone, in the manner of original thought.

The relation between *immediacy* and *mediation in consciousness* is to be discussed explicitly and in more detail below. Here we must just provisionally draw attention to the fact that even if both moments *appear* to be distinct *neither* can *be missing* and that they exist in *inseparable* connection with one another.—Thus the knowing of God, as of everything *super*senuous in general, essentially contains an *elevation* above sensuous sensation or intuition. Hence it contains a *negative* action against this first condition, but therein *mediation*. For mediation is a matter of beginning and having proceeded to a second condition, in such a way that this second condition only exists insofar as it has been arrived at from an other opposed to it. At the same time, though, the knowing of God is no less independent of that empirical side, indeed it essentially gives itself its independence through this negation and elevation.—If one construes the mediation as conditionedness and focuses on it in a one-sided fashion, one can say, though this is not to say much, that philosophy owes its initial emergence to experience (to the *a posteriori*)—thought is in fact essentially the negation of something immediately present—as much as one owes eating to food, since without food one would not be able to eat. In this relation eating is, it must be admitted, conceived as ungrateful [undankbar], for it is the consumption of that to which it is supposed to owe [verdanken] its own existence. Thought is in this sense no less ungrateful.

Thought's own but, because inwardly reflected, inwardly mediated *immediacy* (the *a priori*) is *universality,* thought's being-by-itself in general. In it thought is satisfied in itself, and to this extent indifference toward *particularization,* and hence toward its own development, is native to it. Just as religion, whether more developed or less cultured, whether cultivated to scientific consciousness or kept in artless faith and sentiment, has an equally intensive character of satisfaction and bliss. If thought gets no further than the *universality* of ideas—as is necessarily the case in the first philosophies (e.g., the *being* of the Eleatic school, the *becoming* of Heraclitus, and so forth)—then it is proper to accuse it of *formalism.* Even in the case of a developed philosophy it can happen that only the abstract propositions or determinations—e.g., that in the Absolute all is one, the identity of the subjective and the objective—are grasped and that these are only repeated in connection with the particular. In relation to the initial abstract universality of thought it is correct and well-founded to say that philosophy's *development* is owed to experience. On the one hand, the empirical sciences do not stop at the perception of the *individual details* of appearance, but through thought they have worked up their material in the direction of philosophy, by finding the universal determinations, genera, and laws; in this way they prepare that content of the particular so that it is capable of being taken up into philosophy. On the other hand, the empirical sciences thereby constrain thought to proceed itself to these concrete determinations. The taking up of this content, in which process the still attached immediacy and givenness get sublated by thought, is at the same time a *development* of thought out of itself. By owing its development to the empirical sciences in this way, philosophy gives to the content of these sciences the most essential form of the *freedom* (the *a priori aspect*) of thought and the *validation* of *necessity*—instead of a certification of discovery and of experienced fact—so that the fact becomes a representation and an imitating after-formation [Nachbildung] of the original and completely independent activity of thought.

Par. 50
This unification admits of *two routes* or forms; it is possible to begin from *being* and to make the transition from there to the *abstraction of thought,* or conversely the transition may be effected from the *abstraction* to *being.*

In the former beginning with being, being, as the immediate, presents itself as a being with infinitely multiple determinations, a filled world [erfüllte Welt]. This world can be more precisely determined as a collection of infinitely many contingencies in general (in the *cosmological* proof) or as a collection of infinitely many *purposes* and *purposive* relations (in the *physicotheological* proof). To *think* this filled being means to strip it of the form of individual details and contingencies and to grasp it as a being which is universal, necessary in and for itself, and self-determining and active in accordance with universal purposes, and which is different from that initial being—as God. The main thrust of the criticism of this procedure is that it is an inference, a transition. That is to say: in that the *perceptions* and their aggregate, the world, do not exhibit in themselves as such the universality into which thought purifies this content, this universality does not hereby receive confirmation through this empirical representation of the world. Thus the *Humean* standpoint gets invoked in opposition to the ascent of thought from the empirical representation of the world to God (as in the paralogisms—see par. 47)—the standpoint which declares it to be impermissible to *think* the perceptions, i.e., to extract what is universal and necessary from them.

Because man is a thinking being, healthy common sense will no more than philosophy ever allow itself to be denied the right to elevate itself *from* and *out of* the empirical intuition of the world to God. This elevation has as its foundation nothing other than the *thinking*—not merely sensuous and animal—observation of the world. For thought and *only* for thought, the *essence,* the *substance* is the world's *universal power* and *source of purpose* [Zweckbestimmung]. The so-called proofs of God's existence are to be considered only as the *descriptions* and analyses of the inward *course of the mind* which is a *thinking* mind and thinks the sensuous. The *elevation* of thought above the sensuous, thought's *transcendence* of the finite to reach the infinite, the *leap* which is made into the supersensuous with a breaking off of the sequences of the sensuous—all this is thought itself, this transition is *only thought.* To say that such a transition should not be made is to say that there should be no thought. And in fact animals make no such transition; *they* get no further than sensuous sensation and intuition; they therefore have no religion. Two points should be noted both in general and particularly concerning the criticism of this elevation of thought. *First*, if this elevation is put into the form of *inferences* (so-called *proofs* of God's existence), the *starting-point* is nevertheless the intuition of the world, determined in some way or other as an aggregate of contingencies or of purposes and purposive relations. It may seem that in thought, to the extent that thought makes *inferences*, this starting-point *remains* and is *allowed to remain* a *firm foundation* and just as empirical as this material is to begin with. In this way, the relation of the starting-point to the end-point to which the advance is made is represented as only *affirmative*, as an inference from *one thing* that *exists* and *remains* to an *other* that likewise *exists as well*. However, the great mistake is to want to know the nature of thought only in this form belonging to the Understanding. To think the empirical world means instead essentially to alter its empirical form and to change it into something universal; thought at the same time exercises a *negative* action on that foundation; the perceived material when determined through universality *does not remain* in its initial empirical form. The inner *content* of what is perceived gets extracted through removal and *negation* of its covering (cf. pars. 13 and 23). The metaphysical proofs of God's existence are inadequate expositions and descriptions of the elevation of the mind from the world to God because they do not express, or rather do not extract, the moment *of negation* which is contained in this elevation; for the very fact that the world is *contingent* [zufällig] implies that the world is only *something that collapses* [ein Fallendes], something apparent, something in and for itself *null* [Nichtiges]. The meaning of the elevation of the mind is that the world has being, to be sure, but this being is only illusion not true being, not absolute truth, that absolute truth is rather only beyond that appearance in God, God alone is true being. In being a *transition* and *mediation* this elevation is just as much a sublation [Aufheben] of the *transition* and mediation, for that through which God might seem to be mediated, the world, is rather pronounced to be null; only the *nullity* of the world's *being* binds the elevation, so that what exists as the mediator vanishes and hence in this mediation even the mediation gets sublated.—It is particularly to that relation which is only *affirmatively* conceived as a relation between two existing things that *Jacobi* clings when he attacks the Understanding's proofs. He objects to these proofs with justice that in them *conditions* (the world) are sought for *the unconditioned,* that the *infinite* (God) in this way gets represented as *grounded* and *dependent*. But that elevation as it takes place in the mind corrects this illusion itself; or rather, its whole content is the correction of this illusion. However, Jacobi did not recognize this true nature of essential thought, that in its mediation it sublates the mediation itself, and in consequence he falsely considered the objection which he rightly levels against the merely reflective Understanding to be one which applies to thought in general, and hence also to rational thought.

    In order to throw light on the failure to see the *negative* moment, one can for example cite the objection raised against *Spinozism* that it is a form of pantheism and atheism. To be sure, Spinoza's *absolute substance* is not yet absolute *Spirit*, and it is rightly demanded that God must be determined as absolute Spirit. But when Spinoza's determination of God is represented as a confounding of God with nature, with the finite world, and a turning of the world into God, a presupposition is here being made that the finite world possesses true actuality, *affirmative reality*. On this presupposition it is true that in a unity of God and the world God is simply made finite and reduced to the mere, finite, external manifoldness of existence. Apart from the fact that Spinoza does not define God as the unity of God and the world but as the unity of *thought* and extension (the material world), it is already implied in this unity, even if it is understood in that first and quite inadequate way, that in the Spinozistic system the world is rather determined as only a phenomenon lacking in actual reality, so that this system should rather be regarded as *acosmism*. A philosophy which claims that God and *only* God *exists* ought at least not to be called atheistic. After all, people still ascribe religion to those nations who worship the ape, the cow, stone and bronze statues, and so forth as God. But according to the representation in question it is still much more unacceptable to give up its own presupposition that this its aggregate of finitude which is called *the world* has actual reality. People readily regard it as quite impossible that—as the representation in question might perhaps put it—*there is no world*, or at least as much less possible than that one should entertain the thought that *there is no God*. People believe, and not at all to their own credit, much more readily that a system denies God than that it denies the world; they find it much more intelligible that God is denied than that the world is denied.

The *second* remark concerns the criticism of the *content* which that thinking elevation wins initially. This content, when it consists only of the determinations the *substance* of the world, the *necessary essence* of the world, a *purposively ordering and directing cause*, etc., is to be sure not adequate to the meaning which the term *God* has or should have. But apart from [the dubiousness of] the practice of presupposing a representation of God and judging a result by this presupposition, those determinations do certainly have great value and are necessary moments in the idea of God. In order to bring the content in its true determination, the true idea of God, before thought on this path, one must not, to be sure, take an inferior content as one's starting-point. The *merely contingent* things of the world are a very abstract determination. Organic forms and their purposive determinations belong to the higher sphere, *to life*. But besides the fact that the consideration of living nature and of other relations of existing things to *purposes* can be polluted by triviality in the purposes, indeed through appeals to purposes and their relations which are even childish, merely living nature is not in fact yet itself an adequate basis for understanding the true *determination* of the idea of God; God is more than living, he is Spirit. *Spiritual* nature alone is the worthiest and truest *starting-point* for thought of the Absolute, to the extent that thought takes a starting-point for itself and wishes to take the one which is closest.

Appendix XVIII: *Science of Logic,* Second Edition (1831)—Extract

[In the substantially revised second edition of the *Science of Logic* from 1831 Hegel reprinted his remarks concerning the *Phenomenology* from the 1812 edition's preface and introduction with only very minor alterations (see appendix XV). However, his remarks on the *Phenomenology* in the section "With What Must Science Begin?" underwent thorough rewriting, and I therefore include here a translation of their rewritten version—the counterpart to the original version from 1812 translated in appendix XV. Since much of the interest of this later version lies in seeing how much its takes over from, and how much it adds to, the earlier version, I have marked with angular brackets (⟨ ⟩) material taken over more or less unchanged from the earlier version, thereby also showing the material not so marked to have been newly added in 1831. The reader can form a more precise idea of the similarities and differences between the two versions by comparing this extract with its counterpart in appendix XV.—Text translated from Hegel, *Wissenschaft der Logik* (Frankfurt am Main: Suhrkamp, 1983), vol. 1.]

From "With What Must Science Begin?"

⟨The consciousness has first arisen in recent times that it is a problem to find a *beginning* in philosophy and the source of this problem and the possibility of solving it have been much discussed. The beginning of philosophy must be either something *mediated* or something *immediate,* and it is easy to show that it can be neither the one nor the other. Hence both ways of beginning find their refutation.⟩

A philosophy's *principle* no doubt expresses a beginning as well, but not so much a subjective beginning as an *objective* one, the beginning *of all things.* The principle is a *content* determined in some way or other: water, the one, *nous,* the Idea, substance, monad, etc.; or if the principle refers to the nature of cognition and hence is supposed to be more just a criterion than an objective determination—thought, intuition, sensation, I, subjectivity itself—then here likewise it is the determination of the content that is the point of interest. In contrast, the process of beginning as such remains unconsidered and a matter of indifference, as something subjective in the sense of a contingent manner of introducing the presentation, and consequently the need for the question with what the beginning should be made remains insignificant in comparison with the need for the principle, as that in which alone the interest of *the matter* [der Sache] seems to lie, the interest as to what is the *true,* the *absolute ground* of everything.

But the modern embarrassment concerning the beginning arises from a further need, a need with which those are still unacquainted who in a dogmatic manner see it as the task to prove the principle or who in a skeptical manner see it as the task to discover a subjective criterion against dogmatic philosophizing, and which those deny completely who would begin from their inner revelation, from faith, intellectual intuition, etc. as from a pistol and would claim to be excused from *method* and Logic. When formerly abstract thought to begin with takes an interest only in the principle as *content* but is driven with the advance of culture to pay attention to the other side, to the operation of *cognition,* then *subjective* activity is grasped as an essential moment of objective truth as well, and the need arises that the method be united with the content, the *form* with the *principle.* Hence the *principle* should also be the beginning and what thought takes to be the *first fact* [das Prius] should also be the *first* in the *process* of thought.

Here we have only to consider how the *logical* beginning appears. Both ways in which this beginning can be approached have already been mentioned—either

Appendix XVIII

in a mediated fashion as a result or in an immediate fashion as a real beginning. The question which seems so important to our modern culture, whether the knowing of the truth is an immediate knowing which makes an unconditional beginning, a faith, or rather a mediated knowing, is not to be discussed here. To the extent that such a consideration can be undertaken *in advance* [vorläufig] this has happened in another place (in my *Encyclopaedia of the Philosophical Sciences*, third edition, in the "introduction," pars. 61 ff.). Here we may adduce just the following point from that treatment: that there *is* nothing, nothing in heaven or in nature or in Spirit or anywhere else, which does not contain immediacy just as much as mediation, so that these two determinations prove to be *unseparated* and *inseparable* and the opposition mentioned proves to be a nullity [ein Nichtiges]. As far as the *scientific discussion* is concerned, on the other hand, it is in each logical posit [Satz] that the determinations of immediacy and mediation, and hence the discussion of their opposition and of their truth, occur. To the extent that this opposition receives the more concrete shape of immediate and mediated *knowing* in relation to thought, knowing, and cognition, the nature of cognition in general is considered within the Science of Logic, and in addition cognition in its further concrete form falls within the Science of Spirit and within the Phenomenology of Spirit. But to want already to come to a clear understanding of cognition *before* Science means to demand that cognition be discussed *outside* Science. *Outside* Science this cannot be achieved, at least not in a scientific way, which is our sole concern here.

The beginning is *logical* in that it is to be made in the element of thought which is freely for itself, in *pure knowing*. The beginning is hence *mediated* due to the fact that pure knowing is the final, absolute truth of *consciousness*. It was noted in the introduction that the *Phenomenology of Spirit*, the science of consciousness, is the representation of the fact that consciousness has the *Concept* of Science, i.e., pure knowing, as its result. To this extent the Logic has the science of appearing Spirit as its presupposition, which contains and demonstrates the necessity of the standpoint of pure knowing, and hence the proof of this standpoint's truth, along with this standpoint's mediation in general. In this science of appearing Spirit the beginning is made from the empirical, *sensuous* consciousness, and this is the properly *immediate* form of knowing; what this immediate knowing amounts to is discussed at that point. Other types of consciousness, such as the belief in divine truths, inner experience, knowing through inner revelation, etc., show themselves upon slight reflection to be very improperly paraded as examples of immediate knowing. In the *Phenomenology of Spirit* the immediate consciousness is also what is first and immediate in the science, and hence the presupposition; but in the Logic the presupposition is what had proved itself to be the result from the *Phenomenology of Spirit*'s investigation, namely, the Idea as pure knowing. ⟨The *Logic is the pure Science*, i.e., pure knowing in the full scope of its development. But this Idea has determined itself in the said result as the certainty which has become truth, the certainty which, on the one hand, no longer stands in opposition to the object but has made the object internal, knows the object as itself, and which, on the other hand, has given up the knowledge of itself as something which is in opposition to and only the destroyer of the objective, has externalized itself from this subjectivity[21] and is a unity with its externalization.⟩

Now in order that, proceeding from this determination of pure knowing, the beginning of pure knowing's Science should remain immanent one must do nothing but consider—or rather, setting aside all other reflections, all other opinions that one has, just take up—*what is present.*

⟨Pure knowing, qua *compacted into this unity*, has sublated all relation to an other and to mediation.⟩ It is that which lacks distinctions. This something lacking distinctions hence ceases of itself even to be knowing [hört somit selbst auf, Wissen zu sein]. ⟨There is only *simple immediacy* present.

"Simple immediacy" is itself an expression of Reflection and refers to the distinction from what is mediated. Truly expressed this simple immediacy is therefore *pure being.*⟩ Just as *pure* knowing should be called nothing but knowing as such, quite abstractly, so also pure being should be called nothing but ⟨*being* in general; being, nothing more, without any further determination or content.⟩

Here being, what begins, is represented as having arisen through mediation, more precisely through that mediation which is at the same time a sublation of itself—with the presupposition of pure knowing as the result of finite knowing or of consciousness. But if no presupposition is to be made, if the beginning is itself to be taken *immediately*, then it only determines itself through the fact that it is supposed to be the beginning of Logic, of autonomous thought [des Denkens für sich]. All that is present is the resolve, which can also be regarded as an arbitrary choice, to consider *thought as such*. ⟨Hence the beginning must be an *absolute* or, what in this context means the same, an abstract beginning; and consequently it may *presuppose nothing*, must be mediated by nothing, and must have no ground; it should rather itself be the ground of the whole Science. It must therefore simply *be* an immediate or rather just *the immediate* itself. Just as it cannot have a determination in contrast to an other, it also cannot contain a determination within itself, it can contain no content; for that sort of thing would be a distinguishing and a relating of different things to one another, and hence a mediation. The beginning is therefore *pure being.*⟩

After this simple explanation of what to begin with belongs only to this itself most simple thing, the logical beginning, the following additional reflections can be furnished as well. However, they cannot so much be supposed to serve for purposes of clarifying and confirming that explanation, which is complete in itself. Rather, they are only occasioned by opinions and reflections which may block our path in advance, but which like all other initial prejudices must be disposed of in Science itself, and which should therefore really be requested to have the patience to wait for this.[22]

⟨The insight that the absolutely true must be a result, and conversely that a result presupposes something first and true, which, however, because it is a first,

---

21. Reading, as in the first edition: *sich entäußert hat.*
22. Reading: *wären.*

is, considered objectively, not necessary, and, on the subjective side, not known—has in recent times given rise to the thought that philosophy can only begin with a *hypothetical* and *problematic* truth and that philosophizing can hence to begin with only be a search.⟩ This is a view which *Reinhold* has much advocated in the later periods of his philosophical activity, and one must do it the justice of acknowledging that a true interest underlies it concerning the speculative nature of the philosophical *beginning*. The treatment of this view is at the same time an occasion to introduce a provisional understanding concerning the meaning of logical advance in general, since this view immediately includes a concern with the process of advance. This view indeed presents the process of advance in this manner: ⟨that the advance forward in philosophy is rather a movement backward and a grounding through which it first emerges that what the beginning was made with is not merely something arbitrarily assumed but in fact, on the one hand, the *true* and, on the other hand, the *first true*.

It must be admitted that it is an essential observation—which will emerge more precisely within the Logic itself—that the advance forward is a *return* into the *ground*, to what is *original* and *true*, on which that with which the beginning was made depends, and by which it is in fact brought forth [hervorgebracht wird].—In this way consciousness, on its path from the immediacy with which it begins, gets led back to absolute knowing as its innermost *truth*. This last thing, the ground, is, then, also that from which the first thing comes forth [hervorgeht], though the latter initially made its appearance as something immediate.⟩—In this way it is still more so that absolute Spirit, which emerges as the concrete truth and the last and highest truth of all being, gets recognized as externalizing itself with freedom at the *end* of the development and releasing itself to the shape of an *immediate* being—resolving on [sich entschließend] the creation of a world which contains everything which fell within the development which preceded that result and which together with its beginning gets changed due to this reversed position into something dependent on the result qua the principle. ⟨What is essential for Science is not so much that something purely immediate be the beginning, but that the whole of Science is a circular course within itself in which the first thing becomes also the last and the last thing also the first.

Therefore, on the other side, it proves to be just as necessary to consider that into which the movement returns, as into the first's *ground, as a result*. From this point of view, the first is just as much the ground and the last something deduced; in that the beginning is made from the first and the last is arrived at as the ground through correct inferences, this ground is in fact a result. Moreover, the advance from what makes the beginning is only to be seen as a further determination of it, so that what makes the beginning remains at the basis of everything that follows and does not vanish from it. The advance does not consist in a deduction of something merely *other* or in a transition to something which is truly other—and to the extent that this transition does happen, it just as much sublates itself again. Hence the beginning of philosophy is the foundation which is present and preserves itself in all the developments which follow, it is that which remains entirely immanent to its further determinations.

Through this advance, then, the beginning loses the one-sidedness which it has in this determination of being something immediate and abstract in general. It becomes something mediated, and the line of the scientific advance thereby makes itself *into a circle.*—At the same time, it turns out that what makes the beginning, since in its beginning it is what is still undeveloped and contentless, is in the beginning still not truly known and that only Science for the first time, and indeed Science in its whole development, is the complete, contentful, and for the first time truly grounded cognition of it.

But because the *result* appears for the first time as the absolute ground, the advance of this cognition is not something provisional, nor something problematic and hypothetical, but it must be determined by the nature of the matter [Sache] and the content itself. Neither is that beginning something arbitrary and only provisionally assumed, nor is it something which appears arbitrary and is presupposed only through special pleading, of which it however turns out in what follows that one was right to make it the beginning. The situation here is not like in the constructions which one is instructed to make for the purpose of proving a geometrical proposition, where it only emerges afterwards from the proofs that one did right to draw in these constructions precisely these lines, and then to begin the proofs themselves with the comparison of these lines or angles—this is not intelligible from this line-drawing or comparing independently.⟩

Appendix XIX: Note for the Second Edition of the *Phenomenology* (1831)

[The final text included here is a short note which Hegel wrote in 1831 in connection with his plan to publish a second edition of the *Phenomenology*—a project on which he was still working at the time of his death in the same year.—Text translated from Hegel, *Phänomenologie des Geistes,* ed. J. Hoffmeister (Hamburg: Felix Meiner, 1952), "Zur Feststellung des Textes."]

re preface
Phenom[enology of Spirit]
first part, in fact

a) In advance of Science
   to bring consciousness to this standpoint.

b) Make the object develop independently [für sich],
   the Logic is *behind* consciousness

c) Distinctive earlier work, do not change [umarbeiten],
   —relative to the former time of its composition
   —in the preface: the *abstract Absolute* held sway at that time.

Index

Absolute Spirit, 11; and philosophy of mind, 99, 101n208; and time, 99, 245n90, 291–92; and unity, 11, 43, 79–81, 193–204; as a self, 194–95; as a self-developing conceptual hierarchy, 11–12; chronological history of expressions of, 196, 296–97, 456–62; identity with man/nature, 67n125, 81–83, 101n208, 196–204; realization of, and (self-)knowledge, 12, 14, 15n7, 104n211, 193–204, 245n89, 293–94, 432n157, 560–65, 569n24
action (*Tun*), 89, 255, 335–38, 340–42, 346n127, 350
activism, Hegel's, 102n210, 486–97
Acton, H.B., 445n169
Aeschylus, 32n42, 34n47, 47n78, 48n80, 314, 315n49
Agrippa, 130n11, 152–60, 167–68, 192
alienation (*Entfremdung*), 61n105, 63–67, 83
allgemein, 206n29, 224
Anaxagoras, 25n24, 64
Annas, J., 52n91
appearance (*Erscheinung*): as category of Logic, 260–61; of Science, *Phenomenology* as, 102n210, 115, 225, 259–69, 275, 277, 284, 287, 482n31, 485, 495, 497, 551–55, 566; versus mere *Schein*, 263n7, 264n9
architectonics, 1–7
Aristophanes, 32n42, 34n47, 53n91, 315n49, 462
Aristotle, 167n92, 378n40, 446n171, 490; and everyday views, 105, 122n249; and logic, 407n113; and man/nature dualism, 27, 28n32, 45; and meaning, understanding, interpretation, 52n91, 400–404, 407n113; and mind/body dualism, 41, 94n193; and moral motivation, 35n48; and realized virtue / happiness, 38n57, 56n95; and tragedy, 52n91, 403; and universals, 213, 216n49
Arnold, M., 398n85
art (*see also* Greek comedy; Greek gods and poetry; Greek gods and sculpture; Greek tragedy), 12, 47n78, 225
aufheben/Aufhebung, 23n16, 186n125, 203n23, 237n77, 265, 356; and dialectic, 186n125, 265; and skeptical paradox / skeptical solution, 237n77; of consciousness, 144n43, 195n6; of *Phenomenology* to Science, 282–88, 551–53

647

Bacon, F., 28, 45, 82, 327
Baillie, J.B., 178n111, 188, 271n3, 275n9
Bayle, P., 189
behavior(ism) (*see also* materialism, eliminative; naturalism, Hegel's): and language, meaning, conceptual understanding, 95–100, 205–22, 239–40, 337–38, 346n127, 387; and mind, 94–102, 107n221, 116n240, 145, 196n7, 198, 207, 335–38, 341, 346n127, 387
belief (*see also* cognition; dualisms, fact and volition / theory and practice): ancient skeptical attack on, 129–52; and behavior, 95–99, 100n206; and shapes of consciousness, 119–23; as "cognition"/"knowledge," 90n185, 163n87; as historically localized, 90n186; overcoming of, 90–91, 350; /theory as internal to meaning, 106–7, 119–21, 167n92, 201–2, 237–38, 381–85, 400–402, 407n113, 419; historical variations in, and interpretation, 360–419
Bergson, H., 367n12
Berkeley, G., 105, 133–34, 149
Berlin, B. and P. Kay, 368, 409–13
Bloor, D., 465n3, 477n22
Böckh, P.A., 366, 415n128, 434n159
Bodammer, T., 84n175
body. *See* behavior(ism); dualisms, mind and body; physicalism
Breazeale, D., 117n241
Burnyeat, M.F., 130n12, 137, 146

causal explanation (*see also* explanation; forces; naturalism, Hegel's), 4, 64–67, 133n17, 462n21
charity, in interpretation, 381–404
Charles, D., 400n90
Cherniss, H., 52n91, 403, 404n105
Christianity (*see also* Judeo-Christian tradition; *Phenomenology of Spirit*, *Unhappy Consciousness*), 312–13, 417, 419; and Jesus, 26n27, 40, 75n149, 81n166, 92n191, 199, 230n70; as a shape of consciousness, 324–26, 351–52; critique of, 5, 22–78, 226–27; Hegel's own, 11–12, 26n27, 81–82, 92n191, 193–204, 562–65; social explanation of, 25–28, 30, 35–38, 44n75, 54–55, 59–60, 318–22, 461, 469–72
Churchlands, P. and P., 145
cognition (*see also* belief): and volition, 18n5, 31–33, 51–54, 71, 89–91, 93n192, 339–47, 350; /knowledge as terms, Hegel's use of, 90n185, 144n41, 163n87; finite versus infinite, 109–13, 181
coherence, of *Phenomenology*, 2–4
comedy. *See* Greek comedy
common sense, 100n206, 105–7, 202–3, 208–9, 213, 232–37, 240–41, 349, 405
communal (*see also* community): conceptual articulation of Science, 14, 204–5, 223–26, 274, 560–65; consensus, establishing for Science, 14–15, 244–47, 274, 486–97, 560–65; consensus, historical development of, 86, 89–90, 92, 247–55, 331–32; consensus theory of truth/reality, 5, 14–15, 18n5, 69–70, 84–93, 176n107, 226–43, 339–47, 350, 419n136, 560–67; identification/solidarity, 20, 21n11, 28–30, 45–49, 67–70, 72–75, 83–87, 89–93, 244–50, 313; /individual dualism, 28–30, 45–49, 67–70; nature of language/meaning/concepts, 4–5, 14, 83–84, 93n192, 204–26, 239–40, 338–39, 346n127, 347, 566; nature of self, 83–87, 93n192, 338–39, 346n127; underpinning for Science, 204–55, 477–97

community (*see also* communal): and family, 72–75; and God, 199; and Oedipus cycle, 29, 46n77, 47n78, 48; as an end, 28–30, 45–48, 67–69, 72–73, 83–85

concept-instantiation problem (*see also* concepts-reality distinction/identity [and skepticism]; epistemology), 160–61

Concept, the. *See* Absolute Spirit

concepts (*see also* behavior[ism]; communal; meaning): comprehending one's own through history, 430–45; /conceptions of self, object, and representation, in shapes of consciousness, 84n174, 116–23, 194–97, 299–300, 421; novelty of Hegel's, 100n206, 104n212, 105–7, 195n6, 202–3, 209, 223–26, 233, 236–37, 243n87, 360n1; of finite cognition, discrediting of, 110–14, 116, 121–23, 177, 181; paradox as a mechanism of change in, 425–30; radical differences in, and interpretation, 360–419; -reality distinction/identity (and skepticism), 14–15, 30–31, 49–51, 70–71, 87–88, 149–52, 160–61, 166–67, 174–77, 214–16, 303, 323–24, 347n128, 378n40, 425–30, 548, 565–66; /thought, dependence on corresponding language, 83–84, 93n192, 96, 205–7, 337–38, 366n10, 374n32, 390, 413n124

conceptual schemes, 360–413

conceptual understanding. *See* behavior(ism); communal; concepts; meaning

consciousness (*see also* shapes of consciousness): Absolute/God as a, 144n43, 194–95; and "in itself" / "for itself" distinction, 194n2; essential structure of, 116–21, 144, 194–97, 299–300; "experience" of, 163n87; individual, discrediting of, 114n238, 143–44, 145n44; strata of, 354–57, 421–24

Cook, D.J., 84n175

correspondence theory of truth. *See* fact; representation

cosmopolitanism, 73nn145–46, 419n136

criterion (*Maßstab*): and epistemology, 45, 67n125, 131, 137, 154, 159–60, 163n87, 168–69, 177n109, 220n53, 228–31, 241n84, 333–34, 346n127, 419n136; and interpretation, 414; behavioral, 99n202, 207, 219nn51–52

Davidson, D., 366–409

Democritus, 141, 143, 145, 147, 308, 310

Descartes, R.: and equipollence skepticism, 189–90; and mechanistic science, 28; and mind/body dualism, 42n73, 59n99, 94n193; and preemptive skepticism, 127–28, 154–55, 188n129, 189–90; and "veil of perception" skepticism, 134, 137n27, 142nn38–39, 148

desire (*see also* dualisms, duty and desire): satisfaction of, and happiness, 19–21; in *Self-consciousness* chapter, 20–21, 250–55, 312–15

Detienne, M., 385n48

DeVries, W.A., 94n193

dialectical method, 114–16, 123, 169–72, 175, 182–87, 265–67, 270–81, 293, 425–30, 442–45, 548

Diderot, D., 451, 471nn11,13

Dilthey, W., 14n6, 294n11, 348, 366, 415, 474n15, 479n27

disenchanted nature, 27–28, 44–45, 63–67, 82–83

Dove, K., 274n8

dualisms: and division of labor / class divisions, 31n40, 476n21; and Hegel's monistic cure for, 78–102, 477–97; and modern unhappiness, 61–78; and social basis in antiquity, 25–60, 314n43, 465–70; and social basis in modern Germany, 473–76; duty and desire, 33–38, 54–55, 71–75, 91–92, 93n192, 313–14, 315n51, 469–70; fact and volition / theory and practice, 31–33, 51–54, 71, 89–91, 93n192, 313–14, 340–42, 466–67; God and man/nature, 5n8, 23–26, 28, 43–44, 61–63, 81–82, 194–204, 312–14, 324–25, 417–19, 469–72; individual and community, 28–30, 45–49, 67–70, 83–87, 93n192, 204–55, 313–14, 331–32, 338–40, 466–67, 469; man and nature, 27–28, 44–45, 63–67, 82–83, 313–14, 326–29, 469; mind and body, 40–42, 57–60, 64n115, 76–78, 93–102, 313–15, 335–38, 346n127, 466–67, 469; self/thought and reality, 30–31, 49–51, 70–71, 87–88, 90–91, 93n192, 149–52, 166–67, 174–76, 313–14, 323–24, 326, 378n40, 466–67; virtue and happiness, 38–40, 55–57, 76, 92–93, 313–14, 469–70

Dummett, M., 392n72

Düsing, K., 13n3

duty. *See* dualisms, duty and desire; Kant, and duty/desire dualism; morality; virtue

Egypt, Pharaonic, 304, 310–11, 315n50, 351–52, 449n3, 457

empiricism (*see also* naturalism, Hegel's; natural science; nature): model of meaning (Locke/Hume), 217–18; methodological, and intellectual historicism, 229–30, 361–63, 366–413

Encyclopaedia, G.W.F. Hegel (*see also* Logic, Hegel's, later), 3, 6–7, 11–13, 67n125, 81–83, 84n174, 91, 95nn194–95, 96n196, 97n200, 101n207, 102n209, 104n212, 105n214, 123–24, 126n3, 132nn15–16, 134n21, 154, 157n74, 158–59, 172n103, 180n115, 194n3, 200–201, 203n24, 205n28, 234, 237, 243n88, 276–77, 285–87, 301, 317, 320, 322, 354, 359n154, 448, 541–43, 548–55, 556–70

Enlightenment, the (see also *Phenomenology of Spirit, The Enlightenment*), 19n7, 199n14, 455

epistemology (*see also* concept-instantiation problem; equipollence; skepticism): and certainty, as aim, 88, 180; and dialectical method, 184–87; Hegel-Schelling technique of "critique," 127, 157–58; Hegel's defense against concept-instantiation problem, 14–16, 88n183, 160–61, 166–67, 174–77, 269n14, 565–66; Hegel's defense against equipollence problem, 14–16, 159–60, 164–66, 167–74, 267–69, 565–66; Lambert-Kant, 126, 155–57; Romantic immediate knowledge, 128, 153–54; transcendental arguments, 161–63; universal ad hominem proof of Science, 177–84

equipollence (*see also* epistemology; presuppositions; skepticism): and continental tradition, 189–92; and Descartes, 154–55, 189–90; and early Logic, 167–70; and Fichte, 191–92; and fourth trope of Agrippa, 152–60, 167–68; and Kant, 157, 190–91; attack on current mental states, 138–48;

method of, 129–33, 138–48, 152–58
Euben, J.P., 47n78
Evans-Pritchard, E.E., 367, 372n28, 396
explanation (*see also* causal explanation; teleology): of behavior, 100n206, 220n53, 222n57; mechanistic / efficient causal versus teleological, 27–28, 44–45, 64–67, 82–83, 459–65; of thought in terms of social context, 460–65

fact (*see also* dualisms, fact and volition / theory and practice): -representation correspondence concept(ion) of truth, 88, 156n73, 176n107, 232–38, 419n136, 566–67; of consciousness, 133–34, 143, 147n54, 163n87
fate, 491n52
Feuerbach, L.A., 5, 63nn112–13, 445n171, 486–87
Feyerabend, P., 145, 367n12
Fichte, J.G., 453n8, 481n30; and consciousness, 116–17, 119n247, 196n7, 197; and dualism, 31, 33, 42, 54n92, 59, 94n193; and *Geschichte*, 301n12; and skepticism, 128, 137n28, 189, 191–92
Findlay, J.N., 291n2, 312n40
Finley, M.I., 320n64
Fischer, K., 15n7
Flay, J.C., 161n84
forces (*see also* causal explanation; naturalism, Hegel's; *Phenomenology of Spirit*, Force and the Understanding), 64–67, 215, 220n53, 222n57, 307–11, 338n109, 358
Foucault, M., 431, 465n3
fourth trope. *See* Agrippa
Fränkel, E., 367, 374n33, 396, 398n84
Frede, M., 130n12

Frederick the Great, 90, 254n102, 330–31, 453
freedom/oppression (*see also* Greek freedom/oppression; *Phenomenology of Spirit*, Lordship and Bondage), 20–21, 25–26, 30, 35–40, 44n75, 45, 48–51, 54–55, 59–60, 69–70, 72–75, 77–78, 84–87, 89–93, 199n14, 237n78, 238n81, 242, 245–55, 315n51, 316–22, 466–72, 488, 569n24
French Revolution (see also *Phenomenology of Spirit*, Absolute Freedom and Terror), 102n210, 199n14, 451, 453, 455, 465n2, 483n38, 487–88
Fritz, K. von, 385n48
Fulda, H.F., 3, 15n7, 172n103, 259n1, 268n11, 271n3, 273n6, 274n7, 278n14, 280n18, 503–4, 511–21, 529, 531, 549–55
Furley, D.J., 427n144

Galen, 147
Galileo, 28, 45, 82, 327
genetic fallacy, 445–46
German Constitution, The, G.W.F. Hegel, 102n210, 461, 474–82, 488–94
Geschichte (*see also* history), 301n12, 355
God (*see also* Absolute Spirit; Christianity; community; consciousness; dualisms; Judeo-Christian tradition; morality; naturalism, Hegel's): identity with man/nature, 5, 23–24, 81–82, 194–204, 312–13; epistemic accessibility of, 24–25, 43–44, 63, 81
Goethe, J.W. von, 19, 69, 76n155, 89, 329, 452
Goldhill, S., 47n78
Goodman, N., 98
Gorgias, 51n87, 141, 160n81, 323n70, 425, 428–30

Graeser, A., 126n2, 144n41
Gray, J.G., 26n25, 91n189
Greece, ancient (historical periods): Homeric, 304, 309–11, 315n50, 351–52, 439–40; ideal fifth-century, 312–15, 317–19, 322n68, 325, 351–52; late fifth-century, 317–22, 325, 351–52; Hellenistic, 322–26, 351–52
Greek (*see also* morality, communal Greek; Greek gods): comedy, 32n42, 34n47, 51n89, 53n91, 315n49, 458–59, 462; culture, as ideal, 18–102, 226–27, 312–15; freedom/oppression, 315–21; rationalism, 304, 308–9, 311, 315n50, 351–52, 358–59, 423, 439–40; tragedy, 29, 32n42, 34n47, 46–49, 52n91, 314–15, 318, 449, 454, 458, 462; views on duty and desire, 34, 36n55, 38–39, 55–56, 91–93, 313–15; views on fact and volition, 31n41, 32, 51–53, 90n186; views on the soul, 40–42, 58, 102, 313–15
Greek gods: and poetry, 51–52, 309–10; and sculpture, 23n17, 32, 51n88; epistemic accessibility of, 23–25; proximity to man/nature of, 23–24, 27–28, 44–45, 61–62, 82n168, 202n22, 309–10
Grice, H.P., 406n112
Guthrie, W.K.C., 60n104, 404n105

Habermas, J., 278n13, 280n18, 284n10, 550nn6,8
Haering, T., 3, 286, 501–3, 507, 508–9, 517n12, 531, 533n36, 540, 549–57
Hamann, J.G., 206
happiness (*see also* dualisms; unhappiness): and deepest aspirations of man, 19–21, 69–71, 84–87, 92–93, 245, 247; and truth, 17–18, 125; as goal of philosophy, 18–21, 70n132, 78–81

Hardin, C.L., 368, 409
Harris, H.S., 14n6, 18, 22n12, 25n22, 26n25, 74n147, 132n15, 315n49, 354, 520n16
Haym, R., 3, 15n7, 123n253, 268n11, 302n15, 353, 357–58, 501–2
Heinrichs, J., 276n10, 503–4, 511–21, 524n21, 529, 534
Herder, J.G.: and anthropology, 415n129; and Christianity, 26n27, 335n101; and communality of language/thought/self, 93n192, 209, 221–22, 338–39, 346n127; and fragmented, pathological modernity, 22n12, 31n40, 71, 474n16, 476n21; and historicism, 170n99, 230n69, 294n9, 361, 363n6, 366; and history / historical methodology, 25n24, 170n99, 230n96, 311, 351, 361, 366, 414n126, 415n128, 420n137, 424n140; and language/thought, 206–7, 366; and *Maßstab*, 333–34, 346n127, 414n126; and Machiavelli, 478n26; and pedagogy, 110n228; and philosophy of mind, 94n193, 335–38; and resolutions of modern dualisms, 89–90, 93n192, 102n210, 453; and skepticism, 170n99; and truth as communal, 233, 238, 240n83, 246n91, 255, 339–40, 343–45, 346n127; and universals, 305n21; *Spiritual Animalkingdom* as standpoint of, 89–90, 209, 221–22, 238, 240n83, 241, 248, 255, 332–48, 528–29
Herodotus, 23n17, 29, 39n58, 52n90, 404n104
Historical School, 366, 415n218
historicism, 291–94, 360–446, 459–97, 543
history (see also *Geschichte*; historicism; shapes of consciousness): and dualisms, development and overcoming of, 22–102, 312–50; and

Index 653

enduring communal consensus / truth / freedom, 247–55; and historical methodology, 25n24, 413–24; and Lordship and Bondage, 247–55, 316–22; and relativity of *Phenomenology*, 556–70; and relativity of Science, 569n24; chronological, of consciousness, 296–359, of social contexts, 296–97, 447–56, of expressions of God/Absolute, 296–97, 456–60
Hoffmeister, J., 355n147, 535, 540
Hölderlin, F., 61, 79n159, 89n183, 117n243, 195n6, 348n130
Holy Roman Empire, 461, 474–75, 478, 484
Homer, 23n17, 34n47, 36n55, 38n57, 41, 42n71, 52nn90–91, 309–10, 315n49, 412, 423, 435, 439–40, 491n52, 563
human nature, 5, 229–31, 361–63; and animals, 222n56, 332–33, 346n127
Humboldt, W. von, 106n219, 206, 361, 366, 415n129, 416n131, 417n133
Hume, D., 65; antihistoricism of, 362–63; and *Logical and Psychological Laws*, 58, 217, 328; and nature of concepts/thought, 206, 210, 217–19; and skepticism, 128, 132–35, 149, 161–62, 176, 190, 192n140
Hyppolite, J., 1n2, 15n7, 102n210, 270, 298, 300n10, 317n56, 329n93, 353, 448n2, 456n14, 491n52

identity (*see also* monism; unity): of identity and non-identity, 79n160, 80, 195n6, 199–204
inclination. *See* desire
India, ancient, 304, 307, 311, 351–52, 457
individual (*see also* communal; individualism): and community, 28–30, 45–49, 55–56, 67–70, 83–87, 89–92, 93n192, 204–55, 313–14, 328–33, 338–40, 346n127, 350, 453, 466–96; consciousness versus Science, 114n238, 144; existence/identity dependent on language and community, 83–84, 93n192, 338–39, 346n127; language/meaning not possible, 205–22, 338–39, 346n127; modern Hegelian, as overcoming fact/volition dualism, 89–91
individualism (*see also* individual), 18, 28–30, 45–49, 328–29; costs of, 67–70; Hegel's cure for, 83–87; modern/Hegelian synthesis with communalism, 330–33, 338–40, 346n127, 350; of cultures, 333–35, 346n127
interpretation (*see also* charity, in interpretation; radical interpretation; translation), 229–30, 360–424
Inwood, M.J., 22n14, 65n119, 84n175, 243n88, 279n15
Irwin, E., 412nn120,123
Irwin, T., 400n91

Jaeger, W., 52n91, 373n30, 403
Jebb, R., 48n80, 415n129
Judeo-Christian tradition (*see also* Christianity; dualisms; freedom/oppression; God; morality; *Phenomenology of Spirit*, Lordship and Bondage, Unhappy Consciousness): pre-Christian Judaism, 24n21, 25n22, 28, 32, 36, 42n71, 44n75, 63n113, 72, 74–75, 90n186, 92n191, 461
judgment: agreement in, and truth, 69–70, 84–93, 176n107, 226–47; forms of, and finite cognition, 111–12, 116, 169–70

Kainz, H.P., 88n182, 171n101, 298–99

Kant, I., 26n27, 39n58, 40n63, 105, 132n16, 286n13, 292n3, 417n32, 442, 481n30, 483n34, 486–87; and concept-instantiation problem, 150n61, 160; and consciousness, 116–17, 197; and duty/desire dualism, 35, 37–38, 54, 57, 72–75, 92n191, 107, 249n97; and equipollence skepticism, 130, 189–91; and fact/volition dualism, 33, 53–54; and historicism, 228–31, 293–94, 361, 363; and mind/body dualism, 59, 206; and system, 170–71, 173; and things in themselves, 156; and transcendental arguments, 161–63; and truth, 156–57, 228–32; and universal intersubjective agreement, 228–32; and virtue/happiness dualism, 57, 76; -Lambert epistemological conception, 126, 155–57; *Reason as Testing Laws* as standpoint of, 332n96, 349–50, 453n8

Kelly, G.A., 248n93, 249, 255, 353n141

Kierkegaard, S.A., 187, 192, 435n161

knowledge. *See* Absolute Spirit; belief; cognition; epistemology; Science; truth

Kojève, A., 248–50, 255, 271n3

Kripke, S.A., 98, 176, 207–9, 212n40, 219n52, 385n50, 390n69, 404n107

Kuhn, T.S., 367n12, 370n21, 378n39, 396n82

Lambert, J.H., 126, 155–57, 263nn7–8

language (*see also* behavior[ism]; communal; concepts; individual; interpretation; translation): Hegel's philosophical, 100n206, 104n212, 105–7, 195n6, 202–3, 209, 223–26, 233, 243n87, 360n1

Lavater, J.K., 94, 217, 219n51, 328

law: human versus divine, 29–30, 35–38, 46–49; individual versus communal, 29–30, 55–56, 86n178, 87n181, 91–92, 329–32, 350, 453

Leibniz, G.W., 362n5

lekta, 50, 151n63, 216, 323, 429–30

Locke, J., 58, 206, 210, 217–18, 219n51, 328

logic, formal: skepticism concerning, 130, 162–63; and interpretation, 407n113

Logic, Hegel's: early, 7, 12–13, 67n125, 105n213, 108–16, 123–25, 143–44, 167–70, 174–81, 263–65, 282–83, 286–87, 515–24, 527; later, 6–7, 11–13, 66n122, 88, 104n212, 105, 114n238, 117n242, 124, 166n89, 169, 172n103, 178–80, 200–201, 260–61, 268–69, 270–72, 276–81, 283–86, 501–4, 508–9, 511–39, 548–55, 557–70; underlying *Phenomenology*, 503–4, 511–33, 537–39; knowledge of, not presupposed by *Phenomenology*, 270–81, 503n7

Long, A.A., and D.N. Sedley, 42n69, 429n150

Loraux, N., 47n78

love, 72–75, 79, 92n191, 93n192, 340

Lukács, G., 3, 292, 296–99, 302, 354n144, 447–48, 450, 455, 456n14, 482–86, 549

Machiavelli, N., 478n26, 491
MacIntyre, A., 94n193, 416n130
Maker, W., 282n1
Mannheim, K., 293, 465n3
Marx, K., 5, 22, 94n193, 445nn169,171, 462, 464n1, 465n3, 471n13, 486–87, 489n49
materialism, eliminative, 100n206, 107n221, 145–48

McGinn, C., 384, 395n81
meaning (*see also* behavior[ism]; belief; communal; concepts; individual; language), 205–22, 386–407; holism of, 369, 386, 389; in life, 72–75; private (*meinen*), refutation of, 83n173, 95–96, 205–22
meinen, 206n29
mind (*see also* behavior[ism]; dualisms; materialism, eliminative; naturalism, Hegel's): as active, 89–91, 137n28, 196n7, 335–38, 340–42, 346n127; divine, 99, 101n208, 194–204
modern culture. *See* dualisms
monism (*see also* Absolute Spirit; dualisms; identity; unity): Hegel's, 4, 11–12, 59n99, 78–107, 194–204, 477–96; of ideal Greek culture, 22–78, 312–15; of Plato's *Parmenides*, 143, 174, 308
Montaigne, M.E. de, 189
Moore, G.E., 134
morality (*see also* Christianity; dualisms; Judeo-Christian tradition; Kant; law; *Phenomenology of Spirit, Morality*; virtue): communal Greek, 24, 29, 34, 36n55, 38–39, 46–49, 55–56, 86n178, 91n190, 92–93, 227, 230n70; divine-command (positive), 23n16, 26, 29–30, 32–39, 45–46, 54–57, 74–75, 86, 90n186, 461, 469, 488; individual secular, 85–86, 329; modern communal, 85–86, 91–93, 330–50

Napoleon, 455, 479–84, 496, 549
naturalism, Hegel's, 4–5; concerning causation/forces, 64–67, 215, 220n53, 222n57, 338n109; concerning God, 81–82, 99–102, 197–204; concerning language/meaning, 95–100, 205–22; concerning mind, 64n115, 94–102, 107n221, 145, 198, 335–38, 346n127
natural science (*see also* causal explanation; disenchanted nature; explanation; forces), 27–28, 44–45, 63–67, 82–83, 311n36, 326–29, 358–59, 405–7, 438–40
nature (*see also* disenchanted nature; dualisms; natural science): as purposive/personal, 27–28, 44–45, 57–58, 63–67, 82–83, 312–13; transcendence of, 4–5, 27–28, 44–45, 59–60, 62–63, 65–67, 197–204, 214–15
necessity: and fate, 491n52; and history, 173–74, 243, 292–94, 442; dialectical, 184–87, 265; of transitions between shapes of consciousness, 113–16, 169–74, 182–87, 265–67, 270–81, 292–94, 425–30, 442–44, 548
Newman, F.W., 398n85
Newton, I., 65, 67n124, 311n36, 354, 358
Nietzsche, F.W., 5, 26, 36n55, 63n113, 293, 294n10, 431, 432n156, 438n164, 444, 445nn168,171
Norman, R., 1n2, 466n4

Oedipus cycle. *See* community; Sophocles
oppression. *See* freedom/oppression
Oresteia. *See* Aeschylus
Orphic-Pythagorean-Socratic-Platonic tradition, 41, 42nn71,73, 58, 59n99, 60n104, 77
Owen, G.E.L., 427n144

Parmenides, 166n89, 284, 308, 310, 425–30, 442, 444
Pericles, 29, 315, 318–19, 325
Persia, ancient, 304–5, 311, 351–52, 457
personal identity, 72, 83–84, 93n192, 338–39, 346n127

Phenomenology of Spirit, G.W.F. Hegel: Preface, 11, 13, 17, 43, 49, 80, 98, 105–7, 109–10, 115, 123, 126, 128, 144, 153–55, 158–59, 163n87, 166–67, 177n109, 178, 182, 186n125, 193–97, 201, 204, 216n49, 223, 225, 227, 237n79, 243n88, 245–46, 253n101, 260–63, 271–73, 275–76, 283, 285, 291, 293, 301, 303, 356, 419n136, 420n137, 422, 431–45, 464, 480–86, 495–97, 517, 523, 553–55, 558, 567–68; Introduction, 11, 20, 71, 90n185, 114–24, 126–28, 144, 154–61, 163n87, 168–71, 177–78, 185–87, 210, 233–35, 259–62, 268, 271–72, 275–78, 283, 293, 300, 301n12, 348, 413–14, 503, 505–7, 511–14, 523–24, 529–33; *Consciousness*, 296–311, 351–462, 501–43; *Sense-Certainty*, 49–50, 83n173, 96, 119n248, 163n87, 171–72, 182–83, 205–12, 216n48, 219, 235–36, 240, 300, 303–7, 311, 352, 356–57, 359n154, 365, 421, 424, 439, 449n3, 451, 457, 460, 509, 524–25, 530, 538–39, 547–48; *Perception*, 49–50, 119n248, 120, 213–14, 216, 219, 272, 279–80, 300, 303–4, 306–7, 309, 311, 352, 354, 356–57, 365, 421, 423–24, 439–40, 449n3, 451, 457, 460, 525, 530, 547; *Force and the Understanding*, 50, 65–67, 120, 214–16, 219, 220n53, 261, 272, 280, 303–4, 307–11, 315n50, 317–18, 352, 354, 356, 358, 365, 421, 423, 438–40, 449, 451, 457, 460, 525, 530, 547; *Self-Consciousness*, 19–21, 43–78, 247–55, 296–302, 311–26, 351–470, 501–43; *Life (and Desire)*, 20–21, 43–44, 57–58, 250–55, 312–22, 352, 449, 451, 457–58, 460, 525, 530; *Lordship and Bondage*, 5, 26n26, 44n75, 45, 48–51, 54–55, 59–60, 76, 86, 89, 92, 248–55, 312, 314n43, 315n51, 316–22, 325, 352, 449, 451, 458, 460, 466–72, 525, 530; *Stoicism*, 43, 45, 50, 52–53, 58, 60, 70, 150, 160, 210, 216, 219, 312, 314n43, 317–25, 352, 425, 449, 451, 458–60, 466–68, 525–26, 530, 548; *Skepticism*, 70, 150, 188n128, 312, 314n43, 317–18, 322n68, 323–24, 326, 352, 449–51, 458–60, 468n8, 526, 530; *Unhappy Consciousness*, 5, 43–46, 54–58, 61–63, 76–78, 81, 179n114, 198, 254n102, 312, 314n43, 316n51, 317, 319, 322n68, 324–26, 352, 417–19, 449–51, 459–60, 469–70, 526, 530; *Reason*, 18–21, 86–87, 89–93, 296–302, 326–462, 464, 473, 501–43; *Observing Reason*, 44–45, 65–67, 82–83, 124, 179n114, 326, 450–52, 454, 459–60, 526–27, 530, 541; *Observation of Nature*, 44–45, 65–67, 82–83, 326–27, 352, 526, 530; *Logical and Psychological Laws*, 58–59, 82–83, 93–94, 124, 210, 216n48, 217–19, 327–28, 352, 501, 507, 526–27, 530; *Physiognomy and Phrenology*, 45n76, 59, 82–83, 93–102, 124, 207, 210, 215, 216n48, 217–21, 222n57, 328, 352, 527, 530; *The Actualization of Rational Self-consciousness through its Own Activity*, 18–21, 29n34, 328–29, 527–28, 530, 540; *Pleasure and Necessity*, 19, 69, 89, 329, 352, 452–53, 530; *The Law of the Heart*, 329, 352, 453, 530; *Virtue and the Way of the World*, 90, 254n102, 298n4, 330–31, 352, 453, 530; *Individuality which takes Itself to be Real in and for Itself,*

331–32, 528, 530, 532–33, 539; *The Spiritual Animalkingdom,* 89–90, 94–101, 176, 208–10, 221–22, 224, 233, 235–38, 240–41, 248, 255, 298n4, 332–48, 352, 453, 528–30; *Reason as Lawgiver,* 87n81, 241n84, 298n4, 332n96, 348–49, 352, 530, 532, 534; *Reason as Testing Laws,* 87n181, 241n84, 332n96, 349–50, 352, 453n8, 530; *Pars.* 435–37, 69–70, 86–87, 89–92, 102n210, 227, 241, 248, 332n96, 346, 350, 352, 529–30, 533, 538–39; *Spirit,* 19n7, 46–49, 73, 84–85, 124, 199n14, 296–97, 302, 304n14, 309, 315, 318, 447–73, 501–10, 519, 532–43, 547; *Ethical World,* 46, 309, 313, 315, 318, 448–51, 457–58, 460, 538–39, 547; *Ethical Action,* 46–48, 448–51, 458, 460; *Legal Status,* 48, 50, 448–51, 458–60, 468, 470; *Culture and Faith,* 5, 84, 448, 450–52, 459–60, 470–72; *Pure Insight,* 450–52, 459–60; *The Enlightenment,* 19n7, 199n14, 450–55; *Absolute Freedom and Terror,* 102n210, 199n14, 254n102, 451–53, 455, 459n18; *Morality,* 53–54, 57, 124, 453n8, 538–39; *Religion,* 51–52, 124, 296–97, 300, 303, 305, 307, 310–11, 315, 447, 454, 456–60, 462 63, 501–10, 519, 532, 534, 536–39, 541–43, 547; *Natural Religion,* 457, 460; *God as Light,* 305, 457, 460, 538–39; *Plant and Animal,* 307, 457, 460; *The Artificer,* 310, 457, 460; *Religion of Art,* 47n78, 51–52, 310, 315, 457–60; *Revealed Religion,* 198–99, 417–19, 459–60; *Absolute Knowing,* 99, 124, 172, 245n90, 268n12, 285, 296–97, 447, 454, 456, 462n21, 501–14, 525, 529–39, 542–43, 547, 552

Philo, 325n76
Philosophy of Right, G.W.F. Hegel, 19n7, 21n11, 47n78, 73–74, 87n181, 99, 101n207, 102n210, 321n66, 349n133, 419n136, 472n14, 482, 484–86, 491–95, 497
physicalism. *See* behavior(ism); materialism, eliminative; naturalism, Hegel's, concerning mind
Pippin, R.B., 161n84, 283n8
Plant, R., 22n14, 25n24, 28n30, 79n160, 476n21, 479n29, 491n52, 564n19
Platner, E., 301n12, 355
Plato(nism), 315nn49–50, 462, 567n23; and duty/desire dualism, 35n48, 72; and fact/volition fusing in tragedy, 52n91; and Hegel's early Logic, 112n234, 143, 174; and Hegel's epistemology, 143, 174, 180n116; and man/nature dualism, 64–65; and meaning-individualism, 213–16, 219; and mind/body dualism, 41, 59n99, 60n104; and rationalism of *Force and the Understanding,* 308–10; and theory of meaning/forms, 4, 49–51, 70, 213–16, 219, 220n53, 303–4, 308–9, 323n70, 548; and thought/reality dualism, 50, 51n87, 70, 213–16, 303–4, 308–9, 323n70, 548
Platts, M., 392n72
Plotinus, 325n76
Pöggeler, O., 3, 224n59, 262n6, 270–71, 275n9, 299, 301n12, 311n38, 326n78, 355n147, 502, 508–9, 516, 518n14, 534, 550–55
polytheism, ancient. *See* Greek gods
Popkin, R.H., 189n130
Popper, K.R., 293
Popularphilosophen, 241n84, 332n96, 348–49
positive. *See* morality

Positivity of the Christian Religion, The, G.W.F. Hegel, 23–26, 28–30, 34–40, 45–46, 49, 55, 56n95, 59–60, 62n109, 68, 72, 226–27, 228–31, 237, 243n88, 318–19, 321, 322n68, 361, 363, 461, 469–70, 474n15, 488n47
presuppositions (*Voraussetzungen*), 114n238, 152–60, 285–87
private language. *See* communal; individual; meaning
Protagoras, 160n81
Purpus, W., 271n3, 297n2, 304n16, 503n7
Putnam, H., 367n12, 404n107
Pyrrhonism, 128–92

Quine, W.V.O., 367n12, 387nn56,58,60, 388n61, 391n71, 406, 407n113
radical interpretation, 387–88, 394
reality. *See* communal; concepts; dualisms; fact; monism; shapes of consciousness; skepticism; truth
Reformation, 326, 461, 465n2, 485
Reinhold, K.L., 116–17, 126n3, 157n74, 194, 197
Reitemeier, J.F., 248–49, 320
Relation of Skepticism to Philosophy, The, G.W.F. Hegel, 70, 112n234, 128–67, 188–89, 286
religion. *See* Absolute Spirit; Christianity; dualisms; God; Greek gods; Judeo-Christian tradition; morality
representation (*see also* consciousness, essential structure of; shapes of consciousness): -fact distinction, and truth as correspondence, 88, 156n73, 176n107, 232–38, 419n136, 566–67
Rist, J.M., 141n33
Ritter, J., 483n38
Roman Empire, 40, 48, 59–60, 68, 317, 321–26, 351–52, 449, 468–72, 488

Romantics, 128, 154, 359n154, 453n8
Root, M., 376n37
Rorty, R., 20, 238n81
Rosen, S., 271n3, 554n19
Rosenkranz, K., 17n1, 104n212, 105n213, 106n218, 179n113, 481n30, 482n31, 496n56, 517–18
Rosenzweig, F., 452n6, 479n27, 482–83, 491nn51–52
Rousseau, J.J., 22n12, 199n14, 255n103, 451
Royce, J., 14n6, 119n247, 329n93
Russell, B.A.W., 67n124

Sache selbst, 89n184, 340–45
Sapir, E., 367n12, 380
Schacht, R., 61n105
Schelling, F.W.J. von, 117n243, 166n90, 348n130; and Absolute, 80n163, 195n6, 196n7, 197n9; and epistemology, 127, 157; and everyday versus philosophical views, 105, 107–9; and *Geschichte,* 301n12, 355, 420n137, 422n138, 424n140; and truth as communal, 228n67
Schiller, J.C.F., 292n3, 348n130; and curing of dualisms, 92n191, 102n210, 496n55; and duty/desire dualism, 33–38, 71n141, 72nn143–44; and fact/volition dualism, 31n41; and God / man and nature dualism, 23–25, 61–63; and Hegel's historical schema, 80n164; and *Lordship and Bondage,* 249, 253n99; and man/nature dualism, 27–28; and pathologically dualistic modernity, 22n12, 23n16, 31n40, 476n21; and *The Law of the Heart,* 329, 453
Schleiermacher, F.D.E., 6, 206, 366, 374nn33–34, 398, 413n125, 415, 423n139, 434n159
Schmitz, H., 503n7

Schulze, G.E., "Aenesidemus," 128, 130–32, 134, 150n61, 160
Science (*see also* appearance; aufheben/Aufhebung; Encyclopaedia; Logic, Hegel's): as all truth, 158–59; as cure for dualisms/unhappiness, 78–102; as opposed to everyday views, 104–7; as philosophical system, 11; independence of *Phenomenology* from, 270–81; *Phenomenology* as effecting conceptual articulability of, 14, 223–26; *Phenomenology* as establishing communal consensus/truth for, 14–15, 244–47; *Phenomenology* as "introduction" to, 11–15; *Phenomenology* as justification of, 14, 126–84; *Phenomenology* as pedagogy in, 14, 17–125; *Phenomenology* as provisional presentation of, 14, 113, 115, 123–25, 262–69, 541, 567–68; relativity to historical context of, 569n24
Science of Logic, G.W.F. Hegel, 7, 11–13, 88, 104n212, 105, 114n238, 117n242, 169, 172n103, 178–80, 200–201, 260–61, 271–72, 283, 285–86, 518, 549, 553–54, 556–63, 570
Scruton, R., 188
sculpture. *See* Greek gods and sculpture
Segal, C., 47n78
self. *See* communal; concepts; consciousness; dualisms; individual; shapes of consciousness
self-consciousness. *See* Absolute Spirit, realization of, and (self-)knowledge; consciousness, essential structure of; shapes of consciousness
self-contradictions: as approximating truth, 113, 115, 263–69; as mechanism of conceptual change, 425–30, 442; in early Logic's concepts, forms of judgment, forms of syllogism, 112–14, 116, 168–70, 174n105, 177, 181; in *Phenomenology*'s shapes of consciousness, 115–16, 121–23, 169, 175–77, 182–85, 213–14, 234–35, 260–67, 442
Seneca, 58, 429
Sextus Empiricus, 51n87, 129–47, 150–52, 160, 170n97, 177n109, 284, 324n73, 428
shapes of consciousness (*see also* consciousness; necessity; self-contradictions): and conceptions/concepts of reality, self, and representation, 116–23, 213–14, 299–300, 304–11, 342–44, 364–65; and conceptions of truth as correspondence, 232–36; and expressions of God / shapes of religion, 296–97, 456–62, 505–8, 513–14; and individualistic conceptions of meaning, 210–20; and social contexts / shapes of a world, 296–97, 302, 447–56, 459–72, 505–8, 513–14; as appearance of Science, 260, 262–64; as developing cumulatively, 356–59, 420–22; as entire system / complete, 170–74, 175–76, 178, 183, 211n38, 234, 269; as strata of modern consciousness, 354–59, 421–24; chronological history of, 102n210, 119n248, 170n99, 174, 209, 211n38, 233–35, 296–359, 506–7, 537, 543; correspondence with categories of Logic, 124, 268–69, 271–72, 277–78, 503, 511–15, 521–30, 537–39
Shklar, J.N., 46n77, 102n210, 348n131, 349n134
skepticism (*see also* concept-instantiation problem; epistemology; equipollence; presuppositions; Pyrrhonism), 14; ancient, superiority over modern, 5, 128–33, 188–89, 192; and despair, 20, 70–71, 88, 114; Cartesian preemptive, 127–28,

skepticism (*continued*)
154–55, 188n129, 189–90; concerning current mental states, 130–48, 155, 162–63, 188n129; concerning formal logic, 130, 162–63; Humean, 128, 132nn15–16, 133n17, 134–35, 149, 176, 190, 192n140; modern, dogmatism of, 131–52; modern, "veil of perception" problem, 133–52, 160; *Phenomenology* as itself, 177n109; skeptical paradox, skeptical solution, 176, 207–22, 231n71, 232–38, 346–47

Skinner, B.F., 387n56

slavery. *See* freedom/oppression; *Phenomenology of Spirit, Lordship and Bondage*

Smart, J.J.C., 367n12

Smith, S.B., 22n14

Smyth, H.W., 427n145

social contexts (*see also* history; shapes of consciousness): and origination/underpinning of dualistic Stoic/Christian thought, 465–72; and origination/underpinning of dualistic thought of modern Germany, 473–76; and origination/underpinning of Hegel's monistic thought, 477–86; Hegel's activism regarding, 486–97

Socrates, 38n57, 40–41, 42nn71,73, 49n81, 50, 58–60, 64–65, 180n116, 315n49, 318, 403, 461n19, 465n2, 497, 567n23

solidarity. *See* communal identification/solidarity

Solomon, R.C., 1n2, 2–3, 15n7, 18n4, 47n78, 48n80, 188, 195n4, 198n11, 292, 298, 302, 317n56, 349n134, 354n143, 419n135, 448n2, 456n14, 556n1

Solon, 29, 39n58, 99

Sophism, 51n87, 160n81, 315n49, 323n70, 425–30, 548

Sophocles, 29, 46n77, 47n78, 48, 52n91, 315n49, 454, 462

Spinoza, B., 113n235, 166nn89–91, 167n92, 194–95, 197n9

state (*see also* communal; community; social contexts), 452n6, 455n10, 470–72, 477–84, 489

Stocking, G.W., 415n129

Stoicism (see also *Phenomenology of Spirit, Stoicism*), 38n57, 42–45, 50, 51n87, 52–53, 56n95, 58–60, 70, 86, 150, 151n63, 160, 210, 216, 219, 312, 314n43, 317–19, 322–25, 425–30, 449, 451, 458–60, 466–68, 548

Strawson, P.F., 119n247, 406n112

syllogism: forms of, and finite cognition, 111–13, 116, 169–70, 264–65

system. *See* Science; shapes of consciousness

Taylor, C., 1n2, 15n7, 22n14, 28n32, 73n146, 79n160, 94n193, 100n206, 102n210, 152n65, 161–63, 197n10, 198nn11,13, 199n14, 207n33, 302n15, 348, 353n142, 452n6, 455n10, 491n52, 497n59

teleology (*see also* explanation), 27–28, 44–45, 63–67, 82–83, 173–74, 293–94, 461–63

Terror, Jacobin (see also *Phenomenology of Spirit, Absolute Freedom and Terror*), 103n210, 199n14, 453, 488

thought (*see also* concepts; dualisms; explanation; historicism; meaning; shapes of consciousness; social contexts): as *bekannt* versus *erkannt*, 431–32; history of, and self-comprehension, 430–45

time, 99–100, 245n90, 291–92, 560n8, 569n24

tragedy. *See* Greek tragedy
transcendental arguments, 152n65, 161–63
translation, 370–78, 390n70, 397–99, 413n125
Trede, J.H., 275n9
Troeltsch, E., 170n99, 293
truth (*see also* communal; correspondence theory of truth; fact; representation; Science): and creative volitions, 18n5, 31–33, 51–54, 71, 89–91, 237n78, 238n81, 340–42, 350; as a whole, 158–59; knowledge of, as aim, 17–18, 20, 21n11, 63–67, 69–71, 81, 83n172, 87–88, 92, 125, 245–47

unconditional commitments, 72–75
understanding, conceptual. *See* behavior(ism); communal; concepts; meaning
Understanding, the. *See* appearance of Science, *Phenomenology* as; cognition, finite versus infinite; dualisms; *Phenomenology of Spirit, Force and the Understanding*
unhappiness (*see also* dualisms; happiness), 22–104
unity (*see also* dualisms, monism): of Life, 312–15; of unity and nonunity, 79n160, 80, 195n6, 199–204; psychic, 31–42, 51–60, 89–102, 249; self-world, 23–31, 43–51, 81–88; social, 473–97

Ur-*Phenomenology, Phenomenology*'s expansion from, 172n103, 247, 297, 501–43, 547

"veil of perception" problem. *See* skepticism
Vernant, J.P., 47n78, 385n48
Vidal-Naquet, P., 47n78
virtue (*see also* dualisms; Kant; morality; *Phenomenology of Spirit, Virtue and the Way of the World*), 38–40, 46, 55–57, 72, 76, 92–93, 313–14, 469–70
volition. *See* dualisms, fact and volition; mind, as active; truth
Voltaire, 362–63

Westphal, M., 1n2, 13n5, 22n14, 198n11, 452n6
Whorf, B.L., 367n12, 370n21, 378n39, 380
Williams, B.A.O., 75nn152–53, 78n158, 142n38
Windelband, W., 73n145
Wirklichkeit, 341, 346n127
Wittgenstein, L.J.J., 96n198, 97n199, 99n202, 100n206, 105, 167n92, 176, 192, 205, 207–9, 211–12, 219n52, 239n82, 284, 372n26, 390n69
Wood, A.W., 21, 73n146, 87n181, 119n247

Zoroastrianism, 305, 457